Law Practice Management

Fifth Edition

Law Practice Management

Cynthia Traina Donnes, J.D., M.A.

Fifth Edition

Australia • Brazil • Canada • Mexico • Singapore • United Kingdom • United States

Law Practice Management, **Fifth Edition**
Cynthia Traina Donnes, J.D., M.A.

SVP, Product: Erin Joyner

VP, Product: Thais Alencar

Portfolio Product Director: Jason Fremder

Portfolio Product Manager: Emily Olsen

Product Assistant: Bridget Duffy

Content Manager: Arul Joseph Raj, Lumina
Datamatics, Inc.

Digital Project Manager: Mark Hopkinson

VP, Product Marketing: Jason Sakos

Product Marketing Manager: Neena Bali

Content Acquisition Analyst: Erin McCullough

Production Service: Lumina Datamatics, Inc.

Designer: Gaby McCracken

Cover Image Source: 1297672676/John Baggaley/
Getty Images

For product information and technology assistance, contact us at
**Cengage Customer & Sales Support, 1-800-354-9706
or support.cengage.com.**

For permission to use material from this text or product, submit all
requests online at **www.copyright.com.**

Library of Congress Control Number: 2022918858

ISBN: 978-0-357-76740-5

Cengage
200 Pier 4 Boulevard
Boston, MA 02210
USA

Cengage is a leading provider of customized learning solutions. Our employees
reside in nearly 40 different countries and serve digital learners in 165 countries
around the world. Find your local representative at **www.cengage.com.**

To learn more about Cengage platforms and services, register or access your online
learning solution, or purchase materials for your course, visit **www.cengage.com.**

Notice to the Reader

Publisher does not warrant or guarantee any of the products described herein or perform any independent analysis in connection with any of
the product information contained herein. Publisher does not assume, and expressly disclaims, any obligation to obtain and include information
other than that provided to it by the manufacturer. The reader is expressly warned to consider and adopt all safety precautions that might be
indicated by the activities described herein and to avoid all potential hazards. By following the instructions contained herein, the reader willingly
assumes all risks in connection with such instructions. The publisher makes no representations or warranties of any kind, including but not
limited to, the warranties of fitness for particular purpose or merchantability, nor are any such representations implied with respect to the
material set forth herein, and the publisher takes no responsibility with respect to such material. The publisher shall not be liable for any special,
consequential, or exemplary damages resulting, in whole or part, from the readers' use of, or reliance upon, this material.

Printed in Mexico
Print Number: 1   Print Year: 2022

To my supportive family, friends, and colleagues

Brief Contents

Contents

Contents

3 Ethics and Malpractice 102

4 Client Relations and Communication Skills 146

Contents

5   Legal Fees, Timekeeping, and Billing   177

8 Legal Marketing 295

9 File and Law Library Management 314

Preface

Another class, another boring textbook. Right? Wrong! *Law Practice Management* is a constantly evolving area and a great class to prepare new lawyers and paralegal staff members to handle a law practice efficiently and effectively. You will learn about real-life problems encountered on the job and how to deal with them successfully. You will understand the importance of performing quality work for clients. You will learn methods for improving your communication skills and your ability to work with clients successfully. You will be shown how to track and bill your time correctly, and how to use your time effectively. You will find explanations throughout the textbook on how to avoid ethical problems that may come up. *Law Practice Management* is anything but boring.

The goal of *Law Practice Management* is to educate lawyers and paralegal students regarding law office management procedures and systems. Law firms, as well as lawyers and paralegals, must have good management skills to survive in today's competitive marketplace. This textbook is written for the students who want to understand effective law practice management techniques and systems, whether or not they will go on to become a law office administrator.

This textbook is not intended to be an "armchair" textbook on the theories and principles of management, nor is it a textbook on how to set up a law office. Rather, this textbook presents a practical discussion of law office management with realistic applications.

The information presented is national in scope and assumes no prior knowledge of management or the legal field. Sociology, theories, and jargon are kept to an absolute minimum. To present a flavor of how a real law office operates, step-by-step explanations, "how-to" tips, practical charts, recent trends in law office management and software, as well as practical ideas on law office management are provided. Information is presented in a manner that encourages students to think independently and to learn by participating.

This textbook will help the students manage themselves, in addition to learning basic law office systems, such as timekeeping and billing, docket control, financial management, file and library management, technology, and more. If students take the time to learn the management systems in this textbook, they will perform tasks more efficiently, with greater accuracy, and with less work. Sound too good to be true? That is what good management is all about.

A textbook on law office management has inherent limitations because there are many different management styles, techniques, and philosophies, depending on the size and type of firm (e.g., small-, medium-, and large-sized firms, corporate legal departments), location of the firm (urban, rural, east, west), and so forth. In addition, law office management is such a diverse area that most people cannot agree on all the topics that should be covered. Considering these inherent problems, a vast and varied amount of information from many different angles is presented.

Ethics

The importance of ethics is stressed throughout the textbook. Assuring a high ethical standard in the law office is a major function of law office management. It is very important to your career that you are educated regarding ethical issues and adopt a high ethical standard as a way of life. Each textbook chapter has a discussion on ethics along with ethical-related cases covering points from the chapter from real-life, actual settings.

Organization of Text

The textbook is organized into nine chapters. Chapter 1 is an introduction to the legal environment, including a discussion about members of the legal team found in most law offices, information about the different sizes and types of law practices as well as law firm governance. Chapter 2 is a broad introduction to law office management and covers 11 major areas regarding the topic, giving students a broad "30,000-foot view" of law office management and an excellent framework for the rest of the book. However, from Chapter 2 onward, the chapters stand on their own and do not depend on the preceding chapter(s). Thus, instructors can assign the chapters in whatever order they believe is appropriate.

Changes to the Fifth Edition

The fifth edition of *Law Practice Management* offers a noticeable change over the fourth edition: it has a revised title, reflective of text material changes, geared to appeal to a broad spectrum of legal professionals. The textbook revisions continue to provide updated management practices and technological advances including the following:

- The textbook has updated lessons for ethics/conflict of interest checks, docket control and client management, time and billing, as well as trust accounting and Excel exercises.

- For every chapter, the textbook has On the Web Exercises, Practical Applications, Helpful Web Sites, ethical cases included at the end of most chapters, and Suggested Reading. The text really tries to be *practical* and *hands-on* to offer the student many learning opportunities.

- The textbook continues to have the most current charts and graphs related to each chapter's subject matter.

- The textbook continues to have a strong ethical foundation that is covered in every chapter and with many of the exercises. All the ethics citations have been updated to include any revisions with states' rules of professional conduct that follow the current *Model Rules of Professional Conduct* from the American Bar Association.

- The textbook continues to cover current technological advances throughout chapters.

Special Features

- Strong, practical coverage of ethics throughout the text
- Ethical cases regarding law office management topics in most chapters
- Citations to states' rules of professional conduct including recent updates based on the *Model Rules*
- Introductions that "set the stage" for most chapters
- Up-to-date charts, figures, and graphs to illustrate concepts
- Key terms/concepts defined in the margin
- List of websites by topic for each chapter
- List of suggested reading for each chapter
- Practical applications and exercises at the end of each chapter
- Chapter objectives listed for each chapter
- "On the Web Exercises" for each chapter
- A semester group project, "Opening a Law Office" (Chapter 2), to incorporate the learning objectives of the textbook.

Supplemental Teaching Materials

Additional instructor resources for this product are available online. Instructor assets include an Instructor's Manual, Educator's Guide, PowerPoint® slides, and a test bank powered by Cognero®. Sign up or sign in at **www.cengage.com.** to search for and access this product and its online resources.

To the Student

Law Practice Management is exciting and ever changing. It is my hope that you will find this book useful as a reference tool in your professional career and that you will use some ideas from this book to climb the ladder of success. Remember that just because you graduated, you do not get to start at the top. You should not be surprised if you will likely have to start at an entry level position and work your way up. The experience you will gain is priceless, and through hard work and determination, you will move up more quickly than you think, being the better for it because you will have earned it. Also, remember to help your coworkers. You will not be able to succeed without their help. Treat them like you would like to be treated, put the interests of your law office ahead of your own, and you will go far.

If you have an interesting idea, have solved some problem in law office management, or just have a story to tell and you would not mind me using it as an example in a subsequent edition of this book, please do not hesitate to contact me. I am always interested in learning from you. I wish you the best of luck in your endeavors. Cynthia Lee Traina Donnes, J.D., New Orleans, LA.

Acknowledgments

A special part of writing a book is acknowledging those invaluable people that worked on this project. Many thanks for all your help and support.

Reviewers Thanks to the reviewers of this fifth edition for their time and suggestions to improve the text.

Keisha D. Hudson, JD

Lawrence Joel

Cengage Learning

A special thanks goes to the wonderful people at Cengage Learning, including Emily Olsen, associate product manager, whose help with keeping me on task was invaluable. To Jennifer Ziegler, senior product manager, whose patience and understanding during some very difficult time constraints was so appreciated. Without her support and encouragement, which was invaluable and so appreciated during this undertaking, completing the book would not have been possible. Also, to Arul Joseph Raj and the people at Lumina for their wonderful work with the book edits and reviews. It was a pleasure to work with everyone involved with this project.

Colleagues and Friends

Thanks go to my lifelong friends for their support and encouragement to pursue this textbook. As well, many colleagues have provided invaluable input and suggestions, especially members of the School of Professional Advancement (SOPA) at Tulane University. I am truly grateful to be affiliated with an organization that is open-minded and promotes creativity. Many thanks to Robyn Ice, Kathryn Beachy, and Sallie Davis, for all their support during this project.

Family

A special thanks goes to my family (husband, Bert and our children Dominic, Erin (Dennis), Antonia (Troy), David (Brittany), Louis (Leila) and Sara) for their loving support and inspiration. They are the driving forces that give me the courage to pursue my dreams and never give up, no matter the obstacles. One of those dreams was completing law school and passing the bar, which was accomplished this year. I could not have done this without all of you. And, of course...love to my grandchildren (Saul, Sylvie, Ariail, Adelaide, Trey, Sonny, and #7 on the way).

Cynthia Lee Traina Donnes, J.D.
New Orleans, LA

The Legal Team, Law Practices, and Law Firm Governance

1

Chapter Objectives

After you read this chapter, you should be able to:

- Explain the titles and duties of each member of the legal team.

- Identify the different types of law practices.

- Explain alternative law office organizational structures.

L aw offices are organizations that provide legal services to clients, but they are fundamentally a business. Like any business, their function is to make money, operate at a profit, and earn income for their owners. This chapter introduces you to the legal team members who provide services to clients and management to a law office; salary trends of attorneys and paralegals; different types of law practices that operate in the legal field; and various organizational structures used by law firms.

The Legal Team

In a law office, many people make up the legal team. The **legal team** consists of attorneys, administrators, law clerks, librarians, paralegals, secretaries, clerks, and other third parties (see Exhibit 1-1). Each person provides a distinct range of services to clients, and each has their place on the legal team. The positions and job duties in any law office depend on the type and size of the office. A list of job titles and a general description of common duties and responsibilities are provided in this section. It should be noted that job titles are just that—they are "titles" only. Attorneys and law office administrators are far more impressed with a person's actual performance than with a job title.

legal team
A group made up of attorneys, administrators, law clerks, librarians, paralegals/legal assistants, secretaries, clerks, and other third parties. Each provides a distinct range of services to clients and has a place on the legal team.

Attorney

Attorneys, sometimes referred to as counselors, advise clients regarding their legal rights, represent them in litigation, and negotiate agreements between them and others. Once licensed, they can legally represent clients in court—keep in mind, though, that every state, through its respective bar association, regulates the practice of law. A licensed attorney is responsible for providing competent representation and ensuring that all members of the legal team are aware of the ethical duties owed to the client. Depending on the size of the law office, attorneys may also have administrative duties. There are several kinds of attorneys.

Partner/Shareholder A **partner or shareholder** is an attorney-owner in a private law practice who shares in its profits and losses. In the partnership form of business, an owner of the business is called a partner. In the corporate form of business, an owner is called a shareholder. Partners and shareholders serve primarily the same purpose; it is only the legal structure that is different. For simplicity, "partner" will be used to refer collectively to partners and shareholders, but the term "shareholder" could also have been used.

Partners attend partnership meetings and vote in the management decisions of the firm. Partners must also make monetary contributions to the firm if the need arises. Partners are sometimes called equity partners, since they share in the profits or losses of the firm. To become a partner, an attorney must either be an attorney who founded the firm or be voted into the position by the existing partners. Typically, partners do not receive a "salary" but may receive a periodic draw, which is an advance against future profits.

In some firms, a **managing partner** is chosen by the partnership to run the firm, make administrative decisions, and set policies. The managing partner reports to the partnership on the progress of the firm. Managing partners are typically elected to serve for a set amount of time, such as one or two years. Depending on the size of the firm, a managing partner may spend part or all of his or her time on management duties. In smaller law offices, a managing partner will practice law in addition to running the firm, while in large firms, managing the practice is typically a full-time job.

Associate Attorney An **associate attorney** does not have an ownership interest in the law firm and does not share in the profits. The associate is an employee of the firm who only receives a salary and has no vote regarding management decisions. Associates can be hired directly out of law school or come from other firms. Associates who are hired from other firms are known as lateral hires or lateral hire associates. Associates who are candidates for a future partnership are said to be on a partnership track. An associate is usually with the firm between 5 and 10 years before he or she is a candidate for a partnership position, depending on the size of the firm. In large metropolitan firms, the time may be longer. An associate passed over for partnership may or may not leave the firm to practice elsewhere. Sometimes, to keep good associate attorneys who have nevertheless been passed over for partnership, the firm creates a position known as a non-equity partner. A **non-equity partner** does not share in the profits or losses of the business but may be included

---

attorney
A licensed professional who counsels clients regarding their legal rights, represents them in litigation, and negotiates agreements between them and others.

partner or shareholder
An owner in a private law practice who shares in its profits and losses.

managing partner
An attorney in a law firm chosen by the partnership to run the firm, make administrative decisions, and set policies.

associate attorney
Attorney who is a salaried employee of the law firm, does not have an ownership interest in the firm, does not share in the profits, and has no vote regarding management decisions.

non-equity partner
One who does not share in the profits or losses of the firm but may be included in some aspects of management and may be entitled to certain benefits.

staff attorney
An attorney hired by a firm with the knowledge and understanding that he or she will never be considered for partnership.

in some aspects of the management of the firm and may be entitled to other benefits not given to associates. A **staff attorney** is another type of associate. A staff attorney is an attorney hired by a firm with the knowledge and understanding that he or she will never be considered for partnership. Finally, a **contract attorney** is an associate attorney who is temporarily hired by the law office for a specific job or period. When the job or period is finished, the relationship with the firm is over.

contract attorney
An attorney temporarily hired by the law office for a specific job or period. When the job or period is finished, the relationship with the firm is over.

Exhibit 1-1 The Legal Team

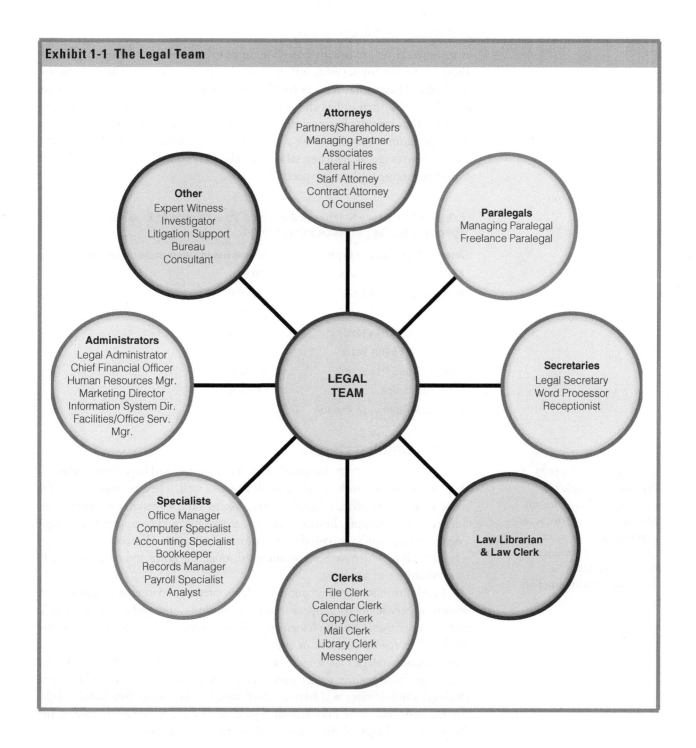

of counsel
An attorney affiliated with the firm in some way, such as a retired or semi-retired partner.

Of Counsel The "of counsel" position is a flexible concept but generally means that the attorney is affiliated with the firm in some way, such as a retired or semiretired partner. Of counsel attorneys lend their names to a firm for goodwill and prestige purposes, in order to attract additional clients and business to the firm. An of counsel attorney may be paid on a per-job basis or may be an employee of the firm. He or she does not usually share in the profits of the firm. The of counsel arrangement is also used when an attorney is considering joining a firm as a partner and wants to work on a trial basis first.

Attorney Compensation

Attorney salaries are usually based on an hourly rate and billable hours, even though the fee for services will be calculated using one of three common methods: (1) fixed-flat fee; (2) contingency fee-percentage; or (3) hourly rate. Law firms will often utilize all types of fee structures with clients and will need to factor that into the business structure to balance lawyer compensation along with operating expenses to have a successful law practice. Exhibit 1-2 provides a current average of attorney salaries in the United States based on years of experience along with some specialized areas.

Exhibit 1-2 Attorney Salaries in the United States Based on Experience/Specialization (https://www.salary.com/)	
Attorney Type (Years of Experience)	**Annual Based Salary in the United States**
Attorney Type 1 (0–2 years)	$98,580
Attorney Type 2 (2–4 years)	$129,836
Attorney Type 3 (4–7 years)	$159,849
Attorney Type 4 (7+ years)	$179,516
Attorney Type 5 (10+ years)	$201,391
Attorney Type 6 (12+ years)	$211,502
Magistrate/Judge	$171,708
Real Estate Attorney (2–4 years)	$154,375

Legal Administrators

legal administrators
Persons responsible for some type of law office administrative system, such as general management, finance and accounting, human resources, marketing, or computer systems.

Legal administrators are usually found in medium and large firms, although they are beginning to be used in small firms as well. They are responsible for some type of law office administrative system such as general management, finance and accounting, human resources, marketing, and computer technology. Legal administrators are typically non-attorneys who have degrees in business or related fields or who have been promoted through the ranks; most report directly to a committee or a partner.

Legal administrators draft annual budgets, prepare and interpret management reports, supervise the fiscal operations of the business, hire and fire support staff, and are responsible for implementing effective systems. In actuality, managers are hired to relieve partners or managing committees of operational burdens. Experienced paralegals are sometimes promoted to become law office managers, which can be a positive career move. Depending on the size of the law firm, the legal administrator will have a varied range of job duties (see Exhibit 1-3). An excellent source of information regarding law office administration is the Association of Legal Administrators (ALA) [http://www.alanet.org].

Exhibit 1-3 Legal Administrator Job Description

Summary of Responsibilities

Handles the law office's overall business functions and operations, including facilities management, systems management, accounting and billing, human resources and data/record organization and maintenance. The legal administrator will report to a management committee, chairman of the board, or managing partner and participates in management meetings as well as sharing strategic planning, marketing, and practice management with the appropriate partners for cost-effective management throughout the organization.

The legal administrator, whether directly or indirectly through a management team, is responsible for all of the following:

Management of Facilities

Responsibilities: Handles office design and space planning, mail and messaging systems (paper and electronic), file and data storage maintenance, telecommunications, and other facility operations.

Management of Systems

Responsibilities: Handles computer systems including office automation and updates for the legal practice and litigation support, digital operations oversight including cybersecurity, records management including electronic data storage, as well as library and research management. Also serves as a liaison between technical staff and legal staff for office equipment and litigation support.

Management of Finances

Responsibilities: Billing and other accounting oversight including banking and trust accounting, billing and collections, payroll, vendor payments, pension plans, tax reporting, office supply budgets, facility maintenance and other expenses for daily operations. Also includes profit analysis, budgeting, and planning.

Management of Human Resources

Responsibilities: Hires, trains, and supervises legal staff including paralegals and support staff. Handles recruitment, employee selection, training and development, motivational resources, employee performance and evaluation, salary administration, and employee relations, including counseling, disciplinary actions, and discharge. Also handles job design, personnel data systems and resource allocation.

Legal administrators are members of the business's management team. They either manage or contribute to the following:

Practice Management

Responsibilities: Recruitment of lawyers and paralegals, provide training and development for new hires. Also responsible for supervising paralegals, overseeing work product, professional standards, substantive practice systems, and other practice management duties.

General Management

Responsibilities: Business and organizational development, tactical and strategic firm planning, quality control, risk management, and other management duties.

Marketing

Responsibilities: Legal services marketing to enhance the firm's visibility and image for preferred practice areas, which includes client development and management, business opportunity forecasts, client development, and profit analysis.

Source: Association of Legal Administrators.

Paralegals

Paralegals, sometimes referred to as legal assistants, are a unique group of people who assist attorneys in the delivery of legal services. Through formal education, training, and experience, paralegals have knowledge and expertise regarding the legal system to perform substantive legal work under the supervision of a lawyer, either employed or retained by lawyers and/or law

paralegals
As defined by the ABA, is a person, qualified by education, training, or work experience, who is employed or retained by a lawyer, law office, corporation, government agency, or other entity and who performs specifically delegated substantive legal work for which a lawyer is responsible.

firms, corporations, governmental agencies, or other entities. According to the U.S. Bureau of Labor Statistics most paralegals and legal assistants have some kind of college education In addition to some college (either an associate degree or certificate), paralegals will take certification exams. Both NALA and the National Federation of Paralegal Association (NFPA) have voluntary certification exams, and some states offer certifications as well.

There are parts of the country as well as some legal organizations that still use the terms *paralegal* and *legal assistant* interchangeably, while others consider the two terms distinguishable. In 2020, the American Bar Association (ABA) adopted the Standing Committee on Paralegals' recommendation to replace the 1997 definition, by removing the term "legal assistant" and to only use "paralegal" in order to reflect a more accurate description of the substantive work performed. The ABA's 2020 definition of paralegal has also been adopted by both NFPA and the NALA, along with the American Association for Paralegal Education (AAfPE).

The ABA has also recognized the contribution of paralegals and legal assistants to the legal profession by creating an associate membership category for them, which allows them to participate in relevant activities and join sections and divisions of the ABA. Many state and county bar associations also allow paralegals and legal assistants to participate as associate members in their organizations. Paralegals and legal assistants have two of their own national professional associations—NFPA and NALA—among others that they may join, which offer paralegals many resources and benefits

Although paralegals perform many tasks, they are strictly prohibited from giving legal advice to clients, from representing clients in court proceedings, from accepting client cases, and from setting a fee in a matter. This is covered in more detail in Chapter 3.

Traditionally, a paralegal works under the direct supervision of an attorney and is accountable to that attorney. Some paralegals, however, work independently as **freelance** or **contract paralegals**; they are self-employed, marketing their services to the legal community on a per-job basis, enjoying the freedom to set their own hours and be their own bosses. Freelance paralegals often work off-site for a number of attorneys or legal organizations at the same time, while still working under the supervision of attorneys. They control time scheduling that is coordinated with the attorneys and the clients. The most important concern is that the work is done. The paralegal or legal assistant can determine the rate for their services, which is paid to them by the attorney. It's a win–win situation.

Independent legal assistants or **legal technicians** present some complicated issues with paralegals/legal assistants, in particular, ethical issues concerning unauthorized practice of law, discussed further in Chapter 3. Independent legal assistants provide services to clients, which involves the law, generally providing self-help services to the public. However, these individuals are not accountable to a lawyer. A **limited license legal technician**, in states where legislation has been passed, is a person qualified by education, training, and work to engage in the limited practice of law in the approved practice area as per the state's laws. In 2013, the state of Washington passed legislation allowing non-attorneys, under carefully regulated circumstances, with specialized training and certification to practice law in a limited capacity. Washington State Rule 28—Limited Practice Rule for Limited License Legal Technicians (LLLT). However, in June 2020, the Washington State Supreme

freelance or **contract paralegals**
Works as an independent contractor with supervision by and/or accountability to an attorney; is hired for a specific job or period.

independent legal assistants or **legal technicians**
Services provided to clients in which the law is involved, but individuals providing the services are not accountable to a lawyer.

limited license legal technician
In states where legislation has provided, a person qualified by education, training, and work to engage in the limited practice of law in the approved practice area as per the individual state's rules.

Court voted to sunset the LLLT program. Those already licensed and in good standing may continue to provide limited legal services, and any persons in the process of being licensed as of June 2020 must complete the program prior to July 2021. In 2018, Utah launched the Licensed Paralegal Practitioner to conduct limited practice in only specified areas of law upon meeting certain educational/experiential qualifications as well as continuing legal education requirements. Rule 14-802 of the Rules Governing the Utah State Bar, and Rules Governing Licensed Paralegal Practitioner 15-703. Other states such as California, Oregon, Colorado, New Mexico, and Montana have formed task forces to consider the adoption of limited license legal technician or similar limited practice forms to address the needs for affordable and quality legal assistance without hiring an attorney, while still protecting the public interest.

Some larger legal organizations have **paralegal managers** who oversee the firm's paralegal program and are responsible for administering all firm policies pertaining to paralegals. The firm's paralegals report either directly or indirectly to the paralegal manager. Paralegal managers develop work plans and standards, prepare staffing plans and bill rates, recruit and hire, provide training and development, monitor workloads, and conduct evaluations of the paralegals.

paralegal managers
Oversee a paralegal program in a legal organization, including preparing work plans, hiring, training, and evaluating paralegals.

Paralegal Roles, Responsibilities, and Employment

People unfamiliar with the legal profession might assume that paralegals spend a great deal of time in court; this is a common misconception. A considerable amount of the paralegal's time is spent researching background information, plowing through reams of files, summarizing depositions, drafting pleadings or correspondence, and organizing information. It is not always exciting, but it is essential work with every case; often, the facts gathered, researched, and presented determine a case's outcome. Depending on the law firm's size or structure, an attorney may have paralegals assist them in discovery, trial preparation, and transactional work, such as real estate closings. In some, for example, in Louisiana, a Notary Public is responsible for performing Acts involving real estate closings, as well as other sales and transfers. Although a licensed attorney in Louisiana can automatically apply for their Notary Public commission, non-attorneys must sit for a statewide exam to obtain a Notary Public commission. However, once they pass the exam, a non-attorney Notary Public has the same authority to perform those Acts as licensed attorneys. This position can be very useful in a law office or title company that routinely performs real estate closings.

Defining a paralegal's job duties is not an easy task, given the wide variety and versatility of the profession. Exhibit 1-4 shows some of the more frequent duties paralegals perform in a law office. Of those duties, assisting at trial is on the lower end. The majority of paralegals/legal assistants are utilized by attorneys to draft letters and case correspondence, work with and manage files and cases, calendar and keep track of case deadlines, work with computer systems, draft pleadings and formal court documents, work on miscellaneous office matters, and work with clients on a daily basis.

Most paralegals practice in a particular area of the law. For the most part, attorneys utilize paralegals in the area of civil litigation, family law, personal injury, and government. These practice areas provide many employment opportunities for paralegals within the legal profession. Paralegals may also be utilized in different kinds of legal organizations. Most paralegals are employed by attorneys in private law offices, and the size of the law office will have an effect on the paralegal's job duties and salaries. In small law offices, paralegals usually compose and draft their own documents on a computer and do their own secretarial tasks. In larger firms, paralegals may supervise secretarial personnel or share secretary staff with other legal professionals. That said, attorneys are still responsible to supervise the work of non-attorneys on their staff.

Exhibit 1-4 Paralegal Duties – Most to least common task				
Duty	Daily	Weekly	Monthly	Occasionally
Case management	Daily			
Draft correspondence	Daily			
Calendar deadlines	Daily			
Automation systems/computers	Daily			
Draft pleadings		Weekly		
Client Assistance		Weekly		
Research/Fact checking			Monthly	
Document analysis/summary			Monthly	
Court filings			Monthly	
Investigation				Occasionally
Personnel management				Occasionally
Client/witness interviews				Occasionally
Train employees				Occasionally
Cite checking				Occasionally
Prepare/attend closings				Occasionally
Law library maintenance				Occasionally
Deposition summaries				Occasionally
Prepare/attend depositions				Occasionally
Assist/attend mediations				Occasionally
Assist at trial				Occasionally

Functions and Duties/Frequencies.

Paralegal Compensation

According to the U.S. Bureau of Labor Statistics the median annual wage paralegal/legal assistants as of May 2021 was $56,230 per year. It reported that paralegal/legal assistants employed by the federal government or those employed in finance and insurance receive higher compensation on average than paralegals/legal assistants in state government and legal service areas. It also reported paralegals working in the far west and New England/eastern areas earned higher compensation than those working in other areas of the United States, and (3) paralegals working in smaller firms tended to make less money than paralegals working in large law firms. Exhibit 1-5 reflects that average paralegal salaries according to the U.S. Bureau of Labor Statistics.

Exhibit 1-5 Paralegal Compensation Statistics

By Years of Legal Experience	Average Total Compensation
1–4 years	$44,000
5–9 years	$51,000
10–19 years	$56,000
Over 20 years	$61,000

By Region	Average Total Compensation
Far West – California	$70,290
New England – New York	$63,270
Southwest – Texas	$56,030
Southeast – Florida	$53,940
Great Lakes – Illinois	$60,920

Exempt v. Nonexempt   The **Fair Labor Standards Act (FLSA)** is a federal law that sets minimum wage and overtime pay requirements for employees. It requires that overtime pay (one-and-one-half times their normal rate) be paid to employees who work in excess of 40 hours per week. Employees do not need to be paid overtime if they fall into one of the four "white-collar" exemptions: executive, administrative, professional, or outside sales. If an employee is **exempt**, he or she is not required to be paid overtime wages. If an employee is **nonexempt**, he or she is required to be paid overtime wages.

> Employment of paralegals and legal assistants is projected to grow 12% from 2020 to 2030, faster than the average for all occupations.
>
> As law firms try to increase the efficiency of legal services, and reduce billing costs as clients push for less-expense services, they are expected to hire more paralegals and legal assistants. Paralegals can be less costly alternatives to lawyers, performing a wide variety of tasks once done by entry-level lawyers. Although law firms will continue to be the largest employer of paralegals, many large corporations are increasing their in-house legal departments to cut costs. This will lead to an increase in the demand for legal workers in a variety of settings, such as finance and insurance firms, consulting firms, and health care providers.
>
> *Bureau of Labor Statistics, U.S. Department of Labor, Occupational Outlook Handbook, 2020 Edition, Paralegals and Legal Assistants, on the Internet at https://www.bls.gov/ooh/legal/paralegals-and-legal-assistants.htm*

The issue of whether paralegals should be exempt or nonexempt is hotly debated. The U.S. Department of Labor, which administers the FLSA, has long taken the position that paralegals are nonexempt and are thus entitled to overtime pay for hours worked in excess of 40 per week because their "duties do not involve the exercise of discretion and independent judgment required by the regulations" (see Wage & Hour Opinion Letters available at https://www.dol.gov/agencies/whd/opinion-letters/request/existing-guidance dated March 20, 1998; February 19, 1998; April 13, 1995; February 10, 1978). As recently as 2005 (see Wage &

Fair Labor Standards Act (FLSA)
Federal law that sets minimum wage and overtime pay requirements for employees.

exempt
The employee is not required to be paid overtime wages over 40 hours per week.

nonexempt
The employee is required to be paid overtime wages (time and a half) over 40 hours per week.

Hour Opinion Letter dated January 7, 2005, FLSA2005-9), the Department of Labor stated that a paralegal was not exempt from the FLSA even if the paralegal possessed a four-year degree, had a paralegal certificate, had taken continuing legal education classes, and had been practicing as a paralegal for 22 years. The Department relied on 29 CFR § 541.301(e)(7), which states that "[p]aralegals and legal assistants generally do not qualify as exempt learned professionals because an advanced specialized academic degree is not a standard prerequisite for entry into the field. Although many paralegals possess general four-year advanced degrees, most specialized paralegal programs are two-year associate degree programs from a community college or equivalent institution."

The advantage of this long-held position by the Department of Labor is that if a paralegal is deemed nonexempt, then he or she is entitled to overtime pay, which can be an attractive benefit. Unfortunately, the ruling arguably diminishes the profession by holding that it is not of a prestigious enough nature to warrant exempt status. The ruling from the Department of Labor was criticized by many that felt it failed to consider the advanced education and continuing legal education of paralegals and legal assistants, the profession's status as well as the substantive duties performed by paralegals and legal assistants for which independent judgment is routinely exercised. In 2019, FLSA issued an opinion letter *See* Wage & Hour Opinion Letter dated July 1, 2019) addressing the paralegal profession pointing out particulars that would help define duties and compensation that would determine "exempt" for paralegals. In particular, it noted that the employee is exempt if "compensated on a salary or fee basis at a rate of not less than $455 per week," (2) the employee's "primary duty" is "office or non-manual work directly related to the management or general business operations of the employer or the employer's customers"; and (3) the employee's "primary duty includes the exercise of discretion and independent judgment with respect to matters of significance." *See* 29 C.F.R. § 541.200(a) (2016). It additionally noted an "exempt" status qualifies if the employee qualifies for the highly compensated exemption by: (1) the employee's "primary duty includes performing office or non-manual work"; (2) the employee receives total annual compensation of at least $100,000;3 and (3) the employee "customarily and regularly performs any one or more of the exempt duties or responsibilities of an executive, administrative or professional employee." *See* 29 C.F.R. § 541.601 (2016). Given these two explanations, "exempt" status for paralegals will continue to be determined by duties, responsibilities, and salaries, as opposed to the profession.

Interestingly, many law firms still do not pay overtime compensation to paralegals/legal assistants, even after the rulings by the Department of Labor on the subject.

The Judicial System's Recognition of the Paralegal Profession

The U.S. Supreme Court case of **Missouri v. Jenkins**, 491 U.S. 274, 109 S.Ct. 2463, 105 L.Ed. 2d 229 (1989), established that the paralegal profession had come of age. In that case, the plaintiff was successful on several counts under a federal statute in a civil rights lawsuit that was attempting to recover attorney's fees from the defendant. The federal statutory language allowed the prevailing party to recover "reasonable attorney's fees" from the adverse party. The plaintiff argued for the right to recover the time that both attorneys and paralegal had spent working on the case. The defendant argued that paralegal time was not "attorney's fees." Alternatively, the defendant argued that if required to pay for paralegal time, the amount should be about $15 an hour, a representation of the overhead costs to the firm of a paralegal.

The Court found that paralegals carry out many useful tasks, and that "reasonable attorney's fees" refers to a reasonable fee for the work produced, whether by attorneys or paralegals, and could be compensable as long as the work was not of a clerical nature. The Court also found that under the federal statute, paralegal time should be compensable at the prevailing market rates. The Court noted that the prevailing rate at that time for paralegal in that part of the United States was about $40 an hour and held that the plaintiff was entitled to receive that amount for paralegal hours expended on the case. This important case defined a paralegal position not as a secretarial or clerical position but as a professional, fee-generating profession.

Former Chief Justice Warren Burger stated that the "expanded use of well-trained assistants, sometimes called 'paralegals,' has been an important development. The advent of the paralegal enables law offices to perform high quality legal services at a lower cost. Possibly we have only scratched the surface of this development."

While ***Missouri v. Jenkins*** was a landmark decision for paralegals, the case involved a federal court interpreting a specific federal statute, the Civil Rights Act. Because fee questions occur in many different situations, it is possible for a court under a different statute to reach a different conclusion. Since ***Missouri v. Jenkins***, many federal and state courts have allowed for recovery of paralegal billable hours [see ***Baldwin v. Burton***, 850 P.2d 1188, 1200-01 (Utah 1993), ***Cooper v. Secretary of Dept. of Health and Human Services***, No. 90-608V, 1992 WL 63271 at 3 (Cl. Ct. March 11, 1992), ***Consolo v. George***, 58 F.3d 791 (1st Cir. 1995), ***Department of Transp., State of Fla. v. Robbins & Robbins, Inc.*** 700 So. 2d 782, Fla. App. 5 Dist. (1997), ***Guinn v. Dotson*** (1994) 23 Cal. App. 4th 262, ***In re Mullins***, 84 F.3d 459 (D.C. Cir. 1996), and ***Taylor v. Chubb Group of Insurance Companies***, 874 P.2d 806 (Ok. 1994). ***Role Models American, Inc. v. Brownlee***, 353 F.3d 962 (C.A.D.C., 2004)].

Paralegal Profitability for Law Offices

The use of paralegals is a financially profitable proposition and represents a win–win situation for both the law office and client. Law offices charge clients for paralegal time. Paralegal billing rates are substantially more than the salaries law offices pay them, so law offices make a profit by billing paralegal time. In addition, clients are typically very willing to pay for paralegal time because the billable rate is substantially less than what an attorney would charge to do the same work.

Office Manager

Office managers are typically found in smaller firms. They handle day-to-day operations of the law office, including activities such as timekeeping and billing, supervision of the clerical support staff, assisting the managing partner in preparing a budget, and making recommendations with regard to changes in systems and purchases. Office managers typically do not have degrees in business. They are usually not given as much decision-making power as administrators and, unlike administrators, usually assist a managing partner in

office managers
Manager who handles day-to-day operations of the law office, such as accounting, supervision of the clerical support staff, and assisting the managing partner.

11

managing the law office. Nonetheless, good office managers are important for the survival of smaller firms. Experienced paralegals are sometimes promoted to office manager positions.

Law Clerk

law clerk
A law student working for a law firm on a part-time basis while he or she is finishing a law degree. Law clerk duties revolve almost exclusively around legal research and writing.

A **law clerk** is usually a student who works for a law firm on a part-time basis while he or she is finishing a law degree. Law clerk duties revolve almost exclusively around legal research and writing. Law clerks perform research, write briefs and motions, and prepare memorandums of law.

Law Librarian

law librarian
A librarian responsible for maintaining a law library, conducting legal research, and managing library resources.

A **law librarian** conducts legal research using both computerized and manual methods; acquires and preserves library materials; is an expert in legal and nonlegal research methods/tools; advises attorneys and legal professionals on legal research methods; maintains, classifies, indexes, and stores library materials; manages the library/legal research budget, and may coordinate the use of electronic resources, such as Westlaw, LexisNexis, and other services.

Legal Secretaries

legal secretaries
Employees who provide assistance and support to other law office staff by preparing documents, composing correspondence, scheduling appointments, and performing other tasks.

Legal secretaries provide a variety of services to attorneys and paralegals. Typical duties include preparing documents, composing routine correspondence, proofreading, reading and routing mail, scheduling appointments, organizing material, filing, answering the phone and screening calls, faxing, copying, responding to e-mails, responding to clients, and other tasks. Secretaries include legal secretaries, receptionists, and word processing secretaries. Competent legal secretaries have highly specialized skills and perform many services for law firms. Legal secretaries, like paralegals, have their own local, regional, state, and national associations. It is not uncommon for a person to start employment with a law office as a legal secretary and work his or her way up to paralegal, office manager, or another position. Receptionists are commonly found in all law offices, and their duties include answering the phone, greeting clients, opening the mail, and making photocopies. Word processing secretaries are commonly found in larger law offices. They type, format, and produce documents using word processing software.

It is not uncommon for friction to exist between paralegals and secretaries. Problems may occur in law offices where there are no clear descriptions of job duties, where paralegals are required to do some clerical or administrative work, and where secretaries perform higher-level research or case management from time to time. This blurring of the lines sometimes causes confusion about who is supposed to do what; when this happens, pressure is added to the working relationship. Some secretaries also resent paralegals performing higher-level work than they themselves are allowed to perform. In addition, some secretaries refuse to perform or resist performing clerical work for paralegals because they view paralegals as peers. In any case, paralegals and secretaries must work together as members of the same team. They must put the needs of the team first and always support their coworkers, because eventually they will need their help.

Clerks

Clerks provide support to other staff positions in a variety of functions. Law offices may have a wide variety of clerks, including mail clerks, copy clerks, file clerks, process servers, messengers, calendar clerks, and billing clerks. Much of their work involves data entry and physically handling files and documents.

clerks
Employees who provide support to other staff positions in a variety of miscellaneous functions.

Other Legal Team Members

A variety of other people and organizations make up the legal team. Other team members may include expert witnesses, investigators, litigation support bureaus, and consultants. An **expert witness** is a person who has technical or scientific expertise in a specific field and agrees to give testimony for a client at trial. Professional investigators are sometimes hired to gather facts and evidence regarding a case. Litigation support service bureaus may be used in cases that have hundreds or thousands of documents to organize and records to computerize for trial. Specialists may also be hired, such as computer specialists, accountants, bookkeepers, records managers, payroll specialists, and analysts. Some large firms employ analysts who are experts in their fields, such as biologists, chemists, and others. These analysts advise the firm and their clients on extremely complex cases. Law offices use business, marketing, and other types of consultants to give them advice on how to run their operation efficiently. Law offices may also use temporary or permanent staffing firms and may outsource jobs, projects, or services as needed, including copying, mail services, and records management.

expert witness
A person who has technical expertise in a specific field and agrees to give testimony for a client at trial.

Types of Law Practices

To a certain extent, how law office management operates depends on the type of law office. Therefore, it is necessary to review the different types of law practices and their functional effect on management. Usually, people think of the private law firm as the only type of law practice, but there are others, including corporate law, government, and legal service practices.

Corporate Law Practice

Some businesses, including large corporations, banks, retailers, manufacturers, transportation companies, publishers, insurance companies, and hospitals, have their own in-house legal departments. Attorneys employed by a corporate law department are often referred to as in-house counsel. In a corporate legal department, attorneys and paralegals have just one client: the business itself. However, some corporate legal departments see each division or department in the corporation as an individual client for whom they must provide quality legal services.

Corporations with their own legal departments are generally large, with millions of dollars in assets. Unlike private law firms, a corporate legal department is not involved in many administrative functions, such as accounting, since the corporation itself provides these services. Corporate legal departments do not record billable hours, since all costs are covered by the corporation. However, corporate legal departments must still budget,

general counsel
The chief for a corporate legal department.

track, and plan activities, and they are responsible for the overall efficiency of their department. Corporate law departments handle a variety of legal concerns in such areas as contracts, labor relations, employee benefits, federal tax laws, intellectual property, environmental law issues, Security Exchange Commission filings, general litigation, real estate law, and workers' compensation claims, among others.

Most corporate legal departments are too small to handle all the legal needs of the corporation, so the law departments hire private law firms that specialize in the additional areas they need. This is sometimes referred to as having "outside counsel." The chief attorney for a corporate legal department is called the **general counsel**. The general counsel, in addition to having legal duties, may also be the corporate secretary. The general counsel typically reports to the chief executive officer and interacts closely with the board of directors of the corporation. Many corporate law departments have practice groups that specialize in certain areas, such as litigation, regulatory work, taxes, contracts and intellectual property work, and more.

Staffing in corporate legal departments includes secretaries, paralegals, law clerks, administrators, and attorneys (see Exhibit 1-6). Most corporate legal departments employ one or more paralegals. The job duties a paralegal performs in a corporate legal department are similar to those performed in other types of practices and may include preparing deposition summaries, performing legal research, and drafting documents. Like paralegals in private law firms, paralegals in corporate legal departments might also specialize in specific areas, such as litigation, real estate, or business law.

Government Practice

Government attorneys, like corporate attorneys, have just one client. In most local, state, and federal agencies, a legal department represents the interests of *each* particular agency. Government attorneys representing agencies or governmental bodies may be involved in contract law, bankruptcy law, tax law, employment law, property law, and environmental law, to name a few. Each state also has an attorney general's office; the attorney general operates as the state's chief law enforcement officer and attorney. In many instances, when a state or state agency is sued, the attorney general's office represents the state. In addition, many other types of government attorneys exist, including local district and city attorneys, state attorney generals, and U.S. attorneys.

In many ways, practicing law for the government is similar to practicing law for a large corporation. Government attorneys, like corporate attorneys, do not record billable hours and are not responsible for as many management duties as are their counterparts in private law firms. Government practices differ from corporate legal department practices in that politics plays a role; government attorneys and paralegals are also paid according to their civil service classification. Staffing for government legal departments consists of secretaries, investigators, paralegals, law clerks, and attorneys. The job duties of paralegals in government practices vary depending on the area of practice, and these duties may be tested in various civil service exams that are a prerequisite to hiring.

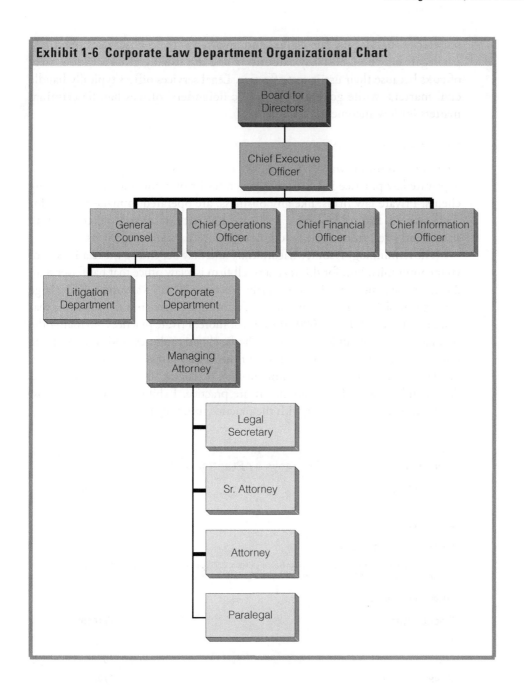

Exhibit 1-6 Corporate Law Department Organizational Chart

Legal Services Offices

A **legal services office**, sometimes called a legal clinic or legal aid office, is a not-for-profit law office that receives grants from the government and private donations to pay for representation of disadvantaged persons who otherwise could not afford legal services. In some cases, legal services offices or clinics are operated by law schools, bar associations, or other nonprofit entities as a public service to the community. Clients pay little or no fees for legal services. Legal services offices typically represent the disadvantaged in areas relating to child support, child custody, disability claims, bankruptcies, landlord-tenant disputes, and mental health problems. Staffing for legal services offices includes

legal services office
A not-for-profit law office that receives grants from the government and private donations to pay for representation of disadvantaged persons who otherwise could not afford legal services.

secretaries, paralegals, law clerks, and attorneys. In legal services practices, paralegals may be used fairly extensively and are usually given a wide variety of tasks because their use is cost effective. Legal services offices typically handle civil matters, while government public defenders' offices handle criminal matters for low-income clients.

Private Law Practices

The most common way that attorneys practice law is in a private law firm. A private law practice is a firm that generates its own income by representing clients. Private law firms, like any business, are operated to make a profit for their owners. Private law firms represent a variety of clients and come in all shapes and sizes, from a sole practitioner to international megafirms.

The terminology is somewhat arbitrary and may depend on the relative size of your community, but, for this text, a small firm is a law office that has fewer than 20 attorneys; a medium-size firm usually has from 20 to 75 attorneys; and a large firm can employ from 75 to hundreds of attorneys. There are also megafirms that employ between 500 and 1000 attorneys or more. Private practices, no matter the size, have their own unique styles, methods, clients, cultures, and ways of doing things. According to the ABA's Profile of the Legal Profession Report conducted in March 2021, there were 1.3 million-plus practicing attorneys in the United States, and 75% of them were in private practice. Exhibit 1-7shows the most common practice areas along with the practice sizes they join.

Exhibit 1-7 Percent of Attorneys by Practice Area/Size

Practice Type	Percent
Litigation	27%
Estate Planning	20%
Real Estate Transactions	16%

Source: *The Lawyer Statistical Report,* American Bar Foundation, 2005 Edition, updated in 2012. (Note: The 2012 statistics are consistent with current data from various employment and law journal resources.)

Private Practitioners

Practice Type	Percent
1	26%
2–9	30%
10–49	17%
50–99	5%
100–499	10%
More than 500	12%

Sources: The American Bar Association

Sole Practitioner

A sole practitioner is an attorney who individually owns and manages the practice. Anyone who works for the attorney is considered an employee. Sole practitioners sometimes hire another attorney as an employee, who is not entitled to any share of the practice's profits. Although the sole practitioner has the advantage of freedom and independence, he or she is also ultimately responsible for all, or nearly all, of the legal work and management duties of the law office. It is important that overhead costs stay as small as possible, if the sole practitioner is to succeed. Overhead costs are the expenses incurred month after month and include such things as rent (thus the term "overhead"), utilities, the lease of equipment (such as copiers and computers), and support staff salaries. These are costs incurred whether the attorney is serving one client or 100. Sole practitioners typically have small offices with a very small law library.

Sole practitioners are typically generalists, meaning they handle a wide variety of cases, such as probate, family law, criminal law, and personal injury. The sole practitioner typically refers a case outside of his or her area of expertise to another attorney who is skilled in that matter. Sole practitioners need good management skills for their practice to survive. This may pose a problem, because management duties take the sole practitioner away from the actual practice of law, which is the activity that brings in the money.

Staffing can include a secretary, paralegal, law clerk, and possibly an associate attorney; these positions may even be part-time. Paralegals working in a sole practitioner's office enjoy a great deal of responsibility and diversity in their jobs. Duties include conducting legal research, drafting pleadings and discovery materials, word processing, and interviewing witnesses. Because sole practitioners are generalists, their paralegals work in many areas of the law. In a solo practice, the paralegal has the opportunity to learn firsthand about law office management and to perform management functions.

Law Firms

Law firms have two or more attorneys in practice together. There are 446,887 law firms in the United States (not counting sole practitioners), according to the ABA. While there is not as much freedom as in sole practice, law firms do not incur as much risk. If a sole practitioner becomes ill, loses a large client, or faces other such catastrophes, the sole practitioner's income may be endangered. These problems may be alleviated in law firms, because more than one attorney is available. Law firms are usually categorized as small, medium, or large.

The Small Law Firm   The small law firm usually has fewer than 20 attorneys. Notice in Exhibit 1-7 that nearly 73% of all attorneys in the United States practice as either a sole practitioner or in a small firm. Most small firms have a staff member—such as an office manager or an administrator—who helps with the day-to-day operations of the business. However, a partner or managing partner is usually responsible for major management decisions such as hiring, firing, distributing profits, and setting salaries. Small firms usually concentrate in a few areas of the law but may also have attorneys who are general practitioners.

A small law office that specializes in only one or two areas of the law is sometimes called a **boutique firm**. The boutique firm normally has several attorneys who practice in the same specialty. Paralegals who work for boutique firms also usually become specialists in that particular area of the law.

Disadvantages that hinder small firms include cash-flow problems; lack of time to recruit, hire, and train new staff; little time for management; and long hours. Staffing positions include clerks, secretaries, paralegals, office managers, law clerks, and attorneys. Small firms offer paralegals a relatively large variety of tasks to perform.

boutique firm
A small law office that specializes in only one or two areas of the law.

The Medium-Size Firm   The medium-size firm usually has from 20 to 75 attorneys. Typically, medium-size firms are organized into subject-area departments. Medium-size firms differ from small firms in that most medium-size firms have professional administrators who manage many aspects of the business. Administrators usually report to a managing partner or a committee that has overall management responsibilities. Medium-size firms typically have multiple offices, and it is not uncommon for them to have sophisticated computer systems. Staffing often consists of administrators, law librarians, receptionists, secretaries, paralegals, law clerks, and attorneys. Paralegals in medium-size firms have a more structured existence than in smaller firms; the diversity of duties and areas of practice are not as broad. However, the legal assistant may learn a particular area of law in greater depth. In addition, the internal structure and lines of communication are more intense and more important than in small firms, where colleagues tend to be more familiar with one another.

The Large Firm   The large firm has between 75 and several hundred attorneys. A few large firms, sometimes called "megafirms," have 500–1000 or more attorneys. Most large firms have practice groups or departments. A large firm might have 15 or more different practice groups, including antitrust, bankruptcy, environmental, estate planning, intellectual property, international, labor/employment law, litigation, patents, trademarks, copyright, property, and tax. The internal structure of these firms is more similar to the structure of business corporations than to other types of law firms. Staffing in large firms typically includes various classes of paralegals, law clerks, and attorneys, in addition to the other business office personnel such as accounting, human resources, IT/data processing, equipment management, and facilities management to name a few. Large firms often have large corporations as clients. Many have offices throughout the United States, and some have international offices. Large firms also tend to have resources such as large law libraries, a word processing department, and extensive, technologically advanced computer systems connecting all their offices for information exchange.

Disadvantages encountered by large firms include recruiting and retaining good employees in the vital areas of the practice, getting departments to communicate and work together, and controlling the bureaucracy itself. Large law firms usually employ a large number of paralegals and treat them formally and professionally, requiring them to attend department meetings, assist attorneys in depositions, and travel as needed. The physical space occupied by a large firm is more lavish than in small- and medium-size firms, usually occupying several floors in a large office building.

Plaintiff/Defense Firms

Private law practices may categorize themselves as either more or less plaintiff or defense oriented, no matter what the size of the law office. Plaintiff-oriented firms, as the name implies, represent clients who bring claims against others. Plaintiff-oriented firms tend to be smaller, not as well funded, and have fewer employees than defense-oriented firms. Cash flow in plaintiff firms may not be as stable as in defense-oriented firms because, in many cases, they take clients on a contingency fee basis; that is, the law office recovers fees for the case only if it wins.

Defense-oriented firms, on the other hand, have the luxury of billing defendants—who are typically businesses—according to the time spent on the case. This gives defense-oriented firms a more stable cash flow, enabling them to hire more personnel, purchase advanced equipment, and spend more on litigation services, such as hiring expert witnesses and taking as many depositions as needed. Nonetheless, effective management is needed in both plaintiff- and defense-oriented firms.

No matter the type of legal organization, good management, including sound financial management, cost-efficient hiring and training of personnel, efficient use of equipment, and overall leadership, is important.

Law Firm Mergers and Acquisitions

Law firm mergers are commonplace in the U.S. legal market and occur for many different reasons. A law firm might merge as a growth strategy, in order to quickly expand their personnel and client base. A law firm might merge in order to create a presence in a new geographic area or to move into a new practice specialty. A merger might take place in order to create a national or international practice. A law firm merger may also occur in order to save what's left of the practice when it is financially weak or if key partners have left or are retiring. Law firm mergers can be complicated for a number of reasons, including conflict of interest problems (if the firms are representing different parties in a legal action), law office culture differences, staffing issues, financial resources, client satisfaction, computer compatibility, political power struggles, and other issues. Nonetheless, they occur regularly among private law practices throughout the United States.

Geographic Service Areas

In years past, a law firm operated in a single location, and the office typically attracted clients within a limited geographic area around that location. That model no longer works in the current legal marketplace. The Internet, sophisticated computer networks that can tie offices together from across the country or around the world, and large, multi-office law firms have changed that paradigm. Many law firms have developed a geographic strategy regarding business expansion and how they define where and what their marketplace and client base will be. Geographic service strategies include local, statewide, regional/multistate, national, international, and industry specific. When considering law practices, size is just one factor; it is also important to take geographic and business strategy into account, along with where they see themselves going in the short and long terms. Geographic and business strategies are also important in that they play a significant part in how firms are managed and operated, and these issues can cause a great deal of disagreement and problems between the owners of a firm who may not see eye to eye on these issues.

Law Practice Organization Structures

Law practices have different organization or management structures. Private law practices are managed by a powerful managing partner, by all partners, or by committees. Corporate and government law practices have either a centralized or decentralized management structure.

Legal Forms of Private Law Firms

Management structures of law firms are affected by the firm's legal status. A law firm can be formed as a sole proprietorship, partnership, corporation, or, in some states, a limited liability company. Before the management structure of law offices can be considered, the legal status of those law offices must be explained.

Sole Proprietorship   In a sole proprietorship, the proprietor, in this case an attorney, runs the business, receives all profits, and is personally responsible for all losses and liabilities of the law office. However, a sole proprietorship is a distinct type of legal structure, and a sole practitioner does not have to use the sole proprietorship form; many sole practitioners are incorporated.

Partnership   The partnership's legal structure allows two or more attorneys to associate themselves together and to share in the profits or losses of the business. Many group practices use this structure. When a law office is established as a partnership, the founding attorneys are usually named as partners. As growth takes place, the partnership may hire additional associate attorneys.

All the partners are jointly and severally liable for the actions of the firm. This means if one partner commits malpractice and injures a client, each partner may be held individually or jointly responsible. Partners are also personally liable for the debts of the partnership. Partnerships typically use committees to make policy decisions, and partners meet regularly to discuss partnership business.

Professional Corporation   The professional corporation allows a single shareholder or a group of shareholders from the same profession, such as attorneys, to join together to share in the outcomes of a business. When a law office is established as a professional corporation, the founding attorney or attorneys receive shares in the business. As in a partnership, associates are not owners and are only paid a salary. Shareholders can vote to offer additional shares of the business to associates and expand the ownership of the law firm. All attorneys are employees of the corporation and are paid a salary. Besides a salary, shareholders are also paid a dividend. The amount of the dividend depends on the profitability of the corporation and on the number of shares owned. Shareholders are not personally responsible for the debts of the professional corporation. The corporate form requires the election of officers and a board of directors.

Limited Liability Company   The limited liability company (LLC) is a hybrid form of legal structure; it is a combination of the corporate and partnership forms. The LLC form of structure is valid in many states. The main advantage of an LLC is that it allows for limited personal liability of company debts for its owners (like a corporation) but is treated like a partnership for income tax purposes.

Private Law Firm Management Structures

The type of management or governing structure used to manage the business aspect of the firm is the choice of the firm itself, but the legal structure of the business may dictate some of that management structure. For example, a corporation—by law—must have a board of directors. Many law practices struggle with the problem of determining who runs the firm and who has the final say on firm decisions. Possible management structures include one powerful managing partner, rule by all partners/shareholders, and rule by management committee or board.

The Powerful Managing Partner In a **powerful managing partner** management structure, a single partner manages the firm. The managing partner is responsible for day-to-day operations of the partnership, while partners vote on major firm decisions (see Exhibit 1-8). The managing partner may have a specific term of office. In some firms, the position is rotated among the practicing partners. In many firms, the managing partner spends anywhere from 60% to 100% of his or her time on management responsibilities. This form allows other partners to spend more time practicing law, but it places the managerial duties on one partner and reduces the managing partner's time to practice law. The powerful managing partner structure is autocratic: power rests with only one person. In some cases, the other partners may feel that they are without a voice in the management of the firm.

The strong managing partner structure works well in small- to medium-sized law practices where the managing partner is well regarded and well liked; makes sound business decisions so that the firm is profitable and stable; is an effective delegator, leader, and manager; and where the practice is not expanding rapidly. One benefit of this structure is that decisions are made relatively quickly and decisively because the power principally lies with one person. The managing partner structure tends to break down, however, when the managing partner makes an unpopular decision, when there is not enough partner oversight to satisfy the other partners, when the firm is not profitable, or where there is substantial conflict or questions about the direction of the firm.

powerful managing partner
A management structure in which a single partner is responsible for managing the firm.

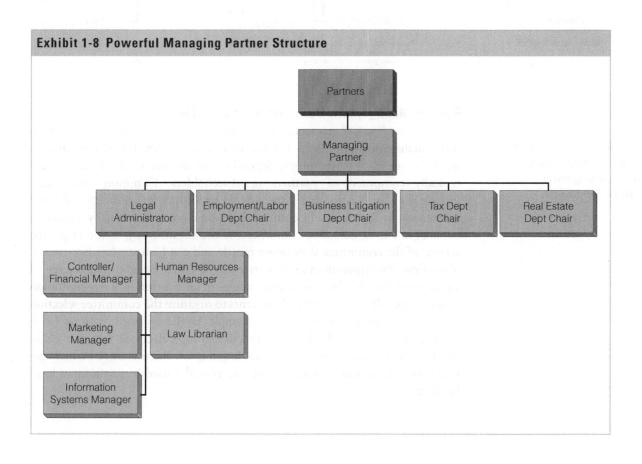

Exhibit 1-8 Powerful Managing Partner Structure

rule by all partners/ shareholders

A management structure in which all partners/ shareholders are included in decisions that affect the firm.

Rule by all Partners/Shareholders Rule by all partners/shareholders is a management structure in which all partners/shareholders make decisions that affect the firm (see Exhibit 1-9). All the partners or shareholders meet whenever management policies or decisions need to be made. This is a democratic structure, since all the partners have a say in firm decisions and policies. Although this structure allows partners'/shareholders' involvement in all decisions of the firm, as the number of partners/shareholders increases, the effectiveness of the group may decrease; a larger group may foster indecision and a lack of direction.

Exhibit 1-9 Rule by All Partners/Shareholders

rule by management committee/board

Management structure that uses a committee structure to make management decisions for the firm.

Rule by Management Committee/Board The **rule by management committee/board** management structure uses a committee structure to make management decisions for the firm (see Exhibit 1-10). Committees are made up of 5–10 members, depending on the size of the firm, and are typically composed of partners or shareholders. Common committees include the library committee, automation or technology committee, finance committee, and personnel committee. These committees usually report to a management or executive committee. If the committee gets too large, the actions of the committee slow down greatly and can hamper the effectiveness of the firm. Participation in a committee can be simply based on the interest of a partner or shareholder, a seniority system, or an election or a representation system, depending on how the firm wants to organize the committee selection process. A representation system, for example, is where a practice group (such as an employment and labor law practice group) elects or selects a chair, and that chair then represents the whole group on the executive or management committee. Committee systems are typically used in medium to large law firms.

Exhibit 1-10 Rule by Management Committee Structure

Corporate, Government, and Legal Aid Organization Structures

Corporate and government law practices have different organizational and management structures than private law firms. Corporate law departments can be centralized or decentralized. In the past, many—but not all—were centralized, meaning they were usually located in the firm's corporate headquarters but provided legal services to the whole company. Many government practices take a decentralized approach; most state and federal agencies have their own legal departments that provide legal services only to that particular agency. Like most private law firms, corporate and government practices can have different divisions within the practice, such as litigation or labor law. Although many corporate departments are centralized and many government practices are decentralized, the choice depends on the type, size, and dynamics of the organization.

The management structure of corporate and government practices is dependent upon the corporation's or agency's own organizational structure as well. Many corporate and government departments have a general counsel responsible for the overall management of the department (see Exhibit 1-10). The power of the general counsel is similar to that of the powerful managing partner in private law firms. However, the power is diluted, since the general counsel must still act under the auspices of the overall corporate structure or of the legislative or other public body in the government practice.

Legal services practices, because they are usually nonprofit corporations, are overseen by a board of directors (see Exhibit 1-11). The board of directors might be made up of law professors, attorneys in private practice, judges, and other interested persons. The board usually hires an executive director who is responsible for the day-to-day operations of the practice. The executive director has attorneys, paralegals, clerical staff, and administrators who report to him or her.

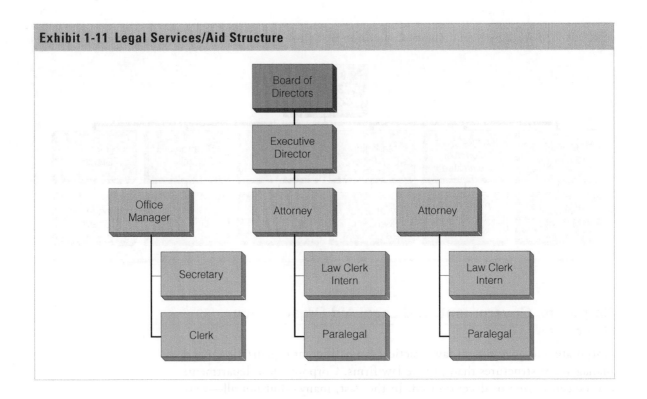

Exhibit 1-11 Legal Services/Aid Structure

Summary

Many people make up a law office legal team, including attorneys, administrators, paralegals/legal assistants, law librarians, legal secretaries, and clerks, among others. An attorney is a licensed professional who counsels clients regarding their legal rights. A partner or shareholder is an attorney-owner in a private law practice. A managing partner is an attorney who runs the firm in some law practices. An associate attorney is a paid employee of the law firm who does not, however, share in the profits of the business. An "of counsel" attorney is a lawyer who is affiliated with a law practice in some way, such as being semiretired, or who is paid by the firm on a per-job basis.

A legal administrator is responsible for a certain type of law office administrative system, such as general management, human resources, finance and accounting, marketing, or computer systems. Legal administrators typically have degrees in business or related fields.

Paralegals/legal assistants are a unique group of persons who assist attorneys in the delivery of legal services. They have knowledge and expertise regarding the legal system and substantive and procedural law that qualifies them to do work of a legal nature under the supervision of an attorney. The Department of Labor has consistently found that paralegals/legal assistants are nonexempt under the Fair Labor Standards Act and are thus entitled to overtime pay (one-and-one-half times their normal rate) for work in excess of 40 hours per week.

Law librarians conduct legal research, acquire and preserve library materials, advise attorneys and legal assistants on research strategies, classify and index materials, and maintain the law firm library.

Law practices include corporate law departments, government practices, legal service/aid practices, and private law firms. Corporate legal departments are found in large corporations and are usually headed up by a general counsel, the attorney responsible for the in-house legal services provided to the company.

Government law practices include attorneys who work in local, state, and federal agencies, as well as in state attorney general offices, and criminal prosecutors who work in all levels of government, among others.

Legal services/aid offices provide legal services to disadvantaged persons who otherwise could not afford it. Legal services/aid offices are nonprofit organizations and are funded by government and private donations.

Most attorneys practice in private law offices; approximately 30% of all attorneys are sole practitioners who own and manage their own law practices. Law firms come in all sizes, including small firms with fewer than 20 attorneys, medium-sized firms with 20–75 attorneys, and large firms with 75 to as many as 1000 attorneys. Many practices distinguish themselves either as plaintiff or defense firms, and law firm mergers are commonplace in the U.S. legal market. Through business strategy and technology, law firms can have different geographic service areas, including clients who are local, statewide, regional/multistate, national, international, or industry specific.

Law firms can take different legal forms, including a sole proprietorship, partnership, professional corporation, or limited liability company. Law firms can also use different governance structures, including a powerful managing partner structure, ruled by all partners/shareholders, or ruled by management committee.

Key Terms

associate attorney	legal services office
attorneys	legal team
boutique firm	limited license legal technician
clerks	managing partner
contract attorney	non-equity partner
exempt	nonexempt
expert witness	"of counsel"
Fair Labor Standards Act (FLSA)	office manager
freelance or contract paralegals	paralegal manager
general counsel	Paralegals
independent legal assistant or legal technician	partner or shareholder
	powerful managing partner
law clerk	rule by all partners/shareholders
law librarian	rule by management committee/ board
legal administrators	
legal secretaries	staff attorney

Practical Applications

1. Compare and contrast ***Missouri v. Jenkins***, 491 U.S. 274, 109 S.Ct. 2463, 105 L.Ed. 2d 229 (1989) and ***Role Models American, Inc. v. Brownlee,*** 353 F.3d 962 (C.A.D.C., 2004), which allowed recovery of paralegal fees, with ***Joerger v. Gordon Food Service, Inc.***, 224 Mich.App. 167, 568 N.W.2d 365 (Mich.App., June 13, 1997), which did not allow recovery.

2. Paralegal/Legal Assistants—Exempt or Nonexempt under the Fair Labor Standards Act: Research and write an in-depth report regarding the question of whether paralegals/legal assistants are exempt or nonexempt under the Fair Labor Standards Act (FLSA). Your report should, at a minimum, include answers to the following questions.

   - What is the FLSA?
   - What is the difference between an exempt and a nonexempt employee?
   - What are the so-called white-collar exemptions to the FLSA?
   - What is the position of the U.S. Department of Labor regarding the exemption status of legal assistants under the law, and why?
   - What positions do the national paralegal/legal assistant associations take on the matter?
   - What is your opinion regarding this matter?

There is a tremendous amount of information on the Fair Labor Standards Act. Starting points for research on this subject include the National Association of Legal Assistants https://nala.org/ the National Federal of Paralegal Associations [http://www.paralegals.org], the United States Department of Labor FLSA compliance page https://www.dol.gov/agencies/whd/industry-resources and the U.S. Department of Labor FLSA Opinion Letters [http://www.dol.gov/whd/opinion/opinion.htm] (see January 7, 2005, FLSA2005-9). If you have access to Westlaw, LexisNexis, or case law, you may also find these resources helpful in researching this issue.

3. Interview two legal professionals in your area. Find out about their jobs and the firms that they practice in, such as how many attorneys each firm has, what practice areas they specialize in, what types of jobs/positions are included in their "legal team," whether or not they use paralegals in their practice (and if so, what tasks the paralegal perform), what is the legal structure of the firm (e.g., partnership, professional corporation, etc.), how the firm is managed, and what type of clients the firms serve or target. Prepare a report regarding your findings.

On the Web Exercises

1. **Law Firm Web Sites** In this exercise, you will find three law firm Web sites on the Internet, review them, and research information about the firms. Start your research by going to http://lawyers.findlaw.com or to www.findlaw.com and clicking on the "Find Lawyers" button. Click on "Law Firms" and then select any city or state you would like. You do not need to select a specialty. Then, click "Search." Alternatively, you can use any general search engine, such as http://www.google.com or http://www.yahoo.com, to search for law firms. Try to find three law firms, such as a solo practitioner, a small- to medium-size firm (2–75 lawyers), and a large law firm (75 or more attorneys). View the "Profile" on Findlaw, go to the firm's Web site, and complete the table below or enter the table into a word processor. If you have difficulty finding large law firms, try using a general search engine to search for "large law firm."

Question	Law Firm 1	Law Firm 2	Law Firm 3
Web address			
Law firm name			
What is the total approximate number of attorneys in the entire firm?			
What is the total number of offices the firm has?			
What is the geographic service area for the firm (local, state, regional, national, or international)?			
What is the number of practice areas the firm has?			
List a few of the main practice areas in which the firm specializes.			
What is the firm's legal structure (if listed) (e.g., sole proprietorship, partnership, professional corporation [PC], or limited liability company [LLC])?			
What kind of attorneys does the firm have ("of counsel," partner, associate, etc.)?			
In addition to marketing information, does the site contain resources, articles, or other information clients or members of the public might find helpful?			

2. **Legal Service/Aid Offices** In this exercise, you will find a legal services/aid office near you. Start by going to http://www.lsc.gov and clicking on the map of the United States. Click on your state and find the closest legal services offices. Go to the office's Web site, if there is a link to it. Alternatively, you can use a general search engine to search for "(state name) legal services aid office." Refer to the office's Web site to learn about their mission, the total number of attorneys, what kind of matters the office handles, the funding level of the office, and other general information. Type a one-page summary of what you found.

Case Review

In the Matter of a Member of the State Bar of Arizona, JEFFREY PHILLIPS, Attorney No. 13362, 244 P.3d 549 (2010)

244 P.3d 549 (2010)

(Cite as: 244 P.3d 549)

Supreme Court of Arizona

In the Matter of a Member of the State Bar of Arizona, JEFFREY PHILLIPS, Attorney No. 13362

No. SB-10-0036-D

December 16, 2010, Decided

PELANDER, Justice

P1 We granted review in this attorney disciplinary case to determine whether the Hearing Officer erroneously used a vicarious liability standard in finding that Petitioner Jeffrey Phillips violated Arizona Rules of Professional Conduct ("ERs") 5.1(a) and 5.3(a), and whether the recommended suspension of six months and one day was appropriate. Although we accept the Hearing Officer's determination that Phillips violated ERs 5.1(a) and 5.3(a), we reduce the suspension to six months.

I. Facts and Procedural Background

P2 Phillips is the founder and managing attorney of Phillips & Associates ("P&A"), a large law firm based in Phoenix. A self-styled "consumer law firm," P&A handles a high volume of cases, having represented approximately 33,000 clients between 2004 and 2006. At the time of the disciplinary proceedings, P&A employed 250 people, including thirty-eight lawyers. The firm's practice was limited to criminal defense, bankruptcy, and personal injury.

P3 Phillips no longer represents clients, but instead supervises and manages the firm. His duties include setting firm policy on billing, accounting, and intake procedures. Although Phillips has general control over the firm, during the relevant period he had delegated primary responsibility for the criminal division to Robert Arentz, and for the bankruptcy division to Robert Teague.

P4 In 2002, Phillips was the subject of disciplinary proceedings resulting in his conditionally admitting to violations of ERs 5.1, 5.3, and 7.1, and agreeing to a censure and two-years' probation. The judgment and order entered in 2002 included detailed probationary terms relating to the management of P&A. Those terms required specific changes to P&A's intake procedures, accounting procedures, and ethics training. Among other things, the 2002 order required the following:

> Prior to entering into a written attorney/client agreement for the firm, an Arizona licensed attorney must speak with the client and approve the legal fees to be charged and retention of the Firm [sic] by the client.
>
> …
>
> Bonuses paid to intake personnel cannot be based exclusively on either the number of clients who retain the firm or on the amount of fees received from those clients. The criteria for determining bonuses must be provided to the intake personnel in writing.
>
> …
>
> All attorneys and other billable staff members who work on criminal cases shall keep contemporaneous time records to enable the firm to conduct a "backward glance" at the conclusion of a case in order to determine whether a refund is due.
>
> …
>
> The firm shall provide a written accounting of time spent and fees incurred within 15 days of a request by a client. When a client terminates the firm's representation in a criminal case and the firm has been permitted to withdraw by the court, the firm shall, within fifteen (15) days following receipt of the Order permitting withdrawal, provide to the client a written accounting of the time spent, fees incurred, and when appropriate, a refund of unearned fees.

Phillips successfully completed his probation in 2004.

P5 Between August 2006 and May 2008, the Bar issued a series of probable cause orders against Phillips and Arentz. The Bar filed a formal complaint against them in October 2007 and, after several amendments, ultimately charged twenty-two counts, alleging violations of ERs 1.1, 1.2, 1.3, 1.4, 5.1, 5.3, 7.1, and 8.4.

P6 A hearing was held over eleven days in 2008. The Hearing Officer heard testimony from many witnesses, including former P&A clients, current and former P&A attorneys, and experts for both Phillips and the Bar.

P7 In detailed findings of fact, conclusions of law, and recommendations, the Hearing Officer found that Phillips had violated ERs 5.1(a), 5.3(a) and 7.1, and Arentz had violated ERs 5.1(a) and (b), 5.3(a) and (b), and 1.5(a). Phillips had a total of twelve. The Hearing Officer found that all the clients involved in the matters giving rise to the allegations were unsophisticated. He recommended that Arentz be suspended for sixty days, and that Phillips be suspended for six months and one day. The Hearing Officer also recommended that Phillips and Arentz be placed on two years' probation upon reinstatement.

P8 The Hearing Officer's findings regarding Phillips's ethical violations can be generally categorized as follows:

A. Caseloads of Bankruptcy Attorneys

P9 The Hearing Officer found that Phillips violated ER 5.1(a) as alleged in Counts 3 and 4, which related to the caseloads of P&A's bankruptcy attorneys, each of whom carried as many as 500 cases at a time. A former P&A attorney testified that, upon joining the firm, she was immediately responsible for 540 cases. Counts 3 and 4 involved circumstances in which clients' needs were not met because of the high volume of cases assigned to bankruptcy attorneys. In both counts, the Hearing Officer also found that, because of the number of attorneys handling a given case, inadequate attention was paid to the problems presented in the case and the client was confused and not adequately informed.

P10 Count 3 specifically involved a breakdown in communication between the attorney and the client, missed hearings by the attorney, and a failure to keep the client reasonably informed. Count 4 involved P&A's practice of having one attorney handle all of the firm's "341 meetings," which are short, informal meetings that debtors are required to attend after filing a bankruptcy petition under Chapter 7 or Chapter 13 of the federal Bankruptcy Code. The P&A attorney handled forty files per day and at times would have six to seven 341 meeting within thirty minutes. Count 4 included a client's complaint that a P&A attorney had missed a 341 meeting and failed to act with reasonable diligence. The Hearing Officer concluded that Phillips violated ER 5.1(a) in both counts for establishing and maintaining a business model in which such ethical violations were likely to occur.

B. Intake and Retention Procedures

P11 Another category of violations related to P&A's intake and retention procedures. Prospective clients who visit the firm's offices do not immediately meet with an attorney. Instead, they are provided a blank fee agreement and a general questionnaire. After completing the questionnaire, the prospective client meets with a P&A legal administrator, a nonlawyer tasked with retaining clients. Legal administrators are paid a base salary and monthly bonuses, based, in part, on the number of cases that the legal administrator retains. After obtaining general information from the client, the legal administrator meets with a lawyer who sets the fee. After the fee agreement is prepared, the client speaks with a lawyer to make sure the client understands the fee agreement, who the lawyer will be, and the scope of P&A's representation. The Hearing Officer found that this process, known as "closing," was often not completed by an attorney knowledgeable in the relevant practice area.

P12 On Counts 9, 12, and 17, the Hearing Officer found P&A's retention policies, as implemented, impeded potential clients from obtaining the information needed to make informed decisions about retention. With respect to Counts 9 and 12, the Hearing Officer found that a P&A legal administrator gave a client's family member unreasonable expectations about the representation, suggesting that the firm would be able to reduce the client's sentence in criminal proceedings.

P13 In Count 9, the client's father was told that the firm should be able to reduce his son's sentence. An attorney signed a fee agreement describing the scope of the services as "mitigation of sentencing." The client, however, had already entered into a plea agreement with a stipulated sentence, and no one at P&A advised the client or his father of the unlikelihood of mitigating the sentence. Despite the client's expectations, the client's sentence was not reduced.

P14 In Count 12, a client's mother signed a fee agreement after being told by a legal representative that the firm should be able to help reduce her son's sentence. As the firm was aware, however, the client had already stipulated to a particular sentence. The client's mother met with a bankruptcy attorney, who did not know what a stipulated plea agreement was. A criminal attorney did not meet with her until the day of sentencing, when she was informed that her son would receive the sentence stipulated in the plea agreement.

P15 The Hearing Officer found that Phillips and Arentz violated ERs 5.1(a) and 5.3(a) in both counts because the firm's retention practices did not require a knowledgeable attorney to speak with the potential client before entering into a fee agreement, and the firm used nonlawyers in its retention process. Similarly, in Count 17, a client with a suspended driver's license met only with a bankruptcy attorney and a legal administrator before hiring P&A to represent him. The client wanted to have his license reinstated but also had an unadjudicated DUI charge. The scope of services set forth in the fee agreement did not match the client's expectations. The firm did not follow the client's decisions regarding the scope of the representation, and the firm waited weeks before telling the client his driver's license could not be reinstated until the DUI charge was resolved. The firm also failed to inform the client prior to retention that the firm could not accomplish his goals. The Hearing Officer found that both Phillips and Arentz violated ER 5.1(a).

C. Conduct by Legal Administrators

P16 The Hearing Officer also found violations of ER 5.3 arising from P&A's providing legal administrators with bonuses based, in part, on the number of clients retained. Count 8 involved a legal administrator who used "high pressure tactics" to attempt to dissuade a client from terminating P&A's representation. Count 19 involved a client who retained the firm for defense of a DUI charge and, as the firm was aware, was also in the process of becoming a United States citizen. When the client asked to terminate P&A's representation after meeting with a legal administrator and a bankruptcy attorney, the client was subjected to intimidation and false statements from a P&A employee. At one point, the employee warned the client that he was "looking to lose his citizenship," and the employee insinuated that if the client stopped payment on the retainer check, the firm could have the police investigate his immigration status. After making several unsuccessful attempts to obtain documents he had furnished to P&A, the client was only able to recover the papers after hiring new counsel.

P17 Although the P&A employees' tactics violated P&A's policies, the Hearing Officer concluded that Phillips and Arentz violated ER 5.3(a) in both counts because legal administrators' bonuses were tied, in part, to client retention. These incentives provided "the motive for the misconduct." The words in the firm's policy manual prohibiting such conduct were insufficient to insulate managers and supervisors from ethical responsibility when the actual ongoing practices were to the contrary.

D. Refund Policy

P18 In Count 11, the Hearing Officer found that P&A employees failed to act promptly on a client's termination request. The firm took more than five months to refund money to the client despite repeated requests for a refund. The Hearing Officer found that both Arentz and Phillips violated ERs 5.1(a) and 5.3(a) for failing to have practices in place to prevent difficulty in obtaining a refund. [1]

FN1. The Hearing Officer also found (in Count 20) that Phillips negligently violated ER 7.1 by writing and using a materially misleading television advertisement in 2007 regarding P&A's DUI defense services and a new DUI law. But the Hearing Officer found that violation did not "warrant significant discipline" because it was neither knowing nor actually injurious; rather, his recommended sanction was based solely on Phillips's knowing violations of ERs 5.1(a) and 5.3(a).

E. Disciplinary Commission Decision

P19 On review, pursuant to Rule 58, Arizona Rules of the Supreme Court, the Disciplinary Commission considered the parties' objections to the Hearing Officer's decision and held oral argument. In December 2009, by a vote of 6-2, the Commission adopted the Hearing Officer's findings of fact, conclusions of law, and recommendations. The two dissenting Commission members found no basis for disturbing the Hearing Officer's factual findings but concluded that "the recommended discipline is too severe" and that lesser sanctions were appropriate - suspensions of thirty days for Arentz and ninety days for Phillips.

P20 Phillips and Arentz jointly petitioned for review. This Court granted review on only two discrete issues Phillips raised: whether the Hearing Officer erroneously applied a vicarious liability standard in finding ethical violations by Phillips, and whether the recommended sanction for him is appropriate. We denied review of any issues raised by Arentz, thereby leaving undisturbed his sixty-day suspension. The Bar did not file a cross-petition for review to challenge the recommended sanction for Arentz. We therefore limit our discussion to the two issues regarding Phillips on which review was granted.

II. Managerial and Supervisory Liability

P21 Phillips first argues that the Hearing Officer used an improper standard of vicarious liability in finding violations of ERs 5.1(a) and 5.3(a) because his analysis was based solely on the ethical breaches of other firm employees. We disagree.

P22 HN1Go to this Headnote in the case. Ethical Rule 5.1(a) provides that a partner or an attorney with comparable managerial authority "shall make reasonable efforts to ensure that the firm has in effect measures giving reasonable assurance that all lawyers in the firm conform to the Rules of Professional Conduct." Similarly, ER 5.3(a) provides that a partner or a lawyer with comparable managerial authority must make "reasonable efforts to ensure that the firm has in effect measures giving reasonable assurances that" nonlawyers employed by the firm or associated with the lawyer comply with the professional obligations of the lawyer.

P23 These duties require not only supervision, but also that the supervising attorney establish "internal policies and procedures" providing reasonable assurances that lawyers and nonlawyers in the firm conform to the Rules of Professional Conduct. ERs 5.1 cmt. 2; 5.3 cmt. 2. The size of the firm is relevant in determining what is "reasonable," and in a large firm such as P&A, "more elaborate measures may be necessary." ER 5.1 cmt. 3.

P24 HN2 Go to this Headnote in the case. The rules imposing managerial and supervisory obligations, however, do not provide for vicarious liability for a subordinate's acts; rather, they "mandate an independent duty of supervision." In re Galbasini, 163 Ariz. 120, 124, 786 P.2d 971, 975 (1990). Nor is a supervising attorney of a nonlawyer assistant "required to guarantee that that assistant will never engage in conduct that is not compatible with the professional obligations of the lawyer." In re Miller, 178 Ariz. 257, 259, 872 P.2d 661, 663 (1994).

P25 The Hearing Officer expressly recognized these legal principles in his decision and did not apply an incorrect vicarious liability standard when finding that Phillips violated ERs 5.1(a) and 5.3(a). Although he found on many of the counts that P&A attorneys' and staff members' conduct violated various ethical rules, the supervisory and managerial breaches for which Phillips was found liable under ER 5.1 or 5.3 were independent. For each violation of ER 5.1 or 5.3, the Hearing Officer found that Phillips had personally failed to engage in the required supervision of either lawyers or nonlawyer personnel.

Indeed, on a number of counts (for example, Counts 5 and 6), the Hearing Officer found that someone at P&A had violated an ethical rule, but that Phillips had not personally violated the rules requiring supervision. Had the Hearing Officer or the Commission applied a vicarious liability standard, Phillips would have been held liable for those violations as well.

P26 In contesting the findings that he violated ERs 5.1(a) and 5.3(a), Phillips refers to the "mountain of undisputed evidence" adduced at the hearing of P&A's supervisory efforts and the "relatively rare" occurrence of ethical breaches by other P&A employees. But the prior modification of firm policies, made pursuant to the 2002 judgment and order, did not alleviate Phillips's ongoing duty to ensure that his subordinates complied with the revised policies and ethical rules. Because the Hearing Officer clearly understood and correctly applied the law by carefully not conflating vicarious liability with managerial and supervisory liability, we find no error in his determination, adopted by the Disciplinary Commission, that Phillips violated ERs 5.1(a) and 5.3(a).

III. Sanction

P27 We next address Phillips's argument that the recommended six-months and one-day suspension was disproportionate and excessive. HN3Go to this Headnote in the case. We review recommended sanctions de novo. In re White-Steiner, 219 Ariz. 323, 327 ¶ 25, 198 P.3d 1195, 1199 (2009). Although we independently review a recommended sanction, we give "serious consideration to the findings and recommendations" of the Commission. In re Pappas, 159 Ariz. 516, 518, 768 P.2d 1161, 1163 (1988) (citing In re Neville, 147 Ariz. 106, 108, 708 P.2d 1297, 1299 (1985)).

P28 HN4Go to this Headnote in the case. "Attorney discipline serves to protect the public, the legal profession, and the legal system, and to deter other attorneys from engaging in unprofessional conduct." In re White-Steiner, 219 Ariz. at 325 ¶ 9, 198 P.3d at 1197 (citing In re Scholl, 200 Ariz. 222, 227 ¶ 29, 25 P.3d 710, 715 (2001)). Another purpose is to instill public confidence in the Bar's integrity. In re Horwitz, 180 Ariz. 20, 29, 881 P.2d 352, 361 (1994) (citing In re Loftus, 171 Ariz. 672, 675, 832 P.2d 689, 692 (1992)).

P29 HN5Go to this Headnote in the case. In determining sanctions, we are guided by the American Bar Association's Standards for Imposing Lawyer Sanctions (2005). In re Van Dox, 214 Ariz. 300, 303 ¶ 11, 152 P.3d 1183, 1186 (2007). Several factors are relevant in determining the appropriate sanction: (1) the duty violated, (2) the lawyer's mental state, (3) the potential or actual injury caused by the lawyer's conduct, and (4) the existence of aggravating or mitigating factors. Id. (citing ABA Standard 3.0). We may also consider any similar cases to assess what sanctions are proportionate to the unethical conduct. Id. at 307 ¶ 39, 152 P.3d at 1190.

A. Duty Violated

P30 HN6Go to this Headnote in the case. ABA Standard 7.0 provides sanctions for violations of duties owed as a professional. The Hearing Officer and the Commission concluded that ABA Standard 7.0

governed this case because the violations of ERs 5.1 and 5.3 involved duties owed to the legal profession. Although these violations also implicate duties owed to the client, ABA Standard 7.0 will guide our analysis because we find no error on this point and because Phillips does not challenge the applicability of that standard. See In re Lenaburg, 177 Ariz. 20, 23, 864 P.2d 1052, 1055 (1993) (applying ABA Standard 7.0 to supervisory violations); In re Rice, 173 Ariz. 376, 377, 843 P.2d 1268, 1269 (1992) (same).

B. Mental State

P31 HN7Go to this Headnote in the case. A lawyer's mental state affects the appropriate sanction for ethical violations. Intentional or knowing conduct is sanctioned more severely than negligent conduct because it threatens more harm. In re White-Steiner, 219 Ariz. at 325 ¶ 13, 198 P.3d at 1197.

P32 HN8Go to this Headnote in the case. ABA Standard 7.0 provides the following guidelines with regard to sanctions:

7.1 Disbarment is generally appropriate when a lawyer knowingly engages in conduct that is a violation of a duty owed as a professional with the intent to obtain a benefit for the lawyer or another, and causes serious or potentially serious injury to a client, the public, or the legal system.

7.2 Suspension is generally appropriate when a lawyer knowingly engages in conduct that is a violation of a duty owed as a professional and causes injury or potential injury to a client, the public, or the legal system.

7.3 Reprimand is generally appropriate when a lawyer negligently engages in conduct that is a violation of a duty owed as a professional and causes injury or potential injury to a client, the public, or the legal system.

P33 The Hearing Officer expressly found that both Phillips's and Arentz's violations of ERs 5.1 and 5.3 were "knowing." Although Phillips challenged that finding in his petition for review, we did not grant review of that issue and, therefore, accept as established that Phillips knowingly violated ERs 5.1(a) and 5.3(a).

C. Actual or Potential Injury

P34 The Hearing Officer found actual injury in each of the client-related counts. P&A clients were misled and improperly advised by unqualified lawyers, had difficulty obtaining refunds, and were misinformed about the reasonable objectives of the representation. Clients were also financially harmed, having paid unreasonable fees or retainers without a full understanding of the likely results of the representation. The record supports these findings.

D. Aggravating and Mitigating Factors

P35 Because Phillips's knowing conduct caused actual injury to clients, we agree with the Hearing Officer that the presumptive sanction in this case is suspension. See ABA Standard 7.2. The Hearing Officer and the Commission found the following aggravating and mitigating factors apply to Phillips:

Aggravating Factors:

1. Prior disciplinary offense
2. Selfish motive
3. Multiple offenses
4. Refusal to acknowledge wrongful nature of conduct
5. Vulnerability of victim
6. Substantial experience in the practice of law

Mitigating Factors:

1. Full and free disclosure to the Bar
2. Delay in disciplinary proceedings
3. Willingness to remedy practice
4. Character

P36 We find none of these findings clearly erroneous. And we agree with the Hearing Officer that the aggravating and mitigating factors, in conjunction with Phillips's knowing misconduct, further support suspension as an appropriate sanction. See In re Galbasini, 163 Ariz. at 121, 125-26, 786 P.2d at 972, 976-77 (adopting recommended six-month suspension of attorney for knowingly failing to supervise nonlawyer employees who engaged in debt collection and improperly solicited clients in attorney's name); Davis & Goldberg v. Ala. State Bar, 676 So. 2d 306, 307-08 (Ala. 1996) (upholding two-month suspension of two partners for implementing policies designed to minimize expenses and maximize profits, to clients' detriment, when firm's practices resulted in unmanageable caseloads and permitted non-lawyers to perform legal services); Att'y Grievance Comm'n of Md. v. Kimmel, 405 Md. 647, 955 A.2d 269, 292-94 (Md. 2008) (holding that violations of ethical rules requiring adequate supervision warranted a ninety-day suspension when attorneys had no prior disciplinary record).

E. Proportionality Review

P37 HN9Go to this Headnote in the case. We may consider the sanctions imposed in similar cases "to preserve some degree of proportionality, ensure that the sanction fits the offense, and avoid discipline by whim or caprice." In re Dean, 212 Ariz. 221, 225 ¶ 24, 129 P.3d 943, 947 (2006) (quoting In re Struthers, 179 Ariz. 216, 226, 877 P.2d 789, 799 (1994)). The Hearing Officer cited two cases for comparison purposes, but they are distinguishable and not very helpful. [2] Nor have the parties cited any authorities that bear on whether the recommended length of suspension is appropriate here. Although we have sometimes engaged in comparative analysis, see In re Van Dox, 214 Ariz. at 307-08 ¶¶ 39-42, 152 P.3d at 1190-91, we agree with the Hearing Officer that this case, involving a "consumer law firm" and a high volume practice, is difficult to compare with others. In any event, "[proportionality review … is 'an imperfect process' that, as here, often provides little guidance. In re Dean, 212 Ariz. at 225 ¶ 24, 129 P.3d at 947 (quoting In re Owens, 182 Ariz. 121, 127, 893 P.2d 1284, 1290 (1995)).

FN2 See In re Lenaburg, 177 Ariz. at 24, 864 P.2d at 1056 (imposing public censure with probation on attorney who negligently violated ER 5.1, causing lack of communication with clients and failure to refund fees in four separate cases); In re Rice, 173 Ariz. at 377, 843 P.2d at 1269 (imposing censure and probation on attorney with no prior disciplinary record who negligently failed to adequately supervise staff during firm's rapid expansion, resulting in sloppy office procedures and mismanagement).

P38 In assessing the duration of Phillips's suspension, however, we must also consider internal proportionality, in particular the length of his suspension in relation to Arentz's. We considered internal proportionality in In re Dean, 212 Ariz. at 225 ¶ 25, 129 P.3d at 947. That case involved a romantic relationship between a prosecutor and a superior court judge. *Id*. at 221 ¶ 2, 129 P.3d at 943. We reduced from one year to six months the Commission's recommended suspension for the prosecutor in part because the judge had not been disciplined. *Id*. at 225 ¶ 25, 129 P.3d at 947. The prosecutor's ethical violations involved the same conduct as the judge's, and we concluded that a reduced sanction for the prosecutor was warranted to avoid a disparity in treatment. *Id*. Without minimizing the seriousness of the attorney's misconduct, we determined that "the interests of justice" required reconsideration of an otherwise suitable sanction. *Id*. Although the judge's immunity from lawyer discipline in that case had resulted inadvertently from this Court's prior action, see *Id*., the rationale employed there also applies here.

P39 In this case, the Hearing Officer found, and the Commission affirmed, that Arentz had a total of nineteen ethical violations (eighteen of which were found to be knowing), compared to Phillips's twelve violations (eleven of which were found to be knowing). The Hearing Officer consistently found that Arentz, but not Phillips, violated subsection (b) of ERs 5.1 and 5.3 based on Arentz's having had direct supervisory authority of P&A's criminal department. [3] Arentz was also directly involved in approving excessive fees, as alleged in Counts 8, 9, and 12, in violation of ER 1.5. In contrast, as the dissenting Commission members noted, the Hearing Officer did not find that Phillips had direct personal knowledge of any of the specific conduct giving rise to the allegations of ER 5.1 or 5.3 violations until after the conduct occurred. Yet Arentz received a suspension of only sixty days compared to Phillips's six-month and one-day suspension. Neither the Hearing Officer nor the Commission addressed or explained this disparity.

FN3. Ethical Rule 5.1(b) requires that a lawyer having direct supervisory authority over another lawyer make "reasonable efforts to ensure that the other lawyer conforms to the Rules of Professional Conduct." Similarly, ER 5.3(b) requires that a lawyer having direct supervisory authority over a nonlawyer make "reasonable efforts to ensure that the person's conduct is compatible with the professional obligations of the lawyer."

P40 Moreover, a six-month and one-day suspension is not actually completed in that time period.HN10Go to this Headnote in the case. Under Rule 65(a), Arizona Rules of the Supreme Court, any suspension exceeding six months requires the lawyer to go through formal reinstatement proceedings. That process extends the effective length of a suspension considerably. An applicant for formal reinstatement must provide an array of personal and financial information and prove by clear and convincing evidence his or her rehabilitation, compliance with all disciplinary orders and rules, fitness to practice, and competence. See Ariz. R. Sup. Ct. 65(a)-(b).

F. Appropriate Sanction

P41 Although Arentz had more violations than Phillips and was more directly involved in the underlying ethical violations of P&A employees in his department, we conclude Phillips's conduct and disciplinary history warrant a more severe sanction for him than Arentz received. Unlike Phillips, Arentz has no prior disciplinary record. We take Phillips's prior disciplinary record seriously, considering it involved the same type of supervisory shortcomings at issue here. HN11Go to this Headnote in the case. The goal of attorney discipline is to protect the public. In re Rivkind, 164 Ariz. 154, 157, 791 P.2d 1037, 1040 (1990). Neither the Hearing Officer nor the Commission erred in determining that the 2002 discipline did not adequately rehabilitate Phillips and was insufficient to protect P&A clients.

P42 We also recognize that Phillips, as managing partner of a law firm representing more than 10,000 clients per year, was in a position of greater supervisory authority than Arentz. Phillips, not Arentz, had full power and control over P&A's policies and practices. As such, he was better able to effect positive change and insist on full compliance with ethics standards. Conversely, Phillips's lapses in these areas might potentially cause greater harm. Phillips's apparent delegation of responsibility and hands-off approach does not make his policies any less of a danger. Indeed, the decisions he makes directly affect the public, the profession, and the integrity of the legal system.

P43 Although attorney partners and supervisors are not guarantors of their employees' conduct, they must take reasonable steps to ensure that firm practices, not merely policies, actually comply with ethical rules binding all lawyers practicing law in this state. Phillips's failure to do so, particularly in view of his disciplinary history, warrants a significant period of suspension followed by a lengthy probation term with strict conditions.

P44 A longer suspension for Phillips is therefore justified. But we do not believe that a sanction at least six times harsher than Arentz's is proportional in this case. [4] Rather, as the two dissenting Commission members observed when recommending a ninety-day suspension for Phillips, a lesser sanction against him would appropriately address the violations found here while deterring future misconduct and thereby protecting the public. We therefore reduce Phillips's suspension to six months. In doing so, we do not minimize the seriousness of Phillips's misconduct. But we believe a six-month suspension avoids an unjust disparity in treatment between him and Arentz.

FN4. Rule 64(e)(1), Arizona Rules of the Supreme Court, permits a lawyer who has been suspended for more than six months to apply for reinstatement no sooner than ninety days prior to the expiration of the suspension. Rule 65(b)(1), as amended this year and effective to reinstatement proceedings commencing after January 1, 2011, provides that a Bar hearing panel will hold a hearing within 150 days of the filing of the application. Within thirty days after completing the hearing, the hearing panel must file a report with this Court containing findings of facts and recommendations concerning the reinstatement. Ariz. R. Sup. Ct. 65(b)(3). The Court must "promptly" review the report and decide whether the applicant is qualified for reinstatement, a process that typically takes about two months. *Id.* at 65(b)(4). Thus, the reinstatement process for Phillips would, at the very least, last five to six months after his suspension is complete, effectively extending his suspension to a total of twelve months, six times longer than Arentz's suspension.

P45 The Hearing Officer and the Commission recommended that Phillips's two-year probation term and conditions of probation begin and take effect after Phillips's suspension is fully served. We accept that recommendation. Although Phillips is prohibited from practicing law or holding himself out as an active attorney during his suspension, he is permitted and strongly encouraged during that time to work with the Bar to immediately address the issues and rectify the problems that led to the violations of ERs 5.1 and 5.3 in this case. Otherwise, P&A would be left with many of its current problems and no immediate solution during Phillips's period of suspension.

P46 During the suspension, however, Phillips's name may not be used in firm advertisements, letterhead, or other communications. [5] Nor is Phillips entitled to receive any income generated by the firm during his suspension. [6]

FN5. See ERs 5.5(b)(2); 7.1; 7.5(a) and (d); see also State Bar of Ariz. Comm. on Rules of Prof'l Conduct, Formal Op. 02-07 (2002) (concluding that a law firm should not continue to use attorney's name in the firm name, letterhead, business cards, or stationary while the attorney is on disability inactive status, and noting that "a suspended partner's name must be dropped in all communications with the public"); Wash. State Bar Ass'n, Formal Op. 196 (2000) (prohibiting use of suspended lawyer's name in firm name or business communications).

FN6. See ER 5.4(a) [***29] ("A lawyer or law firm shall not share legal fees with a nonlawyer."); Disciplinary Counsel v. McCord, 121 Ohio St. 3d 497, 2009 Ohio 1517, 905 N.E.2d 1182, 1189 (Ohio 2009) (concluding that lawyer's receipt of attorney fees while suspended from practice of law was improper and actionable as ethics violation); Office of Disciplinary Counsel v. Jackson, 536 Pa. 26, 637 A.2d 615, 620 (Pa. 1994) (noting a suspended attorney is a "'non-lawyer' within the meaning of the rules"); Comm. on Prof'l Ethics, State Bar of Tex., Op. 592 (2010) (prohibiting a lawyer from sharing legal fees with suspended attorney); cf. West v. Jayne, 484 N.W.2d 186, 190-91 (Iowa 1992) (allowing lawyer in breach of contract action against fellow associate to collect portion of fee, but suggesting that attorney would not be entitled to fees for any work done after he was suspended from practice of law).

P47 In addition to reducing Phillips's suspension to six months, we remove from the Commission's recommended terms of probation term number 13, which would have permitted the Bar to send at random times unidentified "testers" to P&A to check the firm's compliance with required intake procedures. The Bar did not request that particular term and, at oral argument in this Court, acknowledged that it was not warranted. We adopt the Commission's probation terms in all other respects, as set forth in the appendix, as well as the restitution amounts it ordered.

IV. Conclusion

P48 For the foregoing reasons, we modify the recommended length of Phillips's suspension, but otherwise accept the Commission's recommendations. The probation terms and conditions prescribed by the Commission as set forth in the appendix to this opinion shall apply.

A. John Pelander, Justice

CONCURRING: Rebecca White Berch, Chief Justice
Andrew D. Hurwitz, Vice Chief Justice,
Jon W. Thompson, Judge*

*Pursuant to Article 6, Section 3 of the Arizona Constitution, the Honorable Jon W. Thompson, Judge of the Arizona Court of Appeals, Division One, was designated to sit on this matter.

Appendix

1. Phillips shall refrain from engaging in any conduct that would violate the Rules of Professional Conduct or other rules of the Supreme Court of Arizona.

2. Phillips shall contact the director of LOMAP within from the filing date of this opinion and shall schedule and submit to a LOMAP audit within forty-five (45) days thereafter. Following the audit, the director of LOMAP shall formulate and include recommendations based on the audit in a Probation Contract to be executed and implemented by Phillips. The director of LOMAP shall also monitor the terms of probation.

3. Before entering into any written attorney/client fee agreement for the firm, an Arizona licensed attorney must speak with the client and approve the legal fees to be charged and retention of the firm by the client. The attorney meeting with the potential client must be knowledgeable in the practice area, and issues that relate to the retention and retention decision must be discussed before a decision is made on the retention. Retention attorneys shall review all paperwork and ensure that appropriate information is given to the client even if the client lacks the sophistication or knowledge to ask the right questions.

4. Any nonlawyer personnel conducting initial consultations with clients must clearly and affirmatively identify themselves as nonlawyers to prospective clients.

5. Respondent shall ensure that nonlawyer staff shall not give legal advice to clients and shall not make predictions or guarantees as to the outcome of a case.

6. Standard intake forms including a standard fee agreement shall be utilized. The firm shall participate in fee arbitration whenever it is requested by the client and the firm has been unable to resolve the dispute directly with the client.

7. A standardized training manual for intake procedures shall be provided to each intake employee.

8. Pursuant to ER 5.3, Phillips or other attorneys with supervisory authority in the firm (over whom Phillips has direct control) will be responsible for compliance by all intake personnel and nonlawyer staff with applicable ethical rules.

9. When accepting payment of a client's fees in a form other than cash, the firm shall not accept payment without signed, written consent (which may be evidenced by a check, electronic signature, credit card authorization, or other writing) from the party making the payment.

10. A one-time ethics training program, not to exceed three (3) hours, shall be given to all administrative staff including intake and collection personnel. The program shall be provided by the director of LOMAP or designee, and shall be given at a time within the first six (6) months of the probationary terms and in a manner that does not disrupt the firm's practice. The program may be repeated or additional programs may be given during the probationary period if needed as determined by the director of LOMAP. The initial program shall be taped and shown to any new personnel hired during the probationary period.

11. A one-time Continuing Legal Education ethics program, not to exceed three (3) hours, shall be given to all attorneys employed by Phillips's firm. The program shall be provided by the director of LOMAP or designee, and shall be given at a time within the first six (6) months of the probationary period and in a manner that does not disrupt the firm's practice. The program may be repeated or additional programs may be given during the probationary period. The initial program shall be taped and shown to any new lawyers hired during the probationary period.

12. The firm shall utilize a fee review process, consistent with In re Swartz, 141 Ariz. 266, 686 P.2d 1236 (1984), and ER 1.5, at the conclusion of all cases in order to determine whether a refund is due. All attorneys and other billable staff members who work on criminal cases [8] shall keep contemporaneous time records to enable the firm to conduct a "backward glance" at the conclusion of a case in order to determine whether a refund is due.

    FN8. The record indicates that P&A has sold its criminal department. Assuming that P&A no longer offers services in criminal law, this term and others relating to P&A's criminal department no longer apply.

13. The firm shall provide a written accounting of time spent and fees incurred within fifteen (15) days of request by a client. When a client terminates the firm's representation in a criminal case and the firm has been permitted to withdraw by the court, the firm shall, within fifteen (15) days following receipt of the Order permitting withdrawal, provide to the client a written accounting of time spent, fees incurred, and when appropriate, a refund of any unearned fees.

14. If Phillips's firm uses client testimonials in advertisements, the client must acknowledge in writing that he or she is not receiving any money benefit (or the equivalent) for the appearance.

15. Phillips shall develop a system in which he is promptly advised of all client complaint(s) against the firm or lawyers employed by the firm, which implicate the provisions of ERs 5.1 and 5.3. Phillips shall document, in writing, his or the firm's response to each such complaint, and shall maintain a file of such complaints and responses.

16. Phillips shall make reasonable and good faith efforts to ensure compliance with these probation terms and shall respond directly or through his counsel to inquiries concerning the implementation and compliance with these probationary terms.

17. Before conducting a screening investigation into any new complaint(s) relating to practices covered by these terms and conditions of probation, the State Bar, when appropriate and consistent with its normal practice, will first attempt to resolve the complaint(s) through A/CAP and Central Intake, or will, when appropriate, consistent with its normal practice and pursuant to Rule 54(b)(1), Arizona Rules of the Supreme Court, refer the matter for mediation. Nothing in this paragraph is intended to limit the jurisdiction or power of the State Bar disciplinary agency.

18. Bonuses to legal administrators shall not be based, in whole or in part, on the number of clients retained, the amount of fees generated, the number of clients who cancel, or the amount of fees refunded.

19. The firm shall keep accurate records for all work done on a case.

20. Phillips shall pay all costs incurred as a result of these probationary terms.

21. In the event that Phillips fails to comply with any of the foregoing conditions and the State Bar receives information thereof, bar counsel shall file with the imposing entity a Notice of Non-Compliance, pursuant to Rule 60(a)(5), Arizona Rules of the Supreme Court. The Hearing Officer shall conduct a hearing within thirty (30) days after receipt of said notice, to determine whether the terms of probation have been violated and whether an additional sanction should be imposed. In the event there is an allegation that any of these terms have been violated, the burden of proof shall be on the State Bar of Arizona to prove noncompliance by a preponderance of the evidence.

CONCUR BY: SHELDON H. WEISBERG (In Part)

DISSENT BY: SHELDON H. WEISBERG (In Part)

WEISBERG, Judge, concurring in part and dissenting in part

P49 As the majority explains, the impact of a suspension of six months and one day is a great deal more than the impact of a suspension of only six months. Here, however, even allowing for the subjectivity that creeps into the "imperfect process" when considering proportionality, I must respectfully dissent from the majority's decision to reduce Phillips's suspension from the six months and one day recommended by the Hearing Officer. I do so because, unlike the majority, I conclude that a six-month and one day suspension is internally proportionate to the two-months suspension meted out to Arentz.

P50 The majority's conclusion is understandably not based on a general proportionality review. Not only is that approach no longer favored, but it is of little benefit here because Phillips's firm is a fairly unique "consumer" law firm with accordingly tailored practices. The disciplinary cases referenced by the parties are just not comparable enough to be helpful.

P51 In this case, it is enough that Phillips's violations are the sort for which the relevant ABA Standard mandates a suspension. Specifically, ABA Standard 7.2 provides that "[suspension is generally appropriate when a lawyer knowingly engages in conduct that is a violation of a duty owed as a professional, and causes injury or potential injury to a client, the public, or the legal system." Phillips's conduct clearly falls within that described by the ABA Standard. I therefore consider next whether Phillips's recommended suspension of six months and one day would be proportionate to Arentz's two months. I conclude it would.

P52 To begin, Phillips is not being sanctioned for his second ethics violation. He is being sanctioned for his ethics violations eighteen through twenty-nine. I am not aware of any other attorney in Arizona who has committed twenty-nine violations and received only a six-month suspension for his twenty-ninth. While Arentz was arguably punished too lightly for having committed nineteen violations, and Phillips's latest violations number twelve, Phillips had committed seventeen earlier violations. This comparison alone supports the recommended six months and one day suspension. [7]

FN7. I also note that these most recent twelve violations of Phillips involved separate complaints by nine of P&A's clients, while Arentz's complaints involved only six clients.

P53 Second, Arentz's sanction consisting of a two-month suspension and two years of probation represents his first such sanction. It is to be hoped and presumed that this sanction will be sufficient to prevent further violations by him. Phillips, on the other hand, was punished for his earlier violations and completed that probationary period. Unfortunately, he has reoffended multiple times. Thus, a greater penalty that includes a six-month and one day suspension is both warranted and proportionate.

P54 Finally, Arentz committed his ethical violations while working in a system that was developed, implemented, and supervised by Phillips. It was Phillips's decision as to what P&A resources would be devoted to meet its attorneys' ethical responsibilities to their clients. He clearly did not attach sufficient importance to those ethical responsibilities. As the attorney in sole charge of P&A, his fault was therefore far greater than that of Arentz.

P55 For the foregoing reasons, and although I concur with all else in the majority's opinion, I must respectfully disagree with its decision to reduce the period of Phillips's suspension.

SHELDON H. WEISBERG, Judge*

*Pursuant to Article 6, Section 3 of the Arizona Constitution, the Honorable Sheldon H. Weisberg, Judge of the Arizona Court of Appeals, Division One, was designated to sit on this matter.

Case Review Exercises

1. Discuss the court's reasoning for handling each attorney's suspension differently.
2. Referring to Exhibit 1-6, analyze what the attorneys did correctly and incorrectly in terms of the responsibilities of law firm management.
3. How could the attorneys have corrected their management strategy?
4. What issues did the court address concerning legal administrators?

Helpful Web Sites

Organization	Description	Internet Address
American Bar Association (ABA)	Association for attorneys. The site contains a large amount of information and publications relevant to individuals working in the legal profession.	http://www.americanbar.org/
ABA Law Practice Division	ABA site devoted to law practice management issues and concerns, including management publications, articles, and resources.	http://www.americanbar.org/groups/law_practice
ABA Standing Committee on Paralegals	ABA site devoted to the use of paralegals/legal assistants in legal organizations. Contains publications, articles, and other useful information for paralegals and legal assistants.	http://www.americanbar.org/groups/paralegals
American Association for Paralegal Education	Association for paralegal educators. Contains position papers on the paralegal profession and information on how to find quality paralegal programs to attend.	http://www.aafpe.org
Association of Legal Administrators	National association for legal administrators. Contains resources and information related to law office management and legal administration.	http://www.alanet.org
National Association of Legal Assistants Paralegals	National association for paralegals. Contains many resources for paralegals students and practicing paralegals. Includes articles, utilization surveys, and other helpful information.	http://www.nala.org

Suggested Reading (links are regularly updated – use resource name if inoperable).

1. *Law Practice* magazine, published by the American Bar Association Law Practice Management Section https://www.americanbar.org/groups/law_practice/publications/law_practice_magazine/.

2. *Paralegal Today* magazine, published by Conexion International Media, Inc. https://www.legalassistanttoday.com.

3. Lavelle, Kerry M. (2015). The Business Guide to Law: Creating and Operating a Successful Law Firm. American Bar Association.

4. Grella, T. C., & Hudkins, M. L. (2005). *The Lawyer's Guide to Strategic Planning: Defining, Setting, and Achieving Your Firm's Goals.* American Bar Association.

Legal Administration and Technology

2

Chapter Objectives

After you read this chapter, you should be able to:

- Explain the difference between office administration and practice management.

- Identify the functions of legal administration.

- Explain total quality management.

- List and explain major federal employment laws.

- Identify major technology issues in law offices.

Over the past several decades, the legal profession has experienced a dramatic growth, not only with the increased number of lawyers and paralegals entering the profession but also with technological advances that have revolutionized the practice of law. Now more than ever, effective legal administration is essential to the success of any type of law office structure. For lawyers and law firms to thrive, they must embrace this new technology, integrating it with routine duties, representing clients, drafting legal documents and filing lawsuits, conducting research, and preparing for trials and negotiation settlements. Like many other professions, lawyers know their craft but often lack the time and/or the skills for management. A strong support team is an integral part of an effective legal administration, which is necessary to ensure that lawyers and paralegals successfully compete in today's law practice.

Legal Administration Principles

This chapter covers the full spectrum of law office management and legal administration principles, terms that are used interchangeably yet in fact have distinct responsibilities associated with them. Legal administration is complex and broad in scope. Some legal administration topics will be covered in more detail in later chapters, while others will only get brief coverage in this chapter.

There was a time, not so long ago, when legal administration was viewed as unimportant. Attorneys viewed oversight responsibilities as something that got in the way of providing legal services to their clients. In truth, some of this view still exists. This is why a competent paralegal, capable of taking over legal administration responsibilities, is a valuable member of the legal team. Today, the highly competitive nature of the legal field and the need to control costs make legal administration an important topic. If a law practice is going to be successful in serving clients as well as providing a quality workplace for its employees, efficient operations and profits for its partners, along with good administration and management practices, are a must, regardless of the size or type of law firm.

During the last 30 years, there has been a computer and automation revolution that has forever changed legal administration. Before that, law offices were generally unconcerned with computers, word processing, computerized accounting and billing, mobile computing, the "paperless office," the Internet, e-mail, and much more. Now, virtually every aspect of legal administration is computerized in some way. Law offices have spent hundreds of millions of dollars to implement these new technologies.

Dispelling a Myth

A particular myth about attorneys needs to be dispelled. Many people assume that attorneys automatically make good managers; this is simply not true. Truth be told, law office management and practicing law are not synonymous. Although lawyers have gone to school to learn about practicing law, most have no management skills or training. They may realize that management skills are important, but that does not necessarily mean they are proficient at it. As you read this chapter, keep in mind that many attorneys practicing today have never taken a course like this one. There are several national and local bar associations offering some training or education for law office management; because there is a general lack of this type of training, paralegals with good administrative skills can be very useful to law firms.

In today's medium- and large-sized law firms, the situation is alleviated somewhat with the use of professional administrators. Unfortunately, small-sized law firms generally do not have the resources to hire administrators and must rely on attorneys, paralegals, and other staff members to deal with problems as well as their other duties. Given the increasing competitiveness of the legal market, effective legal administration will be a prime concern for law firms for years to come.

The Importance of Legal Administration

Good legal administration affects attorneys, paralegals, and other law office staff alike. The law firms that are unsuccessful in legal administration must close, merge, or even lay off staff. The operating costs of running a law office are extremely high, so attorneys and paralegals depend on the viability of the law office for their economic survival. Practicing good management is hard; it takes time and teamwork, but it is well worth the effort. Some signs of poor management include frustrated and unhappy staff members and clients, daily "crises," reduced attorney effectiveness, higher costs, low employee job satisfaction, high employee turnover, increased use of employee sick leave, and low staff morale.

Practice Management versus Administrative Management

The law office structure basically has two major aspects: practice management and administrative management. **Practice management** (i.e., substantive or case management) refers to management decisions about how a law office will practice law and handle its cases (see Exhibit 2-1). Practice management decisions include determining the general types of cases the law office will specialize in, how many cases the law office should accept in a given area, and which clients should be accepted or rejected. Practice management is sometimes called case management or file management because this type of management centers on managing and controlling client files and client cases.

practice management
Management decisions about how a law office will practice law and handle its cases.

Exhibit 2-1 Practice Management versus Administrative Management

Practice, Case, or Substantive Management

- What type of cases should we specialize in?
- Which cases should we accept?
- How will case files be organized?
- How will documents for each case be indexed for retrieval later?
- What form files will need to be created for each type of case?

Administrative or Office Management

- Purchasing equipment and supplies for the law office
- Hiring and evaluating law office staff
- Sending out invoices for the law office
- Managing the finances and profitability of the law office
- What administrative structure is the most efficient for the law office?

The cases and clients a law office takes on directly affect the profitability of the law firm. If a law office undertakes to represent a number of client cases that do not generate any profits because the client does not pay, the contingency case is lost, or the fees received are unexpectedly low, the economic effects on the law office are quite harmful. Also, if law office staff do not manage and organize cases effectively, then there may be poor-quality legal services, reduced profitability, unhappy clients, and ethical complaints.

Administrative management (i.e., office management) refers to management decisions relating to operating or managing a law office, including financial and personnel matters. This text largely covers administrative management topics, but some practice management areas are also introduced.

administrative management
Management decisions relating to operating or managing a law office, including financial and personnel matters.

management
The administration of people and other resources to accomplish objectives.

Functions of Legal Administration

Management is the administration of people and other resources to accomplish objectives. In private law practices, the primary objective of management is to provide efficient, high-quality legal services that please clients while earning a reasonable profit for the firm. In a corporate or government legal department, where generating a profit is not applicable, the objective of management is to provide efficient, high-quality legal services to its client at a reasonable cost.

The functions of legal administration (see Exhibit 2-2) include practice management, leadership, controlling, financial management, human resources management, planning, marketing management, organization/policies/systems, facilities management, office services management, and technology or information systems management. Each of these areas will be discussed in this chapter. Two areas, financial management and marketing, have one or more chapters devoted to them later in the text, so they are only introduced in this chapter. All of these functions are essential to successful legal administration regardless of the size of the law office. The people who perform these tasks vary, depending on the management structure of the firm; it could be a sole practitioner, a managing partner with the help of an office manager, committees with the help of professional administrators, or all of the partners or shareholders in a law firm.

Exhibit 2-2 The Functions of Legal Administration

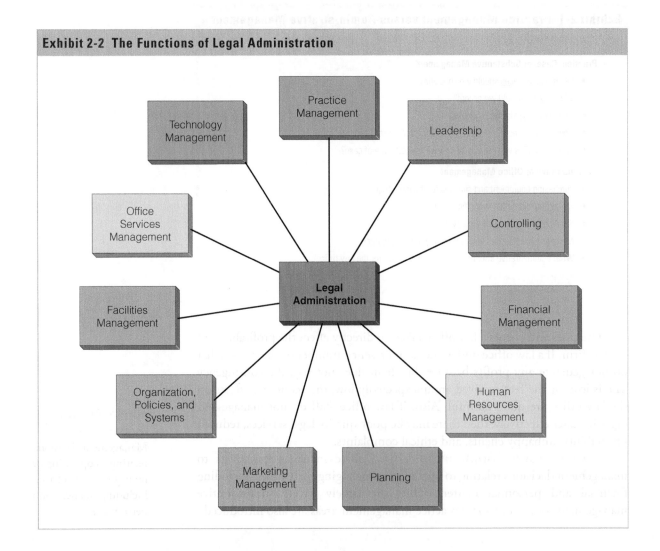

Practice Management

As defined earlier, practice management refers to management decisions about how a law firm will practice law and provide legal services to clients. In the end, every law practice must be able to provide their clients with prompt, competent, and courteous legal services that satisfy and add value to the client, and that are priced at a cost that clients are willing to pay. Law firms are service providers, and if clients do not receive quality legal services, they *will* go somewhere else to get them; it is currently easier than ever to do so, given the intense level of competition in the legal marketplace. A firm's lifeblood is the ability of management to prudently choose the type of clients it serves, to keep existing clients, and to gain new clients for the future. To do this, law firms must define what practice areas and clients to focus on, what legal services they will provide to those clients, and what practice systems and resources they will need to provide those services to the clients. Every law firm must deal with these types of practice management issues.

Defining the Law Firm's Practice

Every law practice must define who it is they will serve. Exhibit 2-3 shows fundamental questions that every law practice must answer and basic decisions that management will need to make. Most of these questions must be answered by the law firm's owners. None of the questions are easy, and all of them will dramatically affect who the law firm will serve and how it will provide services to its clients. There are two basic and important practice management maxims to understand: (1) the practice of law is so broad that even megafirms with 1000 or more attorneys cannot possibly practice in all subspecialty areas of law; therefore, specialization is absolutely required, and (2) successful law practices do not take all of the clients or cases that come to them. Successful law practices weed out good clients from bad clients and strong cases from poor ones. Not all clients are created equal; some clients are easier to work with than others. Some clients have financial resources to pay for legal services, and some do not. Some clients are honest and trustworthy, and some are not. A successful law firm will decide which clients are right for them. Likewise, some cases have true merit to them and some are frivolous or without legal foundation. Again, successful law firms and attorneys are able to decide which cases are the best for them and which ones to refuse.

Exhibit 2-3 Practice Management—Defining the Law Firm's Practice

- Who are our primary clients (businesses, individuals, governments)?
- What market segments will we serve?
- What legal services will we provide?
- What resources will be needed to provide those services?
- What services do our clients need or want? What will we need to add or delete in order to be successful?
- What types of cases do we want to take? What is the long-term projection for those cases?
- In what legal areas will we specialize? Should we focus on area subspecialties?

(continued)

- How many practice areas will we have? How much can we do well with the resources we have?
- Who will champion the practice areas and lead their development?
- Should we focus on providing services to an industry?
- What geographic area will we serve?
- How will we attract clients?
- How will we ensure that the clients receive quality services?
- How will we hold on to the clients (what will be our basis for competition to differentiate our services from the next firm)?

Defining the Law Firm's Services

Once a law firm has decided upon areas of practice and which clients to serve, it must decide and define what services will be provided. For example, if a solo practitioner has decided to practice in the general area of decedent estates, that person must decide whether he or she will (1) draft trusts, (2) advise clients on complex tax issues, (3) perform estate planning, (4) draft wills (including whether to write only simple wills or to draft complex wills involving millions of dollars in assets), (5) probate estates, and so forth. The law firm must decide what specific services they are willing to provide and what services they should refer to other attorneys or decline to take because they lack particular expertise. The answers to these questions are important to the practice management of every law firm.

Defining the Law Firm's Practice System Needs

Once the law firm has decided which clients they want to serve and what services they want to provide, the firm must then determine what types of practice systems are needed to provide and implement those services. Law firms have nearly endless choices regarding the types of practice systems and tools they can use to provide legal services to clients. Exhibit 2-4 contains some examples of different practice systems and options that are available. Technology had virtually no role in how law was practiced 30 years ago; at that time, technology mainly impacted "back office" functions, such as timekeeping, billing, and administrative systems. This is no longer the case. Attorneys and paralegals use practice management technology every day in the practice of law. There is almost no area of law practice that has not been profoundly changed by technology. For more than 200 years, lawyers exclusively used files and file cabinets for records management. Now, many law firms have moved to "paperless offices," where all documents coming into or going out of the firm are scanned and saved in an electronic format for later retrieval without a hard copy. Likewise, legal research has taken the same route. Law books that take up large amount of expensive space and quickly become outdated have mostly been replaced with CD-ROMs or electronic services such as Westlaw, LexisNexis, the Internet, and others. Law practices must also provide practice systems that set standards for things such as ethics, internal law practice policies for providing service, and quality. And, of course with a virtual law office, cloud computing provides real-time and file-sharing capabilities for remote collaboration by the members of the legal team.

Exhibit 2-4 Defining the Law Firm's Practice Systems

Practice Systems	Choices
Document preparation	Pen/paper, typewriter, computer, word processor
File/records management	File cabinets, computer/paperless office
Legal research	State or county law libraries, personal collection of books, Westlaw, LexisNexis,
Docket control	Paper calendars, computer calendars (Outlook), legal docket control, full case management programs
Specialty-specific software	Word processors and general tools or costly but efficient and sophisticated specialty software
Litigation support	Manual methods, computerized litigation support programs, outsourcing to litigation support vendors, e-discovery
Computer systems	Stand-alone systems, hardwired network systems, wireless networks, the Internet, intranet, extranet, desktop computers, laptop computers, personal digital assistants (PDAs) and smart devices.
Communication systems	Telephone systems, voice mail, mobile phones, e-mail, e-filing and VoIP (Voice over Internet Protocol)

Quality and Total Quality Management (TQM)

Ensuring that clients receive quality legal services is one of the most important practice management responsibilities of any law firm partner or administrator. There simply is no substitute for having a quality product, particularly in the legal field.

What Is TQM?

Some might say that **total quality management (TQM)** is outdated and has little to do with a legal organization or a practicing paralegal. Others would say that quality never goes out of style. Because legal organizations must provide quality legal services to stay in business and please clients—whether a megacorporation in litigation, an ordinary person needing a will, or a corporate legal department—that quality must always be the object of focus for a law firm. Legal organizations provide quality legal services through their staff, including their paralegals. There will always be a market for paralegals who look out for the client and provide quality legal services. Quality is what distinguishes poor or average paralegals from exceptional ones. There is also a strong connection between quality and loyalty when it comes to clients. When a client is receiving quality legal services, he or she is usually willing to pay a higher price for those services and has no reason to look elsewhere for a different service provider.

total quality management (TQM) Management philosophy of knowing the needs of each client and allowing those needs to drive the legal organization.

Why would a client risk moving his or her business to another law firm (and have to pay to educate that firm on his or her business) when his or her current firm, current attorneys, and current legal assistants provide outstanding quality legal services that always meet or exceed his or her expectations?

TQM is a management philosophy that is based upon knowing the needs of each client and allowing those needs to drive the legal organization at all levels of activity, from the receptionist to the senior partner. From the outset of this book, you have been introduced to the importance of meeting client needs and providing quality legal services to clients. TQM is just an expansion on this basic idea. The TQM philosophy of allowing clients' needs to drive an organization, instead of the other way around, was taught to major Japanese corporations in the 1950s by W. Edwards Deming.

The TQM philosophy focuses on the idea that businesses should compete based on the quality of the service that is provided, as opposed to price or other factors. Exhibit 2-5 shows the difference between management decisions based on client needs and those based on what is easiest for the law practice to provide.

Exhibit 2-5 Product-Centered versus Client-Centered Philosophies in a Law Office

Product-Centered Philosophy	Client-Centered Philosophy
1. Inner forces control the law office.	Client forces control law office decision making.
2. Emphasis is on short-run productivity.	Emphasis is on long-range planning for quality and client satisfaction.
3. Law office decisions are forced upon clients.	Law office decisions are made based on client input and meeting clients' needs.
4. Law office provides services they already have.	Law office develops new services and modifies existing services based on clients' needs.
5. Law office provides services but does not survey clients to ensure satisfaction.	Law office surveys clients before, during, and after services are rendered to ensure client satisfaction and makes appropriate changes based on clients' needs.
6. Law office focuses on short-term profitability and financial success.	Law office focuses on long-range profitability by putting the priority on meeting clients' needs and providing quality legal services.

What Are Specific TQM Philosophies?

TQM has many nuances and subtleties, but there are several main points to the TQM philosophy.

1. **Management has an overriding duty to ensure that the law firm provides quality legal service.** Management must make decisions based on how the decision will affect the quality of the legal services being provided. The distribution of law firm assets, including purchases, contracts, and staff employees, must be viewed from the client's perspective and be based on how these decisions will affect the *quality* of the services the firm provides. Likewise, when an attorney or paralegal makes a decision or participates in making a decision about a case, he or she must view that decision in terms of how the decision will affect the quality of legal services, such as deciding what copy service, litigation support bureau, or software to use.

2. **Quality service involves every person in the law firm, and everyone must be involved and committed.** Providing quality services begins and ends with everyone. It encompasses the idea of putting dedication and commitment into everything that is done; it requires integrating quality methods into the daily work routine of every member of the staff; and it begins with every person taking pride in his or her work.

3. **Quality service is based not on management's or our own perception of quality, but on the perceptions of the client.** In the end, the only person who is going to bring business back to the firm, or refer your services to other businesses, is the client. Therefore, only the client's perception of quality is what counts. Because it is the client's opinion that counts, law firms must regularly poll or survey their clients to find out what they are doing right, what they are doing wrong, and how they can provide better services to the client. This can be done by interviewing current clients and mailing out client surveys when matters have been resolved, but it is the client's opinions that motivate the firm to change. For a TQM policy to be effective, the firm must be willing to *listen* to the client and to institute *change* to meet the needs of the client. Keep in mind that client needs are constantly changing, so to keep up, the firm must also be willing to change.

   Attorneys and paralegals do not have to wait until the end of a case or matter to ask a client whether or not he or she is pleased with the services provided or if there is anything else you can do to be of assistance. Clients will not always volunteer that kind of information; you may have to ask.

4. **Quality service depends on the individual's, the team's, and ultimately the organization's performance.** In the end, the client will judge the quality of a law firm's job based on his or her experience. Thus, everyone involved must be committed to the idea of quality and must be able to share in the financial or other types of benefits the firm receives. TQM eliminates the "we versus they" mentality and rewards all members of the team who contribute. TQM uses project teams to identify and solve problems and increase efficiency.

   It is critical for attorneys, paralegals, and team members to work on a client's case. If you see another team member struggling, about to make a mistake, or unable to complete a task in a timely fashion, you have to be willing to help.

5. **Improve systems constantly.** Along with ensuring high-quality services, there is also a focus on increasing performance and productivity by constantly improving the systems and ways in which services are provided. This may include purchasing technology, rethinking the ways in which work is performed or routed, removing repetitive tasks, or taking further actions that will increase productivity and efficiency. This is a vigorous process that never ends.

What Are the Benefits of the TQM Philosophy?

The TQM philosophy offers many benefits:

- **Increased client satisfaction**—The ultimate benefit is that clients are satisfied beyond their expectations, and, based on this satisfaction, they will entrust all their legal services and refer new clients to the law firm.

- **Unity among the management, attorneys, and staff**—TQM breaks down the barriers among competing groups in a law practice by focusing everyone on the same goal (unity of purpose) and by allowing all involved to share in the profits of the business. This can be done by awarding bonuses, giving awards, or recognizing outstanding performance. The "we versus they" mentality is a thing of the past.

- **Seek to continuously improve performance and productivity**—TQM seeks to improve the quality of legal services to clients by increasing staff efficiency and productivity, not just once or twice a year but constantly, in order to improve the system. This involves all members of the staff checking the quality of their own work, learning advanced technologies, and doing whatever is necessary to provide the client with the best service.

How Is TQM Implemented?

TQM can be implemented by hiring professional consultants to develop systems for obtaining client feedback and to educate staff members on TQM techniques.

Some law firms include a TQM policy in their staff manual. For example, the American Bar Association publishes a sample manual that includes TQM; it addresses the importance of the entire legal team providing high-quality service to every client throughout the representation in the most cost-effective method.

To a lesser degree, TQM also can be implemented by reading about the subject, by simply accepting the principles of TQM, by being responsive to client needs, and by recognizing the effect management decisions have on the quality of the legal services being provided. In effect, TQM serves as a reminder that quality services are what everything else in the law firm depends on.

Leadership

leadership
The act of motivating or causing others to perform and achieve objectives.

Another function of legal administration is leadership. **Leadership** is the act of motivating or causing others to perform and achieve objectives. Effective leaders inspire others; they set a clear mission, vision, and goals for an organization, and they provide direction and guidance. Good leaders are forward thinking, set clear objectives, measure results, inspire trust, are innovators, and make quality decisions. For any law firm or practice to be truly successful, quality leadership must exist, whether it be from the partnership, a managing partner, legal administrators, committees, or other individuals or groups. Exhibit 2-6 shows a more complete list of effective leadership practices in a law office.

Exhibit 2-6 Effective Law Office Leadership

Effective Law Office Leadership
- Establishes a vision of a positive and successful future for the law practice.
- Enlists others in generating the firm's mission statement, goals, and objectives.
- Develops a written strategic plan incorporating the input, values, and ideas of others.
- Anticipates what can go wrong and acts proactively.

(continued)

- Acts consistently to support the legal team in carrying out the firm's mission.
- Stresses goal attainment in day-to-day activities.
- Rewards team members based on their achievements of goals and objectives.
- Reports and tracks goal attainment data at partnership and law firm meetings.
- Shows confidence in and respect for all legal team members.
- Defuses rumors by keeping all legal team members informed of matters that are relevant to them or the practice.
- Never represents facts or divulges information given in confidence.
- Insists that all team members have strong ethics and high integrity.
- Is trusted by others in the practice.
- Creates a supportive environment for learning, coaching, and developing staff; takes interest in team members as human beings; and is not overly critical of mistakes.
- Takes time to listen to others, no matter who they are, and makes a concerted effort to be responsive.
- Effectively communicates with team members so that they are given continuous, specific feedback regarding progress toward their goals and clearly know what is expected of them.
- Consistently makes difficult decisions without procrastinating and seeks appropriate input from others.

Controlling

Controlling is the process of determining whether the law practice is achieving its objectives, holding stakeholders accountable for their goals, and making strategy adjustments as necessary so that the law firm achieves the objectives. Management must determine whether the law office is achieving its short- and long-range goals. Management must also make stakeholders accountable for meeting objectives and should assist in adjusting strategies so goals can be met. Exercising control is a fundamental aspect of management; this is done via financial audits, budgets versus actual reporting, operational audits, risk management, analysis of financial reports, and the progress tracking of short- and long-range plans.

controlling
The process of determining whether the law practice is achieving its objectives, holding stakeholders accountable for their goals and making strategy adjustments as necessary so the firm achieves its objectives.

Financial Management

Financial management is the oversight of a firm's financial assets and profitability to ensure overall financial health. Financial management is important in any business; a business that does not earn a profit will quickly cease to exist. There are many different aspects of the financial management of a law firm. Timekeeping and billing, which include tracking time spent on clients by attorneys and paralegals and billing clients, is a particularly crucial area, as is trust accounting, which entails the ethical responsibilities of keeping track of client monies paid but not yet earned by the firm. Budgeting and tracking firm expenses, revenue, and profitability, as well as making payments (accounts payable) and tracking firm receipts (accounts receivable), are also important to the overall success of the firm. Other areas of financial management include setting billing and hourly rates, purchasing high-quality goods and services at the least expensive cost, tracking the assets of the firm

financial management
The oversight of a firm's financial assets and profitability to ensure overall financial health.

(including equipment and furniture), properly investing firm monies that are not currently being used, having a good relationship with a bank to secure loans as necessary, tracking tax liabilities, and having proper insurance to protect the firm's assets, payroll, and cash flow. Chapters 5 and 6 cover these topics in detail.

Human Resources Management

human resources management
Hiring, evaluating, compensating, training, and directing law office personnel.

Human resources management refers to hiring, evaluating, compensating, training, and directing law office personnel. While law firms use technology to serve clients more efficiently, for the most part, legal services are delivered to clients by a firm's staff. Therefore, the quality management of that staff is of great concern to most law offices. Firms must recruit, select, and hire staff who are trained and competent in their areas of expertise. Managers must also effectively evaluate staff to let them know how they are doing in terms of meeting the expectations of their jobs, and coach and counsel staff if there are performance problems. Firms must provide compensation and benefits that will appropriately reward and motivate staff so that they are able to retain the employees they have. Furthermore, the staff must be trained regarding changes in the law, technology, and client needs. The firm must also direct staff and periodically review its organizational structure, job designs, and how services are provided to clients, in order to make adjustments that ensure effectiveness.

The Hiring Process

At some point in your career, you may be required to hire someone, such as a another lawyer or another paralegal, a law clerk, legal secretary, or investigators. It is important that you hire the right individual for the job the first time. A poor hiring decision can cost a law office thousands of dollars in wasted salary, training expenses, time, and potential malpractice problems. In addition, if the right person is not hired the first time, the firm must hire another individual and incur the cost of advertising and training all over again.

The hiring process is fairly detailed. Typically, a detailed job description is drafted, ads are placed in newspapers (or recruitment is started), resumes and employment applications are analyzed, candidates are interviewed, references are checked, and a final selection is made.

Writing Job Descriptions   The first step in the hiring process is to write a detailed job description that explains the duties of the position. Exhibit 2-7 provide a Paralegal Job Description Sample. If an employer does not know what the new hire is going to do, there is no way he or she can recognize the best person for the position. A detailed job description lets the employer match the strengths of candidates to the particular position that is being filled. Job descriptions also help the employee to understand his or her role in the firm and what will be expected. Most job descriptions include a job title, a summary of the position, a list of duties, and minimum qualifications that the new employee must have.

Exhibit 2-7 Sample Litigation Paralegal Job Description

Job Description

JOB TITLE: **PARALEGAL** (Litigation)

EXEMPT:	Non-Exempt	**GRADE LEVEL:**	11
DIVISION:	Legal	**LOCATION:**	Headquarters
DEPARTMENT:	Litigation		
INCUMBENT:			
REPORTS TO:	Attorney		

SUMMARY:

Under attorney supervision, provide a broad range of professional and technical litigation duties. Perform factual investigations including gathering documents, researching records, and interviewing witnesses/clients. Work with the supervising attorney and client to prepare and answer discovery documents in draft form. Prepares deposition summaries, witness summaries, and case chronologies or timelines. Manages and organizes litigation files and exhibits. Prepares drafts of pleadings and correspondence. Conducts legal research as needed. Manages the computerized litigation support for each case as needed.

ESSENTIAL DUTIES AND RESPONSIBILITIES (and other duties as assigned):

1. Performs factual investigations including gathering, analyzing, and organizing documents such as medical records, police records, birth and death records, motor vehicle records, incorporation records, and other documents using a variety of sources including the Internet, government agencies, and other contacts. Compiles and summarizes data as necessary. Conducts interviews with clients and witnesses as needed. Works with expert witnesses as needed.

2. Performs a variety of tasks related to discovery under the supervision of an attorney including preparing drafts of interrogatories, requests for admissions, and requests for production of documents. Works with the attorney and client to prepare and coordinate drafts of discovery responses. May prepare drafts of deposition questions, coordinate deposition scheduling, and prepare case chronologies and timelines as necessary. Prepares deposition and witness summaries.

3. Organizes and maintains litigation files, prepares trial notebooks, and assists in organizing, maintaining, and indexing trial exhibits. Performs case management, docketing, scheduling, and planning as needed.

4. Conducts drafts of legal research memorandums using the Internet, Westlaw, LexisNexis, CD-ROM databases, and the law library as needed.

5. Prepares drafts of a variety of litigation-related legal documents under the supervision of an attorney including pleadings, motions, discovery documents, and general correspondence.

6. Reviews, analyzes, organizes, and indexes discovery documents and all case-related documents, including managing the computerized litigation support for each case.

MINIMUM EDUCATION AND EXPERIENCE:

Bachelor's degree (B.A.) from four-year college or university (major: paralegal); or one to two years of related experience; and/or training or equivalent work experience.

LICENSES/CERTIFICATIONS REQUIRED:

Paralegal certificate

KNOWLEDGE, SKILLS, AND ABILITIES REQUIRED:

Knowledge of the principles and procedures of legal research. Strong interpersonal and communication skills and the ability to work effectively with a wide range of constituencies in a diverse community. Skill in the use of personal computers and related software applications. Ability to draft legal documents, such as pleadings, legal responses, affidavits, position statements, and briefs. Ability to develop and maintain recordkeeping systems and procedures. Database management skills. Ability to gather and organize legal evidence. Knowledge of litigation and civil procedure helpful. Knowledge of planning and scheduling techniques. Skill in organizing resources and establishing priorities. Ability to maintain confidentiality of records and information. Excellent customer service skills required.

(continued)

REASONING ABILITY:
Ability to define problems, collect data, establish facts, and draw valid conclusions. Ability to interpret an extensive variety of legal instructions in different areas of the law and deal with several abstract and concrete variables.

LANGUAGE ABILITY:
Ability to read, analyze, and interpret legal documents. Ability to write legal documents and legal/business correspondence. Ability to effectively present information and respond to clients, attorneys, witnesses, opposing counsel, and the general public.

Advertising and Recruiting   After a detailed and accurate job description is drafted, organizations begin the actual hiring process. This includes either promoting from within the organization or recruiting candidates from outside the organization. The process of recruiting candidates can include the use of newspaper advertisements, candidate interviews at specific schools or institutions, employment agencies and search firms, professional associations, the Internet, or candidate referrals from the organization's own employees.

Employment Applications and Resumes   Once an employer has drafted a detailed job description and advertised the position, the next step is to review the employment applications or resumes received.

In many cases, an organization will receive a resume first and subsequently have the individual fill out a formal application for employment. An application for employment is a good idea, because resumes are inconsistent and may not provide all the information needed to make a quality decision.

Employment applications must comply with legal requirements and may not ask for information that the employer is not entitled to have, such as information regarding race, religion, or age.

Interviewing   Once resumes and employment applications have been analyzed and the field of candidates narrowed, the next step is the interview process. The interview is typically the most dynamic part of the hiring process. This is the point where the interviewer decides which applicant is the most qualified and will "fit" with the organization. Below are some general insights regarding interviews.

Screen Applicants to Be Interviewed   A common problem that occurs during the interview is the discovery that a candidate who looked good on paper is, in fact, a bad "fit" for the organization. In this case, the whole interview is a waste of both the employer's and the applicant's time. One way to avoid this is to conduct a casual phone screen of all applicants. By asking some salient questions over the phone, an interviewer can determine whether it is appropriate to have the applicant come in for a formal interview.

Ensure That All Interviews Are Consistent   It is extremely important that all interviews conducted for a position are done consistently. The interviewer must make sure that all candidates are asked the same questions and that all candidates are treated fairly. If interviews are not performed consistently, an interviewer may be giving preference or special treatment to one candidate over another. The more consistent the interview is, the less likely an organization will be susceptible to a discrimination complaint.

The Interviewer Should Talk Less and Listen More   The interviewer should talk as little as possible. Any time the interviewer is talking, he or she is giving up the opportunity to hear from the candidate, which is the whole purpose of the interview. Interviewers should avoid filling in pauses or completing sentences for candidates.

Ask Open-Ended and Behavioral-Based Questions   Most questions in interviews today are open-ended in that no specific answer is hinted at or suggested by how the interview question is asked. The applicant must decide how to answer the question. For example, a typical open-ended question might be "Can you review your work experience for me and tell me how it prepares you for the position you have applied for?" A behavioral-based question is another type often asked in interviews; this type of question asks the candidate to provide a specific example from his or her past. For example, a typical behavioral-based question is "Can you tell me about a time you had a particularly difficult legal ethics problem and how you handled it?" Many organizations use behavioral-based questions because it is more difficult for an applicant to rehearse these answers beforehand. Good interviewers will ask candidates a variety of open-ended and behavioral-based questions that call for concrete examples relating to the candidate's personality, job history, education, and experience related to the potential job.

Avoid Discriminatory Questions   Particular caution should be used when deciding what interview questions to ask. There are many questions that should be avoided because they might be considered discriminatory (see Exhibit 2-8). Exhibit 2-8 is not an all-inclusive list, as many states and local governments have additional antidiscrimination laws. As a rule, if a question is not directly relevant to the position or job performance, an interviewer should not ask it. There is no reason to take unnecessary risks. Personal or family-related questions should be avoided; the problem with most personal questions is that they relate to the applicant's race, color, religion, sex, national origin, age, or disability. Many city statutes and ordinances prevent discrimination on the basis of sexual orientation, so questions related to this should be avoided as well.

Reference Checks   Once the employer has narrowed the list to two or three final candidates, the only thing left to do is check references. Checking references is an important part of the hiring process and should never be left out. Researchers have found that nearly 30% of all resumes contain exaggerated statements or misstatements about education or employment history. In addition, employers have been held liable for negligent hiring. **Negligent hiring** is when an employer hires an employee without sufficiently and reasonably checking the employee's background. In one case, an apartment complex was found liable after a new manager used a passkey to enter an apartment and rape a tenant. The apartment complex had failed to check the new manager's references and reasonably investigate the person's background for felony convictions, fighting, and other criminal activity. Thus, references should always be checked, and gaps in employment and other indicators of problematic behavior should be investigated.

negligent hiring
Hiring an employee without sufficiently and reasonably checking the employee's background.

Exhibit 2-8 Interview Questions That Should *Not Be* Asked

Race/Color/Religion/Sex

Any question that is related to a candidate's race, color, religion, sex, national origin, age, disability, sexual orientation, or veteran status

Name/Marital Status

- What was your maiden name?
- Have you ever used another name?
- Are you married? (permissible after hiring)

Ancestry

- Where were you born?
- Where does your family come from?

Residence

- How long have you lived at this address?
- Do you own your house?

Family/Personal

- How many children do you have?
- How will you provide child care?
- Are you pregnant?

Credit/Financial

- Have you ever filed for bankruptcy?
- Have your wages been garnished?

Age

- What is your date of birth? (permissible after hiring)
- When did you graduate from elementary or high school?

Organizations

- What organizations do you belong to? (You can ask this if you instruct them to delete organizations related to race, religion, color, disability, age, and so forth.)

Religion

- What church do you belong to?

Medical

- Are you disabled or taking medication regularly? (You can ask whether they have the ability to perform the essential functions of the job.)

The following are some tips on how to get good information when performing reference checks.

Call Past Employers/Supervisors   Typically, the most relevant information an employer can gather is from the candidate's last employer or supervisor. Call these people first. Although some will refuse to give out any information for fear of being sued for defamation if they say something negative, many will still answer your questions. A way around this problem is to ask potential candidates to sign a release or waiver that allows the past employer to talk to you openly and freely without fear of being sued for defamation. Ask specific questions about the candidate's dates of employment, job duties and responsibilities, quality and quantity of work, disciplinary problems, work attitude, communication skills, dependability, ability to be a team player, and reason for leaving. Also ask whether the former employer would rehire the person.

Call Institutions/Schools   If a candidate lists graduation from a school or institution, call the school and confirm it. This usually does not take a great deal of time. This is seldom done, and many candidates claim that they have finished degrees when, in fact, they have not.

Call Character References Last   Candidates only give potential employers character references who will give them a glowing recommendation. Expect this, but ask specific questions as well.

Fair Credit Reporting Act   The **Fair Credit Reporting Act** is federal legislation that governs the use of "consumer reports" in all employment decisions. "Consumer reports" are defined very broadly and include reference checks, education checks, credit history reports, and criminal background checks, when an employer hires a third party to conduct these checks. If an employer conducts these checks personally, compliance with the Fair Credit Reporting Act is not required; however, if a third party is used, the organization must comply. The employer must give prior written notice to the applicant before procuring the consumer report and obtain prior written authorization by the applicant before obtaining the consumer report. Before "adverse action" is taken against the applicant (such as not hiring the applicant based on the consumer report), the applicant must be provided with a copy of the report and notified of his or her legal rights.

Fair Credit Reporting Act
Federal legislation that governs the use of consumer reports in all employment decisions.

Performance Evaluations

Timely performance evaluations are a strong human resource development technique. Employees need to know—on a regular basis—what they are doing right and where they need to improve. Performance evaluations allow employees to know where they stand and help them to grow and progress. A performance evaluation should not be viewed as a heavy object with which to beat or threaten employees, but rather as a part of the process of working toward a common goal.

If done correctly, evaluations can strengthen ties with employees by allowing them to participate in the evaluation process. In the end, a well-defined evaluation process can make the organization more efficient. Employee evaluations should be conducted privately, and, when possible, the evaluation itself should be given to the employee before meeting so that he or she is prepared to talk about the evaluation and its findings. The evaluation should always be performed in writing and should be kept in the employee's personnel file.

Evaluations Should Be Done Regularly   Evaluations should be done on a regular basis in order to be effective. Some law offices evaluate employees quarterly, biannually, or annually. Quarterly or biannually evaluations are recommended, because criticism or praise usually has more effect soon after an incident has happened.

Evaluations Should Be Objective and Match Ratings with Performance   Evaluations should be based on objective performance by an employee and not on any personal likes or dislikes of the employer. It is particularly important to match ratings with performance and to always remain fair. It is also important that employers communicate with employees on a regular basis and take a "hands-on" approach to knowing whether or not employees really deserve a certain rating. Using objective criteria and actual examples of the employee's performance will help in this process. Examples of how the employee earned an "excellent" or "average" performance rating will help identify what he or she is doing correctly or incorrectly.

Elicit Open Communication and Set Mutual Goals for Improvement
Any evaluation method must allow the employee to participate in the process by communicating how he or she feels about the evaluation, including what he or she likes or dislikes and what both parties can do to help solve problems. There must be a give-and-take relationship in the evaluation process to make it work. One technique is to ask the employee how he or she feels the year went: what went right or wrong? Let him or her do the talking. This will put the employee at ease and will let the person feel that he or she has taken part in the process. Setting realistic goals to solve any problems also helps to communicate what is expected of the employee in the future. One way of doing this is by having both the employer and the employee set certain goals.

Coaching Technique—Ongoing Evaluation   One way to help an employee succeed in his or her job is to coach and counsel him or her on a daily, ongoing basis. The **coaching technique** focuses on the positive aspects of the employee's performance and explores alternative ways to improve performance. Most people are more willing to listen to advice from a "friend" who is interested in their well-being than from a disinterested and heavy-handed "boss." The coaching technique is borrowed from sports, where a coach works with an individual to overcome deficiencies through counseling and by explaining any problems to the person.

The coaching technique works best when the supervisor has had direct experience in the employee's position. This allows the supervisor to give concrete tips, examples, information, and opinions that the employee can use. Employees typically are more willing to accept advice if the supervisor has been in the same position. When discussing areas that need improvement, try not to be judgmental, but instead give advice on exactly how to correct a deficiency. This technique is especially useful when an employee lacks knowledge about a situation. One of the most positive aspects of the coaching technique is that it does not place blame on the employee; the employee is able to retain his or her self-esteem, which can be lost when an employee is simply reprimanded. Exhibit 2-9 explains how the coaching technique works. The coaching technique is not a substitute for a regular evaluation, but it is a technique for helping an employee to be successful in his or her job.

General Performance Evaluation Form   Exhibit 2-10 contains a general performance evaluation form that could be used for many law office support jobs. This type of evaluation is straightforward and quick to prepare. However, the checklist is not job specific and does not allow a great deal of interaction on the part of the employee. If possible, the employee should be allowed to make comments and be an active participant in the evaluation process.

coaching technique
Counseling that focuses on the positive aspects of the employee's performance and explores alternative ways to improve his or her performance.

Exhibit 2-9 The Coaching Technique

1. **Event**—Describe exactly what happened; do not be negative, just state the facts.
2. **Effect**—Describe the impact of the event, including who or what was adversely affected and why; be specific. Let the employee know why the behavior should be changed.
3. **Advice**—Describe exactly how the employee can improve performance in the future.
4. **Remind**—Emphasize that you believe the employee is competent and that this was just a lapse.
5. **Reinforce**—Monitor the employee's performance. If the employee corrects the mistake, let the person know that he or she is doing it right. Reinforce the positive change he or she made.

Exhibit 2-10 Performance Evaluation

PERFORMANCE EVALUATION

Name: _____ Title: _____

Evaluation Type: Probation   Six-Month   Annual   Special: _____

Date: _____   Evaluation Period: _____

Evaluate the staff member's performance using the following rating criteria and make comments as necessary:

Rating: Description:

5   **Outstanding:** Employee's performance is exceptional and far exceeds normal expectations.

4   **Above Average:** Employee's performance is very good and exceeds expectations.

3   **Average:** Employee performs to normal expectations of the position.

2   **Below Average:** Employee's performance falls below acceptable levels from time to time.

1   **Unacceptable:** Employee's performance is completely unacceptable.

1. Competence in the Law Office
_____   a. Is technically competent in all areas of work.
_____   b. Other staff members have confidence in and trust the employee's work.
_____   c. Continuously strives to learn and expand his/her competence level.
Comments: _____
_____
_____

2. Quality of Work
_____   a. Is accurate in all work.
_____   b. Is thorough and complete in all work.
_____   c. Takes pride in work.
_____   d. Work is consistently of high quality.
Comments: _____
_____
_____

(continued)

3. Dependability

_____ a. Highly dependable.
_____ b. Work is always turned on time.
_____ c. Can be counted on in a crisis.
_____ d. Works independently without need of supervision.

Comments: _____
_____
_____

4. Work Habits/Attitude

_____ a. Has excellent work habits.
_____ b. Has a positive and enthusiastic attitude.
_____ C. Acts as a team player.
_____ d. Gets along with other staff members and supervisors.

Comments: _____
_____
_____

5. Communication/Relationships

_____ a. Treats clients professionally.
_____ b. Treats other staff members professionally.
_____ c. Can write effectively.
_____ d. Has good grammar skills.
_____ e. Listens effectively.
_____ f. Can make self-understood orally.

Comments: _____
_____
_____

6. Judgment

_____ a. Makes sound judgment calls.
_____ b. Exercises appropriate discretion.
_____ c. Intelligently arrives at decisions.
_____ d. Thinks through decisions.

Comments: _____
_____
_____

7. Initiative

_____ a. Accepts new assignments willingly.
_____ b. Takes on new responsibilities without being asked.

Comments: _____
_____
_____

General Comments: _____
_____
_____

Employee's Strengths: _____
_____
_____

Areas That Need Improvement: _____
_____
_____

OVERALL RATING: **Outstanding, Above Average, Average, Below Average, Unacceptable**

(continued)

Employee Comments: _____

_____

_____

Supervisor Signature: _____ Employee Signature: _____

Date: _____ Date: _____

Employee signature only verifies that this evaluation has been discussed and does not indicate agreement with the evaluation.

EMPLOYEE SELF-APPRAISAL:

A. What were your achievements this year?

B. List any goals you would like to achieve next year.

C. What strengths do you have in performing this position?

D. What areas do you think you can improve upon?

E. What can your supervisor do to help you reach your goals?

F. Overall, how would you rate your own performance level?

Goal Setting and Management by Objectives   Another type of performance system is based on goal setting, also commonly referred to as "management by objectives" (see Exhibit 2-11). In a **management by objectives** performance program, the employee and employer agree upon the employee's goals at the beginning of the evaluation period. Target dates for reviewing the employee's progress toward the goals, and a determination for how it will be decided if the goals were achieved or not, are also included in the objectives. An accomplishment report is prepared detailing which goals were accomplished, and rewards or incentives are given for meeting the goals. For example, a goal might be to reduce nonbillable hours by 5% or increase billable hours by 50 hours during the fourth quarter.

management by objectives
A performance program in which the individual employee and the employer agree on goals for the employee.

Compensation and Benefits

Another aspect of human resources management is paying law practice employees and providing them with benefit packages. Most firms set compensation for positions based on the "market salary" for the job in the

---

Exhibit 2-11 Management by Objectives Process

1. Employee and supervisor agree on the employee's major performance objectives for the coming period, including target dates for accomplishing each part of them.

2. Employee and supervisor agree on how the objectives will be measured and how it will be decided if the objectives have been met.

3. Employee and supervisor meet periodically to discuss the employee's progress toward meeting the goals.

4. An accomplishment report is prepared at the end of the period, stating which objectives were met or not met.

5. Awards or incentives are given, depending on whether the objectives were met.

---

marketplace. Some firms may be "above market" while others are "below market." To determine the appropriate compensation and benefits for a position, law practices will consider job description and the education and experience requirements, and will use the average market salary as a benchmark (see Exhibit 1-8 in Chapter 1 for paralegal salary data). According to the 2015 National Utilization and Compensation Survey Report, a paralegal's annual compensation averaged $58,410; paralegals paid bonuses average $4581 annually. Many firms also offer benefit packages to attract and retain paralegals. According to the 2015 survey, 89% received some form of health insurance, 79% received some kind of retirement benefit, 75% received some form of life insurance, 82% had professional association dues paid either entirely or partially by their employer, and 68% received some form of dental coverage.

Training and Development

Some law practices offer training and development opportunities for new professional staff, including attorneys and paralegals. This is usually offered in large-sized law firms where a structured development program is instituted. Specific learning experiences are planned and progress is measured. In many small- to medium-sized firms, little training is provided, and new attorneys and paralegals learn through experience. Many firms, of all sizes, offer continuing education programs to staff. Some of these may be offered through in-house training programs within large-sized firms or by sending staff to external continuing education programs at the firms' expense in small- to medium-sized firms.

Personnel Policies

personnel handbook
A manual that lists the formal personnel policies of an organization.

One of the most useful things a law office of any type can do to effectively manage its human resources is to create a comprehensive and up-to-date personnel handbook. A **personnel handbook** (sometimes called an employee handbook) lists the formal personnel policies of an organization. Personnel handbooks (1) establish formal policies on personnel matters so staff members will know what to expect of management and what management expects of them regarding personnel issues; (2) establish a standard so that all employees are treated fairly and uniformly; and (3) help to protect the law office if it is involved in litigation regarding personnel matters and to avoid government-compliance problems.

Current Personnel Law Issues

Personnel-related issues are highly regulated and often litigated. The following is a sampling of some of the more important areas related to federal personnel/labor law. Exhibit 2-12 contains a summary of federal employment laws.

Employment-at-Will Doctrine

The **employment-at-will doctrine** states that an employer and employee freely enter into an employment relationship, and that either party has the right to sever the relationship at any time without reason. If an employee is covered by a union collective-bargaining agreement, employment contract, or civil service regulations, the employment-at-will doctrine does not apply, and the employer must comply with the terms of the contract or regulations. Employment-at-will typically happens when an employee works for an employer without any type of written agreement or reference to how long the employee will work. For example, suppose a law office hired a legal secretary in an employment-at-will state. The legal secretary did good work, but the firm subsequently changed its mind and decided that it did not need the extra position and terminated the secretary. This would be perfectly acceptable, and the secretary would have no basis for a lawsuit against the law office. For another example, suppose that the legal secretary gets a better-paying job at another law office and quits without giving notice. This also would be acceptable under employment-at-will status.

employment-at-will doctrine
Doctrine that states that an employer and employee freely enter into an employment relationship, and that either party has the right to sever the relationship at any time without reason.

Exhibit 2-12   Partial List of Federal Employment-Related Laws

Law	Description
Family and Medical Leave Act of 1993	Provides that eligible employees be allowed up to 12 work weeks of unpaid leave within any 12-month period for (1) the birth, adoption, or placement of a child for foster care; (2) the care of a child, spouse, or parent with a serious health condition; and (3) the employee's own serious health condition.
Civil Rights Act of 1991	Relaxes the burden of proof in discrimination claims and allows for greater recovery of damages.
Civil Rights Act of 1964	Prohibits discrimination against employees on the basis of race, color, religion, sex, or national origin. The Equal Employment Opportunity Commission (EEOC) was established to enforce this law.
Americans with Disabilities Act of 1990 (ADA)	Prohibits employers from discriminating against persons with disabilities in several different areas.
Age Discrimination in Employment Act of 1967 (ADEA) (Amended 1978)	Prohibits employers from discriminating against persons age 40 or more on the basis of their age unless age is a bona fide occupational qualification.
Equal Pay Act of 1963	Prohibits employers from basing arbitrary wage differences on gender.
Fair Labor Standards Act of 1938	Sets minimum wage and maximum basic hours of work for employees and requires overtime pay for nonexempt employees.

Organizations should be careful when drafting their personnel handbook to state that the policies therein are not a contract or that employees will be retained for a certain amount of time. For example, an employer should not include language such as "If you do your work satisfactorily, you will always have a job here." If a court finds that the employer gave the expectation to an employee that he or she would have a job forever (as long as the work were satisfactory), or that the policies in the personnel handbook were a type of contract, this would upset the normal expectation of employment-at-will. Personnel handbooks should contain a simple employment-at-will statement, typically near the front, that states the following:

> **Employment-At-Will**
> It is understood that these personnel policies and any other firm documents do not constitute a contract for employment, and that any person who is hired may voluntarily leave employment without proper notice, and may be terminated by the firm any time and for any reason.

In addition, some employers require employees to sign a statement like the one above, or they place the statement on the employment application form.

The employment-at-will doctrine does, of course, have limitations. Courts have found that at-will employees may have legal rights against employers, even though the employer is supposed to be able to terminate the employee without any reason. Instances include when the employer violates public policies, such as firing an employee for filing a workers' compensation claim, firing an employee for refusing to commit perjury, or terminating an employee to avoid paying retirement benefits or sales commissions. Other instances include terminating an employee based on discrimination or terminating an employee when the employer promised to retain the employee as long as the employee does a good job. Thus, although employment-at-will is a doctrine that works in favor of employers, it is by no means absolute. Some states even limit the employment-at-will doctrine by statute, so any organization should be familiar with its own state laws.

When employment-at-will is not in effect, or if there is an employment contract in place, the typical standard is "just cause." An employment contract is a contract between the employer and an employee, setting forth the terms and conditions of the employment relationship. "Just cause" means that before an employer can terminate an employee, the employer must have a just, reasonable cause to do so. Just cause can include many things, such as violating the company's rules and regulations, insubordination, and dishonesty.

The Family and Medical Leave Act of 1993

The **Family and Medical Leave Act of 1993 (FMLA)** applies to employers with 50 or more employees and provides that eligible employees be allowed up to 12 workweeks of unpaid leave within any 12-month period for (1) the birth or adoption of a child or placement of a child for foster care; (2) the care of a child, spouse, or parent with a serious health condition; and (3) the employee's own serious health condition. To be eligible for FMLA,

Family and Medical Leave Act of 1993 (FMLA)
Legislation that allows employees in certain circumstances to receive up to 12 workweeks of unpaid leave from their jobs for family- or health-related reasons.

an employee must have one year of service with the organization and have worked at least 1250 hours in the last year. The FMLA requires that an employee granted leave under the act be returned to the same position held before the leave or be given one that is equivalent in pay, benefits, privileges, and other terms and conditions of employment. The employee also is entitled to health-care benefits during the leave. The purpose of the FMLA is to assist workers to better balance the demands of the workplace with the needs of their families.

Fair Labor Standards Act

The Fair Labor Standards Act sets minimum wage and maximum hours of work for employees. It also requires that overtime pay (one- and one-half times their normal rate) be paid to employees who work in excess of 40 hours a week. Employees do not need to be paid overtime if they fall into one of the four "white-collar" exemptions: executive, administrative, professional, or outside sales.

If an employee is exempt, it means that he or she is not required to be paid overtime wages. If an employee is nonexempt, it means that he or she is required to be paid overtime wages. Whether paralegals are exempt or nonexempt is a hotly debated issue (see Chapter 1 for a detailed discussion).

Equal Employment Opportunity

Equal employment opportunity requires employers to make employment-related decisions without arbitrarily discriminating against an individual. This is a statement that is often seen in want ads, employment applications, and other employment-related documents. Federal laws, including the **Civil Rights Act of 1964**, prohibit employers from discriminating against employees or applicants on the basis of race, color, national origin, religion, or gender. The **Americans with Disabilities Act of 1990 (ADA)** prohibits employers from discriminating against employees or applicants with disabilities (see the following section on the ADA). The **Age Discrimination in Employment Act of 1967** prohibits employers from discriminating against employees and applicants on the basis of age where the individual is 40 or older. The **Equal Pay Act of 1963** prohibits employers from paying workers of one sex less than the rate paid to an employee of the opposite sex for work on jobs that require equal skill, effort, and responsibility and that are performed under the same working conditions. There are several other federal laws that legislate in this area. Most of the laws cited here make it unlawful for an employer to arbitrarily discriminate against employees or applicants.

Every personnel handbook should have a policy stating the law office's position on equal employment opportunity, such as the following:

Equal Employment Opportunity Statement
It is the policy of the firm to apply recruiting, hiring, promotion, compensation, and professional development practices without regard to race, religion, color, national origin, sex, age, creed, handicap, veteran status, or any other characteristic protected by law.

equal employment opportunity
Concept that requires employers to make employment-related decisions without arbitrarily discriminating against an individual.

Civil Rights Act of 1964
Legislation that prohibits employers from discriminating against employees or applicants on the basis of race, color, national origin, religion, or gender.

Americans with Disabilities Act of 1990 (ADA)
Legislation that prohibits employers from discriminating against employees or applicants with disabilities.

Age Discrimination in Employment Act of 1967
Legislation that prohibits employers from discriminating against employees and applicants on the basis of age when the individual is 40 or older.

Equal Pay Act of 1963
Legislation that prohibits employers from paying workers of one sex less than the rate paid to an employee of the opposite sex for work on jobs that require equal skill, effort, and responsibility and that are performed under the same working conditions.

bona fide occupational qualification
An allowable exception to equal employment opportunity, for example, for an employee to perform a specific job, the employee must be of a certain age, sex, or religion.

An exception to equal employment opportunity is when age, sex, or religion is a **bona fide occupational qualification** (BFOQ). A BFOQ means that to perform a specific job adequately, an employee must be of a certain age, sex, or religion. A BFOQ does not apply to race or color; an example of a BFOQ would be for a position as a Catholic priest. The employer could reasonably discriminate against non-Catholics because the candidate must believe in and have knowledge of the Catholic religion in order to qualify. In general, BFOQs have been narrowly construed by most courts, and there are few positions in a law office—if any—that would qualify.

Americans with Disabilities Act

The Americans with Disabilities Act of 1990 (ADA), among other things, makes it unlawful to discriminate in employment against qualified applicants and employees with disabilities. Under the ADA, a person has a "disability" if he or she has a physical or mental impairment that substantially limits a major life activity, such as seeing, hearing, breathing, speaking, walking, performing manual tasks, working, or learning. This does not include a minor impairment of short duration, such as a broken limb, infection, or sprain. An individual with a disability also must be qualified to perform the essential functions of the job, with or without reasonable accommodation; that is, the applicant or employee must be able to satisfy the job requirements, including education, experience, skills, and licenses, and be able to perform the job. The ADA does not interfere with an employer's right to hire the best-qualified applicant but simply prohibits employers from discriminating against a qualified applicant or employee because of his or her disability.

reasonable accommodation
Accommodating a person with a disability, which may include making existing facilities readily accessible, restructuring the job, or modifying work schedules.

The ADA also requires that employers "reasonably accommodate" persons with disabilities. An employer must make **reasonable accommodation** for a person with a disability, which may include making existing facilities readily accessible, restructuring the job, or modifying work schedules. The ADA provides that individuals with disabilities have the same rights and privileges in employment as employees without disabilities. For example, if an employee lounge is in a place inaccessible to a person using a wheelchair, the lounge might be modified or relocated, or comparable facilities might be provided in a location that would enable the individual to take a break with coworkers. Persons who have been discriminated against because of a disability can receive back-pay damages, reinstatement, punitive damages, and other remedies.

Sexual Harassment

sexual harassment
Unwelcome sexual advances, requests for sexual favors, and other verbal or physical conduct of a sexual nature that create an intimidating, a hostile, or an offensive working environment. Exhibit 2-13 contains a sample antiharassment policy.

Sexual harassment includes unwelcome sexual advances, requests for sexual favors, and other verbal or physical conduct of a sexual nature that creates an intimidating, hostile, or offensive working environment.

Many people typically think of sexual harassment as a male supervisor sexually coercing a female subordinate in order for her to keep her position or to be promoted. Sexual harassment is much broader than this, however. Sexual harassment can include unwelcome sexual jokes, inappropriate sexual remarks, inappropriate e-mails, innuendos, insults, leering, subtle forms of pressure for sexual activity, vulgar or indecent language, sexual propositions, displaying sexually oriented photographs, and unwelcome and inappropriate touching, patting, and pinching.

Exhibit 2-13 Antiharassment Policy (Contents)

ANTIHARASSMENT

We have a strong commitment to provide fair employment opportunities and provide a work environment free from all types of discriminatory behavior. Harassment of any persons employed or doing business with us will not be tolerated.

Harassment includes unwelcomed advances of a verbal, physical, or sexual nature by an employee or any individual (including customers, vendors, or suppliers) that shows hostility and aversion or denigrates an employee and/or his or her relatives, friends, or associates because of his or her race, color, sex, religion, age, national origin, handicap or disability, veteran status, sexual orientation, or other status protected by law, and which

1. has the purpose or effect of unreasonably interfering with an individual's work performance,
2. has the purpose or effect or creating an intimidating, a hostile, an abusive, or an offensive working environment,
3. otherwise adversely affects an individual's work performance.

This includes acts that are intended to be "jokes" or "pranks" but that are hostile or demeaning with regard to race, color, religion, gender, national origin, age, handicap or disability, veteran status, sexual orientation, or other status protected by law.

As part of this antiharassment policy, no employee or any other individual (including customers, vendors, or suppliers) may sexually harass any employee. Sexual harassment includes unwelcome sexual advances, sexual jokes or comments, requests for sexual favors, or other unwelcome verbal or physical conduct of a sexual nature. This policy is violated when

1. submission to such conduct is made, either explicitly or implicitly, a condition of employment.
2. submission to or rejection of such conduct is used as a basis for employment-related decisions such as promotion, discharge, performance evaluation, pay adjustment, discipline, work assignment, or any other condition of employment or career development.
3. such conduct otherwise unreasonably interferes with work performance or creates an intimidating, abusive, or offensive working environment, even if it leads to no adverse job consequences.

We encourage any employee who has a question, concern, or complaint of discrimination, including harassment based on race, color, sex, religion, age, national origin, handicap or disability, veteran status, sexual orientation, or other protected status, to immediately notify his or her supervisor or manager. If for any reason the employee would feel uncomfortable discussing the situation with his or her supervisor or manager, or if he or she feels further discussion is needed, the employee should contact the human resources manager.

All reports of inappropriate conduct will be promptly and thoroughly investigated to ensure that any improper conduct will cease immediately and corrective action will be taken to prevent a recurrence. Any employee who violates this policy will be subject to disciplinary actions, up to and including termination of employment. The complaining employee will be informed concerning resolution of the complaint as appropriate.

Complaints will be treated confidentially to the extent practical for an effective resolution. No adverse employment consequences will be suffered by the employee as a result of making a good faith complaint or taking part in the investigation of a complaint. Any person who knowingly alleges a false claim against a manager, supervisor, other employee or individual will be subject to disciplinary actions, up to and including termination of employment.

Sexual harassment does not have to involve a subordinate and a supervisor; it also can take place between persons at the same job level. Sexual harassment can involve clients as well; it has been reported that clients sometimes sexually harass law office staff. The law office has as a duty to investigate a client harassing a staff member, since the law office may be liable if it does not take appropriate action to protect its employees. Finally, although the majority of sexual harassment cases involve male employees harassing female employees, women also have been accused of sexually harassing male subordinates. Regardless of who is involved, the employer is responsible for taking corrective action. Both attorney and paralegal managers play a key role in preventing harassment by communicating policies and keeping the door open to complaints

Planning

planning

The process of setting objectives, assessing the future, and developing courses of action to achieve these objectives.

Planning is the process of setting objectives, assessing future needs, and developing a course of action to achieve the objectives. Planning is the road map for meeting the firm's goals. Law firms should have short-range and long-range plans or goals. A short-term plan for a law office might include increasing profitability by 10%, while a long-term plan might include opening additional offices in other cities or expanding the practice into new legal areas. Without a plan, the law office goes about its business with no real direction. Successful law practices only happen with careful planning and the execution of good management decisions.

Why Paralegals Need to Learn to Develop Plans

As a paralegal's career expands, he or she will be given more complex assignments, duties, and tasks. As the complexity of assignments increases, the ability to develop and execute plans is crucial. The following are some plans that paralegals may prepare:

- Budgets for a paralegal department
- Case budgets for a particular case (i.e., how much the law office will expend to bring a case to trial)
- Case plans (in conjunction with a supervising attorney), including which witnesses need to be deposed; which interrogatories, requests for production, and requests for admissions need to be issued, and to whom; which experts need to be hired; which strategies the law office should pursue; what further investigation needs to be conducted, and so forth
- Large projects, such as developing a litigation-support database in cases that have thousands of documents (paralegals and others must plan how the documents will be entered into the computer, what program, service bureau, or technique will be the most successful, and so forth)
- Administrative projects that require planning, including computerizing a law office's time and billing system from a manual system, implementing a computerized docket control system, or setting up a new filing system or law library
- The office's mission statement and some strategic plans (in small-sized law offices)
- Their own career plans (where they want to be in two to five years and how they are going to get there)

The Mission Statement and Strategic Plans

mission statement

A general, enduring statement of the purpose or intent of the law practice.

A mission statement is a particular type of plan. The **mission statement** is a general, enduring statement of the purpose or intent of the law practice.

It is a plan or vision stating what the firm is about and what are its goals and objectives. It puts forth the fundamental and unique purpose that sets it apart from other firms, identifies the firm's scope, and explains why it exists. For examples, see the mission statements in Exhibit 2-14.

All law practices need a vision: they need to know where they have been and where they are going. They need to have a few guiding principles and philosophies that motivate and determine the direction of the firm. The mission statement represents the foundation for priorities and all other plans. If the firm you work for has a mission statement, memorize and use it. Every idea, new client, new employee, equipment purchase—everything you do should be judged by whether it advances the mission of the firm. If it does not advance the mission, then it may not be right for the firm.

Mission statements may include when the firm began; who founded the firm; the philosophy of the founder(s); the nature of the practice (areas of experience and expertise); the geographic service area; the departments in the practice; the philosophies toward costs, income, growth, technology, client services, and personnel; and who the firm's clients are. Mission statements are not static; they should be changed and updated as long as everyone in the firm understands the change. A mission statement is a vision that keeps the firm headed in the right direction. Without one, a law practice may spend a considerable amount of time never knowing where it is headed.

> Strategic planning has always been important, but the present circumstances make it imperative for law offices to consider strengths and weaknesses, evaluate the competition, and devise a game plan that will set the course to the future.

Exhibit 2-14 Law Office Mission Statements

Large-sized law firm	*The mission of the Adams & Lee law firm is to deliver high-quality legal services to business clients nationwide through personalized, value-added service and a strict adherence to the highest ethical standards.*
Corporate law department	*The A & L law department seeks to offer the corporation the best legal services available while keeping costs to a minimum. The law department will utilize four divisions: labor, environmental, litigation, and general business. The use of in-house staff will be maximized. Only matters of vital importance to the corporation will be contracted out. The other departments of the corporation will be defined as our* **"clients."** *Our clients will be given the same high-quality legal services as provided by outside counsel. Our clients will be surveyed on an annual basis, and we will obtain a* **90 percent** *average approval rating.*
Small-sized law firm	*Adams & Lee is a full-service, client-centered law firm. Our goal is to provide outstanding, responsive services to our clients at a reasonable cost. We represent clients as we ourselves would want to be represented. We use a team approach to provide legal services to our clients, including attorneys, paralegals, and office associates to ensure a professional level of response to our clients' needs.*

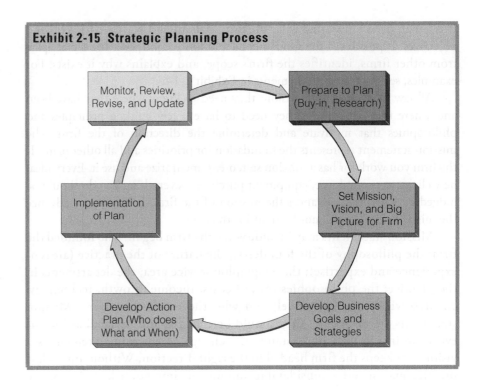

Exhibit 2-15 Strategic Planning Process

- Monitor, Review, Revise, and Update
- Prepare to Plan (Buy-in, Research)
- Set Mission, Vision, and Big Picture for Firm
- Develop Business Goals and Strategies
- Develop Action Plan (Who does What and When)
- Implementation of Plan

strategic planning
Determining the major goals of a firm and then adopting the courses of action necessary to achieve those goals.

Strategic planning is the process of determining the major goals of a firm and then adopting the courses of action and allocating resources necessary to achieve those goals. Exhibit 2-15 shows a diagram of the strategic planning process. For instance, a strategic plan may include expanding a firm's practice into additional areas of the law, such as adding a tax or labor law department. Before you can sell a legal service to someone, though, you must have a buyer; that is, you should not focus on what you want to sell but rather on what the buyer or the client wants to buy. Strategic plans usually answer the questions contained in Exhibit 2-16.

Ideas on How to Plan Effectively

The following are some ideas on how to plan effectively.

- **Gather timely, relevant information.** It is axiomatic that, without good information, you cannot possibly make an effective plan. Too many times, people make plans based on faulty information. Gathering timely and relevant information is one of the most important things you can do to make sure your plan will succeed. You can gather information from public libraries; law libraries; the Internet; Westlaw; LexisNexis; the American Bar Association (ABA); local, state, and national bar associations; law office surveys; consultants; other firms; and historical records from your own firm. Good information is a key to making good decisions.

- **Write all plans.** Goals and plans should be in writing as constant reminders of where you are supposed to be headed.

- **Involve everyone in the planning process.** Always ask for comments from anyone who would be affected by the plan. You want to build a consensus so that everyone will have input into the plan and will support it when

Exhibit 2-16 Key Questions a Law Office Strategic Plan Should Answer

- Who are our clients and what legal services will we provide? (See all of the questions regarding practice management in Exhibit 2-3.)
- Who will manage the firm? Is our governing structure still adequate? Evaluate the current methods used to set and implement firm policy.
- Assess the effectiveness of the executive committee, managing partner, planning committee, compensation committee, and legal administrator.
- What are the general goals of the firm? Rank them in order of importance.
- What new geographic area of the country/world will we enter?
- What sources of finance will we use?
- Will we rent or purchase office space and equipment?
- What kind of technology and systems will we use to provide our legal services to clients?
- What marketing channels will we use to attract clients?
- How will we achieve continual growth?
- What was the firm's growth rate over the past three years? Can the projected growth rate for the next three years be established with any degree of certainty?
- Does the firm have established bill rate requirements for legal staff? Are they adequate or should they be revisited?
- What is the capability of the firm to meet its future needs within existing practice areas? Which areas need improvement?
- What is the culture of the firm? Does it suit the firm well?
- What kinds of insurance will we need to purchase (health, disability, life, malpractice)?
- How many employees will we need and in what positions?
- Should we use alternatives to permanent staff such as temporary workers, contract workers, or should we use outsourcing techniques?
- How will we recruit, train, and retain the right people for our firm?
- Will the firm merge with another firm to obtain a competitive advantage?
- Environmental Analysis—Consider demographic, political, and economic factors when considering strategic planning. How will these factors affect how the firm will serve the clients?
- Industry Analysis—Consider the legal environment as a whole, including surveys of other law firms, average profit margins, growth rates, costs, and so on. How does the firm compare to industry averages?
- Competitive Analysis—Who are the firm's major competitors? What are their strengths and weaknesses? What are your competitors' business strategies?
- Internal Analysis—Compare your strategies with those of your major competitors, and compare your strengths and weaknesses to those of your competitors.
- Determine Threats and Opportunities—Consider what new markets are the most attractive for the firm and then analyze the firm's competitive position in the marketplace, identify any threats that competitors may have, and identify opportunities resulting from market conditions or a competitor's weakness.

it comes time to implement it. People promote plans that they perceive as being their own, either in part or as a whole. This is the "ownership" concept. Soliciting input from others opens the lines of communication and allows all firm members to feel that they have a stake in the action, that their thoughts are important, and that they are needed. When you are involving others in the process, do not judge their suggestions; listen to them and consider them. Your job is to facilitate communication and to provide a nonthreatening environment in which everyone can participate.

- **Stick to the plan.** It takes an amazing amount of patience to stick to a plan and follow through with what you started. It does a firm little good to make a detailed and wonderful plan and then scrap it two months later. It takes commitment from everyone involved to give the plan a chance to succeed.

- **Recognize that planning is a continuous process.** Planning is a continuous process of making improvements; it is not a onetime effort in which you develop a plan and then never revisit it. If all you do is make a plan and never follow it up or monitor it, you have wasted the firm's time.

- **Monitor the plan and communicate the results to others.** Always monitor the progress of the plan. One way to do this is to make a timeline or Gantt chart to track the expected progress over time. A **Gantt chart** is a plan or timeline of the projected begin and end dates of a project. A Gantt chart breaks a large project down into specific jobs or items that must be accomplished. As an item is finished, it can be marked completed (see Exhibit 2-17). Gantt charts are also good at simplifying and communicating complicated projects. Most people find charts more reader friendly than straight text.

Gantt chart
A plan or timeline of the projected begin and end dates of a project.

Periodically, you should check the progress of the project to determine whether the plan needs to be revised or completely overhauled to accomplish its objectives. One way to do this is to hold monthly planning meetings or to otherwise communicate the progress of the plan to others by keeping them informed about how the project is going. If possible, you should build into the plan quantifiable means of progress so others can see that the plan is working as expected and resources are not being wasted.

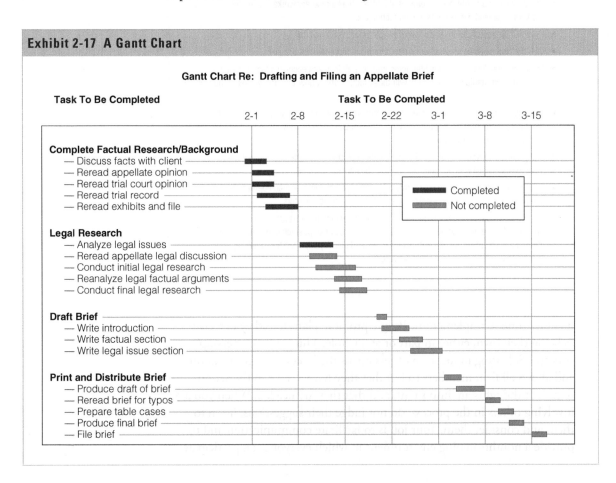

Exhibit 2-17 A Gantt Chart

Gantt Chart Re: Drafting and Filing an Appellate Brief

Marketing Management

Marketing is the process of educating consumers about the legal services the law office provides. It is not enough to simply service existing clients. Law firms, like other businesses in a competitive environment, must continue to bring in new business in order to grow and survive. Marketing has become an important element of management in today's law office. Marketing efforts include market research, discovering and developing a market niche regarding a client need that has previously been unrecognized or unmet, creating a "brand" name for the firm so that it is recognized by potential clients, and advertising efforts through brochures, word-of-mouth/referrals, networking, television, radio, and the Internet. Chapter 7 contains a full chapter on legal marketing.

marketing
The process of educating consumers on the quality legal services that a law office can provide.

Organizing, Policies, and Systems

Organizing is the process of arranging people and physical resources to carry out plans and accomplish objectives. Effective legal administrators create order through setting policy and creating effective systems for accomplishing tasks. A **system** is a consistent or an organized way of doing something. A system allows you to create a set procedure for doing something as opposed to dealing with activities or problems in an ad hoc manner. Without a system, each time a legal service or an administrative function is performed, the person performing the task would rely solely on his or her memory to complete the task. Productivity and accuracy suffer when staff must recreate processes each time a task is done. By developing a system, staff members can take advantage of the experience and expertise of others in the law office. A system collects experience and expertise and passes it on to others. Systems preserve the procedures that have worked successfully in the past, but must be reviewed periodically to allow for future evolution. Systems guarantee quality because the same mistakes are not made twice.

organizing
The process of arranging people and physical sources to carry out plans and accomplish objectives.

system
A consistent or an organized way of doing something.

Systems can be used for both substantive tasks and administrative tasks. A **substantive task** is a task that relates to the process of actually performing legal work for clients. An **administrative task** (or a business-related task) is one that relates to the internal practices and duties involved with operating or managing a law office.

Substantive systems include using form files, checklists, and detailed instructions to standardize many types of legal tasks. Certain areas of the law are particularly suitable for systems because of their routine nature, including bankruptcy, divorces, adoptions, probate, estate planning, and workers' compensation.

Administrative tasks such as docket control, timekeeping and billing, purchasing, and human resource management can also be set up using an established system of procedures. A staff manual establishes administrative policies and procedures and documents how things will be accomplished administratively.

substantive task
A task that relates to the process of actually performing legal work for clients.

administrative task
A task relating to the internal practices and duties involved with operating or managing a law office.

Law Practice Policies and Procedures—the Staff Manual

Read and digest any staff manual provided.

One of the main systems is a law office staff manual, also called a policy and procedures manual. The purpose of a staff manual is to set out in writing the standing policies and procedures of a law office. The types of policies covered by the staff manual depend on the law office, but they can range from personnel policies and how files will be maintained to how letters and pleadings will be formatted (see Exhibit 2-18). Staff manuals establish and document an efficient and cost-effective way of handling the day-to-day operations of the firm. The manual allows everyone to operate under the same procedures and to quickly find consistent answers to common questions. Without a staff manual, each person develops his or her own particular method for accomplishing tasks. Law offices need uniformity so that elements are not missed or forgotten. Staff manuals can be used to guarantee each client the same high-quality legal services, every time.

Staff manuals are particularly helpful when training new employees. New employees can immediately get a feel for how the firm operates and what procedures are to be followed just by reading the manual. This makes the orientation process quicker and less difficult. The idea that staff manuals are only needed in large-sized firms is a misconception. Small-sized law offices, legal aid offices, and government and corporate law departments need written procedures as well.

What Systems or Subjects Are Included in the Staff Manual?

Exhibit 2-18 contains a list of systems that are often found in staff manuals. Staff manuals usually cover such items as how the office is organized, ethical and confidentiality policies, personnel-related policies, the use of office equipment, and office procedures for opening new files. Staff manuals can be adapted to the needs of the specific law practice. In general, if management has to reiterate a policy more than once or twice on a matter of importance, the policy should be put in writing.

Drafting Policies and Procedures

Staff manuals can contain both policies and procedures. Although the concepts are similar, they also are very different from each other. A **policy** is a specific statement that sets out what is or is not acceptable (see Exhibit 2-13). A **procedure** is a series of steps that must be followed to accomplish a task. Some firms have separate manuals for policies and procedures. All policies and/or procedures should be detailed, accurate, and succinct; procedures should be clearly stated, easy to read, and should assign specific responsibilities, stating *who* is responsible for the tasks. In addition, whenever possible, a due date also is included so that staff members know exactly *when* items are due. When writing policies and procedures, a balance should be struck between having too many details (i.e., overregulating) and having too few. The aim is not to make a bureaucratic, detail-ridden manual, but to have a usable, practical guide.

Staff Manuals from an Ethics Perspective

Staff manuals also are important from an ethical point of view. The manual allows management to draft policies that will deter ethical violations. For instance, a common ethical problem is neglect of client matters. A manual can address this by stating which person is responsible for keeping the calendar,

policy
A specific statement that sets out what is or is not acceptable.

procedure
A series of steps that must be followed to accomplish a task.

Exhibit 2-18 Sample Law Office Staff Manual—Table of Contents

Section 1

Employment Policies

1.1   Classifying Employees
1.2   Employment-At-Will
1.3   Employment of Relative and Minors
1.4   Introductory Period
1.5   Privacy and Confidentiality
1.6   Personnel Records and Employee References

Section 2

Office Policies

2.1   Equal Opportunity Employer
2.2   Diversity
2.3   Policy on Sexual Harassment
2.4   Americans with Disabilities Act of 1990 (ADA)
2.5   The Family and Medical Leave Act of 1993
2.6   Quality Management/Client Relations
2.7   Office Hours
2.8   Overtime
2.9   Weekly Time Report
2.10 Code of Personal and Professional Conduct
2.11 Professional Attitude
2.12 Personal Appearance

Section 3

Employee Benefits and Services

3.1   General Information
3.2   Recruitment and Hiring
3.3   Training
3.4   Worker's Compensation
3.5   Unemployment Insurance

Section 4

Legal Document Preparation Guidelines

4.1   Prepare Letters and Memoranda
4.2   Prepare Draft and Legal Documents
4.3   Prepare Legal Opinion Letters

Section 5

Security and Emergency Procedures

5.1   Data Protection
5.2   Emergency Procedures
5.3   Medical Emergencies, Accidents or Work Injuries
5.4   Disaster Planning and Recovery

Section 6

Financial Management Guidelines

6.1   Trust Account
6.2   Receipts
6.3   Disbursements
6.4   Petty Cash
6.5   Billing Procedures
6.6   Timekeeping Records

Section 7

File System

7.1   The File Opening Form and Worksheet
7.2   Opening a New File

(continued)

7.3 Removal of Files from the Record Room
7.4 Returning Files to the Record Room
7.5 Closing Files
7.6 Form Files
7.7 Electronic Files

Section 8

Technology

8.1 Policy on the Use of Technology
8.2 Training
8.3 Dealing with Computer Viruses
8.4 Handling Computer Crashes
8.5 Network
8.6 Word Processing
8.7 Docket/Calendar Software
8.8 Time/Billing Software
8.9 Fax/Modems/Internet
8.10 LexisNexis/Westlaw
8.11 Security

Section 9

Library Policies

9.1 The Function and Use of the Library
9.2 Library Organization and Functions
9.3 The Librarian
9.4 Use by Non-Firm Personnel
9.5 Library Copies of the Firm's Work Product
9.6 Client Charges

Source: Adapted from Wert, R., & Hatoff, H. (2004). *Office Policy and Procedures Manual* (4th ed., p. iii). American Bar Association.

how items will be put on the calendar, and what steps will be taken to avoid missing the deadline. In addition, the staff manual can be used to set out policies on ethical situations, such as the need for strict confidentiality of client information.

Staff Manuals on the Law Office Intranet

intranet
An internal information distribution system used only by a law firm staff.

An **intranet** is an internal information distribution system based on Internet technology. In short, it is a private "Internet" that is used only by law firm staff. When the staff manual is on an intranet, it is immediately accessible to all staff with access to a computer; it can be updated electronically; and it can save thousands of dollars in reduced paper and copying costs.

An intranet can also be used to provide information related to

- Accounting and billing—Access to client time/billing records, firm accounting policies, and accounting forms.

- Law library resources—Access to form files, brief banks, CD-ROM products, Westlaw, LexisNexis, and links to many legal sites on the Internet.

- Human resources and benefits—Human resource information, including job openings, compensation plans, legal postings, benefit plans, and links to benefit-provider sites.

- Continuing legal education (CLE)—Information related to upcoming CLE seminars and links to local and national bar associations.
- Client tracking—Client directories, matter lists, contact information, matter numbers, and other client-related information.
- Practice areas—Separate pages can be created for each of a firm's departments and specialties. Each specialty can have information specifically related to that area of the law, including Internet links to government regulations and statutes, case law, discussion groups, and resources developed by the firm itself to assist practitioners.

Facilities Management

Facilities management encompasses planning, designing, controlling, and managing a law office's building or office space. Facilities management includes a variety of subject areas, such as property acquisition, moves/construction/remodeling, space planning/office design/furniture, parking, cleaning/maintenance/grounds, common areas, environmental considerations (lighting, electrical, climate, and plumbing), and security/safety/disaster recovery.

facilities management
Encompasses planning, designing, controlling, and managing a law office's building or office space.

Property Acquisition

Property acquisition refers to acquiring space in which the law office will be housed, including purchasing a building/property or leasing office space. Property acquisition is an important and expensive proposition for any law office, whether it is a large-sized law firm looking for a long-term lease for a number of floors in a downtown office building (to be near business clients) or a sole practitioner who concentrates on family law and might purchase a house or small building near a residential area. Depending on the office, the practice may want to be on public transportation routes, accessible from major highways, and other such considerations.

Moves/Construction/Remodeling

Facilities management also includes moving from one location to another, constructing a whole new office from scratch, or constructing/remodeling existing office space to meet new needs or demands. All of these areas include a great deal of planning and organizing.

Space Planning/Office Design/Furniture

Office space is important for many reasons; office space and decor help define the law office's image. The facility should be functional and practical, and it should work for the particular law office's structure and needs.

One of the first aspects of space planning that must be considered is the organization of the law office. Law office management must decide upon the needs of the office. For example, management must decide whether practice groups will be grouped together or apart; whether computers, files, and other equipment will be centralized or decentralized; what types of offices are needed (e.g., number and size of conference rooms, kitchen area, and separate postage and copy areas); and whether the office will need to expand in the near future. An effective way of determining needs is to survey the staff members, ask them what they think they need, and then use that information in the planning process. Some offices, especially medium- to large-sized offices, hire consultants and architects to help with these as well as other issues.

Furniture should not only project an office's image but also provide sufficient work surfaces, be comfortable and usable, and efficiently use the space within the law office. There are thousands of different styles of furniture, including traditional (wood and plastic laminate); contemporary (wood, metal, and laminate); high-tech (glass, wood, and metal); and ergonomic (laminate, wood, and metal).

Many law offices use system furniture or module design, including movable partitions or panels, and work surfaces, file cabinets, and drawers that attach to the partitions instead of interior walls. The panels typically have electric cabling that runs through the bottom of each of the electrical outlets. In this way, law offices can be completely flexible and use their space more wisely than ever before. The major disadvantages of interior landscaping are increased noise and decreased privacy. Interior landscaping has gained in popularity because of the increased cost of office space; minimizing the amount of space a law office uses reduces rent and maintenance costs.

Some studies have shown that the most negative feature of interior landscaping is not the increased noise but the lack of personal privacy, especially when short partitions that allow people to see over the top are used, and when the entryways face out, allowing others to see into the work space.

Correlation between Space and Cost   Any law office administrator will tell you that there is a direct correlation between the amount of office space needed and the cost. Office space has become increasingly more expensive, especially in metropolitan areas. Lease payments represent a large overhead expense, which can put pressure on cash flow because it is a fixed cost, meaning that it is incurred every month without relation to whether the office is having a good month, financially speaking. Thus, offices have struggled to become physically smaller and more compact and to use the space they have wisely.

Parking

Adequate parking for both employees and clients should be taken into consideration when choosing office space. Poor parking is a common complaint of the law offices in downtown business districts.

Cleaning/Maintenance/Grounds

Facilities management also includes having the facility cleaned (typically through a cleaning service), repairing or replacing items that break, and being responsible for the office grounds, including lawn care, snow removal, and more.

Common Areas

Facilities management may also include being responsible for common areas in the law office, such as waiting room, kitchen areas, conference rooms, bathrooms, and storage rooms, to name a few.

Environmental Considerations

Environmental considerations include a variety of important topics such as lighting, electrical, climate, and plumbing. Depending on the size of the law office and the number of employees, each of these areas can be extremely technical and involve government standards, and many are operated by sophisticated computer systems. Many law offices hire a facilities management company to provide maintenance and other services regarding environmental matters.

Security and Workplace Violence

Law office security and safety is an extremely important aspect of facilities management. Tragically, violence to attorneys, paralegals, court personnel, and other legal professionals happens quite frequently. Disgruntled clients assault all kinds of law offices all over the country, from the rural solo practitioner to large downtown law firms in skyscrapers.

> On December 8, 2006, Joe Jackson, a disgruntled client, forced a security guard at gunpoint to bring him to the 38th floor of a downtown Chicago building and the offices of Wood, Phillips, Katz, Clark & Mortimer. Once inside the firm's offices, he chain-locked the entrance doors and began shooting, killing three people before he was killed by a sniper.

There are many ways to provide security, including installing security systems, limiting access to private areas of the law office using locked and secure doors that open only with security cards, installing locking doors with buzzers at reception areas, hiring security guards, installing security cameras, issuing identification and/or building passes, and limiting elevator service after certain hours. Law offices simply cannot afford to ignore the security issues that face them. Exhibit 2-19 lists suggestions for tightening security. The type of security you use depends on the size of the law firm, the type of building, and many other factors.

Exhibit 2-19 Strengthening Law Office Security

- **Never allow free access throughout your office**—The golden rule of security is to **never** allow people free access throughout your office. Access to your office can be limited by restricting points of entry. If you are in a small building, lock the back door and do not allow the public to use it. Require the public to use the front door and have a receptionist there at all times, monitoring the entrance with a panic button that will contact the police or others in the case of an emergency.
  If your office is in a high-rise building, security stations and/or a receptionist can be posted at the entrance to the building or your suite.
- **Limit the public to a waiting room with a locked door to inner offices**—A good way to limit access to your office is to secure your waiting room. Simply put, the door from your waiting room to your inner offices should be locked and have a buzzer installed. By having a locked door to your inner offices, you restrict access and require the visitor to check in with the receptionist. This is similar to many doctor's offices, where a receptionist sits behind a sliding window and sounds a buzzer that enables the visitor to enter the internal part of the office.
- **Issue security badges**—Another way to limit access in large-sized offices is to issue security cards or badges to personnel, and to require visitors to check in and be issued a visitor badge.
- **Use security cards**—Many offices use electronic locked doors that use a keyless entry system. If a person does not have a security card, he or she cannot open the locked door.

(continued)

- **Monitor entrances**—Entrances to the building or suites should be monitored, when possible, by using security cameras, buzzers, security guards, keyless entry systems, or other such methods.
- **Remind staff about security issues and issue policies**—Always remind staff about the importance of security issues, and draft policies regarding security issues. Always be prepared.
- **Train staff members on security issues**—Whenever possible, staff members should be trained regarding safety awareness and security issues.
- **Large buildings may install metal detectors**—Metal detectors may be installed in large-sized law offices.

Law offices also need formal policies on security and workplace violence issues, such as the following:

Doors
The doors between interoffice access and the reception area should be locked at all times.

Admission of Visitors and Strangers
No persons, other than employees, shall be allowed within the main law firm office area without being escorted by an employee. Anyone not authorized in the office area must identify themselves and their purpose for being in the office. Please contact the receptionist if you encountered unauthorized persons in the office; if it is after normal business hours, contact the local police.

Workplace Violence
The firm's policy prohibits any acts or threats of violence by any party against any employee in or about the firm's facilities or elsewhere at any time. There is a zero-tolerance policy regarding any firm. The firm is committed to:

1. *provide a safe and healthy work environment;*
2. *take prompt remedial action against anyone who engages in any threatening behavior or acts of violence or who uses any abusive or threatening language or gestures on the firm's premises or while on firm business;*
3. *take appropriate action when dealing with employees, former employees, or visitors to the firm's facilities who engage in such behavior. Action may include disciplinary action including termination, notifying the police, and prosecuting violators of this policy to the maximum extent of the law;*
4. *prohibit employees, former employees, and visitors, other than law enforcement personnel, from bringing firearms or other weapons onto the firm's premises.*

Safety   Safety issues include ensuring the building has a sprinkler system, fire alarms, emergency power/lighting, fire escapes, and similar features. All law offices should also have an evacuation plan and policies in their firm's staff manual regarding what to do in case of a fire, earthquake, or bomb threat. A policy should be in place regarding what to do in case of a medical emergency, a work injury, or an accident. It is also prudent for the law office to have safety-related items such as bandages, gauze, and related items on hand. Large-sized law offices may have oxygen and more advanced medical supplies as well. Occasional fire drills (and related drills) are also prudent and advised.

Disaster Recovery Planning   Disaster recovery planning also tends to fall under the scope of facilities management. All law offices should have a disaster recovery plan in place that can be implemented in the case of a disaster. The **disaster recovery plan** includes information on how the law office will rebuild and recover from a total disaster. Copies of the disaster recovery plan should be kept off-site. It is important to have information and plans in place that can be implemented at a moment's notice.

Typical information contained in a disaster recovery plan would include the following:

- Who is in charge of overseeing implementation of the disaster recovery operation? What key individuals make up the disaster recovery team, and what are their functions and responsibilities? Who will be contacted, and how? Where is the designated meeting place (and an alternative) if the whole facility is unavailable?

- What services/areas/departments have been determined as vital to the recovery operation? What are the steps, components, and alternative strategies for making each area/department operational? What will each department require in terms of resources (computers, minimal office space, desk, chairs, information, etc.) to be operational? All of this must be put in writing, and a copy should be maintained off-site.

- How do firm personnel obtain information and instructions on what to do when a disaster happens?

- Where are important papers and computer backup data located? Important documents should always be maintained off-site in the case of a disaster. These include copies of leases; names, addresses, and phone numbers of all staff; bank account information; copies of insurance policies; a listing of all clients, including contact information for the client and opposing counsel in cases; complete firm-wide inventory list (computers, furniture, art, library books, fixtures, etc.); disaster recovery plans for each department; and computer backup tapes.

- In the case of a disaster, what vendors and companies have been identified in advance who can help to assist with restoration, and who are the contact people for these vendors?

If you wait until the disaster occurs to start planning, it's too late. By that time, you could lose everything. If everything *is* lost, can the firm recover? Can the law office continue as a business? What are the ethical problems with losing everything related to a client's case? If a law office of any size loses everything in a disaster, there is a good chance that it will not be able to recover; that's why disaster recovery planning is so important.

Office Services Management

Office services management refers to a number of internal systems and services in a law office. Office service responsibilities include management of the mail room, copiers and copy facility, file/records management (discussed in Chapter 9), telecommunications (including telephone systems, voice mail, fax machines, and video conferencing), among others.

disaster recovery plan
A disaster recovery plan includes information on how the law office will rebuild and recover from a total disaster.

office services management
It refers to the administration of a number of internal systems and services in a law office. These include mail, copy, fax, and telecommunication services, among others.

Mail Room

Medium- and large-sized law offices have mail rooms that manage and sort incoming mail. They also weigh and place postage on mail with either a postage meter device or electronic means. They may also coordinate overnight delivery services. In small-sized law offices, a clerk, receptionist, or legal secretary may perform these services.

Copy Machines

Copy machines are a staple of every law office, regardless of size or type. Law offices must routinely copy documents for internal files, clients, courts, opposing counsel, and others. While the delivery of documents through electronic means is popular, there is no end in sight for the copier's usage. It is not uncommon, even in a solo practitioner's office, to make tens of thousands of copies a year. Some large-sized law offices have a centralized copy center or department that has its own staff. Other law offices have one or more self-serve copy machines located throughout the office while some have both a centralized department, which handles large documents, and self-serve copy machines for smaller jobs.

As an alternative to the high cost of purchasing and maintaining copy machines, some law offices outsource this function to a vendor. The vendor provides the copy machine, maintenance, supplies, and personnel. In many cases, the vendor is given office space and provides these services on-site.

Billing for Client Copies Making sure that clients are properly billed for copies made for their case can be problematic, given the large number of cases and copies. Some law offices have staff members complete expense slips detailing which client the copies were made for, how many copies were made, and why. Some copy machines allow the user to enter a client identification number, which then tracks the number of copies to be billed to each client, while other machines use client copy cards to calculate the number of copies.

File/Records Management

Law offices of all types must have an effective file/records management system that allows the practice to store, track, and retrieve information about cases in a logical, efficient, and expeditious manner. File/records management is covered in detail in Chapter 9.

Telecommunications

Telecommunications is a rapidly evolving area that has many aspects important to law offices. Among these are telephone systems, voice mail, fax machines, video conferencing, and voice communications through Internet known as VoIP (Voice over Internet Protocol).

Telephone Equipment Telephones are vital to any law office because they are the means by which staff members communicate with clients, opposing counsel, courts, witnesses, and one another.

Telephone systems for law offices can cost from $1000 to $100,000 or more, depending on the number of phone stations and outgoing lines needed.

Voice Mail   Voice mail is a computerized telecommunications system that stores and delivers voice messages. Callers are able to leave a detailed message directly, without going through a secretary or other individual where messages can be distorted or miscommunication can take place. An individual can then retrieve his or her messages—either on-site or off-site—by dialing his other "mailbox." Voice mail is available 24 hours a day, so clients can leave messages for people even when the law office is not open. Voice mail is an integral part of many law offices.

Fax Machines   Fax machines are used by most law offices. Fax machines allow a user to electronically transmit a document's image to a receiving fax machine at another location, which prints the document that was sent. Fax machines are easy to operate and come in hundreds of styles with many features. Some fax machines work in conjunction with a computer system and allows a user to fax a document, such as a word processing file, from his or her computer.

Faxes have become so accepted in the legal community that many courts allow documents to be faxed if the documents are not more than 10–15 pages long.

Faxes and Confidentiality   Faxes should be sent very carefully because an improper or a misdirected fax transmission can lead to breach of client confidentiality, loss of attorney–client privilege, and legal malpractice. All fax cover pages for law offices should have some kind of confidentiality disclaimer on them, such as the following:

CONFIDENTIALITY NOTICE—This fax message contains legally confidential and privileged information intended for the sole use of the individual(s) or organizations named above. If you are not the intended recipient of this fax message, you are hereby notified that any dissemination, distribution, or copy of this message is strictly prohibited. If you have received this fax in error, please notify us immediately by telephone and return this fax to us by mail.

Other precautions that can be taken to ensure fax information stays confidential include ensuring that everyone using the fax machine knows how to use it correctly; making sure that everyone operating the fax machine understands that a misdirected fax can destroy client confidentiality and the attorney–client privilege and can result in charges of malpractice; and requiring the sender to check to make sure the material has been received.

Telecommunications and Client Confidentiality   Client confidentiality should always be considered when dealing with phone systems. This is especially true considering the amount of time that paralegals spend on the phone. Users should never broadcast client names over the law office's intercom/paging system; users should also be very careful about who is in the room when a client's case is being discussed on the phone. Conversations on mobile phones, particularly those that include confidential or sensitive information, should be limited, if possible. Some radios/scanners have the ability to pick up these frequencies.

Video Conferencing

Video conferencing allows users in remote sites to see and hear one another via a monitor and speaker using telephone lines, computer equipment, and a camera. Medium- and large-sized law offices may have these internally. Small-sized law offices can use a vendor for video conferencing. Video conferencing may be used internally to connect remote offices for a meeting and, on occasion, may be used for depositions, among other things.

Technology and Information Systems Management

It is difficult to overestimate the impact that technology has had on the practice of law in the last 25 years. Technology, computers, networks, mobile computing, and information systems in general have completely changed the way that legal professionals practice law and run a law office business. There is virtually no aspect of how legal services are delivered to clients and how a law office is operated that has not been affected. While technology has greatly increased productivity and efficiency, enhanced systems for communicating, and made researching and finding information easier and more accessible, all this has come at a price. Many large- and small-sized law offices struggle to keep up with technology advancements and with finding the money and resources to continue to enhance their technology. Recent surveys found that, on average, firms annually spend between $8000 and $17,000 per attorney. The commitment to and reliance on technology at medium- and large-sized firms are substantial.

Most law offices, even small ones, must now have dedicated staff to support the myriad of computer systems in a typical law practice. Most medium- and large-sized firms must have a host of computer professionals, including a chief information officer, who are solely responsible for the firm's technology. Exhibit 2-20 shows a partial list of common technology in law offices. The list grows every year as new technology is introduced.

Technology and the Legal Staff

Attorneys, paralegals and other members of the legal team, use common electronic resources such as e-mail, the Internet, smart devices, word processing, calendar/docket control, and time and billing programs on a daily basis. Most law offices are equipped with network computers, and paralegals, especially those with technology training, are consulted concerning technology decisions made at their firms.

Hardware

The selection of currently available computer hardware is overwhelming. Law offices can choose from many different types of computer hardware and manufacturers, depending on the type of operation and objectives they have. Options include desktop, laptop, handheld, wireless, and mobile technology. Due to the wide selection of available hardware and the fact that computer technology prices continue to fall, all law firms have access to adequate technology to operate their office in today's electronic business environment.

Exhibit 2-20 Partial List of Typical Technology in a Law Office

Hardware (and Software) Used by Technical Staff	Software Used by Legal Professionals or Administrators	Telecommunications
Desktop or laptop computer, monitor, speakers, storage devices, and mouse for every staff member	Word processing	Internet
Networked or stand-alone printer	Spreadsheet	Intranet
Networked or stand-alone color printer	Database	Extranet
Multifunction printer (printer, fax, scanner, copier)	Presentation	Westlaw/LexisNexis/other online service
Local network servers, cards, wireless, etc.	E-mail	Instant messaging
Wide-area network servers Laptop computers PDAs (personal digital assistants, handheld computers)	Internet browser Docket control/calendar Litigation support	Blogs
Mobile phones, Smart Devices Scanner Operating system software on every computer, laptop, and handheld device	Time and billing Accounting Case management	
Virus protection software Digital projector Digital camera Digital video camera Portable printer Firewall	Document assembly Document management Electronic discovery Knowledge management PDF creation Scanning/optical character recognition	
Central storage devices backups Digital printers Computerized telecommunication equipment Computerized security systems Web design/development software Web site management Document sharing software	Speech recognition Trial presentation Legal-specific programs Graphic/illustration programs Project management Citation checking Conflict checking Transcript/deposition management	
Portable hard drives Remote access software	Contact management	

Mobile computing is also changing the way legal professionals practice. Attorneys and paralegals have nearly constant access to their firms and information via networks, wireless technology, and the Internet. Legal professionals can access data from the courthouse, their homes, the road, and nearly anywhere else in the world. Court-bound lawyers can now take entire cases with them on a laptop, including pleadings, transcripts of arguments and proceedings, court records, depositions, discovery, and millions of documents, all accessible and ready to be retrieved.

Software

Law offices have a wide selection of software that includes general business and productivity programs, general legal programs (such as time and billing), legal programs designed for a specific type of practice (such as software designed for professionals practicing in the area of taxes or bankruptcy) and legal programs designed to perform electronic discovery and trial presentations.

Electronic Mail Electronic mail is the single most used software application by legal professionals.

Electronic mail (e-mail) allows users to send and receive messages using a computer. When an Internet account is opened, the user is given an e-mail address and can then send and receive messages. Hundreds of millions of people use e-mail to communicate every day.

There are many advantages to using e-mail, such as that messages can be sent, almost instantaneously, nearly anywhere in the world; e-mail is very inexpensive (the cost of an Internet account); word processing, sound, and graphic files can be attached to e-mail messages; messages can be sent, read, and replied to at the user's convenience; e-mail prevents telephone tag; messages can be sent to groups of people at the same time; users can get their messages from anywhere; and messages can be saved, tracked, and managed electronically. A common client complaint is that legal professionals are often very busy and hard to reach. E-mail allows legal professionals and clients to communicate with one another quickly and conveniently.

E-Mail in the Legal Environment

E-mail is now a major means of communicating with clients, other attorneys, and courts, and most paralegals use e-mail in their jobs every day. E-mail is being used in legal organizations for everything from routine correspondence to billing, newsletters, and filing court papers. Most clients now demand e-mail access to their lawyers and paralegals. The security of e-mail has long been a concern to legal professionals, but given the dramatic increase with confidential and privileged communications/documents sent via e-mail, security is now critical. The issue of security can be handled in a number of ways, including requiring clients to provide oral or written consent to sending confidential information via e-mail, adding a confidentiality statement at the end of all e-mails, using encryption software, or simply not using e-mail to send confidential documents. In addition, new uses of e-mail arise often; the service of process by e-mail has even been approved by a few courts.

E-Mail Encryption and Digital Signatures

Because e-mail can pass through many network servers before it reaches its destination, it is subject to being read by system administrators, hackers, or others. E-mail is often considered to be more like a postcard than a sealed letter in this respect. Some legal organizations use encryption software to protect confidential e-mails sent to others. Encryption software is used to lock e-mail so that it can be opened only by the intended recipient.

Business E-Mail Etiquette and Tips Most people are familiar with e-mail. However, there is a difference between using e-mail for personal use and business use. In business, you must be very careful about your e-mail usage. The following points provide some important tips for using e-mail in a law office setting.

- *Be succinct and clear, and use short paragraphs*—Whenever possible, keep your e-mails short and to the point. You should be as clear as possible in your messages so that the reader does not have to ask for clarification regarding something you wrote. Use paragraphs liberally. Long paragraphs are hard to read on a computer screen, and it is easy to lose your place, particularly if you have to scroll up and down the message.

- *Spell-check and reread your e-mails*—Most e-mail programs have a spell-check function; use it whenever possible. Many users send e-mails full of spelling and grammar errors that may change the meaning of the message. Before sending your e-mails, reread them to make sure they make sense. Remember, you will be using e-mail to correspond with clients, so it should not be sloppy.

- *Be careful to treat e-mail as business correspondence*—E-mails cannot be retrieved once they are sent. They are written records that are kept by the recipients, so be extremely careful about what you send and make sure that you can live with the message. When in doubt, do not send it. Also, remember that the recipient cannot see your body language or interpret your tone, so be careful how you phrase things.

- *If a message is unclear, ask for clarification*—If you are unsure about a message someone has sent you, ask for clarification and do not assume you know the answer.

- *Be careful of "Reply All"*—Sometimes users get e-mail with 20 other people copied on it. If the user selects "Reply," only the sender of the original e-mail will get a response, but selecting "Reply All" will send a reply to all 20 of the other recipients. Far too often, a user intends to send a personal message to the sender of the e-mail and mistakenly selects "Reply All." Before you select "Reply All," make sure you really want to send your e-mail to everyone on the original message.

- *Do not use e-mail to communicate with clients regarding sensitive information*—Since Internet e-mail can pass through many network servers where the e-mail can be read, it is probably better not to use e-mail at all for communicating with clients about sensitive information; if in doubt, always ask the client first.

- *Double-check the recipient of your e-mail*—Often users intend to send e-mail to one person and accidentally select the wrong person. Always double-check the e-mail address to make sure you entered the correct one.

- *Limit each e-mail message to one topic*—It is difficult to decide where to file multiple-topic e-mails, and it is sometimes difficult to follow-up on them. There could be multiple follow-up actions buried in one e-mail.

- *Always password-protect word processing and other documents sent to clients*—By password-protecting documents, you add some degree of security to the attachment with minimal effort.

Problems with E-Mail   While e-mail is inexpensive and convenient, it is not perfect. Keep the following considerations in mind when using e-mail:

- *Do not assume that an e-mail was read just because you sent it*—Like any other form of written communication, e-mail can be lost, unopened, or accidentally deleted.

- *E-mail relies on computer technology that fails from time to time*—E-mail works only if the computer networks, telephone lines or other technology, and the recipient's computer hardware and software are working correctly. If any of these fail, your message will not reach the recipient.

- *Be careful what you say in e-mails, since they can be forwarded to others*—The nature of an e-mail is that it can be easily forwarded to another person. For example, you may send an e-mail to X about Y, and X can immediately forward it to Y.
- *E-mail security can be breached*—As noted before, e-mail is not necessarily confidential, and e-mail security can be breached in many ways, including the following:
- Leaving confidential e-mails open on your computer screen for others to read over your shoulder
- Leaving your office for lunch or a break while signed into your e-mail program
- Printing e-mails that others can find (such as at a network printer)
- Using a password such as "password" or names of family members that would be easy for others to guess

E-Mail Errors

It is important to be careful when using e-mail. Errors can happen in several different ways and may result in malpractice claims against the lawyer and/or the legal organization. Some common errors include the following:

- *Sending an ill-conceived e-mail to a client or others before it is carefully considered*—Unlike a letter placed in the outgoing mailbox that can be retrieved a few hours later, once the user presses the "Send" button, e-mail is gone.
- *Sending e-mail to unintended parties*—It is easy to use the "Reply All" command to send a private message to a group of people unintentionally, or to click on the wrong e-mail address. Depending on the content of the message, errors like these can damage a client's case, particularly when e-mail is sent to the opposition.
- *Sending the wrong attachments*—Since files can be sent as attachments to e-mails, it is particularly important to ensure that the correct file is attached. It is easy to attach a wrong file to an e-mail that might be devastating to a client's case. This can be avoided by opening the file after it is attached to the e-mail to make sure it is the correct one.
- *Typing errors*—Typing errors, such as leaving words out, can substantially change the meaning of a sentence. For example, in a client e-mail you might intend to type "We don't recommend that you do this," but instead you type "We recommend that you do this." While you have left only one word out, that word could be crucial to how the client proceeds.

E-Mail Confidentiality

As discussed earlier, confidentiality while using e-mail to communicate with clients is an important issue. Attorneys have duty to protect client information pursuant to their respective state's rules of professional conduct, modeled from the *ABA Model Rules of Professional Conduct.* The ABA Ethics Committee looked at the confidentiality of e-mail exchanges between attorneys and clients and concluded that an attorney can communicate with clients over e-mail without encryption. The Ethics Committee stated that e-mail affords users a reasonable standard of expectation of privacy, similar to that of a telephone call, and that unencrypted e-mail could be used to communicate with a client.

However, the ABA also found that an attorney had a duty to consider the sensitivity of the issue being communicated, what it would mean to the client's representation if the communication were disclosed, and the relative security of the contemplated means of communication. Arguably, the ABA wants legal professionals to use a commonsense standard when using e-mail or other forms of communication with clients. If communication with a client is highly sensitive, then the legal professional should check with the client about whether a more secure form of communication is warranted.

Practical considerations for using e-mail ethically include the following:

- Having a policy for the legal organization regarding the use of e-mail and how it will be used to communicate with clients

- Consulting clients about what type of information they want to communicate via e-mail, how often the client receives or responds to e-mail, and other information about the particulars of the client's specific e-mail system or habits

- Making sure the e-mail addresses are accurately entered so that client communication is not sent to others by mistake

- Sending a test e-mail to a client to ensure the right e-mail address is being used

- Adding a confidentiality statement to all client e-mails—this is similar to statements accompanying many fax cover pages that state that the information is intended solely for the recipient and any third party who receives it should immediately forward it or destroy it

- Not using e-mail at all for particularly sensitive information

Word Processing/Spreadsheets/Database Management/Presentation Software   Word processing, spreadsheets, databases, and presentation software are some of the most commonly used software by legal professionals. They are used to draft documents and correspondence, make financial calculations and projections, track and organize documents, and present information to fact finders.

Docket Control/Calendaring/Case Management   Docket control, calendaring, and case management are covered in detail in Chapter 7; these programs are generally used to track, organize, and manage many appointments and deadlines in a law office.

Time and Billing   Timekeeping and billing software automate the process of tracking a timekeeper's billable hours, billing clients, and posting payments to a client's account. Timekeeping and billing are covered in detail in Chapter 5.

Document Management   Document management software organizes, controls, distributes, and allows for extensive searching of electronic documents typically in a networked environment. Document management software allows a legal organization to file documents electronically so they can be found by anyone in the organization, even when there are hundreds of users spread across offices

document management software
Organizes, controls, distributes, and allows for extensive searching of electronic documents, typically in a networked environment.

throughout the country. Document management software goes far beyond the file management capabilities in operating system software. It is the electronic equivalent of a filing room with rows and rows of filing cabinets. If a legal organization is going to move to a "paperless office," the office will have to have a document management program to manage the electronic files. Document management software also provides for extensive searching capabilities and allows users to add a profile of every document that can be easily searched on later.

document assembly software
Creates powerful standardized templates and forms.

Document Assembly   **Document assembly software** creates powerful standardized templates and forms. Instead of having to open an existing client's word processing document and edit it for a new client, it allows the user to create a template than can be used over and over. Document assembly programs have more powerful commands and capabilities than templates found in word processing programs.

Litigation Support   Litigation support software organizes, stores, retrieves, and summarizes information that is gathered in the litigation of a lawsuit. Litigation support programs are powerful database management programs that have been designed specifically for litigation. They can store thousands and even millions of records, search for and retrieve the requested records, summarize and track important case information, and much more.

Electronic Discovery   Electronic discovery programs have the ability to store, search, and retrieve electronic documents in a case, such as e-mails, word processing files, spreadsheets, and other attachments and electronic data produced during discovery. For 200 years, documents have been produced as hard copy, but this is no longer the case. In many legal matters, the parties need the ability to search, sort, track, and organize electronic data. People communicate via e-mails, attachments, and electronic files, and legal professionals need a way to search this information to find data that will assist them in representing their clients.

Legal-Specific Software   Legal-specific software includes programs developed for a legal specialty area. For example, an attorney who practices criminal law might purchase a program that automates and tracks information about criminal cases. The software might track each individual criminal count against a defendant, automate the scheduling of the case, automate the documents in the case (such as witness lists), track restitution, track evidence, and much more.

Trial Software   Trial software assists litigators in preparing for and presenting information to a jury or fact finder. They can work closely with automated courtrooms where judges and juries have computer screens in front of them to receive evidence. The programs typically provide sophisticated presentation graphics features, outline and organize information that will be presented to the fact finder, and include the ability to organize information by legal issue; organize, track, and display trial exhibits; and generate and display complex timelines.

Telecommunications

Law Office Web Sites   Many law offices now have home pages on the Internet, and almost all the U.S. law offices have Web sites. Most offices use their Web site for marketing information, but some are expanding the content to include such things as client intake questionnaires, real-time consulting with prospective clients, and self-help information and research. Some firms have in-house staff and a variety of computer programs to design, develop, and host their own sites, while others outsource these tasks.

Internet Access   Nearly all law offices provide access to the Internet for a variety of purposes, including factual research, legal research (including access to Westlaw and LexisNexis), purchasing, marketing, communicating with clients, and much more. With this access comes a host of security issues, such as hackers, viruses, spyware, and so forth.

Intranet   As defined earlier, an intranet is an internal distribution system used only by a law firm staff. It disseminates information to internal staff using a Web browser and the look and feel of the World Wide Web. An intranet provides information to internal users in the same way the Internet provides information to the public. Typical information a firm might include on its intranet site includes office policies and procedures, links to law-related Web sites, training material, contact lists, links to form files or brief banks, and much more.

Extranet   An **extranet** is a network designed to provide, disseminate, and share confidential information with clients. A client with a Web browser can access the law practice's extranet, go through security and ID/password protections, and access his or her case plans, documents, strategies, billing information, and other data.

extranet
A network designed to provide, disseminate, and share confidential information with clients.

Legal Weblogs   A weblog, or "blog," is a Web site with information contained in posts that are arranged in reverse chronological order. Blogs resemble diary or journal entries in a notebook, and they can contain links to other Web sites or articles. There are many law-related blogs on the Internet, including specific blogs on certain type of law, such as immigration or taxes.

Summary

Legal administration is important to the survival of every law practice. Legal administration covers the following subject matters: practice management, leadership, controlling, financial management, human resources management, planning, marketing, organization/policies/systems, facilities management, office services management, and technology or information services management.

Practice management refers to management decisions regarding how a law office will practice law and handle cases. Administrative management refers to management decisions regarding how a firm will operate as a business, such as how it will handle financial or human resources matters.

Practice management decisions include defining the law office's practice (what cases it will take), services, and the practice systems necessary to provide legal services to clients. Another aspect of practice management is the quality of services that it provides to clients. Quality and TQM is a management philosophy that is based on knowing the needs of each client and allowing those needs to drive the legal organization. This includes the ideas (1) that management has the duty to make sure the firm provides quality legal services to clients; (2) that quality service involves every person in the firm; (3) that clients determine what constitutes "quality services"; (4) that quality depends on individual, team, and organizational performance; and (5) that there is a focus on constantly improving services.

Leadership is the act of motivating or causing others to perform and achieve objectives. Controlling is the process of determining whether the law practice is achieving its objectives, holding stakeholders accountable for their goals, and making strategy adjustment so the firm achieves its objectives. Financial management is the oversight of the firm's financial assets and profitability to ensure overall financial health.

Human resources management refers to hiring, evaluating, compensating, training, and directing law office personnel. Important federal employment laws include the Family and Medical Leave Act, the Fair Labor Standards Act, the Civil Rights Act of 1964, the Americans with Disabilities Act, and the Age Discrimination in Employment Act, among others.

Planning is the process of setting objectives, assessing the future, and developing courses of action to achieve the objectives. Marketing is the process of educating consumers on the quality of legal services that a law office can provide. Organizing is the process of arranging people and physical resources to carry out plans and accomplish objectives. A system is a consistent way of performing a task. A policy is a specific statement that sets out what is or is not acceptable. A procedure is a series of steps that must be followed to accomplish a task. A law office staff manual contains the firm's policies and procedures related to legal and administrative work.

Facilities management includes planning, designing, controlling, and managing a law office's building or office space. Facilities management includes areas such as property acquisition, moves/construction/remodeling, space planning/office design/furniture, parking, cleaning/maintenance/grounds, common areas, environmental considerations (lighting, electrical, climate, and plumbing), security, safety, and disaster recovery planning. Maintaining a secure and safe environment is an extremely important aspect of facilities management. Locked doors, security systems, limited access to interior halls, security passes, and other initiatives help to keep a law office secure. A disaster recovery plan includes information on how the law office will rebuild and recover from a disaster.

Office services management refers to internal systems and services in a law office. The services include management of the mail room, copiers and copy facilities, file/records management, and telecommunications (including telephone systems, voice mail, fax machines, and video conferencing).

Technology has had a large and continual impact on how legal professionals practice law. Law offices have a myriad of choices when it comes to computer hardware and software. Electronic mail is used more by legal professionals on a daily basis than any other application. Other applications that legal professionals use include docket control, time and billing, document management, document assembly, litigation support, electronic discovery programs, and others. Telecommunication services that legal professionals use include law office Web sites, Internet access, intranets, extranets, and legal blogs.

Key Terms

administrative management

administrative task

Age Discrimination in Employment
 Act of 1967

Americans with Disabilities
 Act of 1990 (ADA)

bona fide occupational
 qualification

Civil Rights Act of 1964

coaching technique

controlling

disaster recovery plan

document assembly software

document management software

employment-at-will doctrine

equal employment opportunity

Equal Pay Act of 1963

extranet

facilities management

Fair Credit Reporting Act

Family and Medical Leave
 Act of 1993 (FMLA)

financial management

Gantt chart

human resources management

intranet

leadership

management

management by objectives

marketing

mission statement

negligent hiring

office services management

organizing

personnel handbook

planning

policy

practice management

procedure

reasonable accommodation

sexual harassment

strategic planning

substantive task

system

total quality management (TQM)

On the Web Exercises

1. Compare, contrast, and print out mission statements for three law offices. Some law firms may call them core values, firm philosophy, or a purpose statement, while some include their purpose or their mission in a general introductory statement; large-sized law firms typically include this on their Web site. Start by going to a general search engine like http://www. google.com or http://www.yahoo.com and search for "global law firms" or "large law firms." The Findlaw site, http://www.findlaw.com, has features that allow users to search for lawyers and law firm Web sites as well. Research law-related blogs on the Internet. Find five legal blogs, including at least one on either law office technology or law practice management or administration. Print a few pages of the blogs that you found and write a paragraph explaining each Web site. Again, start by going to a general search engine, such as http://www.google. com or http://www.yahoo.com, and type "legal blog."

Projects

1. Group Project: Opening a Law Office

Your group will act as the Law Practice Management Committee of Adams and Lee Attorneys at Law, a new firm specializing in corporate and insurance law that expects to begin practicing law this year. This project will be done throughout the course.

Your job as the Law Practice Management Committee is to put together a strategic management plan for the first year of operation. You need to take great care in preparing the plan, since the plan will guide your firm for the first year of operation and will also be given to your bank to secure financing. You are to submit one copy of the strategic management plan, which will be reviewed for accuracy, completeness, and logic. Each member of your group will receive a grade. You will also evaluate each other regarding the work done on the project.

The Adams and Lee law office will have two partners and two associate attorneys. The partners expect to make $100,000 a year, and associates expect to make $70,000 a year. You must determine what other staff will need to be hired and at what pay rate. You have no budgetary constraints.

Use the Web sites listed in the Web Links section of this chapter, or a general search engine, to find resources, information, and checklists that would assist an attorney in opening a new law practice.

Your strategic management plan should include the following sections:

A. **Physical location of the building:** You must choose an actual office site for the business. You will need private offices for each of the attorneys and appropriate office space for the other staff. You will also need a reception area, library, and conference room. You must give a narrative description of the office site and include cost (leased or purchased) and justification as to why this site has been chosen.

B. **Layout of the office and furniture:** You must decide how the office interior will be laid out. A layout of the office should be provided, including a narrative description of each office and its accompanying furniture, and an explanation as to why the office was laid out in the particular manner.

C. **Technology/equipment:** Appropriate technology/equipment should be researched. Assume the attorneys want to purchase all new equipment typically found in a law office, including computers, software, printers, Internet access, fax machine, copiers, and so forth. A narrative description of the items to be purchased (and their cost) should be included, as well as the justification for the purchase. Also include a detailed list of computer hardware and software that might be needed.

D. **Staff employment:** Explain what additional staff positions will be needed to support the two partners and two associates. Draft job descriptions for each of the positions. Use a general search engine to find job descriptions for a legal secretary, paralegal or legal assistant, attorney, legal administrator, and law librarian. The attorney is a general practitioner and employs a legal secretary and a paralegal. Compile a detailed list, including pricing and some background on why each item is necessary.

E. **Law library:** An appropriate library for insurance and corporate law must be purchased. Please explain what will be purchased, why, and the cost.

F. **Budget:** A detailed budget should be included for both income and expenses (see Chapter 6). Please indicate the billing rates and hours to be billed for the partners, associates, and any paralegals hired (see Chapter 5). The rates and hours should reflect the common market rates and hours for the area. When considering expenses, do not forget to add 25% to associate and staff salaries to cover fringe benefits. The budget should provide the partners with the income they expect and include the typical expenses found in most law offices.

Practical Applications

1. Interview an attorney and get answers to the following questions: What is the mission of his or her firm? How does he or she define his or her practice? Who are his or her primary clients? What primary services does he or she provide? What practice systems does he or she use to support the legal services provided to clients? Does he or she prefer practice or administrative management?

2. Research and write an in-depth report on disaster recovery plans. Obtain a minimum of five different resources. Information covered in the report should include why they are important, which major sections or areas a disaster recovery plan has, how they are used, and information related to why disaster recovery plans are particularly important in law offices. In addition, write a disaster recovery plan for yourself (e.g., if your apartment or residence has caught fire and everything you had has been destroyed).

3. Research and write a detailed report on total quality management. At a minimum, the report should include who is credited with developing it, where it originated and became popular, what specific ideologies it includes, and how it can be implemented in any business, including a law office.

4. Research and write a one-page detailed summary on each of the following federal employment laws: Civil Rights Act of 1964, Family and Medical Leave Act, Americans with Disabilities Act, and Age Discrimination in Employment Act. At a minimum, include why the law was passed, major provisions of the law, what agency is responsible for enforcing it, and other relevant information about it.

5. Write a mission statement for yourself. What is important to you? What are your goals and objectives? Develop a five-year strategic plan for yourself. Where do you see yourself in five years? What will you have to do to reach your goals and objectives?

Case Review

Bednar et al v. CT Corporation, No. 02-3646 JMR/JSM (D. Minn. filed Sept. 16, 2002)

West's Minnesota Jury Verdict Reports

Thomas Bednar worked for CT Corporation System as a customer specialist. CT is a nationwide legal document service company. The company offers various services to attorneys and law firms and has offices in several states. There are approximately 300 customer specialists employed by CT. Until August of 2002, the customer specialists were compensated on a salary or "exempt" basis, and as such, were ineligible for overtime pay for any hours worked in excess of 40 hours per week. After August 2002, customer service specialists were reclassified as nonexempt. In 2003, Bednar filed a class action complaint against CT in a Minnesota federal district court, alleging the classification of customer specialists as exempt violated the federal Fair Labor Standards Act, 29 U.S.C. 207(a)(1) and various state wage and hour laws. The complaint sought reimbursement for unpaid overtime, liquidated damages, and an award of attorney's fees and costs. The parties agreed to settle the case on December 15, 2003 for a total payment not to exceed $2,825,000, including attorney's fees. Under the terms of the settlement agreement, each member of the class who chose to participate in the settlement would receive back overtime pay based on the actual excess hours that individual worked, in addition to a payment of $4066. The additional payment was deemed to cover any potential state law violations, liquidated damages, and various other damages.

Questions

1. Were you surprised that this FLSA violation happened to a company that works in the legal industry and works with attorneys and law firms every day?

2. Notice in this case that it was only *after* the defendants figured out that they had wrongly misclassified the customer service specialists—and, in fact, corrected the matter—that the plaintiffs discovered the error and filed the class action to recover damages when they were misclassified. Is that fair?

3. Notice also that what may have started as one person, Thomas Bednar, having a single claim against the defendant turned into a full-blown class action costing the firm $2.8 million dollars in damages alone. Did it surprise you how much the case was settled for and how quickly it was litigated?

Case Review

Littell v. Allstate Insurance Co., 177 P.3d 1080 (N.M. Ct. App. 2007).

177 P.3d 1080

(Cite as: 177 P.3d 1080)

Court of Appeals of New Mexico,

Patricia LITTELL, Plaintiff-Appellee, v. ALLSTATE INSURANCE COMPANY, Defendant-Appellant.

No. 26,268.

November 21, 2007

{1} Defendant Allstate Insurance Co. appeals from a judgment on a jury verdict in favor of Plaintiff Patricia Littell on her claims of hostile work environment sexual harassment and retaliatory constructive discharge. Allstate argues that: (1) the district court abused its discretion in admitting certain, evidence; (2) there was no evidence supporting either of Plaintiff's claims or the jury's award of compensatory damages for alleged emotional injuries; (3) the issue of punitive damages should not have been submitted to the jury; and (4) the award of punitive damages manifested the influence of passion and prejudice and, therefore, violates due process. We affirm. We also remand to the district court the issue of whether Plaintiff is entitled to an award of attorney fees for this appeal.

Background

{2} Plaintiff began work as a paralegal in Allstate's Albuquerque Staff Counsel Office in 1996. In October 1998, Todd Aakhus joined the office as lead counsel. At this point, according to Plaintiff, conditions at the office changed. Aakhus regularly made sexual innuendoes and told dirty jokes that were demeaning to women. Aakhus allegedly engaged in sexual discussions and flirted with female employees, inappropriately touched female employees, commented about other employees' sexual preferences, and tolerated similar conduct by other office employees. When Plaintiff reported these occurrences anonymously to Allstate's hotline for employment disputes, Allstate investigated, but Plaintiff did not feel that Allstate did anything to resolve the situation. Also according to Plaintiff, Aakhus began treating her differently after she complained to the Allstate hotline. He became more aggressive,*1083 disciplined Plaintiff for pretextual reasons, and berated and belittled her publicly. Ultimately, when Aakhus refused to give Plaintiff a leave of absence so that she could deal with a "family crisis," Plaintiff resigned.

{3} Plaintiff sued Allstate and asserted claims for violations of the New Mexico Human Rights Act, intentional infliction "of emotional distress, prima facie tort, retaliatory discharge, and punitive damages. The district court entered summary judgment in favor of Allstate on Plaintiffs claim for intentional infliction of emotional distress and on her claim under the Human Rights Act to the extent it was predicated on retaliation. The case went to trial before a jury, and at the close of Plaintiffs evidence, the district court granted judgment as a matter of law in favor of Allstate on Plaintiffs claim for prima facie tort. After deliberating, the jury returned a verdict in favor of Plaintiff on her claims of hostile work environment sexual harassment and retaliatory discharge. The jury awarded Plaintiff $360,000 in compensatory damages and $1 million in punitive damages. The district court denied Allstate's subsequent motion for judgment notwithstanding the verdict or, in the alternative, for remittitur or a new trial. This appeal followed. We provide additional facts in our discussion.

Discussion

{4} Allstate makes the following arguments on appeal: (1) the district court abused its discretion by admitting evidence of incidents of which Plaintiff was not aware, of Allstate's discipline of Aakhus, and of other matters that occurred after Plaintiff left Allstate's employ; (2) there was no evidence supporting the jury's determinations (a) that Allstate violated the Human Rights Act by allowing a hostile work environment to exist in the office, (b) that. Allstate subjected Plaintiff to retaliatory constructive discharge, And (e) that Plaintiff was entitled to compensatory damages for alleged emotional injuries in the amount of $200,000 to $250,000; (3) the district court should not have allowed the issue of punitive damages to go to the jury because (a) Aakhus was not acting in a managerial capacity or in the scope of employment and (b) Allstate did not authorize, ratify, or participate in Aakhus's misconduct; and (4) the punitive damages award manifested the influence of passion and prejudice, was excessive, and violates due process. We address each argument in turn.

I. The District Court Did Not Abuse Its Discretion in Admitting Evidence

{5} Allstate argues that the district court abused its discretion in admitting two categories of evidence, including: (1) testimony about incidents that Plaintiff was not aware of, and (2) evidence of matters that postdated Plaintiffs employment with Allstate, including Allstate's disciplining and discharge of Aakhus. We review the district court's admission of evidence for abuse of discretion, *Coates v. Wal-Mart Stores, Inc.,* 1999-NMSC-013, ¶ 36, 127 N.M. 47, 976 P.2d 999, and conclude that the district court's admission of this evidence was within the sound exercise of its discretion.

A. Incidents of Which Plaintiff Was Purportedly Not Aware

{6} Allstate contends that the only evidence admissible on Plaintiffs claim of sexual harassment was evidence regarding incidents of which Plaintiff was aware or made aware during her employment. Allstate further argues that Plaintiff failed to lay a foundation that she was aware of several incidents about which fellow employees Maureen Reed and Margie Lang testified. These incidents included Reed's testimony that Aakhus reported a story in the office concerning a physician putting his hand in a woman's vagina, Reed's testimony regarding a twenty-minute discussion at lunch about a female attorney's breasts, Reed's testimony that a female attorney in the office would squat in her office "with her crotch open to the area," Lang's testimony that Aakhus gave her a book of erotica, and Lang's testimony about a staff meeting at which a female attorney discussed her breasts.

{7} We agree with Allstate that there is case law supporting the view that Plaintiff could rely only on evidence relating to harassment of which she was aware during the time of her employment. See *Hirase-Doi v. U.S. W. Commc'ns, Inc.*, 61 F.3d 777, 782 (10th Cir.1995) (explaining that the plaintiff in a hostile environment sexual harassment suit under Title VII "may only rely on evidence relating to harassment of which she was aware during the time that she was allegedly subject to a hostile work environment"). Consistent with this view, the district court ruled that evidence of events not witnessed by Plaintiff would be admitted if the events "occurred prior to the time of [Plaintiffs] departure, which she learned of essentially contemporaneously." Our review of the trial transcript establishes that sufficient foundation was laid for introduction of the specified testimony.

{8} Reed testified that Plaintiff "knew about" Aakhus's story regarding the doctor putting his hand in a woman's vagina, and that Plaintiff was probably at the lunch where the female attorney talked about her breasts. Lang testified that she told Plaintiff about the book of erotica Aakhus had given her, and that she was sure that Plaintiff was made aware of the staff meeting where the female attorney discussed her breasts. Given this foundational testimony, we cannot say that the district court abused its discretion in admitting the evidence.

B. Evidence of Matters Postdating Plaintiffs Employment with Allstate

{9} Allstate also contends the district court should have excluded evidence of events that occurred after Plaintiff resigned. That evidence consisted of a complaint to Allstate management about Aakhus, Allstate's subsequent investigation of that complaint, and Allstate's disciplining and discharge of Aakhus. Allstate maintains this evidence was inadmissible under Rule 11-407 NMRA. This rule provides:

> When, after an event, measures are taken which, if taken previously, would have made the event less likely to occur, evidence of the subsequent measures is not admissible to prove negligence or culpable conduct in connection with the event. This rule does not require the exclusion of evidence of subsequent measures when offered for another purpose, such as proving ownership, control or feasibility of precautionary measures, if controverted, or impeachment. *Id.*

Allstate further relies on *Spina v. Forest Preserve of Cook County*, No. 98 C 1393, 2001 WL 1491524 (N.D.Ill. Nov.23, 2001) (mem. and order), in which a federal district court, citing Federal Rule of Evidence 407, excluded evidence of the defendant employer's disciplinary actions against the alleged perpetrators of sexual harassment against the plaintiff. *Id.* at *11. We are not persuaded that Rule 11-407 mandated exclusion of this evidence.

{10} Plaintiff offered evidence of post-resignation events for a purpose other than to prove negligence or culpable conduct. Plaintiff argued to the district court that this evidence was relevant to show that Allstate management did nothing substantive in response to Plaintiffs and other employees' complaints of sexual harassment by Aakhus and to show Allstate's state of mind for purposes of punitive damages. The district court agreed with Plaintiff and further noted that the evidence was relevant to Allstate's affirmative defense that it "exercised

reasonable care to prevent and correct promptly any sexual harassment in the workplace." Consequently, the evidence fell within the exception contained in the second sentence of Rule 11-407. See 23 Charles Alan Wright & Kenneth W. Graham, Jr., Federal Practice and Procedure § 5290, at 148-49 (1980) ("The list of permissible uses in Rule 407 is illustrative, not exclusive; evidence of subsequent repairs may be admitted for any purpose that does not require an inference to the negligence or culpable conduct of the repairer, whether as an ultimate fact or intermediate inference." (footnotes omitted)).

{11} In addition, we do not consider Spina to be persuasive authority. Although the federal district court in that case excluded evidence of the suspension of the plaintiffs superiors, it did so without any significant analysis and in reliance on *Wanke v. Lynn's Transportation Co.*, 836 F.Supp. 587, 595 (N.D.Ind.1993) (mem. and order), which was a wrongful death case, not an employment discrimination case. See Spina, 2001 WL 1491524, at *11. We are similarly unpersuaded by the other cases upon which All-state relies. *Maddox v. City of Los Angeles*, 792 F.2d 1408, 1417 (9th Cir.1986), like *Wanke*, did not analyze the issue. *Hull v. Chevron U.S.A., Inc.*, 812 F.2d 584, 587 (10th Cir.1987), was a personal injury action, in which the policy reasons for excluding subsequent remedial measures (i.e., to encourage the undertaking of measures that enhance safety, see *Couch v. Astec Industries, Inc.*, 2002-NMCA-084, ¶ 26, 132 N.M. 631, 53 P.3d 398) have primary significance. In *Jumper v. Yellow Corp.*, 176 F.R.D. 282, 285 (N.D.Ill. 1997) (mem. and order), the federal district court reserved judgment on whether the subsequent measures would be admissible at trial.

{12} We therefore conclude that the district court did not abuse its discretion in admitting evidence of events that occurred after Plaintiff resigned her position.

II. There Was Substantial Evidence to Support Plaintiffs Claims of Hostile Work Environment and Retaliatory Constructive Discharge, and to Support the Jury's Award of Compensatory Damages

{13} Allstate argues that there was no evidence supporting Plaintiffs claims of hostile work environment sexual harassment and retaliatory discharge, and that there was insufficient evidence justifying the jury's award of compensatory damages for Plaintiffs emotional distress. "In reviewing a sufficiency of the evidence claim, this Court views the evidence in a light most favorable to the prevailing party and disregard[s] any inferences and evidence to the contrary." *Weidler v. Big J Enters., Inc.*, 1998-NMCA-021, ¶ 30, 124 N.M. 591, 953 P.2d 1089 (alteration in original) (internal quotation marks and citations omitted). We defer to the jury's determination regarding the credibility of witnesses and the reconciliation of inconsistent or contradictory evidence. *Id.* "We simply review the evidence to determine whether there is evidence that a reasonable mind would find adequate to support a conclusion." *Id.* We reject Allstate's contention that the "clearly erroneous" standard of review, which is employed by the federal courts, applies in this state court action. See *Bovee v. State Highway & Transp. Dep't*, 2003-NMCA-025, ¶ 17, 133 N.M. 519, 65 P.3d 254.

A. Hostile Work Environment

{14} Allstate contends that Plaintiff failed to introduce evidence on the claim of hostile work environment that Aakhus's conduct rose to the level of extreme offensiveness required by the applicable law. Allstate maintains that Plaintiffs evidence demonstrated nothing more than "a smattering of incidents" that occurred over Plaintiff s three-year employment in the office.

{15} Our Supreme Court, interpreting the New Mexico Human Rights Act, NMSA 1978, §§ 28-1-1 to-14 (1969, as amended through 2007), established what constitutes sexual harassment under a hostile work environment theory in *Ocana v. American Furniture Co.*, 2004-NMSC-018, 135 N.M. 539, 91 P.3d 58. Analogizing to federal law regarding a similar cause of action under Title VII, the Court stated that such a claim "is actionable … when the offensive conduct becomes so severe and pervasive that it alters the conditions of employment in such a manner that the workplace is transformed into a hostile and abusive environment for the employee." *Id.* ¶ 24, 135 N.M. 539, 91 P.3d 58. The fact finder must look at the totality of the circumstances, including the frequency of the discriminatory conduct; its severity; whether it is physically threatening or humiliating, or a mere offensive utterance; and whether it unreasonably interferes with an employee's work performance. The work environment must be both objectively and subjectively offensive—one that a reasonable person would find hostile or abusive and one that the employee did perceive as being hostile or abusive. *Id.* (internal quotation marks and citation omitted). In the present case, the district court instructed the jury in accordance with Ocana.

{16} Plaintiff introduced the following evidence in support of her claim. Plaintiff testified that she was very happy working for Allstate and that there were no discussions of sex or foul language in the office prior to the hiring of Aakhus. However, things changed when Aakhus was hired in October 1998. On his second day in the office, Aakhus came into Plaintiff's office, got physically very close to her, and, using profanity, told her a joke about President Clinton, Monica Lewinsky, and oral sex. Plaintiff said she felt shocked and "absolutely terrified" because the joke was so demeaning to women. The next day Plaintiff told Aakhus she did not want him to tell her, that kind of joke again and that what he had done was against Allstate policy.

{17} Plaintiff testified that, while Aakhus never told her a joke again, the sexual behavior never stopped, and Aakhus continued to tell dirty jokes in Plaintiffs presence over the next three years and four months. This behavior occurred almost daily. Most often, the jokes, which were both written and oral, were demeaning to women and frequently referred to sex acts. Aakhus used profanity and made comments about male and female genitalia. At Halloween, Aakhus commented that a witch on a broomstick looked as if she must be male and referred to the broomstick as a male body part. Aakhus also frequently followed Plaintiff closely, pointing at Plaintiff and berating her in public. Although he did not actually touch her, Plaintiff felt assaulted. Aakhus frequently "flip[ped] people off." Once, Aakhus referred to a news reporter as "Dicks Sniffing" and this offended Plaintiff. In addition, Aakhus frequently used the phrase "bite me."

{18} In 1999 Plaintiff complained to Allstate's Resolution Line, which is a hotline for Allstate employees to use to complain anonymously about their job-related concerns. An employee would complain, the complaint would be investigated, and the people investigating would get back to the complaining employee. Soon thereafter other employees began to complain about Aakhus's sexual jokes and comments. A secretary in the office, Lou Wise, told Plaintiff that Aakhus had said that Wise's daughters must be homosexual because they were not married, and this offended Wise.

{19} Plaintiff became more stressed and tried to avoid being alone with Aakhus, and she observed other employees changing their behavior as well. For example, Plaintiff and Wise, who often worked after 5:00, agreed that neither would leave the other alone and that they would stay until both could leave at the same time. Meanwhile, Plaintiff had received nothing in writing regarding her complaint to the Resolution Line. Several times, she called Allstate's employee assistance program, which provided confidential counseling to employees.

{20} Aakhus became more aggressive and gradually more temperamental. Going into 2000, Aakhus's sexual innuendoes and aggressiveness escalated. Employee complaints to the Resolution Line continued. People from Allstate's human resources department showed up at the office, and Plaintiff tried to communicate to them her understanding of the office atmosphere. Plaintiff was still frightened. Every time she called the Resolution Line, she was told to call back, and when she called back, she was told either that the matter was still under investigation or that the case was closed and to call someone else for further assistance. Plaintiff just wanted Aakhus to stop his behavior, but he would not, and no one at Allstate would make him stop.

{21} In 2000, there were several new hires in the office, including a new paralegal and a new secretary. Plaintiff noticed Aakhus flirting with the paralegal, and the two engaged in sexual discussions and told sexual jokes. The new secretary would touch Aakhus at meetings, and the two would leave the office together, which Plaintiff found demeaning and embarrassing. Two of the female employees discussed explicit details of the sexual acts required to conceive babies, the best time of the month to get pregnant, and said they would be meeting their spouses on company time to try to conceive, noting that their return to the office would be delayed because they would have to elevate their legs. Aakhus participated in these discussions, and he used a rubber chicken to demonstrate elevation of the legs. Several of the female employees, "who played along with [Aakhus's] sexualization of the office," dressed provocatively, displaying cleavage and wearing short, tight skirts.

{22} Plaintiff testified that the office was divided between those who engaged with Aakhus in sexual conversation and those who did not. The people who went along with Aakhus received special privileges and came and went as they pleased.

{23} Secretary Lou Wise testified that when she first began working at the office, Aakhus handed her two to three pages that included content that was "of a sexual nature having to do with oral sex." Wise further testified that "[i]t was constant from Todd Aakhus as far as lewd jokes."

Every joke Aakhus told was sexual. Due to the open, area in the office, Wise could hear Aakhus talking dirty and engaging in sexual banter. After Wise objected to Aakhus, his behavior changed. The episodes of a sexual nature increased and Aakhus would raise his voice so that Wise could hear what he was saying, "which was always of a sexual nature." Plaintiff was aware of all of this having occurred.

{24} Wise observed Aakhus hanging over Plaintiffs desk many times, talking in a very loud voice and pointing his finger at her. Wise observed instances of Aakhus's physical presence being very close to Plaintiff, and she saw Aakhus following Plaintiff, right on her heels. Aakhus's sexual talk got worse in 2000, and Wise saw Aakhus approach Plaintiff more often. Aakhus's criticism of Plaintiff intensified, and Wise saw Plaintiff crying or on the verge of tears many times. This affected Plaintiffs work because she seemed to be afraid of what Aakhus would do next.

{25} Wise reported Aakhus's behavior several times to Allstate's human resources department and to Larry Vogel, an Allstate attorney in the Denver office who was Aakhus's boss. According to Wise, Allstate "corporate" was aware of what was going on. Despite these reports to Allstate, Aakhus did not stop his behavior.

{26} Maureen Reed, who worked for eleven years as an attorney in Allstate's Albuquerque Staff Counsel Office, testified that Aakhus got sexual jokes off the Internet and passed them around to people in the office. Everyone was very shocked and upset by this, and this information was imparted to Plaintiff. Reed said that Aakhus's "sexual references never stopped for the whole time he was there." During team meetings each week, Aakhus made "constant sexual references." Reed reported that "[Aakhus's] thing was talking about sex in front of people…. He loved it, couldn't stop himself for some reason. So it was always sex." All of this kind of talk in a professional setting was "demeaning to women." Plaintiff was aware of all of these incidents.

{27} The sex talk continued at office lunches, which generally occurred when Aakhus's boss, Larry Vogel, was present. Reed heard a female attorney talk about her breasts for twenty minutes at one of these office lunches attended by Vogel. Reed thought Plaintiff was probably at this lunch. Reed also recalled that at a team meeting, one of the female attorneys said she had to go get medicine for her "ta-ta."

{28} Reed described the unprofessional conduct she observed, including "sexualizing the office, constant references to sex, either by innuendo, jokes that you tell, jokes that you pass out." Aakhus once told her a story that included "graphic detail about some doctor on the [witness] stand testifying about putting his hand up into some woman's vagina, in graphic detail." Plaintiff knew about this story.

{29} Allstate's human resources department came to the office, and Reed participated in at least two of these' investigations. Following these investigations, Vogel told the employees that Aakhus "might have a few little problems, … but it's the rest of you's [sic] problem, and you need to take care of yourselves." Aakhus then told the employees that they were not to call Vogel, and that he, Aakhus, "could do whatever he wanted." Reed said that this "was horrible and it was frightening."

She testified that there was a division in the office between Aakhus's employee friends whom he had hired and the employees who complained about Aakhus. She said that "at times, you could cut the tension with a knife. I mean, it was very tense and very hostile."

{30} Reed further testified that Plaintiff would become very upset when Aakhus was particularly abusive or did something outrageous. "[Plaintiff] was, obviously, under a huge amount of stress." By 2001, Aakhus "was totally angry and totally taking his anger out on the people who he believed were complaining." Plaintiff would tell Aakhus when he did something that she did not think was right, and "[t]his made him crazy with her…. So he was totally angry and abusive to [Plaintiff]." Reed testified that "[a]s things escalated, [Aakhus] was unreasonably trying to manage [Plaintiff's] time, making false accusations … about her work quality." In addition, Aakhus "followed [Plaintiff] around on her heels out in the open area in front of everyone." He would "hang over those dividers, and that's what he would do, yelling at her, with his face bright purple." Reed said "it was totally, totally scary."

{31} Margie Lang, a senior legal assistant in the office at the time, also testified. She said that Aakhus told blonde jokes and sexual jokes, many of which had to do with women. Shortly after Aakhus started working in the office, he gave Lang a book to read. The book was erotica. When she discovered the nature of the book, Lang gave it back to Aakhus. She told Plaintiff about this. Lang also testified that at one of the office's staff meetings, there was a discussion about the breasts of one of the attorneys. Plaintiff was made aware of this after the meeting. Lang believed that Vogel and human resources were aware of the complaints about Aakhus's behavior, but she did not observe a change in Aakhus's behavior.

{32} Exhibits introduced at trial showed that Allstate had first received complaints about Aakhus making "inappropriate, unprofessional and sexual comments in the office" in 2000. Allstate's investigation confirmed the validity of the complaints and Aakhus received formal counseling in August 2000. Plaintiff knew nothing about this. In May 2002, Allstate placed Aakhus on "Job in Jeopardy" status for making such comments. Allstate then discovered in August 2002 that Aakhus had violated the terms of the Job in Jeopardy notice by continuing to make such comments. Allstate terminated Aakhus on October 3, 2002. Then, in December 2002, Allstate rescinded its termination of Aakhus and reinstated him as an employee.

{33} Considering this evidence in the context of the applicable law, we conclude there was sufficient evidence to support Plaintiff's claim of hostile work environment sexual harassment. We evaluate the evidence with reference to the language of the jury instructions given, which constitute the law of the case. *Atler v. Murphy Enters., Inc.,* 2005-NMCA-006, ¶ 13, 136 N.M. 701, 104 P.3d 1092. The testimony of Plaintiff, Wise, Reed, and Lang established that Plaintiff was "subjected to offensive conduct of a sexual nature" and that "the conduct was unwelcome." In addition, the evidence gave rise to a reasonable inference that "the harassment occurred because of [Plaintiff's] sex." Both Plaintiff and Reed testified that Aakhus's sexual commentary was demeaning to women.

{34} The evidence also supported the conclusion that Plaintiff "perceived the working environment to be abusive or hostile" because she testified that Aakhus's conduct caused her to feel "assaulted" and "frightened." As time went by, she became more stressed and avoided being alone with Aakhus. Wise testified that Aakhus's conduct affected Plaintiff's work because she seemed to be afraid of what Aakhus would do next. Reed testified that Plaintiff "was, obviously, under a huge amount' of stress." In addition, given Wise's testimony that she reported Aakhus's behavior to Allstate several times, Reed's testimony that "you could cut the tension with a knife" in the office, and all the testimony regarding the frequency of profanity and sex-related conversation, a jury could reasonably conclude that "a reasonable wom[a]n in [Plaintiff's] circumstances would consider the working environment to be abusive or hostile."

{35} Allstate argues that the witnesses' generalized and conclusory testimony that Aakhus's comments "never stopped" and were "constant" is insufficient as a matter of law to establish a hostile work environment. In support, Allstate cites several cases, which we do not find persuasive. For example, the issue in **Woodward v. City of Worland**, 977 F.2d 1392 (10th Cir.1992), was limited to the question of whether the district court had properly denied the defendants' motion to dismiss on the basis of qualified immunity. *Id.* at 1396. Thus, the court's discussion regarding generalized and conclusory testimony focused on the lack, of time-specific evidence tying the alleged harassment to a time when the law was clearly established that sexual harassment violated equal protection rights. *Id.* at 1398. Allstate's reliance on that case is inapposite. The other cases cited by Allstate are equally unpersuasive. See **Miranda v. Wis. Power & Light Co.**, 91 F.3d 1011, 1018 (7th Cir.1996) (affirming summary judgment against the plaintiff because her assertions of a hostile work environment consisted of vague, conclusory allegations); **Ceasar v. N. Star Steel Tex., Inc.**, 69 F.Supp.2d 858, 867 (E.D.Tex.1999) (granting summary judgment against the plaintiff because her allegations constituted only her subjective perception of discrimination and suggested nothing more than a bad working relationship with her superior); **Leskinen v. Utz Quality Foods, Inc.**, 30 F.Supp.2d 530, 533 (D.Md.1998) (granting summary judgment to the defendant because the plaintiff's generalized statements of harassment did not establish that any violations of Title VII occurred within the limitations period).

{36} Allstate contends that there was no evidence that Aakhus's "conduct was sufficiently severe or pervasive to alter the conditions of [Plaintiffs] employment." In support, Allstate cites to **Baskerville v. Culligan International Co.**, 50 F.3d 428 (7th Cir.1995), where the Seventh Circuit Court of Appeals reversed a jury verdict in favor of the plaintiff on her claim of sexual harassment. In that case, the manager called the plaintiff "pretty girl," made a grunting noise at her, suggested she was "hot," talked about "los[ing] control" around pretty girls, and made a gesture suggesting masturbation. *Id.* at 430. The court stated, "We do not think that these incidents, spread over seven months, could reasonably be thought to add up to sexual harassment." *Id.* The court noted that the manager never touched the plaintiff, never invited her to have sex or a date, and he never threatened her, exposed himself, or showed her a dirty picture. *Id.* at 431. Allstate argues that Aakhus never did any of these things either.

{37} We are not persuaded that this case is like Baskerville. The jury in this case was instructed that [w]hether the environment constituted a sexually hostile work environment is determined by looking at the totality of the circumstances, including the frequency of the discriminatory conduct, the severity of the conduct, whether the conduct was physically threatening or humiliating or a mere offensive utterance, and whether it unreasonably interfered with an employee's work performance. There was evidence that Aakhus's profanity and his sex-related comments and jokes occurred almost daily, that it was "constant" and increased over time, that it occurred at office lunches and staff meetings, and that Aakhus became more aggressive as time passed. Plaintiff, Wise, and Reed testified that Aakhus frequently followed Plaintiff close on her heels, pointed his finger at her, and yelled at her "with his face bright purple," and Reed said that Aakhus "was totally angry and abusive" to Plaintiff. Plaintiff testified that Aakhus became critical of her work and that his criticisms were completely unfounded, that Aakhus told her that he knew she had reported him to management, that Aakhus began sabotaging her computer, and that she was operating at an extremely high stress level.

{38} The jury could reasonably consider the totality of these circumstances and conclude that the environment in the office was hostile. See **Nava v. City of Santa Fe,** 2004-NMSC-039; ¶ 15, 136 N.M. 647, 103 P.3d 571 (holding that there was sufficient evidence of harassment even though each incident by itself "may not have been severe enough to support a hostile work environment claim" but "in their aggregate, the incidents reflect[ed] the severity and pervasiveness of the harassment"). While Allstate presented evidence that could be viewed as inconsistent with such a conclusion, "[t]he question is not whether substantial evidence exists to support the opposite result, but rather whether such evidence supports the result reached." **Las Cruces Prof'l Fire Fighters v. City of Las Cruces**, 1997-NMCA-044, ¶ 12, 123 N.M. 329, 940 P.2d 177. We therefore conclude that substantial evidence supported the jury's verdict in favor of Plaintiff on her claim of hostile work environment sexual harassment.

B. Retaliatory Constructive Discharge

{39} Allstate contends the evidence did not support Plaintiff's claim of retaliatory constructive discharge. It makes two arguments on this issue. First, it argues that Plaintiff was not constructively discharged because a reasonable person in Plaintiff s situation would not have felt compelled to resign. See **Ulibarri v. State,** 2006-NMSC-009, ¶ 14, 139 N.M. 193, 131 P.3d 43 (explaining that in order to show constructive discharge, a plaintiff "must show that the employer made working conditions so intolerable, when viewed objectively, that a reasonable person would be compelled to resign" (internal quotation marks and citation omitted)). Second, Allstate asserts that, even if Plaintiff was constructively discharged, she failed to prove that her discharge was in retaliation for an act she performed that public policy would authorize or encourage.

1. Constructive Discharge

{40} Allstate maintains that Plaintiff failed to prove constructive discharge. At most, according to Allstate, Plaintiff presented evidence of (1) a hostile work environment, (2) arguably unfair criticism of her work, (3) being forced to relinquish her private office for a carrel, and (4) an unfounded denial of her request for a leave of absence. According to Allstate, this evidence does not rise to the "extraordinary and egregious" level necessary "to overcome the normal motivation of a competent, diligent, and reasonable employee to remain on the job." *Turner v. Anheuser-Busch, Inc.,* 7 Cal.4th 1238, 32 Cal.Rptr.2d 223, 876 P.2d 1022, 1026 (1994) (in bank), overruled on other grounds in *Romano v. Rockwell Int'l, Inc.,* 14 Cal.4th 479, 59 Cal.Rptr.2d 20; 926 P.2d 1114 (1996).

{41} Again, we assess the sufficiency of the evidence in the context of the jury instructions given. The district court instructed the jury:

> You may consider that [Plaintiff] was constructively discharged from her employment if you find that Defendant Allstate Insurance Company made her working conditions so intolerable, when viewed objectively, that a reasonable person would be compelled to resign, and she had no other choice but to quit. Our review of the transcript convinces us that the jury could have reasonably found that Allstate constructively discharged Plaintiff.

{42} As discussed previously in this opinion, there was substantial evidence supporting the conclusion that Allstate subjected Plaintiff to hostile work environment sexual harassment consisting of pervasive sexual commentary and innuendo. In addition, there was evidence that Aakhus subjected Plaintiff to aggressive, physically intimidating conduct, such as his frequently following her closely on her heels, pointing his finger at her, and shouting at and berating her in public areas of the office. Plaintiff testified that after she reported Aakhus to Allstate's Resolution Line, Aakhus began criticizing her work and that the criticisms were inaccurate and outrageous. Then, in 2000, after Allstate's human resources department conducted an investigation of the various complaints about Aakhus, he told Plaintiff he knew she had reported him, and he became more aggressive. Plaintiff testified that Aakhus began deleting the "ticklers" on her computer. Ticklers were computerized reminders of deadlines in the various cases handled by the office. In 2001, Aakhus formally disciplined Plaintiff by giving her a "requires improvement" notice. Plaintiff testified that the notice was "absolutely full of false accusations." Notably, the evidence of unfair criticism was not solely Plaintiff's testimony of her subjective views. Several witnesses, including two attorneys who worked closely with Plaintiff, testified that Plaintiff was very competent and her work was excellent.

{43} There was also evidence that Plaintiff and others made many complaints about Aakhus to Allstate, apparently to no avail. Plaintiff first complained to the Resolution Line in 1999, and others also complained. Plaintiff received no response to her initial complaint indicating that Allstate had looked at the matter, and she was told that the case was closed. She spoke several times with Allstate's employee assistance program to try to figure out how to get Aakhus to stop his

behavior. There were many complaints about Aakhus to the Resolution Line in 2000. Ultimately, Allstate sent two people from human resources to the office, and Plaintiff spoke to them. Allstate disciplined Aakhus, but Plaintiff did not know at the time that this had occurred. Every time she called the Resolution Line she was told to call back on a specific date, but when she did so, she was told the matter was still under investigation and to call back.

{44} In May 2001, Aakhus was very agitated and told Plaintiff she had to move out of her office into a work carrel area, even though there was vacant office space. This exposed her to more of the sexual talk and innuendo. In 2002, Plaintiff's father died, and her 95-year-old, infirm grandfather was "crushed." Plaintiff, who believed she had a leave of absence available to her, asked Aakhus for leave, and he denied it. Plaintiff begged Aakhus because she "was at [her] wits' end." She testified that this "was the worst day of [her] professional life" and that she "had absolutely no alternative but to give [her] notice."

{45} Allstate presented evidence that was inconsistent with Plaintiff's testimony. However, "when there is a conflict in the testimony, we defer to the trier of fact." *Buckingham v. Ryan,* 1998-NMCA-012, ¶ 10, 124 N.M. 498, 953 P.2d 33. The jury apparently found Plaintiff's evidence to be more credible than that submitted by Allstate, and we will not second guess that determination.

{46} Allstate analogizes this case to *Gormley v. Coca-Cola Enterprises*, 2005-NMSC-003, 137 N.M. 192, 109 P.3d 280, in which the Court affirmed summary judgment in favor of the defendant on the plaintiff's claim of constructive discharge because the plaintiff failed to show that his working conditions rose to the necessary level. *Id.* ¶ 1, 137 N.M. 192, 109 P.3d 280. The plaintiff based his claim on criticism of his job performance, loss of overtime, reduction in pay, and loss of a lighter duty position, which the plaintiff contended jeopardized his safety. *Id.* ¶¶ 13, 17, 137 N.M. 192, 109 P.3d 280. The Court held that the plaintiff's claim of criticism was too generalized, in that he had never received any written discipline; that loss of overtime was not material because it did not result in a reduction in base pay; that the reduction in pay was not extreme; and that he failed to provide record support for his claim that his change in duties jeopardized his safety. *Id.* ¶¶ 14-18, 137 N.M. 192, 109 P.3d 280.

{47} We do not agree that the evidence presented in Gormley was equivalent to Plaintiff's evidence in the present case. Plaintiff introduced proof establishing hostile work environment sexual harassment and evidence that her supervisor physically intimidated her, sabotaged her computer, and falsely accused her of inadequate work performance. The actions of the plaintiff's employer in Gormley were not nearly so egregious.

{48} Allstate's additional arguments on this issue in effect ask us to reweigh the evidence. It cites numerous cases for the propositions that criticism is expected by employees, that denial of leave or movement from an office to a carrel are not egregious enough to constitute constructive discharge, and that giving notice of resignation rather than quitting on the spot demonstrates voluntary termination of employment. We are not persuaded. These contentions are more in the nature of closing argument than legal reasons for concluding that the evidence was insufficient. It is not our role to reweigh the evidence or substitute our judgment for that of the jury. *Id*. Consequently, we conclude that the evidence, when considered in its totality, could have reasonably supported the jury's conclusion that Allstate made Plaintiffs working conditions so intolerable that a reasonable person in her position would have been compelled to resign.

2. Retaliation for an Act Public Policy Has Authorized or Encouraged

{49} Allstate argues that, even if Plaintiff proved that she was constructively discharged, she failed to prove that her discharge was in retaliation for an act that public policy has authorized or encouraged. It contends that it is unclear what act' Plaintiff claimed was the reason for her discharge, that she failed to prove a causal connection. between the act and the discharge, and that there was no retaliation as a matter of law because the district court granted Allstate's pretrial motion for summary judgment on Plaintiff's claim under the Human Rights Act to the extent it was predicated on retaliation. We disagree.

{50} First, the jury instructions provide the answer with respect to Allstate's claim that the evidence did not establish what act of Plaintiff was authorized or encouraged by public policy. The district court instructed the jury that 'lilt is the public policy of the State of New Mexico to prohibit sexual harassment in the work place and to encourage employees to report sexual harassment."

{51} Second, in light of (a) our holding that there was sufficient evidence to support the jury's finding of sexual harassment, (b) Plaintiff's public-policy-sanctioned reporting of that harassment, (c) the evidence that Aakhus indicated that he knew Plaintiff had reported him and that he became more aggressive afterward, and (d) Plaintiff's testimony about what caused her to resign her job, it would be reasonable for the jury to infer that there was a connection between the harassment, the reporting of the harassment, and the discharge.

{52} Third, the district court granted summary judgment to Allstate on Plaintiff s retaliation claims under the version of the Human Rights Act that was in effect at the time because she failed to make her claims within 180 days of each retaliatory act of discipline she alleged. See § 28-1-10(A) (1995) (amended 2005) (requiring complaints of unlawful discriminatory practice to be filed with the human rights division within 180 days after the alleged act was committed). When these claims were argued on summary judgment, they did not include the ultimate claim of retaliatory constructive discharge that ripened on February 15. These statutory claims were distinct from Plaintiffs claim of retaliatory constructive discharge, which is a common law claim. See Gormley, 2005-NMSC-003, ¶ 9, 137 N.M. 192, 109 P.3d 280 (explaining that "constructive discharge is a doctrine that permits an employee to recast a resignation as a de facto firing, depending on the circumstances surrounding the employment relationship and the employee's departure"). We fail to see how the untimely filing of specific statutory claims under the Human Rights Act translates into

the substantive failure of Plaintiff's claim of retaliatory discharge, and the district court did not rule that the facts surrounding the ultimate retaliatory discharge claim were untimely because that matter was not before it.

C. Compensatory Damages for Alleged Emotional Injuries

{53} The jury awarded Plaintiff $360,000 in compensatory damages after being instructed that, if it found in favor of Plaintiff, it should calculate the amount of damages by considering:

[(1) t]he benefits Plaintiff would have earned, less the amount Plaintiff could through exercise of reasonable diligence have earned, in the time made available as a result of the conclusion of her employment with Allstate, from employment of the same quality as her employment with Allstate[,] . . . [and (2) an amount of money that will reasonably and fairly compensate her for any emotional distress caused by the violation.

Allstate surmises that the portion of the total damages awarded that is attributable to Plaintiff's economic damages is between $105,000, which was the amount Plaintiffs counsel requested in closing argument as compensation for loss of pension benefits, and $159,349, which was the amount Plaintiff s expert economist testified was the total amount of pension benefits lost. Consequently, Allstate continues, the remaining amount of damages—between $200,651 and $255,000—must be attributable to Plaintiff's emotional injuries. Allstate claims that this amount is excessive and that the district court should have granted remittitur because Plaintiff offered no corroborating evidence in the form of medical diagnosis or treatment, or in the form of testimony that Plaintiff missed work or looked' for another job while Aakhus was employed at Allstate.

{54} Allstate's argument is partly that there was insufficient evidence supporting the damages award, and to that extent we employ the substantial evidence standard of review recited earlier in this opinion. Allstate also argues that the district court should have ordered remittitur. In determining whether a jury verdict is excessive, we do not reweigh the evidence but determine whether the verdict is excessive as a matter of law. The jury's verdict is presumed to be correct. When a [district] court denies a motion for a remittitur, we defer to the trial court's judgment. ***Ennis v. Kmart Corp.,*** 2001-NMCA-068, ¶ 27, 131 N.M. 32, 33 P.3d 32 (citations omitted).

{55} We first observe that Allstate may be wrong about the amount the jury attributed to Plaintiff's economic damages. Plaintiffs expert economist based the present value of Plaintiffs lost pension on the assumption of a normal life expectancy of age 81. It is possible that the jury concluded that Plaintiff would live longer than age 81.

{56} More importantly, Allstate has not cited any authority for the proposition that a plaintiffs testimony of emotional distress' must be corroborated before the plaintiff is entitled to be compensated for such distress. Allstate relies on the Nava case to support its position, and points to language in that sexual harassment case emphasizing that the plaintiff had not presented any "evidence of concrete damages, such as counseling expenses or lost time from work." 2004-NMSC-039, ¶

18, 136 N.M. 647, 103 P.3d 571. However, in that case our Supreme Court was reviewing a district court's order granting remittitur. *Id.* ¶ 3, 136 N.M. 647, 103 P.3d 571. The Court properly deferred to the district court's determination, just as we must defer to the district court's denial of remittitur in the present case. See *Id.* ¶ 20, 136 N.M. 647, 103 P.3d 571.

{57} There was substantial evidence upon which the jury could base an award of damages for emotional distress. Plaintiff and her co-employees testified about the stress Plaintiff suffered as a result of the sexual atmosphere in the office and the conduct of Aakhus. Plaintiff testified that she was frightened for her job, that she feared being alone with Aakhus and took steps to avoid such a scenario, and that Aakhus publicly belittled and berated her. Her co-workers testified that Aakhus sometimes followed Plaintiff closely and yelled at her and that they saw Plaintiff crying or on the verge of tears many times. Aakhus formally disciplined Plaintiff after she complained about him, and several witnesses testified that Plaintiffs work was exemplary.

{58} Allstate has failed to meet its burden of establishing "that the verdict was infected with passion, prejudice, partiality, sympathy, undue influence, or some corrupt cause or motive." *Ennis*, 2001-NMCA-068, ¶ 27, 131 N.M. 32, 33 P.3d 32 (internal quotation marks and citation omitted). We will not reweigh the evidence and substitute our judgment for that of the jury.

III. The District Court Properly Allowed the Jury to Consider Punitive Damages

{59} Allstate argues that the district court should have granted its motion for directed verdict on the issue of punitive damages because Allstate did not have the culpable mental state that is a prerequisite to an award of such damages. See *Allsup's Convenience Stores, Inc. v. N. River Ins. Co.,* 1999-NMSC-006, ¶ 53, 127 N.M. 1, 976 P.2d 1 (explaining that an award of punitive damages must be based on "a culpable mental state indivisible from the conduct constituting liability" (internal quotation marks omitted)). When we review a district court's ruling on a motion for directed verdict, "any conflicts in the evidence or reasonable interpretations of it are viewed in favor of the party resisting the directed verdict." *Hedicke v. Gunville*, 2003-NMCA-032, ¶ 9, 133 N.M. 335, 62 P.3d 1217. "The sufficiency of evidence presented to support a legal claim or defense is a question of law for the trial court to decide. This Court reviews questions of law de novo." *Id.* (internal quotation marks and citations omitted).

{60} Allstate advances two sub-arguments: (1) that Allstate cannot be vicariously liable for the acts of Aakhus because Aakhus was not acting within the scope of employment when he was engaged in sexually harassing conduct and because Aakhus was not employed in a managerial capacity; and (2) that Allstate did not authorize, ratify, or participate in Aakhus's misconduct. See *Weidler*, 1998-NMCA-021, ¶ 42, 124 N.M. 591, 953 P.2d 1089 (listing two methods of holding a principal liable for punitive damages: by establishing that "the principal has in some way authorized, ratified, or participated in the wanton,

oppressive, malicious, fraudulent, or criminal acts of its agent" or by establishing that "the agent was employed in a managerial capacity and was acting in the scope of his employment" (internal quotation marks and citation omitted)): We need not address the first sub-argument because we conclude that the evidence supported the view that Allstate authorized, ratified, or participated in Aakhus's misconduct. See *Atler*, 2005-NMCA-006, ¶ 16, 136 N.M. 701, 104 P.3d 1092 ("When the jury instructions provide two alternative bases for awarding punitive damages, we will uphold the jury verdict if there is substantial evidence in the record to support either.").

{61} There was testimony at trial that Aakhus's boss, Larry Vogel, was present for some of the "sex talk" that occurred in the office and apparently did nothing to stop it. Although Allstate reprimanded Aakhus for "unprofessional behavior" in August 2000, the employees in the office did not know this, and it appeared that the reprimand had no effect because Aakhus's behavior never improved. On the contrary, it worsened, despite numerous complaints to Allstate over the three-year period when Plaintiff's employment overlapped with Aakhus's. Indeed, Reed testified that Vogel told employees that Aakhus "might have a few little problems … but … you need to take care of yourselves." When others in Allstate management wanted to impose additional discipline on Aakhus, Vogel resisted because he did not think there was sufficient evidence for such discipline and because the Albuquerque office was performing well.

{62} Viewing the reasonable interpretations of this evidence in favor of Plaintiff, see *Hedicke,* 2003-NMCA-032, ¶ 9, 133 N.M. 335, 62 P.3d 1217, we conclude there was sufficient evidence to submit the issue of punitive damages to the jury. We agree with the district court that Vogel's failure to act after observing Aakhus's misconduct firsthand "could constitute authorization, participation in, or ratification. There's also a question for the [j]ury as to whether the disciplinary actions taken were adequate or whether they represent in some way authorization of … Aakhus's conduct."

IV. The Punitive Damages Award Did Not Violate Due Process

{63} Allstate contends the punitive damages award reflects passion and prejudice and, consequently, violates due process. See *Aken v. Plains Elec. Generation. & Transmission, Coop., Inc.,* 2002-NMSC-021, ¶ 17, 132 N.M. 401, 49 P.3d 662 (explaining that punitive damages awards are reviewed under a de novo standard "as a matter of federal constitutional imperative"). We conduct an independent, de novo assessment of the award. *Id.* ¶ 19, 132 N.M. 401, 49 P.3d 662. In effect, we are reviewing the award for reasonableness. *Chavarria v. Fleetwood Retail Corp.*, 2006-NMSC-046, ¶ 36, 140 N.M. 478, 143 P.3d 717. In undertaking this review we consider three criteria: (1) the reprehensibility of the defendant's conduct, or the enormity and nature of the wrong; (2) the relationship between the harm suffered and the punitive damages award; and (3) the difference between the punitive damages award and the civil and criminal penalties authorized or imposed in comparable cases. *Id.*

{64} With respect to the first criterion, the reprehensibility of the conduct, Allstate argues that there was no evidence that Allstate engaged in a pattern of threatening employees with their jobs if they reported sexual harassment, or that Allstate "persisted in a course of conduct after it had been adjudged unlawful on even one occasion, let alone repeat occasions." Our Supreme Court in Aken noted that in retaliatory discharge cases "evidence of repeated engagement in prohibited conduct knowing or suspecting it is unlawful is relevant support for a substantial award." 2002-NMSC-021, ¶ 21, 132 N.M. 401, 49 P.3d 662 (internal quotation marks and citation omitted).

{65} Plaintiff presented evidence that, even after Allstate privately reprimanded Aakhus in August 2000 for what it called "unprofessional behavior," Aakhus's misconduct intensified, and employees continued to make complaints to Allstate's Resolution Line and its human resources department. Although Allstate management investigated these complaints, it did nothing further about Aakhus until nearly two years later, in May 2002. There is no question that Allstate knew that sexual harassment, and specifically Aakhus's conduct, was unlawful, because it distributed to its employees a pamphlet stating that "[i]t is [Allstate's] policy to maintain a working environment free from discrimination and sexual advances or harassment which may affect an employee's terms or conditions of employment." That pamphlet cited, as an example of sexual harassment, "[w]ritten material, photos and/or any other items of a sexual nature." Given this and the testimony of various employees that they reported Aakhus's misconduct many times over a period of years, we conclude that the jury reasonably could have found that Allstate demonstrated consciousness of wrongdoing. See *Id.* (finding support for award of punitive damages in light of evidence showing that "[the defendant's] behavior exhibited consciousness of wrongdoing"). And, like the Court in Aken, "we conclude that a substantial award was necessary to meet the goal of punishing [Allstate] for its conduct and deterring it, and others similarly situated in the future, from engaging in such conduct." *Id.*

{66} As for the second criterion for assessing the reasonableness of the award, the relationship between the harm suffered and the award, we must consider whether the amount of the award is "so unrelated to the injury and actual damages proven as to plainly manifest passion and prejudice rather than reason or justice." *Id.* ¶ 23, 132 N.M. 401, 49 P.3d 662 (internal quotation marks and citation omitted). Although the United States Supreme Court has suggested that due process is most likely satisfied if there is "a single-digit ratio between punitive and compensatory damages," *State Farm Mut. Auto. Ins. Co. v. Campbell*, 538 U.S. 408, 425, 123 S.Ct. 1513, 155 L.Ed.2d 585 (2003), the Court has also indicated the need for a flexible approach. *Id.* Here, the ratio of punitive damages to compensatory damages is 3.6 to 1. This is within the range deemed by the Supreme Court to be consistent with due process. See *Id.*

{67} Allstate contends that the punitive damages award is in some ways duplicative of the compensatory damages awarded for emotional distress because both awards derive from the outrage and humiliation suffered by Plaintiff. This argument is somewhat speculative, and "[a]ny doubt in the mind of the appellate court concerning the question of what appropriate damages may be in the abstract, or owing to the coldness of the record, should be resolved in favor of the jury verdict." *Aken*, 2002-NMSC-021, ¶ 19, 132 N.M. 401, 49 P.3d 662.

{68} The third criterion, comparing the punitive damages award to civil and/or criminal penalties imposed for comparable Misconduct, "has been criticized as ineffective and very difficult to employ." *Id.* ¶ 25, 132 N.M. 401, 49 P.3d 662. This is in part because there may be some categories of conduct for which there is no significant statutory guidance as to what sanctions should be imposed for the conduct. *Id.* As a result, our Supreme Court has characterized this criterion as "the least important indicium." *Id.* We can find no legislative guidance as to the civil or criminal sanctions that might be imposed for sexual harassment or retaliatory discharge. We doubt that Aakhus's misconduct could be characterized as any type of crime, but this does not render his behavior less reprehensible. On the civil side, the legislature, via the Human Rights Act, has clearly condemned discrimination, but it has not attempted to place a monetary valuation on recovery for violations of the Act. See § 28-1-7 (listing the various forms of discrimination that are deemed unlawful); § 28-1-11(E) (permitting human rights commission to award "actual damages"); § 28-1-13(D) (permitting district court to award "actual damages"). This does not signify to us that discriminatory behavior is considered to be minimally sanctionable. To the contrary, it indicates the legislature's willingness to leave the assessment of reasonable compensation to the fact finder, whether the fact finder is the human rights commission or a court of law. Consequently, we deem the third criterion to be neutral. Because the other two criteria convince us of the reasonableness of the punitive damages award, we affirm the award.

V. Plaintiff's Request for Attorney Fees

{69} Pursuant to Rule 12-403 NMRA (permitting appellate court to award attorney fees where allowed by law) and Section 28-1-13(D) (allowing award of attorney fees to prevailing party in an appeal under the Human Rights Act), Plaintiff asks us to award attorney fees for this appeal, or to remand to allow the district court to make this determination. We remand this issue to the district court to determine whether to make such an award and, if so, in what amount.

Conclusion

{70} For the foregoing reasons, we affirm the judgment of the district court.

{71} IT IS SO ORDERED. WE CONCUR: LYNN PICKARD and JAMES J. WECHSLER, Judges.

Exercises

1. If the Allstate employee, in fact, made repeated sexual advances and comments about others to the paralegal, do you believe this constitutes sexual harassment?
2. Based on the facts of the case, do you believe the defendants discharge was a retaliatory?
3. Did you agree with the court that the work environment was hostile? Explain your answer.
4. Did you generally agree or disagree with the decision?

Helpful Web Sites

Organization	Description	Internet Address
ABA Law Practice Today	ABA site devoted to law practice management and legal administration.	http://www.abanet.org/lpm
ABA Legal Technology Resource Center	ABA site devoted to technology. Includes resources and articles.	http://www.abanet.org/tech/ltrc/home.html
Alabama State Bar—Law Office Management Assistance Program	Articles on a variety of law office management topics, including a disaster recovery kit.	http://www.alabar.org/
Association of Legal Administrators	National association for legal administrators. Contains resources and information related to law office management and legal administration.	http://www.alanet.org
Maryland State Bar Association—Law Practice Management Assistance	The site has a wide variety of law office management topics, including a number of articles and excellent resources.	http://www.msba.org/
New Jersey State Bar Association—Law Office Management Articles	Articles on a variety of law office management topics.	http://www.njsba.com/
New York State Bar Association – Attorney/Practice Resources	The site is extremely in-depth and has a collection of some of the best law office management-related articles and information on the Internet. The articles are also arranged by folders according to subject matter.	http://www.nysba.org/
South Carolina Bar—Practice Management Section	The site has a wide variety of law office management topics, including a number of articles and excellent resources.	http://www.scbar.org/
State Bar of Georgia—Law Practice Management Articles	Articles on a variety of law office management topics.	http://www.gabar.org/
State Bar of New Mexico—Law Office Management Site	Miscellaneous law office management and legal administration topics and links.	http://www.nmbar.org/

Suggested Reading

1. American Bar Association. (2021). *American Bar Association Legal Technology Surveys*.
2. Schultz, S. S., & Schultz, J. S. (2006). *The Complete Guide to Designing your Law Office*. American Bar Association.
3. Wert, R. C., & Hatoff, H. I. (2006). *Law Office Policy & Procedures Manual* (Revised and Updated 5th ed.). American Bar Association.
4. *Law Practice* magazine, published by the American Bar Association Law Practice Management Section [http://www.abanet.org/lpm].
5. Grella, T. C., & Hudkins, M. L. (2005). *The Lawyer's Guide to Strategic Planning: Defining, Setting, and Achieving Your Firm's Goals*. American Bar Association.

3

Ethics and Malpractice

Chapter Objectives

After you read this chapter, you should be able to:

- Explain the importance of ethics and professionalism in the practice of law.

- Explain what the unauthorized practice of law is and identify factors that are used to determine whether an attorney or paralegal is "practicing law."

- Identify the voluntary ethical codes established by national paralegal and legal assistants associations.

- Explain the attorney–client privilege and to whom it applies.

- Explain what a conflict of interest is and what a law office can do to limit conflict of interest problems.

The E. Eric Guirard law firm primarily handled personal injury cases. The firm employed attorneys, case managers, and other nonlawyer staff, such as investigators and receptionists. The court concluded that the attorneys had a large-volume personal injury practice where delegated tasks to nonlawyers included negotiations and settling client matters. The firm's standard practice in handling cases was to

- Pay investigators and case managers fees for "signing up" clients.
- Case managers, not attorneys, were present on a daily basis to handle client matters.
- Case managers spoke to new prospective client, not the attorney, and made the decision to accept or reject the cases.
- Investigators, not the attorney, would sign-up the clients for a fee.
- Case managers were incentivized (received a commission) if cases were settled versus filing litigation.

In most instances, the only time the clients met with the attorneys was when the settlement check was disbursed. The court found that the nonlawyers performed many services that constituted the unauthorized practice of law. Adapted from *In re Guirard*, 11 So.3d 1017 (La.2009), included at the end of this chapter.

Why Is Ethics So Important in the Legal Profession?

The importance of high ethical standards and of following your state's ethical rules cannot be overemphasized. Clients must have total confidence that attorneys, paralegals, and all members of the legal team understand the many ethical problems that might arise in the practice of law. Ethical problems routinely encountered by attorneys and paralegals include the unauthorized practice of law, conflict of interest problems, and confidentiality problems. Unethical behavior of attorneys and paralegals can cause an attorney to lose a case, destroy client confidence in the entire law office, or lead a client to dismiss the attorney. Unethical behavior on the part of any member of the legal team could lead to sanctions, fines, and disciplinary action against the attorney, and it can cost a paralegal his or her job. It also could result in damaging publicity for the law office and may even lead to criminal charges being filed against the attorney. Consequently, attorneys as well as paralegals must know how to work through and solve tough ethical problems.

Attorneys and paralegals must perform careful, high-quality work in everything he or she does. An error can be very costly and can subject an attorney or a law office to a malpractice claim. Malpractice occurs when an attorney's or a law office's conduct does not meet the professional standard for the area and injures a client. Malpractice claims can result in a law office being liable for thousands of dollars of damages to injured clients. Paralegals must clearly understand how malpractice occurs and how it can be prevented.

Legal Ethics and Professional Responsibility

Legal ethics is an increasingly important and difficult topic for attorneys and paralegals in every type of law practice. There are many treatises that cover this topic in depth. This section will cover ethics from both the attorney's and the paralegal's perspective, providing insight into common ethical problems likely to arise.

It is important to understand ethics, not only because a law office or an attorney can be disciplined for violating ethical rules, but also because ethics bears on whether quality legal services are being provided to clients. If a law office or its employee engages in unethical conduct, the reputation of the office will be affected, and clients will lose confidence in it. The unethical behavior does not necessarily have to be directly detrimental to the client or the client's case. If a client senses that the attorney or paralegal is acting unethically toward an adversary, the client may suspect that the attorney or paralegal could be guilty of the same type of practice toward him or her. The issues of trust and ethics are closely related and bear directly upon the attorney–client relationship.

When clients lose confidence, they may move their business to another law office, cease referring new clients to the law office, or even sue. Nearly 70% of all new business a law office receives comes from referrals. When a client takes business elsewhere, it has an immediate as well as a long-term effect on the firm, since that source of revenue is also gone for future years. In short, legal ethics has a direct bearing on the law office's bottom line and on the long-term success of the firm. Thus, paralegals and attorneys have both an incentive and a duty to act ethically and to develop systems that stress the importance of legal ethics on a daily basis.

Ethical Standards for Attorneys

ethical rule
A minimal standard of conduct.

An **ethical rule** is a minimal standard of conduct. An attorney may not fall below the standard without losing his or her good standing with the state bar. Attorneys who violate ethical rules may be disciplined; being disciplined for unethical conduct may include permanent disbarment from practicing law, temporary suspension from practicing, public censure, private censure, or an informal reprimand. Exhibit 3-1 shows a procedural example of ethical rules at work. The client initiates the inquiry in most instances of attorney misconduct, typically by sending a letter of complaint to the state's disciplinary administrator. The state disciplinary administration is in charge of enforcing the state's professional licensing standards for attorneys.

Exhibit 3-1 Example of Ethical Violation and Subsequent Ethical Proceedings against an Attorney	
The facts:	An attorney represented a client who was selling a piece of real estate. It was agreed that the attorney's fees would be $6500. After completing the sale, the proceeds of the sale were placed into the attorney's trust account (i.e., a holding account for client funds). The attorney paid some proceeds to the client, withdrew $14,000 for himself, would not provide an accounting of the funds to the client, and would not respond to many messages left by the client.
The client:	The client, becoming increasingly frustrated with the attorney, calls the local courthouse and asks how to complain about the conduct of the attorney. The client is told to send a letter of complaint to the state's disciplinary administrator in the state's judicial branch. The client is told that the letter should clearly explain who the attorney was and exactly what happened. The client then sends the letter.
The disciplinary administrator:	The state's disciplinary administrator receives the client's letter. The administrator determines that if everything the client says is true, the attorney may have violated Supreme Court Rule 4-1.5 for his state, which says that "an attorney shall not charge an illegal or clearly excessive fee." The administrator sends a letter to the attorney asking for his side of the story but never receives a reply.
Investigation:	The disciplinary administrator then refers the matter to the State Bar's Investigation Committee, which investigates the matter, including interviews with both the client and the attorney. The Committee, after a full investigation, recommends that formal charges be filed before the state's bar court to discipline the attorney.
State's bar court/state's supreme court:	The disciplinary administrator files formal charges and prosecutes the attorney for the ethical violations before the state's bar court, an arm of the state's supreme court. A hearing or trial is held where both sides present their evidence. The bar court determines that the attorney violated Rule 4-1.5 and disciplines the attorney by suspending him from the practice of law for two years, and orders him to pay restitution to the client.

Ethics has had a long-standing place in the American legal system. In 1908, the American Bar Association (ABA), a voluntary association of attorneys, adopted the Canons of Professional Ethics. In 1969, the ABA updated and expanded the canons into the *Model Code of Professional Responsibility*. The *Model Code* was updated in 1983 and is now called the *Model Rules of Professional Conduct*.

In the late 1990s, the ABA convened the Ethics 2000 Commission on evaluation of the rules of professional conduct to undertake a comprehensive review and rewrite of the *Model Rules*; in 2002, the ABA adopted the newly revised *Model Rules* after several years of work and 50 days of open meetings, including numerous public hearings and free debate. The ABA continually meets to determine what revisions are necessary to keep up with changes in the legal practice. The last big revision to the model rules was in 2013. The rules were revised to address advances in technology and the global aspect of practicing law.

Today, nearly all states base their ethical rules on the ABA *Model Rules*. Attorneys in each state are regulated by their individual state bar association and state court system. Although state courts are free to create their own rules of conduct for attorneys, most simply modify either the ABA *Model Code* or ABA *Model Rules* to reflect the specific ethical conditions in their own states. For this text, the ABA *Model Rules* is most often referenced, even though some states still model their ethical/disciplinary rules on the older ABA *Model Code*.

Model Code of Professional Responsibility/Model Rules of Professional Conduct
Self-imposed ethical standards for ABA members, but they also serve as a prototype of legal ethics standards for state court systems.

Attorney Ethical Rules Not Directly Applicable to the Paralegal

State canons of ethics, the *Model Code of Professional Responsibility*, or the *Model Rules of Professional Conduct* do not apply directly to paralegals, but to attorneys only. However, attorneys can be disciplined for the acts of their staff members, including paralegals, because attorneys have the duty to adequately supervise their staff, as shown in Exhibit 3-2, illustrating Louisiana's Rule 5.3 (identical to the *ABA's Rule 5.3*).

Exhibit 3-2 State Example: Louisiana's Rules of Professional Conduct, Rule 5.3

RULE 5.3 RESPONSIBILITIES REGARDING NONLAWYER ASSISTANTS

With respect to a nonlawyer employed or retained by or associated with a lawyer:

(a) a partner, and a lawyer who individually or together with other lawyers possesses comparable managerial authority in a law firm shall make reasonable efforts to ensure that the firm has in effect measures giving reasonable assurance that the person's conduct is compatible with the professional obligations of the lawyer;

(b) a lawyer having direct supervisory authority over the nonlawyer shall make reasonable efforts to ensure that the person's conduct is compatible with the professional obligations of the lawyer; and

(c) a lawyer shall be responsible for conduct of such a person that would be a violation of the Rules of Professional Conduct if engaged in by a lawyer if:

(1) the lawyer orders or, with the knowledge of the specific conduct, ratifies the conduct involved; or

(2) the lawyer is a partner or has comparable managerial authority in the law firm in which the person is employed, or has direct supervisory authority over the person, and knows of the conduct at a time when its consequences can be avoided or mitigated but fails to take reasonable remedial action.

Source: State of Louisiana.

This section of the **Model Rules** is important to paralegals and other non-lawyers because it requires attorneys to ensure that their staff members operate within the bounds of these rules. If a paralegal is found to be acting unethically, especially when there is a pattern and practice of doing so, the attorney has an affirmative duty to remedy the situation, even if that means terminating the paralegal's employment. Thus, there are many incentives for paralegals to act ethically and to comply with the same rules as attorneys. In addition, this section of the rule ensures that an attorney cannot avoid the ethical rules and accomplish an unethical act by delegating or allowing a staff member to do it.

So, although a paralegal cannot be disciplined by state regulatory bodies for violating state ethical rules, he or she would be held accountable by the attorney who hired or supervised him or her. Paralegals must understand and abide by any ethical rules governing the conduct of attorneys.

Voluntary Ethical Codes Established by Paralegal Associations

Paralegals remain largely unregulated. There are, however, self-imposed, *voluntary* ethical standards set out by national or local paralegal and legal assistants associations. The National Association of Legal Assistants (NALA)–The Paralegal Association and the National Federation of Paralegal Associations (NFPA) have adopted ethical canons for their members. These rules are intended to assist attorneys and paralegals in the expectation of performance in the paralegal profession. Exhibits 3-3 and 3-4 show the codes of ethics for both associations. Paralegals cannot be disciplined for not following such voluntary codes. However, following such a code will help the paralegal avoid ethical problems.

Exhibit 3-3 NALA–The Paralegal Association—Paralegals Code of Ethics and Professional Responsibility

NALA Code of Ethics and Professional Responsibility (Summary of the Canons)

NALA – The Paralegal Association members agree to adhere to the ten (10) cannons listed below and understand membership could be cancelled if the cannons are not followed. (*See Model Standards and Guidelines for Utilization of Legal Assistants, Section II* for the exact wording.)

The NALA cannons apply to the organization and must be taken into consideration along with Court rules, agency rules, and statutes.

In 2020, the ABA adopted the revised paralegal definition as recommended by the Standing Committee on Paralegals. NALA – The Paralegal Association also adopted the revised definition of paralegal, which reads as follows:

A paralegal is a person, qualified by education, training or work experience who is employed or retained by a lawyer, law office, corporation, governmental agency or other entity who performs specifically delegated substantive legal work for which a lawyer is responsible.

Canon 1. Paralegals may not perform attorney duties.

Canon 2. Paralegals may perform certain types of attorney tasks, but those tasks must be under the direct supervision of an attorney who is ultimately responsible to the client and the work product.

Canon 3. Paralegals must not perform acts that are considered unauthorized practice of law, establish an attorney-client relationship, set fees, represent clients, unless authorized to appear before certain agencies, give legal advice or opinions, or take actions that would assist or involve the attorney violating professional ethics.

(continued)

Canon 4. Paralegals must perform their duties consistent with their knowledge and experience, without rendering an independent judgment that should only be done by an attorney.

Canon 5. Paralegals must clearly identify themselves as a paralegal and ensure that their assistance with clients is within the scope of their duties as a paralegal.

Canon 6. Paralegals must maintain the integrity of the profession through education and training in substantive law areas, rules and in the legal practice to properly assist lawyers in the legal profession.

Canon 7. Paralegals must protect client confidential information and the attorney–client privilege regarding conversations and work product of the attorney.

Canon 8. Paralegals must disclose to employers any potential client conflicts from prior employments with other legal professionals or businesses.

Canon 9. Paralegals must perform their duties in such a way as that the ethics and responsibilities of the legal profession are maintained as defined by law or rules.

Canon 10. Paralegals' conduct is promulgated by the ABA and each state's code of ethics and professional responsibility.

NALA – The Paralegal Association Cannons (The Full Version); Copyright 2007; Adopted 1975; Revised 1979, 1988, 1995, 2007. This Exhibit is an example of NALA's 10 canons. The full version is located on the NALA website.

Exhibit 3-4 NFPA Model Code of Ethics and Professional Responsibility

NATIONAL FEDERATION OF PARALEGAL ASSOCIATIONS, INC. MODEL CODE OF ETHICS AND PROFESSIONAL RESPONSIBILITY AND GUIDELINES FOR ENFORCEMENT (Summary of the Rules)

NFPA members agree to maintain the integrity of the paralegal profession by following the eight (8) rules and their subparts developed by the organization.

The Model Code of Ethics and Professional Responsibility (*Model Code*) was adopted by NFPA in May 1993.

The Model Disciplinary Rules (*Model Rules*) were adopted by NFPA in April 1997. It was later determined that the *Model Code of Ethics and Professional Responsibility* should be the code followed by all paralegals. **NFPA MODEL DISCIPLINARY AND ETHICAL RULES**

1.1 PARALEGALS SHALL SUSTAIN HIGH LEVELS OF COMPETENCY
Through education, training, work and continued education in the law and its developments.

1.2 PARALEGALS SHALL SUSTAIN HIGH LEVELS OF INTEGRITY
through communications with court, clients, and other litigation parties.
through maintaining accurate time records and billing.
through honest and proper maintenance of client funds.

1.3 PARALEGALS SHALL SUSTAIN HIGH LEVELS OF PROFESSIONALISM
through dignity and decorum before the courts, as well following rules of the court and litigants, and through remaining fit to be a part of the paralegal profession and not aide or assist with acts that would violate the model rules or codes.

1.4 PARALEGALS SHALL AID WITH IMPROVING THE LEGAL SYSTEM AND SERVING THE PUBLIC INTEREST
through pro bono, community services, including quality legal service, etc.

1.5 PARALEGALS SHALL SUSTAIN HIGH LEVELS OF CONFIDENTIALITY
through following all rules of confidentiality governed by legal authority.

(continued)

1.6 PARALEGALS SHALL DISCLOSE CONFLICTS OF INTEREST
through notification to past present and future employers.

1.7 PARALEGALS SHALL PROPERLY IDENTIFIED THEMSELVES
through clearly identifying their title as paralegal in all documentation including business cards, letterhead, and other documentation.

1.8 PARALEGALS SHALL REFRAIN FROM THE UNAUTHORIZED PRACTICE OF LAW
through complying with all applicable laws and rules.

This exhibit is an example of NFPA'S 8 Rules. The full version is located on the NFPA website.

Criminal Statutes Regarding the Unauthorized Practice of Law

There are criminal statutes in nearly every state that provide sanctions for nonlawyers who engage in "practicing law," which usually includes providing legal advice to the public or representation of a client in a court of law.

There is no direct regulation of paralegals, but they are indirectly regulated through state ethical standards for attorneys, nonbinding paralegal association ethical standards, and criminal statutes barring non-attorneys from practicing law.

The Unauthorized Practice of Law

Most states have a criminal statute that prohibits a layperson from practicing law. The reason behind such a statute is to protect the general public from individuals who are not qualified to give legal advice because they do not have the proper educational training, have not passed the bar exam, or are not fit to practice law. In Florida, for example, an unauthorized practice violation results in a third-degree felony charge and up to a $5000 fine.

Besides criminal prohibitions, there are ethical prohibitions as well. Rule 5.5 regarding the rules of professional conduct prohibits an attorney from assisting a person who is not a member of the bar in an activity that would constitute the unauthorized practice of the law. This rule draws a line that paralegals cannot cross. A paralegal is permitted to assist an attorney as long as the activity does not, in itself, constitute "practicing law."

The real question is: at what point does one actually "practice law"? The ABA, as well as most states, have been unwilling to give a specific definition of exactly what the "practice of law" is, preferring to consider the matter on a case-by-case basis.

Although what constitutes the practice of law is established by each jurisdiction, Exhibit 3-5 explains what types of actions are typically referred to in court decisions as the "practice of law." Exhibit 3-5 also defines "other work" in a law office. Notice in Exhibit 3-5 that there are many other professional duties that a paralegal can perform that do not constitute the practice of law.

Giving Legal Advice

Only attorneys may give legal advice. Paralegals may not directly advise a client regarding a legal matter. Throughout the years, courts have used

Exhibit 3-5 The "Practice of Law" versus "Other Work" in a Law Office

"Practice of Law"	"Other Work" in a Law Office
Giving legal advice	Obtaining facts from a client
Representing clients in court	Communicating information to the client
Proceedings	Interviewing witnesses
Performing legal analysis and preparing legal documents	Performing limited legal research to assist an attorney with legal analysis
Evaluating a case and selecting an appropriate course of action	Obtaining documents. Preparing drafts of requests for production of a document
Accepting or rejecting a case	Preparing drafts of interrogatories
Setting a fee	Preparing drafts of responses to requests for production of documents
Sharing a fee with an attorney	Preparing drafts of responses to interrogatories Preparing drafts of pleadings Preparing correspondence Organizing documents and evidence Preparing case chronologies Preparing deposition summaries Preparing exhibit lists Organizing and tracking deadlines Conducting factual research on the Internet Designing/entering litigation support database Working with e-discovery requests/software Preparing presentations

several methods to distinguish between giving legal advice and simply providing legal information. The purpose for this is to protect the public from unethical people that prey on unsuspecting individuals. In determining what constitutes legal advice, the court focuses on the context in which the advice is given.

- **Was a particular legal skill or knowledge used for the advice given?** The issue here is whether the information given was based on specific advice involving the operation of law or the process regarding a legal matter.

- **Was a specific direction involving the individual's rights or consequences provided for the advice given?** The issue here is whether the advice given explained legal rights or the law as it pertains to the issue. Although it is clearly understood that paralegals may not give legal advice, most courts do recognize a properly supervised paralegal is not practicing law when they convey the attorney's answer to a client's legal question; the paralegal may not convey their own opinion regarding the attorney's answer.

For example, in **In re Houston**, 127 N.M. 582, 985 P.2d 752 (N.M. 1999), clients came to an attorney's office when a van they had recently purchased had serious mechanical problems that the dealer refused to repair. The firm filed a lawsuit against the dealer. Approximately 18 months later, the car dealer filed for bankruptcy. The law firm received the bankruptcy notice but never told the clients. The clients discovered the bankruptcy from someone else and called the law firm. The attorney's legal assistant handled the call and told the clients that the bankruptcy would not affect the case. The clients were never told that their claim could be lost if a discharge was entered in bankruptcy without an objection to discharge being granted for their claim. After the bankruptcy was closed, the district court dismissed the clients' claim as barred by the discharge in bankruptcy. At no time, from when the clients initially came to the law firm until just before the case was dismissed, did the clients meet with an attorney. The legal assistant gave legal advice specifically related to the effect of bankruptcy on the clients' case. The advice required legal skill and knowledge, arguably included advising the clients of their rights (the conclusion that the clients did not need to do anything because the bankruptcy would have no effect). In addition, the court found that having a legal assistant conduct all meetings with the clients, during which the clients' objectives and the means for pursuing them were discussed and decided, raised serious questions regarding the unauthorized practice of law. The attorney was suspended for 18 months. In another case, the Oregon state attorney general's office is presuming a $25,000 fine for an unauthorized practice of law validation of a paralegal. The unauthorized practice of law violation is for "continued possession of immigration law materials in his business office, representation to consumers of expertise of special knowledge about immigration matters, and use of the Internet to provide information related to immigration matters to consumers."

- **Was the advice given considered an action by the nonlawyer that would be outside the scope of normal business activity?** There are several professions such as real estate agents, financial advisors, accountants, and engineers that provide legal related advice as it pertains to conducting their business. It generally will not constitute practicing law.

Misrepresentation of Status

Another factor that sometimes becomes an issue with giving legal advice is whether or not the person giving the information to the client, or third party, clearly identified himself or herself as a paralegal. Unless otherwise told, a client may rightly assume that he or she is talking to an attorney when, in fact, he or she is not. In such instances, the client may rely on the information from the paralegal as legal advice. To avoid misunderstandings, paralegals should always disclose their status as a paralegal and nonlawyer. NALA Code of Ethics and Professional Responsibility, Canon 5, speaks to this issue, noting that paralegals should always disclose their position as a "paralegal" when dealing with any of the parties (including the general public) concerning client representation or affiliation with lawyers and law firms (*see* Cannon 5; Exhibit 3-3).

Representing Clients in Court Proceedings

Paralegals generally cannot appear in federal or state courts or legal proceedings, such as a deposition, on behalf of a client; the rights and interests of the parties are more fully safeguarded with licensed attorneys who have extended training. Attorneys may not appear before a court in which they have not been admitted, which likely will take place when an attorney would perform legal services in a foreign jurisdiction, such as a state they are not admitted to practice in through its bar association. Without court authorization, they cannot appear in court to represent clients. There are, however, some administrative agencies that do allow a paralegal to appear on behalf of a client. Some federal and state agencies require nonlawyers to satisfy certain requirements before appearing before them, while others do not. Some jurisdictions allow paralegals to make limited appearances, such as in uncontested matters and small claims court. Attorneys and paralegals should carefully check the rules of his or her jurisdiction before nonlawyers make an appearance in a proceeding.

Performing Legal Analysis and Preparing Legal Documents

Paralegals cannot draft legal documents such as wills, briefs, motions, pleadings, or contracts without the supervision of an attorney, unless specifically authorized by that state's rules. For example, Louisiana Notary Publics are commissioned with authority to prepare legal documents. Paralegals routinely draft these types of documents; the distinction is that they do so properly under the direction and supervision of a member of the bar. The attorney is ultimately responsible for the legal documents; legal documents affect the legal rights of clients and parties and therefore require the oversight of an attorney. As long as a paralegal is actively working under the supervision of an attorney, and the attorney maintains a relationship with the client, the paralegal may interview witnesses or prospective clients, perform legal research, draft pleadings and briefs, and investigate the facts of cases without being accused of the unauthorized practice of law.

Evaluating a Case, Selecting or Rejecting a Case, and Selecting an Appropriate Course of Action

The act of evaluating a fact pattern, applying it to the law, considering possible courses of action based on that factual and legal analysis, and working with the client to strategize the best outcome for the client is reserved exclusively for an attorney. It is a fundamental duty of practicing law for an attorney to perform these functions. Paralegals may, of course, participate in this process, but they must do so under the auspices of an attorney. Also, the act of accepting or rejecting the representation of a client is usually reserved by an attorney, because the process includes the evaluation of the case and the potential giving of legal advice to the client. In *Cincinnati Bar Association v. Bertsche*, 84 Ohio St.3d 170, 702 N.E.2d 859 (Ohio 1998), an attorney allowed a paralegal to operate a satellite office without adequate supervision. The paralegal interviewed clients, obtained information, prepared documents, operated bank accounts, secured signings of bankruptcy petitions and other documents, and presumably (though not specifically stated) accepted cases (given that it was a satellite office). From time to time, the attorney would visit the office, interview clients, and oversee the signing of documents. The court concluded that the attorney's delegation of such matters to the paralegal and his lack of supervision over that assistant violated a disciplinary rule regarding a lawyer not neglecting an entrusted legal matter.

Setting a Fee and Sharing a Fee

The attorney is the only person allowed to establish fees with the client; a paralegal may not set fees. Additionally, the attorney may not share fees with anyone other than another attorney; a paralegal may not share fees with an attorney. A paralegal can provide information regarding fees to a client at the attorney's direction, but the paralegal should be careful to explain that the setting of the fee was done by the attorney. Rule 5.4 regarding the rules of professional conduct specifically addresses fee setting and fee sharing.

In *In re Soulisak*, 227 B.R. 77 (E.D. Va. 1998), a lawyer and a nonlawyer worked together to provide legal services in bankruptcy cases. In addition, they agreed to split the legal fees. The agreement was to charge bankruptcy clients $650; $400 was paid to the attorney, and $250 was paid to the nonlawyer to cover paralegal, clerical, and operating expenses. The court found that the non-lawyer provided many of the services to the clients, thereby committing a UPL violation. The court also found the fee agreement to be improper fee sharing.

Legal Technicians, Freelance Paralegals, and the Unauthorized Practice of Law

legal technicians
People who market their legal services directly to the public.

Recently, a new class of paralegals, sometimes called "legal technicians," has emerged. What separates **legal technicians** from paralegals is that they market their services directly to the public and do not work under the supervision of an attorney. Bar associations across the country have argued that since legal technicians do not work under the supervision of a licensed attorney but represent clients directly, they clearly violate criminal statutes regarding the unauthorized practice of law. Legal technicians argue that they simply provide forms that have been written by attorneys and help the clients fill in the forms. However, as mentioned in Chapter 1, limited licensed legal technician laws were passed in Washington State but were recalled in 2020. However, other states have contemplated allowing non-attorneys, with specialized training and certification, to practice law in a limited capacity. For now, decisions regarding this issue are being decided on a case-by-case basis, with many courts limiting or greatly restricting what services legal technicians can provide.

Freelance paralegals were also defined in Chapter 1 as self-employed paralegals who market and sell their services to law offices on a per-job basis. Freelance paralegals are less likely to be accused of the unauthorized practice of law, since they should be acting under the supervision of an attorney. However, in instances where the freelance paralegal is removed from the attorney, and where supervision is limited or nonexistent, unauthorized practice of law problems can occur.

How to Avoid the Unauthorized Practice of Law

- **A supervising attorney should always approve paralegals' and nonlawyers' work.** No matter how routine a legal document is, an attorney should always review it. Remember, a paralegal and other nonlawyers can do many types of activities as long as they are done under the supervision of an attorney, so take advantage of this and get everything approved. A paralegal should never let an attorney approve his or her work without reading it. If the attorney says, "I do not have time to review it; I'll sign it and you just send it out, I trust you," bring the document back at another time or find a tactful way to suggest to him or her that the document needs to be approved the right way.

- **Never let clients convince paralegals and nonlawyers to give them legal advice.** Most paralegals and nonlawyers never intend to give a client legal advice; however, it is easy to do when a client presses for information immediately and the attorney is unavailable. Legal advice might include telling the client what he or she should or should not do, answering a legal or statutory question, or telling the client what defense or legal argument he or she should make. The client should be informed that as a paralegal or nonlawyer, you are unable to provide legal advice or commentary, and they must speak with the attorney directly. If a paralegal or nonlawyer does give legal advice and things go wrong, for any reason, many clients will not hesitate to turn on you and say that they relied on your advice; therefore, this issue is extremely critical. What a paralegal can do is provide general broad information on the procedural aspects of the matter and suggest that the client seek the advice of an attorney.

- **A paralegal or nonlawyer should never begin sentences with "You should" or "I think."** When on nonlawyer hears themselves say "You should" or "I think," they should immediately stop and realize that they are probably about to give legal advice. Again, it's not worth the risk.

- **Always clearly identify yourself as a paralegal.** When you talk to clients or send letters out on law office or company letterhead, *always* identify yourself as a paralegal. It is very easy for a client to say, "Well, I thought he was an attorney" to a disciplinary administrator or in a malpractice case.

  Never represent to others, either directly or indirectly, that you are an attorney. Paralegals are allowed to have business cards and sign letters on the law practice letterhead in many states, as long as the title of "paralegal" or "legal assistant" is included.

- **Management should develop ethical guidelines and rules.** From a management perspective, law office managers should publish rules regarding the unauthorized practice of law, tell staff members what they can and cannot do, and provide a policy on the responsibilities of supervising attorneys.

- **Management should make periodic checks of ethical standards.** It is not enough to simply establish rules and then never monitor them to see if they are being followed. Occasionally, management must monitor its staff regarding compliance with law practice rules and state guidelines to ensure compliance. Management should keep staff members up-to-date on changes or clarifications in ethical standards by circulating recent ethical opinions. Publications of paralegal associations also report on recent ethical opinions. When appropriate, these should be called to the attention of management for general circulation. Another option is for law office management to hold workshops or seminars on ethics. Attorneys, paralegals, and staff members should be constantly reminded about ethics.

Competence and Diligence

Attorneys and paralegals must perform legal services in a competent and diligent manner. Rule 1.1 regarding the rules of professional conduct speaks to the issue of competence. As noted throughout the text, nearly every state's rules of professional conduct are modeled after the ***ABA's Model Rules of Professional Conduct***. Exhibit 3-6 illustrates Minnesota's Rule 1.1 (identical to the ***ABA's Rule 1.1***), which states that an attorney must be competent in order to represent the client; that is, he or she must reasonably know the

Exhibit 3-6 State Example: Minnesota's Rules of Professional Conduct—Rule 1.1

RULE 1.1 COMPETENCE

A lawyer shall provide competent representation to a client. Competent representation requires the legal knowledge, skill, thoroughness and preparation reasonably necessary for the representation.

Comment:

Legal Knowledge and Skill

[1] In determining whether a lawyer employs the requisite knowledge and skill in a particular matter, relevant factors include the relative complexity and specialized nature of the matter, the lawyer's general experience, the lawyer's training and experience in the field in question, the preparation and study the lawyer is able to give the matter and whether it is feasible to refer the matter to, or associate or consult with, a lawyer of established competence in the field in question. In many instances, the required proficiency is that of a general practitioner. Expertise in a particular field of law may be required in some circumstances.

[2] A lawyer need not necessarily have special training or prior experience to handle legal problems of a type with which the lawyer is unfamiliar. A newly admitted lawyer can be as competent as a practitioner with long experience. Some important legal skills, such as the analysis of precedent, the evaluation of evidence, and legal drafting, are required in all legal problems. Perhaps the most fundamental legal skill consists of determining what kind of legal problems a situation may involve, a skill that necessarily transcends any particular specialized knowledge. A lawyer can provide adequate representation in a wholly novel field through necessary study. Competent representation can also be provided through the association of a lawyer of established competence in the field in question.

[3] In an emergency a lawyer may give advice or assistance in a matter in which the lawyer does not have the skill ordinarily required where referral to or consultation or association with another lawyer would be impractical. Even in an emergency, however, assistance should be limited to that reasonably necessary in the circumstances, for ill-considered action under emergency conditions can jeopardize the client's interest.

[4] A lawyer may accept representation where the requisite level of competence can be achieved by reasonable preparation. This applies as well to a lawyer who is appointed as counsel for an unrepresented person. See also Rule 6.2.

Thoroughness and Preparation

[5] Competent handling of a particular matter includes inquiry into and analysis of the factual and legal elements of the problem, and use of methods and procedures meeting the standards of competent practitioners. It also includes adequate preparation. The required attention and preparation are determined in part by what is at stake; major litigation and complex transactions ordinarily require more extensive treatment than matters of lesser complexity and consequence. An agreement between the lawyer and the client regarding the scope of the representation may limit the matters for which the lawyer is responsible. See Rule 1.2(c).

Maintaining Competence

[6] To maintain the requisite knowledge and skill, a lawyer should keep abreast of changes in the law and its practice, engage in continuing study and education and comply with all continuing legal education requirements to which the lawyer is subject.

Source: State of Minnesota.

area of law that the client needs representation in and, assuming the attorney does know the area of law, that he or she takes the preparation time to become familiar with the case in order to represent the client adequately.

The purpose of this rule is to ensure that an attorney does not undertake a matter that he or she is not competent in, and to ensure that the attorney has had "adequate preparation." The amount of adequate preparation depends on the type of legal matter the client has; major litigation will require far more preparation time than, say, the amount of time it takes to prepare a will. A legal professional should not undertake to represent a client if he or she does not have the skill or preparation time necessary to do so. Paralegals must have a basic understanding of the law in each area in which they are working. Additionally, they must be able to analyze, organize, and prepare the factual and legal data obtained to perform their job competently.

Rule 1.3 regarding the rules of professional conduct requires that an attorney act with a reasonable degree of diligence and promptness in pursuing the client's case. Further insight is found in Comment [3] of the rule. It notes that attorneys should carry through to conclusion all legal matters undertaken for a client unless the relationship is properly and clearly terminated. The purpose of this rule is to ensure that attorneys put forth reasonable effort and diligence in representing a client. Attorneys and paralegals cannot adequately represent the interests of clients if they ignore the case, if they are lazy and do not work the case, or if they negligently handle the case.

Attention to detail is an extremely important skill for both attorneys and paralegals. Exhibit 3-7 provides examples of how paralegals failed to perform

---

Exhibit 3-7 Examples of Nonlawyers Failing to Act Competently and Diligently

Paralegal/Legal Assistant's $92 Million Dollar Error

A paralegal/legal assistant at Prudential mistakenly left off the last three zeros on a mortgage used to secure a $92,885,000 loan made by Prudential to a company that filed for bankruptcy. Because of the mistake, Prudential had a lien for only $92,885; the error left Prudential's lien $92,792,115 short.

Prudential Ins. v. Dewey, 170 A.D.2d 108 (N.Y. App. Div. 1991)

Paralegals/Legal Assistants Sued for Negligence

Unsupervised paralegals engaged in the unauthorized practice of law:
When she represented three clients regarding their auto accident claims, the paralegal's negligence was the proximate cause of clients' injuries, and attorneys and paralegal were jointly and severally liable for damages.

Tegman, et al., v. Accident Medical Investigations, Inc., 107 Wn.2d. 102, 75 P.3d 497 (2003).

Paralegal/Legal Assistant Fails to File Document, Leads to Dismissal of Case

See *Ortiz v. Gavenda*, 590 N.W.2d 119 (Minn. 1999).

Israel Ortiz was severely injured on September 24, 1993 when the motorcycle he was driving collided with a truck driven by Bryan Gavenda and owned by Gavenda's employer, Frito Lay, Inc. Israel Ortiz died from those injuries on December 11, 1993. On June 6, 1995, his widow, Frances Ortiz (Ortiz), served a complaint on Gavenda and Frito Lay (collectively Gavenda) asserting a wrongful death claim and seeking damages as the trustee for the heirs of Israel Ortiz. Gavenda's answer to the complaint denied liability and alleged that Ortiz's claim "failed to comply with the provisions of Chapter 573 of Minnesota Statutes"—the chapter governing wrongful death actions.

On November 15, 1995, Ortiz signed a petition to have herself appointed trustee for the next of kin of her deceased husband as required by Minn. Stat. § 573.02, subd. 3 (1998). Although the petition and an accompanying consent and oath form were properly signed and duly notarized, a legal assistant for Ortiz's attorney inadvertently failed to submit the documents to the court and, as a consequence, Ortiz was not appointed trustee. The mistake went unnoticed when Ortiz's complaint was filed with the Anoka County District Court on December 6, 1995. The oversight came to light and Ortiz filed her petition to be appointed trustee on January 8, 1997, but by then more than three years had elapsed since her husband's death. The Minnesota Supreme Court dismissed the action due to the document not being filed on time by the legal assistant.

competently—not by failing to know the law, but rather by being disorganized or failing to pay attention to details. Ultimately, the supervising attorneys in those cases were responsible to check over their work, and the failure to supervise cost their clients money and rights.

Confidentiality and the Attorney–Client Privilege

client confidentiality
Keeping information exchanged between a client and law office staff confidential.

Another basic ethical concept is that of client confidentiality. **Client confidentiality** refers to the need to keep information exchanged between a client and law office staff, including attorneys and paralegals, confidential. In addition to the ethical rules of maintaining client confidences, there is a rule of evidence, generally called the attorney–client privilege, that an attorney or a paralegal may invoke to avoid revealing the secrets of a client. The purpose of both the privilege and the ethical rules is to ensure that clients can consult with their attorneys without the fear that such statements will be passed to others or used against them later. If clients knew that what they told their attorney could be repeated to others, clients would be reluctant to tell their attorneys the truth. The attorney–client privilege and the ethical rules on confidentiality complement one another to achieve the same end.

The Attorney–Client Privilege Rule of Evidence

attorney–client privilege
A standard that precludes the disclosure of confidential communications between a lawyer and a client by the lawyer.

Generally, the **attorney–client privilege** precludes the disclosure of confidential communications between a lawyer and a client by the lawyer. Thus, if a criminal defendant confessed a crime to his attorney, the attorney–client privilege prevents the prosecutor from calling the attorney to the stand to testify about the confession. In addition, courts have applied the attorney–client privilege to paralegals. For the privilege to be invoked, the communication must have been made in confidence between the client and the attorney for the purpose of obtaining legal advice.

Ethical Prohibitions on Revealing Client Communications

There are several ethical rules that address attorneys preserving client communications, including Rule 1.6 regarding the rules of professional conduct. Rule 1.6 states that an attorney cannot reveal information relating to the representation of a client unless the client has consented to the release of that information.

Canon 7 of the NALA *Code of Ethics and Professional Responsibility* (see Exhibit 3-3) and Section 1.5 of NFPA's *Model Code of Ethics and Professional Responsibility* (see Exhibit 3-4), although not enforceable, prohibit paralegals from revealing client confidences.

Again, the purpose of these ethical rules is to encourage clients to be completely honest with their attorneys. Note that there are many nuances regarding the attorney–client privilege and ethical rules, however, including some exceptions to the rules.

Attorneys and paralegals have an absolute duty to preserve the confidences and communications of clients. All information must be kept confidential and should not, under any circumstances, be revealed in casual conversations with anyone outside the workplace. In addition to the moral and ethical reasons for not disclosing client communications, there also is the issue of quality service to the client. If a client learns that his or her communications have been revealed to outside sources, by whatever means, even if it is by accident, the client may lose confidence in the entire firm. If a client cannot trust his or her attorney, the client will quickly move on to another firm. If confidential information gets out, it could compromise the client's case.

How Attorneys and Paralegal Can Avoid Confidentiality Problems

- **Resist the temptation to talk about what goes on in the office, whether or not it is client related.** There is always a temptation to talk about office politics and other office matters with people outside the firm. Resist this temptation. If you do this, it will only make it easier to talk about client-related matters. Consider that you are a professional and that both your firm and your clients demand anonymity.

- **Only talk about client matters to office personnel on a need-to-know basis.** Never go around your office talking about a client's case to employees who do not have a reason to know about it. You must get in the habit of keeping information to yourself. Why tell someone about client-related matters, even if it is a fellow employee, unless he or she needs to know for some legitimate reason? Even if you are talking to someone who has a need to know, avoid doing so in public places, such as waiting rooms, elevators, and restaurants, where your conversation can be overheard.

- **Never discuss the specific facts or circumstances of a client's case with anyone, not even friends or relatives.** There is a specific temptation to talk with friends and relatives about interesting cases you have worked on, because you trust them. However, many client secrets have been unwittingly revealed by friends and relatives who have repeated information they never should have been told. The statement "I promise I won't tell anyone" does not work. People do tell. Former girlfriends or boyfriends may reveal knowledge you told them in order to spite you. Mothers, fathers, brothers, sisters, or friends may inadvertently reveal a confidence you told them that gets back to the client, adverse party, or a member of your law office. When this happens, you will hear about it one way or another, and the repercussions can be severe. Do not take the chance; it is simply not worth losing a client or a job. You should not even reveal the fact that an individual is or may be a client of your law office.

- **Always clear your desk of other case files when meeting with clients.** If case files are left in the open, other clients can read the files and access confidential information. Be very careful with any case files taken away from the law office.

- **Do not take phone calls from other clients when meeting with a client.** Taking phone calls from other clients while a client is in your office can expose confidential information. Be aware of who is in your office when talking about confidential information on the phone, and, when possible, keep your door closed when meeting or talking with clients.

Exhibit 3-8 Law Office Confidentiality Policy

Confidential Nature of Client Matters

All matters relating to any clients or office matters are completely confidential. Nothing that occurs in the office should be discussed with family, friends, other clients, or anyone else. Particular care should be taken with papers that are transmitted in the office. Papers should not be examined and matters should not be discussed in public places such as restaurants, lobbies, or elevators, where other persons can peruse such papers or overhear conversations. Particular care should be exercised in commuter trains, buses, or any public area where much law office talk still continues to be overheard on a daily basis. Even after a case has become a matter of public notice by virtue of its having been filed in court or reported in the press, assume that it is still confidential and do not discuss it publicly.

Staff members should be careful, even in the office, not to leave confidential papers in open or public areas, nor should they leave computer monitors on in places where they can be easily seen by passersby. It is the policy of the firm not to use a client's name for the purpose of surveys or in materials that are prepared to describe the firm without the permission of the billing lawyer(s).

The paper shredder located in (provide location in office) should be used for confidential material that must be destroyed; however, such material should not be destroyed without the prior approval of the billing lawyer(s). The use of a confidentiality notice on facsimile (telecopier) transmissions should also be considered as appropriate. Likewise, care must be exercised in dealing with all computer disks, tapes, and other media that contain privileged material.

Care should be taken when dealing with vendors as well. A confidentiality agreement may exist between the firm and a vendor or potential vendors making proposals to the firm.

- **Management must create policies and systems to ensure confidentiality.** Law office managers also have a duty to create systems that ensure confidentiality. Some of these systems may include locking file cabinets that contain client files, limiting access to client files on a need-to-know basis, requiring files to be checked out, having law office policies on client confidentiality, and developing procedures to ensure that the confidential information of clients is maintained (see Exhibit 3-8). Most law offices limit staff members from revealing to persons outside the office that a particular individual is being represented; even revealing the names of clients can give the appearance that the law office does not take confidentiality seriously. Although there is an affirmative ethical duty to maintain client confidentiality, there is also the potential for malpractice liability for firms that violate confidentiality. Under a legal malpractice theory, if a law office (through its employees) reveals client confidences, accidentally or intentionally, it could be legally liable to the client for damages that result.

- **Be careful when responding to discovery requests.** Many times, paralegals are involved in responding to discovery document requests. It is important that all confidential files (including electronic files) are labeled and identified appropriately, that each piece of documentation that is to be submitted to the opposing party is carefully reviewed to ensure that confidential client information is not given out, and that such information is discussed with the supervising attorney.

- **Be particularly careful when using fax machines, e-mail, mobile telephones, and related services.** There have been many instances where confidential information conveyed over these media has been inadvertently revealed to others. It is particularly easy to accidentally reveal confidential information via fax machine and e-mail. An improper or misdirected fax transmission can lead to breach of client confidentiality. Faxes should be sent very carefully. All fax cover pages for law offices should have some kind of confidentiality disclaimer on them. The confidentiality of e-mail is also a concern. From the client's perspective, there are many advantages to using e-mail to communicate with legal professionals. The problem with e-mail was addressed in Chapter 2.

Conflict of Interest

Conflict of interest problems are an important ethical concept. A **conflict of interest** occurs when an attorney or a paralegal has competing personal or professional interests with a client's case that would preclude him or her from acting impartially toward the client.

Conflict of interest problems typically occur when:

- The attorney or paralegal has a personal, financial, or other interest in a case.
- The attorney or paralegal is a substantial witness in the case.
- The law office, attorney, or paralegal sometime in the past represented a client who is now an adverse party in a current case.
- The attorney and a client enter into business together.
- When the attorney is asked to advocate a position on behalf of a client that is contrary to the position of another of the firm's clients (an issue conflict).
- When law firm mergers or acquisitions occur.
- When legal professionals change jobs/firms.

conflict of interest
A competing personal or professional interest that would preclude an attorney or a paralegal from acting impartially toward the client.

If, for instance, an attorney represented a husband and wife in a legal action and then, several years later, the husband approaches the attorney to sue the wife for divorce, the attorney has a conflict-of-interest problem because he had at one time represented both parties. Not only would he have a question as to which client he should be loyal to, but the attorney may have during the first representation been privy to confidences and secrets of the wife that could be used in the divorce case against her.

Rule 1.7 regarding the rules of professional conduct speaks to conflicts of interest, whereby an attorney would be unable to represent a client when a conflict exists. According to Rule 1.7, a conflict exists if an attorney's representation of one client directly and adversely affects another client. The rule allows the attorney to represent the clients where the attorney can provide competent representation of each client, it is not prohibited by law, both clients give informed written consent, and the attorney is not representing both parties in the same litigation where the parties are asserting claims against each other.

Most case law in this area presumes that if a firm has represented both parties in the past, there is an actual conflict of interest. It is not necessary to prove that confidences and secrets were exchanged during the first representation. Usually, but not always, when an actual conflict of interest occurs, the whole firm, not just the attorney involved, is prohibited from entering the case.

Rule 1.8 regarding the rules of professional conduct speaks to the conflict-of-interest issue. It states, among other things, that attorneys cannot enter into business transactions with a client that are adverse to the client unless a number of specific conditions are met. Rule 1.8 also prohibits an attorney from using information related to the representation of a client to the disadvantage of the client unless the client has given informed consent. Under the rule, generally, attorneys cannot solicit substantial gifts from clients as well.

Exhibit 3-9 Conflict of Interest Examples

- Using Client Information to Harm the Client
  An ambitious associate attorney regularly defends the X insurance company. Client comes into attorney's office and wants to sue X insurance company for a major personal injury claim, not knowing that the attorney has represented the company before. Attorney, in an effort to help X insurance company, intentionally lets the statute of limitations run and then pays the client $2500 from his own pocket, telling him that the insurance company settled. Attorney had a clear duty to tell the client of his conflict of interest. Attorney was disbarred and the law firm was sued for malpractice.

- Financial Interest
  Attorney is an employee of the county government's water district. Attorney uses his position of authority to influence the water board's decision to purchase a piece of land that he owns through a partnership. Attorney also delays $300,000 of sewer connection fees to another of his pieces of land until after the sale of land is completed to a third party. Attorney had a clear conflict of interest in both cases. Attorney was suspended for two years for the practice of law and pled guilty to using his official office to influence a governmental decision.

Attorneys and paralegals should be loyal to their clients and have no alternative motives that might influence their independent professional judgment to represent the clients. Exhibit 3-9 provides a few more examples of conflict-of-interest problems.

As noted before, there are different types of conflicts, including an issue conflict. In an issue conflict, an attorney or a firm takes different positions on the same issues for different clients. The *Model Rules* generally prohibits this; however, if each client gives an informed consent, then the firm can most likely continue representing the clients. Also, if the legal matters are in different jurisdictions and the firm reasonably believes neither party will be adversely affected, then most likely the firm can continue representing the clients.

Conflict Checking

Because law offices and attorneys typically represent a large number of clients, it is often difficult for them to remember every client. As a result, it is possible for an attorney to have a conflict of interest but simply not remember the former client. Thus, it becomes the responsibility of management to ensure that before new cases are taken, a conflict check should take place. A written policy regarding conflict checking is prudent.

Many law offices maintain a list of all their former clients and adverse parties so that when a new case is being considered as to whether it should be accepted, the firm will routinely check this list to ensure that there are no conflict-of-interest problems.

Most law firms now use a computer program to search for conflicts; some firms use a computerized database program to do conflict checking. A database program is application software that stores, searches, sorts, and organizes data. When using a database, it is advantageous to include the client's date of birth or Social Security number; otherwise, a misspelled name may not be picked up by the program. Some accounting, billing, docket control, and case management programs can also be used to perform conflicts checking. Exhibit 3-10 shows some case-specific conflict of interest designs. If a firm practices in a certain area, a more specific design would be beneficial.

Exhibit 3-10 Fields to Track in a Case-Specific Conflict of Interest Check

Type of Legal Matter	Fields to Track
Administrative law	• Adverse party • Counsel • Investigator • Witnesses
Bankruptcy	• Debtor(s) • Creditor(s) • Other interested parties • Counsel
Corporate	• Owner(s) • Officers • Partners • Shareholders • General counsel • Affiliates/subsidiaries
Criminal	• Defendant(s) • Prosecutor • Victim(s) • Witnesses • Experts
Estates, trusts, probate	• Testator • Heirs • Children • Spouse • Trustee • Conservator • Power of attorney • Personal representative • Beneficiaries • Counsel
Family law	• Spouse • Children • In-laws • Counsel • Guardian
Litigation	• Client • Adverse parties • Witnesses • Expert • Insurer
Real estate	• Buyer • Seller • Agent • Counsel

(continued)

(continued)

| Workers' compensation | • Client
• Employer
• Insurer
• Health-care provider |
| Other | • Firm lawyers
• Firm paralegals/legal assistants
• Spouses/parents/siblings
• Employees
• Current/past clients
• Prospective clients |

Exhibit 3-11 A Case Upholding the Ethical Wall Theory

The plaintiff in this case is represented by Lee J. Rohn (Rohn) of the Law Offices of Lee J. Rohn. Defendants are represented by Kevin Rames, Esq. (Rames) of the Law Offices of Kevin Rames. This motion revolves around Eliza Combie (Combie), who worked as a paralegal at the Rames law office from October 30, 2000 to March 26, 2004. Her work at Rames's office involved working with several litigation matters, including this case. On March 26, 2004, Combie began work with the Rohn law firm. During Combie's interview with Rohn, they discussed the possible conflicts raised by Combie's possible employment. Combie was told that should she accept employment with the Rohn firm, she would be barred from contact with those cases. Rohn states that on Combie's first day of work with Rohn, she submitted the list of cases. The list was circulated to all employees and a memo informing employees to refrain from discussing those cases in her presence was circulated and posted in common areas of the office. Combie and Rohn state that no one in the office has discussed any of the relevant matters with Combie. They also state that Combie is locked out of the electronic files and does not work in close proximity to them or to Rohn.

Rames invokes ABA Rules of Professional Conduct 5.3, 1.9, 1.16, and 1.10 to argue that Rohn and the entire law firm must be disqualified because during Combie's previous employment with Rames, she obtained confidential information regarding pending matters which she may divulge to Rohn. The Court is satisfied that the procedures employed by Rohn's office to shield Combie from the files supports a finding that any information obtained at the Rames law firm will not be disclosed. It is important that nonlawyer employees have as much mobility in employment opportunity consistent with the protection of clients' interests. To so limit employment opportunities that some nonlawyers trained to work with law firms might be required to leave the careers for which they have been trained would disserve clients as well as the legal profession.

In light of the foregoing, disqualification is not warranted. In addressing ethical problems created by nonlawyers changing employment from a law firm representing one party to a law firm representing an adverse party, courts must fashion rules which strike a balance between the public policy of protecting the confidentiality of attorney–client communications and a party's right to representation by chosen counsel. Accordingly, any restrictions on the nonlawyers' employment should be held to the minimum necessary to protect confidentiality of client information. The Court finds that plaintiff's counsel has rebutted the presumption of improper disclosure by presenting evidence of the "Chinese Wall" ["or Ethical Wall"] implemented in that regard. Accordingly, disqualification is not warranted and the defendants' motion will be denied at this time.

Source: *Lamb v. Pralex*, 333 F.Supp.2d 361 (2004 D. Virgin Islands).

Some insurance companies that issue malpractice insurance to attorneys also require that the firm must have and consistently use a conflict-checking device before the policy is written.

The Ethical Wall

Although it is the general rule that courts tend to disqualify a whole firm when a conflict-of-interest problem arises, some courts have carved out an alternative to disqualification. The alternative is called the **Ethical Wall**, which occurs when a firm effectively isolates the attorney, paralegal, or other legal team members with a conflict of interest from having anything whatsoever to do with the case, thus creating an Ethical Wall around him or her (see excerpts of the *Lamb v. Pralex* opinion in Exhibit 3-11). This is typically done by instructing staff members not to talk to the attorney in question about the case, not to disclose any information acquired at the previous firm and limiting any access the attorney might have to the files of the case by locking file cabinets and placing passwords on computer files.

If the Ethical Wall is created and the court agrees, it will limit disqualification to the specific attorney, paralegal, or other personnel. Not all courts accept the Ethical Wall theory. Again, it would be the duty of management to ensure that the office locks up the files, and to segregate the attorney or paralegal with the conflict from the rest of the staff. Law offices must also effectively limit access to computers and client data files to build an effective Ethical Wall.

Ethical Wall
Term for a technique used to isolate the paralegal or attorney with a conflict of interest from having anything to do with a case.

Paralegal Conflict of Interests

Many courts have extended the conflict-of-interest issue to paralegals as well as attorneys. Conflict-of-interest problems usually occur when a paralegal changes employment. For instance, in *In re Complex Asbestos Litigation*, a paralegal worked for a law firm defending major asbestos litigation claims. He worked with discovery documents, was a part of the defense team for three years and attended defense strategy meetings. Subsequently, he was hired by a firm representing asbestos plaintiffs. The defendants moved to disqualify the plaintiff's attorney because of the paralegal's conflict of interest (he had knowledge of confidential information gained over several years). The motion was granted by the court.

Paralegals should be ready to answer questions about their previous employers when interviewing for jobs to avoid conflict-of-interest problems. The ABA Committee on Ethics and Professional Responsibility issued an opinion regarding this matter. It pointed out that effective screening of non-lawyers, such as a paralegal, could help to avoid disqualification, when a paralegal might have worked on a common case at their previous law firm employment. The paralegal's diligence in providing potential conflict information to the new law firm employer is the key to avoiding the problems associated with disqualifications.

The paralegal should be alert to situations that might present a potential conflict of interest because of information gained in past employment and should disclose any questionable situation to the employer.

How Attorneys and Paralegals Can Avoid Conflicts of Interest

- **When changing jobs, bring up the issue of potential conflicts in the interview.** Tell the firm whom you have worked for and what types of cases you have worked on. It is better to deal with potential conflict problems up front than for an employer to hire you and then find out there are problems.

- **Be absolutely honest about your past.** Do not hide or deceive employers about potential conflict of interest problems. Honesty is always the best policy.

- **If you later find out you may have a conflict, immediately inform your supervising attorney or paralegal manager and do not have anything to do with the case.** If you find out after you have been hired by a new firm that you may have a conflict problem, immediately raise the issue with your supervising attorney. Do not volunteer information to the new firm regarding the matter. If you can, approach your former employer and ask for an informed and express written waiver giving consent for you to work for the other firm. Verbal consent is hard to prove, so get it in writing.

- **Management must ensure that conflict-of-interest problems are checked.** It is also the duty of management to ensure that employees are not hired who have substantial conflict of interest problems, or if they do have such problems that the firm knows about them up front. For instance, management might want to add a question to its employment form that asks potential employees to state any conflict problems, in addition to establishing the conflict-checking system mentioned earlier.

Resolving Ethical Problems

There is nothing easy about resolving an ethical problem. Typically, ethical issues are complex and messy; they are rarely "black and white." However, the following ideas can help you deal with ethical problems.

- **Talk to your supervising attorney or paralegal manager regarding ethical problems.** When you encounter an ethical problem, the first thing you should do is to talk to someone else about it to get a different perspective. Typically, this will be the supervising attorney, or in the case of a paralegal, possibly a paralegal manager. However, this is sometimes hard to do when the supervising attorney is the one asking you to do something you think is unethical or if the attorney is him- or herself doing something unethical. One way to approach the issue is to discreetly ask the attorney if he or she thinks this might be a problem; it is important not to be accusatory, but to simply inquire into the issue and to present your point as objectively as possible. You always have the option, no matter how difficult, to say no if you are asked to do something that you know is unethical. Also, be sure to check your firm's personnel policy manual. Ethical problems and procedures for handling them are sometimes covered in this type of manual.

- **Talk to another attorney or paralegal in the firm regarding ethical problems.** If you have a hard time talking to your supervising attorney about an ethical problem, talk to another attorney, paralegal, or ethics committee, if the firm has one. It is important when dealing with ethical problems to take counsel with others, to bounce ideas off others, and to talk about them. Other people may have more experience than you might have previously dealt with a similar situation. When talking to another attorney in the firm, use the same non-accusatory approach. Be sure that you are talking to a person you can trust for sincere advice on how to handle the situation; you do not want to be perceived as spreading rumors or stirring up trouble. In large-sized firms, you also have the option of asking to be transferred.

- **Join a professional association.** Professional associations offer a good way to share information and experiences with others, including information about ethical problems. Most professional attorney organizations will include county/parish bar associations along with the state bar organization that for most attorneys is a mandatory membership organization. For paralegals, in addition to NALA and NFPA, most states and county/parishes have paralegal organizations to provide guidance on ethical concerns. Use these resources to help you solve your ethical problem.

- **Be familiar with the ethical rules of your state.** It is always a good idea to have a copy of the ethical rules used in your jurisdiction and to review them from time to time.

- **Subscribe to periodicals that cover ethical issues.** Many national attorney and paralegal publications routinely carry articles on ethical concerns. Some even have a regular column on the issues of ethics. This kind of timely information can be helpful when dealing with ethical problems.

- **Report ethical violations to the state bar association as a last resort.** If you have tried to work out an ethical problem to no avail, you always have the option of reporting the violation to the state bar association. This is a very difficult decision to make because you may lose your job as a result. Ethical problems are not easy to deal with, and you must be able to live with whatever decision you make.

- **When considering ethical questions, think conservatively.** When you are faced with a hard ethical question, be conservative and do what you know is right, no matter how much it may hurt.

- **Do not ignore the ethical problem.** A common way to handle ethical problems is to simply ignore them and hope they will go away. Unfortunately, this approach rarely works. In many instances, it simply makes the situation worse. For example, if you see a staff person charging time to a client's case when he or she is not working on that case, it is better to bring the issue to the forefront right away than wait for him or her to do the same to 20 clients. Ethical problems are better handled when they first occur as opposed to letting them fester and become far more complicated.

Ethical Questions Regarding Paralegal/ Nonlawyers Employment Services

The following is a list of questions and answers to common ethical issues arising with the employment of paralegals and other nonlawyer professionals. The answers are based on general statements of law, so an answer may be different depending on your particular jurisdiction.

- **May paralegals have business cards, and may their names appear on law firm stationery?** In many states, the answer is yes. For business cards, care must be taken to ensure that the nonlawyer status of the cardholder is displayed prominently on the card. Regarding firm stationery, the name of the paralegal(s) must be set apart from the lawyers' names, and the paralegal's title must be shown clearly. Some firms print lawyers' names on one side of the stationery and print paralegals' names on the other side.

- **May a paralegal sign letters prepared on firm stationery?** Yes, provided (1) the letter contains no direct legal advice or opinions, and (2) the paralegal's status is shown clearly. The best practice is to include the title "Paralegal" or "Legal Assistant to X" directly below the typed name in the signature block of the letter.

- **May a paralegal discuss fee ranges with a client on a preliminary basis, leaving the final discussion and decision to the supervising attorney?** All discussions related to fees must be deferred to the attorney. Even when a firm uses an internal fee schedule, it generally serves as a guideline only. It is solely the attorney's responsibility to measure the situation presented by each case and to set the fee.

- **How often and in what way must a paralegal identify his or her nonlawyer status?** There is no single, correct way to identify the paralegal's status. It seems prudent to do so at the beginning of all telephone conversations and at the beginning of every initial conference with a client or witness. For example, regarding a telephone call, one might say, "Hello. This is Jack Samson, Jane Mitchell's paralegal." If it appears that the other party thinks the paralegal is a lawyer, that impression should be corrected right away. The issue is not how often identity must be clarified to comply with the rules; it is how often identity should be clarified to protect the paralegal from charges related to the unauthorized practice of law.

- **May a paralegal counsel a close friend or a relative about a legal matter when the friend or relative knows that the paralegal is not a lawyer and when the paralegal is not paid for the advice?** Other than suggesting that the friend or relative see a lawyer, the paralegal cannot give advice or comment in any way that may be taken as a legal opinion. The problem arises most frequently at family dinners, parties, and other social events. Friends and relatives can create an extremely uncomfortable situation. Whether the paralegal is paid or not is irrelevant; legal advice cannot be given by the paralegal under any circumstances.

Malpractice and Malpractice Prevention

legal malpractice
Possible consequence when an attorney's or a law office's conduct falls below the standard skill, prudence, and diligence that an ordinary lawyer would possess or that is commonly available in the legal community.

Legal malpractice occurs when an attorney's or a law office's conduct in representing a client falls below the standard skill, prudence, and diligence that an ordinary lawyer would possess or that is commonly available in the legal community.

Exhibit 3-12 lists the most common types of errors that result in a malpractice claim being filed. Notice in Exhibit 3-12 that "substantive errors" account for 47% of malpractice claims and that failure to know or properly apply the law represented the most common reason for all malpractice claims.

Exhibit 3-13 provides some excellent suggestions for helping to avoid costly malpractice claims. Engagement and disengagement letters are another way to avoid malpractice claims. Clients sometimes think attorneys are representing

Exhibit 3-12 Profile of Legal Malpractice Claims

Type of Alleged Error	2016–2019
ADMINISTRATIVE	**PERCENTAGE**
Failure to calendar properly	4.3
Procrastination in performance/follow-up	9.7
Failure to file document (no deadline)	3.1
Failure to react to calendar	2.3
Clerical error	3.5
Lost file/document evidence	7.5
SUBSTANTIVE	
Failure to know/properly apply law	13.6
Failure to know/ascertain deadline	6.9
Inadequate discovery/investigation	7.4
Conflict of interest	4.3
Planning error (procedure choice)	7.8
Error in public record search	3.0
Failure to understand/anticipate tax	1.4
CLIENT RELATIONS	
Failure to obtain consent/inform client	7.0
Failure to follow client's instruction	5.7
Improper withdrawal of representation	1.9
INTENTIONAL WRONG	
Malicious prosecution/abuse of process	3.4
Fraud	4.5
Libel or slander	1.0
Violation of civil rights	1.3

Source: 2016–2019, American Bar Association Standing Committee on Lawyers' Professional Liability.

Exhibit 3-13 Tips to Prevent Legal Malpractice

1. Gather factual information from the client to determine the basis of any legal claim and immediately determine and track when the statute of limitations takes effect.
2. Give the client a copy of the written fee agreement specifying the terms of employment and the basis of the attorney's fees in the case.
3. Conduct a thorough conflict of interest check before the client's case is accepted and immediately notify the client in writing if a conflict or a potential conflict is discovered.
4. Investigate the facts of the client's case and the law regarding the case diligently and promptly.
5. Keep the client informed regarding the status of his or her case by providing routine status reports; always inform the client of all developments that might affect the client's rights; and ask for his or her participation throughout the case.
6. Charge a reasonable and fair fee for services performed and provide the client with clear and detailed accounting of the basis for the fees charged.
7. Carefully and thoroughly proofread all documents and e-mails before they go out for mistakes and, whenever possible, send a copy of the document to the client for his or her approval and review.
8. Immediately tell the client of problems or mistakes as they happen and offer solutions.
9. Do not overestimate the firm's capacity to take on cases outside its expertise and always determine whether there is sufficient time to handle the matter properly.
10. Provide the client with written notice upon the attorney's withdrawal from representation (obtain court approval in matters involving litigation) and promptly provide the client with his or her file and other property he or she is entitled to.

them when, in fact, they are not. Law offices should always send an engagement letter or a contract that clearly sets out when a case is taken, what the firm is going to do, and on what the fees will be based.

In addition, law offices should routinely send out disengagement letters for any type of case or legal matter, even if the only thing the law office did was to meet with the client in an initial interview (see Exhibit 3-14). The purpose of the disengagement letter is to clearly set out in writing that the attorney–client relationship was not formed or has ended. A client may not understand that the firm is not pursuing the matter, then come back months or even years later claiming that the attorney committed malpractice against him or her by not following up on the case.

Exhibit 3-14 Disengagement Letters

Example 1: Disengagement Letter—New Client Where Case Was Not Accepted

Subject: Potential Claim of *Client v. Smith*

Dear Client

Thank you for coming into our office on Thursday, February XX, 201, regarding your legal matter. We are interested in your concerns and appreciated the opportunity to meet with you. However, after further consideration we have decided to decline representation of your interests in the captioned matter.

We have not made a legal opinion as to the validity or merits of your case. You should be aware that any action in this matter must be filed within the applicable statute of limitations. We suggest that you consult with another attorney concerning your rights in this matter.

Again, we will not be representing you in the captioned matter and are closing our file.

Thank you again, and we wish you the best.

Kindest Regards,

Example 2: Disengagement Letter Following Representation

Subject: *Client v. Smith*

Dear Client

Thank you for allowing us the opportunity to serve you regarding the captioned matter. The case is now closed, and we are removing the case from our active file status. We will be archiving the file shortly. If you would like evidence or other material that you have provided to us returned, please give me a call so I can get it to you.

We are interested in knowing how you feel about the quality of legal services you received from our firm. We would appreciate it if you would complete the enclosed client survey questionnaire. We are always interested in knowing how we can serve you better in the future.

Again, the captioned case is now closed, and we greatly enjoyed representing your interests.

If you have any questions, please feel free to give me a call.

Kindest Regards,

Summary

An ethical rule is a minimal standard of conduct required by attorneys. An attorney may not fall below the standard without losing his or her good standing with the state bar. The ***Model Rules of Professional Conduct*** are ethical rules for attorneys that are promulgated by the American Bar

Association. Ethical rules for attorneys do not apply directly to paralegals. However, attorneys can be disciplined for the acts of their staff, including paralegals. In addition, paralegals themselves can lose their jobs and face criminal charges and fines for practicing law without a license, among other things, so it is important that attorneys and paralegals act in an ethical manner.

Attorneys are directly responsible for the acts of all members of the legal team, including paralegals. Under the **Model Rules,** attorneys must make reasonable efforts to ensure that their conduct is compatible with the ethical rules. Paralegals and legal assistants have two national associations that they may belong to, the NALA – The Paralegal Association and the National Federation of Paralegal Associations (NFPA). Both associations have voluntary model codes of ethics for paralegals/legal assistants.

All states have statutes regarding the unauthorized practice of law by lawyers and nonlawyers. Paralegals that "practice law" can be criminally charged under these statutes. Paralegals and attorneys not authorized to practice in a particular jurisdiction are prevented from giving legal advice. The factors involved in making this determination include (1) whether advice given requires legal skill or knowledge, (2) whether the person was advised of his or her legal rights, and (3) whether the advice is not normally given by a nonlawyer as part of another business or transaction (such as a tax consultant). A non-barred lawyer or paralegal also may not misrepresent his or her status so that others believe that he or she is an attorney; they must clearly state his or her title and that he or she is not an attorney nor authorized to practice. Paralegals are not allowed to represent clients in court proceedings, perform legal analysis and prepare legal documents (without supervision of an attorney), set or share a fee, or evaluate a case regarding whether to accept or reject it.

Attorneys—and, therefore, paralegals—are required to act in a competent manner for their clients. They must reasonably know and understand the area of the law they are working in, and they must adequately prepare for the representation of the client. Attorneys and legal professionals must also act diligently, including acting promptly and without undue delay.

Attorneys and paralegals are required to maintain client confidentiality. The duty of confidentiality is an important part of the client–attorney relationship; the attorney–client privilege is a part of that relationship. The privilege precludes the disclosure of confidential communications between a lawyer and a client by the lawyer. The privilege also extends to paralegals and all members of the legal team.

Attorneys and paralegals are prohibited from representing a client where they have a conflict of interest. A conflict of interest is a competing personal or professional interest that would preclude an attorney or a paralegal from acting impartially toward the client. An "Ethical Wall" is a technique used to isolate the attorney and/or paralegal with a conflict of interest from having anything to do with a case; the Ethical Wall can sometimes be created so that an entire firm does not have to be disqualified from representing a client because of the conflict with one staff member, such as a paralegal.

Legal malpractice occurs when an attorney's conduct in representing a client falls below the standard skill, prudence, and diligence that an ordinary lawyer would possess or that is commonly available in the legal community.

Key Terms

ABA *Model Code of Professional Responsibility*

ABA *Model Rules of Professional Conduct*

attorney–client privilege

client confidentiality

conflict of interest

ethical rule

Ethical Wall

legal malpractice

legal technicians

Practical Applications

1. You are employed at a law firm that is representing a company in the process of negotiating a deal to merge with a competitor. You inadvertently mention the possibility of the merger to your father. Without your knowledge, your father purchases a large sum of stock in the company you represent, knowing that when the merger becomes public, the price of the stock will substantially rise. Several months after the transaction, your father gives you a check for $5000 and explains how he made the money. He tells you that he only did it for your benefit. Disregarding the criminal statutes that have been violated, how would you handle the situation and how could the problem have been avoided?

2. You work for a government agency and are responding to a plaintiff's request for production of documents. One of the requests specifically asks for any notes or memoranda arising out of the facts of the case. In one of the boxes of material the agency has collected on the matter, you find a particularly incriminating memorandum that will virtually win the case for the plaintiffs if it is produced. What do you do?

   Assume you go to your supervising attorney about the matter. The attorney responds that he or she will take care of the matter and thanks you for your diligent work. Several months go by and you are now working on preparing the case for trial. You quickly realize that the document was never produced to the plaintiffs. How would you resolve this situation?

3. You are working on a client's case when the client's accountant calls and asks you for information about the client. You have worked with this particular accountant before and know the accountant is trustworthy. Is there any problem with revealing the information to the accountant? How would you handle it?

4. Your law office just signed an agreement to represent a famous athlete in contract negotiations with his team. A reporter from **Sports Illustrated** calls and asks if your firm is representing the athlete. You read **Sports Illustrated** all the time and are impressed that one of its reporters called your firm. In fact, you are caught off guard by the question. Being typically honest and forthright, you begin to answer. What is your answer?

5. Your law office represents a nonprofit corporation. The executive director of the nonprofit corporation calls you when your supervising attorney is out of the office. The executive director states that an employee is demanding overtime pay, since she has worked for more than 40 hours last week, and is saying that if she is not paid overtime, she will immediately file a wage-and-hour complaint with the appropriate state agency. The attorney will not be in the office the whole week but may call in. You recollect from previous experience that the Fair Labor Standards Act generally states that employees should receive overtime pay for hours worked in excess of 40 hours a week, though you are not sure about exceptions to the rule. The executive director presses you and says that he absolutely has to have an answer immediately and that if your firm cannot respond to emergencies, then maybe he will take his business elsewhere. How would you resolve the situation? Give options.

6. One of the job duties of the paralegal is to screen clients. The paralegal routinely sees new clients and reports the facts of each client's case to one of the attorneys. The attorneys then decide which cases they have time to take on. On Monday, a client comes into the office. The client has no money but appears to need an attorney. The client informs the paralegal that she has been sued and needs legal counsel to represent her for a hearing in the state district court on Friday at 10:00 a.m. before Judge Smith. The paralegal is sure the attorneys do not have the time to accept this case. After listening to the client, the paralegal respectfully tells the client that they do not think the office will be able to represent her. The client leaves, and the paralegal prepares a memo to the attorneys. The attorneys subsequently decide not to handle the matter and file is closed.

On Friday at 10:15 A.M., the office receives a phone call from Judge Smith. Judge Smith tells the receptionist that an attorney from the office has five minutes to get over to her courtroom to represent the client or she (Judge Smith) will hold the office/attorneys in contempt of court and levy a fine against the office. Apparently, the client told Judge Smith that she had met with a representative from the legal aid office and had told the representative about the hearing. It was the client's understanding that an attorney from the legal aid office would represent her. Explain how this matter could have been avoided.

On the Web Exercises

1. Start by going to the search engines, such as http://www.google.com or http://www.yahoo.com; search for all of the lawyer disciplinary agencies for the 50 states. A number of them have Web sites. Visit five of the Web sites and compare what kind of information is available to clients that are having difficulty with an attorney.

2. Visit three state bar association Web sites on the Internet and compare the information on ethics for each one. Several Web sites are listed in the Web Links section of this chapter and also of Chapter 2. Alternatively, you can search for state bar associations using http://www.google.com or http://www.yahoo.com. Most of the disciplinary administrator Web sites found in Exercise 1 use the state bar association Web sites as well, so if you completed that assignment, you should have already found most of them.

3. Visit the NALA and NFPA Web sites on ethics that are listed in the Web Links section of this chapter. What kind of information do they offer, and is it helpful?

4. Go to CLIO Case Management System (either set up individually or by the course instructor): Review instructions for (1) Entering Contacts to understand adding new contacts; and (2) Conflict of Interest Searching to understand the CLIO feature to perform search queries and conflict checks.

Case Review

In re Hrones, 933 N.E.2d 622 (Ma. 2010).

Supreme Court of Massachusetts.

In re: Hrones
OPINION
SPINA, J. This bar discipline matter is before us on a reservation and report, without decision, from a single justice of this court. The respondent, Stephen Hrones, is an attorney who practices law and maintains a law firm in Boston. The Board of Bar Overseers (board) has recommended that he be suspended for one year and one day, for, among other violations, forming a business arrangement with a nonlawyer and assisting a nonlawyer in the unauthorized practice of law. The respondent argues (1) that his actions did not amount to assisting a nonlawyer in the unauthorized practice of law, and (2) that a three-month suspension is the appropriate sanction. For the reasons that follow, we conclude that the respondent did assist a nonlawyer in the unauthorized practice of law, and a suspension from the practice of law for one year and one day is the appropriate sanction for this and his other violations.

1. Background. The following facts are drawn from the findings of a hearing committee, which were adopted unanimously by the full board. See Matter of Brauer, 452 Mass. 56, 57, 890 N.E.2d 847 (2008). We have supplemented the hearing committee's findings with undisputed facts contained in the record on appeal. See id.

The respondent was admitted to the practice of law in this Commonwealth on December 14, 1972. At the time of the misconduct, the respondent operated a law firm in Boston, employing an associate, a secretary, and an intern. The respondent's legal practice was concentrated in the areas of criminal defense and civil rights cases.

Around September, 2001, the respondent was introduced to Lionel Porter, a law school graduate who had not passed the bar examination. Porter was knowledgeable in employment discrimination law and had appeared before [1] the Massachusetts Commission Against Discrimination (MCAD) on behalf of the National Association for the Advancement of Colored People. Porter was looking for work, and the respondent agreed that Porter would share office space with respondent's law firm and utilize the firm's support staff. Relying on the law firm's name and the respondent's license to practice law, the respondent and Porter agreed that Porter, working as a paralegal, would develop a practice in employment discrimination cases before the MCAD and the United States Equal Employment Opportunity Commission (EEOC). They agreed that the firm would enter into contingent fee arrangements with Porter's clients, and all fees and retainers would be paid to the firm. The respondent would then give Porter two-thirds of any fees collected and retain one-third. The respondent listed Porter on the firm's letterhead as a paralegal, and he permitted Porter to use a firm business card that identified him as a paralegal.

FN1. See 804 Code Mass. Regs. § 1.10 (1)(c) (1999) (allowing MCAD complaints with the Massachusetts Commission Against Discrimination [MCAD] to be filed by nonprofit organizations "whose purposes includes the elimination of the unlawful practice[s]") and 804 Code Mass. Regs. § 1.13(5)(b) (1999) (claimant may be accompanied to an informal investigative conference "by his/her attorney or other representative").

The respondent's firm generally did not handle employment or other discrimination cases, and the respondent himself had little or no experience in discrimination cases. The respondent intended that Porter would operate a virtually independent discrimination law practice, without substantial supervision by the respondent or any other attorney at the firm. No one in the office was assigned to, or did, supervise Porter's work.

Prior to his employment, Porter told the respondent that he was not required to be a member of the Massachusetts bar to practice before the MCAD. The respondent and Porter reviewed an unidentified statute or regulation that the respondent believed confirmed Porter's representation regarding nonlawyer practice at the MCAD. However, the respondent also understood that Porter could represent clients at the MCAD only pursuant to an appearance of an attorney of record; therefore, the respondent gave Porter authorization to sign his name to appearance forms, administrative complaints, and other filings before the MCAD and the EEOC, without requiring that the respondent review them before filing.

Porter identified prospective clients by reviewing the MCAD's list of pro se complainants and sent each a letter on firm letterhead. The letter stated that "[p]ersons at [respondent's] firm have had several years handling discrimination complaints and the firm is generally known for its civil rights advocacy." Porter marketed his practice and exercised sole discretion in deciding to accept discrimination cases. He determined fee arrangements, executed fee agreements, and collected fees. In conducting the cases, Porter filed complaints, drafted pleadings, conducted discovery, counselled clients as to their legal rights, settled cases, and performed all other legal work on the cases. Porter carried out these functions and operated the firm's discrimination practice with virtually no supervision by the respondent or another lawyer in the firm.

The respondent left to Porter's discretion whether and when a case should be removed from the MCAD or EEOC to State or Federal court. The respondent and Porter did not make any arrangements to handle such a contingency, and the respondent did not make any arrangements requiring Porter to seek his authorization before removing a case – in the respondent's name – to State or Federal court. In at least two instances, Porter actually removed cases to State or Federal court, without the respondent's knowledge. The record does not show whether Porter ever appeared at an oral argument or before any State or Federal court.

In June, 2003, the MCAD assessed sanctions against the respondent, as attorney of record, in connection with misconduct by Porter. The respondent learned of the sanctions in June, but took no action. Porter subsequently concealed a September, 2003, warning that the respondent's failure to pay sanctions would result in his suspension from practice before the MCAD. In November, 2003, the respondent received a notice from the MCAD suspending the respondent, his firm, and Porter from practice before the MCAD for one year for failure to pay the sanctions. The order required the respondent to withdraw as counsel or remove all cases to a court within twenty-one days. The respondent did not investigate the charges, review Porter's case files, withdraw his appearances in any cases, or notify Porter's clients that the firm had been suspended from practice before the MCAD. [2] Approximately forty cases were pending at the time of the suspension, and the respondent did not instruct Porter to take any action in response to the order. The respondent did not do anything at this time to protect the rights of the firm's discrimination clients.

FN2. In light of the notice, the respondent did request hearings before the MCAD and the office of Bar Counsel (bar counsel). The MCAD did not grant a hearing.

Despite the sanctions, the respondent did not terminate his relationship with Porter. Around the same time, the respondent learned that Porter had removed a case from the MCAD to Federal court, under the respondent's name. The respondent reprimanded Porter, but did not terminate the relationship or investigate whether other suits were filed in court under his name. In early October, 2004, the respondent learned that Porter had filed an untimely complaint in Federal court under the respondent's name, without the respondent's authority. In addition, between February and October, 2004, the respondent received multiple complaints of neglect, lack of communication, misrepresentation, and other misconduct by Porter, including complaints filed by clients with the office of Bar Counsel (bar counsel).

In October, 2004, the respondent learned from Bar Counsel that Porter had not remitted a client's fee payment and he fired Porter in response, for violating their agreement that Porter would run all fees through the respondent's accounts. At this point, the respondent notified Porter's clients of the termination, refunded retainer fees to some of them, and acknowledged that in a number of cases, the firm had missed key deadlines and otherwise mismanaged the cases. He directed an associate to review the files to determine which claims were viable, and contacted outside attorneys to see if they would be interested in taking some of the cases.

2. Procedural history. Bar counsel's third amended petition for discipline brought eight counts against the respondent. Count I set out general charges arising from the respondent's alleged misconduct. Counts II through VI alleged misconduct specific to five clients, all as a result of Porter's mismanagement of their cases. In each of those cases, Porter failed to meet mandatory filing deadlines, which resulted in dismissal of the clients' underlying claims. Counts VII and VIII concerned unrelated violations of the rules regarding IOLTA accounts and the provision of financial assistance to clients.

The case was heard by a hearing committee in April, 2008, and the hearing committee recommended that the respondent be suspended for six months and one day. The hearing committee determined that the respondent improperly split fees with Porter, failed to supervise Porter, failed to communicate adequately with the discrimination clients, failed to provide competent and diligent representation to those clients, failed to keep adequate trust records, advanced financial assistance to clients, and entered into a business transaction with one client.

On appeal, the board adopted the hearing committee's subsidiary findings, but modified the report by adding conclusions that the respondent had assisted in unauthorized practice, formed a business entity with Porter, made false, deceptive, or misleading communications, and made unauthorized disclosure of confidential client information. The board recommended that the respondent be suspended for one year and one day.

3. Standard of review. "In bar discipline cases that have been reserved and reported, we 'review the board's findings and reach our own conclusion.'" Matter of Wainwright, 448 Mass. 378, 384, 861 N.E.2d 440 (2007), quoting Matter of Fordham, 423 Mass. 481, 487, 668 N.E.2d 816 (1996), cert. denied, 519 U.S. 1149, 117 S. Ct. 1082, 137 L. Ed. 2d 216 (1997). We accept "subsidiary facts found by the board" if they are "supported by substantial evidence, upon

consideration of the record." S.J.C. Rule 4.01, § 8 (4), as appearing in 425 Mass. 1309 (1997). The findings and recommendations of the board, although not binding on this court, are entitled to great weight. Matter of Murray, 455 Mass. 872, 879, 920 N.E.2d 862 (2010), and cases cited. The board's findings here, adopting all the hearing committee's findings, are supported by the evidence, and we accept those findings.

4. Assistance in the unauthorized practice of law. The respondent argues that he did not assist in the unauthorized practice of law, but instead failed to supervise Porter adequately, a lesser violation of the Massachusetts Rules of Professional Conduct. The respondent argues that assistance in the unauthorized practice of law requires more than the negligence or omissions present in this case and also requires the lawyer to possess a specific intent to assist in the unauthorized practice of law. Bar counsel argues that, not only did Porter engage in the unauthorized practice of law, the respondent assisted him in such practice.

Rule 5.5(b) of the Massachusetts Rule of Professional Conduct, 426 Mass. 1410 (1998), which was in effect through December 31, 2006, prohibits an attorney from "assist[ing] a person who is not a member of the bar in the performance of activity that constitutes the unauthorized practice of law." [3] Only attorneys may represent parties in court and give legal advice. See Goldblatt v. Corporation Counsel of Boston, 360 Mass. 660, 665, 277 N.E.2d 273 (1971); Opinion of the Justices, 289 Mass. 607, 613-614, 194 N.E. 313 (1935). Although this court has observed that "[i]t is not easy to define the practice of law," Lowell Bar Ass'n v. Loeb, 315 Mass. 176, 180, 52 N.E.2d 27 (1943), we have stated that the practice of law includes:

FN3. Effective January 1, 2007, the rule was reworded and restructured, but its substance is unchanged. See Mass. R. Prof. C. 5.5 (a), as appearing in 447 Mass. 1302 (2007). In this opinion, we cite to the former rule, as it was in effect during the incidents at issue.

"directing and managing the enforcement of legal claims and the establishment of the legal rights of others, where it is necessary to form and to act upon opinions as to what those rights are and as to the legal methods which must be adopted to enforce them, the practice of giving or furnishing legal advice as to such rights and methods and the practice, as an occupation, of drafting documents by which such rights are created, modified, surrendered or secured."

Matter of an Application for Admission to the Bar of the Commonwealth, 443 Mass. 1010, 1012 n.4, 822 N.E.2d 1206 (2005), quoting Matter of the Shoe Mfrs. Protective Ass'n, 295 Mass. 369, 372, 3 N.E.2d 746 (1936). We also have held that the practice of law may involve "either rendering legal advice to or soliciting... clients, or... engaging in a legal contest in a Massachusetts forum." Matter of Chimko, 444 Mass. 743, 752, 831 N.E.2d 316 (2005). Finally, we have held that "an attorney should not permit lay persons even to appear to form the attorney-client relationship with a prospective client, because that is part of the practice of law." DeVaux v. American Home Assurance Co., 387 Mass. 814, 820, 444 N.E.2d 355 (1983).

The appropriate inquiry is whether the actions by Porter, "viewed individually or as a whole, are actions only a lawyer is entitled to perform on behalf of another in the circumstances." See Matter of the Shoe Mfrs. Protective Ass'n, supra.

Here, Porter's discrimination practice included determining fee arrangements and executing fee agreements, counselling clients about their legal rights, drafting and filing pleadings, conducting discovery, negotiating settlements, and deciding whether and when to remove cases from the MCAD or EEOC for filing in State or Federal court. In Matter of Jackman, 20 Mass. Att'y Discipline Rep. 263, 267-268 (2004), S.C., 444 Mass. 1013, 830 N.E.2d 1083 (2005), the single justice determined that the unauthorized practice of law occurred when an attorney's staff member handled and settled personal injury cases with inadequate supervision or oversight. Similarly, many of the activities undertaken by Porter in this case fall within the definition of the "practice of law."

The respondent argues that "the vast majority of Porter's activities fall within the ambit of permissible paralegal work." While many tasks performed by an attorney may also be performed by a paralegal, we require that an attorney supervise a paralegal's performance of such work. See comment 1 to Mass. R. Prof. C. 5.5 (b) (rule "does not prohibit a lawyer from employing the services of paraprofessionals and delegating functions to them, so long as the lawyer supervises the delegated work and retains responsibility for their work"). Here, respondent did not supervise Porter in Porter's discrimination law practice. In addition, much of Porter's practice of law before the MCAD was unauthorized, as practice by nonlawyers before the MCAD is confined to the filing of complaints by a qualifying organization and participation in some informal conferences. [4] See 804 Code Mass. Regs. § 1.10 (1)(c) (1999) (allowing MCAD complaints to be filed by nonprofit organizations "whose purposes include the elimination of the unlawful practice[s]"); 804 Code Mass. Regs. § 1.13(5)(b) (1999) (claimant may be accompanied to an informal investigative conference "by his or her attorney or other representative"). Porter's discrimination law practice at the respondent's firm was not covered under the regulation regarding nonprofit organizations, as he was not acting on behalf of a qualified organization; accordingly, Porter handled each of his cases at the MCAD under the appearances he filed in respondent's name, but without any supervision from the respondent or another attorney at respondent's firm. In addition, Porter's unsupervised activity at the MCAD went far beyond appearing at informal investigative conferences.

FN4. The respondent relies on testimony by a former MCAD commissioner to support his argument that Porter was authorized to practice before the MCAD. The former commissioner testified that, while there was no regulation allowing law firm paralegals to engage in the practice of law at the MCAD, it was common for paralegals to engage in some activities at the MCAD during his tenure. See 804 Code Mass. Regs. § 1.13(5)(b) (claimant may be accompanied to an informal investigative conference "by his/her attorney or other representative"). He did testify that hearings on probable cause,

interrogatories, depositions, and public hearings at the MCAD were expected to be handled by attorneys.

The respondent argues that, even if Porter's activities consisted of the unauthorized practice of law, he did not offer any assistance to Porter in violation of Mass. R. Prof. C. 5.5(b). Specifically, the respondent contends that (1) because the hearing committee determined his conduct was negligent, and consisted mostly of omissions, the more accurate violation is failure to supervise under Mass. R. Prof. C. 5.3(b), 426 Mass. 1408 (1998); and (2) in order to have assisted in the unauthorized practice of law, the respondent must have had a more active role and the specific intent to assist in practice which he knows to be unauthorized. Despite the respondent's arguments, we conclude that the total effect of his conduct was to assist Porter in the unauthorized practice of law.

The hearing committee determined that the respondent merely failed adequately to supervise a nonlawyer assistant under Mass. R. Prof. C. 5.3(b), which states that "a lawyer having direct supervisory authority over the nonlawyer shall make reasonable efforts to ensure that the person's conduct is compatible with the professional obligations of the lawyer." In support of this theory, the respondent relies on Matter of Holzberg, 15 Mass. Att'y Discipline Rep. 264, 266 (1999) (Holzberg), wherein an attorney was held to have failed to supervise his support staff, but not to have assisted in the unauthorized practice of law, when he allowed a paralegal to handle a client's tort claim. Holzberg can be distinguished in that it only involved a single instance of misconduct, and the paralegal was not responsible for an unsupervised ongoing practice. Id. Moreover, the attorney in Holzberg did not allow the paralegal to file actions in court under his name. Id. The facts here go far beyond those presented in Holzberg, and support the board's finding that the respondent not only failed to supervise Porter adequately but also assisted Porter in the unauthorized practice of law.

Lawyers who employ nonattorneys are required to supervise the delegated work and retain responsibility for the nonattorney's work. The Massachusetts Rules of Professional Conduct indicate that failure to do so could result in a charge of assistance in the unauthorized practice of law. See comment 1 to Mass. R. Prof. C. 5.5. See also Restatement (Third) of the Law Governing Lawyers § 4 comment g (2000) ("[L]awyers and law firms are empowered to retain nonlawyer personnel to assist firm lawyers in providing legal services to clients. In the course of that work, a nonlawyer may conduct activities that, if conducted by that person alone in representing a client, would constitute unauthorized practice. Those activities are permissible and do not constitute unauthorized practice, so long as the responsible lawyer or law firm provides appropriate supervision… and so long as the nonlawyer is not permitted to… split fees…"). In Matter of DiCicco, 6 Mass. Att'y Discipline Rep. 83, 89-91 (1989), the single justice held that, where an attorney formed a business with a paralegal to represent prison inmates experiencing administrative problems and listed the paralegal on letterhead as "Of Counsel," and then failed to supervise the paralegal's activities, the attorney assisted in the unauthorized practice of law. Similarly, in Matter of Jackman,

20 Mass. Att'y Discipline Rep. 263, 267-268 (2004) (Jackman), the respondent was held to have provided the "necessary 'assistance'" to a nonmember of the bar to conduct the unauthorized practice of law when he agreed to allow the nonlawyer to manage the day-to-day operations of an office in which nonlawyers handled and settled personal injury cases, arranged to split legal fees from the business with the nonlawyer, and then failed to provide adequate supervision or oversight. The differences between Jackman and this case are minor: in Jackman, the nonlawyers operated from a separate office; here, Porter ran a separate practice within the respondent's office. In addition, the respondent allowed Porter to run his own unsupervised discrimination law practice from the respondent's law office, understanding that people would "assume that Porter was employed by [the firm] as a paralegal, despite the reality that Porter was carrying on his own practice." The total effect of the respondent's conduct was to facilitate Porter's unauthorized practice of law by creating an environment in which it could exist. Here, the respondent allowed it to flourish.

The respondent's efforts to curb Porter's conduct, by holding Porter out as a paralegal, instructing Porter on fee agreements, requiring Porter to turn over all fee payments to the firm, and minimally reprimanding Porter when he was informed of Porter's missteps, are not sufficient to avoid a charge of assistance in the unauthorized practice of law. See, e.g., Matter of Jackman, supra at 268 (finding it immaterial that nonattorneys did not hold themselves out as members of bar).

The respondent's final argument is that, because he had no specific intent to assist Porter in the unauthorized practice of law, the decision by the board cannot stand. The hearing committee found that the respondent had a good faith belief that Porter was permitted to practice before the MCAD, [5] based on an unidentified regulation that he believed permitted such practice; therefore, the respondent argues that he had no specific intent to assist Porter in the unauthorized practice of law. The board rejected this argument, noting that nothing in Mass. R. Prof. C. 5.5 suggests a requirement of specific intent, in contrast with other rules that explicitly require that a lawyer "knowingly" engage in prohibited conduct before receiving disciplinary sanctions. [6] It is clear that the respondent was aware of the nature and the extent of Porter's unsupervised discrimination practice, which was unauthorized. Our caselaw has not addressed specifically the issue of the necessary intent, and we need not address it in this case. However, no cases support the addition of a requirement that the attorney know that the practice is unauthorized. See Matter of Jackman, supra at 264 (merely stating that Jackman "knew that [the nonlawyer] was handling personal injury claims and managing the office without adequate supervision"). See also Matter of Luongo, 416 Mass. 308, 311, 621 N.E.2d 681 (1993) (not requiring knowledge element on charge of assisting in unauthorized practice, but using Luongo's "knowing participation" as matter in aggravation on issue of appropriate sanction).

FN5. However, the respondent also testified that he understood Porter could only represent clients at the MCAD pursuant to an attorney's appearance and allowed Porter to sign the respondent's name on all appearances. Furthermore, even after the MCAD sent a letter stating that Porter's appearances before the MCAD were not allowed, he did not fire Porter or arrange for attorney supervision of Porter's discrimination practice.

FN6. See, e.g., S.J.C. Rule 1.8(a), 426 Mass. 1338 (1998) (lawyer shall not knowingly acquire pecuniary interests adverse to client); S.J.C. Rule 3.3, 426 Mass. 1383 (1998) (lawyer shall not knowingly engage in conduct that violates requirement of candor before a tribunal); S.J.C. Rule 3.4 (c), 426 Mass. 1389 (1998) (lawyer shall not knowingly disobey obligation under rules of tribunal).

Similar to Jackman, the respondent was aware of the extent of Porter's practice before the MCAD, was aware that Porter's practice was unsupervised, did not arrange for his actions to be supervised, and was aware that Porter was not an attorney. At best, the respondent's defense is that, because he was not aware that Porter's activities, as permitted and arranged by the respondent, amounted to the unauthorized practice of law, he cannot be held liable for assisting in that practice. This is not a sufficient defense. See Matter of the Discipline of an Attorney, 392 Mass. 827, 835, 468 N.E.2d 256 (1984) ("There have been, and will be, few cases of unethical conduct where we consider it relevant that an offending attorney was not aware of the disciplinary rules or their true import").

Here, the respondent's conduct in knowingly facilitating Porter's unsupervised discrimination practice clearly falls within the ambit of assistance in the unauthorized practice of law, and this holding upholds the purpose of the rule forbidding an attorney from assisting in the unauthorized practice of law -- that is, the protection of the public from the rendition of legal services by unqualified persons. Comment 1 to Mass. R. Prof. C. 5.5.

5. Sanctions. The board recommended a term suspension of one year and one day. In reviewing the board's recommended sanction, we consider whether the recommended sanction "is markedly disparate from judgments in comparable cases." Matter of Finn, 433 Mass. 418, 423, 742 N.E.2d 1075 (2001). See Matter of Kerlinsky, 428 Mass. 656, 664, 704 N.E.2d 503, cert. denied, 526 U.S. 1160, 119 S. Ct. 2052, 144 L. Ed. 2d 218 (1999). Regardless, "[e]ach case must be decided on its own merits and every offending attorney must receive the disposition most appropriate in the circumstances." Matter of the Discipline of an Attorney, supra at 837. The consideration of the cumulative effects of several ethical violations is proper when determining the appropriate sanction. Matter of Saab, 406 Mass. 315, 326-327, 547 N.E.2d 919 (1989).

The respondent argues that the appropriate sanction for his disciplinary violations is a three-month suspension. He claims that because he merely failed to supervise Porter adequately, instructed him on the appropriate use of fee agreements and the handling of client funds, took steps to determine whether Porter's practice at the MCAD was allowed, and made efforts to identify Porter as a paralegal, the sanction recommended by the board would be disproportionate to other similar cases. Conversely, bar counsel argues that the board's recommended sanction of one year and one day is the minimum required to address the respondent's misconduct.

We agree with the board's recommended sanction of one year and one day, as it is not disparate from sanctions imposed in similar cases. The board, in affirming the subsidiary findings of the hearing committee and adding conclusions that the respondent assisted in the unauthorized practice of law, formed a business entity with Porter, and made false, deceptive, or misleading communications, determined that the respondent violated several of the rules of professional conduct in connection with collaboration with Porter; and further violated other rules of professional conduct on unrelated charges involving the respondent's trust account records, financial assistance to clients, and business transactions with clients. These conclusions are well supported by the record.

The sanction for similar cumulative misconduct in previous cases has varied, depending on the severity of the misconduct. In Matter of Jackman, 444 Mass. 1013, 1014, 830 N.E.2d 1083 (2004), this court stated that "with respect to the misconduct involving fee splitting, inadequate supervision of nonlawyers, and assisting in the unauthorized practice of law, a term suspension is warranted." See Matter of Luongo, 416 Mass. 308, 311, 621 N.E.2d 681 (1993) ("standing alone, the attorney's knowing participation in the practice of law with [a nonlawyer] warrants at least a suspension from the practice of law, where the attorney obtained financial gain from the association and clients were defrauded"). Jackman was suspended for two years for his improper association with nonlawyers and negligent misuse of client funds, each of which caused harm to clients and warranted a term suspension. Matter of Jackman, supra at 1014-1015. As noted by both the respondent and bar counsel, the misuse of client funds as a result of Jackman's inaction is a significant difference between Jackman and the respondent's case. See Matter of Wysocki, 16 Mass. Att'y Discipline Rep. 437 (2000) (two-year suspension for assisting disbarred lawyer's practice [without fee split or financial benefit], taking cases from disbarred lawyer without consent, neglect, commingling, and record-keeping violations); Matter of DiCicco, 6 Mass. Att'y Discipline Rep. 83, 89 (1989) (two-year suspension for assisting in unauthorized practice of law by paralegal, including representing that paralegal was "of counsel," neglect of cases, and other misconduct). Conversely, the

respondent's infractions were less egregious, particularly in light of his belief, albeit misguided, that all of Porter's actions were sanctioned by the MCAD. Accordingly, we conclude that a suspension of less than two years is appropriate, as the cases imposing a two-year suspension involve conduct more severe than the respondent's actions in this case.

The respondent relies on cases where the sanction for similar misconduct was less than one year. In Matter of Dash, 22 Mass. Att'y Discipline Rep. 179 (2006), the attorney was suspended for six months and one day for setting up a tort practice with a paralegal, letting the paralegal manage and settle cases, letting the paralegal control his IOLTA account, and failing to supervise the paralegal. In contrast to the respondent's case, the misconduct at issue in Dash did not result in any loss or injury to the rights or interests of any client, the arrangement with the paralegal only lasted for a matter of months, and there were no additional instances of misconduct separate from Dash's arrangement with the paralegal. Id. at 179-180. In Matter of Holzberg, 15 Mass. Att'y Discipline Rep. 264, 265-267 (1999), an attorney received a public reprimand for allowing a paralegal to manage one client's case with very little supervision, and the paralegal mishandled the client's money. The client was not prejudiced by the paralegal's actions. Id. at 266. In contrast, the respondent here engaged in misconduct that spanned three years, involved at least forty clients, and resulted in prejudice to the claims of numerous clients. See Admonition No. 00-23, 16 Mass. Att'y Discipline Rep. 482, 483 (2000) (attorney assisted in unauthorized practice of law; however, no clients interests were harmed, fees were not shared with paralegal, and representation by paralegal was limited to Social Security claims). Each case relied on by the respondent is distinguishable from the respondent's case and supports the conclusion that the respondent's conduct in connection with Porter, which resulted in injury and prejudice to multiple clients, in addition to his recordkeeping and other violations, warrants the suspension of the respondent for the recommended sanction of one year and one day.

6. Disposition. A judgment shall enter suspending the respondent from the practice of law in the Commonwealth for one year and one day.

So ordered.

Case Review Exercises

1. Did you feel that the respondent had a valid argument to support his position that the sanction should be failure to supervise instead of assisting with the unauthorized practice of law? Explain.
2. Do you feel that a business relationship was formed between a lawyer and nonlawyer in this case? Explain.
3. Describe the nonlawyer's conduct that constituted unauthorized practice of law. Do you agree? Explain.
4. Was there an ethical arrangement that could have existed between the attorney and the nonlawyer?

Case Review

In re Guirard, 11 So.3d 1017 (La. 05/05/09),

(Cite as 11 So.3d 1017)

Supreme Court of Louisiana.

In re E. Eric Guirard and Thomas R. Pittenger.

ATTORNEY DISCIPLINARY PROCEEDINGS

PER CURIAM * Retired Judge Philip C. Ciaccio, assigned as Justice ad hoc, sitting for Associate Justice Chet D. Traylor, recused.

This disciplinary matter arises from formal charges filed by the Office of Disciplinary Counsel ("ODC") against respondents, E. Eric Guirard and Thomas R. Pittenger, attorneys licensed to practice law in Louisiana.

UNDERLYING FACTS

Respondents are partners in a law practice operating under the name of E. Eric Guirard and Associates, P.L.C. (the "law firm" or the "firm"). The law firm, which has offices in Baton Rouge and New Orleans, has operated since July 1994 and handles primarily plaintiff's personal injury cases. [FN1] In 2000, the ODC began investigating respondents' employment of five "case managers." all nonlawyers, who assisted in the processing of the personal injury claims being handled by the firm prior to litigation. One of the primary issues under investigation concerned the compensation of the case managers. These employees were paid their compensation by regular bi-monthly payroll from the firm's general operating account as a commission computed as a percentage of the firm's gross legal fees collected on the individual settled cases that the individual case manager worked on and settled during [Pg 2] the payroll period. [FN2] In 2000, the following nonlawyer personnel were paid their compensation as commissions on the firm's gross legal fees collected on the settled cases, in the following percentages and amounts, on the following number of settlements made:

FN1. The law firm was originally located in Baton Rouge; the New Orleans office was added in June 1999. At that time, the only employee resident in New Orleans was a case manager, Verna Schwartz, although respondents made an effort to go to the office at least one day a week. In the summer of 2000, respondents hired an attorney to work full-time in the New Orleans office.

FN2. Most of the case managers were paid their compensation on a straight commission basis, but at least one case manager was paid on a salary/draw plus commission basis.

Case manager Michelle Clouatre was paid her compensation as commissions on the firm's gross legal fees at a basic rate of 17% on cases to which she was assigned; 8.5% on cases which were transferred to her from another case manager and subsequently settled; and 5% (unless otherwise noted on the payroll records) on some of the cases to which she was assigned which were ultimately transferred to a litigation attorney and then settled. She was paid approximately $ 81,492.58 as her compensation in commissions for her work on approximately 261 settled cases.

Case manager Lisa Kaplan was paid her compensation as commissions on the firm's gross legal fees at a basic rate of 15% on cases to which she was assigned; 7.5% on cases which were transferred to her from another case manager and subsequently settled; and 5% (unless otherwise noted on the payroll records) on some of the cases to which she was assigned which were ultimately transferred to a litigation attorney and then settled. She was paid approximately $ 68,303.66 as her compensation in commissions for her work on approximately 231 settled cases.

Case manager Trina McAlister was paid her compensation as commissions on the firm's gross legal fees at a basic rate of 15% on cases to which she was assigned; 7.5% on cases which were transferred to her from another case manager and subsequently settled; and 5% (unless otherwise noted on the payroll records) on some of the cases to which she was assigned which were ultimately transferred to a litigation attorney and then settled. She was paid approximately $ 57,060.28 as her compensation in commissions for her work on approximately 258 settled cases.

Case manager Robin Tucker-Holland was paid her compensation as commissions on the firm's gross legal fees at a basic rate of 15% on cases to which she was assigned; 7.5% on cases which were transferred to her from another case manager and subsequently settled; and 5% (unless otherwise noted on the payroll records) on some of the cases to which she was assigned which were ultimately transferred to a litigation attorney and then settled. She was paid approximately $ 39,908.17 as her compensation in commissions for her work on approximately 179 settled cases.

Case manager Verna Schwartz was paid a base salary of $ 1,384.62 per pay period. On May 17, 2000, she was paid her base salary plus a 5% commission on the firm's gross legal fees on a case that she managed which was settled. On or about May 18, 2000, a $ 10,000 quota was instituted for Ms. Schwartz, with an 8% commission being paid only after the quota amount of legal fees had been collected on the settled cases that she managed. She was paid approximately $ 27,211.31, of which about $ 3,673.39 represented commissions for her work on approximately 34 settled cases.

Additionally, in the year 2000, and no later than January 31, 2001, the firm's officer manager, Kim Gautreaux, was paid as her compensation a 1% commission of the firm's total gross legal fees collected on all settled cases, in addition to her salary. She was paid $ 63,679.23 as compensation in the year 2000, of which about $ 28,169.84 represented commissions on approximately 1,100 settled cases.

Benita Zombo was employed by the firm as a legal assistant to attorney Joseph Durio. During the year 2000, but not later than January 31, 2001, Ms. Zombo was paid her compensation as a salary of $ 840 per pay period, plus either a 6% or a 6.5% commission on the firm's gross legal fees on the cases assigned to Mr. Durio. Ms. Zombo was paid $ 49,470.80 as compensation in the year 2000, including about $ 28,169.79 in commissions on the firm's gross legal fees on Mr. Durio's cases, which included approximately 137 settled cases.

During the course of the ODC's investigation, respondents were advised that the compensation plan as described above appeared to violate the Rules of Professional Conduct. Respondents thereupon ceased this compensation plan as of January 2001.

The ODC also investigated the activities of the case managers and the law firm's investigators with regard to the unauthorized practice of law. Specifically, the ODC sought to determine whether these nonlawyer employees were properly supervised by respondents or whether the nonlawyers were actually performing the duties of an attorney in violation of the Rules of Professional Conduct.

At respondents' firm, the receptionist typically transferred telephone calls from new prospective clients to the case manager on duty to receive such calls. If the phone call came in after business hours, an answering service paged the duty case manager. The duty case manager spoke to the new prospective client, and decided if the case was one that the firm would be interested in handling. The duty case manager gathered certain information and gave it to one of the law firm's investigators, who in turn met with the prospective client at his or her home and had the prospective client sign an attorney-client contingency fee contract. The investigator also obtained other signed forms from the client, including releases for medical records and employment and wage information, and took photographs, if needed. The investigator returned the signed contract and other information to the law firm's office, and was thereupon paid $ 50 for the visit. [FN3] The investigator also received additional compensation if he obtained signed contracts for additional clients while visiting the initial client. [FN4]

FN3. The investigator was paid a lesser sum of $ 25 if he returned to the office without a signed contract.

FN4. The investigator was paid $ 15 if he obtained a contingency fee contract signed by a member of the original prospective client's household, and $ 50 if he signed up a claimant involved in the same accident but who resided outside of the original client's household.

After the signed contract and other information was returned to the law firm, the material was reviewed by either Mr. Guirard or Mr. Pittenger. In most cases the file was then assigned to a case manager, who processed the file pursuant to instructions contained in the law firm's Case Manager Manual. [FN5] After the client completed medical treatment, the case manager prepared an evaluation of the case on a form used by the firm. The completed form and the case file were forwarded to either Mr. Guirard or Mr. Pittenger, who would approve a high dollar value and a low dollar value on the case for purposes of making a settlement demand. [FN6] The file was then returned to the case manager, who would send a demand letter signed by a lawyer. The case manager was responsible for contacting the insurance adjuster and negotiating a settlement. When a settlement was reached, the case manager notified the client, arranged for the client to come to the office to pick up the settlement check, and prepared the settlement disbursement statement. Mr. Guirard typically met with the client to disburse the settlement funds.

FN5. As stated in the manual, the firm had "developed a process to handle any size personal injury case in a systematic manner. The name for it is 'The Case Manager System.' The Case Manager System relies heavily on the use of a well trained staff to manage the majority of the tasks associated with a personal injury case."

FN6. The Case Manager Manual stated that the evaluation form would provide a "bottom line settlement" amount set by either Mr. Guirard or Mr. Pittenger, and "the Case Manager does not have authority to settle the case for less than this amount."

During the course of the ODC's investigation, respondents were advised that the case manager system appeared to violate the Rules of Professional Conduct. [FN7] In 2001, each lawyer in respondents' firm was assigned to supervise one case manager (in contrast to the case manager system in which respondents, as well as four to five additional lawyers, together supervised the case managers). Sometime in early 2004, a single lawyer assumed primary responsibility for supervising all of the case managers. The case manager system was completely abolished in November 2004.

FN7. Respondents hired the first case manager in 1997. From 1994, when the firm opened its doors, until 1997, the firm did not utilize the case manager system.

DISCIPLINARY PROCEEDINGS

In February 2004, the ODC filed two counts of formal charges against respondents jointly. In Count I, the ODC alleged that respondents paid their case managers percentage commissions on gross legal fees, and thereby improperly shared legal fees with nonlawyers, in violation of Rules 5.4(a) and 8.4(a) of the Rules of Professional Conduct. The ODC further alleged that this impermissible fee sharing arrangement created a conflict between the interests of the law firm, particularly the case managers, and the clients whose cases were being handled by the case managers, in violation of Rule 1.7(b). In Count II, the ODC alleged that respondents have employed a "business first" model in operating their law firm, [FN8] resulting in a situation in which their nonlawyer employees have engaged in the unauthorized practice of law, either by design, or by respondents' failure to supervise, or by some combination of the two. Accordingly, the ODC alleged that respondents' conduct violated Rules 5.3(a) (responsibilities regarding nonlawyer assistants), 5.5(a) (engaging in the unauthorized practice of law), 5.5(b) (assisting a person who is not a member of the bar in the performance of activity that constitutes the unauthorized practice of law), 8.4(a) (violation of the Rules of Professional Conduct), 8.4(b) (commission of a criminal act, especially one that reflects adversely on the lawyer's honesty, trustworthiness, or fitness as a lawyer in other respects), [FN9] 8.4(c) (engaging in conduct involving dishonesty, fraud, deceit, or misrepresentation), and 8.4(d) (engaging in conduct prejudicial to the administration of justice) of the Rules of Professional Conduct. The ODC further alleged that the actions of the law firm's nonlawyer employees operating in the "business first" format established by respondents have, particularly when combined with the fee sharing arrangement in Count I, resulted in and/or created a conflict between the interests of the law firm and the clients whose cases were being handled by the law firm, in violation of Rule 1.7(b).

FN8. The record reflects that in November 2003, Mr. Guirard was quoted by the Baton Rouge newspaper as stating, "We always have approached this as a business first and a law firm second."

FN9. La. R.S. 37:213 makes it a crime to engage in the unauthorized practice of law.

Respondents, through separate counsel, answered the formal charges and denied any misconduct.

Prior to the hearing in this matter, the parties entered into a joint stipulation of facts setting forth the case managers' compensation plan, as discussed in detail above. The parties also stipulated that in 2000, "there is no evidence that any case manager or other non-lawyer personnel ever appeared as counsel in court or at a deposition."

Formal Hearing

The formal hearing of this matter commenced on September 23 and 24, 2004. The ODC presented evidence in support of the formal charges and rested. The hearing was then continued indefinitely while the parties discussed the possibility of resolving the formal charges by consent discipline. However, the parties ultimately decided for various reasons not to pursue consent discipline. Accordingly, the [Pg 8] hearing committee reconvened on May 9, 2007. At this hearing, respondents presented evidence on their own behalf.

Hearing Committee Report [FN10]

FN10. In the section of its report captioned "Introduction," the hearing committee stated that "the Louisiana Supreme Court ultimately rejected the agreed upon consent discipline and remanded the matter for further proceedings," This statement is in error, as no petition for consent discipline was ever filed with this court. The hearing committee's misstatement was corrected by the disciplinary board in its recommendation to this court.

After considering the evidence and testimony presented at the 2004 and 2007 hearings, the hearing committee made the following factual findings:

In Count I, the committee adopted the joint stipulation of facts. As stipulated, a commission was paid to nonlawyer employees that was computed as a percentage of the firm's gross legal fees collected on specific individual settled cases. The testimony of respondents also makes it clear that, for the most part, if the case managers did not settle cases within a particular amount of time, the cases would be transferred to litigation, and the case managers would receive zero compensation for the work they had put into the case, unless a special bonus was assigned. The committee noted that the case managers were compensated on a percentage of the gross fees for each individual file; they were not compensated on a percentage of net profits of the firm.

Based on these factual findings, the committee found that respondents violated Rules 1.7(b), 5.4(a), and 8.4(a) of the Rules of Professional Conduct. The committee specifically rejected respondents' assertion that the percentage compensation paid to the case managers is a form of profit sharing and therefore ethically permissible, [FN11] agreeing with the ODC that under In re Watley, 01-1775 (La. 12/7/01), 802 So.2d 593 [Pg 9], [FN12] the splitting of legal fees with a nonlawyer on the gross fee received from a particular file constitutes a violation of Rule 5.4(a). The committee commented that this is not a situation in which the case managers are paid a percentage of net profits at the end of the year on the general business of the law firm; rather, "each nonlawyer receives a piece of the action if the case is [settled] by them. This is fee splitting and always has been." Moreover, the committee found the arrangement creates a clear conflict of interest between the law firm (particularly the case managers) and the clients. The nonlawyer case manager is being paid on a successful settlement of a claim; if the file is turned over to litigation, the case manager receives nothing, or, at most, a discretionary percentage. Under these circumstances, the committee found the case manager has an "overwhelming motive to settle a claim at any price" before losing control over the file.

FN11. Rule 5.4(a)(3) of the Rules of Professional Conduct is an exception to the general rule that a lawyer shall not share legal fees with a nonlawyer. It provides that nonlawyer employees may be included "in a compensation or retirement plan, even though the plan is based in whole or in part on a profit-sharing practice of law."

FN12. In Watley, the court found the respondents guilty of violating Rule 5.4(a) by entering into a fee sharing contract with a non-attorney. Specifically, the parties created an arrangement whereby the respondents' law firm agreed to pay a paralegal service 40% of the attorney's fees earned on personal injury cases and 60% of the fees earned on cases referred by the paralegal service. The court found the agreement to constitute intentional fee sharing, illustrated by the fact that the firm attempted to hide the arrangement through misleading invoices. Although the court found no indication of direct harm to a client, it cautioned that the arrangement had the potential to cause harm "because once non-lawyers were given a financial interest in respondents' legal fees, there was a possibility they could interfere with respondents' independent judgment in the case." The court concluded this potential harm to clients and to the legal profession warranted discipline in the form of a one year and one day suspension from the practice of law.

In Count II, the committee found that during the year 2000, the case managers negotiated directly with insurance adjusters, reached settlement agreements during telephone conversations when negotiations took place, and dealt directly with clients concerning settlement offers. The committee also found that an attorney in the firm established parameters of a high and a low within which to settle a case, and that the case managers were then allowed to negotiate a settlement between these two figures, independently of any supervision by an attorney.

Based on these factual findings, the committee found that respondents violated Rules 1.7(b), 5.3(a), 5.5(a) and (b), 8.4(a), 8.4(b), 8.4(c), and 8.4(d). Nonlawyers would initiate the attorney-client relationship and the case managers would advise clients whether they had a viable claim. They also advised prospective clients regarding the execution of legal documents, the attorney-client contract, medical releases, and other documents. In addition, the case managers were given leeway in settling individual cases using their own judgment without supervision from an attorney. The committee acknowledged that an attorney established the highs and lows for settlement purposes, but concluded it was the case manager who utilized the professional judgment in settlement. [FN13] The case managers also had great leeway in managing the file, including obtaining settlement authority from the client, determining liability, determining probable insurance coverage, and determining an applicable prescription date.

FN13. Respondents testified that when they established the parameters of the settlement, then they have in effect approved whatever settlement occurs. As the committee observed, "The problem with this is that the attorney is not involved in the negotiating process but leaves that to the case manager once the parameters have been established."

Respondents argued that in Louisiana State Bar Ass'n v. Edwins, 540 So. 2d 294 (La. 1989), [FN14] this court placed only three qualifications on the employment of lay personnel, stating that it was a violation for a nonlawyer to engage directly in the practice of law, to appear in court, or exercise a lawyer's professional judgment. The committee found, however, that even if the case managers employed by respondents did not hold themselves out as attorneys, they were nonetheless exercising the "professional judgment" of a lawyer:

FN14. In Edwins, Rallie Edwins, a Baton Rouge attorney, entered into an arrangement with a paralegal, Rob Robertson, to use Mr. Robertson's paralegal office in New Iberia as Mr. Edwin's branch law office. Mr. Robertson met with a personal injury client and led the client to believe he was an attorney. Mr. Robertson entered into an attorney-client contract with the attorney, but later advised the client that he

would be represented by Mr. Edwins. Subsequently, Mr. Edwins was hospitalized, and authorized Mr. Robertson to sign his name to various pleadings. Mr. Edwins admitted that he never saw the client's file. The personal injury case was later settled for $ 9,000; of this amount, Mr. Edwins turned over $ 8,000 to Mr. Robertson.

This court, in an opinion by Justice Dennis, held that for purposes of considering whether an attorney has aided a paralegal or other nonlawyer assistant in the unauthorized practice of law, a lawyer may delegate various tasks to paralegals, clerks, secretaries and other non-lawyers; that he or she may not, however, delegate to any such person the lawyer's role of appearing in court in behalf of a client or of giving legal advice to a client; that he or she must supervise closely any such person to whom he or she delegates other tasks, including the preparation of a draft of a legal document or the conduct of legal research; and that the lawyer must not under any circumstance delegate to such person the exercise of the lawyer's professional judgment in behalf of the client or even allow it to be influenced by the non-lawyer's assistance.

Applying these principles, the court found that Mr. Edwins assisted Mr. Robertson in the unauthorized practice of law:

The respondent attorney in the present case, in our opinion, knowingly assisted the non-lawyer, Robertson, to engage in the unauthorized practice of law. Even if Edwins was unaware that Robertson had held himself out as an attorney, we are convinced that he knowingly allowed Robertson to perform the functions of a lawyer in advising prospective clients as to their claims, entering employment contracts with them, preparing and filing lawsuits, motions and briefs for them, counseling them on the advisability of the settlement of their cases, and receiving, distributing and accounting for their settlement funds. Moreover, in all of these respects Edwins delegated the exercise of his professional judgment to Robertson, adopting the non-lawyer's decisions as his own with little or no supervision by the attorney.

We are convinced further that Edwins assisted Robertson in the unauthorized practice of law with the intent to obtain a benefit for himself and the non-lawyer. Edwins allowed Robertson to hold his paralegal office out to the public as the attorney's branch law office and paid part of the expenses of its operation. Edwins clearly intended to profit and did profit from the attorney fees that were generated by the unauthorized services performed by Robertson. Likewise, the arrangement intentionally benefitted Robertson by enabling Edwins to compensate Robertson for his work in connection with cases that Edwins may not have been able to handle without the unauthorized legal assistance of Robertson.

The court concluded that "disbarment is the prima facie appropriate sanction for the respondent's aiding unauthorized practice violation, . . ." In light of the numerous aggravating factors present, and considering the absence of mitigating factors, the court disbarred Mr. Edwins.

... [T]he leeway given the case managers, their flexibility in settling cases with the client, and their interaction with the client, even if they did not hold themselves out as attorneys, is, at the very least, the exercising of professional judgment. If this is not, then Respondents have gone right up to the edge. However, the Committee thinks that the case managers did exercise professional judgment in the administration of these files in violation of the Rules of Professional Conduct.

The committee determined that respondents violated duties owed to their clients, the public, and the legal profession. The committee found respondents acted intentionally but they "were of the sincere belief that they were following professional guidelines and were not in violation of the Rules of Professional Conduct. In this regard, their actions were more negligent than they were intentional." The committee found no evidence of any harm to respondents' clients (but noted that "it would be almost impossible to determine that at this stage in the proceedings"), and concluded that the applicable baseline sanction in this matter is suspension.

In aggravation, the committee found a pattern of misconduct, multiple offenses, and substantial experience in the practice of law. The mitigating factors found by the committee are the following: absence of a prior disciplinary record, absence of a dishonest or selfish motive, timely good faith effort to rectify the consequences of the misconduct, full and free disclosure to the disciplinary board and a cooperative attitude toward the proceedings, and good character and reputation.

The committee concluded:

The Committee is of the belief that a suspension of one year and a day is appropriate. This is based upon clear factual evidence that the Respondents, during the year 2000, engaged in fee splitting with nonlawyers distributing a portion of attorney fees to the case managers as compensation. In addition, the Committee is also of the belief that the evidence indicates that the case managers participated in the unauthorized practice of law in the handling of each individual file and in particular the negotiation of a settlement without the proper supervision of a supervising attorney.

Based on this reasoning, the committee recommended that respondents be suspended from the practice of law for one year and one day.

Both the ODC and respondents filed objections to the hearing committee's report and recommendation. The ODC objected to the leniency of the sanction recommended by the committee and asserted that disbarment is appropriate. Respondents took issue with the committee's finding that they violated the Rules of Professional Conduct. Alternatively, respondents argued that even assuming the rule violations alleged in the formal charges were proven by clear and convincing evidence, the sanction recommended by the committee is too harsh in light of the significant mitigating factors present. Notwithstanding these arguments, however, respondents subsequently filed a brief with the disciplinary board in which they admitted their misconduct as charged in the formal charges and "ask[ed] for appropriate measure of discipline," which they suggested was either

a public reprimand, or, at most, a fully deferred suspension with supervised probation.

Following the filing of the hearing committee's report, and prior to the submission of the matter for oral argument before a panel of the disciplinary board, respondents and the ODC filed a pleading captioned "Joint Supplementation of the Hearing Committee Record." In this pleading, the parties stipulated to the steps taken by respondents to conform their firm's practices and procedures to the Rules of Professional Conduct. The changes implemented in good faith by respondents included, among others, the payment of fixed salaries to the firm's nonlawyer staff as of January 2002.

Disciplinary Board Recommendation

After review, the disciplinary board determined that the hearing committee's factual findings are not manifestly erroneous. The board noted that respondents have now admitted their misconduct as charged in the formal charges, but that for clarity's sake it would nevertheless make specific determinations concerning the alleged violations of the Rules of Professional Conduct:

Rule 1.7 is the general rule dealing with conflicts of interest. The applicable version of this rule provides in subsection (b) that a lawyer shall not represent a client if the representation of that client may be materially limited by the lawyer's responsibilities to another client or to a third person, or by the lawyer's own interests, unless the lawyer reasonably believes the representation will not be adversely affected and the client consents after consultation. The board found that the system in place at respondents' law firm in which the case managers were permitted, within a specified time period, to settle cases within "high" and "low" limits created a conflict of interest between the clients and the law firm, particularly the case managers of the firm, because the case managers were being paid based upon a successful settlement of the claim within a certain time frame. If the file was turned over to the litigation section of the firm, the claims manager received nothing, or, at most, a discretionary percentage. As noted by the hearing committee, this created an overwhelming motive to settle a claim at any price before the case manager lost control over the file. The board agreed that this situation created a conflict pursuant to Rule 1.7(b).

Rule 5.3(a) provides that with respect to a nonlawyer employed or retained by or associated with a lawyer, a partner in a law firm shall make reasonable efforts to ensure that the firm has in effect measures giving reasonable assurance that the person's conduct is compatible with the professional obligations of the lawyer. Here, respondents allowed the case managers to improperly settle cases, which was not compatible with respondents' professional obligations pursuant to Rules 5.5(b) (a lawyer shall not assist a person who is not a member of the bar in the performance of activity that constitutes the unauthorized practice of law) and 1.7(b). The board agreed that respondents violated Rule 5.3(a).

Rule 5.4(a) provides, in part, that a lawyer or law firm shall not share legal fees with a nonlawyer, except that a lawyer or law firm may include nonlawyer employees in a compensation or retirement plan, even though the plan is based in whole or part on a profit-sharing practice of law. The board found this rule was violated because the case managers were paid by a commission method of compensation based upon the gross attorney's fees of a particular file and not the firm's net profits. The record also indicates that the firm's office manager and at least one secretary of the firm were paid commissions on the firm's gross legal fees collected on various cases.

Rule 5.5 provides that a lawyer shall not (a) practice law in a jurisdiction where doing so violates the regulation of the legal profession in that jurisdiction; or (b) assist a person who is not a member of the bar in the performance of activity that constitutes the unauthorized practice of law. Respondents violated both subsections because they allowed the case managers to give legal advice to the firm's clients concerning the settlement of their cases, and allowed the case managers to negotiate the clients' claims with insurance adjusters, after giving the case managers latitude to determine the correct settlement amount within a high-low range. Moreover, respondents violated these subsections by allowing their investigators to engage in the unauthorized practice of law. These individuals, upon the initial meeting with the prospective clients, advised the clients regarding the execution of legal documents, including a contract of employment, medical releases, an insurance search disclosure form, employment and wage information releases, and conflict of interest releases.

Rule 8.4(a) states, among other things, that it is professional misconduct for a lawyer to violate or attempt to violate the Rules of Professional Conduct. By their conduct in violation of the other rules of Professional Conduct, respondents have violated Rule 8.4(a).

Rule 8.4(b) states that it is professional misconduct for a lawyer to commit a criminal act, especially one that reflects adversely on the lawyer's honesty, trustworthiness or fitness as a lawyer in other respects. Here, the board found that Rule 8.4(b) was violated because respondents assisted their case managers and investigators in the unauthorized practice of law, which is a felony.

Rule 8.4(c) states that it is professional misconduct for a lawyer to engage in conduct involving dishonesty, fraud, deceit, or misrepresentation. The board found respondents violated this rule because the firm's clients were not specifically advised that their cases would be negotiated or settled by case managers. Having the case managers negotiate and settle the cases was a misrepresentation by omission to the clients, particularly considering that clients were given the "E Guarantee," which implied that a lawyer, not a case manager, would handle the case. [FN15]

FN15. The "E Guarantee" promised that "Your case will be assigned to an attorney!"

Rule 8.4(d) provides that it is professional misconduct for a c to engage in conduct that is prejudicial to the administration of justice. The board found Rule 8.4(d) was violated because the case managers and investigators engaged in the unauthorized practice of law.

In addition to these rule violations, the board found there was sufficient evidence presented to find respondents engaged in improper client solicitation, in violation of Rule 7.2, a violation not charged by the ODC in the formal charges.

Rejecting the hearing committee's finding that respondents confected the law firm's procedures and compensation plan in a "negligent" fashion, the board determined that respondents' conduct was intentional. The board found that the law firm's office procedures were carefully crafted and documented in forms and in a Case Manager Manual, and that respondents expected their employees to follow these procedures, notwithstanding any suggestion by Mr. Guirard to the contrary. [FN16] The board determined that although no actual harm was proven as to any specific client, the potential for harm to clients, the public, the legal system, and the profession was immeasurable. By allowing nonlawyers to practice law, respondents ran the risk of having cases settled improperly and proceedings later being declared nullities. By implementing the compensation plan at issue, the potential for conflict between the client's interests and the case managers' interests was also great. [FN17] Further, by improperly paying their case managers and investigators bonuses for "signing up" clients, the reputation of the legal profession and the legal system has undoubtedly been marred. The board found the applicable baseline sanction is disbarment.

FN16. In his testimony, Mr. Guirard attempted to minimize the significance of the Case Manager Manual, claiming that for the most part, his employees put the manual in their desk drawers and forgot about it.

FN17. As further evidence of this conflict, the board observed that respondents ran contests in which the case managers were rewarded with trips to Cancun or the Beau Rivage Resort on the Mississippi Gulf Coast if they reached a certain level of fees generated from the settlement of cases during designated time periods.

In aggravation, the board found a pattern of misconduct, multiple offenses, substantial experience in the practice of law, and illegal conduct. The mitigating factors found by the board are the following: absence of a prior disciplinary record, timely good faith effort to rectify the consequences of the misconduct, full and free disclosure to the disciplinary board and a cooperative attitude toward the proceedings, and good character and reputation. [FN18]

FN18. The board specifically rejected the committee's finding that respondents lacked a dishonest or selfish motive and did not cause harm to their clients.

The board then turned to a discussion of the prior cases involving misconduct similar to respondents'. With respect to respondents' failure to supervise and facilitation of the unauthorized practice of law by their nonlawyer staff, the board cited In re Sledge, 03-1148 (La. 10/21/03), 859 So. 2d 671. In Sledge, the respondent operated a high-volume personal injury practice as a solo practitioner. Mr. Sledge's staff included two nonlawyers, Lil Lalumandier and Wendy LeBleau, who were employed as his office manager/litigation supervisor and his legal assistant, respectively. Non-litigation matters ordinarily went to Ms. LeBleau, who would oversee the clients' medical treatment, verify insurance, correspond with insurance adjusters, and prepare demand letters seeking sums based on guidelines used in all cases. Following her preparation of a demand letter, Ms. LeBleau would direct the matter to Ms. Lalumandier, who would negotiate and settle the matter directly with the insurance adjuster. At no point during this process did Mr. Sledge directly supervise or review the work of his staff; indeed, in most cases, he had not even met the client his firm was representing. In the litigation files, all petitions and other pleadings were drafted by various non-attorney employees using general pleading forms. The staff signed the pleadings and correspondence with Mr. Sledge's signature or used a rubber stamp to do so, even if he was present in the office. In most instances, Mr. Sledge did not review the pleadings or correspondence that left his office; by all accounts, he simply participated in depositions and made court appearances. Mr. Sledge's law office operated in this fashion from 1996 to 1998, during which Mr. Sledge was absent from his office for several months at a time.

This court found that Mr. Sledge had neglected his law practice and failed to exercise any meaningful supervision over his nonlawyer assistants, thereby allowing them to engage in the unauthorized practice of law. The ODC also proved that Mr. Sledge made cash payments to three individuals for client referrals. The court imposed disbarment for this misconduct. In support, the court cited In re: Brown, 01-2863 (La. 3/22/02), 813 So. 2d 325, in which it held that disbarment was the appropriate sanction for an attorney who completely delegated the exercise of his professional judgment to a nonlawyer and exercised no supervision over the nonlawyer. [FN19] The court also reaffirmed its holding in Edwins, supra, that disbarment is the prima facie appropriate sanction for facilitating the unauthorized practice of law by a nonlawyer.

FN19. In Brown, Tyrone Brown worked as an attorney for the East Baton Rouge Parish Public Defender's Office. In the course of his employment, Mr. Brown met Robert Matthews, a convicted felon who was later pardoned, who worked as an investigator for the public defender's office. Although Mr. Matthews was not licensed to practice law, he apparently "represented" various personal injury clients and obtained settlements on their behalf from insurance companies. Mr. Matthews was successful in his activities, and many insurance adjusters mistakenly believed he was an attorney. However, his activities later came under suspicion, and Mr. Matthews became the subject of a fraud investigation by the Louisiana State Police.

In order to continue his activities, Mr. Matthews approached Mr. Brown with a scheme whereby Mr. Matthews would act as Mr. Brown's paralegal. Mr. Brown agreed to the scheme and provided Mr. Matthews with blank, pre-signed letters of representation on Mr. Brown's letterhead stationery, which purported to authorize Mr. Matthews to deal with the insurance companies. Additionally, Mr. Brown provided Mr. Matthews

with pre-signed letterhead stationery which was otherwise blank. Mr. Brown also agreed to pay Mr. Matthews an undetermined fee based on the amount of the fee generated by each case.

The board found respondents' conduct was similar to that seen in Sledge, Brown, and Edwins. Like Mr. Sledge, respondents delegated tasks to nonlawyers which included the negotiating and settling of client matters. Respondents also paid investigators and case managers fees for "signing up" clients. The board acknowledged that respondents likely exercised more supervision over the employees in their Baton Rouge office than Mr. Sledge did over his office; however, that was not the case in respondents' New Orleans office. In New Orleans, respondents had no resident lawyer present from June 1999 until July or August 2000. Rather, only a case manager, Verna Schwartz, was present on a daily basis to handle clients' cases in the manner similar to the procedure used by the case managers in Baton Rouge. [FN20] One of the respondents traveled to work in the New Orleans office only one day a week. Moreover, like the respondents in Brown and Edwins, respondents have aided their nonlawyer employees in the unauthorized practice of law.

FN20. Mr. Guirard testified that there was one extra layer of protection in the New Orleans office. Once Ms. Schwartz effected a settlement within the parameters given to her by respondents, she was required to get the "okay" from respondents concerning the settlement amount before she could relay or finalize the settlement.

As to the Rule 5.4 violation, the board found Watley, supra, instructive. Like the respondents in Watley, respondents in the instant matter have engaged in improper fee splitting with nonlawyers in violation of Rule 5.4. Also similar to the situation in Watley, respondents' compensation arrangement with their case managers and office staff had the potential to harm their clients. Once the nonlawyers were given a financial interest in respondents' legal fees, there was the obvious possibility that the interests of the nonlawyers could interfere with respondents' independent judgment in the case.

The board found the foregoing misconduct warrants serious discipline. Citing Guideline 6 of the permanent disbarment guidelines (insurance fraud, including but not limited to staged accidents or widespread runner-based solicitation), the board recommended that respondents be permanently disbarred.

Respondents filed an objection to the disciplinary board's recommendation. Accordingly, the case was docketed for oral argument pursuant to Supreme Court Rule XIX, § 11(G)(1)(b).

DISCUSSION

Bar disciplinary matters fall within the original jurisdiction of this court; La. Const. art. V, § 5(B). Consequently, we act as triers of fact and conduct an independent review of the record to determine whether the alleged misconduct has been proven by clear and convincing evidence. In re: Quaid, 94-1316 (La. 11/30/94), 646 So. 2d 343; Louisiana

State Bar Ass'n v. Boutall, 597 So. 2d 444 (La. 1992). While we are not bound in any way by the findings and recommendations of the hearing committee and disciplinary board, we have held the manifest error standard is applicable to the committee's factual findings. See In re: Caulfield, 96-1401 (La. 11/25/96), 683 So. 2d 714; In re: Pardue, 93-2865 (La. 3/11/94), 633 So. 2d 150.

Respondents do not contest that they have violated the Rules of Professional Conduct as alleged in the formal charges. Their misconduct involves conflicts of interest, failure to supervise their nonlawyer staff, impermissible fee sharing with nonlawyers, and facilitation of the unauthorized practice of law. Thus, the only issue before us is the appropriate sanction to be imposed.

In considering that issue, we are mindful that disciplinary proceedings are designed to maintain high standards of conduct, protect the public, preserve the integrity of the profession, and deter future misconduct. Louisiana State Bar Ass'n v. Reis, 513 So. 2d 1173 (La. 1987). The discipline to be imposed depends upon the facts of each case and the seriousness of the offenses involved considered in light of any aggravating and mitigating circumstances. Louisiana State Bar Ass'n v. Whittington, 459 So. 2d 520 (La. 1984).

The disciplinary board's recommendation of permanent disbarment has no support in the record, as it is premised entirely on the conclusion that respondents engaged in runner-based solicitation. However, the ODC concedes that it did not allege or prove runner-based solicitation. The record does not corroborate a finding of solicitation. Accordingly, we reject the board's finding and the corresponding recommendation of permanent disbarment.

Our prior decisions in Sledge, Brown, and Edwins establish that the baseline sanction for the facilitation of the unauthorized practice of law by a nonlawyer is disbarment. In cases involving fee sharing with a nonlawyer, we have imposed a suspension of one year and one day. In re: Watley, 01-1775 (La. 12/7/01), 802 So. 2d 593. For respondents' misconduct involving both facilitation of the unauthorized practice of law and fee sharing, the overall baseline sanction is disbarment.

As aggravating factors, we recognize a dishonest or selfish motive, a pattern of misconduct, and substantial experience in the practice of law (Mr. Guirard was admitted in 1987; Mr. Pittenger was admitted in 1992). In mitigation, we find the following factors are supported by the record: absence of a prior disciplinary record, timely good faith effort to rectify the consequences of the misconduct, full and free disclosure to the disciplinary board and a cooperative attitude toward the proceedings, and good character and reputation.

Having considered these factors in light of the record in its entirety, we decline to deviate from the baseline sanction of disbarment. Respondents delegated the handling of their clients' cases to their nonlawyer staff. This was a systematic practice as part of the "business first" model knowingly employed by respondents. By structuring their law firm in the manner in which they did, respondents harmed their clients, who, as we noted in Sledge, "were deprived of the benefit of a thoughtful, individualized and professional legal analysis of their cases." Respondents then motivated the nonlawyers to settle the clients' claims as quickly as possible in order to collect a paycheck. Of course, these egregious practices profited respondents as well.

We conclude we would be remiss in our constitutional duty to regulate the practice of law if we were to impose any sanction in this case less than disbarment. Therefore, respondents are hereby disbarred.

DECREE

Upon review of the findings and recommendations of the hearing committee and the disciplinary board, and considering the record, briefs, and oral argument, it is ordered that E. Eric Guirard, also known as Eric J. Guirard, Louisiana Bar Roll number 18242, be and he hereby is disbarred. His name shall be stricken from the roll of attorneys and his. license to practice law in the State of Louisiana shall be revoked. It is further ordered that Thomas R. Pittenger, Louisiana Bar Roll number 21819, be and he hereby is disbarred. His name shall be stricken from the roll of attorneys and his license to practice law in the State of Louisiana shall be revoked. All costs and expenses in the matter are assessed against respondents in accordance with Supreme Court Rule XIX, § 10.1, with legal interest to commence thirty days from the date of finality of this court's judgment until paid.

Case Review Exercises

1. What were the main factors listed by the court that persuaded them that the services performed by the nonlawyer personnel violated the unauthorized practice of law statutes?

2. What were the formal charges against the attorneys? Evaluate the Hearing Committee basis for the charges/counts determined in the report.

3. The attorneys argued that the percentage compensation was a form of profit sharing and therefore ethically permissible. How did the court handle this argument? Whose argument did you find more persuasive: the court's or the lawyers'? Why?

4. The court concluded that the attorneys delegated the handling of their clients' cases to their nonlawyer staff. Explain/describe the court's view of the egregious practice in place.

5. For each issue raised by the court regarding the unauthorized practice of law by the case managers, what new procedural system would you put in place to avoid violations?

Helpful Web Sites

Organization	Description	Internet Address
American Bar Association (ABA) Center for Professional Responsibility	The Web site has a number of excellent resources regarding ethics, including the full version of the *Model Rules of Professional Conduct*, summaries of ABA ethical opinions, and more.	http://www.americanbar.org
California State Bar	State bar Web site with a number of state and national resources related to ethics.	http://www.calbar.ca.gov (http://ethics.calbar.ca.gov/)
FindLaw—Ethics and Professional Responsibility practice area	The Web site has a number of resources, articles, and links to a variety of ethics issues.	http://www.findlaw.com
LegalEthics.com	An excellent Web site for updated cases and information related to legal ethics.	http://www.legalethics.com
Michigan State Bar	State bar Web site with a number of state and national resources related to ethics.	http://www.michbar.org (http://www.michbar.org/opinions/ethicsopinions)
The Paralegal Association	National association for legal assistants–paralegals. Contains many resources for paralegals/legal assistants, including ethics-related articles and model ethics rules.	http://www.nala.org
National Federation of Paralegal Associations	National association for paralegals. Contains many resources for paralegals/legal assistants, including ethics-related articles and model ethics rules. The Web site also has a page related to ethics.	http://www.paralegals.org

Suggested Reading

1. *The Model Rules of Professional Conduct*, American Bar Association, 2022. https://www.americanbar.org/groups/professional_responsibility/publications/model_rules_of_professional_conduct/model_rules_of_professional_conduct_table_of_contents/.

2. Kaufman, K. (2014). *Legal ethics*, 3rd ed. Clifton Park, NY: Cengage Learning.

3. *Model Code of Ethics and Professional Responsibility*, National Federation of Paralegal Associations. http://www.paralegals.org.

4. *NALA Code of Ethics and Professional Responsibility*, published by the National Association of Legal Assistants–Paralegals. http://www.nala.org.

5. *NALA Model Standards and Guidelines for Utilization of Paralegals*, published by the National Association of Legal Assistants–Paralegals. http://www.nala.org.

6. *The Ethical Wall—Its Application to Paralegals*, The National Federation of Paralegal Associations, 2009. http://www.paralegals.org. Direct link is currently https://www.paralegals.org/files/THE_ETHICAL_WALL.pdf.

4

Client Relations and Communication Skills

After you read this chapter, you should be able to:

- Identify factors that will promote effective client relationships.

- Explain ethical duties owed to clients.

- Explain the importance of good communication skills.

- Identify the pros and cons of using groups to make decisions.

A poorly served client often feels neglected and disrespected. The client expects to receive some evidence of work performed when they have paid the attorney for services. Constant unreturned phone calls by the attorney along with no correspondence or copies of prepared documents is frustrating, not to mention unethical. The client sought a qualified attorney (one authorized to practice—registered with the state bar association) because the law is complicated, and most laypersons lack the ability to adequately represent themselves. That said, the attorney's failure to communicate leaves a client with the worst fear—the attorney is not doing their job. And they are most likely correct. The client's recourse at this point is with the bar association. Poor client communications create poor client relations, which may lead to disciplinary actions against the attorney.

***

On the other hand, a well-served client will generally appreciate the efforts put forth by the attorney, even if the outcome is not in his or her favor. A reasonable client wants to be informed concerning his or her case status and receive a fair and honest projection regarding the outcome of the case. When the attorney along with the members of the legal team stays in contact with the clients, providing them with copies of the relevant documents, billing details for services performed, and prompt communications about hearings, negotiations, and rulings, the client feels respected. In turn, the client will generally respect the hard work performed by the attorney and his or her staff. Good communications make for good client relations.

The Importance of Good Client Relationships and Effective Communication Skills

Fostering positive client relationships and communicating effectively with others is an important aspect of practice management and is an absolute necessity for attorneys and paralegals to be successful. Customer service and satisfaction are very important to the practice of law, especially considering the number of law offices and the fierce competition that exists. Attorneys and paralegals who mishandle client relationships by not putting the client first will cause clients to go elsewhere for legal services. Nearly every task performed requires communication skills such as writing correspondence, drafting briefs, interviewing clients and witnesses, and legal research/writing. The ability to effectively exchange ideas and information with others is an essential part of the legal profession.

This chapter will explore ethical duties to clients and a basic but practical explanation of communication, along with ideas for how communication skills can be improved. This includes related communication topics, such as leadership qualities, the advantages and disadvantages of working with groups, and how to conduct client interviews.

Ethical Duty to Communicate with Clients

Although much of this chapter covers how to provide clients with excellent customer service as it relates to providing quality legal services, there is also a strong ethical duty regarding the need to regularly communicate with clients. Keeping a client informed about his or her case, keeping him or her abreast of changes, developing strategy with him or her, and keeping him or her involved in the progress of a case—including communicating settlement offers—is fundamental to the practice of law. Attorneys and paralegals are bound by this ethical duty. Clients cannot make informed decisions about their cases if they do not know what is happening.

Rule 1.4, regarding the rules of professional conduct, requires an attorney, within reason, to promptly comply with the client's requests for information, to keep the client informed about the status of their legal matter(s), to consult with the client, and to provide the client with an explanation of their matter(s) so that the client can make informed decisions.

Rule 1.4 specifically requires the attorney to act "reasonably" with the client when it comes to explaining general strategies, providing information, and consulting about their legal matters. The "reasonableness" of the situation will depend on the facts and circumstances of the particular case.

The comment to *Rule 1.4* discusses the guiding principle for a lawyer to consider in fulfilling the client's expectation in a reasonable manner that would be consistent with the duty to act in the client's best interests, and the client's overall requirements as to the character of representation.

Clients become extremely frustrated when they pay for legal services and the attorney or paralegal refuses to take their calls, answer their letters, or otherwise communicate with them in any way.

The duty to communicate derives in part from the attorney's fiduciary duty of utmost good faith to the client. Exhibit 4-1 explains the specific duties of an attorney to communicate with clients as decided by case law.

Exhibit 4-1 Duties of an Attorney to Communicate with a Client

Client communication includes a duty of an attorney to:

- Routinely inform a client concerning the status of their case.
- Promptly inform a client about important information.
- Never cover up a matter if the attorney failed to carry out the client's instructions.
- Notify a client if he or she is stopping work on a client's case, leaving a firm, or quitting the practice of law.
- Explain the law as well as the benefits and risks of alternative courses of actions for a client.
- Promptly notify and communicate settlement offers to a client.

Duty to Timely Respond to a Client's Request for Information   There is an absolute duty for an attorney to respond to reasonable requests for information. Although this seems basic, many attorneys still do not return client phone calls, respond to client letters, respond to client e-mails, or show up for client appointments. There are thousands of state bar disciplinary opinions where attorneys have been reprimanded, suspended, and disbarred for failing to respond in a timely fashion to their clients.

Duty to Promptly Inform a Client About Important Information   An attorney may not withhold important information that affects a legal matter without telling the client. For example, cases have held that an attorney has a duty to promptly tell a client that the client was named as a defendant in a civil action; an attorney cannot wait for six months to tell an incarcerated defendant that the attorney had been appointed to represent the client; and an attorney has to tell a client that a case was set for docket and later dismissed for failure to prosecute.

Duty to Never Cover Up a Matter If the Attorney Failed to Carry Out the Client's Instructions   If an attorney fails to carry out the instructions of a client by either neglect or design, the attorney has a duty to be up front and communicate this to the client. Many attorney discipline cases have been filed because an attorney agreed to file a claim and then did not, either due to negligence or because the attorney later changed his or her mind and then told the client the case was, in fact, filed. This type of behavior is also prohibited by *Rule 1.4*.

Duty to Notify a Client If He or She Is Stopping Work on a Client's Case   An attorney cannot cease working on a client matter without affirmatively telling the client, because doing so without the client's consent or knowledge could injure the client's legal interests. The withdrawal from a client matter should preferably be in writing, in the form of a letter to the client. If formal representation has been made in court, the attorney must file a motion to withdraw.

Duty to Notify a Client If an Attorney Is Leaving the Firm or Quitting the Practice of Law   An attorney has a duty to tell a client that he or she is leaving the firm and, therefore, representation of the client's case will be handled by someone else. The same holds true if the attorney is going to stop practicing law. The client needs to be made aware of this fact so that he or she can get his or her file returned and secure other counsel.

Duty to Explain the Law as well as the Benefits and Risks of Alternative Courses of Action   An attorney has a duty to help the client make an informed decision about the client's matter. This may include explaining legal theories to the client, explaining the effects of contracts and other documents, advising a client on the consequences of accepting one alternative over another, and generally giving advice and counseling the client regarding the legal matter.

Duty to Promptly Notify and Communicate Settlement Offers to a Client   An attorney has a duty to notify a client of all settlement offers, including explaining the terms and conditions of the offer and the ramifications to the client. An attorney cannot ordinarily, without the prior direction of the client, unilaterally decline or accept a settlement offer.

The Paralegal's Role in Communicating with Clients   Paralegals can play an active role in communicating with clients. Paralegals are often more accessible to clients than attorneys and therefore may have many opportunities to work with clients and to keep them informed. This is admirable and encouraged as long as the attorney is actively involved with the case, is reviewing all documents prepared by the paralegal, is the only party giving legal advice to the client, and meets with the client as needed.

Client Relationships

A fundamental aspect of law office management is the commitment to provide quality legal service to clients. This is true whether you work in a private law firm or legal aid office with many clients, or in a corporation or government practice where you have only one client; service is the key. Providing quality legal services begins with a good working relationship with each client, and this relationship is not just for attorneys. Everyone in the office, including paralegals, should be committed to this. Remember, the client always comes first; he or she is the one paying your salary in the end. Clients may not have the legal background to know whether or not they are receiving good legal representation. However, clients do know whether their phone calls are being returned, whether documents in their cases are poorly written and have typographical errors, whether deadlines are missed, or whether they are being treated respectfully. Merely providing good technical legal skills is not enough to please clients. Most clients are referred to attorneys and law offices by previous clients; if you provide poor service to existing clients, you will be depriving your firm of the best way to expand the practice.

Fostering Positive Client Relationships

Exhibit 4-2 shows a list of things that clients like and dislike about attorneys and law office staff. These likes and dislikes determine whether a client will come back for future business or refer others to the firm. Notice that the issue of winning or losing a case is not included in either list.

Exhibit 4-2 What Clients Like and Dislike

What Clients Like	What Clients Dislike
Friendliness	Being talked down to
Competence	Arrogance
Promptness	Staff acting bored or uninterested
Being able to reach attorneys/staff on the first try	Impatience
Excellent follow-up	Rudeness
Not being billed for every two-minute phone call	Calls and e-mails not returned
Attorneys/staff taking extra time to explain the legal process in layperson's terms	Incorrect billings
Listening and paying attention to what the client has to say	Being forgotten, treated as unimportant, or taken for granted
Demonstrating genuine interest in the client's problems and concerns year in and year out	Confidentiality breaches
Honesty	Errors
Good financial stewardship	Poor-quality work
Completing work on time	Multiple staff billing for the same event
	Waiting in the waiting room when they have an appointment and they are on time

It is important to note that many of the items listed next are the opinions of how a client perceives the legal professionals.

- Does the client see you as friendly and willing to help, or inattentive and impersonal?
- Do you come across to the client as prompt and businesslike, or indifferent?
- Do you show common courtesy to the client, or do you come across as rude?
- Are you respectful of the client and what he or she is going through, or do you have a superior and condescending attitude?
- Do you, at every possible opportunity, let the client know what is going on with his or her case and establish a feeling of trust and cooperativeness, or is the client ignored?

Each of these areas is critical to the success of the client relationship. Fail in any of these areas, and the relationship is undermined. This section will provide you with some ideas about how to foster excellent client relationships (see Exhibit 4-3).

Exhibit 4-3 Fostering Positive Relationships with Clients—"Clients for Life"

Description	Behavior
Know your client	• When dealing with the client, take into account his or her emotional/mental/physical state (consider how you would feel in the same circumstances), understand that many clients are anxious or nervous about seeing a legal professional and, based on this, respond and ask questions appropriately. • Establish basic trust in the relationship at every opportunity by listening to their needs, being honest, and being respectful. • Ask your client what his or her concerns are about the matter. • Ask the client what his or her business is about. • Do your own research about the client's business and industry. • Ask how the client prefers to be communicated with (in person, e-mail, telephone, or voice mail). • Ask the client how often he or she wants to be communicated with. • Ask how you can serve them better periodically.
Treat each client as if he or she is your only client	• When you meet with a client, only have that person's file on your desk. • Never take another call when meeting with a client, and let others know not to disturb you. • Never talk about how busy you are or about other cases to clients. • Particularly with new clients, it is important that the initial meeting go well and that law office staff is immediately available after a referral is made. • Particularly with new clients, be sure to mention whether the firm has handled similar cases in the past. Clients like to know that the firm is experienced regarding the subject matter of their case.
Send copies of all documents to clients	• Always send copies of documents to the client. This lets them know what you have been working on and keeps them informed. If the document is not particularly sensitive, attach it to an e-mail to the client; it's cheaper and faster.
Do not use legalese	• Talk to clients in layperson's terms and refrain from using jargon.
Return all phone calls and reply to e-mails and voice mails immediately	• Always return phone calls, e-mails, and voice mails immediately, no later than the end of the day.
Be courteous and professional	• Always be courteous, professional, and empathetic with clients. This is extremely important to most clients. • Dress professionally.
Respond to clients' requests and keep promises	• Always respond to client requests in a timely manner; if you make a promise to get something to a client, make sure you get it done on time and contact the client to let him or her know the status.
Give periodic updates	• Be proactive and periodically give updates to a client on the status of his or her case, whether or not the client specifically asked for it.
Never share personal problems or complain to clients	• Avoid sharing personal problems with clients. Clients are there to receive a service. • Do not complain to clients at all, especially about how hard you are working on their case. They are paying the firm a significant fee.
Preserve client confidences	• Maintaining client confidentiality is critical to maintaining the foundation of trust in the relationship.
Survey clients	• Use formal client surveys to find out what clients think about your services.
Management must help promote good client relations	• Work with management to let them know how to better support positive client relationships.
Publish a client manual	• Publish a client manual to help clients understand what to expect from the law office and how the judicial system functions regarding their type of case.
Take conflicts of interests seriously and be ethical	• Ask yourself who the client is, if there is more than one person in your office. • Always do careful conflicts checks, disclose any issues whatsoever, and get any consents to conflicts in writing after full disclosure. • If a client sees you being unethical in any way, that client may assume that you are not ethical with him or her.
Do not procrastinate	• Do not put things off or delay communicating with clients, even when you do not have good news or when work has not been completed. Be honest and up front.

Know Your Client

Knowing your client and your client's individual needs is extremely important. Each client has a unique set of needs, worries, and desires related to his or her legal matter. Firms with outstanding client relations discover what those specific needs are for each client, and then systematically deliver on each need.

Before you can understand a client and his or her needs, it is helpful to understand why a client comes to a legal professional. Like any other relationship, the client relationship is based on trust. Clients come to legal professionals because they need help. Whenever possible, take the client's emotional, mental, and physical state into consideration and empathize with him or her.

By showing the client that you understand and recognize his or her situation and concerns, you establish trust, which is the foundation of the relationship. Another way to establish trust is by being respectful and honest with the client at all times.

Once a relationship of trust is established with the client, it is important to know specifics about that individual, such as what his or her business is, what his or her concerns are about the legal matter, and what you can do to serve his or her needs.

Do not assume that you know what the client needs or wants. You may or may not be right, but you will know for sure if you ask. Because communication is vitally important, ask the client how he or she wants to receive communication. Are office visits the most convenient? Is e-mail the best? Does the client prefer telephone or voice mail? Again, the idea is to ask and then deliver services based on the client's needs.

Treat Each Client as If He or She Is Your Only Client   Every client should be treated individually. Behave as if that client's case is the only thing you are working on and as if their case is the most important one. Everyone at the firm needs to put the client at ease. When you meet with a client, have only his or her file on your desk and give the client your undivided attention. Never take a call when meeting with a client, and let others know not to disturb you. This is a good idea not only because it shows the client that you are interested in his or her case, but also because the confidentiality of your other clients must also be maintained.

Never tell the client how busy you are or how many other cases you are working on; the client's case is the only one he or she is concerned about and the only one you should be talking to him or her about. If a client calls and asks if you are busy, say something such as "I'm never too busy to take a call from a good client" (even if you are swamped). If a client comes in for an appointment, never make him or her wait in the waiting room. A good law practice makes prompt, *personal* service a high priority. Take a personal interest in the client's affairs and be empathetic. It is always best to be personable with clients because this fosters good working relationships that will continue for years to come.

Send Copies of All Documents to Clients As a matter of practice, it should be the policy of the law office to always send copies of all letters, memos, pleadings, and documents to the client. In nearly all cases, the client will appreciate this, and it will increase his or her confidence, satisfaction, and trust; even though this might be just another case to you, this matter is of particular importance to the client. Although many people focus on the results of a case, the documents are a large piece of the product for which the client is paying. Even if the client does not understand everything sent, it still allows him or her to know what is happening in the case and how difficult the theories and complexities of the case are, and it lets the client know that you are actively working on the case. The cost of the copies can be charged to the client's account, so there is no real reason not to do it. Also, if the client has e-mail and the document is not particularly sensitive, attach it to an e-mail and send it directly to the client. Clients are usually more willing to pay their attorney's fees when they have seen the work done on the case and may be frustrated if they do not know what is happening and then receive a bill.

Do Not Use Legalese Do not use legalese or legal jargon when talking with clients. Many clients do not understand legal jargon, and it is confusing and frustrating to them. Some clients may be too intimidated to ask what the terms mean. Try to explain legal concepts in words that a layperson could understand.

Return Client Phone Calls Immediately It is essential that you return client phone calls immediately. If that is not possible, at least return the calls on the same day when they are made. It is not uncommon for clients to call paralegals. Usually, paralegals are easier to reach than attorneys, and paralegals often work with clients quite closely, depending on the type of case. Because paralegals typically are very busy and may be working on many projects at once, you will be inclined to put client calls off, but do not do this. Always return a client's call first and then finish the job at hand. If you do not reach the client on the first try, continue to try to reach the client rather than letting the client call back for you.

Be Courteous, Empathetic, and Professional at All Times Some clients may be abusive at times. Do not take client comments personally. Never become impatient with a client, "snap" at a client, or act rudely. If you have a problem with a client treating you abusively, mention it to your supervising attorney or paralegal manager and let him or her handle it. Act professionally in all situations.

Finally, never allow a secretary or receptionist to let a client stay on hold after calling for you. If you are on another call and cannot get to the client immediately, have the receptionist tell the client you will return the call as soon as you get off the phone, then follow up and call the client. If the client leaves a voice mail, return it as soon as possible.

Respond to Client Requests in a Timely Fashion and Keep Your Promises   It is not enough to simply return client phone calls. When clients request that you answer their questions and send letters, or when they need things from you, you must respond as quickly as possible. If you tell the client that you will have something to give him or her by a particular time or date, keep your promise. If an emergency comes up and you cannot make the deadline, always contact the client and let him or her know and set a new deadline that you can meet.

Give Clients Periodic Status Reports   Some cases can be sitting on appeal for months, waiting for a motion to be ruled on, or facing other things that make them lie in a dormant state. This always frustrates clients, who like quick remedies to their problems. On a weekly or not less than a monthly basis, review your cases, and, with the approval of your attorney, write or e-mail clients letting them know what is happening in their cases. E-mail and word processors can be configured to make this a very quick process by having form letters on file for different situations. If the case is waiting for some kind of action, you should still write the client and let him or her know that you are waiting and have not forgotten the case. If you do not review the case periodically, the case could very well sit for months with no contact with the client. Keeping in touch with the client never hurts; it reiterates that his or her business is important to you.

Do Not Share Personal or Office Problems with Clients   Always keep your personal problems to yourself and never make comments that are derogatory about your supervising attorney, firm, or other staff members. Clients need to know that their legal matters are in good hands and that everything is under control. Also, never complain to a client regarding how hard you are working on his or her case. After all, that is what he or she is paying for.

Preserve Client Confidences   Preserving client confidence is very important and cannot be overemphasized. Apart from the ethics question, you should keep in mind that if release of client information gets back to the client, the relationship is most likely finished.

The Use of Client Surveys   A client survey is a way to find out exactly what your clients think of your services (see Exhibit 4-4). Most client questionnaires are given at the conclusion of a case. Any time you get information directly from a client, you should take it to heart. Most firms allow the client to remain anonymous in completing the questionnaire to ensure truthfulness, and it is usually short, not more than a page long, to make completion as easy as possible.

Management Must Help Promote Good Client Relationships   Management also has a duty to promote good client relationships. Exhibit 4-5 contains a sample client-centered policy that would be found in a law office staff manual.

Exhibit 4-4 Sample Questionnaire

Thank you for participating in the questionnaire and prompt return for our review. It is through your responses that we may continue to provide excellent service to our clients and the community.

With our kindest regards,

1. Case type: —————————————————————————

2. Attorney or paralegal: ———————————————————

3. Were you previously represented by the firm or an attorney located with the firm?
   —————————————————————————————

   If you answered yes, please provide details (month/date/year) ——————

4. For what reason(s) did you choose the attorney and/or the firm? ————

5. Were you informed about the basis of our charges for legal services at the beginning of the case? ————————————————————

6. Did you ever wait for an extended period of time in the waiting room before the attorney or paralegal met with you? ——————————————

   If yes, how many times? ——————————————————————

7. Did members of the legal team and the law firm treat you with courtesy? ——

8. Did the attorney or paralegal provide you with timely notices regarding the case progress? ——————————————————————————

9. Do you feel the fee charged was reasonable? ———————————

10. Do you feel the results obtained in the case were to your satisfaction? ——

    If no, why not? ————————————————————————

11. Would you recommend our law firm? ————————————————

    If yes, why? ——————————————————————————

    If no, why not? ————————————————————————

12. How would you rate the quality of services provided by the firm (please select).
    —————————————————————————————

    (Excellent, Very Good, Good, Fair, Poor) ————————————

13. Please provide comments below: ——————————————————
    —————————————————————————————
    —————————————————————————————

Publish a Client Manual Some law offices publish a manual for their clients, which explains what to expect from a law office, such as how attorney fees are calculated, how the attorney–client relationship works, what discovery is, how to prepare for a deposition, and what to expect at trial. This type of manual is very beneficial and will save the attorney and paralegal from answering the same questions over and over for different clients.

Exhibit 4-5 Sample Service Policy for Clients

Part One: Basic Client Representation Goals

The attorneys and all members of the legal team will strive to focus on client representation in the following manner:

- Maintain a communicative process of client representation.
- Clients are not numbers; clients should be treated individually and personably.
- All members of the legal team should display a sincere concern for the clients' issue(s) when contacting them.
- Priority should be given in responding to client contacts.
- All members of the legal team should maintain a consistent mindset that the client is the focus.

Part Two: Correspondence

Communications may include written correspondence (letters, memos), faxes, or e-mail messages, and in some situations text messages or instant messaging (IM).

- Clients should receive copies of all documents and pleadings, along with a letter explaining the included paperwork in a prompt manner.
- Client e-mails and/or text messages should mostly be used for brief messages, avoiding confidential or privileged information unless communications have security (encryption) to protect the transmitted information.
- Client updates should be received at least monthly unless other arrangements are agreed to by the client.

Part Three: Telephone Communications

Communications should be consistent with the established agreements between the client and the attorney during the client representation meeting.

- Client communication should meet the client's needs and expectations.
- Clients should receive information concerning important changes or events promptly; bad news should be communicated immediately.
- Returning client phone calls should be done within a reasonable time frame. If not by the attorney, then by a member of the legal team explaining the delays and attempting to help the client if immediate attention is needed.
- Attorneys should return phone calls within the same day, which means clients might be called back late into the evening.

Part Four: Billing Process and Communications

The billing process is an effective client communication tool that provides details regarding the attorney's services through billing invoices.

- Monthly bills along with a cover letter briefly describing the services performed by the attorney and future plans should be sent in order to maintain routine status for the client.
- Time entries should provide information concerning substantive work performed for the client on their case.

Part Five: Handling Client Expectations

Throughout the entire representation, the client's expectations must be handled.

- The client should be informed as soon as possible if there are significant changes in the case plan or course of the matter.
- During the course of the matter, the case plan and any fee estimate should be easily accessed and referenced.
- All members of the legal team should work together to manage a case plan within the client's expectation.
- When preparing monthly billings, attorneys should refer to the fee estimates.

(continued)

(continued)

- If the attorneys are unable to meet the fee estimates established, they should adjust the methods for handling the case or contact the client about adjusting the estimates.

- If the monthly bill is higher than the client expected, the attorney should contact them immediately to avoid surprising the client.

Part Six: Recovery

When the client conveys dissatisfaction or a problem concerning the services provided, the situation must be addressed immediately.

- High priority should be given in returning phone calls expressing dissatisfaction with some aspect of services provided.

- Members of the legal team should ensure that messages from clients expressing dissatisfaction should be communicated to the attorney immediately.

- There should be no delays returning a dissatisfied client's phone call either by the attorney or members of the legal team.

Take Conflicts Seriously and Be Ethical Conflicts of interest must be taken seriously, and a careful conflicts check should be done before a case or client is accepted. If there are any possible conflicts found, they should be fully disclosed to the client and the client should consent in writing. It is also important to always act in an ethical manner to clients, *in everything you do*. If a client sees you being dishonest, he or she will infer that you are dishonest to him or her as well.

Do Not Procrastinate A law office is no place for people who procrastinate; procrastination always causes problems and never solves them. Handle client problems when they occur. Deliver bad news to clients or admit that a deadline was missed up front. That way, clients can at least respect you for being honest. Honesty is the best and only policy when it comes to dealing with clients. The whole attorney–client relationship is based on trust; if that fails, the attorney–client relationship will fail as well.

Resolving Client Dissatisfaction

Resolving client dissatisfaction is not an easy task and may not be up to the paralegal to resolve at all. Client dissatisfaction can have many roots, including personality conflicts with the legal staff, disagreement on strategy, misunderstandings, lack of knowledge about the law or facts, or frustration with the legal system. Here are some ideas for how to resolve client dissatisfaction.

Listen to the Complaint; Do Not Interrupt and Do Not Argue When a client has a complaint, the first thing to do is to listen carefully and patiently. Listen with empathy and do not react. Avoid interrupting or arguing with the client; this is rude. In some instances, clients just want to vent about something they do not agree with, that they see as unfair, or that they believe was a mistake. The client may be fully satisfied simply by finding someone who will listen patiently and react in a courteous, professional manner. If the client is satisfied with this, thank him or her for the call, let him or her know that you or the firm will try to correct this in the future, and then pass along the information to the appropriate parties who can prevent the problem from recurring.

Empathically Listen   When speaking with a client regarding a complaint, it helps to acknowledge what he or she is saying and reaffirm that you are listening by saying "Yes" or "Hmmmm" or "I see." Responses like these show that you are actively listening.

Do Not Overstep Your Bounds or Promise Something You Cannot Deliver   A client may try to extract a promise from you to do something that you do not have the authority to do. Do not let a client force you into doing something you are not comfortable with or that you do not have the authority to do. In those instances, say something like, "I will talk to my supervising attorney and get back to you as soon as possible, hopefully by X." Telling the client an exact time you will get back to him or her should alleviate fears that the complaint will be ignored.

Take Notes   Always take careful notes so that you can recount exactly what the complaint is about, including the fine details. This will allow you to relay it to others for the purpose of resolving the matter.

Forward All Complaints to Your Supervising Attorney and Be Honest   All complaints should be immediately referred to your supervising attorney. If a client is calling to complain about a mistake you made and you know it is a mistake, be honest, admit the mistake to your supervising attorney, generate possible solutions to the problem, and put procedures in place to keep it from happening again.

Do Not Ignore the Complaint   If you receive a client complaint, never procrastinate or ignore it. If a client believes he or she has been ignored or his or her comments were summarily disregarded, he or she will only become angrier. Resolving the matter as quickly as possible is the best thing to do.

Recognize That Some Clients Will Always Complain   Some clients are seemingly never happy and always have a complaint to make. Hopefully, the number of clients like this is very small, but nonetheless they do exist. Treat the client as considerately as you can and talk to your supervising attorney. In extreme cases, a firm may decide to simply terminate the relationship and move on.

Work Through Personality Conflicts   Some client complaints may be the result of personality conflicts. In most instances, you should work through personality conflicts; in severe instances, you may be able to request that another staff member handle the matter. This should be asked for as a last resort. You may have to handle the matter anyway, either because there is no one else to take over or there is no one else with your experience regarding that client or the legal/factual issues involved.

Clients and Technology

Clients are demanding technology-based solutions. They demand access to their attorney and law office by e-mail; they want documents to be e-mailed to them immediately, instead of waiting for days before they arrive in the mail; they want law offices to use the same basic software programs they have, so they can access documents of all types, from word processing to spreadsheet to presentation files; and they want electronic access to documents so they can edit them in real time. They want their law offices to offer slick technological solutions from practice-based computer programs; they want everything from electronic discovery to the automated tracking of exhibits on a laptop for trial; they want online billing, so that they can receive their bills immediately and in a format *they* want; they want electronic access to *their* files and information via extranets and other services that are available at all times; and they want their attorney's and paralegal's mobile phone numbers so that they can reach them when *they* have an emergency. It is important, when working with a new client, to understand exactly what the client's expectations for technology are and then meet those expectations. Clients mostly want these things because they result in direct access to their legal professionals; however, some clients demand these things, knowing that more technology means greater efficiency and lower hourly bills.

How to Lose Clients

Losing clients is easy; keeping them for life is hard. Losing a client may result from missing an urgent phone call, making an inappropriate or unprofessional remark, losing an important document, giving legal advice that is not well thought out, lacking trust, or making the client think that you overbilled or that he or she was not treated ethically. There are many reasons why clients leave legal professionals and law offices; the goal is to keep this from happening. The legal professionals who retain their clients year in and year out keep their "eye on the ball" and on what is important to the clients at all times.

Dealing with Difficult Clients

Not all clients are created equal. It was noted in Chapter 2 that successful attorneys and law practices are able to distinguish bad clients and cases from good ones. Some clients may be extremely difficult to work with; some have completely unreasonable expectations about their case; some may have mental impairments; some may be vengeful; some may be violent; some may be dishonest; some may not be able to pay for legal services, and so on. It is up to the attorney to select what kind of clients and cases he or she will accept and work with. Once these decisions are made, it is up to the paralegal to work with the client to the best of his or her ability, even if the client proves difficult.

- **Stay calm and maintain professionalism** Always stay calm when working with a difficult client, no matter what the client does. Maintain a professional demeanor, and never react to a client's outburst with one of your own. If possible, ratchet down the dialogue and try to find common ground with the client. If a client becomes upset or abusive, which is very rare, immediately leave the area and inform the attorney. Some difficult clients are harder on staff than the attorney. It is important that you let the attorney know about the situation.

- **Document conversations** Protect yourself from difficult clients by carefully documenting your conversations with them—e-mail is a great tool for this. It never hurts to send the client an e-mail or a letter confirming an important instruction, just to be sure that all parties are on the same page. Some case management programs provide a place in the program to document all conversations with clients. No matter what tool you use, always save it for future reference.

- **Be courteous, but maintain an arm's-length relationship** Always be courteous to clients, but consider treating a difficult client a little more at "arm's length." You do not need to be "chummy" or friends with clients in order to do your job. Be professional, be competent, and do not let your guard down. You also do not need to share personal information with clients, even if they ask for it. If a client asks for advice or wants to know how you would make a decision regarding something related to his or her case, do not provide an answer—these are decisions that the client must make.

- **Keep the attorney fully informed** It is important, when dealing with a difficult client, to always keep the attorney fully informed of all of your conversations or correspondence with the client. Copying or blind-copying the attorney on e-mails to the client is an effective way to keep the attorney informed. Also, do not fail to let the attorney know if a client shows any unprofessional behavior toward you. It is the attorneys' job to prevent clients from abusing staff.

Communication Skills

Possessing good communication skills is necessary in most professional jobs, but it is especially important in a law office. Paralegals must communicate with clients, opposing counsel, supervising attorneys, office staff, court clerks, and witnesses on a daily basis regarding complex and important matters. Good communication skills also bear directly on the effectiveness of law office management. Communication is an important part of management because, without it, management cannot plan, organize, control, or direct the business. Thus, having good communication skills bears directly on both legal services to clients and law office management.

General Communication

Professionals, such as paralegals and attorneys, typically spend three-fourths of each day communicating. **Communication** is the transfer of a message from a sender to a receiver. Although communication can be quickly defined, it is more difficult to explain why there is so much poor communication in the world.

A **communication barrier** inhibits or prevents a receiver from obtaining the correct message from a sender. These barriers include situations where the sender and receiver have different cultural backgrounds, perceptions,

communication
The transfer of a message from a sender to a receiver.

communication barrier
Something that inhibits or prevents the receiver from obtaining the correct message.

understandings, and ages. The abundance of communication barriers helps to explain why some messages are never properly received. Noise is also a communication barrier; **noise** interferes with or distorts the message being communicated. A good example of noise is when one person is trying to listen to several senders at one time—the messages are distorted because the receiver cannot understand all of the messages at the same time.

Feedback is an important part of effective communication. **Feedback** is information sent in response to the sender's message. There is no way for the sender to know whether his or her information has been properly received without feedback. Feedback allows the receiver to state his or her understanding of the message, and also allows the sender to evaluate the effectiveness of the message and to clarify misunderstood points. Feedback does not have to be verbal; it can be as simple as a puzzled look on the receiver's face.

noise
Any situation that interferes with or distorts the message being communicated.

feedback
Information sent in response to a message.

Nonverbal Communication

Communication is much more than just speech. There are many nonverbal communicators, such as eye contact, facial expressions, posture, appearance, clothing, tone of voice, and gestures. All of these nonverbal means of communication have a hand in determining whether or not a message is properly received.

Improving Your Communication Skills

Listening   Listening is one of the most important features of communicating effectively, and although it sounds easy to do, often it is not. The average person forgets 50% of what was said to him or her within just a few minutes. We have all caught ourselves in the middle of conversations thinking about something unrelated to the conversation. We become "lazy listeners," only minimally listening. Exhibit 4-6 contains some excellent rules on listening. A common problem that attorneys and paralegals are guilty of is that, instead of listening to what another person is saying, they formulate arguments and prepare for when they will speak. This effectively takes the listener out of good listening, and the listener may miss the total message.

Keep It Simple and to the Point   Most people understand more of a message when the sender uses short, direct sentences rather than long, complex ones. You can explain complex issues to others just by using words and phrases they understand. Avoid jargon and legalese when dealing with clients. In the same vein, research has shown that short letters are read sooner than are long ones, and the reader actually remembers the message of the short letter more accurately.

Do Not Become Emotional   Try not to be emotional when communicating. Try to be objective and calm, without being cold and distant.

Consider Your Nonverbal Signals   Realize that when you are communicating with people, they look at you and your message as a total package. They notice how you are dressed, if you are nervous, if you are fidgeting, if you have your hands in your pockets, and if you have confidence in yourself.

Exhibit 4-6 The 10 Commandments to Effective Listening

1. **YOU MUST QUIT SPEAKING.**

   If you are speaking, you are not listening.

2. **YOU MUST MAKE THE SPEAKER FEEL COMFORTABLE.**

   Let the person know he or she can speak freely.

3. **YOU MUST LET THE SPEAKER KNOW YOU ARE LISTENING.**

   Do not read text messages on your phone while someone is speaking. Pay attention and listen attentively.

4. **YOU MUST RELATE TO THE SPEAKER.**

   It is important to recognize the speaker's viewpoint(s).

5. **YOU MUST NOT BE DISTRACTED.**

   Do not read text messages or organize papers. Put your phone on private, silence and shut the office door if possible.

6. **YOU MUST CONTROL YOUR TEMPER WITH THE SPEAKER.**

   If you are upset, it is easy to misunderstand what the speaker said.

7. **YOU MUST BE PATIENT WITH THE SPEAKER.**

   Do not interrupt someone while he or she speaks, begin packing your briefcase, or checking the clock.

8. **YOU MUST NOT ARGUE WITH OR CRITICIZE THE SPEAKER.**

   If the speaker gets defensive, he or she will stop talking. If you argue with the speaker, you do not get anything accomplished.

9. **YOU MUST ASK THE SPEAKER QUESTIONS.**

   When you ask questions, the speaker knows you are listening and this helps address additional issues.

10. **YOU MUST QUIT SPEAKING.**

    It is important to reinforce the silence because all other commandments rely on your ability to listen. Human beings have twice as many tools for listening as they do for speaking and should consider that a hint for developing proper listening behaviors.

Make Eye Contact   Make eye contact with everyone you are talking to, since it conveys honesty and interest. Juries, for instance, often cite the lack of eye contact as a reason that they did not believe a witness.

Be Aware of Your Body Language   Crossed arms usually mean you are feeling defensive, scared, or cold about something; poor posture is sometimes interpreted as lazy or slothful. One kind of body language that is more important than anything else for setting a positive tone is a simple smile. A smile relaxes both your audience and you.

Be Precise and Clear   Always try to be as precise as possible when communicating with others. How often have you heard someone say, "Well, I thought you meant . . . ." Speak clearly and do not leave anything to the imagination. For example, if you tell a delivery person you need something filed at the courthouse, be sure you are precise and tell him or her whether you need it filed at the federal courthouse, the local courthouse, or the state courthouse. These subtle differences can be very important in a law office, so be absolutely clear when you communicate. Look for feedback. If someone has a puzzled look on his or her face, explain your message again or ask him or her to repeat it to you.

Consider Your Audience   Always tailor your communication to the specific audience with which you are communicating. You can have the best message in the world, but if you are delivering it to someone who does not care about it, you have wasted your effort. If possible, find out what is important to your audience, what concerns it has, and then tailor everything you say to address these concerns.

Consider the Timing and Context   Timing is everything; a good communicator must know when to communicate his or her message. Be patient and wait until the time is right. Time your message so that noise and barriers are kept to a minimum. You may want to wait until the receiver is in a good mood or has just heard good news. Communication is an art; people will react to the same message in different ways depending on the timing. You must consider the context in which the communication is being made for your message to be effective. Is the receiver having a bad day? Where is the communication taking place: in a crowded hallway or in a private office? What type of relationship have you had with the receiver? Do you respect each other, dislike each other, or distrust each other?

   Try to consider the other person's perception of your communication. Consider this, when you find yourself in a disagreement with someone: are you more likely to believe that *your behavior is motivated by context* (e.g., you had a bad day, you are tired, and you are stressed out) while you believe that the *other person's behavior is motivated not by context, but by something personal* (e.g., spite, revenge, meanness, or unreasonableness)? This is a normal reaction. Consider the context and the environment in which the other person is viewing your communication; look at it from his or her point of view and be aware of your own biases. This will improve your ability to communicate with others.

Avoid Negatives and Do Not Be Judgmental   Do not start with negative or judgmental comments such as "That probably will not work." This will only make your audience defensive. Try to be positive and explore the conversation in a positive light. If you do not think an idea will work, ask a question about why you think it might not work, such as "Well, have you considered what would happen if this occurred . . . ? Will your idea still be successful?" This allows the other person to consider your side but in a positive, constructive light.

Ask Questions   Never assume something based on unsupported evidence. It is very easy for people to misread or assume things about other people. Instead of assuming something incorrectly, ask questions and talk about it. This will allow you to verify whether or not your initial assumptions were accurate.

Rephrase Ideas   If you are not sure whether you truly understand what someone has told you, try rephrasing. **Rephrasing** is a technique of telling the sender your understanding of the conversation. It allows the sender to clarify information that might not have been understood clearly.

rephrasing
A technique used to improve communication by repeating back to a person your understanding of the conversation.

Recognize the Importance of Good Communication with Third Parties A paralegal deals with many types of people, including witnesses, court personnel, outside agencies, libraries, businesses, and other law offices. You must be professional at all times and have good relationships with these third parties, since they may provide information that will help you to perform your job. When possible, cultivate these relationships.

Use Proper Telephone Techniques

Poor telephone techniques abound in many law offices. Here are some examples of what not to do:

- Office staff: "Law offices."
  - Client: "May I speak to Mr. Smith?"
  - Office staff: "Sure, just a sec."

- Office staff: "Law offices."
  - Client: "May I speak to Mr. Smith?"
  - Office staff: "He's yakking on the other line, you want to hold?"

- Office staff: "Law offices."
  - Client: "May I speak to Mr. Smith?"
  - Office staff: "He's not in. Why don't you call back this afternoon?"

Good telephone techniques are important in any legal organization. Most legal professionals spend a great deal of time on the phone and need courteous telephone skills.

Always Communicate in a Businesslike, Professional Tone Because callers cannot see your body language and facial expressions on the phone, the words you say and the tone you use are very important. Always be calm and professional when talking on the phone. If you have a million things to do and you are flustered or might get short with the caller, then do not answer the phone. Call back when you are calm.

Put the Caller at Ease Listen carefully and make appropriate responses that put the caller at ease whenever possible. You gain nothing by offering quick responses that may alienate the caller.

Refer to the Caller by Name When the caller tells you his or her name, call the person by that name: "Mr. Smith, I'll page her immediately." This puts the caller at ease and lets him or her know that you remember who he or she is. It also communicates personal service.

When Taking a Message, Always Obtain the Telephone Number of the Caller Callers often say that the person whom they are calling already has their number. Obtain a callback number from the caller anyway, just in case the number has been changed recently or has been lost, the caller has a new number, or just because it is more convenient for the person who will return the call.

When Taking a Caller's Name or Phone Number, Always Repeat Back the Information By repeating the information back to the caller, you confirm that you have received the message correctly and that the name and number are accurate. Think how frustrated you get when someone takes a message and does not record the information accurately.

Always Identify Yourself as a Paralegal/Legal Assistant If you are taking a call from a client, an attorney, or a third party regarding a case, always identify yourself as a paralegal/legal assistant early in the conversation.

When Taking a Message, Get a General "Feel" for the Subject It is important to get a general "feel" for what the caller needs when taking a message, because you might be able to handle the matter yourself. If you cannot, then do not ask for too much information, from clients in particular. Some clients do not like to give out details about their problems.

Be Wary of Mobile Phones Be careful that the conversation is not about sensitive client matters when speaking on a mobile phone. Although mobile phones are becoming more secure, it is still prudent to be careful.

When Taking a Message, Explain Briefly Why the Individual Called Is Not In Giving a short explanation as to why someone cannot take a call, such as "Susan is in court this morning," lets the caller know that the person is not ducking his or her call. Avoid saying that the person is "unavailable."

Try to Answer Your Phone When You Are Not with a Client In the era of e-mail and voice mail, sometimes clients want to talk to a person to discuss a matter. Try to answer your phone instead of letting it roll to voice mail whenever possible. Clients can become quite frustrated when they cannot reach someone on the phone, particularly when the client has an emergency.

The following is a client maxim to think about:

- I needed the help of a lawyer or paralegal.
- I could not reach you.
- I reached a competing law office.
- I no longer need you.

Do Not Keep Callers on Hold Except for a Very Short Period of Time Nothing is more frustrating to a caller than to be indefinitely put on hold. If you must place a caller on hold, do so for only a very short period of time. Continually update the caller as to the status of his or her call.

Leadership and Communication

Being a leader takes a special type of communication skill. Leadership was described in Chapter 1 as the act of motivating or causing others to perform and achieve objectives. Leaders give us direction, vision, and motivation. Leadership is an important part of any organization or department. Paralegals need to take leadership roles, and there are opportunities for paralegals who have leadership skills; for instance, paralegals can be paralegal managers or law office administrators. Paralegal "leaders" can take on projects and cases that need innovation and have never been done before. Paralegals with leadership characteristics are sought after and are important to growing law offices.

How Do I Become a Leader? Having determined that leadership qualities are essential for the paralegal, the next question is: "How does one become a leader?" This has been a hotly debated issue over the years. Early leadership theories said that only exceptional people were capable of assuming the leadership role (i.e., you either were or were not born with it). But current research overwhelmingly shows that leaders are not born, they are made. The following are some suggestions on how to become a leader:

1. **Be an expert.** Effective leaders are experts in what they do. They know precisely what they are talking about. People around them have confidence in their abilities and rely upon their knowledge and judgment. They are inventive and ingenious and are able to plan, organize, and manage resources to solve problems. Before they give opinions, they do research and master the subject they are talking about. Leaders must be competent, make good decisions, and be able to evaluate situations and act accordingly.

2. **Be honest.** Effective leaders have a reputation for being extremely honest and forthright and for possessing a high degree of integrity. These are important qualities; subordinates must respect leaders and be motivated, inspired, and willing to follow their directives.

3. **Stay calm.** Good leaders stay cool and collected, even when they are "under fire." They have confidence in their own abilities and are not shaken by disagreement or challenge. Instead, they rise to the occasion.

4. **Trust and support those under you.** Good leaders choose effective and competent subordinates and then support them in their efforts. Subordinates know that they are trusted and that their abilities and skills are appreciated, and thus they work even harder for the leader.

5. **Take risks and do not be afraid of failure.** Effective leaders take calculated risks. They focus on the positive and refuse to think about failure. Failures and mistakes are steps in the learning process and are to be expected. Leaders have the ability to make bold decisions and to stand by them when others are backpedaling.

6. **Encourage honest opinions from others.** Effective leaders encourage subordinates to be honest and to articulate their opinions, even if those opinions are in disagreement with the leader's opinions. Debate sharpens the decision-making process so that all alternatives are considered and evaluated based on their merits. This is the only way situations can be properly evaluated. Leaders encourage others around them to cooperate and communicate with one another by listening to everyone's ideas and opinions.

7. **Set goals and visions.** Effective leaders set goals and have specific visions for the future. The goals and visions inspire and empower others to accomplish the goals and to work toward the common dream.

8. **Be respectful.** Good leaders respect, get along with, and care for other people. They foster meaningful personal and professional relationships with the people around them.

Communication is at the center of leadership. Leaders emerge when a new crisis arises or when a new challenge surfaces. Leaders are able to put together a solution, empower their subordinates to support it, reshape and retool their resources, and come up with a package that meets the new challenge and solves the problem.

Group Communication

Communicating in groups involves a whole different set of variables than communicating one on one. Paralegals must routinely work with groups (including attorneys and paralegals) on trials and similar projects, and with clients and attorneys on cases. Additionally, they serve on committees and associations. The following are some commonly known advantages and disadvantages of group work:

- Groups tend to make more accurate decisions than do individuals. As the adage says, "Two heads are better than one"; that is, there are more points of view to be heard and considered and a greater number of solutions offered and analyzed in a group.

- Once a group has arrived at a decision, there is an increase in the acceptance of the final choice because group members were involved in the process.

- Group members can communicate and explain the group's decision to others because they were included.

- Once a decision has been made by a group, implementation is easier because the group members were involved in the process and have a "stake in the action."

- Decisions by groups take up to 50% longer to make than do decisions by individuals.

- Group decisions are often compromises between different points of view rather than the most appropriate alternative.

- Group decisions can sometimes result in groupthink. **Groupthink** occurs when the desire for group cohesiveness and consensus becomes stronger than the desire for the best possible decision.

- Groups sometimes make more risky decisions than do individuals, especially when there is no one individual responsible for the consequences of the group decision.

- Groups are sometimes dominated by one or more individuals who rank higher in status within the organization.

groupthink
Term for when the desire for group cohesiveness and consensus becomes stronger than the desire for the best possible decision.

Communication in Interviewing Clients, Witnesses, and Third Parties

Interviewing clients, witnesses, and third parties is a specialized communication skill that you need to possess. In many firms, interviews are conducted by experienced paralegals or attorneys. However, new paralegals sit in interviews with an experienced paralegal or attorney to learn good interviewing skills.

The initial client interview is very important, because it is usually the first real contact the client has with the firm. The purpose of the interview is to relax the client, to convince the client that he or she has come to the right firm, and to gather enough information to decide whether your firm and responsible attorney are interested in representing the client or at least finding out more about the case. The following are some suggestions for handling each part of the interview and what you should do when you encounter difficulties. Exhibit 4-7 is an evaluation sheet to assess your interviewing skills. While Exhibit 4-7 is specifically geared toward a client interview, many of the same principles apply to all interviews.

Exhibit 4-7 Client Interviewing Techniques

Client Interview Basics

I. **Preparing for the client interview**

　i. **Common factors in preparing the basic client interview:**

　　a. What is the effective time allocation for an initial interview?

　　b. What is the best meeting arrangement?

　　c. What information should the client receive?

　　d. What can be done to limit interruptions during the interview?

　　e. What attire should be worn during the interview?

　ii. **Common factors in preparing for a specific client interview:**

　　a. A conflict check should be performed.

　　b. A preliminary review and legal research should be performed.

　　c. Determine the necessary documents the client should bring for the interview.

　　　(1) Possibly provide a questionnaire for the client to prepare and provide during the interview.

　　d. Determine a checklist for investigating the areas relative to the client's issue(s).

　iii. **Consider what resources should be gathered to properly prepare for the client interview:**

　　a. Form books

　　b. Checklists

　　c. Questionnaires

II. **Effective interview skills**

　i. **Methods for building client rapport:**

　　a. Allow the client to feel comfortable and speak openly.

　　b. Listen with attention and interest to the client while avoiding being emotional or involved in connection to the issue(s).

　　c. Be receptive to the client and avoid judgmental attitude.

　　d. Avoid interrupting the client, except when necessary.

　　e. Use active listening responses and language that the client understands.

　　f. Be cognizant of communication blocks.

　　g. Encourage client questions.

　　h. Be respectful and avoid condescension to clients.

　　i. Make sure to offer client support.

　ii. **Methods to effectively gather information:**

　　a. Obtain a detailed factual account of the issue(s).

　　b. Identify additional subjects during the interview process.

　　c. Focus on subjects that will produce relevant information.

　　d. Develop questions in a pattern starting with general to specific or using the opposite approach.

　　e. Use leading and open-ended questions when appropriate.

　　f. Avoid diagnosing client issue(s) prematurely.

　　g. Make sure the client understands the questions and the interviewer understands the client's answers.

　iii. **Methods for evaluating and improving interviewing skills:**

　　a. Attend Continuing Legal Education seminars that focus on improving interviewing skills.

　　b. Transcribe and review interview transcripts.

　　c. Review current interviewing skills articles.

III. **Recording and documenting interviews**

　i. **Method to preserve information gathered from interviews:**

　　a. Take accurate notes during the interview.

　　b. Immediately record interview details.

　　c. Provide abundantly clear details for other reviewers to quickly and accurately understand the interview information.

　　d. Prepare for file follow-up and client follow-up, if necessary.

Prepare for the Interview   One of the simplest things you can do to make sure that an interview goes well is to prepare for it. Always try to get as much initial information as possible before the interview. Establish a checklist of questions you want to ask and specific information you want to gather. You must establish what the purpose or goal of the interview is, and then steer the interview toward the direction of the goal. For example, if you routinely interview clients regarding workers' compensation claims, there is certain information that you must have. Establish exactly what information you need and then draft a checklist and an agenda to ensure that you obtain the information.

Many law offices also have an intake form on which the client generally describes why he or she has come to the firm. All this information will help you to prepare for the interview. Whoever is setting up the interview should, in addition, always ask the client to bring in any documentation that may be relevant.

Break the Ice   The beginning of any interview brings apprehension both for the interviewer and interviewee. Ways to break the ice include meeting the client in the waiting room, offering your hand for a handshake, accompanying the client back to your office, and talking to the client about the weather or other neutral topics. Always wear a smile and be warm and friendly. Another interesting way to break the ice is to ask the client or witness about his or her family. This allows you to gain some background information. Some people may think this is nosy; you may tell the person that the questions are not meant to embarrass him or her, but simply to understand who he or she is and to get the "big picture." You also may explain about the confidentiality of everything that he or she tells you.

Always Inform the Person You Are Interviewing of Your Status as a Paralegal   Once the client is relaxed and is ready to talk about why he or she is there, indicate your status as a paralegal. Do not make a prolonged speech, which may demonstrate your lack of confidence; simply state, "I am a paralegal, and I work for Ms. Smith, who is an attorney here." You should also tell the person what you will be doing and what the attorney is going to do: "I will initially be talking to you about your case. I will take down the facts of your case and then prepare a memo to the attorney about it. The attorney will then contact you to discuss it in more depth." Once you have done that, you are ready to begin the interview. Many people begin with an open-ended statement, such as, "Tell me why you are here. Start at the beginning."

Listen Carefully   Listening carefully to the client's story is sometimes hard to do. The client may ramble, talk about events out of sequence, and talk about matters that may be irrelevant to the legal problem. However, refrain from leading the conversation, at least during the first part of the interview. Be patient and let the client tell the whole story in his or her own way. Then go back and fill in the details by asking questions. Do not take too many notes during the first part of the interview. You should give the client your undivided attention and try to make eye contact. Clients need to be reassured that you are interested in their case. As you listen, determine whether the client's story makes sense and think of what facts the client may be leaving out.

Communicate Sincerity For any interview to be successful, you must communicate that you are sincerely interested in the client's problem. Characteristics such as dominance or defensiveness are counterproductive to establishing sincerity. One of the best ways you can communicate sincerity is to show you are really listening to what the person is saying by asking thoughtful questions. Avoid appearing as if you are "grilling" a client.

Be Empathetic Be empathetic with the client, letting him or her know that you feel for him or her and for the situation he or she is in. Empathy is distinguished from sympathy, which is feeling sorry for the individual. However, be sure to keep your objectivity. Sometimes the client may have to describe very personal, traumatic, or embarrassing information. In that case, you need to be extra sensitive and inform the client that everything said is confidential and is necessary so that you understand what happened.

Organize the Information Once you have listened to the client tell his or her story the first time through, you are ready to organize the information. A common way to organize the client's story is to build a chronology of events that starts at the beginning of the problem and works forward. This helps the client relive the facts in a particular order and may cause the client to remember more exact details. However, be aware that clients seldom remember things in exact order, so it usually takes several times through before your chronology is accurate.

Ask Appropriate Questions When you want to get detailed information about a particular event, remember to ask who, what, when, and where questions. Do not ask leading questions that might suggest a particular answer, such as, "You saw the traffic light as you were going through and it was green, right?" Ask your questions carefully. A better approach might be to say, "Describe the intersection before the accident."

In addition, avoid compound questions that ask the client to answer two or more questions; for example, "How many cars were in the intersection and when was the first time you saw the blue car?" Ask your questions one at a time.

Do Not be Judgmental Never be judgmental toward a client. Saying things like "You really need to get a grip on yourself," "You are acting like a child," or "You can't mean that" is the opposite of being empathetic, which is what you ideally want to be. Avoid questions that begin with "Why did you . . . ?" This type of question might be viewed as judgmental and may make the client feels defensive.

Never Say "You Have a Great Case" Be very careful about judging the client's case. Do not make any promises to the client and never tell the client what a great case he or she has, since this may be bordering on giving legal advice. At this stage you do not have enough information to make that determination. Lawsuits are usually too complex for this type of statement.

Leave Fee Discussions to the Attorney Discussions regarding whether the firm is going to take the case and discussions about the amount of the fee should be left to the attorney.

Close the Interview Appropriately   Do not close the interview too quickly. Before you close, be sure to do the following:

- Get copies of all the documentation that the client brought.

- Instruct the client not to discuss the case with anyone else.

- Reassure the client by telling him or her exactly what your office will be doing and when it will be done. For example: "I will draft a memo to the attorney, our office will do some preliminary legal research, and this will be completed by Friday. Our office will call you on Friday to set up an appointment for early next week." Never tell the client that "the attorney will get back to you as soon as he can." Clients want to know exactly what is going to happen and when it is going to happen.

- Get the client's e-mail address.

- Review your checklist to make sure you have obtained all the information you need.

- Have the client sign any release or authorization you might need to get information, such as a medical release for the client's files from a doctor or hospital.

- List everything the client did *not* bring with him or her. Give a copy of the list to the client with a self-addressed return envelope.

- Thank the client for coming into the office, reassure the client that you will be in contact with him or her shortly, and instruct the client that, if they remember anything else that is important, to be sure to give you a call. Give the client your business card.

Summary

Attorneys have an ethical duty to communicate with their clients, and paralegals can play an active role in this process. This duty includes informing client of the status of his or her case, responding to a client's request for information in a timely manner, explaining the law and the benefits and risks of alternative courses of action, and notifying and communicating settlement offers, among other things.

Attorneys and paralegals must also foster positive relationships with clients. This includes knowing your client, treating each client like they are your only client, sending copies of documents to clients, responding to client phone calls immediately, being courteous and professional to clients, giving clients periodic status reports, and preserving client confidences. When resolving client complaints, it is imperative that you listen to the client and forward the complaints to the attorney.

Clients are also demanding the use of technology in the ways legal services are provided. This includes e-mail, attachments, extranets, electronic billing, and more. In dealing with difficult clients, it is important to stay calm and maintain professionalism, document conversations with the client, be courteous but maintain an "arm's-length" posture, and keep the attorney informed.

Attorney and paralegal work is largely based on communication; communication is the transfer of a message from a sender to a receiver.

Any time you communicate, you must be prepared to work through communication barriers, such as noise, terminology differences, background differences, different competence levels, and many other factors. In enhancing communication, a person should consider the timing and the context of the message; do not be judgmental, use rephrasing, and ask questions.

Attorneys and paralegals must also work in group settings. Communicating in a group is different from communicating one on one with another person. Groups take longer to make decisions, tend to make better quality decisions, but can also fall into groupthink, where the desire for group cohesiveness and consensus becomes stronger than the desire for the best possible decision.

Client interviews must be conducted properly. Strategies for conducting a good client interview include preparing for the interview in advance, using an icebreaker to open the interview, clearly informing the client that you are a paralegal, listening carefully, taking notes and organizing the information, asking appropriate questions, and closing the interview.

Key Terms

communication	groupthink
communication barrier	noise
feedback	rephrasing

Practical Applications

1. The executive director of a legal aid office calls you in to advise that he has received complaints from clients regarding paralegals and other staff members being less than courteous on the phone and in person. The executive director gives you one week to begin turning this situation around. He mentions on his way out the door that, in addition to a short-term solution, he wants a long-term solution to the problem. How would you proceed?

2. The executive committee at a medium-sized law office thinks there should be more emphasis on client services. You are a respected part of the firm and the committee thinks you interact with clients exceptionally well. The committee has approved the development of a client manual that will be given to all of its clients. The committee has chosen you to be in charge of developing the manual in the initial stages.

Your task is to prepare a client manual that will be presented to the executive committee within 30 days. In addition, once the committee approves the manual, you also will be in charge of implementing its use. The committee is giving you control over researching and developing the manual.

Assume you have never heard of or developed a client manual before. Assume you can choose to either accept the task or not. Would you accept the assignment? Why or why not? How would you develop the client manual? Would you choose to use a work group or not? What sections or key points would you include in the manual? Give reasons for your answers.

3. As a paralegal in a busy office, you try your best to talk to clients when they call and to pass along information from the client to your supervising attorney, but sometimes you forget. On one such occasion, a client called you because she was unable to talk to the attorney. The client called with vital information that the attorney needed regarding an important aspect

of the case. Unfortunately, you failed to pass the information along. Discuss from an ethics and malpractice standpoint the importance of communication skills.

4. Think about a group or committee that you have worked on. Write down the dynamics of how the group interacted. Who emerged as the leader, and why? Looking back, do you see any evidence of groupthink? Did the group members communicate with each other effectively? Was the group successful at accomplishing its purpose? Why or why not? Did you feel like an active member of the group? Why or why not? If you could have changed one thing about the group, what would that have been?

On the Web Exercises

1. Go to the ABA Center for Professional Responsibility, find the ***ABA Model Rules of Professional Conduct***, and read and print out ***Rule 1.4*** Communication and the accompanying comment.

Depending on your class instructions, access your NSLT subscription to conduct assignments in CLIO. You may also be assigned direct activities in CLIO based on the course structure. CLIO is a web-based office management program that has a free subscription for 365 days. It is a fully functional program and can either be worked on independently or set up by the course instructor to have an integrated CLIO program with your classmates.

Case Review

828 S.E.2d 65 (2019) 419 S.C. 238

Supreme Court of North Carolina.

In re Cornwell Opinion #27864

February 6, 2019 Submitted; April 24, 2019, Refiled.

Case Summary
Overview

HOLDINGS: [1]-The state's highest court accepted an Agreement for Discipline by Consent between an attorney and the South Carolina Office of Disciplinary Counsel disbarring the attorney for violating S.C. App. Ct. R. 407:1.1, 1.3, 1.4, 1.5, 1.15(a), 1.15(b), 1.15(c), 1.16, 3.3(a), 3.4(c), 8.1(a), 8.1(b), 8.4(a) and 8.4(e), S.C. App. Ct. R. 417:1, 2, 3 and 6, and S.C. App. Ct. R. 413:7(a)(1); [2]-The attorney failed to keep his clients reasonably informed as to the status of their cases and to respond to reasonable requests for information; [3]-He failed to respond to initial notices of investigation and Treacy letters; [4]-He failed to respond timely to requests for information from the Court; [4]-He improperly used his trust account, wrote a check from his trust account on insufficient funds, and did not maintain accurate records as required by the rules for financial recordkeeping.

Outcome
Agreement accepted. **Attorney disbarred.**

Opinion
PER CURIAM: In this attorney disciplinary matter, respondent and the Office of Disciplinary Counsel (ODC) have entered into an Agreement for Discipline by Consent (Agreement) pursuant to

Rule 21, RLDE, Rule 413, SCACR. In the Agreement, respondent admits misconduct and consents to a three-year suspension or disbarment. We accept the Agreement and disbar respondent from the practice of law in this state, retroactive to the date of his interim suspension. [FN2] The facts, as set forth in the Agreement, are as follows.

FN2. Respondent was placed on interim suspension on February 17, 2017. In re Cornwell, 419 S.C. 238, 797 S.E.2d 395 (2017).

Facts
Matter I

After being appointed to represent a client in a post-conviction relief (PCR) matter, respondent failed to keep his client reasonably informed of the status of the matter and failed to respond to reasonable requests for information.

Matters II, IV, VI, & VIII[FN3]

Respondent was appointed or retained to represent various clients in PCR matters. During respondent's representation of the clients in Matters II, IV, and VI, respondent failed to keep the clients reasonably informed as to the status of their cases. In Matters VI and VIII, respondent failed to respond to the clients' reasonable requests for information.

Additionally, in Matters II, IV, and VIII, respondent failed to respond to the initial notices of investigation (NOI) and to the *Treacy* [FN4] letters from ODC seeking responses to the complaints. [FN5] In Matter VI, respondent initially failed to respond to the

NOI but later filed a written response to the NOI upon a written inquiry from ODC.

FN3. Respondent appeared before ODC and answered questions on the record as they related to Matters III, IV, V, VI, and VIII.

FN4. In re Treacy, 277 S.C. 514, 290 S.E.2d 240 (1982).

FN5. Regarding Matter II, respondent called ODC about a different matter and ODC informed him that it was waiting for his response to this matter. Respondent stated he had not received a NOI or Treacy letter. ODC resent the NOI and received a response a week later.

Matter III

Although the underlying complaint in this matter was ultimately determined to be without merit, respondent failed to respond to the NOI.

Matter V

In February 2013, respondent was appointed to represent a client in a PCR matter. Following an adverse ruling at an evidentiary hearing, the client mailed a letter seeking an appeal to an incorrect address for respondent. Respondent asserts he did not receive the client's letter. The client later mailed a letter to this Court requesting an appeal and attached a copy of the original letter he sent to respondent. This Court forwarded a copy of the client's request to respondent. Respondent contends he first learned of the request for an appeal when he received this Court's letter. However, respondent did not contact the client or serve the requested notice of appeal.

Additionally, respondent did not respond to the NOI or the Treacy letter from ODC seeking a response.

Matters VII & IX

Respondent was appointed to represent clients in PCR matters, but failed to respond to the clients' requests for information regarding their cases. Additionally, in Matter IX, respondent failed to keep the client reasonably informed as to the status of the case. Both clients' PCR actions were dismissed and they filed pro se notices of appeal.

After receiving the pro se notice of appeal in Matter VII, this Court mailed respondent a letter requesting the date on which respondent received written notice of the order of dismissal of the client's PCR matter. Respondent failed to respond. The Court then directed respondent to respond by January 15, 2016, and to include an explanation as to why he failed to respond initially. Respondent eventually responded to the Court's inquiries but failed to provide the date on which he received written notice of the dismissal of the client's PCR matter. The Court again requested the information and gave respondent ten days to respond. Respondent failed to respond to the Court's inquiry, and the Court dismissed the appeal without prejudice.

After receiving a pro se notice of appeal in Matter IX, this Court notified respondent and requested that he provide an explanation as required by Rule 243(c), SCACR. Respondent informed the Court that he had been relieved as counsel. After determining that respondent had not been relieved as counsel, the Court sent respondent another letter requesting he provide the required explanation. Respondent did not respond within the fifteen-day timeframe. Thereafter, the Court, by order dated September 22, 2016, requested respondent provide a written explanation within ten days of the Court's order. On October 14, 2016, the Court received respondent's explanation, which it found insufficient under Rule 243(c), SCACR. The Court then required respondent to file a response that complied with HN1 Dennison v. State, 371 S.C. 221, 639 S.E.2d 35 (2006) (allowing counsel to inform the Court if counsel is unable to set forth an arguable basis for asserting the PCR court's determination was improper). Respondent did not respond within the ten-day timeframe. The Court relieved respondent as counsel and directed Appellate Defense to represent the client.

Matter X

Respondent was appointed to represent a client in a PCR matter, and a hearing was conducted on April 14, 2015. After the hearing, the client requested a copy of his PCR transcript from respondent and that an order be drafted regarding the hearing. Respondent did not respond to the client's requests.

ODC sent respondent a NOI, followed by a Treacy letter, to which respondent did not respond. Thereafter, ODC sent respondent a notice of additional allegations and requested a response within fifteen days. Respondent did not respond. [FN6]

FN6. Respondent appeared before ODC and answered questions on the record.

Matter XI

In May 2016, respondent was retained to represent a client in a domestic relations action. Respondent failed to (1) adequately communicate with the client regarding the status of the case; (2) comply with reasonable requests for information; and (3) respond to the client's request for a refund of his fee after terminating respondent's representation. In response to the allegations, respondent asserts he did not return the fee because the case was a flat rate case and he had earned the fee. While respondent contends he drafted documents on the client's behalf, he never entered a notice of appearance on behalf of the client or filed any documents on the client's behalf.

Additionally, there was conflicting language in the fee agreement regarding when the fees were due to be paid by the client and when the fees would be treated as earned. The fee agreement also did not include language notifying the client that he might be entitled to a partial or full refund if the agreed-upon legal services were not provided.

Matter XII

In November 2015, BB&T informed ODC that a check was presented against insufficient funds on respondent's trust account. ODC mailed a NOI to respondent requesting the following: (1) a written response; (2) checks related to the overdraft; (3) copies of his bank statements; (4) documentation that funds were fully restored to the trust account; and (5) a complete copy of his trust account reconciliation. Respondent did not respond.

Thereafter, ODC sent respondent a Treacy letter via certified mail to his address on file with the Attorney Information System. However, the letter was returned as unclaimed. ODC later received a response, which failed to include the information requested in the NOI. ODC then subpoenaed BB&T for copies of respondent's bank statements relating to his trust account. Upon ODC's review of the statements, ODC discovered respondent's trust account contained withdrawals for several items made payable to cash as well as payments for personal expenses.

In response, respondent asserted the trust account was set up only for the deposit of a settlement for one case and any additional deposits into the trust account were from earned fees. However, respondent admits he improperly used his trust account. Respondent cannot demonstrate that the funds in his trust account were handled properly because he did not maintain accurate records as required by the rules for financial recordkeeping.

Law

Respondent admits that by his conduct he has violated the following provisions of the Rules of Professional Conduct, Rule 407, SCACR: Rule 1.1 (competence); Rule 1.3 (diligence); Rule 1.4 (communication); Rule 1.5 (fees); Rule 1.15(a) (safeguarding client property); Rule 1.15(b) (commingling funds); Rule 1.15(c) (keeping of unearned legal fees in trust account); Rule 1.16 (declining or terminating representation); Rule 3.3(a) (making a false statement of fact or law to a tribunal or failing to correct a false statement of material fact or law previously made to the tribunal by the lawyer); Rule 3.4(c) (disobeying an obligation under the rules of a tribunal); Rule 8.1(a) (knowingly making a false statement of material fact in connection with a disciplinary investigation); Rule 8.1(b) (failing to respond to a demand for information from a disciplinary authority); Rule

8.4(a) (violating the Rules of Professional Conduct); and Rule 8.4(e) (engaging in conduct prejudicial to the administration of justice).

Respondent further admits he violated the following rules regarding Financial Recordkeeping, Rule 417, SCACR: Rule 1 (financial recordkeeping); Rule 2 (client trust account safeguards); Rule 3 (requiring Rule 1 records to be readily accessible to the lawyer); and Rule 6 (precluding cash withdrawals from trust accounts).

Respondent also admits his conduct constitutes grounds for discipline under the following provision of the RLDE: Rule 7(a)(1) ("It shall be a ground for discipline for a lawyer to: (1) violate or attempt to violate the Rules of Professional Conduct, Rule 407, SCACR, or any other rules of this jurisdiction regarding professional conduct of lawyers . . . .").

Conclusion

We accept the Agreement and disbar respondent from the practice of law in this state. Respondent is ordered to enter into a payment plan with the Commission on Lawyer Conduct to pay the costs incurred in the investigation and prosecution of these matters within thirty (30) days of the date of this opinion. Respondent is also ordered to complete the Legal Ethics and Practice Program Law Office Management School and Trust Account School prior to seeking reinstatement.

Additionally, prior to seeking reinstatement, respondent must demonstrate his compliance with Rule 33, RLDE, Rule 413, SCACR (reinstatement following a definite suspension for nine months or more or disbarment), including completion of Legal Ethics and Practice Program Ethics School within the preceding year.

Within fifteen (15) days of the date of this opinion, respondent shall file an affidavit with the Clerk of Court showing that he has complied with Rule 30 of Rule 413, SCACR, and shall also surrender his Certificate of Admission to the Practice of Law to the Clerk of Court.

Disbarred

BEATTY, C.J. KITTREDGE, HEARN, FEW and JAMES, JJ., concur.

Case Review Exercises

1. Were you surprised at the number and depth of the violations with which the respondent was charged?

2. What could have the respondent done to avoid the sanction?

3. Do you believe disbarment was the appropriate sanction for the respondent? Explain your answer.

Helpful Web Sites

Organization	Description	Internet Address
Alabama State Bar—Law Office Management Assistance Program	Articles on a variety of law office management topics, including a manual on how to keep clients.	https://www.alabar.org/programs/lawpracticemanagement/
ABA Law Practice Management	ABA Web site devoted to law practice management issues and concerns, including management publications, articles, and resources.	http://www.abanet.org/lpm
Paralegal Today	National magazine for paralegals. The Web site has limited information but the magazine itself is full of useful articles, including ethical issues related to paralegals.	http://www.americanbar.org/groups/paralegals
Maryland State Bar Association—Law Practice Management Assistance	The Web site has a wide variety of law office management topics, including using client surveys, tips for enhancing client relations, how to select clients, and much more.	http://www.msba.org
National Association of Legal Assistants—Paralegals	Contains many resources for legal assistants and paralegals.	http://www.nala.org
National Federation of Paralegal Associations	National association for paralegals. Contains many resources for paralegals.	http://www.paralegals.org

Suggested Reading

1. *Law Practice* magazine, published by the American Bar Association Law Practice Management Section. http://www.abanet.org.

2. *Paralegal Today* magazine, published by Conexion International Media, Inc. http://www.paralegaltoday.com.

3. Foonberg, J. (2004). *How to Start and Build a Law Practice*. American Bar Association.

4. Ewalt, H. (2008). *Through the Client's Eyes: New Approaches to Get Clients to Hire You Again and Again* (3rd ed.). American Bar Association.

Legal Fees, Timekeeping, and Billing

5

Chapter Objectives

After you read this chapter, you should be able to:

- Differentiate between timekeeping and billing.

- Identify the major types of legal fee agreements.

- Differentiate between billable and nonbillable time.

- Explain the billing process and value process.

- Differentiate between an earned and an unearned retainer.

When a New York–based law firm submitted its bill of $675,000 in fees, the client refused to pay. The law firm was hired to handle bankruptcy matters involving one of the client's companies. Despite being disqualified to represent the bankruptcy entity due to a conflict of interest, the law firm continued to work behind the scenes and charged the client fees of $675,000 for additional services. When the firm sued the client, he filed a counterclaim alleging he had overpaid and was overbilled for services that were unnecessary, duplicative, and wasteful.

***

During discovery, incriminating e-mails were uncovered that reflected the law firm's bill churning practice. Among those e-mails was the infamous "Churn that bill, baby!" e-mail that was acknowledged by the law firm. The counterclaim filed by the client requested return of the previous fee payment in the amount of $776,000.00 and punitive damages of $22.5 million against the law firm for their alleged wrongdoings. A confidential stipulation was reached.

Source: *DLA Piper, LLP (US) v. Adam Victor*, Index #650374/2012, State of New York, County of New York (filed February 9, 2012).

Understanding the Difference Between Timekeeping and Billing

timekeeping
The process of tracking time for the purpose of billing clients.

billing
The process of issuing invoices for the purpose of collecting monies for legal services performed and being reimbursed for expenses.

In the legal environment, **timekeeping** is the process of tracking time for the purpose of billing clients. The obvious reason private attorneys and paralegals keep track of their time is to bill clients. However, many corporate, government, and legal services/aid practices also keep time records for other reasons. Timekeeping can be used to manage and oversee what cases attorneys and paralegals are working on and whether they are spending too much or too little time on certain cases; it can be used to evaluate the performance of attorneys and paralegals and to help determine promotions and raises; and it also can be used to evaluate what types of cases are the most beneficial and profitable for the office.

Billing is the process of issuing invoices for the purpose of collecting monies for legal services performed and being reimbursed for expenses. The lifeblood of any organization depends on its ability to raise cash and be paid for the services it renders. In most cases, private law practices must be able to generate billings on at least a monthly basis to generate the cash they need to meet their expenses, such as rent, utilities, and salaries. Attorneys and paralegals in corporate and government practices also need to know about billing to ensure that when they hire outside counsel (private law firms), the corporation or government gets the most for its money.

Why the Legal Team Needs to Know Timekeeping and Billing

There are several reasons why members of the legal team need to know about timekeeping and billing. In most private law practices, attorneys and paralegals are required to track their time so it can be charged to the case(s) on which they are working. Most law practices require attorneys, associates, paralegals, and law clerks to bill a minimum number of hours during the year. It is important to remember that private law firms are fundamentally businesses, and like any business, their function is to make money, operate at a profit, and earn money for their owners. Therefore, the billing of time to a firm's clients is crucial to its operations and success as a business. Recent surveys found that attorneys were often expected to bill between 33 and 44 hours per week (1700 and 2300 annually) and paralegals were expected to bill between 26 and 40 hours a week (1352 and 2080 annually). Thus, it is necessary for both attorneys and paralegals to understand how timekeeping and billing works. Sometimes attorneys and paralegals will be discharged from their jobs because they fail to bill the required number of hours. The issue of tracking time and billing a minimum number of hours is very important in many offices.

Many times, paralegals are put in charge of actually running the timekeeping and billing system, including managing the timekeeping process and generating bills. This usually occurs in smaller law offices. In those cases, it is important for paralegals not only to know the process but also to know how to actually run and operate the system. Timekeeping and billing are important issues because the survival of law offices depends on their ability to track and bill time. However, before exploring the fundamentals of timekeeping and billing in depth, you first need a background in legal fee agreements, legal expenses, and trust accounts.

Kinds of Legal Fee Agreements

Legal fees can be structured in many different ways. The kind of legal fee depends on the type of case or client matter, the specific circumstances of each particular client, and the law practice's preference toward certain types of fee agreements. Fee agreements can be hourly rate fees, contingency fees, flat fees, retainer fees, and others.

Hourly Rate Fees

An **hourly rate fee** is a fee for legal services that is billed to the client by the hour, at an agreed-upon rate. For example, suppose a client hires an attorney to draft a business contract. The client agrees to pay $250 for every hour the attorney spends drafting the contract and advising the client. If the attorney spent four hours working on the contract, the client would owe the attorney $1000 ($250 × 4 hours equals $1000).

One of the frustrations for clients regarding legal professionals billing by the hour is that a client has no idea what the total cost of the matter will be. Exhibit 5-1 contains a fee projection worksheet for a case in litigation. Using a tool like this at the beginning of a matter, a client can get an idea what the total cost will be.

Hourly rate agreements can be complicated. Law offices have several specific types of hourly rate contracts, including the following:

- Attorney or paralegal hourly rate
- Client hourly rate
- Blended hourly rate fee
- Activity hourly rate

Some law practices use a combination of these to bill clients.

Attorney or Paralegal Hourly Rate   The **attorney** or **paralegal hourly rate** is based on the attorney's or paralegal's level of expertise and experience in a particular area; Exhibit 5-2 is an example of this type of contract. If a partner or shareholder worked on a case, his or her hourly rate charge might be considerably more than that of an associate or a paralegal's hourly rate charge. Partners typically can earn from $200 to $500 per hour. Paralegals typically charge from $60 to $100 per hour. The difference in price is based on the expertise of the individual working on the case and on locally acceptable rates. In this type of fee agreement, it is possible for a client to be billed at several different rates in a given period if several attorneys or paralegals work on a matter, because they all may have different rates.

hourly rate fee
A fee for legal services that is billed to the client by the hour at an agreed-upon rate.

attorney or paralegal hourly rate
Fee based on the attorney's or paralegal's level of expertise and experience in a particular area.

Exhibit 5-1 Fee Projection Worksheet

Adams & Lee Law Firm **Worksheet—Fee Projection (Civil Litigation)**

Date: _____

Case: _____

Billing Rate		Partner	Associate	Paralegal
		$300	$200	$80
No.	Activity Description	Partner Hours	Associate Hours	Paralegal Others
A.	Initial File Work			
B. C.	Strategic Conference			
D. E.	Factual/Background Investigation Initial Legal			
F.	Research			
G.	Litigation – Lawsuit /Complaint/Answer/ Counterclaim Motions (Nondiscovery)			
H.	Interviews (Parties; Witnesses)			
	Discovery			
	i. Drafting Interrogatories			
	ii. Answering Interrogatories			
	iii. Drafting Discover Requests			
	iv. Reviewing Produced Documents & E-Discovery			
	v. Responding to Document Requests			
	vi. Opposing Party Depos			
	vii. Our Depos			
I.	Motions (Discovery)			
J.	Additional Legal Research			
K.	Motions (Substantive)			
L.	Pretrial Memoranda/Conference			
M.	Settlement Conference			
N.	Trial (includes preparation days and actual trial days)			
O.	Miscellaneous phone calls/strategy			
	Total Hours			
	TOTAL PROJECTED FEES			

Based on: Calloway & Robertson (2002). Winning alternatives to the billable hour (p. 214). American Bar Association.

Exhibit 5-2 Attorney/Paralegal Hourly Rate Contract

HOURLY RATE CONTRACT FOR LEGAL SERVICES

This contract for legal services is entered into by and between Ginger Rogers (hereinafter "Client") and Adams & Lee (hereinafter "Attorneys") on this _____ day of December, 202_. The following terms and conditions constitute the entirety of the agreement between Attorneys and Client and said agreement supersedes and is wholly separate and apart from any previous written or oral agreements.

1. Client hereby agrees to employ Attorneys and Attorneys hereby agree to represent Client in connection with a contract dispute in New Case County District Court of Clients claim against XYZ Corporation.

2. Client agrees to pay a retainer fee of **$10,000.00**, which will be held in Attorney's trust account until earned.

3. Client agrees to pay associate attorneys at **$200** per hour, partners at **$300** per hour, paralegals at **$80** per hour and senior paralegals at **$100** per hour for legal services rendered

(continued)

(continued)

regarding the matter in paragraph one. Attorneys are not hereby obligated to take an appeal from any judgment at the trial court level; if an occasion for an appeal arises, Attorneys and Client hereby expressly agree that employment for such an appeal must be arranged by a separate contract between Attorneys and Client.

4. Client agrees to reimburse Attorneys for all expenses incurred in connection with said matter; and Client agrees to advance all expenses requested by Attorneys during the duration of this contract. Client understands that he is ultimately responsible for the payment of all expenses incurred in connection with this matter.

5. Client understands that Attorneys will bill Client periodically (usually on a monthly or quarterly basis, depending on how quickly the case moves through the system) for copying costs at the rate of $.25 cents per copy, postage and handling costs, long-distance telephone costs, travel costs, and other costs, and that Client is obligated to make payments upon said billing for said fees and expenses described at paragraphs (2), (3), and (4) above, or otherwise satisfy said fees and expenses. Attorneys will also bill Client for all deposition costs incurred and Client is solely responsible for said deposition costs and Client will be required to advance the sum of $2,500 (or more as necessary) for trial costs (including subpoenas, travel costs, and preparation costs) once the case is set for trial.

6. Client understands and agrees that this litigation may take two to five years or longer to complete and that he will make himself available for Attorneys to confer with and generally to assist Attorneys in said matter. Client agrees he will not discuss the matter of his litigation with any unauthorized person at any time or in any way. Client understands and agrees that Attorneys may withdraw from representation of Client upon proper notice. Client further understands that he can apply for judicial review and approval of this fee agreement if he so desires.

7. Client agrees that associate counsel may be employed at the discretion of Attorneys and that any attorney so employed may be designated to appear on Client's behalf and undertake Client's representation in this matter and such representation shall be upon the same terms as set out herein. **Client understands that Attorneys cannot and do not guarantee any particular or certain relief and expressly state that they cannot promise or guarantee Client will receive any money damages or money settlement.**

The undersigned hereby voluntarily executes this agreement with a full understanding of same and without coercion or duress. All agreements contained herein are severable and in the event any of them shall be deemed to be invalid by any competent court, this contract shall be interpreted as if such invalid agreements or covenants were not contained herein. Client acknowledges receiving a fully executed copy of this contract.

_____

Date

_____

Date   LAW FIRM OF ADAMS & LEE

NOTE: THIS IS ONLY AN EXAMPLE AND IS NOT INTENDED TO BE A FORM; CHECK WITH YOUR STATE BAR FOR A PROPER FORM.

Client Hourly Rate   The **client hourly rate** method is based on one hourly charge for the client, regardless of which attorney works on the case and what he or she does on the case. For example, if an insurance company hires a law practice to represent it, the insurance company and the law practice might negotiate a client hourly charge of $225 for attorneys and $85 for paralegals. This means that no matter which attorney or paralegal works on the case, whether the attorney or paralegal has 1 year or 20 years of experience, and regardless of what the attorney or paralegal does (e.g., making routine phone calls or appearing in court), the insurance company would be charged $225 per hour for attorney time or $85 per hour for paralegal time.

client hourly rate
Fee based on one hourly charge for the client, regardless of which attorney works on the case and what he or she does on the case.

blended hourly rate fee

An hourly rate that is set taking into account the blend or mix of attorneys working on the matter.

Blended Hourly Rate Fee   A **blended hourly rate fee** is an hourly rate that is set taking into account the blend or mix of law office staff working on the matter. The "blend" includes the mix among associates, partners, and (sometimes) paralegals working on the matter. Some states only allow the "blend" to include associates and partners, while other states allow paralegals to be included. Billing is simpler, because there is one rate for all paralegal and attorney time spent on the case. The bill is thus easier for the law office to produce and easier for the client to read. Some states will allow paralegals to have their own "blend" and have one rate for all paralegals, whether experienced or inexperienced.

activity hourly rate

Fee based on the different hourly rates, depending on what type of service or activity is actually performed.

Activity Hourly Rate   An **activity hourly rate** is based on the different hourly rates, depending on what type of service or activity is actually performed. For example, offices using this approach might bill attorney time to clients as follows:

Court appearances	$300 per hour
Legal research by attorneys	$225 per hour
Drafting by attorneys	$200 per hour
Telephone calls by attorneys	$150 per hour
Legal research by paralegals	$85 per hour
Drafting by paralegals	$80 per hour

This is sliding-scale hourly fee based on the difficulty of an activity. Hourly rate agreements, no matter what the type, are the most common kind of fee agreement.

Contingency Fees

contingency fee

Fee collected if the attorney successfully represents the client.

A **contingency fee** is a fee that is collected if the attorney successfully represents the client. The attorney is entitled to a certain percentage of the total amount of money awarded to the client. If the client's case is not won, and no money is recovered, the attorney collects no legal fees but is still entitled to be reimbursed for all expenses incurred (see Exhibit 5-3). Contingency fees are typically used in representing plaintiffs in personal injury cases, workers' compensation cases, employment cases, medical malpractice, and other types of cases in which monetary damages are generated. The individual who would like to bring the lawsuit usually has little or no money to pay legal fees up front. Contingency fees typically range from 20% to 50%.

Exhibit 5-3 Contingency Fee Contract

CONTINGENCY FEE CONTRACT FOR LEGAL SERVICES

Date:

Name: D.O.B.

Address: Phone:

1. I hereby employ **Adams & Lee** (hereinafter "attorneys") to perform legal services in connection with the following matter as described below: Personal injury claims arising out of an automobile accident which occurred January 15, 2022, on Interstate I-55.

2. I agree to pay a nonrefundable retainer fee of $2,500 plus

---

(continued)

(continued)

3. I agree attorneys will receive <u>20%</u> of any recovery, if prior to filing suit.

   I agree attorneys will receive <u>25%</u> of any recovery, if prior to pretrial conference.

   I agree attorneys will receive <u>33%</u> of any recovery, if after first trial begins.

   I agree attorneys will receive <u>40%</u> of any recovery, if after appeal or second trial begins.

   Attorneys are not hereby obligated to take an appeal from any judgment at the trial court level; if an occasion for an appeal arises, attorneys and client hereby expressly agree that employment for such an appeal will be arranged by a separate contract between these parties. Further, I agree that attorneys will be entitled to the applicable above-mentioned percentage of recovery minus whatever a court may award, if I am a prevailing party and the court awards fees following my request therefor.

4. As to the expenses of litigation, I agree to reimburse attorneys for all expenses incurred in connection with said matter, and any expenses not fully paid as incurred may be deducted from my portion of any recovery. I agree to advance any and all expenses requested by attorneys during the duration of this contract. I agree to make an advance of expenses upon execution of this contract in the amount of <u>$1,500</u>. I understand that these litigation expenses do not pertain to the retainer fee or percentage of any recovery, and I am ultimately responsible for the payment of all litigation expenses.

5. I understand that attorneys will bill client periodically, and that client is obligated to make payments upon said billing for said fees and expenses described at paragraphs (2) and (4), or otherwise satisfy said fees and expenses.

6. I understand and agree that this litigation may take two to five years (or longer) to complete, and that I will make myself available for attorneys to confer with, and generally to assist attorneys in said matter. I will not discuss the matter of my litigation with an unauthorized person at any time in any way. I understand and agree that attorneys may withdraw from representation of client at any time upon proper notice.

7. I agree that associate counsel may be employed at the discretion of ADAMS & LEE, and that any attorney so employed may be designated to appear on my behalf and undertake my representation in this matter and such representation shall be upon the same terms as set out herein. Attorneys have not guaranteed, nor can they guarantee, any particular or certain relief.

The undersigned herewith executes this agreement with a full understanding of same, without coercion or duress, and understands the same to be the only agreement between the parties with regard to the above matter, and that if any other terms are to be added to this contract, the same will not be binding, unless and until they are reduced to writing and signed by all parties to this contract. I acknowledge receiving a fully executed copy of this contract. Further, the undersigned Client understands that said Client is entitled to apply for judicial review and approval of this fee agreement, if Client so desires.

_____

Date

_____

Date   LAW FIRM OF ADAMS & LEE

NOTE: THIS IS ONLY AN EXAMPLE AND IS NOT INTENDED TO BE A FORM; CHECK YOUR STATE BAR FOR A PROPER FORM.

For example, suppose a client hires an attorney to file a personal injury claim regarding an automobile accident the client was in. The client has no money but agrees to pay the attorney 20% of any money that is recovered (plus legal expenses) before the case is filed, 25% of any money that is recovered after the case is filed but before trial, 33% of any money recovered during trial, and 40% after appeal or second trial. Suppose the claim is settled after the case is filed but before trial for $10,800. Suppose, also, that the legal expenses the attorney incurred were $800. Under most state laws, legal expenses are paid first and then the contingency fee is calculated. The attorney would deduct the expenses off the top and the remaining $10,000 would be divided according to the contingency fee agreement. Because the suit was settled after the case was filed but before the trial, the attorney would be entitled to receive 25% of any recovery. The attorney would be entitled to $2500 and the client would be entitled to 75%, or $7500 (see Exhibit 5-4).

Contingency fee agreements must be in writing. Exhibit 5-3 contains a sample contingency fee contract. Some states put a cap or a maximum percentage on what an attorney can collect in areas such as workers' compensation and medical malpractice claims; for example, some states prevent attorneys from receiving more than a 25% contingency in a workers' compensation case. Contingency fees, by their nature, are risky—if no money is recovered, the attorney receives no fee. However, even if no money is recovered, the client must still pay legal expenses, such as filing fees and photocopying. Contingency fees and hourly fees also may be used together; some offices reduce their hourly fee and charge a contingency fee.

Exhibit 5-4 Contingency Fee Example

Written Contingency Fee Agreement Provisions
Attorney receives

- 25% of any money recovered (plus legal expenses) before case is filed.
- 33% of any money recovered (plus legal expenses) after case is filed or during trial.
- 40% of any money recovered (plus legal expenses) after trial or second trial begins.

Settlement
Case is settled for $10,800 after case is filed, but before trial.
Attorney has $800 worth of legal expenses.

Calculation of Contingency Fee

1. Legal expenses are paid first.

Settlement of	$10,800
Minus legal expenses	−800
Balance	$10,000

2. Contingency fee is calculated as follows:

Total recovery minus legal expenses		$10,000
Attorney's 25% contingency fee	($10,000 × 25% = $2500)	−2500
	TOTAL TO CLIENT	$7500

3. Total fees and expenses to attorney

Reimbursement of legal expense		$800
Contingency fee		$2500
	TOTAL TO ATTORNEY	$3300

Flat Fee

A **flat fee** is a fee for legal services that is billed as a flat or fixed amount. Some offices have a set fee for handling certain types of matters, such as preparing a will or handling an uncontested divorce, a name change, or a bankruptcy (see Exhibit 5-5). For example, suppose a client agreed to pay an attorney a flat fee of $500 to prepare a will. No matter how many hours the attorney spends preparing the will, the fee is still $500. Flat fee agreements are usually used when a legal matter is simple, straightforward, and involves few risks.

Exhibit 5-6 shows a comparison of different methods of billing for drafting a routine or standard will. Flat rates will typically be the least expensive for the client in routine matters. In addition, flat rates and the blended methods are typically the easiest types of bills to both prepare and read.

Retainer Fees

The word "retainer" has several meanings in the legal environment. Generally, retainer fees are monies paid by the client at the beginning of a case or matter. However, there are many types of retainers. When an attorney or a paralegal uses the term "retainer," it could mean a retainer for general representation, a case retainer, a pure retainer, or a cash advance. In addition, all retainer fees are either earned or unearned.

flat fee
A fee for legal services that is billed as a flat or fixed amount.

Exhibit 5-5 Flat Fee Price List

⌐ **PRICE LIST** ⌐

Initial Consultation with Branch Lawyer.............$100.00

REAL ESTATE

Divorce - Uncontested...................................1000.00
Domestic contracts and family litigation vary according to time involved.

REAL ESTATE

Purchase or Sale of House............................1000.00
Each Mortgage—Additional............................300.00
Each Discharge of Mortgage—Additional..........200.00
Refinancing...700.00

WILLS & ESTATES

Basic Will..500.00
Estates, administrations, and estate litigation vary according to time involved

BUSINESS

Consultation..200.00
Incorporation...2000.00
We provide many other business services, including:
- *Commercial Leases*
- *Purchase and Sale of Businesses*
- *Trade Marks & Copyright*

ADDITIONAL SERVICES

Collection—demand letter.............................200.00
Notarization (per signature)...........................20.00
Power of Attorney / Promissory Note.................50.00

⌐ **PAYMENT POLICY** ⌐

We require a retainer before commencing work on your behalf, which amount is paid into trust. We then draw checks on the retainer to pay out-of-pocket expenses made on your behalf and our fees.

We will advise you of completion of our services to you and ask you to come in and pick up the documentation involved and pay any balance owing at the same time.

In real estate transaction the balance must be paid prior to closing. In litigation and criminal matters, any outstanding account and the estimated fee for the appearance must be paid prior to the court appearance.

ETHICAL NOTE: Even if the firm has a price list, matters involving fees should be limited to discussions with the attorneys and their clients.

Exhibit 5-6 Comparison Legal Fees to Prepare a Will

Activities Provided:

1. Paralegal interviews client (office conference) regarding the law office drafting a will for client.

    Paralegal gets background information including financial holdings, heirs, family tree, etc. .... 1.50 hours

2. Paralegal drafts memo to associate attorney, itemizing the conference with client .... 0.25 hours

3. Associate attorney reads the paralegal's memo and talks with client on the telephone .... 0.25 hours

4. Associate attorney conducts legal research and prepares a draft of the will that meets the expectations of the client .... 0.50 hours

5. Associate confers with senior partner regarding the will .... 0.50 hours

6. Client reviews will, holds office conf. with associate attorney, associate attorney discusses client's changes to the will, makes client's changes to the will, and the will is executed, witnessed, and notarized .... 1.0 hours

    TOTAL HOURS .... 4.0 hours

- CLIENT HOURLY RATE

Assume attorney agrees to charge the client to prepare the will for his/her time as follows:

- $275 per hour for all attorney's time
- $90 per hour for his/her paralegal's time

TOTAL COST $845.00

(Paralegal 1.75 hours × $90 = $157.50; Attorney 2.50 × $275 per hour = $687.50; $157.50 + $687.50 = $845.00)

- ATTORNEY/PARALEGAL HOURLY RATE
- Assume the senior partner's normal hourly rate is $350.
- Assume the associate attorney's normal hourly rate is $250.
- Assume the paralegal's normal hourly rate is $80.

TOTAL COST $752.50

(Paralegal 1.75 hours × $80 per hour = $140; Associate attorney 1.75 hours × $250 per hour = $437.50; Senior partner 0.50 hour × $350 per hour = $175; $140 + $437.5 + $175 = $752.50)

- **BLENDED (Attorneys and Paralegal) HOURLY RATE**
- Assume blended hourly rate for all attorney and paralegal time is $175 per hour.

TOTAL COST $700 (4 hours × $175 per hour = $700).

ACTIVITY HOURLY RATE

Assume:

- Paralegal office conference rate is $70 per hour and for attorney is $200 per hour.
- Paralegal time for drafting memo is $80 per hour and for attorney is $225 per hour.
- Attorney time for phone conferences is $150 per hour.
- Attorney time for drafting pleadings, will, legal research, and conferring with other partners is $225 per hour.

TOTAL COST $587.50

1.5 × $70 = $105; 0.25 × $80 = $20; 0.25 × $150 = $37.50; 0.50 × $225 = $112.5; 0.50 × $225 = $112.50, 1.0 × $200 = $200; Total $587.50

FLAT FEE RATE

Assume attorney and client agree on a flat rate of $500 to prepare the will.

TOTAL COST $500.00

CONTINGENCY RATE $0.00 (No monetary recovery—not applicable)

Earned v. Unearned Retainers   There is a very important difference between an earned retainer and an unearned retainer. An **earned retainer** means that the law office or attorney, who has earned the money, is entitled to deposit it in the office's or attorney's own bank account, and can use it to pay the attorney's or law office's operating expenses, such as salaries, immediately upon deposit.

For example, suppose an attorney agrees to take a products liability case on a contingency fee basis but requires that the client pay a nonrefundable (earned) retainer of $2000. The attorney drafts a contract and both parties sign it; the contract clearly states that the $2000 is nonrefundable. The earned, nonrefundable retainer is an incentive for the attorney to accept the case on a contingency basis. The attorney may deposit the $2000 in his or her law office checking account and pay operating expenses out of it. This is an example of a case retainer, which is discussed in more detail later in this section.

An **unearned retainer** is money that is paid up front by the client as an advance against the attorney's future fees and expenses as a kind of down payment. Until the monies are actually earned by the attorney or law office, they belong to the client. According to ethical rules, unearned retainers may not be deposited in the attorney's or law office's normal operating checking account; unearned retainers must be deposited into a separate trust account and can be transferred into the firm account as it is earned.

For example, suppose a business client wants to sue his or her insurance company for failing to pay a claim submitted by the business. The business signs a contract with the attorney to pay a (unearned) retainer of $10,000. The contract states that the $10,000 will be held in trust and paid to the attorney as the attorney incurs fees and properly bills the client. This is an example of a cash advance retainer, which is covered in more detail in the next section.

A **trust** or **escrow account** is a separate bank account, apart from a law office or an attorney's operating checking account, where unearned client funds are deposited. Client trust accounts are covered in detail in Chapter 6. As an attorney or a law office begins to earn an unearned retainer by providing legal services to the client, the attorney can then bill the client and move the earned portion from the trust account to his or her own law office operating account.

The written contract should set out whether the retainer is earned or unearned. However, in some instances the contract may be vague on this point. Typically, when a contract refers to a "nonrefundable retainer," this means an earned retainer.

Additionally, flat fee rates, as discussed earlier, are said to be "nonrefundable" in many contracts, and thus are treated as earned. However, some state ethical rules regulate this area heavily and hold that all flat fees are a retainer, have been unearned, and must be placed in trust until they are earned. Whether a retainer is earned or unearned will depend on your state's ethical rules and on the written contract.

Cash Advance Retainer   One type of retainer is a **cash advance**, unearned monies that act as an advance against the attorney's future fees and expenses. Until the cash advance is earned by the attorney, it actually belongs to the client. The cash advance is a typical type of unearned retainer.

Suppose a client wishes to hire an attorney to litigate a contract dispute. The attorney agrees to represent the client only if the client agrees to pay $200

earned retainer
Term for the money the law office or attorney has earned and is entitled to deposit in the office's or attorney's own bank account.

unearned retainer
Monies that are paid up front by the client as an advance against the attorney's future fees and expenses. Until the monies are actually earned by the attorney or law office, they belong to the client.

trust or escrow account
A separate bank account, apart from a law office's or an attorney's operating checking account, where unearned client funds are deposited.

cash advance
Unearned monies that are the advance against the attorney's future fees and expenses.

187

per hour with a $2500 cash advance against fees and expenses. The attorney must deposit the $2500 in a trust account. If the attorney deposits the cash advance into his or her own account (whether it is the firm's account or the attorney's own personal account), the attorney has violated several ethical rules. As the attorney works on the case and bills the client for fees and expenses, the attorney will write himself or herself a check out of the trust account for the amount of the billing. The attorney must tell the client that he or she is withdrawing the money, and keep an accurate balance of how much the client has left in trust. If the attorney billed the client for $500, the attorney would write himself a check for $500 from the trust account, deposit the $500 in the attorney's or the firm's own bank account, and inform the client that there was a remaining balance of $2000 in trust. If the case ended at this point, the client would be entitled to a refund of the remaining $2000 in trust. Look closely at the payment policy in Exhibit 5-5; the firm retainer requires a cash advance before it will take any case.

Retainer for General Representation   Another type of retainer is a **retainer for general representation**. This type of retainer is typically used when a client such as a corporation or entity requires continuing legal services throughout the year. The client pays an amount, typically up front or on a prearranged schedule, to receive these ongoing services. For example, suppose a small school board would like to be able to contact an attorney at any time with general legal questions. The attorney and school board could enter into this type of agreement for a fee of $5000 every six months; the school board could contact the attorney at any time and ask general questions; and the attorney would never receive more than the $5000 for the six-month period. Retainers for general representation allow the client to negotiate and anticipate what his or her fee will be for the year. This type of agreement usually only covers general legal advice and would not include matters, such as litigation (see Exhibit 5-7). Depending on the specific arrangements between the client and the attorney, and on the specific ethical rules in your state, many retainers for general representation are viewed as being earned because the client can call at any time and get legal advice. Retainers for general representation resemble a flat fee agreement. The difference is that in a flat fee agreement, the attorney or law office is contracted to do specific work for a client, such as prepare a will or file a bankruptcy. In the case of a retainer for general representation, the attorney is agreeing to make himself or herself available to the client for all nonlitigation needs.

Case Retainer   Another type of retainer is a **case retainer**, which is a fee that is billed at the beginning of a matter, is not refundable to the client, and is usually paid to the office at the beginning of the case as an incentive for the office to take the case. As an example, say that a client comes to an attorney with a criminal matter. The attorney agrees to take on the case only if the client agrees to pay a case retainer of $2000 up front plus $200 per hour for every hour worked on the case. The $2000 is paid to the attorney as an incentive to take the case and, thus, is earned. The $200 per hour is a client hourly basis charge. Because the case retainer is earned, the attorney can immediately deposit it in the office's own bank account.

retainer for general representation
Retainer typically used when a client such as a corporation or entity requires continuing legal services throughout the year.

case retainer
A fee that is billed at the beginning of a matter, is not refundable to the client, and is usually paid at the beginning of the case as an incentive for the office to take the case.

A case involving a contingency fee presents another example of a case retainer. Suppose a client comes to an attorney to file a civil rights case. The attorney agrees to accept the case only if the client agrees to a 30% contingency fee and a nonrefundable or case retainer of $2000. Again, the earned retainer is an incentive for the attorney to take the case and can be deposited in the attorney's or the office's own bank account.

Exhibit 5-7 Retainer for General Representation Agreement

Ms Ginger Rogers, Chairperson
New Case School District School Board

Subject: General Representation of the NCSD School Board

Dear Ms Rogers:

Thank you for your letter informing us that the School Board would like to place our law firm on a general retainer of $ _____ for the coming year. We will bill on a quarterly basis for the retainer plus any expenses incurred.

The retainer will include general advice concerning business operations, personnel questions, legislative initiative, and attendance at all board meetings. It will not cover litigated matters requiring appearances at boards or commissions, court, or state administrative agencies. Should any of the excluded services appear to be necessary, we shall be happy to discuss the cost of these services with you.

It is our hope that the knowledge that we are ready to serve you under the retainer will provide you with regular advice to avoid any serious problems or litigation. Please sign this letter and return it to us. If you have any questions, please feel free to give me a call.

Kindest Regards,
James Adams
ADAMS & LEE

Accepted for New Case School District School Board by:
_____
Ginger Rogers, Chairperson

Pure Retainer A rather rare type of retainer is a **pure retainer**; a pure retainer obligates the law office to be available to represent the client throughout the agreed-upon time period. The part that distinguishes a pure retainer from a retainer for general representation is that the office typically must agree to not represent any of the client's competitors or to undertake any type of adverse representation to the client.

Retainers for general representation, case retainers, and pure retainers are usually earned retainers; a cash advance is an unearned retainer. However, the language of the contract will determine whether amounts paid to attorneys up front are earned or unearned. The earned/unearned distinction is extremely important, and it is one reason all fee agreements should be in writing.

Court-Awarded Fees

Court-awarded fees are another type of fee agreement. In certain federal and state statutes, the prevailing party (i.e., the party that wins the case) is given the right to recover from the opposing side reasonable attorney's fees. The amount of the attorney's fees is decided by the court; thus, these are called

pure retainer
A fee that obligates the office to be available to represent the client throughout the time period agreed upon.

court-awarded fees
Fees given to the prevailing parties pursuant to certain federal and state statutes.

court-awarded fees. Court-awarded fees are provided for in civil rights law, antitrust, civil racketeering, and in many other instances and statutes as well. The prevailing party must submit to the court, detailed time records showing specifically how much time was spent on the case. If the prevailing law office does not keep such records, the court will not award fees. The purpose of court-awarded fees is to encourage potential plaintiffs in public interest issues to pursue legitimate claims while discouraging frivolous claims. For example, if an employee brings a sexual harassment suit against an employer and subsequently wins the suit, the employee's attorneys would be entitled to receive reasonable attorney's fees from the defendant.

Prepaid Legal Services

prepaid legal services
A plan that a person can purchase that entitles the person to receive legal services either free or at a greatly reduced rate.

A prepaid legal service plan is another type of fee agreement. **Prepaid legal services** is a plan that a person can purchase, which entitles the person to receive legal services (as enumerated in the plan) either free or at a greatly reduced rate. In some cases, corporations or labor unions, for example, provide a prepaid legal service plan to their employees as a fringe benefit. For instance, if a person who is a member of a prepaid legal service plan needs a will drafted, that person would go to either an attorney employed by the prepaid plan—or a private attorney with whom the prepaid plan contracted—and get the will drafted free of charge or at a greatly reduced rate.

Value Billing

Over time, there have been plenty of discussions about why private law practices should stop billing by the hour and use a different billing method instead. The arguments for the change from hourly billing include the following:

- During any stage of the work, the client never knows the total amount they will be charged for legal fees.
- Clients sometimes avoid calling paralegals and attorneys, even it is a simple phone call, because they know they will be charged for the time.
- Clients have trouble seeing the relationship between what is performed by the paralegal or attorney and the enormous fees that can be generated.
- Hourly billing encourages lawyers and paralegals to be inefficient (i.e., the longer it takes to perform a job, the more revenue they earn).
- Many law offices force attorneys and paralegals to bill a quota number of hours a year, which puts a tremendous amount of pressure on the individual paralegal and attorney.

value billing
A type of fee agreement that is based not on the time spent to perform the work but on the basis of the perceived value of the services to the client.

So, what is value billing? The **value billing** concept represents a type of fee agreement that is based not on the time required to perform the work but on the basis of the perceived value of the services to the client. Value billing typically provides that the attorney and client reach a consensus on the amount of fees to be charged. Because of increased competition in the legal environment and because of the power of the client as a buyer, clients are demanding that they have a say in how much they are going to pay for legal services, what type of service will be provided, and what the quality of the legal notice services will be for the price.

The Ethics of Timekeeping and Billing

There are more timekeeping- and billing-related ethical complaints filed against attorneys and law offices than all other types of complaints; thus, attorneys and paralegals should completely understand the ethics of timekeeping and billing. In past years, timekeeping and billing complaints were viewed simply as "misunderstandings" between the client and the law office. Recently, state bars have viewed timekeeping and billing disputes as having major ethical implications for attorneys; that is, such disputes were simply not misunderstandings, but law offices were sometimes flagrantly violating ethical rules regarding money issues.

Billing from the Corporate and Government Perspective

Corporate and governmental law practices sometimes hire outside counsel (private law offices). **Outside counsel** refers to when corporate and government law practices contract with private law offices (i.e., outside of the corporation or government practice) to help them with legal matters, such as litigation, specialized contracts, stock/bond offerings, and so forth. Thus, corporate and government law practices are purchasers of legal services and tend to look at billing from a different perspective.

Corporate and government law practices are concerned with limiting the costs of legal fees. Many corporate clients will state that they will not pay more than a certain amount—perhaps $200 per hour—for any attorney, regardless of experience. If the office wants to maintain the particular client, it will agree to the terms. Because corporations and governments have access to large sums of money and typically are good-paying clients, many offices will reduce their price to get and keep the business.

Corporate and government clients usually require very detailed bills to control costs and what is being done on the case; in some cases, corporations and governments use a competitive bidding process to select outside counsel. Thus, summary billings are usually not accepted. They also will typically limit the type and cost of expenses that are billed to them. For instance, some corporations require that computerized legal research (Westlaw, LexisNexis, etc.), postage, fax costs, and similar expenses be borne by the office.

It is not uncommon for a corporate law practice to publish policies and guidelines covering exactly what outside counsel will charge, when it will charge, how payments will be made, how much and what type of legal expenses will be reimbursed, and so on. Exhibit 5-8 shows the top 10 reasons corporate law departments fail to pay private law offices.

Timekeeping and billing complaints by clients can lead not just to ethical complaints against attorneys; such complaints may also turn into criminal fraud charges filed against attorneys and paralegals.

Ethical Considerations Regarding Legal Fee Agreements

There are several important ethical considerations that need to be stressed about fee agreements. The first is that all fee agreements should be in writing, especially when a contingency fee is involved. Second, contingency fees should not be used in criminal- or domestic-relation matters.

outside counsel
Term referring to when corporate and government law practices contract with law offices (i.e., outside of the corporation or government practice) to help them with legal matters, such as litigation, specialized contracts, stock/bond offerings, and so forth.

Fee Agreements Should Be in Writing

It is highly recommended that, as a matter of course, all fee agreements be in writing. The days of a handshake cementing an agreement between an attorney and a client are long over. There is no substitute for reducing all fee agreements to writing. If the firm and the client have a dispute over fees, the document will clarify the understanding between the parties.

Exhibit 5-8 Reasons Why Corporate Law Departments and Government Legal Departments May Refuse to Negotiate on Legal Bills

Reason	Explanation
Legal services are below standard	The legal services provided were below standard or did not meet the needs of the corporate client. Corporate law departments typically attempt to negotiate down the fees. In these instances, the corporate law department staff must take the time to correct the problems, even though they paid to have it done correctly.
Too many attorneys and paralegals working the case	When multiple timekeepers attend the same deposition or bill for the same work provided, the costs rise quickly. Many corporate law departments try to set limits on the number of timekeepers working on a case at one time. Also, if the attorneys or paralegals who are working on the case change, the client must pay for the new attorneys or paralegals to get up to speed.
Billing lacks detail	Most law departments want to see detailed reports of how timekeepers spent their time and not just "for legal services provided."
Billing is incomplete	A bill does not include previous payments made or is otherwise incomplete.
Billing has numerical errors	The bill does not add up, or wrong billing rates are used.
Sticker shock	The corporate law department expects a bill for $5000 and receives a bill for $25,000.
Attorneys and paralegals conferencing with each other frequently	It is frustrating for a client to receive a bill where attorneys and paralegals are frequently meeting to discuss strategy or otherwise, because this greatly increases the client's bill. This is particularly frustrating for the client when the bill does not say why the staff members working on the case were meeting.
Billing sent to the wrong person	Sending the bill to the wrong person can be frustrating in a large corporation. The bill can literally get lost inside the corporation unless the bill is sent to the correct person.
Billing every little thing	Clients strongly dislike being billed for every five-minute phone call, being billed for the time it takes to prepare the bill itself, or other items that—in the big picture—do not amount to much.
Being billed for another case	Occasionally, a client is billed for time spent on another case. This undermines the whole billing process.
Billing is received late	Corporate clients become frustrated when they receive a bill for services that were delivered five months ago. Not only is the billing late, but it is difficult to remember that far back as to the details of the service.

Rule 1.5(b) regarding the rules of professional conduct states that an attorney is required to provide a client with the rate for fees and expenses along with the basis for charging those rates and communicate the scope of representation. The rule recommends but does not require the communication be written.

Although the rules of professional conduct state that the agreement should "preferably" be in writing, nearly every authority on this subject, as well as most attorneys, will tell you that the agreement absolutely should be in writing to protect both the attorney and the client. Legal fee agreements should be in writing for the following reasons:

1. Clients file more ethical complaints against attorneys and law offices for fee disputes than for any other type of complaint.
2. The client and the attorney may (will) forget what the exact fee agreement was, unless it is reduced to writing.
3. In a factual dispute regarding a fee between a client and an attorney, the evidence is typically construed in the light most favorable to the client.

Contingency Fee Agreement Must Be in Writing   When a contingency fee is involved, most jurisdictions state that the agreement *shall* be in writing for the office to collect the fee. *Rule 1.5(c)* regarding the rules of professional conduct state that the contingency fee agreement must be in writing, state the contingency fee arrangement, along with client responsible expenses and how the expenses will be deducted, and the client must sign the agreement. It also requires the attorney to give the client a final written statement specifically explaining the recovery amount, how it was determined, and the allocation of the monies received.

Even the *Model Rules* makes a distinction between contingency agreements and other types of fee agreements and requires that contingency agreements be in writing. It must be in writing because, in many cases, large sums of money are recovered, and the difference between 20% and 30% may be tens of thousands of dollars. Contingency agreements are risky for the attorney, and they simply must be reduced to writing so that the client and the attorney know what the proper percentage of fees should be. It is also important that the contingency agreement state, and the client understand, that even if there is no recovery in the case, the client must still pay for expenses.

No Contingency Fees in Criminal and Domestic-Relation Proceedings in Some Jurisdictions   Many jurisdictions prohibit contingency fees in criminal and domestic-relation proceedings as a matter of public policy. *Rule 1.5(d)* regarding the rules of professional conduct specifically states that an attorney shall not enter into a contingency fee arrangement regarding domestic relations or criminal matters. For example, suppose that an attorney agrees to represent a client in a criminal matter. The client agrees to pay the attorney $10,000 if the client is found innocent, but the attorney will receive nothing if the client is found guilty. This is an unethical contingency fee agreement; contingency fees in these types of cases appear to be against the public policy and should be prohibited.

Only a "Reasonable" Fee Can Be Collected

No matter what the contract or legal fee agreement is with a client, it is important to keep in mind that attorneys and paralegals can only receive a "reasonable" fee. Unfortunately, there is no absolute standard for determining reasonableness, except that reasonableness will be determined on a case-by-case basis.

Rules 1.5 regarding the rules for professional conduct along with cases on the subject have provided numerous factors to consider in determining reasonableness regarding fees. These factors include the following:

- the amount of time and labor required;
- the novelty or difficulty of the issues raised;
- the skill required to perform the legal services;
- the acceptance of the case and whether it would preclude the attorney from taking other cases;
- the local "going rate" or fee customarily charged in the area for the services performed;
- the end result of the case (how successful the representation was);
- the time limitations imposed by the client or by the circumstances;
- the professional relationship with the client, including past dealings or history with the client;
- the experience of the attorney;
- the attorney's reputation and/or the ability of the lawyer (or lawyers) performing the services;
- the type of fee agreement, including whether the fee was fixed or contingent.

Notably, courts have found certain fee amounts unreasonable, such as a $22,500 fee, pursuant to a written agreement for a real estate matter that was not unduly complex and involved very little time for the attorney.

For many years, it was thought that overbilling and stealing from clients by attorneys was only done by sole practitioners and attorneys in small firms. However, court rulings on this subject indicate these practices happen at all levels.

In John Grisham's modern classic, The Firm, Avery Tolar advises the young lawyer Mitchell McDeere on how to charge clients, explaining that the client should be charged for "every minute spent even thinking about a case." It was this philosophy that got the legal team into trouble. Unethical billing practices do not only exist in legal novels like The Firm but have been a pervasive problem in law firms across the country.

James Dougherty, a Florida attorney was disbarred for five years after turning in padded bills for an insurance investigation and overcharging a client by more than $2 million. The Court found that Dougherty overbilled by $300,000 for his own work, by $1.2 million for the work of his associates, and by over $1.2 million for expenses. The court held that "[f]ederal felony convictions for wire fraud by overbilling [the] client ... warranted disbarment for five years."

— The Florida Bar v. Dougherty, 769 So.2d. 1027 (Fla. 2000).

Many State Bars' Rules Provide for Oversight/Arbitration on Fee Issues

One of the ways that state bar associations and courts have dealt with the abundance of fee disputes is to provide for immediate and informal review/arbitration of fee disputes. Many state ethical and court rules provide that clients have the right, at any time, to request that the judge in the case or an attorney representing the state bar review the reasonableness of the attorney's fees. The attorney is required to inform the client of this right in many states; in those states, the judge or attorney hearing the matter has the right to set the fee and determine what is reasonable under the particular facts and circumstances of the case.

Fraud and Criminal Charges

Intentionally overbilling clients for work not done is called "fraud." You can be criminally prosecuted by government officials and civilly prosecuted by your clients.

Charging an unreasonable fee is no longer simply a matter of ethics. Recently, attorneys and paralegals have been criminally charged with fraud for intentionally recording time and sending bills for legal services that were never provided. **Criminal fraud** is a false representation of a present or past fact made by the defendant, upon which the victim relies, resulting in the victim suffering damages.

Criminal charges for fraud are not filed against attorneys and paralegals when there is simply a disagreement over what constitutes a reasonable fee. Criminal charges are filed when an attorney or a paralegal acts intentionally to defraud clients. This usually happens when the attorney or paralegal bills for time when he or she did not really work on the case, or in instances in which the office intentionally billed a grossly overstated hourly rate far above the market rate.

Interestingly, many of the most recent criminal cases being brought are against well-respected large and small law offices specializing in insurance defense and corporate work. Some insurance companies and corporations, as a matter of course when a case has been concluded, hire an audit firm or independent attorney to go back and audit the firm's billing and files to be sure they were billed accurately. In some instances, these audits have concluded that intentional criminal fraud has occurred and have been referred to prosecutors where criminal charges have been filed. No matter what type of firm is involved, intentionally overstating bills can lead to very big problems.

Ethical Problems

There are several difficult ethical problems with no definite solutions regarding timekeeping and billing that need to be explored. The rule in answering ethical questions such as these is to use your common sense and notions of fairness and honesty.

Billing More Than One Client for the Same Time, or "Double Billing" A situation happens from time to time in which a paralegal or an attorney has the opportunity to bill more than one client for the same time period. For instance,

criminal fraud
A false representation of a present or past fact made by a defendant.

while you are monitoring the opposing side's inspection of your client's documents in case A, you are drafting discovery for case B. Another example is while traveling to attend an interview with a witness in case A, you work on case B.

If you were the client, would you think it fair for the attorney to charge full price for travel time related to your case while billing another case? A reasonable approach is to bill only the case on which you are actively working on, split the time between the cases, or bill the case you are actively working on at the regular hourly rate and bill the case you are inactively working on at a greatly reduced rate. Be fair and honest; your clients, as well as judges and others looking at the time, will respect you for it.

When Billing by the Hour, Is There an Ethical Obligation to Be Efficient? Does the Firm Have to Have a Form File in Lieu of Researching Each Document Each Time? Must an Office Use a Computer to Save Time? These types of ethical questions are decided on a case-by-case basis. Billing by the hour rewards people who work slowly, since the more slowly they work, the more they are paid.

Common sense says that if you were the client, you would want your legal staff to be efficient and not to "milk" you for money. The real issue is whether the attorney or paralegal acted so inefficiently and charged so much—when compared with what a similar attorney or paralegal with similar qualifications would charge in the same community—that the fee is clearly unreasonable. When a judge rules on the reasonableness of fees, there is no doubt that he or she will consider what a reasonably efficient attorney or paralegal in the same circumstances would have charged. Use your common sense and be honest and efficient, because someone in your office might have to justify your time and charges someday.

Should You Bill for Clerical or Secretarial Duties? Law offices cannot bill clients for clerical or secretarial tasks, because these tasks are viewed as overhead costs or are considered a normal part of doing business. An easy but unethical way to bill more hours is for a paralegal to bill time to clients for clerical functions such as copying documents or filing material. Paralegals clearly should not bill for these types of clerical tasks; paralegals bill time for professional services, not for clerical functions.

This issue was addressed in the U.S. Supreme Court case of *Missouri v. Jenkins*, 491 U.S. 274, 109 S.Ct. 2463, 105 L.Ed. 2d 229 (1989). The Court found that when paralegals perform professional level work, these hours are recoverable as "attorney's fees," but services that are merely clerical or secretarial cannot be billed. The Court held

> It has frequently been recognized in the lower courts that paralegals are capable of carrying out many tasks, under the supervision of an attorney that might otherwise be performed by a lawyer and billed at a higher rate. Such work might include, for example, factual investigation, including locating and interviewing witnesses; assistance with depositions, interrogatories, and document production; compilation of statistical and financial data; checking legal citations; and drafting correspondence .... Of course, purely clerical or secretarial tasks should not be billed at a paralegal rate, regardless of who performs them. (p. 288)

If you are unsure about whether a task is clerical, ask your supervising attorney or record the time initially, point it out to the supervising attorney, and let him or her decide.

Should You Bill for the Mistakes of the Law Office? This is another tough problem. People make mistakes all the time. Clients generally feel that they should not have to pay for mistakes, since the reason they went to an attorney was to get an expert to handle their situation. This is a decision that should be left to every law office to decide, but generally the practice of billing for mistakes should be discouraged.

Must a Task Be Assigned to Less-Expensive Support Staff When Possible? Common sense and efficiency will tell you that tasks should be delegated as low as possible. Clients should not have to pay for attorney time when the task could be completed by an experienced paralegal. In addition, this practice is more profitable to the law office because higher paid persons are free to do tasks for which they can bill clients at their normal rates.

Legal Expenses

In addition to recovering for legal fees, law practices are also entitled to recover from the client reasonable expenses incurred by the office in representing the client. For example, in Exhibit 5-9, the office needed to make copies of a motion to compel and mail them to opposing counsels. The cost of making the copies of the motion and mailing them out is directly related to the case, so the office is entitled to be reimbursed from the client for this expense. In most offices, it is important that the client is billed for the expense either through manual records, as in Exhibit 5-9, or some type of computerized or automated system. Such expenses typically include the costs of photocopying documents, postage, long-distance telephone calls, or travel expenses (see Exhibit 5-10).

The expenses alone can run into the tens of thousands of dollars in cases involving litigation. Therefore, the careful tracking of expenses is no trivial matter. Consider the revenues that would be generated if you billed copies at 25 cents and the office made 80,000 copies a year directly related to clients; this would be $20,000. Consider also the additional overhead an office would have if it did not bill clients for the copies.

As a paralegal, you may be required to pay expenses for a case out of your own pocket from time to time. If this happens, be sure to ask for receipts. It also helps to know in advance what specific expenses the office will reimburse you for before they are incurred.

Exhibit 5-9 Expense Slip

Adams & Lee
Expense Slip

Expense Type & Code

1 Photocopies	4 Filing Fees	7 Facsimile	10 Travel
2 Postage	5 Witness Fees	8 Lodging	11 Overnight Delivery
3 Long Distance	6 Westlaw/LexisNexis	9 Meals	12 Other _____

Exhibit 5-10 Expenses Typically Billed to Clients

Court reporter fees (deposition transcripts)
Delivery charges (FedEx, etc.)
Expert witness fees
Facsimile costs
Filing fees
Long-distance phone calls
Photocopying
Postage
Travel expenses
Westlaw/LexisNexis
Witness fees

Timekeeping

Timekeeping is the process of tracking what attorneys and paralegals do with their time. Although this might seem like an incredibly easy task, it is not. Timekeeping is a necessary evil in most law practices. Keeping careful time records is important both for managerial reasons and for producing income.

From a managerial perspective, time records (1) provide the office with a way to monitor the progress of a case, who is working on the case, and/or who is responsible for the matter; (2) allow the office to determine which cases are the most profitable; and (3) allow office management to monitor the efficiencies of law practice staff.

From an income-producing perspective, time records (1) allow offices to bill their time to clients and (2) allow the office to document its fees in probate matters and in cases where legal fees will be decided by a court.

Notice that managerial reasons could apply to any type of law practice, including corporate, government, or legal services/aid. It is also not uncommon for corporate, government, and legal services/aid practices to be given court-awarded attorney's fees from time to time.

Exhibit 5-11 is an example of a manual time sheet. A **time sheet** or **time slip** is where legal professionals record detailed information about the legal services they provide to each client. Timekeeping entries must contain information, such as the name of the case, the date the service was provided, and a description of the service.

Manual Timekeeping

There are many different types of manual timekeeping methods that can be purchased from most legal law office supply catalogs. The time slips are recorded chronologically and are completed by different billing people within the office for a variety of different cases. At some point, typically once a week, the time slips are turned in to the billing department by everyone in the office. Each individual slip can be separated and is often designed with adhesive on the back. Each slip is separated and stuck to each client's time-slip

time sheet or time slip
A record of detailed information about the legal services professionals provide to each client.

page (see Exhibit 5-12); this provides a convenient method for tracking time for each client. All clients' time-slip pages can be stored in a three-ring notebook in alphabetical order by client name, or stored in each individual client's accounting file.

It is important to point out that time records do not automatically get charged to clients. The supervising attorney in the case typically reviews the time records turned in and determines whether they will be charged as is, or whether the time should be adjusted upward or downward. It should also be noted that it is common to have clients with more than one matter pending. Separate records need to be kept for each matter, and typically, separate invoices are generated. Most manual timekeeping systems are being replaced with computerized methods, even in very small law firms.

Computerized Timekeeping

Nearly all timekeeping and billing computer programs can aid in keeping track of time. In some programs, the user enters what case is being worked on and whether the time is billable or nonbillable and then turns the "meter" on. The computer keeps track of the time until the user is completed with the project for that client. The computerized time slip is then stored in the program until a bill is generated. When a bill is generated, the computerized time slip is automatically calculated and included in the client's bill.

Exhibit 5-11 Typical Manual Time Slip/Time Record Form

PC—Phone Conference	R—Review
LR—Legal Research	OC—Office Conference
L—Letter	T—Travel
D—Dictation	CT—Court Hearing

Time Conversion
6 Minutes = .1 Hour   36 Minutes = .6 Hour
12 Minutes = .2 Hour   42 Minutes = .7 Hour
15 Minutes = .25 Hour 45 Minutes = .75 Hour
18 Minutes = .3 Hour   48 Minutes = .8 Hour
24 Minutes = .4 Hour   54 Minutes = .9 Hour
30 Minutes = .5 Hour   60 Minutes = 1.0 Hour

Date	Client/Case	File No.	Services Performed	Attorney	Time Hours	& Tenths
6-18-22	Jones v. United Sales	18294	Summarized 6 depositions; Client; Δ (Defendant) Heler; Δ Barnes, Δ Rosalie; Witness Forham & Johns	JBD	6.	5
6-19-22	Marcel v. Greer Oil	18003	PC w/Client Re: Settlement offer; Discussions w/Attorney; Memo to file Re: offer	JBD	.	3
6-19-22	Jolly v. State	18118	PC w/Client's Mother, PC w/Client; LR Re: Bail; Memo to file; R correspondence	JBD	.	75
6-19-22	Potential claim of Walters v. Leslie Nursery	Not Assigned Yet	OC w/Client; (New client); Reviewed facts; Received medical records Re; accident; Conf. w/atty	JBD	1.	50
6-19-22	Jones v. United Sales	18294	Computerized searches on depositions for attorney	JBD	.	75
9-5-22	Jay Mahoney Bankruptcy	18319	PC w/Creditor, Capital One; Memo to file; Client; LJ to Client	JBD	.	3

(continued)

(continued)

9-5-22	Potential Claim of Walters v. Leslie Nursery	—	LR Slip & Fall cases generally; Standard of care	JBD	1.	00
9-5-22	Marcel v. Greer Oil	18003	Conf. w/atty. & Client Re: Settlement; Drafted & prepared LJ to Δ's Re: Settlement offer	JBD	1.	10
9-5-22	Jay Mahoney Bankruptcy	18319	Drafted Bankruptcy petition; OC w/Client; List of Debts; Fin. Stmt; Conf. w/atty	JBD	1.	00
9-5-22	Jones v. United Sales	18294	Drafted and prepared depo notice to Witness Autumn	JBD	.	25
9-5-22	Seeley Real Estate Matter	18300	Ran amortization schedule to attach to 'Contract for Deed'	JBD	.	25

Exhibit 5-12 Time Sheet Record for a Case

Time Records for Case Name: __Jones v. United Sales__   Case No: __18294__

6-19-22	Jones v. United Sales	18294	Summarized 6 depositions; Client; Δ (Defendant) Heler; Δ Barnes, Δ Rosalie; Witness Forham & Johns	JBD	6.	5
6-19-22	Jones v. United Sales	18294	Computerized searches on depositions for attorney	JBD	.	75
9-5-22	Jones v. United Sales	18294	Drafted and prepared depo notice to Witness Autumn	JBD	.	25

Billable versus Nonbillable Time

billable time
Actual time that a paralegal or an attorney spends working on a case and that is directly billed to a client's account.

nonbillable time
Time that cannot be directly billed to a paying client.

One of the basics of timekeeping is the difference between billable and nonbillable time. **Billable time** is actual time that a paralegal or an attorney spends working on a case and that is directly billed to a client's account. Any activity that an attorney or a paralegal performs further to a client's case, other than clerical functions, is usually considered billable time, including interviewing witnesses, investigating a case, serving subpoenas, performing legal research, drafting, and so forth. **Nonbillable time** is the time that cannot be directly billed to a paying client. Nonetheless, it should still be tracked.

There are typically three types of nonbillable time:

(1) general firm activities

(2) personal time

(3) pro bono work

General firm activities refer to time spent on personnel materials, planning, marketing, client development, staff/committee meetings, library mainte-nance, and professional development. Personal time refers to taking breaks, cleaning and organizing, and taking sick/vacation days. **Pro bono** work is legal services that are provided free of charge to a client who is not able to pay for the services. Pro bono may be required by your firm or by some state bars. Typically, pro bono cases are taken to generate goodwill in the community for the office or to provide a community service. Although handling pro bono cases is a morally proper thing to do, it is still counted as nonbillable time.

Nonbillable time is sometimes referred to as "overhead" or "office hours" because the cost of nonbillable time must be paid for by the office. **Overhead** refers to general administrative costs of doing business; they are incidental costs regarding the management and supervision of the business. Overhead includes costs such as rent, utilities, phones, office supplies, equipment, and salary costs for administrators who manage the business and others. Overhead costs are sometimes defined as any cost not directly associated with the production of goods or services.

pro bono
Legal services that are provided free of charge to a client who is not able to pay for the services.

overhead
General administrative costs of doing business, including costs such as rent, utilities, phone, and salary costs for administrators.

Recording Time

Many law offices have a preoccupation with the billable hour concept and set billable hour quotas that attorneys and paralegals must meet. The minimum number of billable hours depends greatly on the location and size of the law office and on the types of cases it handles.

There are several different ways to record or track your time. One method is to bill time in tenths of an hour, with 0.5 being a half-hour and 1.0 being an hour. Every six minutes is a tenth of the hour, so you would be billing on six-minute intervals. Billing in tenths works out as follows:

0–6 minutes = 0.1 hour

7–12 minutes = 0.2 hour

13–15 minutes = 0.25 hour

16–18 minutes = 0.3 hour

19–24 minutes = 0.4 hour

25–30 minutes = 0.5 hour

31–36 minutes = 0.6 hour

37–42 minutes = 0.7 hour

43–45 minutes = 0.75 hour

46–48 minutes = 0.8 hour

49–54 minutes = 0.9 hour

55–60 minutes = 1.0 hour

As an alternative, some offices will bill using a quarter of an hour as the basis, as follows:

0–15 minutes = 0.25 hour

16–30 minutes = 0.50 hour

31–45 minutes = 0.75 hour

46–60 minutes = 1.0 hour

Although the quarterly basis is easier to use, it is not as accurate as the tenth-of-an-hour system. Suppose you took a five-minute phone call from a client and your average billing rate is $80 per hour. Using the tenth of an hour system, the fee for the phone call would be $8 (0.1 hour $\times$ $80 equals $8). However, using the quarterly system, the fee for the phone call would be $20.00, since 0.25 is the smallest interval (0.25 $\times$ $80 equals $20.00), or more than twice as much.

It is important that you include as much detail as possible when completing your time records, that the language be clear and easily understood, and that the time record itself be legibly written. Clients are usually more willing to pay a bill when they know exactly what service was performed for them. For example, compare these general bill statements.

1. "Telephone conference—0.50 hour $40.00."
2. "Telephone conference with client on Plaintiff's Request for Production of Documents regarding whether or not client has copies of the draft contracts at issue—0.50 hour $40.00."

Which of these statements would you rather receive?

Many clients would prefer the latter, since they are able to see, and hopefully remember, exactly what specific services they received.

Timekeeping Practices

If attorneys on average are required to bill between 1700 and 2300 hours per year, and paralegals are required to bill between 1400 and 1800 hours a year, it is very important that he or she take the timekeeping function extremely seriously. The following are some suggestions to consider regarding keeping track of time.

- *Find out how many hours you must bill annually, monthly, and weekly up front, and track where you are in relationship to the quota*—one of the first things you should do when you start a new paralegal job is to find out how many billable hours you must have. If the office requires that you bill 1400 hours a year, budget this on a monthly and weekly basis, and keep track of where you are so that you will not have to try to make it all up at the end of the year.

- *Find out when time sheets are due*—Another thing you should do when starting a new position is to find out exactly what day time sheets are due so that you can submit them on time.

- *Keep copies of your time sheets*—Always keep a copy of your time sheet or know how to access them electronically for your own file, in case the original is lost or misplaced. Having a record also allows you to go back and calculate your number of billable hours.

- *Record your time contemporaneously on a daily basis*—One of the biggest mistakes you can make is to not record your time as you go along during the day. If you wait until the end of the day to try to remember all the things you did, there is absolutely no way that you will be able to accurately reconstruct everything. In the end, you will be the one suffering, doing work you did not get credit for. So be sure to keep a time sheet handy and fill it out as you go along.

- *Record your actual time spent; do not discount your time*—Do not discount your time because you think you should have been able to perform a job faster. If it took you four hours to finish an assignment and you worked the whole four hours, there is no reason to discount the time. *If the supervising attorneys think a discount is warranted, they can decide that, but it is not up to you to do that.* However, if you made a mistake or had a problem that you do not think the client should be billed for, tell your supervising attorney, and let him or her help you to make the decision.

A daunting task for bankruptcy trustees is preparing a Trustee's Final Account. As a new trustee, it was hard to recall at the end of the day, or that week, the time spent on the cases. Things happen quickly and I am certain that early on, billable time was left out and not compensated. I immediately realized the value of recording time as you go and developed daily time sheets that could later be entered into the computer system to track time and expenses. That is the only way to be accurate.
—Cynthia Traina Donnes

- *Be aware if billable hours are related to bonuses or merit increases*—
  Be aware of how billable hours are used. In some law offices, billable hours are used in distributing bonuses and merit increases and can be used in performance evaluations, so know up front how they will be used.
- *Be ethical*—Always be honest and ethical in the way you fill out your time sheets. Padding your time sheets is unethical and simply wrong. Eventually, wrongdoing regarding timekeeping, billing, or handling client funds will become apparent.
- *Be aware of things that keep you from billing time*—Be aware of things that keep you from having a productive day, such as:
  - People who lay their troubles at your feet or who are constantly taking your attention away from your work. An appropriate approach is to say, "I would really like to hear about it at lunch, but right now I am really busy."
  - Wasted time spent trying to track down other people or trying to find information you need.
  - Constant interruptions, including phone calls. If you really need to get something done, go someplace where you can get the work done, and tell others to hold your calls. However, check in every once in a while, to return client phone calls. Clients should have their phone calls returned as soon as possible.

Billing

To generate the necessary income to operate the firm, special attention must be paid to billing, the process of issuing bills for the purpose of collecting monies for legal services performed and for being reimbursed for expenses.

Billing for Paralegal Time and Profitability

Many law offices bill for paralegal time as well as for attorney time. Clients often prefer this because the paralegal hourly rates are much lower than attorney hourly rates.

For example, assume an associate attorney and a paralegal can both prepare discovery documents in a case and that the task will take seven hours. Assuming the paralegal bills at $80 per hour and the associate bills at $175 per hour, the cost to the client if the paralegal does the job is $560, and the cost if the associate drafts the discovery is $1225. Thus, the client will have saved $665 by simply allowing the paralegal to do the job. The client would still have to pay for the attorney's time to review the paralegal's discovery, but the cost would be minimal. This represents substantial savings to clients.

As mentioned earlier, the question of whether law offices can bill for paralegal time was considered by the U.S. Court in *Missouri v. Jenkins*, 491 U.S. 274 (1989). In that case, the plaintiff was successful on several counts in a civil rights lawsuit and was attempting to recover attorney's fees from the defendant under a federal statute. The statutory language provided that the prevailing party could recover "reasonable attorney's fees" from the other party. The plaintiff argued for recovery for the time that paralegals spent working on the case as well as for the time attorneys spent. The defendant argued that paralegal time was not "attorney's fees." Alternatively, the defendants argued that if they did have to pay something for paralegal time, they should only have to pay about $15 per hour, which represents the overhead costs to the office for a paralegal.

The court found that paralegals carry out many useful tasks under the direction of attorneys and that "reasonable attorney's fees" referred to the reasonable fee for work produced, whether by attorneys or paralegals. The court also found that, under the federal statute, paralegal time should not be compensated as overhead costs to the office but should be paid at the prevailing market rates in the area for paralegal time. The court noted that the prevailing rate for paralegals in that part of the country at that time was about $40 per hour and held that the office was entitled to receive that amount for paralegal hours worked on the case. Thus, it is clear that offices can bill for paralegal time if they choose to do so.

Leveraging and How Hourly Billing Rates Are Determined

leveraging
The process of earning a profit from legal services that are provided by law office personnel (usually partners, associates, and paralegals).

Leveraging is an important concept in law office billing. **Leveraging** is the process of earning a profit from legal services that are provided by law office personnel (usually partners, associates, and paralegals). Leveraging allows the office not only to recover the cost of an attorney or a paralegal's salary but also to pay overhead expenses and even make a profit on each such person. Thus, paralegals are also a profit center for law firms. It is a win–win situation; clients pay lower fees for paralegals over attorneys, and law firms still generate a profit on paralegal time.

Functions of a Successful Billing System

An oft-forgotten aspect of any billing system is that the system must please the firm's customers or clients. A good billing system is determined by whether or not the firm's clients are satisfied with the billings and whether or not they are paying the bills that are sent to them. One quick way a firm can lose a good client is by mishandling the client's money in some way, by overbilling the client, or by giving the client the impression that her or his money is being used unjustly or unfairly. In addition, mishandling a client's money is a top reason that attorneys are disciplined. A good billing system, whether computerized or not, must do several things, including accurately tracking the client's account, providing regular billings, and providing clients with an itemization of the services performed.

Accurately Track How Much a Client Has Paid the Firm   A successful billing system must be able to accurately track how much clients have paid the firm and whether the payments are made in cash, through a trust account, or otherwise. Although this may seem easy, often it is not. Consider how you feel when a creditor has either lost one of your payments or misapplied it in some manner. This is especially important for a law firm because, in many instances, large sums of money are involved. Payments can be lost, not entered into the system, or even applied to the wrong client. The firm must take great care with regard to what goes in and out of the billing system and must ensure that the information is accurate.

Send Regular Billings   Nearly all clients like to receive timely billings. We all expect to receive regular billings for routine things, such as credit cards, utilities, and so forth. Likewise, most clients like to receive billings that are at least monthly. Imagine the frustration of a client who receives a quarterly billing that is four or five times more expensive than expected. Regular billings alert the client on how he or she is being billed and how much needs to be budgeted. In addition, if a client sees timely bills that are more expensive than were planned for, he or she can tell the firm how to proceed so as to limit future bills before costs are incurred. This at least gives the client the option of cutting back on legal services instead of getting angry at the firm for not communicating the charges on a timely basis.

Provide Client Billings That Are Fair and Respectful   Billings that are fair and courteous are essential to a good billing system. If a client believes that the firm is overcharging for services or that the billings are curt and unprofessional, the client may simply not pay a bill or may hold payment. If you ever must speak to a client regarding a bill, always be courteous and respectful, and try to understand the situation from the client's point of view. If a dispute arises, simply take down the client's side of the story, relay the information to the attorney in charge of the matter, and let the attorney resolve the situation.

Provide Client Billings That Identify What Services Have Been Provided   When a client receives a billing, it is important that the client knows what services were received. Bills that simply say "For Services Rendered" are, for the most part, a thing of the past. Although the format of bills depends on the client, it is recommended that you indicate exactly what service was performed, by whom, on what date, for how long, and for what charge. If a client can see exactly what the firm is doing and how hard the staff are working, the client may be more willing to pay the bill.

Provide Client Billings That Are Clear   Finally, billings should be clear and without legalese. They should be easy to read and should provide the information that a client wants to see. Payments on billings that are complicated and hard to read are often held up while a client tries to decipher a bill.

In short, a billing system should satisfy your customers so that they are willing to make payments on time.

Manual Billing Systems

Before legal billing software was widely available, billings were generated manually, using typewriters or word processors and time sheets. Law practices typically would store the time sheets in the accounting file of each case and then periodically send a statement. Although a few offices may still produce billings manually, manual systems have certain inherent limitations. Manual billings typically are slow and cumbersome, are prone to mathematical errors, and can take a great deal of overhead time to generate the bill. Thus, manual billings are sent out less frequently than most offices would like, which can cause cash-flow problems. In addition, management reports on manual systems are burdensome to produce. Computerized billing systems automatically produce management reports that show who is billing the most hours, which clients pay the best, and which types of cases generate the most money.

Computerized Billing Systems

Computerized billing systems solve many of the problems associated with manual systems. Generally, timekeepers still must record what they do with their time on a time slip or time sheet, or record the entry directly into the program. If the time slips are completed manually, then they must be entered into the legal billing software, usually on a daily or weekly basis. It is common for offices using computerized billing systems to produce monthly or even biweekly bills according to the wishes of the client. In addition to solving cash-flow problems, most legal billing software programs produce reports that can help the office make good management decisions (this is covered in more detail later in the chapter). Computerized timekeeping and billing also produce billings that are more accurate than manual methods because all mathematical computations are performed automatically by the computer. Because legal timekeeping and billing software prices have plunged several hundred dollars, nearly any office can afford these types of programs.

The Computerized Timekeeping and Billing Process

Timekeeping and billing software packages differ greatly from one another. However, the computerized timekeeping and billing process for most billing packages is as shown in Exhibit 5-13.

1. **The Client and the Attorney Reach an Agreement on Legal Fees** An attorney can bill for services in many different ways. At the outset of most cases, the client and the attorney reach an agreement regarding how much the attorney will charge for her or his services. Preferably, the agreement is in writing in the form of a contract. After the legal fee has been agreed on, the new matter is set up in the computerized billing package by entering information, including the client's name and address, the type of case it is, and the type of legal fee that has been agreed upon.

2. **The Attorney and Paralegal Perform Legal Services and Prepare Time Slips** When attorneys or paralegals perform work on a legal matter for a client, they fill out a time slip to track the exact services (either using a manual time slip form or entering the information directly into the computer). Many timekeeping and billing programs also support data entry from a handheld personal digital assistant (PDA).

3. **Time Slips and Expense Slips Are Entered into the Computer** If manual time slips are used, they must be entered into the computer. The information is typed into the computer in roughly the same format as it appears on the time slip. It is essential that the information be accurately entered into the computer. In addition, expense slips are also entered into the computer to track the expenses a firm incurs on behalf of a client.

Exhibit 5-13 Computerized Timekeeping and Billing Cycle

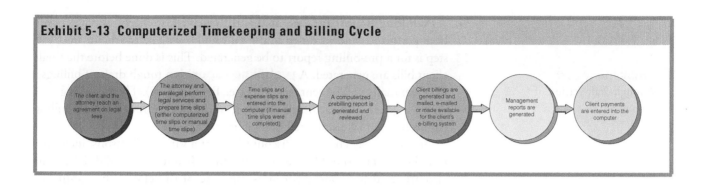

Exhibit 5-14 Prebilling Report

```
                                Adams & Lee
12/15/2021                   Prebilling Report                          Page 1
------------------------------------------------------------------------------
Power Systems, Inc.                          Corporate Matters
Miscellaneous Corporate Matters              Monthly
Case Number: Corp 1002                       Trust Balance: $3,825
P.O. Box 83001                               Case Rate: $125
500 South Peters Street                      Case Attorney: JBD

Malibu, CA  90014
Phone: (213) 553-9342


                                             Previous Bill Owed $470.20


                        —Legal Fees—

12/10/15  JBD   Telephone conference with
                Stevenson re: November minutes      .50 hr      $62.50 JBD

12/13/15  JBD   Preparation of November minutes;
                prepared for review at next
                meeting of the board of directors  1.00 hr     $125.00 JBD

12/14/15  JBD   Conference with Schorr at home      .25 hr      $31.25 JBD

                Total Legal Fees ...........       1.75 hr     $218.75 JBD

                        —Costs Advanced—

12/13/15  JBD   Photocopy documents; October 2010
                minutes (for board meeting)        $.25 ea
                                                   100 items     $25.00

                Total Costs Advanced ........                    $25.00



                        Continued on Page Two
```

prebilling report
A rough draft version of billings.

4. **A Prebilling Report Is Generated and Reviewed** After legal services have been performed and recorded in the time and billing software, the next step is for a pre-billing report to be generated. This is done before the final client bills are generated. A **prebilling report** is a rough draft of billings that eventually will be sent to clients (see Exhibit 5-14). The prebilling report is given to the attorney in charge of the case for review or to a billing committee to make sure the billing is accurate.

    Attorneys may choose to discount bills for a variety of reasons, including thinking the task should have taken less time than it actually did. Discounts also are used for good customers, because of the client's hardship, for professional courtesy or for friends, or because the billing looks unreasonable. This can, however, be very frustrating to a paralegal who has his or her time cut back. Typically, only the amount that is actually billed is counted against the target or minimum billable number of hours.

5. **Client Billings Are Generated and Mailed** Formal client billings are generated, in most cases, by a computer software program (see Exhibit 5-15). Most timekeeping and billing software can produce many different billing formats. The computer automatically prints the bills, and they are subsequently mailed to the clients.

6. **Management Reports Are Generated** Most computerized timekeeping and billing programs have a wide variety of management reports available. Management reports are not used for billing clients; they are used to evaluate the effectiveness of a firm. For example, most programs generate a report that shows how much time is nonbillable (i.e., not chargeable to clients). If a firm has a lot of nonbillable time, it might indicate that the firm is not productive and is losing valuable time from its timekeepers.

    Management reports can also be used to make management decisions, such that particular types of cases are no longer profitable, the firm needs to raise hourly rates, or other types of decisions.

7. **Client Payments Are Entered into the Computer** Finally, payments made as a result of billings must be recorded or entered into the computer, giving clients proper credit for the payments.

Bill Formats

Generating bills is the most important aspect of any timekeeping and billing program. There is no uniform way that all law offices bill clients; the look and format of billings depend on the law office, its clients, the type of law it practices, and so forth. Thus, it is important that any timekeeping and billing system that is used, whether manual or computerized, be flexible in the number of client billing formats that are available. For example, some bill formats contain only general information about the services provided, while others show greater detail. In many computerized systems, the format of the bill is set up when the client's case is first entered into the system.

    Historically, many offices did not itemize their billing, simply stating "For Services Rendered $XXX" on the bill. Although each client is different, most clients like to receive detailed billings of exactly what services are being provided. This allows the client to see what he or she is paying for. This also is beneficial to the office, since clients are more willing to pay the bill when they know what it is for. Producing detailed bills takes work. It requires timekeepers to make accurate, current time slips of what services they have provided. Although this seems enough, it is not. It is very hard to persuade timekeepers to write down each service they perform. Yet, the whole point of billing is to be paid. So, if an office produces a bill that is not itemized and, therefore, the client does not pay it, nothing has been gained. Although itemized billings are sometimes inconvenient for the timekeeper and take longer to produce, the extra work has paid off if the bill is paid in the end.

Exhibit 5-15 Final Client Billing

Adams & Lee
11 Canal Street, Suite 2B
New Orleans, Louisiana 70115
(212) 585-2342

Sara Autumn
Power Systems, Inc.
P.O. Box 83001
500 South Peters Street

Malibu, CA 90014

Billing Date: 01/03/22

Account # 00237
Previous Bal. in Trust
$3,825.00

RE: Power Systems, Inc. Miscellaneous Corporate Matters

DATE	PROFESSIONAL SERVICES	INDIV.	TIME	
12/10/21	Telephone conference with Schorr re: November minutes	JBD	.50	$62.50
12/13/21	Preparation of November minutes: prepared for review at next meeting of the board of directors	JBD	1.00	$125.00
12/14/21	Conference with Schorr at home	JBD	.25	$31.25
TOTAL FOR THE ABOVE SERVICES			**1.75**	**$218.75**

DATE	EXPENSES		
12/13/15	Photocopy documents; November minutes (for board meeting)		$25.00
TOTAL FOR ABOVE EXPENSES			**$25.00**
TOTAL BILLING			**$243.75**
CURRENT BALANCE IN TRUST			**$3,581.25**

Management Reports

Almost all timekeeping and billing software packages produce a wide variety of management reports (see Exhibit 5-16). **Management reports** are used to help management analyze whether the office is operating in an efficient and effective manner. Management reports can be used to track problems an office may be experiencing and to help devise ways to correct the problems. The following are explanations of some common management reports and how they are used by offices.

management reports
Reports used to help management analyze whether the office is operating in an efficient and effective manner.

Exhibit 5-16 Time and Billing—Management Reports

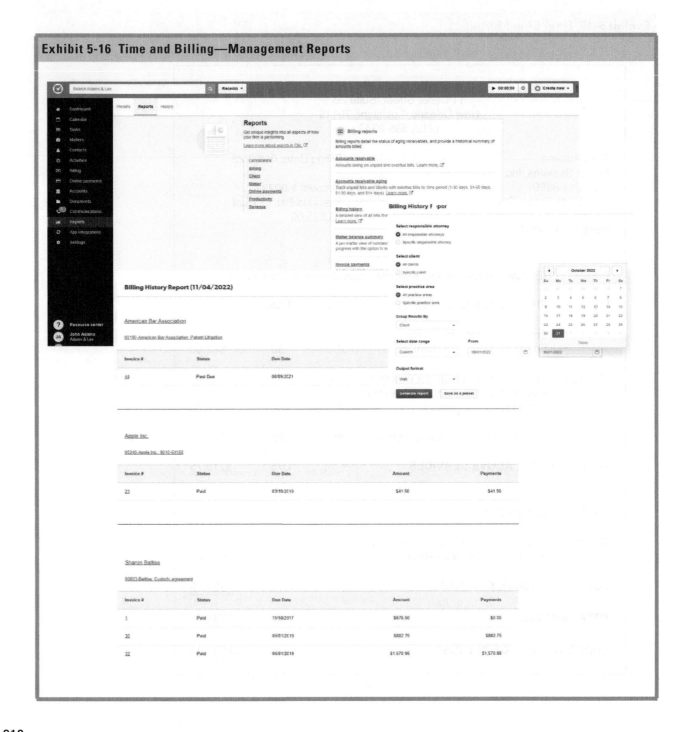

Case/Client List   Most billing packages allow the user to produce a case or client list. A list of all active cases an office has is very important in trying to effectively manage a large caseload. Most reports list not only the client names but also the appropriate account number (also called the "client identification number" by some programs). This is useful when trying to locate a client's identification number.

Aged Accounts Receivable Report   An **aged accounts receivable report** shows all cases that have outstanding balances due to the office and how long these balances are past due. These reports break down the current balances due and the balances that are 30, 60, and more than 90 days past due. Using this type of report, management can clearly see which clients are not paying and how old the balances are. The report is also helpful for following up on clients who are slow in paying their bills. Most programs allow the report to run according to the type of case. Thus, management can also see what types of cases (criminal, divorce, tax, etc.) have the most aged accounts. If one particular type of case has more than its share of aged accounts, it might be more profitable to stop taking that type. So, from a management perspective, this can be a very important report. It should be noted that aged account information should not appear on bills sent to clients. Bills that are more than 30 days old should simply say "past due."

aged accounts receivable report
A report showing all cases that have outstanding balances due and how long these balances are past due.

Timekeeper Productivity Report   The amount of billable and nonbillable time being spent by each timekeeper is shown and can be reflected in a **timekeeper productivity report**. These reports can be used to identify which timekeepers are the most diligent in their work. It lists the billable hours, the total amount billed, and payments received. It also reflects the nonbillable or nonchargeable hours, amounts that are charged off (uncollectible), and amounts that are on hold (not billed). This information helps to determine the deviation between the standard rate billed and the realized rate for the time billed. For example, if team member "A" billed a total of only 77.75 hours for the month of September while team members "B" and "C" billed more than 100 hours, the report would quickly reflect the lesser productive team member. Also, the report will indicate which team member produced the most billable hours and payments received by the office.

Along with reflecting each team members' production, most programs reflect the office billable and nonbillable information. Most importantly, the report should reflect the amount billed against the payments received. Most programs allow for various reporting periods (i.e., monthly, quarterly, annually, etc.).

timekeeper productivity report
A report showing how much billable and nonbillable time is being spent by each timekeeper.

Case Type Productivity Report   A **case type productivity report** will generally show case types (criminal, personal injury, bankruptcy, etc.) and those that are the most profitable (see Exhibit 5-17). For example, note in Exhibit 5-17 that the bankruptcy and family law areas of the law office brought in $36,050.00 and $25,050.00, respectively, for the month of September 2021, or 24.74% and 17.19% of the income earned. This report obviously shows which types of cases are the most profitable and which types are the least profitable. Management will use this type of report to decide which areas to concentrate on to become more profitable.

case type productivity report
A report showing which types of cases (e.g., criminal, personal injury, bankruptcy, etc.) are the most profitable.

electronic billing
When law firms bill clients using electronic means, such as the Internet.

Electronic Billing

Electronic billing is when law firms bill clients using electronic means, such as the Internet. Many large clients—such as Fortune 1000 and other businesses—are demanding that law firms bill them using electronic means. The Legal Electronic Data Exchange Standard specifies a uniform output for law firm time and billing systems to export to e-billing systems. Many of the e-billing vendors are application service providers, third-party vendors that set up the e-billing part of the system, receive data from law firms, and operate the software over the Internet. Clients are able to see bills (from any law firm they use) in a standard format and then customize the reports to meet their particular needs. For large clients, electronic billing is a big enhancement over traditional paper billing.

Exhibit 5-17 Time and Billing—Productivity Report

ADAMS & LEE

Productivity Report by Case Type

September 30, 2015

CASE TYPE	BILLABLE HOURS	BILLED FEES	PAYMENTS	FEE INCOME % TOTAL	HOURS % TOTAL
Admiralty	95.75	$10,053.75	$7,550.75	5.18	6.75
Bankruptcies	245.00	$55,125.00	$36,050.00	24.74	17.26
Civil Matters	128.50	$12,850.00	$8,350.50	5.73	9.05
Corporate Matters	80.75	$12,112.50	$10,112.50	6.94	5.69
Estate Planning	58.75	$14,687.50	$10,487.50	7.20	4.14
Family Law	220.50	$33,075.00	$25,050.00	17.19	15.53
Insurance Defense	108.25	$13,531.25	$9,785.00	6.71	7.63
Labor Law	150.75	$16,582.50	$11,500.00	7.89	10.62
Litigation	125.50	$13,805.00	$10,805.00	7.41	8.84
Personal Injury	25.75	$3,862.50	$2,850.00	1.96	1.81
Taxation Matters	180.00	$19,800.00	$13,200.00	9.06	7.61
September Totals	1,419.50	$205,485.00	$145,741.25		

Summary

Timekeeping is the process of tracking time for the purpose of billing clients. Billing is the process of issuing invoices for the purpose of collecting monies for legal services performed and being reimbursed for expenses.

There are several different kinds of legal fee agreements. An hourly rate fee is a fee for legal services that is billed to the client by the hour at an agreed-upon rate. An attorney or a paralegal hourly rate is based on the attorney's or paralegal's level of expertise and experience in a particular area. A client hourly rate is based on an hourly charge for that particular client; no matter what level of attorney (associate, partner, etc.) works on a case, the client is billed one rate. Similarly, no matter what level of paralegal works on a case (entry level, senior level, etc.), the client is billed one rate. A blended hourly rate is an hourly rate that takes into account the blend or mix of office staff working on the matter. Depending on the state, a "blend" may include paralegals. If a law office charges $175 for all staff (paralegals, associates, senior partners, etc.), this would be a blend. An activity hourly rate means that different hourly rates are charged depending on the type of activity, for example, $150 for telephone calls, $200 for office conference, and $250 for legal research and drafting.

A contingency fee is a fee that is collected if the attorney successfully represents a client. The attorney is entitled to a certain percentage of the money that is recovered. If the client's case is not won, and no money is recovered, the attorney collects no legal fees but is still entitled to recover expenses. Contingency fee agreements must be in writing. A flat fee is a fee for legal services that is billed as a flat or fixed amount, no matter how much time is actually spent on the matter.

An earned retainer means that the money has been earned and can be deposited in the law office's or attorney's operating bank account. An unearned retainer means that the money has not yet been earned and is placed in trust as an advance against the attorney's future fees and expenses. As the money is earned by the law office, the money is removed from the trust and placed in the law office's or attorney's operating account. A trust or escrow bank account is a separate bank account, apart from a law office's or attorney's operating checking account, where unearned client funds are deposited. A cash advance retainer is an unearned retainer.

A retainer for general representation is used when a client such as a corporation requires continuing legal services (not including litigation) throughout the year. The client pays a retainer and is entitled to the legal services without any additional fees. In many states, a retainer for general representation is an earned retainer, because the client can call at any time and receive legal services. A case retainer is a fee paid at the beginning of a matter, is nonrefundable, and is paid as an incentive for the attorney to take the case. Case retainers are earned retainers. A pure retainer obligates the office to be available to represent a client throughout a certain time period, and the firm agrees to not represent any of its competitors. A pure retainer is typically an earned retainer.

Court-awarded attorney fees are given to prevailing parties pursuant to certain federal and state statutes. Value billing is a type of fee agreement that is based on the perceived value of the services to the client.

The rules of professional conduct require that the basis or rate of the fee and expenses for a matter should be communicated to the client, preferably in writing, and that any fee charged should be reasonable. Whether a fee is reasonable depends on a number of factors, including the time and labor required, the novelty and difficulty of the issues raised, the fee customarily charged, the results obtained, the nature and length of the professional relationship, and the experience and reputation of the attorney, among other things.

Attorneys and law offices can charge and be reimbursed for reasonable legal expenses. Billable time is time that a legal professional can directly bill to a client's account. Nonbillable time cannot be billed to a client and includes pro bono work (services that are provided free of charge) and overheard costs such as general management, supervision, client development, and other activities. Paralegals are allowed to bill for their time as long as the work is professional and not clerical in nature. Leveraging is the process of earning profit from legal services that are provided by paralegals and attorneys.

A successful billing system, whether computerized or manual, accurately tracks how much clients have paid, can send out regular billings, and provides clients with fair, respectful, and detailed bills.

The computerized timekeeping and billing process includes a client and an attorney reaching a fee agreement, legal services being provided, times and expense slips entered into the computer, a prebilling report generated, a final bill generated, management reports run, and client payment recorded. Most computerized time and billing systems can produce management reports, including case/client list, aged accounts receivable, timekeeper productivity, and case type productivity reports, among others. Electronic billing is when law offices bill clients using electronic means, such as the Internet.

Key Terms

activity hourly rate	leveraging
aged accounts receivable report	management reports
attorney or paralegal hourly rate	nonbillable time
billable time	outside counsel
billing	overhead
blended hourly rate fee	prebilling report
case retainer	prepaid legal service
case type productivity report	pro bono
cash advance	pure retainer
client hourly rate	retainer for general representation
contingency fee	timekeeper productivity report
court-awarded fees	timekeeping
criminal fraud	time sheet or time slip
earned retainer	trust or escrow account
electronic billing	unearned retainer
flat fee	value billing
hourly rate fee	

Practical Applications

1. Your office is on the same side of the city as a major manufacturing plant. You notice that many of the plant's employees come to your office for routine legal services, such as wills, adoptions, and name changes. Although the office has been charging these clients on an hourly basis, you think that there might be alternatives. You talk to one of the partners, and she suggests that you look into the alternatives. Prepare a memorandum to the partner discussing billing options for this situation.

2. You are interviewing a new client. The client wants to hire your office to help negotiate the purchase of a small business. The seller has offered $20,000. The new client would be willing to pay this amount, although she thinks it is a bit high, but she does not feel comfortable negotiating with the seller and would rather have an attorney involved in the deal for her protection. The new client is suspicious of paralegals and attorneys and is especially concerned about how much her case will cost. You inform the client that the attorney will be the one who actually talks to her about the fee issue, but that typically this type of case is taken on an hourly basis and that the attorney will only be able to give her a very broad estimate of what the total matter will cost. The client states that this would be unacceptable to her because she does not have a lot of money to pay overpriced attorneys. The client also states that she would like this matter to get settled as soon as possible. You must prepare a memorandum to the attorney outlining the facts of the case. What type of fee arrangement would you suggest to the attorney? Please keep in mind the client's anxieties and her particular needs.

3. Recently, your office has found a niche in representing spouses collecting on past-due child support. In most cases, your clients have little money with which to pay you and are financially strapped, as they no longer have the income of their former spouses to support their children and have not received child support. In some cases, large amounts of money are owed, but finding the former spouses has proved difficult. Your supervising attorney decides that the best way to handle these types of cases is on a one-third contingency basis. Your supervising attorney asks for your comments. How do you respond?

4. You have just finished a hectic morning. Before you go to lunch, you fill out your timekeeping report for the day. Although you wanted to record your time earlier, you just could not get to it. Please record your time on a blank piece of paper or a spreadsheet; have columns set up for the date, client/case name, timekeeper, services rendered, billable or nonbillable, and the amount of time spent on the matter (see Exhibit 5-11). For each activity listed, decide whether it is billable or not billable. Record your time, using tenths of hours. You should also fill out expense slips for items that should be charged back to clients. Record the expenses on a blank piece of paper and include date, client/case name, your name, type of expense, and cost. Please total the cost of each expense slip. The firm charges 25 cents each for copies and 50 cents per page to send a fax. Assume long-distance phone calls cost 25 cents a minute.

   As best you can recall, this is how your day went:

8:00 A.M. to 8:12 A.M.	Got a cup of coffee, talked to other law office staff members, reviewed your schedule/things to do for the day, and reviewed your e-mail inbox.
8:13 A.M. to 8:25 A.M.	Talked to your supervising attorney (Jan Mitchell) about some research that she needs to be done on the standards necessary to file a motion to dismiss in *Johnson v. Cuttingham Steel.* Ms. Mitchell also asked you to find a bankruptcy statute she needs for *Halvert v. Shawnee Saving & Loan.*

8:26 A.M. to 8:37 A.M.	A paralegal from another office calls to remind you that the paralegal association you belong to is having a meeting at noon, and that you are running the meeting.
8:38 A.M. to 8:40 A.M.	One of your least favorite clients, John Hamilton, calls to ask you when he is supposed to be at your office to prepare for his deposition tomorrow. You access the weekly schedule electronically and read him the information he needs.
8:41 A.M. to 8:50 A.M.	You find the information you need re: the motion to dismiss in *Johnson v. Cuttingham Steel* in a motion in another case you helped prepare last month. The research is still current, so Ms. Mitchell will be pleased you found it so fast. You note that it took you two hours to research this issue when you did it the first time. You copy the material Ms. Mitchell needed (five pages), put it in her box, and send it to her electronically.
8:51 A.M. to 9:30 A.M.	You get hold of a witness you have been trying to contact in *Menly v. Menly.* The call was long-distance. The call lasted 15 minutes, and the memo to the file documenting the call took 20 minutes.
9:31 A.M. to 9:54 A.M.	Ms. Mitchell asks you to contact the attorney in *Glass v. Huron* regarding a discovery question. You spend 10 minutes on hold. The call is long-distance but you get an answer to Ms. Mitchell's question.
9:55 A.M. to 10:45 A.M.	One of the secretaries informs you that you must interview a new client, Richard Sherman. The person who was supposed to see Mr. Sherman got delayed. Mr. Sherman comes to your office regarding a simple adoption. However, in talking to Mr. Sherman, you find out that he also needs someone to incorporate a small business that he is getting ready to open. You gladly note that your office has a department that handles this type of matter. You take the basic information down regarding both matters. You tell the client that you will prepare a memo regarding these matters to the appropriate attorney and one of the office's attorneys will contact him within two days to further discuss the matter. You also copy 10 pages of information that Mr. Sherman brought.
10:46 A.M. to 10:54 A.M.	One of the secretaries asks you to cover her phone for her while she takes a quick break. Because the secretary always helps you when you ask for it, you gladly cover the phone for a few minutes. Ms. Mitchell asks you to send a fax in *Stewart v. Layhorn Glass*, so you use this time to send the six-page fax.
10:55 A.M. to 12:00 P.M.	You were given the job of organizing some exhibits in *Ranking v. Siefkin* yesterday by Ms. Mitchell. You finally have some free time to organize the exhibits.
12:01 P.M. to 1:00 P.M.	You attend the paralegal association lunch.
1:01 P.M. to 2:00 P.M.	You work on a pro bono criminal case that Ms. Mitchell is representing on appeal. In an effort to become familiar with the case, you read some of the transcripts from the trial.
2:01 P.M. to 5:30 P.M.	Ms. Mitchell hands you a new case. Ms. Mitchell says that the office will be representing the defendant. She asks you to read the petition and client file, analyze the case, and draft interrogatories to send to the plaintiff. You spend the rest of the day working on this case.

On the Web Exercises

1. Go to the ABA Center for Professional Responsibility at http://www.americanbar.org, find the **ABA Model Rules of Professional Conduct**, and read and print out **Rule 1.5** Fees and the comment.

2. Go to CLIO Case Management system (either set up individually or by the course instructor): Review instructions to create Time Records, including use of the Timer Feature, Entering Expense Slips and Producing Prebills, Final Bills, and Reports.

3. Go to the Georgia Bar Association Web site at http://www.gabar.org/ committeesprogramssections/programs/lpm/forms.cfm and find a sample contingency fee agreement. Go to several other state bar association Web sites and try to find another sample contingency fee or hourly rate contract agreements.

4. Go to http://www.findlaw.com and print out and read the U.S. Supreme Court case of **Missouri v. Jenkins**, 491 U.S. 274 (1989). **Click** "Visit Our Professional Site," then **click** "Cases and Codes." Scroll down to US Courts of Appeal – Opinions and Resources and **click** "United States Supreme Court," then **click** "Search by Docket Number or Citation." You should then be able to enter the citation of the case—491 U.S. 274.

5. Go to the ABA Law Practice Management Section home page at http://www.americanbar. org and find timekeeping, billing, fees, and finance-related articles.

Case Review

In the Matter of Disciplinary Proceeding Against W. Russell Van Camp, an Attorney at Law.

257 P.3d 599 (2011) Supreme Court of Washington,

In re Disciplinary Proceeding Against Van Camp No. 200,811-9.

June 16, 2011.

Opinion

C. JOHNSON, J. - This attorney discipline case focuses on an ambiguous written fee agreement, the representation provided in the litigation, and the attorney's conduct during the grievance investigation. Attorney W. Russell Van Camp required a $25,000 initial "retainer" fee to represent a client in an injunction suit, but he did not explain to the client whether it was a nonrefundable flat fee, an hourly fee, or something else. Nor did the fee agreement Van Camp prepared. When the client expressed confusion about the fee, Van Camp asserted it was a flat fee and made no effort to renegotiate in accordance with the client's understanding that he would be charged an hourly rate. In the suit, despite numerous settlement offers from opposing counsel and his client's desire to settle, Van Camp resisted settlement, prolonging the case, and neither communicated nor explained the settlement offers to the client. The client was not consulted or advised concerning the claims against him and the options available to him in resolving the case. After the client filed a grievance with the Washington State Bar Association (WSBA), Van Camp submitted differing and exaggerated time reconstructions based on hours he claimed to have

worked on the case to justify the amount of the fee, despite having little to no work to show for it. We adopt the Disciplinary Board's reconstruction and disbar Van Camp.

FACTS [FN1]

FN1. These facts are mainly taken from the hearing officer's "Findings of Facts, Conclusions of Law and Hearing Officer's Recommendations," as adopted by the Disciplinary Board. While Van Camp assigned error to some of these findings, he did not argue the error in his briefs, so these facts are verities on appeal. **_In re Disciplinary· Proceeding Against Marshall, 160 Wn.2d 317. 330-31. 157 P.3d 859 (2007)_** (citing cases).

Van Camp has been practicing law since 1973. He has handled 37 cases in the United States District Court, Eastern District of Washington, where this client's suit was filed. He practices in Spokane, emphasizing in personal injury law, criminal law, and family law. This proceeding arises out of Van Camp's representation of Randy Honkala, a car enthusiast. Honkala had obtained a "power lease" certificate for $5,000 that gave him purchasing priority for a Shelby Mustang. Honkala purchased the car through his previous employer, Wendie Motors, but it was delivered in poor condition, so Honkala returned it. Honkala expected to realize a profit on the car but lost any expected profit and the $5,000. Then he discovered that Wendie had listed the returned vehicle on an auction site and was reselling it for a profit without disclosing the defects. Honkala contacted the auction's highest bidder to report the problems, which dissuaded the bidder from purchasing the car, and Honkala also made numerous derogatory posts about Wendie on various web sites.

Wendle, represented by Richard Campbell, sued Honkala in federal court in November 2006, seeking injunctive relief to stop the Internet postings but additionally alleging various claims and seeking attorney fees. [FN2] A telephonic temporary restraining order (TRO) hearing was held December 2006, and Honkala appeared pro se. Campbell said he wanted to get the case resolved without going to trial if possible. Honkala agreed to the restraining order so long as it was mutual. Wendle then moved for a preliminary injunction, noted for argument on December 20, 2006. Wendle e-mailed Honkala a proposed stipulation and permanent injunction that would have resolved the case through mutual restraints on defamation, and with all other claims against Honkala dismissed. Exs. Sent to Disciplinary Board Exs. 5, 33 (hereinafter Board Ex.). The e-mail conveyed that Wendle's primary purpose was for Honkala to stop the Internet postings. Honkala did not understand the permanent injunction, so, rather than reply to Wendle, he sought counsel.

FN2. The complaint listed (I) misappropriation of trade secrets; (2) tortious interference with business relations; (3) civil libel, slander, and defamation; (4) a Consumer Protection Act, *chapter 19.86 RCW,* violation; and (5) Lanham Act violations; it sought injunctive relief, affirmative acts by Honkala to protect Wendie's reputation, a money judgment, treble damages, costs, and attorney fees. Disciplinary Board Ex. I.

Honkala found Van Camp's name in a phone book, and met with him on December 15, 2006, bringing the documents Wendle had sent. Van Camp required Honkala to pay him a $25,000 "retainer." Van Camp did not explain how the fee would be calculated or whether it was refundable; Van Camp did inform Honkala that if the case settled within a week, he would return most of the $25,000. Honkala testified they discussed hourly rates. The fee agreement itself lists several items:

A. An earned retainer of:	$25,000
B. An hourly rate, computed as follows:	
Mr. Van Camp, Mr. Deissner	250.00
Mr. Shaw	100.00
Paralegals	50.00
Secretarial	25.00

Board Ex. 6. A small finger icon pointed to "A" on the agreement. The agreement also states, "Monies paid by the client shall be considered as earned towards the ultimate total fee, unless otherwise designated." But the meaning of "earned retainer" is not explained, nor is the scope of representation defined other than to represent and defend Honkala in a suit. Honkala was not given a copy of the fee agreement. He obtained $25,000 through a home equity loan and brought Van Camp a check a few days later.

Van Camp phoned Wendle's counsel, Richard Campbell, that same day, December 15, 2006. He joked that Campbell should send him a box of chocolates to thank him for all the money Campbell would make on this case. Later that day, Campbell faxed Van Camp a letter that mentioned the box of chocolates remark as tongue-in-cheek but communicated Wendle's desire to quickly resolve the case without further litigation. The letter referenced the settlement and proposed permanent injunction

as attached, but evidently it was not transmitted with the letter. Van Camp did not respond to the letter or request the missing attachment, except to call Campbell's office to complain to the answering extern about his displeasure at seeing the chocolates remark in writing.

Little work was done on Honkala's case. Notices of appearance were filed by both Van Camp and his partner, Dustin Deissner. A declaration for Honkala was filed with a memo in opposition to the emergency TRO-which had already been granted; the upcoming hearing was for a preliminary injunction scheduled for December 20, 2006. Deissner represented Honkala in that telephonic hearing, and the preliminary injunction was granted. Van Camp performed no work in response to the preliminary injunction, and there is no evidence that he explained its significance to Honkala.

On February 21, 2007, Campbell sought a response to his December 15, 2006, letter because a status conference was quickly approaching, but Van Camp did not respond. Van Camp participated in a telephonic scheduling conference in March, with a resulting discovery deadline of September 10, 2007. Someone in Van Camp's office answered Wendle's interrogatories in the middle of April, but no discovery was prepared on behalf of Honkala until late August.

In early March, Honkala sent Van Camp a letter expressing his concerns. Board Ex. 14. Honkala reminded Van Camp of his desire that the case be resolved as quickly as possible, given there was no benefit to prolonging it. Second, Honkala requested copies of the documents filed in his case to see what had been done to resolve it and stated he had asked several times, yet received nothing. Third, Honkala requested an itemized bill showing what charges had been made against the $25,000 retainer. A week later, in full, Van Camp replied:

> As to the breakdown of fees, our retainer agreement was for an earned retainer (flat fee), you would not be charged any more attorney fees. You don't have to worry about an additional charge for attorney fees. I do not keep hours on such retainers. If you have any questions let me know.

Board Ex. 17. The request for documents and more communication was repeated the following day by both Honkala and his wife. Honkala additionally sought *any* document stating the $ 25,000 was a flat fee. A packet of materials was sent, but it is unclear what this included. The Honkalas e-mailed again, wishing to discuss the claims against them the steps being taken, and seeking a copy of the retainer agreement. Van Camp did not respond.

On July 20, 2007, Van Camp filed an answer to Wendle's complaint. He included a counterclaim against Wendle seeking the lost contract expectancy regarding the Shelby Mustang and damages for Wendle's defamation of Honkala. Board Ex. 23. Wendle had never moved for default, but Campbell requested an answer before the mediation Van Camp had scheduled for July 25, 2007. At the mediation, Honkala sought the $25,000 in attorney fees he had paid Van Camp, but Wendle rejected any legal responsibility for those fees. When the mediator mentioned the offer of settlement, it surprised Honkala, who was unfamiliar with the offer. The mediation was unsuccessful.

Following the attempted mediation, Honkala again e-mailed Van Camp, seeking copies of anything filed in support of the counterclaim. The e-mail reiterated Honkala's desire to resolve the case quickly. Fallowing receipt of the few documents Van Camp could provide, Honkala sought a copy of the proposed permanent injunction referenced in Campbell's December 15, 2006, letter. Van Camp could not provide this as he never informed Campbell the injunction itself was not attached. Instead, Van Camp replied that this referenced the preliminary injunction already in place. [FN3] Additionally, the copy of Campbell's letter sent to Honkala had been altered by a staff member in Van Camp's office. The altered version did not contain the box of chocolates reference or that it was Wendie's desire to resolve the case quickly through a simple cease and desist agreement. [FN4]

FN3. One of Van Camp's employees finally contacted Campbell, seeking the permanent injunction and settlement offer on August 3, 2007.

FN4. While Van Camp reviewed the package, he did not notice the alteration. The hearing officer found insufficient proof that Van Camp directed the employee to alter the letter, although Van Camp had stated that he did not like the chocolates reference.

Honkala filed a grievance against Van Camp on July 31, 2007. Van Camp received this on August 8, 2007, and sent an apologetic e-mail the next day. He stated there was still a good chance to have the matter resolved in Honkala's favor and asked if he should pursue settlement. In his response to the WSBA, Van Camp stated he had done enough work to have earned most of the fee. But, he stated, if the case settled, he would be happy to review the fee with Honkala, and if he, Van Camp, felt it was unreasonable, he would refund some of it. If Honkala disagreed, then Van Camp would submit the matter to fee arbitration. He did not offer this directly to Honkala.

At the end of August, Van Camp informed Honkala that he had scheduled a deposition of Chud Wendle. Honkala replied that he had not yet seen the permanent injunction and settlement offer, which he thought he should review, and that he wanted to settle. Board Ex. 41. Despite now having a copy of the settlement offer and permanent injunction, Van Camp replied that the only offer was the one previously transmitted directly to Honkala and attached the current preliminary injunction.

The deposition was taken, with Honkala's participation, as Van Camp requested. Van Camp asked only the questions Honkala had provided. This was the only discovery completed on behalf of the counterclaim. Van Camp suggested he would move to extend the discovery cutoff date but never did. He prepared deposition notices for four Wendie employees, but Honkala fired Van Camp the same day these were prepared-August 31, 2007. Honkala sought a statement of actual costs incurred and a refund of the remainder, neither of which he received.

Honkala then contacted Campbell himself in early September and sought $5,000 (the cost of the power lease) to settle, which Wendie refused. Honkala took the proposed permanent injunction to another attorney to review. That attorney charged Honkala $150 per hour, for a total fee of about $500. The lawsuit settled and was dismissed at the end of September 2007.

WSBA INVESTIGATION, HEARING, AND DISCIPLINARY BOARD REVIEW

In October 2007, Van Camp sent a follow-up letter to the WSBA. Regarding the fee agreement, he wrote, "As far as I can tell, Mr. Honkala is a competent adult able to read and write." Board Ex. 65. But he agreed to forgo the flat fee and attached a time reconstruction showing he had earned well over $25,000, so the issue of a refund was moot. In discussing the case, Van Camp gets the procedural history wrong, stating Honkala represented himself at the preliminary injunction hearing-but Honkala was pro se at the TRO hearing and was represented by Van Camp's partner, Deissner, at the preliminary injunction hearing. Van Camp states he never saw nor received a copy of any of the injunctions, despite, at the very least, Campbell's fax in August 2007. He denied receiving any communication from Campbell on December 15, 2006, although this is the date of the chocolates reference being included in the letter sent by Campbell, which, more importantly, sought a permanent injunction and quick settlement.

During the investigation, Van Camp submitted various estimates of hourly charges to justify his retention of the $25,000. Van Camp's paralegal, Christian Barber, who had been directed to create these reconstructed time sheets, testified that he started by using 10th-of-an-hour increments, as he had learned to do in school. This resulted in a total fee between $8,000 and $10,000. Van Camp reviewed this and instructed Barber to use half hour increments for attorney time, in accordance with the fee agreement. The new calculations resulted in a fee between $16,000 and $20,000. Still too low for Van Camp, he directed Barber to add that Van Camp had reviewed every document that came in and went out, and each instance merited at least a half hour on the spreadsheet. This resulted in a total figure of $33,000, which Van Camp submitted to the WSBA.

The WSBA charged Van Camp with nine counts of misconduct, alleging numerous Rules of Professional Conduct (RPC) violations. After a five day hearing, the hearing officer found six of the nine charges proved. She recommended a two year suspension and $15,000 restitution. The charges found proved are as follows:

Count 1

By not abiding by the client's objectives to try to settle the case as quickly as possible, Respondent violated *RPC 1.2(a).*

Count 2

By failing to follow up with attorney Richard Campbell's December 15, 2006 letter and other settlement proposals, Respondent violated *RPC 1.3.*

Count 3

By failing to timely provide the client with copies of letters and settlement proposals, even after repeated requests, Respondent violated *RPC 1.4(a).*

Count 4

By failing to explain clearly at the outset of representation how his fee would be calculated and/or how the client's $25,000 payment would be applied, Respondent violated **RPC 1.4(b)** and/or **RPC 1.5(b)**.

Count 5

By charging $25,000 under the facts of this case, Respondent violated **RPC 1.5(a)**.

Count 9

By misrepresenting in his July 31, 2007 letter to Honkala that Campbell had provided a proposed preliminary injunction with his December 15, 2006 letter, Respondent violated **RPC 8.4(c)**.

Decision Papers at 000002-03 (Findings of Fact). The hearing officer found American Bar Association's **Standards for Imposing Lawyer Sanctions** standard 4.42 (1991 & Supp. 1992), with a presumptive sanction of suspension, applied for counts 1, 2, 3 and 9. The hearing officer found injury to the client and the profession but not serious or potentially serious injury. For counts 4 and 5, the hearing officer applied standard 7.2, also with a presumptive sanction of suspension. Again, she found injury, but not serious injury, to the client. As a mitigating circumstance, the hearing officer mentioned Van Camp's reputation as a successful plaintiff's personal injury attorney. The aggravating factors were more extensive:

(a) **Prior Disciplinary Offenses.** Before this proceeding, Van Camp had been disciplined three times. In 1985, he was censured for charging an unreasonable fee. In 2002, he was suspended for six months for making false statements in his bankruptcy proceeding. In 2005, Van Camp was reprimanded for using the term "earned retainer fee" when the actual purpose of the money, whether for fees, costs, or both, was unclear. This last offense was of particular note because the term "earned retainer" was still included in Van Camp's retainer agreement without additional explanatory language. The hearing officer thought the false statements in the bankruptcy proceeding relevant as reflecting poorly on Van Camp's record for truthfulness and honesty, and "is indicative of a serious disregard for upholding the integrity of the legal system and the profession." She thought the 1985 excessive fee offense was too remote in time to matter.

(b) **Dishonest or selfish motive.** The hearing officer concluded an initial $25,000 fee created a disincentive to defend or pursue the client's case; further, the deliberate withholding of the December 15, 2006 letter and settlement proposals prolonged the litigation with the selfish motive of justifying the fee.

(c) **Bad faith obstruction during disciplinary process.** The WSBA alleged and Van Camp did not contest bad faith in his replies to Honkala's grievance and questions posed by the WSBA, except to dispute knowledge of the altered [chocolates] letter. The hearing officer concluded the time sheet submitted was a "grossly over-inflated fabrication of time and services," and was submitted in bad faith.

(d) **Refusal to acknowledge wrongful nature of conduct.** Despite prior discipline, Van Camp consistently denied any wrongdoing, refused to accept a share of the responsibility, placed blame on an unsophisticated client for giving inconsistent instructions, criticized opposing counsel for his own behavior [chocolates remark], and pointed out his staffs mistakes, lack of diligence and incompetence. Of note was his failure to provide ethical training to his staff, and that he allowed his secretary to accept entire legal responsibility for potentially committing a felony without any willingness to bear the consequences of her action.

(e) **Substantial experience in the practice of law.** Van Camp's extensive experience did not benefit his client, nor did it result in a high level of understanding the RPCs.

Decision Papers at 000026-29.

On review, the Disciplinary Board adopted the findings but increased the presumptive sanction to disbarment because the client, the legal system, and the profession suffered serious injury. The Disciplinary Board added an additional aggravating factor: indifference to making restitution, because three years had passed with no voluntary refund to Honkala. The Disciplinary Board found the aggravating factors outweighed the mitigating factor, justifying disbarment. The Disciplinary Board's vote was seven to three, with the dissenters recommending a three year suspension.

Van Camp challenges the recommendation in this court. He argues procedural errors denied him a fair hearing and requests a new one. Alternatively, he disagrees with the conclusions of law made by the hearing officer and adopted by the Disciplinary Board, and he argues the injury was not serious and that his mental state was mere negligence, so he should only be sanctioned with a suspension of six months or less.

ISSUES

1. Did procedural errors deny Van Camp a fair hearing?
2. Does substantial evidence support the findings of misconduct?
3. Is the recommended sanction of disbarment appropriate?

ANALYSIS

This court has the ultimate responsibility of disciplining lawyers. **In re Disciplinary Proceeding Against Preszler, 169 Wn.2d 1, 15-16, 232 P.3d 1118 (2010)** (citing **In re Disciplinary Proceeding Against Marshall. 160 Wn.2d 317, 329, 157 P.3d 859 (2007))**. We review conclusions of law de novo and uphold them if supported by the findings of fact. **In re Disciplinary Proceeding Against Whitney, 155 Wn.2d 451, 461, [*7981 120 P.3d 550 (2005)** (citing **In re Disciplinary Proceeding Against Curran, 115 Wn.2d 747, 759, 801 P.2d 962 (1990))**.

1. Did procedural errors deny Van Camp a fair hearing?

Van Camp argues that he was denied a fair hearing based on two decisions by the hearing officer. First, he argues the WSBA should not have been allowed to call a rebuttal expert after failing to list any experts on its witness list. His entire defense, he argues, was based on the WSBA's representation that it would not call experts, and after it was allowed to do so, he could not "catch up." Although parties have a right under *Rules for Enforcement of Lawyer Conduct (ELC) 10.1 3(d)* [FN5] to submit rebuttal evidence, he argues this should be limited to exhibits or previously disclosed witnesses. A party should not be allowed to withhold evidence proper to its case in chief, only to cumulatively present it at the end of the defendant's case.

FN5. *ELC 10.13(D), titled* "Witnesses," provides in pertinent part, "The parties have the right to cross-examine witnesses who testify and to submit rebuttal evidence."

The WSBA explains that it initially chose to forgo expert witnesses, reserving the right to call rebuttal witnesses, but then sought to amend after seeing Van Camp's list of three experts to testify concerning the reasonableness of Van Camp's fee. The hearing officer denied the request as untimely, but allowed, as rebuttal evidence, the named expert to testify following Van Camp's expert's testimony. The WSBA analogizes this to character evidence, so that once Van Camp had "opened the door," it had a right to rebut that testimony. Moreover, the WSBA argues, the motion to call the rebuttal expert was granted June 1, 2009, but the expert did not actually testify until July 9, 2009, giving Van Camp sufficient time to obtain discovery about the expert's testimony. Since he chose not to, he cannot establish error. *See State v. Swan, 114 Wn.2d 613. 654-55. 790 P.2d 610 (1990)* (defense had a full day to prepare for rebuttal witness and did not request a continuance or seek to reopen case, therefore no abuse of discretion). We agree.

Evidentiary rulings are reviewed for abuse of discretion. *Marshall, 160 Wn.2d at 341.* Such abuse occurs only when no reasonable person would take the adopted view. *In re Disciplinary Proceeding Against Bonet, 144 Wn.2d 502, 510, 29 P.3d 1242 (2001).* Van Camp does not explain how the hearing officer's decision was manifestly unreasonable. The hearing officer wanted to hear from a rebuttal expert regarding the fee, and without a specific articulation of why no one would think this a reasonable thing to do, we will not overturn her decision.

Next, Van Camp argues he should have been permitted to delve into the mediation because doing so would have revealed Honkala's duplicity. But Van Camp *was* allowed to discuss the mediation. Van Camp was asked by his counsel, Deissner, whether Honkala was told he could settle by walking away, and Honkala still chose not to walk away. Van Camp so testified, and Deissner stated that was the only question he needed to ask. 3 Report of Proceedings (RP) at 726-30. It is unclear what else Van Camp feels should have been discussed to reveal Honkala's alleged duplicity, and again, he does not explain how the hearing officer's limiting the mediation discussion was manifestly unreasonable. As the WSBA points out, Van Camp does not cite to any specific ruling by the hearing officer and does not establish that error occurred. *State v. Riker, 123 Wn.2d 351, 369, 869 P.2d 43 (1994)* (objection to exclusion waived when party fails to seek final ruling following tentative ruling on motion in limine). Van Camp has not established grounds for a new hearing.

2. Does substantial evidence support the findings of misconduct?

The WSBA must prove misconduct by a clear preponderance of the evidence. This is more than a mere preponderance, but less than beyond a reasonable doubt. The Disciplinary Board's ultimate conclusions of misconduct are upheld if supported by substantial evidence in the record, that is, sufficient evidence to persuade a fair-minded, rational person. *Marshall, 160 Wn.2d at 330.*

Count 1

By not abiding by the client's objectives to try to settle the case as quickly as possible, Respondent violated *RPC 1.2(a).*

A lawyer is required to abide by the client's decisions concerning the objectives of the representation, the means by which those are carried out, and whether to accept a settlement offer. *RPC 1.2(a).* The hearing officer concluded Van Camp failed to assist Honkala in making decisions, failed to follow his instructions, and failed to advise him throughout, including not advising Honkala that he could settle the claims against him early in the representation through the permanent injunction. We find sufficient evidence exists to support this finding of misconduct.

The record establishes that Honkala repeatedly indicated he wished for quick resolution of this case, and yet Van Camp never communicated or explained the permanent injunction and offer of settlement to him. In fact, given Van Camp's admissions to the WSBA, it seems Van Camp never reviewed the permanent injunction at all. This failure to review, communicate, and explain the settlement offer is alarming. Van Camp could not abide by his client's decision concerning settlement if the client was never presented with the option of settlement. An attorney must communicate offers of settlement to the client and discuss in meaningful terms the advantages or disadvantages of accepting the proposal. This includes the lawyer's fees and costs associated with the various options. Then the attorney should make recommendations to the client about what is best, but the client controls and decides what to do regarding the claims. Van Camp did none of these things, constituting a violation of his ethical duties as an attorney.

While Van Camp argues Honkala's objectives were unclear because he gave conflicting instructions, that is, to pursue the counterclaims aggressively and to settle quickly, as the WSBA articulates, these are compatible. Aggressive pursuit of the counterclaims might have placed pressure on Wendle to settle with more favorable terms for Honkala. Moreover, Honkala's confusion and somewhat contradictory instructions in this case are, unfortunately, further evidence that Van Camp failed to properly counsel his client.

Van Camp's arguments on this count do him more harm than good. He continues to blame the client as the source of confusion. He argues Honkala understood what the permanent injunction called for right from the beginning-but if this is so, Honkala had no need of Van Camp or his $25,000 in services. [FN6] Van Camp thought Honkala was seeking damages and refers to Honkala's various grievances against

Wendle, but most of these were not made in the counterclaim. He blames Honkala for not settling at the mediation, but Honkala was leery of settlement only because it meant he lost the entirety of money he had paid to Van Camp. Van Camp states there was never a clear instruction from Honkala to settle despite not getting anything in return, but, in the material before us, quotes Renee Honkala's e-mail expressly stating that position. Board Ex. 44. Van Camp repeatedly asserts that an attorney should not be disciplined for failing to tease out what his client really wishes. But, in this record, extensive documentary evidence exists showing Honkala desired quick settlement and an end to the litigation. We therefore agree with the Disciplinary Board that Van Camp violated *RPC 1.2(a)*.

FN6. Van Camp argues he did in fact explain the injunction, accurately, in this way: "that agreeing to the injunction would essentially be giving up and 'admitting you're ugly, too,'" but Honkala just did not like that advice. Van Camp's Br. at 29.

Count 2

By failing to follow up with attorney Richard Campbell's December 15, 2006 letter and other settlement proposals, Respondent violated *RPC 1.3*.

"A lawyer shall act with reasonable diligence and promptness in representing a client." *RPC 1.3*. The Disciplinary Board concluded that Van Camp's failure to respond to Campbell's offers to settle violated *RPC 1.3*. We find that this is also supported by substantial evidence. Campbell sent Van Camp a settlement offer the very day Honkala hired Van Camp. Van Camp received the letter, but not the attachment. The attachment contained the proposed permanent injunction that would have ended the litigation against Honkala. Van Camp did not inform Campbell of the missing attachment, although Campbell specifically requested a response to the settlement offer. Nor did he communicate the offer to Honkala, who, as discussed previously, desired quick resolution. Honkala testified he was surprised to hear of the settlement offer in July 2007, *eight months* after Campbell sent it. Campbell continued to seek settlement throughout that period, and yet Van Camp never responded to those requests, in violation of his duty of diligent representation.

Van Camp argues that Honkala had already rejected a settlement before hiring Van Camp and that a lawyer is not required to communicate (or to even respond to) previously rejected offers. There is no evidence that Honkala rejected the offer; in fact, he sought counsel in order to better understand it. Van Camp additionally argues that he was in fact pursuing settlement, using a technique that had served him well in the past, pushing the case to mediation, and his technique just failed him in this instance. But Van Camp fails to explain why a conversation with Campbell in December 2006 was insufficient, and it was necessary to wait until July 2007 to mediate, when an offer was already on the table. We conclude a violation of *RPC 1.3* has been established in this record.

Count 3

By failing to timely provide the client with copies of letters and settlement proposals, even after repeated requests, Respondent violated *RPC 1.4(a)*.

A lawyer must, under *RPC 1.4(a)*, inform the client of any circumstance requiring the client's consent, reasonably consult with the client regarding the means by which the client's objectives will be accomplished, keep the client reasonably informed about the status of the matter, and promptly comply with any requests for information. The Disciplinary Board's conclusion that Van Camp violated *RPC 1.4(a)* is supported in the record by the numerous requests sent by Honkala seeking status updates and copies of documents. Twice in March Honkala requested copies of the documents filed in his case and mentioned he had repeatedly asked for these and received nothing. Van Camp finally sent some copies in April, but it is unclear what was sent. In August, Honkala was still seeking a copy of the settlement offer and proposed permanent injunction.

Van Camp does not dispute this failure but instead argues he was confused about what documents he had, which is why he did not provide Honkala with what he was seeking. Van Camp alleges his negligence in this regard did not harm Honkala, since the permanent injunction was similar to the preliminary one. But given Honkala's desire, even if conflicted, of quick settlement, this failure could have cost Honkala and his wife months of lawsuit-related stress and expense. Regardless, as to the violation itself, the RPCs do not inquire about harm. There is substantial evidence, including Van Camp's own admission, to show he violated *RPC 1.4(a)*.

Count 4

By failing to explain clearly at the outset of representation how his fee would be calculated and/or how the client's $25,000 payment would be applied, Respondent violated *RPC 1.4(b)* and/or *RPC 1.5(b)*.

The Disciplinary Board found Van Camp violated both *RPC 1.4(b)* and *RPC 1.5(b)*. Under *RPC 1.4(b)*, the lawyer "shall explain a matter to the extent reasonably necessary to permit the client to make informed decisions regarding the representation." Under *RPC 1.5(b)*, the lawyer is required to explain the rate or basis of the fee and the lawyer's billing practices and, if asked, must provide the client, in writing, the basis or rate of the fee. [FN7] The record establishes that Van Camp failed to communicate how the fee would be calculated and applied. Further, the Disciplinary Board found entering into the ambiguous fee agreement itself to be a violation. The agreement was ambiguous because it included both hourly and retainer-type fee arrangements, and it was devoid of any description of the scope of representation. These conclusions are similarly supported by substantial evidence.

FN7. *RPC 1.5(b)* provides, "The scope of the representation and the basis or rate of the fee and expenses for which the client will be responsible shall be communicated to the client, preferably in writing, before or within a reasonable time after commencing the representation, except when the lawyer will charge a regularly represented client on the same basis or rate. Any changes in the basis or rate of the fee or expenses shall also be communicated to the client. Upon the request of the client in any matter, the lawyer shall communicate to the client in writing the basis or rate of the fee."

The hearing officer found that Honkala believed he was retaining Van Camp on an hourly basis because hourly rates were discussed at the first meeting. We give considerable weight to her findings, especially with respect to the credibility of the witnesses. *__In re Disciplinary Proceeding Against Cramer, 165 Wn.2d 323, 332, 198 P.3d 485 (2008).__* Rather than dispute this, Van Camp argues that once it became clear Honkala was confused, in March, he communicated that it was a flat fee, so he complied with his ethical duty. This argument does not address ***RPC 1.4(b),*** in that Honkala needed sufficient information about the matter (including how the fee was being calculated) to make informed decisions concerning his case. Had Van Camp been clear that the $25,000 was a flat fee, Honkala might have sought a different attorney. Van Camp argues that his offer to arbitrate the fee should somehow excuse any violation. But, even if this were so, the offer was never communicated directly to Honkala. Van Camp suggested he would arbitrate the fee dispute to the WSBA, but then claimed he had earned well over $25,000 from the representation.

Van Camp additionally argues that the RPCs did not require a written fee agreement for flat fees at the time. While this is literally true, it does not excuse the confusing nature of his written fee agreement which Van Camp does not dispute. He agrees that a clearer fee agreement would have prevented Honkala's claims of misunderstanding now, continuing to imply that Honkala is misrepresenting himself to the WSBA. Even in those situations where no written fee agreement is required, in order to avoid confusion or later dispute, it is always wise to have one and, if a written fee agreement is used, it should be written in clear language that the client can understand. What is more, Van Camp knew that the phrase "earned retainer" was problematic based on his prior discipline, yet chose to retain that language, prompting this proceeding. We therefore find Van Camp violated both ***RPC 1.4(b)*** and ***RPC 1.5(b).***

Count 5

By charging $25,000 under the facts of this case, Respondent violated ***RPC 1.5(a).***

A lawyer's fee must be reasonable. ***RPC 1.5(a).*** The Disciplinary Board concluded Van Camp violated this by charging $25,000 under the facts of this case. Of particular note were reasonableness factors 1, 4, 7, and 9: (1) the time, labor, novelty, difficulty, and skill required; (4) the amount involved and results obtained; (7) experience, reputation, and ability of the lawyer; and (9) and the terms of the fee agreement, including whether the client received a reasonable and fair disclosure of material elements of the fee agreement and the lawyer's billing practices. This conclusion 1s amply supported by the record. Decision Papers at 000022.

As already mentioned, experts testified for both sides concerning the reasonableness of the fee. Van Camp's expert, Mark Roecks, who obtained his understanding about the nature of the case from Deissner (not through reviewing the case file or pleadings-3 RP at 544), testified that a $25,000 flat fee would not be unreasonable to take the case to trial, at least at the inception of the agreement. He could not testify about the reasonableness of this in relation to the actual work done.

The WSBA's expert, Leslie Weatherhead, who had reviewed all the pleadings and the entire case file, testified without hesitation that the fee was excessive and unreasonable. Weatherhead's testimony raised questions about the quality of representation in relation to the results obtained (factor 4): for example, neither the TRO nor the preliminary injunction gave any legal basis for using the court's power to silence Honkala, and in Weatherhead's mind raised huge issues of prior restraint, yet, since it was not defended, it is basically what Honkala had to settle with. [FN8] Weatherhead questioned Van Camp's procrastination regarding discovery because in his opinion a lawyer working on a flat fee would pursue discovery aggressively up front to demonstrate his seriousness about the case. He questioned the August 31, 2007, discovery preparation since any depositions would not be ready in time for a summary judgment filing on September 10, 2007, the cutoff for dispositive motions. Weatherhead reviewed the time reconstruction and questioned its accuracy. His testimony was extensive and comprehensive, and left little doubt that the fee here was unreasonable.

FN8. Weatherhead testified, "I do have the opinion that Judge Van Sickle would have seriously entertained, had serious doubts about the legitimacy of using the power of the Federal Courts to silence a consumer who was unhappy about a product that he bought or tried to buy.

> . . . Had the court been forced to seriously address the appropriateness of the Lanham Act as applied in that situation, there may well have been a serious question of subject matter jurisdiction. If the preliminary injunction had been refused there's reason for optimism that he would not have settled on those terms." 4 RP at 833, 834, 840.

A review of Van Camp's reconstructed billing statements is extremely troubling and illustrates the unreasonableness of this fee. In describing his process, Barber, the paralegal tasked with the reconstruction, testified he went through the file page by page, building a timeline and accounting for any ***possible*** work that could have been done. For those tasks he was unfamiliar with, he simply guessed at the amount of time. His original estimates were in 10ths of an hour, but Van Camp was unhappy with the resulting $8,000 to $10,000 fee and instructed Barber to use half-hour increments for attorney time. This change bumped the fee up to between $16,000 and $20,000, but Van Camp was "unhappy that the figure was low." 4 RP at 882. Barber advised Van Camp the only way to increase the amount was to show Van Camp had reviewed every document that came in, and Van Camp instructed Barber to do so. The actual response or review time was immaterial, since Barber used the half-hour increment for each, so "if it was a two-sentence letter or if it was a one-page letter, it didn't make any difference." Barber spent four or five days perfecting this time reconstruction, with a final total of over $33,000. But Barber testified that the first version, the $8,000 one, was the fairest estimation of time actually spent on Honkala's representation. 4 RP at 876-92. [FN9] Given this extensive evidence, we conclude Van Camp violated *RPC 1.5(a)*.

FN9. For comparison purposes, it is worth noting that Campbell, Wendie's counsel, billed approximately $27,000, of which $3,000 to $6,000 was legal research, and the majority of billings were for work on the TRO and preliminary injunction. Decision Papers at 000020.

Count 9

By misrepresenting in his July 31, 2007 letter to Honkala that Campbell had provided a proposed preliminary injunction with his December 15, 2006 letter, Respondent violated *RPC 8.4(c)*.

It is professional misconduct for a lawyer to "engage in conduct involving dishonesty, fraud, deceit or misrepresentation." *RPC 8.4(c)*. The hearing officer concluded Van Camp violated this in a letter to Honkala when he misrepresented that the permanent injunction Honkala requested was actually the preliminary injunction Honkala had been served with and which currently in place. This too is supported by the record.

By the time Campbell sent the fax on December 15, 2006, Campbell had already filed the motion for the preliminary injunction and the hearing had been noted for a few days later. Campbell's letter sought to finally resolve the suit through a *permanent* injunction. By July 31, 2007, the preliminary injunction had been in place for eight months, and the parties had been to mediation, where the permanent injunction was referenced. Van Camp may not have possessed a copy of it, but this does not change the nature of the document itself. The hearing officer, who was the judge of Van Camp's credibility, found he knowingly withheld this document to prolong the case and justify his fee. We agree with the hearing officer and the Disciplinary Board, and find Van Camp violated *RPC 8.4(c)*.

3. Is the recommended sanction of disbarment appropriate?

The Disciplinary Board recommended disbarment as the presumptive sanction for counts 4 and 5, those related to the fee. [FN10] The hearing officer recommended two years' suspension. We give more weight to the Disciplinary Board's recommendation based on its unique experience and perspective in the administration of sanctions. *Preszler, 169 Wn.2d at 19* (citing *In re Disciplinary Proceeding Against Cohen, 150 Wn.2d 744, 754, 82 P.3d 224 (2004))*. We affirm the Disciplinary Board's recommendation unless we can articulate a specific reason to reject it. *See In re Disciplinary Proceeding Against Marshall, 167 Wn.2d 51, 90, 217 P.3d 291 (2009)*. We use a three step process when reviewing the recommended sanction. We first consider the ethical duties violated, the lawyer's mental state, and the actual or potential injury caused by the conduct, using the ABA *Standards*. Second,

we determine whether aggravating and mitigating circumstances call for a departure from the presumptive sanction. Third, if raised by the attorney being disciplined, we evaluate the proportionality of the sanction to the misconduct and the extent of agreement among the Disciplinary Board.

FN10. With multiple instances of misconduct, the overall sanction should be consistent with the sanction for the most serious offense. *Preszler 169 Wn.2d at 18*.

The total of Van Camp's ethical violations here is extremely serious. While we have already analyzed these violations, a few points merit further mention. First, Van Camp utilized a confusing fee agreement that he *knew* to be ambiguous. [FN11] The form used the phrase "earned retainer" when Van Camp argues he meant "flat fee." The agreement should have expressly established the basis for the fee. While retainer and flat fee agreements are ethically acceptable, *RPC 1.5(l)*, [FN12] the terms must be clear, in language the client can readily understand, and must be contained in a writing signed by the client. The client must know and understand the agreement. Any ambiguities will most often be construed against the lawyer as the drafter. In this case, adding to the confusion on this form, Van Camp's fee agreement contains both the "earned retainer" phrase and listed hourly rates, which suggests that hourly rates may be charged against the "earned retainer" amount. Further, the agreement did not define the scope of the representation. It should have. And, taking us to our next point, the services agreed upon should actually be performed.

FN11. In 2005, Van Camp was disciplined for violating *RPC 1.4(b)* for using the ambiguous term "earned retainer." During that proceeding, actual injury to the clients was found based on this because the clients were denied sufficient information to allow them to make an informed decision regarding Van Camp's representation.

FN12. A "retainer" is a fee paid by the client to ensure the lawyer is available to the client during a specified period or for a specified matter and may be separate from and in addition to any other fees paid for legal services actually performed. A "flat fee," on the other hand, constitutes complete payment for a lawyer's services. *RPC 1.5(J)(2)*. Numerous requirements for both types are listed in the rule and comments, and if a lawyer does not follow these, any payment is considered an advance fee deposit against future services or costs and must be deposited in the lawyer's trust account. *RPC 1.5* cmt. 12. Washington has diverged from the American Bar Association's *Model Rules of Professional Conduct* regarding these types of fee arrangements. While *RPC 1.S(J)* was not in effect at the time of these violations, Van Camp was aware of and subject to this definition of "retainer" due to prior discipline, as will be discussed below.

The only specification in the fee agreement was that Van Camp would represent and defend Honkala "in a suit." But Van Camp's various ethical violations demonstrate he fell far short of this and his general responsibility to represent his client. A lawyer must advise his client, advocate for his client's interest, and provide representation consistent with his client's needs. In this case, Van Camp did not communicate or explain a settlement offer to his client, despite numerous indications that his client wished to settle. He did not provide his client with diligent representation, for example, by failing to follow up with opposing counsel regarding settlement offers. He did not keep his client informed about his case. And Van Camp misled his client, telling Honkala there was no permanent injunction offer. This emerging pattern of dishonesty is very troubling.

Van Camp's reconstructed time sheets are further significant evidence of his ethical lapses. He does not dispute that this was an attempt to justify his fee. But it was not an honest justification. The entirety of the reconstruction is questionable. For example, it lists 9.5 attorney hours for the first day of the representation, when Honkala initially met Van Camp. This is in addition to listing 27.0 attorney hours for e-mails from and to Honkala. (Worth noting, we disbarred a lawyer largely based on her misrepresentations and falsification of documents to the WSBA during the investigation process. *In re Disciplinary Proceeding Against Whitt. 149 Wn.2d 707. 72 P.3d 173 (2003).)* This falsification of the time sheets indicates that Van Camp knew he was violating the RPCs.

This brings us to an examination of the lawyer's mental state and the injury caused by the misconduct. Under the ABA *Standards,* suspension is appropriate if the lawyer knowingly engages in violative conduct and causes injury or potential injury to the client, the public, or the legal system. ABA STANDARDS std. 7.2. Disbarment, however, is appropriate when the lawyer knowingly engages in violative conduct **with the intent to benefit himself or herself** that causes **serious or potentially serious** injury to the client, the public, or the legal system. ABA *Standards* std. 7.1 (differences emphasized).

The facts before us are sufficient to find the requisite mental state warranting disbarment. We give great weight to the hearing officer's factual findings regarding the lawyer's state of mind. *Cramer, 165 Wn.2d at 332.* The hearing officer found that Van Camp knowingly deceived his client with the ambiguous fee agreement and that the fee arrangement was drafted expressly and knowingly by Van Camp for his own benefit, so the knowledge and intent requirements were met. This is further evidenced by Van Camp's prior discipline, which put him on notice that his fee agreement was problematic, and by his dishonest time reconstruction.

The Disciplinary Board increased the sanction from the hearing officer's recommendation because it thought the injury to Honkala and the legal system was, in fact, serious. We agree. Importantly, the Disciplinary Board noted Van Camp withheld an early settlement offer that could have settled the litigation early and at minimal expense, and he refused to voluntarily refund any portion of the fee. [FN13] The WSBA argues the injury to Honkala was serious due to Honkala's financial situation. Honkala was unemployed because of a disability and had to get a loan to come up with the $25,000, and his family, which includes three children, supported itself mainly on his wife's income so $25,000 was a substantial amount of money to him.

Additionally, Van Camp's failure to diligently represent his client likely cost Honkala any chance he had in prevailing against Wendie on his lost contract expectancy claim, as his counterclaim was included in the litigation that was dismissed with prejudice. Together, these warrant a finding of serious injury.

FN13. In an interesting analogy, the WSBA notes that the intentional deprivation of over $5,000 constitutes first degree theft, a class B felony. *RCW 9.A.56.030.* The hearing officer ordered restitution of $15,000, three times that amount, which Van Camp refused to voluntarily repay. At oral argument in front of the Disciplinary Board, Van Camp's counsel explained the withholding was due to Van Camp's belief that fee arbitration, not a disciplinary action, was the appropriate forum to determine the fee dispute. Van Camp has now paid Honkala $15,000, but this was not part of the record before the hearing officer or the Disciplinary Board.

The extensive aggravating factors present give further support for disbarment. The hearing officer listed (1) prior discipline, (2) dishonest or selfish motive, (3) bad faith obstruction of the disciplinary process, (4) refusal to acknowledge wrongful nature of conduct, and (5) substantial experience in the practice of law as aggravators. [FN14] Additionally, the Disciplinary Board added a sixth factor: indifference to making restitution, after three years passed without Van Camp making any refund of fees. We consider these aggravators to be very serious. *See In re Disciplinary Proceeding Against Cramer, 168 Wn.2d 220, 237-38, 225 P.3d 881 (2010)* (aggravating factors of prior discipline, bad faith obstruction of disciplinary process, substantial experience, and indifference to making restitution would justify disbarment even if not the presumptive sanction).

FN14. The hearing officer considered Van Camp's reputation as a successful plaintiff's personal injury attorney as a potential mitigating factor, but this reputation did nothing to aid Honkala and is insufficient to overcome the extensive aggravating factors.

Of these aggravators, we are concerned with Van Camp's record of similar prior discipline. He has been disciplined three times in the last 25 years for violations similar to those here.

In 1985, Van Camp was censured for charging an excessive fee, engaging in conduct prejudicial to the administration of justice, making misrepresentations to the court and the WSBA, and engaging in potential conflicts of interest by making loans to a client and by having an ex parte hearing without notice to the other party. Restitution for the excessive fee was $29,000. Here, the hearing officer thought this violation too remote to have much bearing upon the present proceeding. The Disciplinary Board correctly disagreed, listing the excessive fee as an aggravator within its discussion of disbarment as a more appropriate sanction than suspension. We agree. We routinely consider misconduct dating back many years as an aggravating factor where the misconduct is similar. *See, e.g., In re Disciplinary Proceeding Against VanDerbeek, 153 Wn.2d 64, 92, 101 P.3d 88 (2004).*

In 2002, Van Camp was suspended for six months for making false statements, under penalty of perjury, in his bankruptcy proceeding. The hearing officer found this to be a poor reflection of Van Camp's record for truthfulness and honesty, and "'indicative of a serious disregard for upholding the integrity of the legal system and the profession'." Decision Papers at 000027. We agree. This violation is somewhat similar to the current misrepresentations to his client, and one of Van Camp's current aggravating factors, bad faith obstruction of the disciplinary process, which involved false statements as well.

In 2005, Van Camp was reprimanded for violating former **RPC 1.4(b)** (1985) by using the term "earned retainer fee" on intake of a potential medical malpractice case. In that case, the agreement was unclear how $1,000 paid by the client would be used, whether for costs, fees, or both, and whether any of it was refundable should Van Camp not pursue the case. There was actual injury to the client because she was denied sufficient information to allow her to make an informed decision regarding Van Camp's representation, similar to the current situation. Finding the evidence close, the hearing officer gave him the benefit of the doubt as to mental state and selfish motive and concluded he was merely negligent. Ultimately, Van Camp was reprimanded and placed on a two year probation, but a review of the hearing officer's recommendation reveals she chose not to recommend suspension because Van Camp was then currently suspended, and she assumed it would run concurrently. There were two terms of the probation:

a. Respondent may not accept earned retainer fees as defined in Formal Opinion 186 [FN15] in cases where he undertakes representation of personal injury victims, regardless of the cause of that injury, be it medical malpractice or otherwise. Respondent must treat all advance fee and/or cost payments as advance fee and/or costs payments, including maintaining them in his trust account until withdrawal is appropriate under [former] **RPC 1.4** (i.e., the fee is earned and due to the lawyer, or the cost is incurred).

FN15. Formal Opinion 186, which has since been withdrawn, discussed the difference between "advance fee deposits" and "retainers." Retainers secure a lawyer's availability, are considered earned at the time of payment, and are nonrefundable regardless of whether the lawyer performs any services provided the client agrees to such an arrangement. The important point was that the client understood and agreed, and a written fee agreement that could be easily referenced in case of questions was recommended. WASH. STATE BAR Ass'N, RESOURCES 450 (2002-2003). Formal Opinion 186 was withdrawn December 9, 2005, following our opinion in *In re Disciplinary Proceeding Against DeRui: 152 Wn. Jd 558. 99 P.3d 881 (2004),* and the subsequent void in guidance regarding retainers was filled with **RPC 1.5(l),** effective November 18, 2008.

b. Respondent must purchase a stamp, which must be used on all documents, pleadings[,] or correspondence received or produced by his office and sent to clients, to evidence the fact that the document has been sent or mailed to the client ....

Board Ex. 71. [FN16] The terms of the probation put Van Camp on notice to more adequately explain his fees and to provide clients with copies. Yet, the conduct in this case is largely the same.

The only aggravating factor Van Camp contests is the similarity of the 2005 discipline, attempting to distinguish his prior misconduct from the present. However, the language of the fee agreement that was found to be ambiguous was the same as used here. While some facts may differ in the present proceeding, what remains is that Van Camp did not learn from his prior discipline and correct the problem. We have disbarred attorneys for repeated behavior indicating the attorney did not learn from the previous disciplinary action. *See In re Disciplinary Proceeding Against Yates, 1 JO Wn.2d 444, 453, 755 P.2d 770 (1988)* (citing *In re Disciplinary Proceeding Against Allper, 94 Wn.2d 456, 617 P.2d 982 (1980); In re Disciplinary Proceeding Against Vetter, 104 Wn.2d 779, 711 P.2d 284 (1985); In re Disciplinary Proceeding Against Selden, 107 Wn.2d 246, 728 P.2d 1036 (1986)).*

Next, we consider the extent of agreement among the Disciplinary Board. "We give deference to the sanction decisions of a unanimous Disciplinary Board." *Cramer, 165 Wn.2d at 331* (citing *In re Disciplinary Proceeding Against Day, 162 Wn.2d 527, 538, 173 P.3d 915 (2007)).* But here the Disciplinary Board was split: seven favored disbarment while three preferred a three year suspension. Van Camp argues a split Disciplinary Board decision vitiates the deference we give, but he cites no authority that supports this proposition. The consideration of a divided Disciplinary Board is merely one aspect of our analysis. One thing is clear: the Disciplinary Board was unanimous in imposing a serious sanction of at least a three year suspension. With this in mind, we consider proportionality.

FN16. Van Camp was suspended in 2002 following the misrepresentations in the bankruptcy proceeding, and it was still 2002 when the charges were brought regarding this third disciplinary matter. Board Ex. 73. We denied Van Camp's petition for discretionary review regarding the third matter on January 6, 2005. The WSBA charged Van Camp with violating the terms of his probation in this current proceeding, but the hearing officer found this charge unproved because the majority of violations here occurred after January 6, 2007.

In conducting this proportionality analysis, we focus on the misconduct, aggravating factors, prior discipline, and the lawyer's culpability to determine whether the sanction here is appropriate. *See In re Disciplinary Proceeding Against Christopher, I 53 Wn.2d 669, 686-87, 105 P.3d 976 (2005).* The lawyer must show the recommended sanction disproportionate, *Marshall, 160 Wn.2d at 349,* and that the recommended "'sanction departs significantly from sanctions imposed in other cases.'" *In re Disciplinary Proceeding Against Hicks, 166 Wn.2d 774, 790, 214 P.3d 897 (2009)* (emphasis omitted) (quoting *In re Disciplinary Proceeding Against Haley, 156 Wn.2d 324. 339, 126 P.3d 1262 (2006)).*

None of the cases provided by Van Camp establish that disbarment would be disproportionate. [FN17] What they do suggest is that had Van Camp's misconduct been less serious, or not involved six counts, or not involved such extensive aggravating factors, or not been coupled with prior discipline, then disbarment might be disproportionate. But the misconduct before us, when considered together in its entirety, does warrant disbarment, and disbarment is not disproportionate.

FN17. *See Hicks 166 Wn.2d at 784-93* (2 year suspension for trust account violations and false statements to client and WSBA with similar aggravators but no prior discipline); *In re Disciplinary Proceeding Against Bohmer. 166 Wn.2d 759. 773-74. 214 P.3d 133 (2009)* (6 month suspension for failure to obtain consent for conflicts of interest and improper disclosure of client confidences); *Cramer 165 Wn.2d at 340* (8 month suspension for knowingly placing client funds in general account when no harm resulted); *In re Disciplinary Proceeding Against Treio. 163 Wn.2d 701. 185 P.3d 1160 (2008)* (3 month suspension for trust account violations coupled with prior discipline); *In re Disciplinary Proceeding Against Holcomb, 162 Wn.2d 563. 173 P.3d 898 (2007)* (6 month suspension for inappropriate financial dealings with client, no prior discipline); *In re Disciplinary Proceeding Against Poole. 156 Wn.2d 196. 125 P.3d 954 (2006)* (6 month suspension for failure to provide accounting and one misrepresentation with similar aggravators but no prior discipline); *DeRui: 152 Wn.2d 558* (12 month suspension for similar violations and aggravators but no prior discipline); *In re Disciplinary Proceeding Against Plumb. 126 Wn.2d 334. 892 P.2d 739 (1995/* (3 year suspension for first degree theft, no prior discipline).

CONCLUSION

The six ethical violations found by the hearing officer and affirmed by the Disciplinary Board are supported by substantial evidence. Van Camp violated his duty to advise and inform his client, to abide by the client's objectives, to act with reasonable diligence, and to be honest with his client. He used a fee agreement he knew to be ambiguous, failed to explain the basis for his fees, and charged an unreasonable fee. He did this knowingly and intentionally for his own benefit. Numerous aggravating factors, including similar prior discipline and bad faith obstruction of the disciplinary process, support the sanction of disbarment. Therefore, we adopt the Disciplinary Board's recommendation and disbar Van Camp.

MADSEN, C.J., and ALEXANDER, CHAMBERS, OWENS, FAIRHURST, J.M. JOHNSON, STEPHENS, and WIGGINS, JJ., concur.

Case Review Exercises

1. Did procedural errors deny Van Camp a fair hearing?
2. Does substantial evidence support the findings of misconduct?
3. Is the recommended sanction of disbarment appropriate?

Helpful Web Sites

Organization	Description	Internet Address
American Bar Association (ABA)	Association for attorneys. The site has a large amount of information and publications relevant to individuals working in the legal profession.	http://www.americanbar.org
ABA Law Practice Division	ABA site devoted to law practice management issues, including timekeeping and billing issues.	https://www.americanbar.org/groups/law_practice/
ABA Legal Technology Resource Center	ABA site devoted to technology. Includes resources and articles.	https://www.americanbar.org/groups/departments_offices/legal_technology_resources/
Association of Legal Administrators	National association for legal administrators. Contains resources and information related to law office management and legal administration.	http://www.alanet.org
Georgia State Bar Association	Articles on a variety of law office management topics, including billing-related articles and information.	http://www.gabar.org
The Paralegal Association	National association for paralegals. Contains many resources for paralegals.	http://www.nala.org
National Federation of Paralegal Associations	National association for paralegals. Contains many resources for paralegals.	http://www.paralegals.org

Timekeeping and Billing Software

Organization	Product/Service	Internet Address
Abacus Data Systems	Abacus Law—accounting and billing program	https://www.amicusattorney.com/abacuslaw
Perfect Practice	Perfect Practice—billing and accounting	https://perfectpractice.com
Clio	Web-based accounting and billing program	http://www.goclio.com
Journyx, Inc.	Journyx Timesheet/e-billing	http://www.journyx.com
PCLaw	PCLaw—Time Matters Legal timekeeping and billing software
Juris—Legal timekeeping and billing software	http://www.lexisnexis.com/law-firm-practice-management/pclaw/
Sage Software, Inc.	Timeslips legal timekeeping and billing software	http://na.sage.com/us/sage-timeslips
Thomas Reuters Elite	ProLaw legal timekeeping and billing software	http://www.elite.com
TimeSolv	Easy time and billing software	http://www.timesolv.com/

Suggested Reading

1. *Law Practice* magazine, published by the American Bar Association Law Practice Management Section. https://www.americanbar.org/groups/law_practice/publications/law_practice_magazine/.

2. *Paralegal Today* magazine, published by Conexion International Media, Inc. https://www.legalassistanttoday.com.

3. Foonberg, J. (2016). *How to Start and Build a Law Practice* (6th ed.). American Bar Association.

4. Greene, A. G., & Roberts, P.D. (2019). *The Lawyer's Guide to Increasing Revenue, E-Book* (3rd ed.). American Bar Association.

5. Robertson, M. A., & Calloway, J. A. (2008). *Winning Alternatives to the Billable Hour* (3rd ed.). American Bar Association.

6. Morgan, J. H., & Foonberg, J. (2003). *How to Draft Bills Client Rush to Pay* (2nd ed.). American Bar Association.

Client Trust Funds and Law Office Accounting

6

Chapter Objectives

After you read this chapter, you should be able to:

- Explain the importance of law office accounting including trust/escrow accounts.

- Describe the ethics rules regarding safeguarding client funds.

- Explain the budgeting process.

- Identify strategies for maintaining strong financial internal controls.

Some 18 months prior to the Office of Disciplinary Counsel's investigation, a lawyer was informed by his partner that proceeds on a claim he settled without the clients' knowledge had been misappropriated and that $1,695,000 owed to clients, Mr. and Mrs. A, was missing from the trust account. The lawyer took no action and instead executed a promissory note to Mr. and Mrs. A, agreeing to pay $12,000 a month until the debt was satisfied. This was one of several cases where client funds where misappropriated; the exact manner that this occurred varied from case to case. The Lawyers' Fund for Client Protection (Lawyers' Fund) received more than $1,286,000 in claims from respondent's clients and more than $3,800,000 in claims from partner's clients. The attorneys and other firm staff members routinely signed client names to settlement documents and endorsed client names on settlement checks. Many clients were unaware that their cases were settled, then discovered that medical bills went unpaid and their credit had been damaged. The lawyer was disbarred for misappropriating client funds by settling cases without the respective clients' knowledge or consent and allowing attorneys and other staff members of the firm to routinely sign the names of clients to settlement documents and endorsed their names on checks.

(*Source: In re Rivers,* 409 S.C. 80, 761 S.E.2d 234 (S.C., 2014).

The Importance of Understanding Law Office Accounting

It is important to have a basic understanding of law office accounting for several reasons. One reason is that attorneys, paralegals, and others office personnel either directly or indirectly work with trust/escrow accounts on a regular basis; they need to understand what trust accounts are and how they work. Another reason is that financial decisions drive the law office. It is important to understand how and why a law office operates and to know some basic accounting concepts. In smaller law offices, paralegals may have some bookkeeping or accounting responsibilities and may help prepare office or department budgets in some firms. Thus, it is important to have at least a basic knowledge of how to prepare a budget.

Client Funds—Trust/Escrow Accounts

A trust account, sometimes called an escrow account or a client account, is an important part of how law practices manage money. A trust or escrow account is a bank account, separate from a law office's or attorney's business or operating checking account, where unearned client funds are deposited. Nearly all private law practices have at least two checking accounts, one account from which normal business deposits and expenses are paid and a separate trust account, typically a checking account as opposed to a savings account, where only client funds are kept (see Exhibit 6-1). Checks used with the trust/escrow account will carry the title of Trust Account, Client Trust Account, or Escrow Account. Deposit slips also will have this designation, and a separate bank statement will be received for the trust account.

No Commingling of Client and Law Office Funds

Ethical rules prohibit the commingling of client funds and law office funds in the same account. This rule cannot be overemphasized, and there is virtually no flexibility regarding it.

Examples of How a Trust Account Is Used

There are times when clients pay a cash advance or an unearned retainer to an office to apply against future fees and expenses. Until the office has actually earned these monies, it must keep these funds in the trust account. The reason is simple: if client funds are commingled in the same bank account with general law practice funds, creditors could seize these funds to repay debts of the law practice.

The cash advance is just one way that the trust account is used. Trust accounts also are used in other ways, such as for distributing settlement checks. A **settlement** occurs when both parties in a dispute mutually agree to resolve the dispute on specified terms, such as for one party to pay to the other party a certain sum of money.

For example, suppose that an attorney represented a client in a personal injury case and the matter was settled out of court for $10,000. Suppose that the defendant issued a $10,000 check made payable to both the attorney and the client, and that the attorney was entitled to $2000 and the client to $8000. The proper way to dispose of the monies would be for both the attorney and the client

settlement
A mutual agreement to resolve a dispute on specified terms.

Exhibit 6-1 Operating and Trust Checks

Law Office Operating Account

BANK **1**

ADAMS & LEE
ATTORNEYS AT LAW
11 Canal Street, Suite 2B
New Orleans, Louisiana 70115
(212) 585-2342

004562

_____ 20____

PAY _____ DOLLARS

To The
Order Of

$ _____

ⅠⅠ˙08526ⅠⅠ2344567432 ⅠⅠ˙234 3ⅠⅠ˙

Authorized Signature

Law Office Trust Account

BANK **1**

ADAMS & LEE
CLIENT TRUST ACCOUNT
11 Canal Street, Suite 2B
New Orleans, Louisiana 70115
(212) 585-2342

000730

_____ 20____

PAY _____ DOLLARS

To The
Order Of

$ _____

ⅠⅠ˙944701ⅠⅠ9349569434 ⅠⅠ˙735 3ⅠⅠ˙

Authorized Signature

to endorse the settlement check. Then, the attorney would deposit the $10,000 settlement check in the trust account and subsequently write an $8000 check from the trust account to the client and a $2000 check from the trust account to the law office.

Ethics and Trust Accounts

Trust Funds and Office Operating Funds Cannot Be Commingled

Every state bar's ethical rules prohibit the commingling of client and law office funds. *Rule 1.15* regarding the rules of professional conduct provides that an attorney must hold the property of a client (such as unearned monies) in a separate account from the attorney's own operating account. An attorney must also maintain complete and accurate records regarding the client's property or monies, and such records must be maintained for five years after termination of the representation. According to the rule, the only time an attorney can deposit the attorney's own money in the trust account is to pay for bank service charges on the trust account. An attorney can only withdraw monies from the trust account as they are earned or actual expenses incurred. An attorney also has an ethical duty under the rule to promptly deliver to a client the monies that are owed to the client and to render to the client a full accounting of the monies in the matter.

It is permissible to use one trust account for all client funds as long as there is sufficient record-keeping to know how much each client has in the trust account. Law practices do not have to have separate trust accounts for every client. In fact, many law offices have only one trust account for all client monies. Large-sized offices may choose to have several trust accounts to help organize and control the large numbers of cases they have.

For example, suppose Attorney A has 25 clients who have monies deposited in one trust account, and each client has differing amounts. This is perfectly acceptable, as long as Attorney A knows—and has records to prove—exactly how much each client has in the trust account and maintains a running ledger to show what money was taken out check by check and deposited for each client (see Exhibit 6-2). This is why good record-keeping regarding trust accounts is crucial. Law offices must know to the penny how much each client has in the trust account so that when it comes time to give the money back to the client, the money will be there. Most state bars require that the bank statement for the trust account be reconciled every month, showing exactly which clients have what amounts in the trust account. A failure of the law office to keep detailed records can result in a finding by the state bar that the attorney is subject to disciplinary action.

Trust Accounts Cannot Be Used to Pay Law Office or Personal Expenses   Ethical rules also prohibit attorneys from using trust funds to pay for general office expenses. For example, if an attorney had client money in the trust account but did not have enough money in the attorney's law office checking account to cover the law office rent, the attorney would be absolutely prohibited from writing the rent check on the trust account.

Sometimes attorneys will say that they are simply "borrowing" money from the trust fund and will pay it back. This, too, is a violation of the ethical rules, even if the money is in fact repaid to the trust account within the same day. Client funds simply cannot be used in any way for the personal use of the law office or attorney.

Under *Rule 1.15(d)* regarding the rules of professional conduct, once the client is entitled to receive monies held in trust, the attorney must deliver the monies promptly. For example, if a client's case is concluded and the client still has money left in trust from a cash advance, the attorney has a duty to promptly return the funds.

Commingling of Client Funds Is a Common Problem

The commingling of client funds with attorney or law office funds is not a trivial or uncommon matter (see Exhibit 6-3). Hundreds of attorneys are

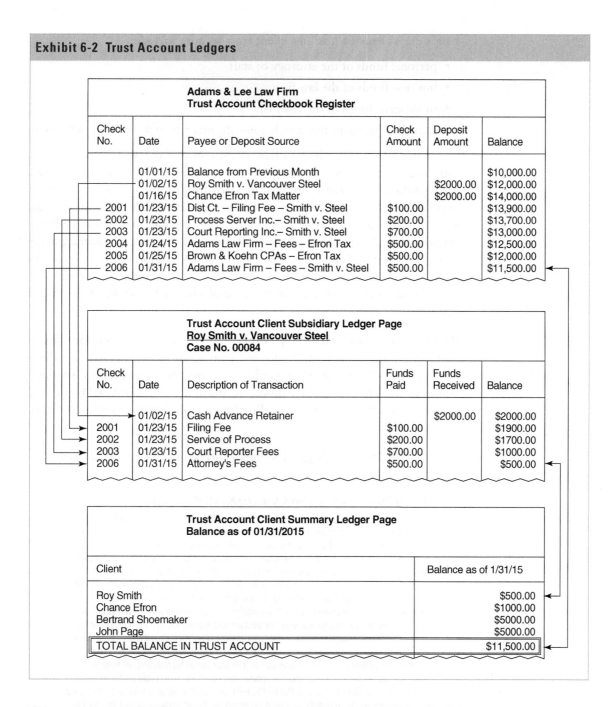

Exhibit 6-2 Trust Account Ledgers

Adams & Lee Law Firm
Trust Account Checkbook Register

Check No.	Date	Payee or Deposit Source	Check Amount	Deposit Amount	Balance
	01/01/15	Balance from Previous Month			$10,000.00
	01/02/15	Roy Smith v. Vancouver Steel		$2000.00	$12,000.00
	01/16/15	Chance Efron Tax Matter		$2000.00	$14,000.00
2001	01/23/15	Dist Ct. – Filing Fee – Smith v. Steel	$100.00		$13,900.00
2002	01/23/15	Process Server Inc.– Smith v. Steel	$200.00		$13,700.00
2003	01/23/15	Court Reporting Inc.– Smith v. Steel	$700.00		$13,000.00
2004	01/24/15	Adams Law Firm – Fees – Efron Tax	$500.00		$12,500.00
2005	01/25/15	Brown & Koehn CPAs – Efron Tax	$500.00		$12,000.00
2006	01/31/15	Adams Law Firm – Fees – Smith v. Steel	$500.00		$11,500.00

Trust Account Client Subsidiary Ledger Page
Roy Smith v. Vancouver Steel
Case No. 00084

Check No.	Date	Description of Transaction	Funds Paid	Funds Received	Balance
	01/02/15	Cash Advance Retainer		$2000.00	$2000.00
2001	01/23/15	Filing Fee	$100.00		$1900.00
2002	01/23/15	Service of Process	$200.00		$1700.00
2003	01/23/15	Court Reporter Fees	$700.00		$1000.00
2006	01/31/15	Attorney's Fees	$500.00		$500.00

Trust Account Client Summary Ledger Page
Balance as of 01/31/2015

Client	Balance as of 1/31/15
Roy Smith	$500.00
Chance Efron	$1000.00
Bertrand Shoemaker	$5000.00
John Page	$5000.00
TOTAL BALANCE IN TRUST ACCOUNT	$11,500.00

disbarred or suspended from practice every year for commingling client funds. In nearly every issue of every state's bar association journal, one can read about an attorney being disciplined for commingling client monies. Funds that ***must*** be held in a client trust account include

- client funds
- third-party funds
- funds that belong partly to a client and partly to an attorney (such as settlement funds)
- retainers for legal services that are unearned and that are the client's property until they are earned

Funds that *cannot* be held in a client trust account include

- personal funds of the attorney or staff
- business funds of the law firm
- investment funds of the law firm
- earned fee payments that have become the property of the attorney or law firm

State disciplinary authorities have taken notice of the problem of attorneys commingling client and business funds and attorneys stealing from their clients. Many jurisdictions now have rules in place that require a bank or financial institution to contact the state disciplinary authorities when any attorney trust account has checks returned as insufficient. When this happens, state disciplinary authorities conduct an audit of the law firm's trust account. In addition, many state disciplinary authorities conduct random audits of attorney trust accounts in an effort to prevent these problems from occurring. Commingling of client funds is a common problem that nearly always results in harsh discipline being levied against the attorney.

Bonding for People Handling Funds   Law offices should routinely buy a dishonesty bond from an insurance company to cover all employees handling client or law office funds. If an employee, covered by an employee dishonesty bond, steals client or law office funds, the insurance company would cover the loss up to the amount of the bond. Bonding is a prudent way to protect funds.

Exhibit 6-3 Commingling and Misappropriation of Client Trust Funds

Anthony Cavuto (In re Cavuto, 160 N.J. 185, 733 A. 2d 1174 (N.J., 1999)

Attorney had practiced law for 33 years. The attorney settled a personal injury claim for a client for $36,000. The settlement proceeds were deposited in the attorney's trust account. The attorney was to pay himself a fee of $12,000, the client's health-care providers a fee of $12,727, and the rest to the client. Within a month of depositing the funds in this trust account, the attorney paid himself 22 checks from the trust account, for a total of $26,259. The attorney never paid the medical expenses. The client did not discover that the medical expenses had not been paid until more than five years later when the doctor refused to treat the client because the client's bill had not been paid. The client complained to the disciplinary authorities and an audit was done. The audit showed that the attorney had very few trust account matters and that the attorney did not keep a trust account receipts journal, a disbursement journal, or client record cards. The attorney did not reconcile his trust account. The attorney tracked his trust account through the running balance on the check stubs. The attorney said that he kept fees in his trust account to keep them from the attorney's spouse, since the spouse had authority to sign checks on the attorney's business account. The attorney said that he had tried to review the file after the client complained, but that the file had been mistakenly purged by his spouse. The attorney then asked the client to bring in the client's records. Still, the attorney could not remember whether the medical providers had been paid. The attorney told the client that he did not have the money to pay the bills at that time, but that he would pay them from another settlement that he was handling for the client. The attorney never paid the medical providers. The attorney suffered from diabetes, depression, fatigue, forgetfulness, and memory loss. The New Jersey Supreme Court found that the attorney knowingly misappropriated client funds and disbarred the attorney. At the time of the disbarment, the actions of the attorney were 13 years old.

Committee on Professional Ethics and Conduct of the Iowa State Bar Association v. Minette, 499 N.W. 2d 303 (Iowa, 1993)

Attorney was client's financial advisor. Client was the recipient of a $40 million trust funded through 842,120 shares of stock. Attorney was authorized to write checks on client's bank account and to approve the sale of stock from the trust when greater funds were needed to pay client's expenses.

(continued)

(continued)

Attorney paid himself $9000 from client's account to settle a professional negligence claim against him and paid himself a $2500-per-month retainer. When the complaint was received, attorney had misappropriated about $88,000 in client funds. Attorney had no written fee agreement to establish any of these payments. Attorney was disbarred.

In Re-Petition for Disciplinary Action Against Erickson, 506 N.W.2d 628 (Minn., 1993)

A bank notified the state bar that an attorney's trust account was overdrawn. The state bar found that the attorney's trust account records were incomplete; that client subsidiary ledgers for several clients had not been timely established; and that, on occasion, the trust account had contained both client and personal funds, because the attorney had not promptly withdrawn earned fees. In three instances where there were no client funds in the trust account, only earned fees, respondent wrote checks on the account for filing fees, thus using the trust account as a personal business account. Attorney was suspended for 60 days.

Trust Account Management   Exhibit 6-4 shows a list of practices and strategies for proper trust account management. Careful and accurate record-keeping is crucial to properly maintaining a trust account. There are many computerized trust account programs available that allow even sole practitioners to inexpensively automate the tracking of a trust account. It is recommended that clients be notified in writing at least monthly regarding all activities in the trust account that affect their case. It is also recommended that the trust account be carefully reconciled every month and a document kept that verifies it. State disciplinary administrators routinely ask for attorney trust account reconciliation reports to prove that an attorney or office has such an account and that it is being properly used and maintained. Records should be kept regarding every deposit and withdrawal, including receipts, statements, and so forth, so that each transaction can be verified. ***Rule 1.15(a)*** regarding the rules of professional conduct requires that client trust account records be maintained for a minimum of five years after termination of the client matter, so it is important that records are carefully maintained even after a client's case is concluded.

Exhibit 6-4 Proper Trust Account Management

- Set up a trust account for all client monies and maintain written, detailed records (journals) of deposits and withdrawals from the trust account.
- On a monthly basis, review individual client balances and notify clients regarding all deposits and withdrawals.
- Unexpended costs and unearned fees should remain in the trust account until spent or earned.
- Promptly disburse funds owed to clients.
- Never commingle attorney/law firm monies in the trust account. Only a managing partner should sign on the account.
- Reconcile the trust account monthly and maintain a written record of the reconciliation.
- Follow the Interest on Lawyers' Trust Account (IOLTA) Rules for your state and retain trust records according to state rules.

Interest on Lawyers' Trust Account (IOLTA)
An interest-bearing account set up specifically to hold trust funds. The interest that accrues on an IOLTA account is given to a state bar foundation or other nonprofit legal organization for the good of the public.

budget
A projected plan of income and expenses for a set period of time, usually a year.

Interest on Lawyers' Trust Account (IOLTA) An **Interest on Lawyers' Trust Account (IOLTA)** account is an interest-bearing account set up specifically to hold trust funds. The interest that accrues on an IOLTA account is given by the financial institution to a state bar foundation or other nonprofit legal organization for the good of the public, such as funding for legal services/aid offices. The exact way that IOLTA programs operate differs from state to state, but most states provide that IOLTA accounts can only be used for client funds that are a nominal amount or that are expected to be held for only a short time. If a large amount of client funds are involved, or if an amount is to be held for a long period, then the attorney should open a separate interest-bearing account for that specific client and the interest should be given to the client. In 2003, the U.S. Supreme Court upheld the use of IOLTA accounts in ***Brown v. Legal Foundation of Washington***, 538 U.S. 216, 123 S. Ct. 1406 (2003).

Budgeting

Budgeting in any kind of law office is a good tool to control expenses and make a profit. Firms that develop and use budgets recognize that the budgeting process allows them to project and manipulate the profitability they want to achieve.

A **budget** is a projected plan of income and expenses for a set period of time, usually a year. Budgets allow firms to plan for the future; to anticipate problems, needs, and goals for the firm; and to allocate and manage resources. A budget also is a management tool used to keep revenues and expenses moving toward the profit goal. Exhibit 6-5 shows an example of a typical law office budget. Notice that the budgeting process involves careful development of planned operating expenses, professional and administrative staff sizes, professional and administrative salaries, desired income, and planned capital expenditures for items such as computers, copiers, and furniture.

Exhibit 6-5 Law Firm Budget—Master Budget

STEP 1—Income Budget	Hours	Rate	Total
R. Adams, Partner	1750	$350	$612,500
C. Lee, Partner	1750	$350	$612,500
J. Brown, Partner	1750	$400	$700,000
J. T. Green, Associate	2100	$250	$525,000
H. Hammond, Associate	2100	$250	$525,000
L. Noland, Associate	2100	$250	$525,000
C. Miller, Paralegal	1700	$90	$153,000
B. Gonzales, Paralegal	1700	$80	$136,000
Other Income			$150,000
SUBTOTAL (Total Billing)			$3,939,000
Time-to-Billing Percentage (actually billed)			95%
TOTAL TO BE BILLED			$3,742,050
Realization Rate			90%
TOTAL GROSS INCOME			**$3,367,845**

(continued)

(continued)

STEP 2—Staffing Plan/Salaries	Expense
EXPENSE BUDGET—SALARY EXPENSES & BONUS	
J. T. Green, Associate	$140,000
H. Hammond, Associate	$120,000
L. Noland, Associate	$120,000
C. Miller, Paralegal	$62,500
B. Gonzales, Paralegal	$52,500
M. Harris, Legal Administrator	$85,000
J. Parks, Computer/Network Specialist	$70,000
J. Inez, Secretary	$47,500
J. Logan, Secretary	$42,000
C. Glazer, Secretary	$40,000
T. Monie, Secretary/File Clerk	$37,500
B. Dover, Bookkeeper/Clerk	$37,500
R. Hopper, Receptionist	$35,000
TOTAL SALARY EXPENSE	**$889,500**

STEP 3—Other Expenses *(continues on next page)*	Expense
Accounting Professional Services	$10,000
Amortization of Leasehold Improvements	$7,500
Association/Membership Dues	$7,500
Client Billings/Write-Offs	$75,000
Continuing Legal Education	$15,000
Copying Costs (not billed to clients)	$45,000
Depreciation	$50,000
Employee Benefits and Taxes	$225,000
Entertainment	$20,000
Equipment Purchase/Computers/Network	$85,000
Equipment Rental	$8,500
Forms, Stationary, Paper	$7,500
Insurance (P/C, Malpractice, etc.)	$125,000
Housekeeping/Cleaning Services	$7,500
Marketing	$30,000
Office Supplies	$25,000
Other Taxes	$10,000
Postage	$14,000
Reference Materials/Library/Westlaw	$40,000
Rent Expense	$200,000
Repairs/Maintenance	$35,000
Telephone/Internet/Communication/Mobile	$50,000
Travel (not billed)	$45,000
Utilities	$100,000
TOTAL OTHER EXPENSES	**$1,237,500**
TOTAL ALL EXPENSES	**$2,127,000**

STEP 4—Determine Acceptable Profit Goal

NET INCOME TO BE DISTRIBUTED TO PARTNERS $1,240,845

It is not uncommon for paralegals to prepare budgets for their department, their office, or, in small firms, for the whole practice.

Budgeting and Planning

Budgeting and planning go hand in hand; a budget is just a specific type of plan. For example, if a firm's long-term strategic and marketing plans call for $30,000 of marketing expenditures, the budget needs to reflect that amount.

Steps in the Budget Process

Step 1. Income budget—One of the first steps in developing a firmwide budget is to draft an income budget (see Exhibit 6-5). An **income budget** estimates how many partners, associates, paralegals, and others will bill for their time, what the appropriate rates of hourly charge should be, and the number of billable hours each timekeeper will be responsible for billing.

When preparing an income budget, you should estimate as close to possible what the actual amount will be. However, if you are unsure of something, it is usually recommended that you be conservative in estimating the income budget; if you overestimate income and then rely on the overestimate in the expense budget and spend it, but income is actually lower than expected, you have a net loss. However, if you underestimate income and then the actual income is above the level (and expenses stay the same as budgeted), the firm makes a larger profit than was estimated and there is no harm done. One way to minimize this problem is to use a "time-to-billing" percentage. The **time-to-billing percentage** adjusts downward the actual amount that will be billed to clients, taking into account the fact that timekeepers are not always able to bill at their optimum levels due to vacations, sickness, and other unforeseeable events. Notice in Exhibit 6-5 that the firm used a time-to-billing of 95%, thus reducing its billing estimate by 5%. The time-to-billing percentage for most firms ranges from 85 to 100%. The purpose of the time-to-billing percentage is to build into the budget the fact that the firm may not bill all the hours it would like to.

Reasons that timekeepers may not bill their required number of hours include the following:

- Extended medical leave of timekeepers
- Too few clients
- Procrastination or other bad work habits
- Disorganization or inefficiencies in case management
- Failure to consistently report all billable hours
- Extensive use of the timekeeper on pro bono or other nonbillable tasks
- Marketing effects not as effective as planned

In some instances, paralegals' and attorneys' actual hours end up being greater than the budgeted hours. The firm makes an even larger profit than expected when this happens, as long as expenses remain as budgeted.

income budget
Estimate of how many partners, associates, legal assistants, and others will bill for their time, what the appropriate rates of hourly charge should be, and the number of billable hours each timekeeper will be responsible for billing.

time-to-billing percentage
System of adjusting downward the actual amount that will be billed to clients during the budget process, taking into account the fact that timekeepers are not always able to bill at their optimum levels.

Realization is also an important concept in budgeting income. **Realization** is what a firm actually receives in income as opposed to the amount it bills. In Exhibit 6-5, the firm anticipates that it will actually receive or collect 90% of what it bills. Some firms strive for a 95% rate, while others are comfortable with a rate as low as 80%.

Notice in Exhibit 6-5 that the firm usually sets the hourly rates for the year at this point. Setting rates in the income budget can be difficult. If a firm sets the rate too high, clients may take their business to a competing firm, but if rates are too low, it could mean a loss of revenue. It also is quite difficult to try to project income if the firm has many contingency fee arrangements. One way to do it is to look at gross income figures for contingency fees for the past several years to help in estimating future contingencies.

Step 2. Staffing plan—A staffing plan should also be established early in the budgeting process. A **staffing plan** estimates how many employees will be hired or funded by the firm, what positions or capacities they will serve, what positions will need to be added, what positions will be deleted, and how much compensation each employee will receive. One of the largest expenses of any professional service is salary costs. Thus, it is important that the firm determine whether positions will be added or cut, or whether existing staff members will receive cost-of-living adjustments or merit increases. A staffing plan also goes hand in hand with preparing the income budget.

Step 3. Estimating overhead expenses—Firms also must accurately estimate their general operating or overhead expenses. This can be fairly tricky because, in many cases, the estimates are covering a period that ends a minimum of a year in advance. For example, if a person was preparing a budget in November 2014, and the budget covered the period of January 2015 to December 2015, the person would not know until 14 months later whether the estimates were accurate. The time problem makes budgeting difficult; if insurance rates go up unexpectedly, if marketing costs rise significantly, or if large equipment breaks down unexpectedly, your budget will be greatly affected. When discussing the income budget, it should be noted that the preparer should be conservative in estimating income. However, when you get to the expense budget, the opposite is true. As always, you should try to be as accurate as possible in estimating expenses. However, if you question the validity of an item, you should be liberal in estimating the expense. This allows the firm to forecast unforeseeable events that might otherwise leave the budget short.

Step 4. Profit margin—The last step is to calculate income and expenses so that the firm budgets the targeted profit margin it needs. That is, if after the draft budget the firm is not happy with the profit margin, the preparer can manipulate and make changes in the budget—such as adding additional profit-making positions or cutting expenses further—to reach the desired goal. The following are some additional suggestions about budgets:

- **Communicate the budget to everyone involved.** For a budget to be effective, everyone in the firm should be aware of it, and there should be a consensus reached by the firm's management on major issues such as desired profits and equipment purchases. For instance, if even one timekeeper fails to charge the number of estimated hours, it can completely throw the budget off. Thus, it is very important that management stress the importance of the budget and communicate it effectively.

realization
Amount a firm actually receives in income as opposed to the amount it bills.

staffing plan
Estimate of how many employees will be hired or funded by the firm, what positions or capacities they will serve in, what positions will need to be added, what old positions will be deleted, and how much compensation each employee will receive.

- **Track budgets year-round and consult them regularly.** For budgets to be useful, they must be taken out of the desk drawer. That is, if a firm wants to purchase a piece of computer equipment, it is important that the budget be consulted to see if the purchase was planned or if there is room in the budget to allow for it.

- **Track the progress of the budget on a monthly basis.** As suggested before, budgets are of little value if they are not updated and used throughout the year. One way to use the budget year-round is to compare "budget" versus "actual." This allows the firm to know whether it is staying in line with its budget or if it needs to make midyear adjustments.

- **Always document your budget.** Always document budgets well, making notes and narrative statements in the budget itself. It is common to make assumptions when formulating a budget, and unless the preparer notes why the assumption was made, he or she may forget its purpose. It also helps in preparing the budget for next year.

- **Use zero-based budgets.** Although it is common for organizations to start the budgeting process for a new year by using the actual figures from the previous year and adding 4 or 5%, this is not an effective way of controlling costs and managing the firm. By using a **zero-based budgeting system**, everyone in the organization must justify and explain his or her budget figures in depth without using last year's figures as justification. In short, each year's budget is taken on its own merit.

zero-based budgeting system
Procedure that forces everyone in the organization to justify and explain his or her budget figures in depth without using prior years' figures as justification.

Collection/Income

Collecting monies that have been billed to clients is an important financial aspect of any law office; this is particularly true in small-sized law offices but can cause problems in large ones as well. Collection and income are closely tied to each other. Most newcomers to the legal field quickly find out that it is easy to bill but much more difficult to actually get paid for legal services rendered. Billing large amounts of time and not getting paid is a direct path to bankruptcy for any law office. The first step in collecting a high percentage of billings is for the attorney to carefully select and weed out what clients' cases he or she will accept in the first place. Attorneys must do a good job of weeding out cases that will not be profitable; there is no substitute for this. Another strategy that many law offices take is to get monies up front using deposits in the form of earned and unearned retainers.

Other strategies law offices use for collecting fees billed include sending regular monthly billings and withdrawing from cases as soon as possible once it is determined the client will not pay. This is sometimes difficult to do since ethical rules put limits on when attorneys can withdraw from cases. *Rule 1.16* regarding the rules of professional conduct provides that an attorney may withdraw from representing a client when:

- the withdrawal can be done without negatively affecting the client's interests;
- the attorney believes that the client's conduct is criminal or fraudulent, or that the client has used the attorney's services to commit a crime or fraud;
- the client persists in a course of conduct with which the lawyer fundamentally disagrees;

- the client has not completed an obligation to the attorney regarding the attorney's services;
- the representation of the client is causing an unreasonable financial burden on the attorney;
- the client is unreasonably difficult to work with;
- there is some other good cause.

In most courts, an attorney must ask for permission to withdraw from the matter. If a court denies an attorney's request to withdraw, the attorney must ordinarily continue to represent the client. For example, if an attorney requests to withdraw from a complex criminal case right before trial, the interests of the client could be affected negatively and a court might reasonably deny the attorney's request to withdraw. If an attorney is permitted to withdraw from a case, the attorney must act prudently to protect the client's interests, such as giving the client reasonable notice, providing the client with his or her file, and refunding unused monies for fees or expenses.

Another strategy to collect on billings is for the attorney to actually sue the client for the fee. This is usually a method of last resort, as no attorney wants to be put in the situation of suing his or her own client; in some instances, however, this is the only option.

Internal Controls

Law offices of every type—private, corporate, government, and legal aid—must establish good internal control procedures. **Internal control** refers to procedures that an organization establishes to set up checks and balances so that no individual in the organization has exclusive control over any part of the accounting system. Internal controls discussions are usually saved for accounting professionals. However, embezzlement by law practice personnel has become a major issue (see Exhibit 6-6) and is quite prevalent. If embezzlement occurs in an organization, it signals that its internal controls are weak and ineffective.

internal control
Procedures that an organization establishes to set up checks and balances so that no individual in the organization has exclusive control over any part of the accounting system.

Exhibit 6-6 Embezzlement Is Common in Law Practices

Legal Assistant Sentenced to Four Years in Prison

A legal assistant with five years of experience stole more than $102,000 by forging the names of attorneys he worked for on settlement checks that should have been deposited into the attorneys' trust account. The legal assistant passed himself off as a lawyer to the attorneys he was working for and kept the monies from 10 personal injury settlements. The legal assistant began the scheme by only taking the attorney's portion of the settlement check and quickly graduated to taking all of the monies in several settlements. The legal assistant was sentenced to four years in a state prison and restitution.

Legal Assistant Allegedly Launders Insurance Rebate Checks

A legal assistant allegedly stole approximately $724,000 from an insurance company over a two-month period. The legal assistant allegedly conspired with another person to issue 34 fraudulent rebate checks to policyholders. The legal assistant allegedly laundered the checks through a number of different accounts. The insurance company realized that something was wrong and started an investigation, but not before nearly three-quarters of a million dollars was gone. The legal assistant was charged with 5 counts of money laundering, 14 counts of embezzlement, and conspiracy and forgery charges.

(continued)

(continued)

Former Paralegal Sentenced in Embezzlement Case

A former paralegal was sentenced to two months of home detention and one year of probation for having embezzled $8,000 in funds belonging to a bankruptcy debtor while employed as a paralegal at an East Coast law firm. The paralegal faced a maximum penalty of five years' imprisonment and a $250,000 fine. The paralegal was custodian of the bankruptcy debtor's account and was responsible for preparing checks for the bankruptcy trustee. The embezzlement was discovered a few months after the paralegal left the firm while he was working at another firm. "We discovered certain irregularities during a routine inventory of accounts and turned the information over to the proper authorities," said one of the firm's directors. The case was investigated by the Federal Bureau of Investigation. At the time of sentencing, the paralegal informed the U.S. attorney's office that he was no longer working at the new firm and that he voluntarily withdrew from law school entirely.

Sources: N. J. paralegal jailed for theft (2004, January/ February). *Legal Assistant Today*, 24; A "clean" getaway . . . almost (1999, May/June). *Legal Assistant Today*, 19; *Legal Assistant Today* (1992, July/August), 27.

Internal controls must be established in both large- and small-sized firms. Interestingly enough, small-sized law offices need internal controls more than large-sized firms do. Why? Because fewer people handle the finances in a small-sized office, and there are typically fewer written and strict procedures. Thus, the opportunity to embezzle tends to be greater in a smaller office. Therefore, it is absolutely critical in a small-sized law office to have exceptionally good internal controls. The downside of internal controls is that it takes time to do them right and they can slow down the financial process (e.g., by requiring a partner to sign all checks instead of having a bookkeeper sign them). This is particularly true in small-sized firms, but it is the only way to ensure that embezzlement and fraud do not take place.

What type of internal control procedures could limit the possibility of embezzlement? There are several.

- **Never allow a bookkeeper or person preparing checks to sign checks or to sign on the account.** Never let the individual who writes the checks sign on the account. In addition, never let any one person record the checks in the checkbook (or equivalent), prepare the checks, obtain signature(s) on the checks, and mail the checks. Embezzlement is more likely to happen in that case. A partner or ranking member of the firm should sign all checks, if possible. An alternative is to require two signatures on all checks.

- **Have careful, unannounced, routine examination of the books.** A partner or other ranking member of the law office with no direct accounting responsibilities should carefully look over the books on a weekly basis. A partner also should account for all monies on a regular basis (once every week or two weeks) by reviewing bank statements and canceled checks for the authenticity of the signatures, reviewing the reconciliation register, ensuring that check numbers out of sequence are not being cashed, and looking through cash disbursement records carefully. These procedures must be done for both the office business account and the trust account.

- **All documents must routinely be read and examined—no exceptions.** Never sign or let someone else sign checks, correspondence, or other important documents without carefully reading the material. It is very easy to hand documents to people and ask for their signature immediately. Do not do this, and do not let someone else do it. Everyone involved should always check all the supporting documentation of a check.

- **All checks should be stored in a locked cabinet.** All checks should be kept under lock and key at all times when not in use, and access for writing checks should be given to as few people as possible.

- **Never let the person signing the checks reconcile the account.** The person writing or signing the checks should not be allowed to reconcile the bank account or even open the monthly bank statement. If the person who is preparing and signing the checks is allowed to reconcile the account, that person will be able to write him- or herself a check, sign it, and destroy the check when it comes in the bank statement. This might tempt even a basically honest person. Oversight is the key. Never let anyone have the opportunity to embezzle; set up good procedures and follow them.

- **Use check request forms.** Check request forms are also used to bolster internal control procedures. If, for instance, an employee or attorney needed a check for a client expense or for an expense charged to the firm, the person would be required to complete a form similar to the one shown in Exhibit 6-7. Small-sized law offices should also use check requests whenever possible.

- **Establish guidelines for how the mail should be opened.** The mail should be opened by someone with no accounting duties, such as a receptionist, secretary, or mailing clerk. When a check is received, the person opening the mail should be instructed to immediately endorse the check on the back with "FOR DEPOSIT ONLY" in ink or with a stamp. If the bookkeeper or someone in accounting opens the mail, there is absolutely nothing to stop that person from taking the check and cashing it. This would be easy to do, because the firm would have no record of it.

- **Use nonaccounting personnel to help with internal controls.** An additional internal control would be for the receptionist, secretary, or another person to prepare the bank deposits, because he or she would be separated from the accounting department and would not have recorded the cash receipts in the accounts receivable system. In this way, all cash receipts and bank deposits are independently verified by someone completely outside the accounting department who has no access to accounting records.

  A very common way embezzlement occurs is through refund checks. For example, it is not uncommon for firms to receive large refund checks from insurance companies and other vendors. If a person in the accounting department opens the mail, he or she could endorse the check and deposit it into his or her own account with little possibility of someone finding out about it. Why? Because the original invoice would be shown as paid on the firm's books, and no one else would know that a refund had ever been received.

- **Require two signatures on checks over $10,000.** Checks over a certain dollar amount might also require a signature by a second individual (i.e., two signatures on the check). This is another example of an internal control; it would limit large checks from going out of the firm with the authority of only one individual.

Exhibit 6-7 Check Request Form

ADAMS & LEE
ATTORNEYS AT LAW
11 Canal Street, Suite 2B
New Orleans, Louisiana 70115
(212) 585-2342

CHECK REQUEST FORM

Client Name and File Number: _____

Date of Request: _____

Request Made By: _____

Bank Account: General Business Account   Trust Account   (Circle One)

Amount of Check: $ _____

Check Should Be Made Payable To: _____

Address of Payee: _____

Detailed Description: _____

_____

_____

_____

_____

Accounting Use Only

Account No./Code: _____

Approved by: _____   Date: _____

- **Stamp invoices "CANCELED."** Once a check has been paid, the invoice should be stamped "CANCELED," so that no one could intentionally resubmit the same invoice for payment.

- **Have an audit done once a year or hire a Certified Public Accountant (CPA) to help you set up internal controls.** A yearly audit by an accounting firm can help find embezzlement, and strengthen and monitor internal control procedures. If your firm cannot justify the cost of an audit, hire a CPA to help you set up good internal controls and have him or her come in once a year to review them.

Lawyers and Nonlawyers Cannot Share Fees

Attorneys are generally barred from directly sharing their legal fees with a nonlawyer, such as a paralegal; in fact, **Rule 5.4** regarding the rules of professional conduct prevents a lawyer from sharing legal fees with a nonlawyer. The sharing of a fee between a lawyer and a nonlawyer could interfere with the lawyer's professional judgment and lead to the nonlawyer being concerned only with profits and not the best interests of his or her clients. Regarding paralegals, this typically arises when a paralegal refers a person to an attorney for representation. The attorney is prohibited from sharing the representation fee with the paralegal or paying the paralegal specifically for the referral. Exhibit 6-8 presents an example of lawyers sharing fees with nonlawyers.

Exhibit 6-8 Lawyers Cannot Share Fees with Nonlawyers

In re Guirard, **11 So.3d 1017 (La., 2009)**. Respondents, E. Eric Guirard and Thomas R. Pittenger were partners in a law firm with locations in New Orleans and Baton Rouge. In 2000, the Office of Disciplinary Counsel (ODC) began its investigation into compensation arrangements for nonlawyers, including case managers, legal assistants, secretaries, and agents.

ODC found that five case managers received compensation as commissions on the firm's gross legal fees at a basic rate of 15% on cases directly assigned to the case manager and 7.5% on cases reassigned to them. The firm manager, a nonlawyer, was paid 1% commission of the firm's total gross legal fees collected on all settled cases in addition to their salary. Legal assistants were paid either 6% or 6.5% of fees paid to the supervising attorney. Investigators were paid $50 for obtaining signed client forms for the law firm and additional compensation if additional clients were signed up while visiting the initial client.

ODC found that the nonlawyer case managers were paid a piece of the action if the case was settled and no commissions if the case was not settled and had to be litigated. Respondents had engaged in fee splitting with nonlawyers in clear violation of **Rule 5.4(a)**, which prohibits lawyers and law firms from sharing fees with nonlawyers. Respondents were disbarred for fee splitting violations, delegating the handling of their clients' cases to their nonlawyer staff, motivating them to settle claims quickly to receive commissions in conflict with the clients' best interest, and misconduct, noting their practices were egregious.

Summary

Ethical rules require that client funds not be commingled with law office operating funds, meaning that a law office must have a trust or escrow account. A trust accounting is a bank account, separate from a law office's or an attorney's operating checking account, where unearned client funds are deposited, such as unearned retainers or the proceeds of a settlement. Attorneys have an ethical responsibility to safeguard client property. Attorneys and law offices must carefully track all clients' funds in a client trust account. This includes having trust account ledgers for all transactions in the account, including ledgers for each individual client. In addition, the only time an attorney can have his or her own funds in the client trust fund is to pay for bank services charges. IOLTA is an acronym meaning Interest on Lawyers' Trust Account; an IOLTA account is an interest-bearing bank account set up specifically to hold client trust funds. The interest that accrues on an IOLTA account is given by the financial institution to a designated state bar foundation or other nonprofit legal organization (in accordance with state rules) for the good of the public.

A budget is a projected plan of income and expenses for a set period of time, usually a year. Most budgets consist of an income budget, staffing plan, general overhead expenses, and an estimated profit.

Collecting monies after they have been billed is an important issue for all law offices. Strategies for collecting monies that are due to an attorney or law office include carefully selecting and accepting cases; obtaining monies in the way of deposits/retainers up front, before legal work on a case has started; withdrawing from cases where a client will not pay (if allowed); and suing clients as a last resort if they do not pay.

Law offices must safeguard their assets by implementing internal control procedures, which establish checks and balances so that no individual in the firm has exclusive control over any accounting system. It is generally unethical for an attorney to share a fee with a nonlawyer.

Key Terms

budget
income budget
Interest on Lawyers' Trust Account (IOLTA)
internal control

realization
settlement
staffing plan
time-to-billing percentage
zero-based budgeting system

Practical Applications

1. You are a paralegal in a five-attorney legal services/aid practice. The office manager, who writes all the checks for the organization, will not be back for several hours. Your supervising attorney asks you to get the checkbook out of the office manager's desk and issue a check that she needs right now. You fill in the manual check stub and type the check. Because the office manager is not there to sign the check, you hand the check to your supervising attorney to sign with several other papers. The attorney quickly signs her name while looking at the other documents. On your way to your office, the receptionist asks you to drop off the office manager's mail in his office. You notice that one of the envelopes appears to be a check from the local bar association that makes contributions to the practice as a community service. You also notice that another of the envelopes appears to be a bank statement and returned checks for the previous month. The office manager uses the returned checks and bank statement to reconcile the bank account. You place all the items on the office manager's desk as requested. Do you see any potential problems? Would it matter if the office manager had been there for 20 years, was extremely trustworthy, and refused to even take a vacation in that it might take him away from work? What recommendations would you make?

2. Your office represented a business client in litigation. During the litigation, the client made several cash advances. The matter has been concluded for approximately two months and the client has a balance in the trust account of about $20,000. The client has requested that the money be returned, but the supervising attorney has not gotten around to it yet. How would you analyze the situation, and what would you do?

3. You have just been given the assignment to begin work on incorporating a new business. At the first meeting with the client, the client hands you a check for $5000 and states that

although no work has been performed on the case, this was the agreement that the client and your supervising attorney worked out last week on the telephone. Later, you hand the check to the supervising attorney. The attorney says to just deposit it in the office's account. What problems would you face, what would you do, and why?

4. As a paralegal in a sole practitioner's office, you sometimes become "burned out" and tired. The attorney you work for is very appreciative of your hard work and would like to give you incentives when possible to keep you motivated. The attorney mentions that she will pay you a bonus equal to 10% of any new client retainers you are responsible for bringing in. How does this sound to you? Analyze this arrangement from an ethics perspective.

5. You are a paralegal in a relatively small office. One day, one of the partners in the office instructs you to transfer $5000 from the trust account into the office's general account. You ask him what case is involved. The partner says "There is no case name, but it doesn't concern you." What would you do? Explain your answer.

6. At 8:00 A.M. on a Monday morning, your supervising attorney rushes into your office. She states that at 10:00 A.M. she has a meeting with one of the firm's administrators to go over her draft version of the proposed budget for her satellite office. Although the office is relatively small, she must submit a budget that will produce a reasonable profit for the firm. Unfortunately, she has a meeting with a client and a court appearance to go to before the 10:00 A.M. meeting. She hands you a list of her notes and asks you to please come through for her on this one. You reluctantly agree, but then remember that your bonus at the end of the year will depend on how profitable your office is. Suddenly, you feel better about the assignment.

Below are the attorney's notes.

- Rent is $5000 a month, but halfway through the year the lease calls for a 5% increase.
- The paralegals will bill at $80 an hour and must work a minimum of 1750 hours. You think that they will do this, since they will not be eligible to receive a bonus unless they work this amount.
- Utilities are included in the lease agreement, so do not worry about these.
- Associates will bill at $225 an hour. You figure that they will bill no less than 1900 hours because if they do not, they will not look good for a partnership position.
- From past history, the firm has determined that its time-to-billing percentage is 98% and the realization rate is 92%.
- Telephone cost is expected to be $4000 a month.
- Staffing is as follows:

  Two paralegals
  Four secretaries
  Three associates

Last year, paralegals were paid, on average, $50,000; secretaries, $40,000; and associates, $90,000. Budget a 3.5% cost-of-living adjustment and a 2.5% merit increase.

- Fringe benefits and taxes are figured at 25% of the total of the salaries.
- Office supplies and stationery expenses will be about $20,000.
- The office must purchase four computers. Your best estimate is that they will cost about $3000 each when all costs are included (installation, cabling, software, printers, network hardware, training, maintenance contract, etc.).
- All other items, such as malpractice/general liability insurance and professional services, will be prorated to your office by the accounting office. You do not need to worry about this now.

  What profit or loss is the office budgeted for?

7. You are a paralegal manager in a small- to medium-sized firm. The firm administrator asks you to prepare a proposed income budget for your department of six legal assistants. You are not required to do an expense budget, as this is handled by the administrators and the accounting department. From past years, you know that you must sit down with each of the paralegals and discuss billable hours, hourly rates, and so forth. You do not relish this much, because the firm has consistently pressed for more and more billable hours. Thus, this topic can be somewhat touchy for you as a manager. Below is the information you obtained to help you. Also, note that time-to-billing percentage is figured at 95%, and the realization rate is also 95%.

Paralegal #1 typically works for one of the firm's general litigators. Because of her extensive background in this area, her hourly charge is about $90. However, during trial and trial preparation, her hourly charge is usually about $100. She figures that about 40% of her time will be spent either in trial or preparing for trial. About 10% of her time is spent traveling to and from trials, finding witnesses, and so on. Her travel time is billed at $60 an hour. She is a very hard worker, and although she billed 1900 last year, she is requesting that her billable hours be lowered to 1800. You tentatively agree.

Paralegal #2 has recently been given a new assignment: to work almost exclusively on insurance defense cases. His typical hourly billing rate was $85. However, you know that the insurance company that he will primarily be working for will only pay a maximum of $75 an hour for paralegal time. In addition, the insurance company is extremely picky about its invoices and absolutely refuses to pay for anything even remotely close to secretarial functions. The paralegal states he thinks that 1750 is a reasonable number of billable hours, considering his present salary. You figure that, based on your experience, the insurance company will either reasonably or unreasonably question about 40 hours that he bills. You reduce your estimate by this amount just to be safe.

Paralegal #3 handles workers' compensation cases. Unfortunately, these cases are almost all taken on a contingency basis. The firm typically recovers 25% of these types of cases. You estimate that the firm will receive about $600,000 in revenues from this gross part of its practice. You also note that about one-third of this is usually allocated to the work of the paralegal.

Paralegal #4 works mainly in the probate area. She typically receives about $70 per hour for her work. You note that although she billed more than 2000 hours last year, she did not take any vacation and took very little time off. Your conversation reveals that she is going to take three weeks off for an extensive vacation and that she may need to take an additional week off for medical reasons.

Paralegal #5 is new to the firm. From your past experience, you do not want to burn him out by putting too many billable hours on him at first. You also recognize that he will have many nonbillable hours during the first several months due to staff training and general unfamiliarity with the firm. You budget him for 1600 hours. He will be a rover, working for many different people, and thus his hourly billing rate is hard to estimate, but you budget $70.00 an hour.

Finally, Paralegal #6: yourself. You have many administrative responsibilities. You would like to set a good example, so you budget yourself at 1400 hours. You bill at $90 per hour. You are responsible for coordinating the efforts of the legal assistants under you, for handling personnel-related issues, and many other duties. You also remember that you are to take a greater role in marketing this year and that approximately 160 hours of your time will be nonbillable while you handle this function.

8. Your managing attorney has asked you to compute the current Balance in Trust for the Singer case for both fees and expenses. She asks you to track each of them separately. Here is what you find in the file:

- January 1, initial deposit/retainer against future fees (unearned) of $20,000 paid by client
- January 1, initial deposit/retainer against future expenses (unearned) of $10,000 paid by client

- February 1, client billed for $3500 in fees and the same amount paid out of the client trust fund to the attorney

- February 1, client billed for $2000 in expenses and the same amount paid out of the client trust fund to the attorney

- February 15, check from the client trust fund for filing fees of $100

- February 21, check from the client trust fund for $200 for service of process

- March 1, client billed for $5500 in fees and the same amount paid out of the client trust fund to the attorney

- April 1, client billed for $10,000 in fees and the same amount paid out of the client trust fund to the attorney

- April 17, check from the client trust fund for court reporting charges of $6000

9. A case settles in the amount of $120,000 for your client. The money has been deposited into the firm's client trust account. Your managing attorney has asked you to calculate the amount owed to all of parties. Below are the facts:

- Your firm is to pay medical expenses of your client out of the settlement of $10,000.

- Your firm has incurred $12,000 in legal expenses.

- Your firm billed hourly on the case in the amount of $40,000 but your managing attorney agreed to reduce the fee to $35,000.

- The client owes the firm $10,000 on another case and has agreed in writing to pay the firm that fee from this settlement.

On the Web Exercises

1. Go to the ABA Center for Professional Responsibility at http://www.americanbar.org. Find the *ABA Model Rules of Professional Conduct*; read and print out *Rule 1.15* Safekeeping Property and the Comment.

2. Visit five state bar association Web sites and find three articles on trust accounting, legal financial management, legal budgeting, law office profitability, or accounting for client funds. The following link will take you to a Web site that connects to all state bar sites: http://www.nationallist.com/resources/associations-state-bar-list.

3. Using a general search engine, such as http://www.google.com or http://www.yahoo.com, or state bar association Web sites, find a model chart of accounts for a law office.

4. Using a general search engine, such as http://www.google.com or http://www.yahoo.com, find a minimum of three sites (they do not need to be law related) that discuss what internal controls are and why they are important. Print out your results.

5. Using a general search engine, such as http://www.google.com or http://www.yahoo.com, find a minimum of three accounting or trust accounting programs (not listed in the Helpful Web Sites section of this chapter) that can be used in a law office.

Projects

1. Using a general search engine, such as http://www.google.com or http://www.yahoo.com, search for trust accounting procedures. Alternatively, go to a library or visit state bar association Web sites, such as the Alabama State Bar Association [http://www.alabar.org], and write a detailed paper on ethical trust account practices.

2. Research the issue of IOLTA accounts. Go to http://www.findlaw.com and print out and read the U.S. Supreme Court case of **Brown v. Legal Foundation of Washington**, 538 U.S. 216, 123 S. Ct. 1406 (2003). Try selecting "For Legal Professionals," scroll until you see "Cases and Codes," and then click on "Supreme Court" and "Supreme Court Opinions." You should then be able to enter the site of the case—538 U.S. 216. Why is the issue of IOLTA so controversial? What did the plaintiffs argue in the case? How did the Court decide? Why was there a descent in the case?

3. Research and write a paper on computerized financial management and trust accounting systems. Visit the American Bar Association Technology Resource Center http://www.americanbar.org/groups/departments_offices/legal_technology_resources.html and state bar association Web sites, as well as other legal technology Web sites, and review helpful articles and materials you find. Also go to the financial and trust accounting software Web sites listed in the Helpful Web Sites section of this chapter. Compare and contrast some of the different products that are available. Which one were you most impressed with, and why?

4. Using a general search engine, such as http://www.google.com or http://www.yahoo.com, search for law office profitability. Alternatively, go to a library or visit state bar association Web sites and write a detailed paper on how law offices can be profitable. Your paper should cover such topics as how to increase revenue, control expenses, increase collections, and related topics.

5. Using a law library, state bar journal magazine, Westlaw/LexisNexis, or the Internet, write a paper that summarizes a minimum of three attorney discipline cases regarding the misuse of client funds, client trust accounts, or related topics. Be sure to include an analysis of the case, what the court found, what ethical rules were at issue, what rules were violated, what discipline was imposed, and why.

Case Review

In the Matter of a Member of the Bar of the Supreme Court of the State of Delaware:

JOHN J. SULLIVAN, JR., Petitioner,

No. 698, 2013

SUPREME COURT OF DELAWARE

Board Case No 2011-0233-B

FILED: December 27, 2013

Submitted: January 16, 2014

Decided: March 7, 2014

Cite as: *In re Sullivan*, 86 A.3d 1119 (Del. 2014)

Before HOLLAND, JACOBS and RIDGELY, Justices.

ORDER

This 7th day of March, 2014, it appears to the Court that the Board on Professional Responsibility has filed a Report on this matter pursuant to Rule 9(d) of the Delaware Lawyers' Rules of Disciplinary Procedure. The Office of Disciplinary Counsel filed no objections to the Board's Report. The Respondent did file objections to the Board's Report. The Court

has reviewed the matter pursuant to Rule 9(e) of the Delaware Lawyers' Rules of Disciplinary Procedure and approves the Board's Report.

NOW, THEREFORE, IT IS ORDERED that the Report filed by the Board on Professional Responsibility on December 27, 2013 (copy attached) is hereby APPROVED and ADOPTED. The Respondent is hereby disbarred effective immediately.

BY THE COURT: Henry duPont Ridgely, Justice.

BOARD ON PROFESSIONAL RESPONSIBILITY OF THE SUPREME COURT OF THE STATE OF DELAWARE

In the Matter of a Member of the Bar of the Supreme Court of Delaware

JOHN J. SULLIVAN, JR. Respondent.

CONFIDENTIAL

Board Case No. 2011-0233-B

BOARD REPORT AND RECOMMENDATION

This is the report of the Board on Professional Responsibility of the Supreme Court of the State of Delaware (the "Board") setting forth its findings and recommendations in the above captioned matter.

The members of panel of the Board (the "Panel") are Wayne J. Carey, Esquire, Yvonne Anders Gordon, Ed.D. and Lisa A. Schmidt, Esquire (the "Chairperson"). The Office of Disciplinary Counsel (the "ODC") was represented by Patricia Bartley Schwartz, Esquire. The Respondent John J. Sullivan, Jr. (the "Respondent") appeared on his own behalf.

I. Procedural Background

On January 14, 2013 the ODC filed a Petition for Discipline. Respondent filed an answer on February 1, 2013. The ODC filed an Amended Petition on April 23, 2013 and a Second Amended Petition on May 9, 2013 (references to the "Petition" herein are to the Second Amended Petition). Respondent answered the Amended Petition on April 23, 2013 (references to the "Answer" will be to the Answer to the Amended Petition). [FN1]

> FN1. The second Amended Petition was presented to the Panel at the May 9 Hearing to correct certain errors and changes intended to be addressed in the Amended Petition. The Respondent did not object and the changes did not require further answer by the Respondent. (Transcript of the May 9, 2013 Hearing ("May 9 Tr.") at 2-3, 143).

A telephonic pre-hearing conference was held on May 3, 2013. The Panel conducted a hearing on liability on May 9, 2013 (the "May 9 Hearing). [FN2] The parties provided the Panel with a Stipulation of Admitted Facts ("Admitted Facts"). At the May 9 Hearing, the Panel heard testimony from 4 witnesses; Ed Tarlov, Roseanne Goldberg, [FN3] Respondent and Sheila Pacheco. In addition, ODC Exhibits 6 through 27 were admitted into evidence. (May 9 Tr. 4) At the conclusion of the May 9 Hearing, the ODC presented an oral closing argument. On June 20, 2013, the Respondent submitted a written closing argument. On July 11, 2013 the ODC submitted a response the Respondent's closing argument.

> FN2. A motion was made by the ODC to consolidate this matter with Board Case No. 2011-0234-B which shares common questions of law and fact. The respondents, in both this case and Case No. 2011-0234B did not object to consolidation. After consideration of the request, the Chair of the Board on Professional Responsibility denied the request noting: "based upon the lack of detailed information about the evidence and positions and defenses contemplated, I feel compelled to err on the side of caution and deny the motion." (Letter dated January 29, 2013). For the sake of economy, it was later determined, with the concurrence of the Chairperson of the Board, that the same Panel of the Board would hear both matters. Despite having several weeks of notice that the same panel would hear both matters, Respondent raised, for the first time at the May 9 Hearing, an objection to having the same Panel hear both matters. The Panel overruled the objection on the basis that the matters would be decided on two completely separate records and each would be decided on the record presented in the individual matter.

> FN3. By agreement of the parties the testimony of Mr. Tarlov was presented by transcript from the hearing in Board Case No. 2011-0234-B and the testimony of Ms. Goldberg via deposition transcript (references to transcript testimony are to "Tarlov _" or "Goldberg_").

On August 7, 2013 the Panel notified the ODC and the Respondent that it planned to recommend to the Delaware Supreme Court that the Respondent violated Delaware Rules of Professional Conduct 4.1(a), 4.1(b), 5.3, 8.4(b), 8.4(c), 8.4(d) and 1.15(a), as alleged in the Petition. On September 11, 2013 the Board reconvened to hear testimony and argument relating to sanctions (the "September II Hearing"). At the September 11 Hearing, the Panel heard testimony from: Kenya Smith, Gloria Henry, Montgomery Boyer, William Cheesman, Sherry Hoffman, John Williams, Christopher McBride, Stephen Dalecki, Mary Kathleen Glenn [FN4] and Respondent, followed by closing arguments. Exhibits 6-27(h) and (i), 29 and 30 were admitted into evidence.

> FN4. The testimony of Mr. Dalecki and Ms. Glenn was presented by transcript from the criminal trial of Mr. Jamaar Manlove. The Panel considered only the non-hearsay aspects of this testimony. Respondent objected to other transcript testimony found at Exs. 28, 31 and 32 on the basis that he did not have an opportunity to cross-examine the witnesses. The Panel sustains the objection. Exhibits 28, 31 and 32 are not admitted into the record.

II. Allegations in the Petition for Discipline

The Petition alleges that Respondent violated Delaware Lawyers' Rules of Professional Conduct ("Rules") 4.1(a), 4.1(b), 5.3, 8.4(b), 8.4(c) and 8.4(d) in connection with residential real estate closings Respondent conducted between 2006 and 2008. Respondent is alleged to have certified that the representations contained in Department of Housing and Urban Development Settlement Statements ("HUD-1 Statement") were a true and accurate account of the transaction when in fact they were not. Specifically, the Petition charges that either the buyers did not bring the financial contribution set forth on the HUD-1 Statement and/or the proceeds from the transaction were disbursed in amounts that differed from those set forth on the HUD-1 Statement. The Petition alleges that the false certifications constitute violations of Rules 4.1(a), 4.1(b), 8.4(b), 8.4(c) and 8.4(d). The Petition further alleges that Respondent failed to ensure that the paralegals, who assisted him in connection with the closings, prepared checks for the disbursement of proceeds as set forth on the HUD-1 Statement in violation of Rule 5.3 relating to the supervision of non-lawyer staff. Finally, the Petition charges Respondent with violating Rule 1.15(a) for using his firm's client trust account to fund all or part of the buyer's contribution.

III. Factual Findings

A. Admitted Facts

Respondent is a member of the Bar of the Supreme Court of Delaware. He was admitted to the Bar in 1984. At all times relevant to this matter, Respondent was engaged in the private practice of law with the firm Sanclemente & Associates, LLC (the "Sanclemente Firm"). Respondent is still presently engaged in the private practice of law in Delaware but not with the Sanclemente Firm. (Petition and Answer 1 and 2, Admitted Facts1, May 9 Tr. 44-46). From 2006 through 2008, Respondent as the closing attorney for the following real estate closings, represented the borrower:

Phyllis Graham 405 Llangollen Blvd. New Castle, DE	405 Llangollen Blvd. Closing	Ex. 6	10/30/08		Derron Bowe 214 East 35th Street Wilmington, DE	214 East 35th Street Closing	Ex. 22	6/22/07
Patricia Singleton 713 E. 7th Street Wilmington, DE	713 E. 7th Street Closing	Ex. 7	8/29/08		Derron Bowe 107 West 30th Street Wilmington, DE	107 West 30th Street Closing	Ex. 23	5/2/07
Lee Price & Tony Coleman 15 Cherry Road New Castle, DE	15 Cherry Road Closing	Ex. 8	8/20/08		Kyle Steed 721 Wood Duck Court Middletown, DE	721 Wood Duck Court Closing	Ex. 24	1/4/07
Gloria Hemy 29 Dallas Road New Castle, DE	29 Dallas Road Closing	Ex. 9	7/18/08		Reginald Johnson 417 E. 10th Street Wilmington, DE	417 E. 10th Street Closing	Ex. 25	11/20/06
Evelyn Anders on Closing 123 Stroud Street Wilmington, DE	123 Stroud Street	Ex. 10	6/19/08		Kyle Steed 133 Sterling Avenue Claymont, DE	133 Sterling Avenue Closing	Ex. 26	2/27/07
Charles & Jamie Holmes 411 Jefferson Street Wilmington, DE	411 Jefferson Street	Ex.11	4/28/08		Theodore Jones 426 Eastlawn Avenue Wilmington, DE 426	Eastlawn Avenue Closing	Ex. 27	2/4/08
Evelyn Anderson 1122 Elm Street Wilmington, DE	1122 Elm Street Closing	Ex. 12	4/1/08					
Craig Williams 1009 W. Seventh Street Wilmington, DE	1009 W. Seventh Street Closing	Ex. I3	3/12/08					
Dwayne & Sheree Manlove 104 Rita Road New Castle, DE	104 Rita Road Closing	Ex. 14	12/27/07					
Anna Bennett 729 E. Tenth Street Wilmington, DE	729 E. Tenth Street Closing	Ex. 15	1/24/08					
Dwayne & Sheree Manlove 230 Channing Drive Bear, DE	230 Channing Drive Closing	Ex. 16	12/10/07					
Larry Manlove 54 University Avenue New Castle, DE	54 University Avenue Closing	Ex. 17	12/3/07					
Gary and Lillian Wilson 314 W. 31" Street Wilmington, DE	314 W. 31" Street Closing	Ex. 18	10/23/07					
Ramon Leak 2921 N. Broom Street Wilmington, DE	2921 N. Broom Street Closing	Ex. 19	9/12/07					
Clifton Coleman 2511 Heald Street Wilmington, DE 2511	Heald Street Closing	Ex. 20	8/30/07					
Clifton Coleman 2142 Culver Drive Wilmington, DE	2142 Culver Drive Closing	Ex. 21	8/15/07					

Collectively these real estate closings are referred to as the ("Sullivan Closings"). (Admitted Facts 'il 2, Exs. 6-27, May 9, Tr. 49, 127) (Respondent confirmed at the May 9 Hearing that he conducted the 133 Sterling Avenue Closing), May 9, Tr. 151-154). Non-lawyer assistants would prepare the HUD-1 Statements and the checks for the Sullivan Closings. (Petition and Answer 'i[7, Admitted Facts 'i[3). The Sanclemente Firm's real estate escrow accounting records show that there were no deposits of funds from the buyers in eighteen of the Sullivan Closings and the buyers' costs were paid by others in nineteen of the twenty-one Sullivan Closings. (Admitted Facts 'il 4, 5). In the Sullivan Closings, funds were not disbursed according to the HUD-1 Statement but were disbursed as reflected in the disbursement statement. (Admitted Facts 'il 6, 7). As such, funds were disbursed to individuals not identified on the HUD-1 Statements. (Admitted Facts 'i[8).

B. Factual Findings from May 9 Hearing and Exhibits Admitted into Evidence.

Respondent has admitted facts sufficient to support a recommended finding that Rules 4.1(a), 4.1(b), 8.4(b), 8.4(c) and 8.4(d) were violated. Specifically, Respondent has admitted that (1) he was the closing attorney in the 22 transactions that form the basis for the allegations in the Petition; (2) that the Sanclemente Firm real estate escrow account records reflect that there were no deposits of funds from the buyers in 18 of the transactions and the buyers' costs were paid by others in 19 of the transactions; and (3) funds were not disbursed according to the HUD-1 Statement. The Panel believes that the factual findings described herein confirm that conclusion, support a recommended finding that Respondent also violated Rules 5.3 and 1.15(a), and assist in determining the appropriate sanction.

1. The Manlove Transactions.

While employed by the Sanclemente Firm, Respondent conducted settlements that involved Mr. Jamaar Manlove, his relatives and associates. (May 9, Tr. 46-49). Respondent became acquainted with Jamaar Manlove when Manlove was a loan broker with Central Fidelity (May 9, Tr. 46). Jamaar Manlove had two organizations known as Master Builders for Christ ("MBFC") and Vision Builders Christian Center ("VBCC") (May 9, Tr. 46-47). Both organizations were used as fronts for an equity stripping scheme. Manlove, his relatives, friends, MBFC and VBCC received payments from the sale proceeds in many of the Sullivan Closings. [FN5]

> FN5. In addition Mark Singleton and his entity MDS Enterprise arranged similar transactions and also received sales proceeds. (May 9 Tr. 114-115, Exs. 7, 10, 11, 12, 13 and 16).

Respondent explained that in the Sullivan Closings, the homeowners were in danger of losing their homes to foreclosure, and Jamaar Manlove would arrange for an investor to purchase the home to help them avoid foreclosure. The seller would remain in the home for a year and then repurchase the home from the buyer. (May 9, Tr. 62). Respondent never asked for any documentation of this purported agreement. (May 9, Tr. 76). Respondent testified that in order to compensate the buyer for the risk and to ensure that they had funds to make their mortgage payments, the seller would pay funds to the buyer at closing. (May 9, Tr. 62-63). Respondent also explained that funds were paid to MBFC and/or VBCC to be held for the one year period to enable the buyer to make their mortgage payments (May 9, Tr. 65). In short, the sellers were stripped of any equity they may have had in their homes in the guise of contributions to MBFC, and/or VBCC and/or some other entities.

The following chart shows the extent of the equity that was taken from some of the sellers in the Sullivan Closings:

Seller	Exhibit No.	Amount of Equity Stripped
Norlyn Ritter	6	$34,710.00
Ferris Properties	7	$30,189.00
Mary Glenn	8	$51,430.00
Michael Fisher	11	$41,456.80
James Moss	13	$13,566.18
Donnell Fisher	16	$34,393.00
Stephen Dalecki	17	$24,906.36
Kenya Smith	18	$21,333.03
Adrienne Spencer	19	$66,727.34
Jamaar Manlove	20	$49,396.44
William Cheesman	21	$26,288.36
Jamaar Manlove	24	$23,073.56
Grace Cuff	25	$51,240.24
Gerald Hackett	27	$96,700.00

Respondent also testified that he initially believed people were contributing to Jamaar Manlove or his church to:

Thank him for saving their home, for–to express commitment to his church and things like that, and that they were paying in order– paying these funds to avoid losing their home at foreclosure.

(May 9, Tr. 74-75). Despite this belief, Respondent did not obtain any documentation indicating that the monies paid to MBFC and VBCC were gifts. (May 9, Tr. 75). Other than going over the entries on the HUD-1 Statement with the parties, Respondent did not question the monies going to the Manlove entities. (May 9, Tr. 81-82).

We find Respondent's position to be disingenuous at best. What was really happening was that the homeowners, who were at risk of losing their homes to a sheriff's sale because their current cash positions were insufficient to allow them to pay current obligations and to refinance their mortgages, were (without their knowledge) selling their homes and the equity that those homeowners had in their properties was diverted to MBFC and/or VBCC. The poor cash positions of the homeowners/sellers, along with the size of the purported donations to MBFC and VBCC should have alerted Respondent to the nefarious nature of the transactions from day one.

2. Buyers Did Not Make the Cash Contributions Reflected on the HUD-1 Statement.

The buyers in eighteen of the Sullivan Closings did not make any cash contribution (Admitted Facts4) despite the fact that checks were received by the Sanclemente Firm from many of the buyers for their HUD-1 Statement contribution amount. (See, e.g., Exs. 11, 12, 14, 16, 22, 25, 27). Those checks were copied and placed in the file to have a record of the buyer contribution but were never deposited. (May 9, Tr. 98, 101) (see, also, May 9 Tr. 113, 114, 124-25, 127, 132). Many of these personal checks were in excess of the $10,000 limit under Rule 1.15(k) and, despite a law firm policy that Respondent should not accept personal funds in excess of $2,000. (May 9, Tr. 113). Respondent admitted that in closings that did not involve Jamaar Manlove or related entities, he would not have accepted large personal checks. (May 9, Tr. 113).

Respondent claimed that he learned "probably sometime in 2007 that the borrowers" checks were no longer being deposited (May 9, Tr. 154), yet in the first of the closings at issue, in November of 2006 (Ex. 25) he collected a personal check from the borrower at closing for $15,000 in violation of Rule 1.15(k) and his firm's policy. [FN6] The acceptance of that check certainly suggests he knew it would never be deposited. Respondent never notified the lender that the buyers were not bringing their financial contribution as reported on the HUD-1 Statements and in some cases were receiving funds in the transaction because he knew that if the HUD-1 Statements were changed to reflect zero contribution from the borrower "it would have created red flags from the lender." (May 9, Tr. 99, 121).

> FN6. Later Respondent testified he could not remember when he learned that the checks he was collecting were a fiction and were not funds from the buyer. (May 9, Tr. 162-63).

3. The Sanclemente Firm's Escrow Account Funds were Used to Cover the Buyer's Contribution.

Respondent admitted that in some instances funds due to the seller or a Manlove entity were disbursed instead to the Sanclemente Finn to meet the buyer's cash contribution. (May 9, Tr. 59-60). This was necessary because funds were being used from the Sanclemente Finn's escrow account to balance or zero out the transaction. The funds to reimburse the Sanclemente Finn's escrow account were taken from proceeds due to another party, either the seller or a Manlove entity. (See Exs. 6, 8 and 27; May 9, Tr. 137-141; 193-196). Respondent viewed this as a "zero balance transaction". He testified, "we took the money out of the escrow account and put it right back into the escrow account. (May 9, Tr. 194-195).

4. Funds were Disbursed to Persons or Entities not Listed on the HUD-1 Statement.

Respondent claimed he was unaware of how the proceeds from the sales were being disbursed because the checks were prepared by a paralegal and given to him in sealed envelopes to disburse. (May 9, Tr. 163). Ms. Pacheco, the former paralegal at the Sanclemente Firm who prepared the documents for closings and "cut the checks for closings" (May 9, Tr. 198) indicated that Jarnaar Manlove would contact Ms. Pacheco directly and have her break down the checks in different ways. (May 9, Tr. 201-202). She indicated there would be no reason for her to tell Respondent about these changes post-closing. (May 9, Tr. 206). Ms. Pacheco testified, however, that when checks were distributed at the closing, the checks would not be placed in envelopes to be handed out by Respondent. (May 9, Tr. 207). Thus, Respondent could see the amounts being disbursed were inconsistent with the HUD-1 Statement.

5. Respondent Becomes Concerned.

Respondent testified that sometime during the period covered by the Sullivan Closings, he became concerned with the transactions involving Mr. Manlove:

Over time, it became clear that there were substantial amounts of money that were being received by Mr. Manlove, by MBFC, by VBCC, by his relatives, his friends, whomever, and that money that was supposed to be going to the seller wasn't going to the seller, but the seller's funds were being used to meet the buyer's obligation or they were being paid to Mr. Manlove or to his associates.

May 9, Tr. 166). Respondent indicated that he discussed the issue with Mr. Sanclemente and it was decided that they would no longer do transactions for Mr. Manlove. (May 9, Tr. 167). Yet, Respondent admittedly continued for some period of time to conduct Manlove closings. (May 9, Tr. 167). He claimed to be relying on Mr. Sanclemente's representations that they had no obligation to the seller. (May 9, Tr. 167).

As long as the seller was an adult and we were going over the settlement statements, that they were voluntarily signing them, and that they knew that they weren't getting the funds, or they were getting zero funds, and they were signing voluntarily, weren't questioning it, that satisfied our obligation. (May 9, Tr. 167).

While Respondent claims it became clear "over time" that large sums were going to Manlove entities, each of the Sullivan Closings followed a similar pattern throughout the two-year period. By way of example in the first closing in issue in November 2006, (Ex. 25) the HUD-1 Statement indicates that Reginald Johnson purchased a property from Grace Cuff for a contract price of $88,000.00. (Ex. 25A). According to the HUD-1 Statement, the buyer was to make a cash contribution of $15,200.71. (Ex. 25A). The seller was to receive cash at closing in the amount of $19,700.00. (Ex. 25A). The seller's proceeds were reduced by settlement charges that included a payment of $66,440.95 to MBFC. (Ex. 25A). According to the HUD-1 Statement, there was no mortgage lien on the property and the remaining settlement charges to the buyer were less than $2,000.00. (Ex. 25A). The buyer wrote a personal check for $15,200.71 (Ex. 25C) which was never deposited. (May 9, Tr. 127). Respondent certified the HUD-1 Statement.

The last closing at issue was conducted by Respondent on October 30, 2008. (Ex. 6). The HUD-1 Statement for this closing reflects a $6,900.50 buyer contribution. (Ex. 6A). The buyer wrote a personal check in that amount which was never deposited. (Ex. 6C). Instead, funds due to another party were disbursed to the Sanclemente Firm to meet the buyer's contribution and cover the shortfall in the escrow account. (May 9, Tr. 58-61). The HUD-1 Statement reflects payments to VBCC [FN7] of $60,500.00 and MBFC of $43,610.68. (Ex. 6A). MBFC received $34,710.00 in part to cover the buyer's contribution. (Ex. 6B, D).

> FN 7. Respondent agreed that the entry on teh HUD-1 Statement for "BBCC" was a typographical error and should have been "VBCC". (May 9, Tr. 64)

6. Respondent Contacts the Department of Justice.

The pattern was consistent throughout the period yet it took more than 2 years before Respondent took any steps to remedy the situation. Respondent testified that:

I came to realize they were stripping equity from these properties.

And it was at that point when I became aware of the fact that there was equity stripping going on, that's when I contacted the Department of Justice and spoke to Sherry Hoffman there because I was concerned about these transactions.

I came in. I met with Ms. Hoffman. I went over a number of the transactions with her. We talked about ways to try to remedy the situation, to try to see if there was a way we could set aside the purchases, to put the homes back in the names of the original sellers. The problem was that the mortgage companies, of course, would not want to release their mortgages unless they were paid. And since Mr. Manlove and his friends and the investors didn't have the money any longer, there wasn't a way to undo the transaction.

(May 9, Tr. 159-60). Respondent indicated that he contacted the Department of Justice after the last closing he conducted related to Jamaar Manlove. (May 9, Tr. 160-61).

There is some question regarding how Respondent carne to discuss the Manlove closings with Ms. Hoffman. John Williams, Esquire, a Delaware lawyer with a real estate practice, testified that the Hackett brothers came to see him about a real estate transaction involving a home they inherited from their mother. (Sept. 11, Tr. 72-73). Mr. Williams indicated that there was a $79,000 payment that he could not explain and the Hackett brothers received very little in the transaction. (Sept. 11, Tr. 73-74, see also Ex. 27). Mr. Williams contacted Respondent who told him that "he felt it was an arm's length transaction and that it involved some kind of lease or something." (Sept. 11, Tr. 74-75). It was after that conversation that Mr. Williams contacted the Department of Justice and went in to meet with Ms. Hoffman. (Sept. 11, Tr. 75-76). Ms. Hoffman testified that she had two meetings with Mr. Sullivan but could not recall who initiated the contact. (Sept. 11, Tr. 66). This testimony raises the question of whether Respondent initiated the contact with Ms. Hoffman.

7. The Lender's Decision to Fund Would Have Been Impacted if the True Facts were Disclosed.

The Sullivan Closings were inconsistent with Respondent's representations to the lenders on the HUD-1 Statement. The funding decisions by the lenders would have been impacted had the HUD-1 Statements been revised to reflect the true nature of the transactions. The ODC presented testimony from Ms. Roseanne Goldberg, Vice President of customer service for Freedom Mortgage, with 25 years of experience in the mortgage industry. (Goldberg 2-3). Ms. Goldberg testified that Freedom Mortgage requires that the HUD-1 Statement be faxed prior to the closing and there should be no changes once it has been approved by Freedom Mortgage. (Goldberg 5-6). Ms. Goldberg indicated that Freedom would want to know if a borrower comes to a closing without funds and if the borrower's contribution is coming out of someone else's settlement disbursement. (Goldberg 8-9). By way of example, Ms. Goldberg reviewed the HUD-1 Statement in Exhibit 14, which reflected a borrower's contribution of $22,466.77. Ms. Goldberg testified that if the borrower did not "come to the table" with money, that would have affected Freedom Mortgage's decision to fund the loan. (Goldberg 20). Similarly, Ms. Goldberg indicated that the fact that the borrower received a $10,000 disbursement at the time of closing would also have affected the decision to fund. (Goldberg 20); see, also, Goldberg 22-25 (similar testimony with respect to Exs. 16, 17, 19, and 20). Finally Ms. Goldberg testified that Freedom Mortgage expects the Delaware attorney who is the closing agent for Freedom Mortgage to ensure that the borrower's contribution is collected as reflected on the HUD-1 Statement. (Goldberg 37).

8. Respondent's Conduct was Inconsistent with His Obligation to Lender.

Mr. Tarlov, a member of the Delaware Bar, was called by the ODC to give expert testimony regarding residential real estate matters and the standard of conducting residential real estate closings in Delaware. (Tarlov 24). Mr. Tarlov has been a member of the Delaware Bar for more than 25 years and has represented the buyer in thousands of residential real estate closings. (Tarlov 23-24). Mr. Tarlov testified that the certification language contained above the lawyer's signature

line on the HUD-1 Statement means that the "HUD-1 is an accurate reflection of the transaction" and "every single penny on the HUD is accurate." (Tarlov 44-45). At closing, Mr. Tarlov indicated that he is representing the borrower, but following the lender's instructions. (Tarlov 49-50). If Mr. Tarlov became aware at closing that the buyer was receiving settlement assistance from the seller he would revise the HUD-1 Statement and notify the lender for approval because "the lender approved the HUD and the HUD is a representation that you're putting cash into the transaction" (Tarlov 34; see also Tarlov 39 ("I would call the lender"); Tarlov 40-41 ("I am going to obey the lender 100 percent"); Tarlov 43 ("the HUD is being approved by the lender … so just want the lender to sign off on my HUD"); Tarlov 60 ("I still would go back to the lender"). [FN8]

> FN8. Mr. Tarlov testified that if the buyer's contribution as listed on the HUD-1 Statement was coming from a third party and not the seller, he would verify that the funds were not a loan, and he would also notify the lender. (Tarlov 40-42).

IV. Standard of Proof

Allegations of professional misconduct set forth in the ODC's Petition must be established by clear and convincing evidence. (Rules of Disciplinary Procedure IS(c)). That burden falls on the ODC. (Rules of Disciplinary Procedure 15(d)).

V. Discussion and Analysis

A. Violation of Rules 4.1(a), 4.1(b), 8.4(b), 8.4(c), 8.4(d).

Respondent had admitted and the extensive record confirms that Respondent certified HUD-1 Statements that were not a true and accurate account of the transactions where the HUD-1 Statements indicated: (i) the buyer(s) made a financial contribution to the transaction when in fact the buyer(s) made no contributions; (ii) the funds were disbursed in amounts different than the amounts certified on the HUD-1 Statement; and/or (iii) the funds were disbursed to persons or entities not identified in the HUD-1 Statement.

Rule 4.1(a) provides it is professional misconduct for a lawyer, during the course of representing a client, to knowingly make "a false statement of material fact or law to a third person." Rule 4.1(b) provides it is professional misconduct for a lawyer, during the course of representing a client, to unknowingly "fail to disclose a material fact when disclosure is necessary to avoid assisting a criminal or fraudulent act by a client." (Delaware Lawyers' Rules of Professional Conduct 4.1(a) and 4.1(b)). The HUD-1 Settlement Statement contains the following certification above the attorney signature line:

The HUD-1 Settlement Statement which I have prepared is a true and accurate account of this transaction have caused or will cause the funds to be disbursed in accordance with this statement.

(Tab A of Exhibits 6-27). In the Sullivan Closings funds were not disbursed according to the HUD-1 Statements. (Admitted Facts 6). In addition, Respondent's clients did not provide funds reflected as "cash from borrower" on the HUD-1 Statement. Both Respondent and his client, the borrower, made false statements on the HUD-1 Statement. Respondent's certification of HUD-1 Statements that were not a true and accurate account of the transaction violates Rules 4.1(a) and 4.1(b).

Rule 8.4 provides that it is professional misconduct for a lawyer to:

(b) commit a criminal act that reflects adversely on the lawyer's honesty, trustworthiness or fitness as a lawyer in other respects; (c) engage in conduct involving dishonesty, fraud, deceit or misrepresentation; (d) engage in conduct that is prejudicial to the administration of justice.

The HUD-1 Settlement Statement contains the following language:

WARNING: It is a crime to knowingly make false statements to the United States on this or any other similar form. Penalties upon conviction can include: a fine or imprisonment. For details see: Title 18 U.S. Code § 1001 and § 1010.

(Tab A of Exhibits 16-27) Respondent knowingly executed HUD-1 Statements that contained false statements in violation of 10 U.S.C. § 1010.

Respondent argues that the ODC did not present any evidence that the HUD-1 Settlement Statements were offered or accepted by the Department of Housing and Urban Development or offered to the department "for the purpose of obtaining any extension or renewal or credit, or mortgage insured by such department or for the acceptance, release or substitution of any security or for the purposes of influencing in any way the action of such department" relying on the language of 18 U.S.C § 1010. Respondent did not offer any support for his interpretation of this provision. Instead, Respondent offered HUD-1 statements for federally insured loans that he knew to be false.

Respondent knew that each HUD-1 Statement was approved by the lender and that lenders were relying on the accuracy of the HUD-1 Statements in funding the loans. Respondent conceded that he never notified the lenders that the buyers did not make the: financial contribution listed on the HUD-1 Statements and that the funds were not disbursed as outlined because it would have raised "red flags" and the loans may not have been funded. In fact, copies of the checks collected from the buyer were made for the file even though Respondent knew the check would never be deposited in the firm's escrow account. In the Panel's view, Respondent's false statement to lenders to ensure loan funding constituted a "criminal act that reflects adversely on the lawyer's honesty, trustworthiness or fitness as a lawyer in other respects" under Rule 8.

As a result of these actions, and the facts outlined above, the Panel recommends a: finding that Respondent's action violated Rules 4.1(a), 4.1(b), 8.4(b), 8.4(c) and 8.4(d).

B. Violation of Rule 5.3.

Rule 5.3 states in part that in employing non-lawyer assistants:

(b) A lawyer having direct supervisory authority over a non-lawyer shall make reasonable efforts to insure that the person's conduct is compatible with the professional obligations of the lawyer; (c) a lawyer shall be responsible for conduct of such person that would be a violation of the Rules of Professional Conduct if engaged in by the lawyer if: (i) the lawyer orders or, with knowledge of the specific conduct, ratifies the conduct involves; or. (ii) the lawyer … has direct supervisory authority over the person, and knows of the conduct at time when its consequences can be avoided or mitigated but fails to take reasonable remedial action.

(Delaware Lawyers' Rules of Professional Conduct 5.3)

The ODC argues that Respondent violated Rule 5.3 (i) by failing to make reasonable efforts to insure that the non-lawyer staff's conduct was compatible with the professional obligations of a Delaware lawyer and/or (ii) by ratifying the non-lawyer staff's conduct with respect to the disbursement of the real estate funds contrary to the HUD-1 Statements and/or (iii) by failing to take reasonable remedial action once Respondent had knowledge of the non-lawyer staff's conduct.

While Respondent denied having any managerial authority at the Sanclemente Firm, he did concede that he had supervisory authority over non-lawyer staff and could direct their conduct. For example, Respondent testified that if he needed a document changed during the preparation for closing he could direct non-lawyer staff to make changes. (May 9 Tr. 51). Respondent also conceded that if he needed something to be changed on the HUD-1 Statement or change the amount of a check during a closing he could direct the non-lawyer staff to make the changes needed. (May 9 Tr. 52, 191). Ms. Pacheco confirmed that if Respondent needed to have documentation changed during closing she would make the changes for him. (May 9 Tr. 207-208). Ms. Pacheco conceded that Respondent could direct her conduct to a certain degree. (May 9, Tr. 208).

Respondent took no action to prevent Ms. Pacheco from issuing checks inconsistent with the disbursement amounts listed on the HUD-1 Statement. Respondent knew that the checks received from the buyers in most instances were never cashed but that the legal assistants made photocopies for the file. Respondent also knew that the lenders were not notified of any of these actions. The Panel recommends a finding that Respondent violated Rule 5.3.

C. Violation of Rule 1.15(a).

Rule 1.15(a) requires, in pertinent part, that a lawyer "shall hold property of clients or third persons that is in a lawyer's possession in connection with a representation separate from the lawyer's own property", and that property of clients or third persons must be appropriately safe guarded. The ODC argues that by using other clients' funds that were in the firm's trust account to fund part or all of the buyer's contribution in certain settlements, Respondent violated Rule 1.15(a).

In three of the Sullivan Closings (Exs. 6, 8, 27), checks were disbursed to the Sanclemente Firm from proceeds from the sale to reimburse the firm's escrow account for the buyer's contribution. (May 9, Tr. 137-41; 193-96). Respondent viewed this as a "zero balance" transaction because they took money out of the escrow account and put it right back into the account. (May 9, Tr. 194-95). The fact that the funds were replaced does not negate the violation of Rule 1.15(a). See In Re Figliola, 652 A.2d 10711, 1076 (Del. 1995) (the Court rioted the issue was not whether the funds could be adequately reimbursed, but rather whether the money should have been taken without authorization) (citing In Re Librizzi, 569 A.2d 257, 261 (N.J. 1990)). The Panel recommends a finding that Respondent violated Rule 1.15(a).

D. The Panel's Recommendation is Supported by Precedent from Other Jurisdictions.

The Panel's recommended findings that Respondent violated Rules 4.1(a), 4.1(b), 5.3, 8.4(b), 8.4(c), 8.4(d) and 1.15(a) of the Delaware Lawyers' Rules of Professional Conduct are supported by case law from other jurisdictions involving similar fact patterns. North Carolina State Bar v. Rose, 10 DHC 17 Feb. 23, 2011; Cincinnati Bar Association v. Powers, 895 N.E.2d 172 (Ohio 2008); and In Re Barbare, 602 N.E.2d 382 (S.C. 2004). In Rose, there was one real estate transaction at issue. In that transaction Rose prepared a HUD-1 Statement reflecting a buyer contribution of $59,652.31 and a seller disbursement of $50,930.29. The Disciplinary Hearing Commission found that the HUD-1 Statement prepared by Rose was false and that the buyer brought no money to the closing and Rose did not disburse funds to the seller. The Commission further found that Rose was responsible for ensuring the HUD-1 Statement accurately recited the receipt and disbursement of funds in the transaction and that the HUD-1 Statement certification was false. The Disciplinary Hearing Commission found that Rose had violated Rules 8.4(b) and 8.4(c) which are identical to the Delaware Rules. Respondent argues that this case is distinguishable because Rose represented both the borrower and the lender. Respondent, however, does not address the fact that Rose was also charged with a violation of Rule 8.4(g) involving intentional prejudice to his client, the lender, during the course of the professional relationship.

The ODC also relies on Cincinnati Bar Association v. Powers, where the attorney was charged with fabricating closing documents on over 300 loans causing lenders to lose nearly $3.5 million and for filing false income tax returns that concealed his profits. While Respondent did not profit from his actions or file false tax returns, there are some similarities with Powers. Mr. Powers knew that the buyer did not bring the down payment but that it was provided by others and that some of the buyers received funds from the sale proceeds. The Court found that these facts were not disclosed to the lenders and that the HUD-1 Statements were falsely certified. The Court found that Powers violated sections of the Ohio Disciplinary Code of Professional Responsibility which are nearly identical to Delaware Rules 8.4(b), (c) and (d).

The ODC also asks the Panel to rely on In Re Barbare. Respondent concedes that the Barbare case is most similar to this matter. (Respondent's Closing Argument at 1f 14). In Barbare the Respondent pled guilty to a violation of 18 U.S.C. § 1010 in connection with his false certification of HUD-1 Statements where he certified that borrowers brought funds to closing when in fact no borrower's contribution had been made. In addition, the Respondent in Barbare

permitted the clients to instruct non-lawyer staff on disbursements which were contrary to the amounts reflected on the HUD-1 Statements. The Court found that the Respondent's conduct violated Rules 4.1, 5.1, 5.3 and 8.4 of the South Carolina Rules of Professional Conduct, which are identical to the corresponding Delaware rules.

The Respondent here argues that in Barbare the Supreme Court of South Carolina found that there were "red flags" which should have alerted Barbare to the criminal activity of third parties in connection with these closings. Respondent argues that he was deceived by Jamaar Manlove in his scheme to defraud the sellers of their homes. The Panel finds that Barbare is not distinguishable on those grounds. Moreover, that Respondent was deceived by Manlove is not credible. Respondent never sought documentation of the alleged buy-back agreements between buyer and seller. Respondent took action to hide the fact that buyers were not making the financial contributions as disclosed on the HUD-1 Statements and also because Respondent admittedly continued conducting closings after he testified that he became concerned with the "equity stripping" being conducted. Red flags were everywhere for Respondent to see.

The ODC also relies on In re Foley, No. BD-2010-005 (March 24, 2010) and provided a copy of the Petition for Discipline filed with the Commonwealth of Massachusetts Board of Bar Overseers and the Order of Tenn Suspension issued by the Supreme Court of the Commonwealth of Massachusetts. Respondent argues that since neither document includes the findings of either a Board of Professional Responsibility or of the Supreme Court for the Commonwealth of Massachusetts, these documents do not represent appropriate precedent to be considered by the Panel and the Panel agrees.

VI. Sanctions.

A. Standard for Imposing Sanctions.

"The objectives of the Lawyer Disciplinary system are to protect the public, to protect the administration of justice, to preserve confidence in the legal profession, and to deter other lawyers from similar misconduct." In Re McCann, 894 A.2d 1087, 1088 (Del. 2005); In Re Fountain, 878 A.2d 1167, 1173 (Del. 2005) (quoting In Re Bailey, 821 A.2d 851, 866 (Del. 2003)). The focus of the lawyer disciplinary system in Delaware is not on the lawyer but, rather, on the damage to the public that is ascertainable from the lawyers' record of professional misconduct. In Re Hall, 767 A.2d 197, 201 (Del. 2001). It is the duty of the Panel to recommend the sanction that will promote those objectives.

In reaching its recommendation of an appropriate sanction, the Panel considered the ABA Standards for imposing lawyer sanctions (the "ABA Standards"):

The ABA framework consists of four key factors to be considered by the Court: (a) the ethical duty violated; (b) the lawyer's mental state; (c) the actual potential injury caused by the lawyer's misconduct; and (d) aggravating and mitigating factors.

ABA Standards for Imposing Lawyer Sanctions, at 9 (1992) (the "ABA Standards"), available at http://www.abanet.org/cpr/regulationlstandards_sanctions.pdf.

B. Application of the Standard.

1. The Ethical Duties Violated by Respondent.

As set forth above, the Panel recommends a finding that Respondent violated Rules 4.1(a), 4.1(b), 5.3, 8.4(b), 8.4(c), 8.4(d) and 1.15(a) of the Delaware Lawyers' Rules of Professional Conduct.

2. Respondent's Mental State.

The Panel must determine the Respondent's mental state in order to determine the level of culpability. The ABA Standards define the most culpable mental state as that of "intent" when the lawyer acts with purpose to accomplish a particular result. A less culpable mental state is that of "knowledge" where the lawyer is consciously aware of the attendant circumstances of his or her conduct but without the objective or purpose to accomplish a particular result. The least culpable mental state is negligence where the lawyer deviates from the standard of care that a reasonable lawyer would exercise in a given situation. (ABA Standards at 6-7). Based on the factual findings described above, the Panel concludes that the Respondent's mental state was intentional. Respondent acted with the intent of facilitating 22 real estate closings that defrauded those who relied on the accuracy of the HUD-1 Statements.

C. Injury Caused by Respondent's Misconduct.

Pursuant to the ABA Standards, the Panel must consider the potential or actual injury caused by the Respondent's action. (ABA Standards at 6-7). At the September 11 Hearing the ODC presented testimony from several witnesses to address the injury caused by Respondent's actions. Ms. Kenya Smith, Mr. Montgomery Boyer and Mr. William Cheesman were all sellers of properties in the Sullivan Closings.

Ms. Smith testified that the closing for her property took five minutes and she was presented with papers to sign but with no accompanying explanation and was in and out in five minutes. (Sept. 11, Tr. 12-15). Ms. Smith did not receive any proceeds from the sale of her home and she did not understand that the buyer was receiving funds as a result of the sale. (Sept. 11, Tr. 10-11). Ms. Smith and her children remained in the home paying rent to the buyer for less than six months when they were evicted by the sheriff. (Sept. 11, Tr. 8-9).

The testimony of Mr. Boyer was similar. Mr. Boyer acknowledged that at the closing for his property the lawyer showed him documents which he could not see due to poor vision nor could he understand the substance of the documents. (Sept. 11, Tr. 43-44). Mr. Boyer did not receive any proceeds in the sale and was unaware that the buyers received $10,000.00 and Jamaar Manlove received $1,700.00. (Sept. 11, Tr. 41). Mr. Boyer further testified that he had no understanding of why MBFC received $34,000 at closing. (Sept. 11, Tr. 48). Mr. Boyer left his home when he could no longer afford the rent the buyers were charging which was more than his prior mortgage. (Sept. 11, Tr. 38-40).

Mr. Cheesman also testified that he was only in Respondent's office for 10 or 15 minutes for his closing and did not recall Respondent going over the HUD-1 Statement. (Sept. 11, Tr. 51-52, 56). Mr. Cheesman received no funds at closing. (Sept. 11, Tr. 53). He also had no understanding that he was making donations to an entity called MMBK and VBCC of more than $57,000 combined. (Sept. 11, Tr. 53-54). No one explained that he was also contributing $4,800 for closing costs. (Sept. 11, Tr. 57). Mr. Cheesman rented his home back from the buyer until it was put up for sheriff's sale. (Sept. 11, Tr. 55-56).

The ODC also presented the testimony of Gloria Henry. Respondent represented Gloria Henry who was the borrower in the 29 Dallas Road Closing. (Ex. 9). The HUD-1 Statement for this closing indicates that the borrower was making a cash contribution of $7,636.35 toward the $90,000 purchase price which Respondent admitted was not received. (May 9, Tr. 111). The HUD-1 Statement also shows payments to VBCC and MBFC of $16,700 and $5,000 respectively. (Ex. 9A). Ms. Henry testified that she did not understand that she was purchasing a home but instead thought that she was co-signing a loan for her nephew. (Sept. 11, Tr. 25, 28). She testified that she remembered signing the papers but did not understand them because she could not read well and no one went over the papers she was asked to sign. (Sept. 11, Tr. 27, 32-33). Ms. Henry indicated that prior to the transaction she had excellent credit which was impacted negatively by the transaction and she can no longer make purchases on credit. (Sept. 11, Tr. 30).

The ODC also offered the testimony of Christopher McBride, the real estate coordinator for the New Castle County Sheriffs Office. (Sept. 11, Tr. 89). Mr. McBride explained the sheriffs sale process and testified regarding 13 properties that were sold in the transactions at issue which were sold at sheriffs sale. (Sept. 11, Tr. 101-119). Mr. McBride explained that when the loans were not repaid and the properties were sold, Fannie Mae and Freddie Mac who guaranteed the loans took a loss on the properties. (Sept. 11, Tr. 38).

D. The Existence of Any Aggravating and Mitigating Circumstances.

The Panel considered whether there were any aggregating or mitigating circumstances which would warrant an increase or a decrease in the sanction.

ABA Standard 9.22 sets forth the following aggravating factors:

(a) Prior disciplinary offenses;

(b) dishonest or selfish motive;

(c) a pattern of misconduct;

(d) multiple offenses;

(e) bad faith obstruction of the disciplinary proceeding by intentionally failing to comply with rules or orders of the disciplinary agency;

(f) submission of false evidence, false statement or other deceptive practices during the disciplinary process;

(g) refusal to acknowledge wrongful nature of conduct;

(h) vulnerability of the victims;

(i) substantial experience at the practice of law;

(j) indifference to making restitution;

(k) illegal conduct, including that involving the use of controlled substances.

Based on the evidence presented, the Panel finds the following aggravating factors:

Respondent has a prior disciplinary record. (ABA Standard § 9.22(a)). Respondent testified that he did have a prior disciplinary history. (Sept. 11 Tr. 144-45). In 1999 he was suspended from the practice of law for eighteen months for violations of Rule 8.4(c)9 In 1996 he received a private probation for violation of Rule 1.4 and in 1995 he received a private admonition for violation of Rules 1.3 and 1.7.

Respondent has engaged in a pattern of misconduct. (ABA Standard § 9.22(c)). The evidence demonstrates that Respondent's misconduct occurred over a period of approximately two years and involved twenty-two separate real estate transactions.

Respondent's misconduct consists of multiples offenses. (ABA Standard § 9.22(d)). The Panel has recommended a finding that Respondent violated Rules 4.1(a), 4.1(b), 5.3, 8.4(b), 8.4(c), 8.4(d) and 1.15(a).

The evidence presented at the September 11 hearing demonstrated that the victims of Respondent's misconduct were vulnerable.

Respondent has been a member of the Delaware Bar since 1984 and has substantial experience in the practice of law.

Lastly, although Respondent was not charged criminally, he falsely certified HUD-1 Statements which is a crime under 18 U.S.C. 1010.

I. Mitigating Factors.

ABA Standard § 9.32 sets forth the following mitigating factors:

(a) Absence of a prior disciplinary record;

(b) Absence of a dishonest or selfish motive;

(c) Personal or emotional problems;

(d) Timely good faith effort to make restitution or to rectify consequences of misconduct.

(e) Full and free disclosure to disciplinary board or cooperative attitude toward proceedings;

(f) inexperience in the practice of law;

(g) character or reputation;

(h) physical disability;

(i) mental disability or chemical dependency including alcoholism or drug abuse when:

    (1) there is medical evidence that Respondent is affected by a chemical dependency or mental disability;

    (2) the chemical dependency or mental disability caused the misconduct;

    (3) respondent's recovery from the chemical dependency or mental disability is demonstrated by a meaningful and sustained period of successful rehabilitation; and

    (4) the recovery arrested the misconduct and recurrence of that misconduct is unlikely;

(j) delay in disciplinary proceedings;

(k) interim rehabilitation;

(l) imposition of other penalties or sanctions;

(m) remorse; and

(n) remoteness of prior offenses.

Based on the evidence presented the Panel finds the following mitigating factors:

Respondent made full and free disclosure to the disciplinary board and had a cooperative attitude toward the proceedings.

Respondent did not have a selfish motive only to the extent that he did not personally profit from the transactions except from the legal fees earned for his employer in connection with the closings.

VII. The Panel's Recommended Discipline.

The ODC argues that disbarment is the appropriate sanction. Respondent asks the Panel to recommend a substantial suspension. The ODC relies on several cases in support of its request that Respondent be disbarred. First, the ODC relies on In re Freebery, 947 A.2d 1121, 2008 WL 1849916 (Del. 2008). There, Ms. Freebery failed to disclose a loan on a personal mortgage application and pled guilty to a violation of 18 U.S.C. § 1014, a felony criminal offense. Ms. Freebery stipulated to a violation of Rule 8.4(b). The Panel in Freebery analyzed whether the mental state that formed the basis for her conviction was "knowing" or "intentional" As the Panel explained:

This distinction is critical, since the recommendations suggested by the ABA Standards are based on the mental state that forms the basis of an attorney's misconduct- i.e., more culpable mental states generally receive more severe sanctions. Specifically, under the ABA Standards, "knowledge" is defined as "the conscious awareness of the nature or attendant circumstances of the conduct but without the conscious objective or purpose to accomplish a particular result." ABA Standards Definitions (emphasis added) Given the language of 18 U.S.C. § 1014, Respondent's contention that her conduct was merely "knowing," and not "intentional," is misplaced. The federal statute under which Respondent was convicted specifically requires that Respondent's false statement be made "for the purpose of influencing … any institution the accounts of which are insured by the Federal Deposit Insurance Corporation." Her guilty plea establishes this wrongful conduct. Respondent purposely omitted her $2.3 million liability to ensure Commerce Bank's expeditious approval of her loan application. While Respondent may not have sought to defraud Commerce Bank, she did intend to have Commerce Bank rely on the erroneous application in granting a mortgage on her new home with favorable terms. Accordingly, her mental state cannot fall within the ABA

Standard's definition of "knowledge", which excludes "the conscious objective or purpose to accomplish a particular result." Rather, the statute, on its face, requires purposeful influencing of a financial institution, a mental state the Panel considers in the context of this disciplinary proceeding to be substantially equivalent to intentional.

In re Freebery, 2008 WL 1849916, (Del. Supr.) In adopting the Panel's Report in Freebery, the Court agreed that disbarment was the appropriate sanction for the conduct that led to a felony conviction and a violation of Rule 8.4(b).

Here while Respondent was not convicted of a felony, his conduct violated Section 1010 and implicates the same "intentional" mental state as found in Freebery, suggesting a more severe sanction under the ABA Standards. Section 1010 provides:

Whoever, for the purpose of obtaining any loan or advance of credit from any person, partnership, association, or corporation with the intent that such loan or advance of credit shall be offered to or accepted by the Department of Housing and Urban Development for insurance, or for the purpose of obtaining any extension or renewal of any loan, advance of credit, or mortgage insured by such Department, or the acceptance, release, or substitution of any security on such a loan, advance of credit, or for the purpose of influencing in any way the action of such Department, makes, passes, utters, or publishes any statement, knowing the same to be false, or alters, forges, or counterfeits any instrument, paper, or document, or utters, publishes, or passes as true any instrument, paper, or document, knowing it to have been altered, forged, or counterfeited, or willfully overvalues any security, asset, or income, shall be fined under this title or imprisoned not more than two years, or both.

18 U.S.C. § 1010. Respondent here admittedly violated 18 U.S.C. § 1010 by certifying HUD-1 Statements that he knew to be false and by failing to cause the funds to be disbursed in accordance with the HUD-1 Statements. He did not change the HUD-1 Statements to reflect that borrowers were not making financial contributions because it would have raised "red flags" with the lenders. Respondent intended for the lenders to rely on the HUD-1 Statement he certified. Although Ms. Freebery made false statements on a loan application for her own benefit and pled guilty to a felony, the Panel does not believe a lesser sanction is warranted here even though Respondent did not obtain any personal benefit other than his closing fees. Respondent made misrepresentations on the HUD-1 Statements in 22 transactions over a 2-year period and caused injury to his client, other parties to the transaction and the lenders.

The ODC also presented other cases in support of its recommended sanction. In re Lassen, 672 A.2d 988 (Del. 1996) (lawyer suspended for three years for multiple rules violations including 4.1(a), 8.4(b), 8.4(c) and 8.4(d) for falsifying invoices to clients); In re Fabrizzio, 498 A.2d 1076 (Del. 1985) (lawyer suspended for two years for violating (now) Rule 8.4(c) for falsifying settlement sheets in connection with one real estate closing); In re Faraone, 772 A.2d 1 (1998) (lawyer suspended for six months for violations of Rules 4.(a), 4.1(b) and 8.4(c) for representations made in connection with two real estate transactions); Cincinnati Bar Assoc. v. Powers, 895 N.E.2d 172 (Ohio 1008) (lawyer disbarred for multiple rules violations in connection with falsifying closing documents on over 300 loans). [FN10]

Respondent did not offer any cases in support of his request that the Panel recommend a substantial suspension.

> FN10. While Powers is distinguishable on the basis that the lawyer personally profited from his actions and also falsified federal tax returns to hide his profit, the Panel believes that the Delaware precedents support the recommended sanction and is not relying on Powers for that purpose.

The Panel has considered the extensive factual record summarized above, the ABA Standards, including aggravating and mitigating factors and precedents of the Delaware Supreme Court and recommends disbarment as the appropriate sanction.

Lisa A. Schmidt (Bar No. 3019)

Wayne J. Carey (Bar No. 2041)

Yvonne Anders Gordon

Case Review Exercises

1. What internal controls were lacking regarding both the trust accounts and supervision of nonlawyer staff?

2. What mitigating circumstances did the court consider when determining Sullivan's sanctions, and what was the result?

3. What did the court address in connection with Sullivan's deposits from the real estate closing and the firm's trust account?

Case Review

In the Matter of James A. Cleland, 2 P.3d 700 (Colo. 2000).

2 P.3d 700 (Colo. 2000)

2000 CJ C.A.R. 2672

(Cite as: *In re: Cleland* 2 P.3d 700)

Supreme Court of Colorado, En Banc.

In the Matter of James A. CLELAND, Attorney—Respondent.

No. 99SA89. May 22, 2000

John S. Gleason, Attorney Regulation Counsel, James C. Coyle, Assistant Regulation Counsel, Denver, Colorado, Attorneys for Complainant.

No Appearance By or on Behalf of Attorney—Respondent.

PER CURIAM.

The respondent in this attorney regulation case, James A. Cleland, admitted that he knowingly misappropriated funds belonging to his clients. We have consistently held that disbarment is the appropriate sanction for this type of misconduct, unless significant extenuating circumstances are present. No such circumstances exist in this case. Nevertheless, a hearing panel of our former grievance committee [1] accepted the findings and recommendation of a hearing board that Cleland should be suspended for three years, rather than disbarred. The complainant filed exceptions to the findings and recommendation, contending that Cleland should be disbarred. On review, we determine that certain of the board's findings are clearly erroneous, and we disagree with some of its legal conclusions. On the other hand, we agree with the complainant that disbarment is the only appropriate sanction in this case. Accordingly, we reject the panel's and board's recommendations and we order that Cleland be disbarred, effective immediately.

> FN1. By order of the Supreme Court dated June 30, 1998, effective January 1, 1999, the grievance committee was superseded by the reorganization of the attorney regulation system. The same order provided: "All attorney discipline cases in which trial has occurred prior to January 1, 1999 before a Hearing Board … shall be reviewed by the applicable Hearing Panel at a final meeting to be held in 1999. …" Order re Reorganization of the Attorney Regulation System (Colo. June 30, 1998), reprinted in 12 C.R.S. at 605 (1999). This case was tried on April 29, 1998, and was reviewed by the hearing panel on February 20, 1999.

I.

James A. Cleland was first licensed to practice law in Colorado in 1989. [2] The amended complaint contained six counts. Count I charged Cleland with commingling his personal funds with a client's funds, knowingly mishandling contested funds, and knowingly misappropriating funds belonging to the client. Count II alleged that Cleland knowingly misappropriated $5000 of his client's funds to reimburse a third party for an earnest money deposit that Cleland was supposed to have held in trust. Count III of the complaint charged that Cleland consistently mismanaged his trust account from September 1995 to February 1996. Count IV alleged that Cleland unilaterally charged his client interest on past-due attorney's fees, without the client's authorization. In Count V, the complainant asserted that Cleland had failed to file a collection matter for a client; that he failed to keep the client reasonably informed about the status of the matter; and that he misrepresented that he had settled the case when in fact he had not. Finally, Count VI charged Cleland with making misrepresentations to one of the complainant's investigators and a paralegal during the investigation of Count V. [3]

> FN2. In an unrelated attorney regulation matter heard after the hearing panel acted in this case, the presiding disciplinary judge and hearing board suspended Cleland for two years, effective October 18, 1999. See In re Cleland, No. GC98B118, slip op. at 14 (Colo. PDJ Sept. 17, 1999).

> FN3. The hearing board found that the charges in Count VI had not been proven by clear and convincing evidence. The complainant did not except to this finding; we therefore dismiss Count VI and do not discuss it further.

The evidence before the hearing board consisted of the testimony of the complainant's and respondent's witnesses (including Cleland himself), documents, and a stipulation of facts contained in the trial management order the parties submitted. As the facts are sometimes complex, we address each count of the complaint separately, together with the hearing board's findings and conclusions pertaining to that count.

A. Count I—The Kasnoff Funds

Cleland represented George M. Kasnoff Jr. and his various business entities. In 1994, however, Cleland and Kasnoff had a disagreement over the attorney's fees Kasnoff owed Cleland. One of the business entities involved was Kas-Don Enterprises, Inc., which was owned by Kasnoff and Don Shank. Kasnoff and Shank decided to dissolve Kas-Don in the summer of 1995; Shank agreed to buy out Kasnoff s interest in the real estate the corporation owned. Cleland was to prepare the documents that were necessary to transfer the property and to terminate Kas-Don. This was completed in August 1995 and the corporation was dissolved.

Because he was on his honeymoon in Europe on the closing date, Kasnoff made arrangements for Cleland to deposit the net proceeds from the closing into Cleland's trust account. The parties agreed that once the funds were in the trust account, they would be disbursed for certain business expenses. In addition, Kasnoff authorized Cleland to pay himself $5,000 for past attorney's fees. Cleland was to deposit the balance of the funds in Kasnoff's bride's bank account.

On August 16, 1995, Cleland deposited proceeds from the closing in the amount of $16,576.56 into his trust account. With his client's permission, Cleland paid certain business expenses that Kasnoff owed with funds from the trust account. On August 17, 1995, Cleland asked Kasnoff to pay attorney's fees over and above the $5,000 that Kasnoff had agreed to pay. Kasnoff did not authorize any additional sums to be taken out. Nevertheless, Cleland paid himself an additional $4,581.94 for legal services, including $600 for fees that had not yet been earned. Cleland deposited these unauthorized funds into his operating account and used them for his own purposes. When Kasnoff called from Europe on August 16, Cleland told him that he had deposited the balance of the funds (including the $4,581.94 he had paid himself without permission) into Kasnoff's wife's bank account. This was untrue.

The hearing board found that Kasnoff frequently paid the attorney's fees he owed Cleland slowly. Cleland also reasonably believed that Kasnoff was in financial difficulties. The exact amount of attorney's fees that Kasnoff owed was in dispute even at the hearing (although after these disciplinary proceedings were underway, Cleland returned the clearly unearned $600 in fees through his lawyer). The hearing board also found that at the time he paid himself the unauthorized funds, Cleland was under considerable financial and personal pressure, and that he was clinically depressed.

The board concluded that Cleland's conduct violated Colo. RPC 1.15(a) (failing to keep the client's property—in this case, the $4,581.94—separate from the lawyer's own property), and 1.15(c) (failing to hold separate any property that the lawyer and another—in this case, the client—both claim an interest in). The board found, however, that the complainant did not prove by clear and convincing evidence that Cleland violated Colo. RPC 8.4(c) (engaging in conduct involving dishonesty, fraud, deceit, or misrepresentation). The complainant did not specifically complain about this finding in his opening brief, and we find it unnecessary to address it.

B. Count II—The Clearly Colorado Matter

On June 19, 1995, about two months before Kas-Don was dissolved, Clearly Colorado, L.L.C. entered into a contract with Kasnoff to purchase the latter's one-half interest in Kas-Don real estate. The contract provided that Clearly Colorado would pay a $5,000 earnest money deposit, and that this would be held in Cleland's trust account. After receiving the $5,000, Cleland used the trust funds for his own use. This was not authorized. [4] The real estate transaction fell through and Clearly Colorado demanded the return of its $5,000 deposit. Because he had already diverted the trust funds, however, the balance in Cleland's trust account on August 3, 1995 was only $66.40. Nevertheless, on August 15, 1995, Cleland wrote a $5,000 check drawn on his trust account as a refund to Clearly Colorado. This $5,000 was paid from the proceeds of the Kas-Don transaction referred to in Count I above.

> FN4. It is unclear why Cleland was not charged with initially misappropriating this $5,000 from his trust account.

The board concluded that Cleland knowingly misappropriated client funds to reimburse Clearly Colorado in violation of Colo. RPC 8.4(c) (engaging in conduct involving dishonesty, fraud, deceit, or misrepresentation).

C. Count III—Commingling and Misappropriation

Count II details numerous transactions that Cleland engaged in with respect to client funds and his trust account. For our purposes here, it is sufficient to note that Cleland admitted to commingling his own funds with those belonging to his clients in his trust account and that he knowingly misappropriated client funds without the authorization or knowledge of the clients affected. [5]

> FN5. The board did find that client funds belonging to Donna Nazario were transferred to Cleland's operating account by mistake, and thus did not constitute commingling or misappropriation.

In particular, the hearing board found that Cleland: (1) knowingly misappropriated $1376.95 of client funds from his trust account to repay another client; (2) commingled personal funds with client funds in his trust account on numerous occasions between November 1995 and August 1996; and (3) disbursed trust account funds belonging to various clients to other clients, without the authorization or knowledge of the clients affected. The board thus concluded that Cleland's conduct violated Colo. RPC 8.4(c).

D. Count IV—Kasnoff Interest

Without his client's consent or agreement, Cleland charged interest on Kasnoff's past-due accounts. The board found that this practice violated Colo. RPC 1.5(a) (charging an unreasonable fee), and 8.4(c) (conduct involving dishonesty).

E. Count V—Robin Caspari

Robin Caspari hired Cleland to prosecute a landlord-tenant dispute, and gave him $91 to file suit against two tenants for past-due rent. The hearing board concluded that Cleland failed to keep Caspari reasonably informed about the status of the matter, in violation of Colo. RPC 1.4(a). In addition, Cleland told the client, falsely, that he had filed an action against one of the tenants, when he had not; that hearings had been set and orders had been entered in the case, when in fact there was no case; and that he had settled the matter with one of the clients for $600, which he then paid to the client. The $600 was actually from Cleland's personal funds. This conduct violated Colo. RPC 1.3 (neglecting a legal matter), and 8.4(c) (engaging in dishonest conduct).

II.

[1] The hearing panel approved the hearing board's recommendation that Cleland be suspended for three years, with conditions. The complainant filed exceptions, claiming that certain of the board's factual and legal conclusions were erroneous, and that the appropriate disciplinary sanction was disbarment. The key to the appropriate discipline is also the most serious misconduct here—the knowing misappropriation of client funds in Counts II and III.

[2] As we have said numerous times before, disbarment is the presumed sanction when a lawyer knowingly misappropriates funds belonging to a client or a third person. "When a lawyer knowingly converts client funds, disbarment is 'virtually automatic,' at least in the absence of significant factors in mitigation." People v. Young, 864 P.2d 563, 564 (Colo. 1993) (knowing misappropriation of clients' funds warrants disbarment even absent prior disciplinary history and despite cooperation and making restitution); see also In re Thompson, 991 P.2d 820, 823 (Colo. 1999) (disbarring lawyer who knowingly misappropriated law firm funds); People v. Varallo, 913 P.2d 1, 12 (Colo. 1996) (disbarring lawyer who knowingly misappropriated client funds); People v. Ogborn, 887 P.2d 21, 23 (Colo. 1994) (misappropriating client funds warrants disbarment even in absence of prior discipline and presence of personal and emotional problems); People v. Robbins, 869 P.2d 517, 518 (Colo. 1994) (converting client trust funds warrants disbarment even if funds are restored before clients learn they are missing but not before the conversion is discovered by the lawyer's law firm).

[3] Consistent with our approach, the ABA Standards for Imposing Lawyer Sanctions (1991 & Supp. 1992) provides that, in the absence of mitigating circumstances, "[d]isbarment is generally appropriate when a lawyer knowingly converts client property and causes injury or potential injury to a client." *Id.* at 4.11. Neither this standard nor our cases require serious injury before disbarment is appropriate. On the

other hand, "[s]uspension is generally appropriate when a lawyer knows or should know that he is dealing improperly with client property and causes injury or potential injury to a client." *Id.* at 4.12.

The hearing board found that the following aggravating and mitigating factors were present. In aggravation, Cleland has prior discipline in the form of a letter of admonition for neglecting a legal matter, see *Id.* at 9.22(a); and multiple offenses are present, see *Id.* at 9.22(d). The board also determined that there was a pattern of misconduct, see *Id* at 9.22(c), but only with respect to Cleland's "continuing recklessness and gross negligence in management of his trust account from approximately mid-1995 to mid-August 1996."

According to the board, mitigating factors included the absence of a dishonest motive or intention on Cleland's part, see *Id* at 9.32(b); Cleland admitted that he committed some of the misconduct and otherwise cooperated in the proceedings, see *Id* at 9.32(e), Cleland was relatively inexperienced in the practice of law, see *Id* at 9.32(f); and he has expressed remorse, see *Id* at 9.32(1). Additional mitigating factors found were the presence of personal financial and emotional problems, see *Id* at 9.32(c); and a timely good faith effort to rectify the consequences of at least part of his misconduct, see id, at 9.32(d). The board noted that Cleland was diagnosed with a depressive disorder that impaired his judgment, concentration, and thinking. The conclusion that Cleland tried to rectify some of the consequences of his misconduct stems from the board's belief that he offered to arbitrate the fee dispute with Kasnoff before he was aware that he was under investigation.

While acknowledging our statement in Varallo, 913 P.2d at 12, that disbarment is the presumed sanction when knowing misappropriation is shown, the board declined to apply what it deemed such a "bright-line" rule to the facts in this case. In particular, the hearing board cited three cases that we decided after Varallo that it believed contradicted a literal reading of the case: People v. Zimmermann, 922 P.2d 325 (Colo. 1996); People v. Reynolds, 933 P.2d 1295 (Colo. 1997); and People v. Schaefer, 938 P.2d 147 (Colo. 1997). However, these cases did not modify Varallo's "bright-line" rule. [6]

> FN6. The virtue of a bright-line rule like this one is not that it is easy to apply, although it is. Rather, such a rule strives to eliminate the disparate treatment of lawyers who have committed serious misconduct, when the unequal treatment may otherwise be based on invidious and irrelevant factors.

We decided Zimmermann three months after Varallo. The respondent in Zimmermann, John Delos Zimmermann, seriously mismanaged the funds in his trust account. He commingled funds that should have been placed in his trust account with funds that should have been deposited in his operating account; he improperly used clients' funds to pay his personal or business expenses; and refunded unearned attorney's fees to clients from funds advanced by different clients. See 922 P.2d at 326–29. We suspended Zimmermann for one year and one day. See *Id* at 330. Zimmermann's misconduct is similar to that charged in Count III of the complaint in this case, with one important exception. That exception serves to distinguish Zimmermann from this case, however, in the same way that we distinguished Zimmermann from Varallo. We stated that:

> The single most important factor in determining the appropriate level of discipline in this case is whether [Zimmermann's] misappropriation of client funds was knowing, in which case disbarment is the presumed sanction, People v. Varallo, 913 P.2d 1, 12 (Colo. 1996), or whether it was reckless, or merely negligent, suggesting that a period of suspension is adequate. People v. Dickinson, 903 P.2d 1132, 1138 (Colo. 1995).

Zimmermann, 922 P.2d at 329 [emphasis added]. However, the hearing board specifically found that Zimmermann's mental state when he was mismanaging his trust account was one of recklessness. See *Id* We noted that although the evidence before the board would have supported a finding that Zimmermann's conduct was knowing, rather than reckless, the board's conclusion found support in the record and we would not overturn it. See *Id* at 329 n. 1. Zimmermann therefore stands for the same proposition as Varallo—the lawyer's actual mental state is the most significant factor for determining the proper discipline. Because the board found that Zimmermann's mental state when he mismanaged his trust and operating accounts was reckless, not knowing, Dickinson (suspension) governed the result, not Varallo (disbarment).

We suspended the respondent in People v. Reynolds, 933 P.2d 1295 (Colo. 1997), for three years. John Kerz Reynolds engaged in an extensive pattern of "neglect of client matters, misrepresentations to clients, dishonesty, misuse of client funds, and assisting a nonlawyer in the unauthorized practice of law." *Id* at 1305. He also failed to account for, or return, unearned advance fees he received from various clients. See *Id* at 1296–1301. The case did not involve the knowing misappropriation of client funds, however. Reynolds was not charged with misappropriation, nor did the hearing board in that case make any findings on the issue. Reynolds is therefore distinguishable.

Finally, in People v. Schaefer, 938 P.2d 147 (Colo. 1997), we suspended Richard A. Schaefer for two years. Citing Zimmermann and Varallo, we concluded that "[t]he hearing board's determination that [Schaefer's] mishandling of his client's funds was negligent rather than intentional is not clearly erroneous and we will not overturn it." *Id.* at 150. Schaefer is thus completely consistent with Varallo.

The present case cannot be distinguished from Varallo. In two separate counts, Cleland admitted, and the hearing board found, that he knowingly misappropriated client funds. The board erred when it did not just accept Cleland's admissions and its own initial findings, and then go on to determine whether the factors in mitigation were weighty enough to justify a sanction less than disbarment. Because there is no evidence in the record that supports the conclusion that Cleland's mental state was merely reckless or negligent, that finding is clearly erroneous, and we reject it.

Having determined that disbarment is the presumed sanction in this case, we must now independently review the record with an eye toward the factors in mitigation. The hearing board first found that Cleland did not have a dishonest motive or intention when he committed the misconduct. As the complainant points out, this is directly contrary to the stipulation and a large part of the evidence. The hearing board specifically concluded that Cleland engaged in conduct involving dishonesty, fraud, deceit, or misrepresentation in Counts II (knowing misappropriation of client funds), III (knowing misappropriation of client funds), IV (unilaterally charging unauthorized interest), and V (misrepresenting the status of a case and that it had settled), in violation of Colo. RPC 8.4(c). The fact that Cleland may not have had a dishonest motive in every single instance of misconduct does not demonstrate that the mitigating factor exists. We reject this as a mitigating factor.

Next, the board found that Cleland's admissions of misconduct and his cooperative attitude in the proceedings were mitigating factors. See ABA Standards, supra, at 9.32(e). We agree that these constitute bona fide mitigating circumstances, but we accord them little ultimate weight, given Cleland's failure to appear and participate in this court, and his noncooperation and default in the proceedings before the PDJ for the misconduct (similar to that in this case because it involved mismanagement of trust funds) that earned him a two-year suspension. The reason we consider mitigating factors at all is so we may gauge the level of danger that an attorney poses to the public and, ideally, to arrive at a disciplinary sanction that adequately balances the seriousness of the danger against the gravity of the misconduct.

Although Cleland's cooperation before the hearing board warrants some consideration, we are troubled by his later noncooperation, and feel that this does not bode well for Cleland's future as a lawyer.

The board also considered Cleland's relative inexperience in the practice of law as a mitigating factor. It is such a factor; but inexperience does not go far in our view to excuse or to mitigate dishonesty, misrepresentation, or misappropriation. Little experience in the practice of law is necessary to appreciate such actual wrongdoing. On the other hand, Cleland's expressions of remorse are mitigating, as the board found. See *Id* at 9.32(1).

The hearing board also considered that the personal, financial, and emotional problems that Cleland was experiencing were mitigating. See *Id*. at 9.32(c). Specifically, the board noted that Cleland had been diagnosed with a depressive disorder that impaired his judgment, concentration, and thinking. However, we deem it worthy of note that, despite the advice of the psychiatrist who testified for him, Cleland had not sought treatment for the disorder. Moreover, we reject the proposition that Cleland's financial difficulties mitigate his misappropriation of client funds in any way. Finally, the board found that by offering to arbitrate the fee dispute with Kasnoff, Cleland made some effort to rectify the consequences of at least part of his misconduct. See *Id*. at 9.32(d). Despite the fact that Cleland's clients may not have suffered significant actual damages, as the hearing board found (a point that is debatable given the record in this case), the potential for injury was nevertheless substantial.

Taking all of the above factors into consideration, we conclude that they are not significant enough to call for any result other than disbarment. However, two members of the court disagree and would approve the recommendation to suspend Cleland for three years. Accordingly, we reject the board's and panel's recommendation, and we order that Cleland be disbarred.

III.

We hereby order that James A. Cleland be disbarred, effective immediately. Should Cleland ever seek readmission to practice law pursuant to C.R.C.P. 251.29, he must first demonstrate that he has complied with the following conditions:

(1) Cleland must pay George M. Kasnoff Jr. any amount awarded in Kasnoff's favor in the fee arbitration proceedings between Cleland and Kasnoff;

(2) Cleland must pay the costs incurred in this proceeding in the amount of $2,188.73, to the Attorney Regulation Committee, 600 Seventeenth Street, Suite 200 South, Denver, Colorado 80202.

END OF DOCUMENT

Case Review Exercises

1. Why did the court disagree with the board's findings that the attorney should only be suspended for three years and instead find that the attorney should be disbarred?

2. How did the attorney "consistently mismanage" his trust account?

3. In the Kasnoff matter (Count I), why could the attorney not place the $600 of unearned fees in his operating account?

4. How did the attorney complicate matters by writing a check in *The Clearly Colorado Matter* (Count II) for $5000 when there was only $66.40 in the account at the time? Apparently, the check cashed because another deposit was made. Where did this money come from?

5. In the Robin Caspari matter (Count V), what was wrong with the attorney taking the $600 from his own personal account, as a client actually received a benefit and no client was harmed?

6. When considering mitigation, was the court persuaded by the fact that the attorney had been diagnosed with a depressive disorder that impaired his judgment, concentration, and thinking? Why or why not?

Helpful Web Sites

Organization	Description	Internet Address
Alabama State Bar—Law Office Management Assistance Program	Articles on a variety of law office management topics, including finance-related articles and information. The Web site has a comprehensive manual on trust funds.	http://www.alabar.org/
American Bar Association (ABA)	Association for attorneys. The Web site has a large amount of information and publications relevant to individuals working in the legal profession.	http://www.americanbar.org
ABA Law Practice Management Section	ABA Web site devoted to law practice management issues and including financial issues.	http://www.americanbar.org/lpm
ABA Legal Technology Resource Center	ABA Web site devoted to technology. Includes resources and articles.	http://www.americanbar.org/groups/ departments_offices/legal_technology_ resources.html
ABA Center for Professional Responsibility	Rules for auditing lawyer trust accounts, maintaining and tracking client funds, and trust account overdraft notification	http://www.americanbar.org/groups/ professional_responsibility.html
Association of Legal Administrators	National association for legal administrators. Contains resources and information related to law office management and legal administration.	http://www.alanet.org
Law Technology News	Excellent periodical for legal technology issues.	https://www.law.com/legaltechnews and http://www.legaltechnology.com/ and https://legaltechnology.com/
State Bar Associations—and The National List of Attorneys	Articles published on individual states' bar association Web sites. There are a variety of law office management topics, including trust funds, fees, and finance-related articles and information. The National List of Attorneys maintains a complete list of state bar association Web sites.	https://www.nationallist.com/industry_ resources/assoc-state-bar-list/ You may also use search engines such as yahoo.com or google.com to reach a particular state's bar association Web site.
National Association of Paralegals	National association for legal assistants. Contains many resources for legal assistants.	http://www.nala.org
National Federation of Paralegal Associations	National association for paralegals and legal assistants. Contains many resources for paralegals/legal assistants.	http://www.paralegals.org

Financial and Trust Accounting Software

Organization	Description	Internet Address
Abacus Data Systems	AbacusLaw—Full-featured legal accounting software.	http://www.abacuslaw.com
Aderant	Time & Billing—Full-featured legal accounting software.	http://www.aderant.com
AppFolio™	MyCase—Full-featured legal accounting software.	http://www.mycase.com
Clio	Full-featured legal accounting software.	http://www.goclio.com
PC/TIME MATTERS	Full-featured legal accounting software.	https://pclawtimematters.com/
Software Technology, Inc.	Tabs3—Full-featured legal accounting software.	http://www.tabs3.com
Thomson Reuters—Elite	ProLaw—Full-featured legal accounting software.	http://www.elite.com/prolaw

Suggested Reading

1. American Bar Association. *ABA Model Rules for Client Protection: Model Rules for Lawyers' Funds for Client Protection*.

2. American Bar Association. *ABA Model Rules for Client Protection: Model Rule for Trust Account Records*.

3. American Bar Association. *ABA Model Rules for Client Protection: Model Rules for Trust Account Overdraft Notification*.

4. American Bar Association. *ABA Model Rules for Client Protection: Model Rule for Random Audit of Trust Accounts*.

5. American Bar Association. *ABA Model Rules for Client Protection: Model Rule on Financial Recordkeeping*.

6. Greene, A., & Roberts, P. (2019). *The Lawyer's Guide to Increasing Revenue* (3rd. ed.). American Bar Association.

Calendaring, Docket Control, and Case Management

7

Chapter Objectives

After you read this chapter, you should be able to:

- Explain how to make docketing entries.

- Identify methods to calculate court deadlines.

- Explain why a poor docket control system is harmful to a law office, including ethical and malpractice issues.

- Differentiate between manual and computerized docket systems.

A client sued her former attorney for legal malpractice involving three different incidents: failure to timely file an appeal with the state appeal board, failure to file an administrative claim, and failure to determine the proper identities of persons to sue through inexpensive discovery methods. The discovery issue was noted by the court as grounds for denying her original action to recover from the auto accident resulting in the client's personal injuries.

The client sought the advice of another attorney and filed a legal malpractice claim against the first attorney. A jury awarded the client $473,000 in damages against the attorney, and after appeals the court reversed the district court's decision, denying interest accrual, remanding it for a determination of additional sums owed.

Source: *Hook v. Trevino*, 839 N.W.2d 434 (Iowa, 2013).

Understanding the Importance of Calendaring, Docket Control, and Case Management

The practice of law is filled with appointments, deadlines, hearings, and other commitments for every case that is handled; considering that a single legal professional can have a caseload between 20 and 100 cases at any one time, just staying organized and on top of what needs to get done is a big job. It is extremely important that these dates be carefully tracked for ethical, customer service, and general business reasons. Most, but not all, legal organizations track these deadlines by computer. This chapter introduces calendaring, docket control, and case management. These terms are somewhat confusing and are often used interchangeably.

Calendaring is typically a generic term used to describe the recording of appointments for any type of business. For example, an accounting or engineering firm might use a generic calendaring or scheduling form that comes with an office suite of software programs to track appointments.

Docket control is typically a law office–specific term that refers to entering, organizing, and controlling all the appointments, deadlines, and due dates for a legal organization. There are many legal-specific software programs and manual systems that perform docket control functions for law offices, corporate law departments, and government law departments.

Case management is also a legal-specific term, but it always means more than just tracking appointments and schedules. The breadth of features in current case management programs seems to grow every day. Some of the features found in case management programs include docket control (scheduling/appointments), things to do, contact information databases (name, address, e-mail, phone, fax, etc.) by case (parties, co-counsel, opposing counsel, judges, etc.), case notes, document assembly, document tracking/management, integrated billing, e-mail, and more. All information is centered around and tied to cases in case management programs. This is very helpful for legal organizations that view and organize most of their data according to the case to which it is tied. This is a different approach than general calendaring/personal information managers or docket control.

As the legal software market has matured, more and more manufacturers have entered the market. In addition, nearly all of the current legal products available in this market have gotten significantly more sophisticated at meeting the needs of attorneys, paralegals, and legal organizations.

A final term sometimes used to describe docket control is *tickler*, because it "tickles" the memory for upcoming events.

In many law offices, paralegals operate the docket control system for the whole office, whereas in others, paralegals only use the system to manage and track cases. Although the calendaring and docketing subject may seem trivial at first, the examples of dire consequences resulting from docketing system failures at the beginning of this chapter should indicate the grave nature and importance of this subject. Thus, it is critical for the attorneys and their legal assistants to know how to use docket control so that important deadlines are tracked and kept.

calendaring
A generic term used to describe the function of recording appointments for any type of business.

docket control
A law office–specific term that refers to entering, organizing, and controlling all the appointments, deadlines, and due dates for a legal organization.

case management
A legal term that usually refers to functions such as docket control, things to do, contact information by case, case notes, document assembly, document tracking by case, integrated billing, and e-mail.

Appointments

A legal professional will have many appointments during the course of a case or legal matter: meetings with clients and co-counsel, witness interviews, interoffice meetings, and so forth. Keeping appointments is very important. Law offices that must constantly reschedule appointments with clients may find their clients going to other attorneys who provide better service. The concept of rescheduling appointments or legal deadlines is often called getting a **continuance** (e.g., the deposition was continued because the witness was sick).

Deadlines and Reminders

The practice of law is filled with deadlines at practically every stage of a legal matter. One of the most important types of deadlines is a statute of limitations, also known as prescription. A **statute of limitations** is a statute or law that sets a limit on the length of time a party has to file a suit. For instance, some states impose a five-year statute of limitations on lawsuits alleging a breach of a written contract. That is, if a lawsuit is brought or filed more than five years after a contract is breached or broken, the lawsuit is barred by the statute, and a court dismisses the action. The purpose of a statute of limitations is to force parties to bring lawsuits in a timely fashion so that evidence is not destroyed, before witnesses leave the area, and so forth. If an attorney allows a statute of limitations to run or expire without filing a case, he or she may be liable for legal malpractice.

There also are many deadlines that are set after a case has been filed. In some courts, the judge and the attorneys on both sides sit down and schedule a list of deadlines that the case must follow. The schedule may look something like the one shown in Exhibit 7-1. These deadlines must be adhered to and tracked; an attorney who does not adhere to the deadlines may be penalized or cause the case to be dismissed. Some courts are very reluctant to continue deadlines once they have been set.

Because attorneys and paralegals are busy, usually working on many cases, the law office must have a system of tracking upcoming deadlines. This is done not only by calendaring the deadline itself but also by creating reminder notices in the calendar so that a deadline does not catch a person by surprise. These reminders are called warnings. For example, regarding the January 31 motion to dismiss in Exhibit 7-1, the attorney or paralegal may want to be reminded 30, 15, and 5 days before the deadline. Therefore, reminder notices would be made on January 1, January 16, and January 26, in addition to the deadline itself being recorded on January 31. It is common for an attorney or a paralegal to request from one to four reminders for each deadline. If reminders are not entered in the docket system, it may make it hard to meet the deadline. Thus, logging reminder notices of upcoming events is crucial to the effective practice of law.

Some deadlines are automatically set by the rules of procedure that are in effect in any given court. Rules of procedure are court rules that govern and tell parties what procedures they must follow when bringing and litigating cases. For instance, in some courts, the rules of procedure hold that after a final decision in a case has been rendered, all parties have 30 days to file an appeal.

continuance
Rescheduling an appointment or a court date.

statute of limitations (also known as prescription)
A statute or law that sets a limit on the length of time a party has to file a suit. If a case is filed after the statute of limitations, the claim is barred and is dismissed as a matter of law.

Exhibit 7-1 A Typical Case Schedule

Deadline Item	Deadline Date
All Motions to Dismiss must be filed by:	January 31
Responses to Motions to Dismiss must be filed by:	March 1
Discovery (depositions, interrogatories, request for production) to be completed by:	December 20
Summary Judgment Motions to be filed by:	February 1
Responses to Summary Judgment Motions to be filed by:	March 1
Pretrial order to be filed by:	June 1
Settlement Conferences to be completed by:	June 30
Pretrial Motions to be completed and decided by:	July 15
Trial to start no later than:	September 1

For a law office that practices in the tax area, April 15, the date that federal income tax returns are due, is an example of an automatic or a procedural deadline that must be tracked. Thus, this automatic or procedural deadline must be tracked by the office's docket system, and appropriate reminders must be made so that returns are not filed late and penalties assessed.

Hearings and Court Dates

Hearings and court dates are formal proceedings before a court. It is extremely important that these dates be carefully tracked. Most courts have little tolerance for attorneys who fail to show up for court. In some instances, the attorney can be fined or disciplined for missing court dates.

In larger cases, especially when the case is being litigated in court, there may be hundreds of entries in the docket system. Exhibit 7-2 includes a list of common docket entries, including both substantive and law office management–related entries.

Receiving Documents, Following Court Rules, and Calculating Deadlines

Receiving documents that need to be calendared, calculating deadlines, and following the local court rules are important aspects of docket control.

Receiving Documents

When documents arrive in the mail, e-mail, or otherwise, response dates and other deadlines should be immediately and systematically entered into the law office's docket system. This includes pleadings, motions, discovery documents, and other documents that require responses within a certain time period.

Suppose that your office received interrogatories (written questions that your client must complete and send back) in the mail for one of your clients. Also, suppose that in the particular court where the suit is filed, interrogatory responses must be answered within 30 calendar days of the date they are received. When the interrogatories are received by the mail department (or whoever opens the mail),

Exhibit 7-2 Common Docket Control Entries

- Expiration dates for statutes of limitations
- Judgment renewal dates
- Employee-benefit annual filings
- Renewal dates for copyrights, trademarks, and patents
- Renewal dates for leases and licenses
- Renewal dates for insurance coverage
- Trial court appearance dates
- Due dates for trial court briefs
- Due dates on various pleadings: answers, depositions, replies to interrogatories and requests for admissions, various motions and notices, etc.
- Due dates in probate proceedings, such as inventory and appraisal dates
- Appearances in bankruptcy proceedings
- Action dates in commercial law matters
- Due dates in corporate or security matters
- Closing dates for real estate transactions
- Due dates for appellate briefs and arguments
- Tax return due dates
- Due dates in estate matters, such as tax return dates, valuation dates, and hearing dates
- Dates of stockholder meetings
- Dates of board of directors meetings
- Review dates for wills
- Review dates for buy and sell valuations of business interests
- Review dates for trusts
- Renewal dates for leases on offices
- Renewal dates for attorney licenses
- Expiration dates on notary certificates
- Renewal dates for malpractice and other insurance
- Personal property tax return dates
- Dates for partner (and other recurring and nonrecurring) meetings
- Review dates for billings and accounts receivable
- Review dates for work-in-process
- Review dates for evaluation of associates and staff
- Review dates for raises and bonuses
- Due dates for quarterly payroll withholding reports

the documents with calendar entries should be routed immediately to someone who has the responsibility to record the deadlines in the docket control system. If there is confusion as to whose responsibility it is to enter the calendar item, or confusion as to when the documents should be calendared (i.e., there is no systematic system), there is an excellent chance that the calendar dates will not be entered into the docket system. If that happens, it is virtually guaranteed that deadlines, response dates, and so forth will be missed and ethical problems will follow.

Know the Local Court Rules

It is imperative to know the local court rules for each court in which your office has cases. Even courts in the same state can have vastly different rules, depending on the internal operating procedures of each court.

Calculating Deadlines

Calculating deadlines depends on the local rules. However, the following are some of the different ways that deadlines can be calculated and some problems that may arise in making calculations.

Calendar Days v. Workdays Some courts make a distinction between calendar days and workdays. For example, if a court rule says that a party responding to a motion has 15 days from the file date to file a response, you need to know if the 15 days refers to all days (i.e., calendar days) or only to workdays.

When calculating deadlines, **calendar days** typically mean literal days, counting all days including weekends and holidays. For example, if a motion is filed on the 1st day and you have 15 calendar days to respond, the response must be filed by the 16th day. When you count days, you count from one day to the next; for example, the 1st to the 2nd day is one day, the 2nd to the 3rd day is two days, and so on. So, you actually start your count on the day *after* you receive the motion. When using the calendar-day method, a deadline may fall on a Saturday or Sunday; in many courts, the due date would simply be the Monday following the Saturday or Sunday. If the deadline falls on a holiday, the deadline is typically the next day the court is open for business.

When calculating deadlines, **workdays** typically refer to only those days when the court is open. Because courts usually are not open on holidays and weekends, these days are omitted from the calculation. For example, if a motion is filed on the 1st day and you have 15 workdays to respond, and assuming the 1st day is a Monday (with no holidays in between), the response would be due on the 22nd day (see Exhibit 7-3).

You need to know whether the court rules are figured on calendar days or workdays because there is a big difference between the two.

File Date versus Document Receipt Date

Court rules will typically state when and/or how deadlines are determined. Deadlines can be calculated either on the date the person actually receives the document or on the date when the document is stamped "FILED" at the clerk's office.

File Date A typical court rule may state, for a civil action, that a party has 30 days from when the judgment is "FILED" to file an appeal. Assume the court files a judgment on the 1st day and that the party receives the judgment on the 3rd day; the deadline is calculated from the file date, and if there were 30 days in the month, the appeal would have to be filed by the 1st day of the next month.

Document Receipt Date Discovery document deadlines typically are calculated by receipt date. For example, a court rule may state that a party has 30 days to answer interrogatories. This is usually calculated from when the document is actually received by the law office needing to respond. So, if the

calendar days
System for calculating deadlines that counts all days including weekends and holidays.

workdays
System for calculating deadlines that refers to only days when the court is open.

Exhibit 7-3 Calendar for Calculating Calendar Days and Workdays Example

Monday	Tuesday	Wednesday	Thursday	Friday	Saturday	Sunday
1 Motion filed	**2**	**3**	**4**	**5**	**6**	**7**
8	**9**	**10**	**11**	**12**	**13**	**14**
15	**16** Response Due if 15 Calendar Days	**17**	**18**	**19**	**20**	**21**
22 Response Due if 15 Workdays						

Sample Event:	Number of days:	Due Date:
Motion filed on 1st	15 Calendar Days	Tuesday, 16th
Motion filed on 1st	15 Workdays	Monday, 22nd

document was mailed on the 1st day and actually received on the 3rd day, then the party will have until the 4th day of the next month to send responses to the opposing side. Thus, it can be very important for the law office to establish when a document was received. Law offices should routinely stamp all documents that come into the office with a received stamp that shows the date the document was received (e.g., "RECEIVED 10/1/2007").

In addition, when a party prepares a court document in a case, there typically is a **Certificate of Service** at the very end of the document. The purpose of the Certificate of Service is to certify and establish when the document was placed in the mail. The "Certificate of Service" must also be signed. This way, the clerk of the court and the involved parties know when a document was placed in the mail.

A **Bates stamp** is sometimes used to number every page of a document. A Bates stamp stamps a document with a sequential number and then automatically advances to the next number. In this way, it is possible to establish the order of every page in a document, particularly large documents such as those that have been produced for evidence.

Certificate of Service
A statement at the end of a court document that certifies or establishes when a document was placed in the mail.

Bates stamp
Stamps a document with a sequential number and then automatically advances to the next number.

Due Date—File Date v. Mail Date

When reading court rules, it is important to know whether documents can be mailed in or if they must actually be "FILED" within the specified deadline. For example, assume you receive a document on the 1st day and the court rule says you have 20 days to respond; the response would be due on the 21st day. In some courts, it is acceptable to put the response in the mail on the 21st day. That is, you do not actually have to get the document stamped "FILED" on the 21st day. Some courts automatically give you three days' mail time before they say the document is late. Different courts have different rules; again, be sure you know if due dates are calculated on file dates or mail dates. This distinction becomes more important in rural areas.

Ethical and Malpractice Considerations

The ramifications of missing deadlines and otherwise failing to track the progress of cases can be severe. In fact, there are two types of negative outcomes that can result from case neglect: an ethical proceeding against the attorney and a legal malpractice claim filed against the attorney or firm. An attorney who neglects a case can be disciplined by a state ethics board. Such discipline in an ethics case may include reprimand, suspension, or even disbarment. In a legal malpractice case, the attorney involved is sued for damages for providing substandard legal work. These types of cases are not remote or obscure. There are thousands of legal ethics and malpractice proceedings filed throughout the country every year alleging case neglect.

Ethical Considerations

Studies of attorney disciplinary opinions have found that the main two reasons that clients file disciplinary proceedings and that courts discipline attorneys are (1) attorneys failing to communicate with their clients and (2) attorneys neglecting or not pursuing client cases diligently. Both of these problems are easily preventable when attorneys and legal assistants use good docket control systems and effective time management.

The ABA *Model Rules of Professional Conduct* gives direct guidance on these issues. The *Model Rules*, adopted and made a part of each states' rules of professional conduct, state that attorneys should be competent in the area in which they are practicing and that they are reasonably prepared to represent the client. The *Model Rules, as adopted by the states*, note that the attorney must act with reasonable diligence and promptness when representing a client, and finally, that an attorney must keep the client reasonably informed about what is going on in the representation of the client. While these ethical rules have been discussed in previous chapters, it is important to include them again in the context of docket control because it is through docket control and organization that a legal professional complies with these rules. Each of these areas is explored in detail.

Competence and Adequate Preparation   The *Rules* regarding professional conduct hold that an attorney must be competent to represent the client; that is, he or she should reasonably know the area of law in which the client needs representation, and, assuming the attorney does know the area of law, he or she should take the preparation time needed to become familiar with the case in order to represent the client adequately.

Rule 1.1 regarding rules of professional conduct states that an attorney must provide competent representation to a client, including reasonable preparation necessary to perform the legal work. The purpose of this rule is to ensure that an attorney does not undertake a matter in which he or she is not competent and to ensure that the attorney has had adequate preparation. The amount of "adequate preparation" depends on what type of legal matter the client has. Major litigation, for example, will require far more preparation time than the amount of time it takes to prepare a will. Attorneys should not undertake to represent a client if, for some reason, they cannot do it with the skill and preparation time necessary. Legal professionals use docket control systems to plan adequate preparation time for cases.

Diligence *Rule 1.3* regarding rules of professional conduct requires that an attorney act with a reasonable degree of diligence and promptness in pursuing a client's case. The rule specifically requires an attorney to act with commitment and dedication when representing a client and to avoid procrastination. Further insight concerning this rule comments that time passage may adversely affect a client's interest and/or destroy the client's legal rights. At the very least, time delays that are unjustified may create unnecessary anxiety for the client and raise questions as to the lawyer's integrity.

Furthermore, as noted by the rule's comment, an attorney should carry through to conclusion all legal matters undertaken for a client unless the relationship is properly and clearly terminated. If there is any doubt about the existence of an attorney–client relationship, the attorney should clarify the situation "in writing so that the client will not mistakenly suppose the attorney is looking after the client's affairs when the lawyer has ceased to do so." The purpose of this rule is to ensure that attorneys put forth reasonable effort and diligence to represent a client. Attorneys cannot adequately represent the interests of clients if they ignore the case, if they are lazy and do not work on the case, or if they do not have the systems in place to manage deadlines, appointments, and things to be done.

Communication with Clients An attorney also must communicate regularly with the client. *Rule 1.4* regarding rules of professional conduct requires an attorney to promptly and reasonably consult with a client, to promptly comply to a client's reasonable request for information, and to keep a client informed about the cases status and legal matters, as well as explain matter(s) to clients so that they might reasonably make informed decisions.

This rule specifically requires the attorney to maintain reasonable contact with a client, explain general strategies, and keep the client reasonably informed regarding case status. "Reasonableness" is dependent upon the facts and circumstance for each case and is determined on a case-by-case basis. As noted in the rule's comment, a lawyer must meet reasonable expectations from the client, which is consistent with the lawyer's responsibility to provide quality representation, acting in the client's best interest.

Exhibit 7-4 shows only a few examples of attorneys and paralegals failing to follow up on client cases. A basic element of due diligence to a client requires an attorney to meet deadlines and limitation periods and appear at requisite legal proceedings. Many of these failures could have been avoided by a good docket control system and attorneys' and legal professionals' willingness to plan, organize, and simply get the work done. There is little excuse for poor organization

Exhibit 7-4 Cases Regarding Lack of Diligence

Paralegal's Heavy Caseload Not an Excuse for Failing to Respond Timely to a Motion to Dismiss—Case Dismissed

An attorney filed an employment action for a client against the client's former employer one day after the statute of limitation. The defendant company moved to dismiss the complaint in August. No response was filed, and in February of the following year the Court granted the motion and dismissed the client's case. In October of that year, more than a year after the Motion to Dismiss was originally filed, the plaintiff's attorney filed a Motion to Set Aside Judgment of Dismissal on the grounds that his paralegal had a heavy caseload and failed to respond to the motion to dismiss. The Court denied the motion and upheld the dismissal. The Court noted that the neglect of the legal assistant was not a reason to set aside the judgment, and that even if a response had been filed, the case was filed outside of the statute of limitations and most likely would have been dismissed anyway. **Deo-Agbasi v. Parthenon Group**, 229 F.R.D. 348 (D. Mass. 2005).

Paralegal Scheduling Clerk Fails to Properly Docket Three Court Appearances for Attorney

An attorney's paralegal neglected to properly docket three court appearances for an attorney. As a result of this, the "answer" that was filed by the attorney for the client was stricken and the Court entered default judgment against the attorney's client. The attorney appealed the default judgment. The appellate court found that when the trial court granted the default judgment, it served to punish the innocent client for the paralegal's neglect. The appellate court reversed and allowed the attorney to file the answer. **Hu v. Fang**, 104 Cal.App 4th 61, 127 Cal.Rptr. 2d 756 (2002).

Attorney Files Suit for Special Education Student and Then Loses Interest

An attorney accepted $4000 to file a suit on behalf of a mother and her daughter, a special education student, so the daughter could be placed in a public school. The attorney then took no action in the case, never sent the client a detailed accounting, and refused to communicate with the client. Three and a half years later, the client received a letter from the attorney stating that in light of his "other business projects," he did not anticipate practicing law any longer. When the client requested the return of the $4000 in legal fees and her file, the attorney denied both requests. The attorney received a one-year suspension followed by a six-month period of supervised probation. **In Re Dunn**, 831 So.2d 889 2002.

and poor docket control in the modern law office. Firms today have access to an unlimited supply of outstanding computerized docket control systems and case management programs made specifically for law firms, and an even greater supply of generic calendaring software that comes with most computers. Even with all these systems and technology, however, failure to properly perform work on time is a major reason that attorneys are disciplined in this country.

Conflict of Interest

Attorneys must take steps to prevent conflict of interest problems. A conflict of interest occurs when an attorney or a paralegal has competing personal or professional interest with a client's case that would preclude him or her from acting impartially toward the client. Before an attorney or a law firm accepts a case, he or she should perform a thorough conflict of interest search. Many attorneys and law firms use computerized software to perform such a conflict of interest search. Many case management programs allow attorneys to perform a conflict of interest search on current clients, past clients, law office contacts, adverse clients, counsel, and much more. A thorough conflict of interest search using computerized software is an effective way of avoiding conflict of interest problems.

Legal Malpractice Considerations

[A] client sued their former attorney(s) alleging that they were negligent with the fraud case that was dismissed by, among other things, failing to file a timely appearance, failing to attend certain depositions and advise of witnesses' testimonies in advance of other depositions, failing to properly prepare the case for trial, and failing to seek a voluntary nonsuit on date of trial, all leading to the client's case being dismissed. The jury returned a verdict for the client in the amount of $2,337,550, finding that but for the attorneys' negligence, the client would have been successful in their breach of contract and contract fraud lawsuit.

Source: Tri-G, Inc. v. Burke, Bosselman and Weaver, 817 N.E.2d 1230, 353 Ill. App.3d 197, 288 Ill. Dec. 580 (Ill. App., 2004).

In addition to the ethical considerations of neglecting a client's legal matter, the client may also have a legal malpractice claim against the attorney for negligence. The general theory in a **legal malpractice** claim is that the attorney breached an ordinary standard of care applicable to a reasonable attorney under those circumstances. In a legal malpractice case, both the plaintiff and defendant must rely on attorneys who are expert witnesses to testify whether the defendant did or did not act like a reasonable attorney would in the same situation.

Exhibit 7-5 shows some common deadlines that, when missed, may lead to malpractice claims. In fact, many malpractice insurers will refuse to write malpractice insurance for a law office that does not have an effective docket control system.

In recent years, the number of legal malpractice claims that have been filed has gone up dramatically. In some cases, the amount of damages can be substantial. Some insurance companies that offer legal malpractice coverage actually meet with staff members who are in charge of docket control to ensure that a docket control system is being used. Thus, attorneys and law offices have two powerful reasons to maintain a quality docket system.

legal malpractice
A claim that an attorney breached an ordinary standard of care that a reasonable attorney would have adhered to in that same circumstance.

Exhibit 7-5 Common Reasons for Malpractice Claims

1. Expiration of the statute of limitations
2. Failure to appear or plead, resulting in a default judgment
3. Dismissal of a lawsuit for lack of prosecution
4. Failure to file tax returns or other documents within the time required
5. Failure to file pleadings or to comply with an order within the time required
6. Failure to answer interrogatories within the time required
7. Failure to give timely notice when such notice is a precondition to a recovery of damages
8. Failure to communicate with clients
9. Not knowing what to do next (i.e., the attorney not being competent in an area)

Manual Docket Control Systems

There are many types of manual docketing systems, including a simple calendar, a card system, and others. Manual docketing systems work best for fairly small law offices. As a law office grows, manual systems become more difficult to manage.

Calendar Small law offices may use simple computer calendar programs or a page-a-day calendaring system. Many calendars provide a section to record "things to do" or reminders, in addition to providing a place to schedule appointments.

As cases or legal matters are opened, deadlines and reminders (i.e., "ticklers") are entered into the calendar. Notices from courts, attorneys, and so forth also are entered. In addition to the due dates or appointment date being entered, reminders also must be manually entered into the calendar. This process of manually entering due dates and reminders can be very time consuming; for instance, if a deadline with two reminders was entered, the whole entry would have to be manually entered a total of three times in three places.

In some offices, each attorney and paralegal maintains his or her own separate calendar. The issue with this approach is that often the attorneys and paralegals fail to coordinate their schedules and calendars. This can be a serious problem.

Finally, if attorneys wanted a short list of things to be done, appointments, or critical deadlines for a day, week, or month, it would have to be compiled and entered into a word processor by a staff member.

Card System A card system (sometimes called a "tickler card system") uses index cards or their equivalent to track deadlines and things to be done. A manual card or form is used for each deadline or task to be completed and includes client name, action to be performed, client number, reminder date, and due date. Cards can be color-coded to indicate different types of deadlines. In most cases, the card or slip of paper is kept in duplicate or triplicate; copies are used as reminders and filed before the actual due date. An index-card holder or expanding file folder with dividers for each month and each day must be maintained to file each card. When the date on a card tickler is reached, the card is pulled and given to the appropriate person to perform the task, or a list of the deadlines and things to do is made.

An individual must check the card system every day in order for it to work properly. However, if a slip is lost or misfiled, the system breaks down. Although computerized systems may occasionally break down as well, manual systems are far more likely to be error prone. In addition, like the manual calendar, any daily, weekly, or monthly card system report must be typed by hand.

Manual calendaring systems also lack the ability to track information by case. For example, if a client asked to see all the upcoming events for his or her case, a staff person would have to go through the calendar and manually put together a list. Depending on the case, there could be many entries. Again, this is a time-consuming process.

Another problem with a manual calendaring system is that successive calendars must be purchased every year (e.g., one for 2020, one for 2021, one for 2022, and so on). It is also difficult to schedule dates far in the future—five years down the road for a statute of limitations entry, for instance—because you will need the appropriate calendar.

Manual calendaring systems are prone to error and are time consuming to administer. Because the process is slow and tedious, it encourages users to make as few docket entries as possible. Further, manual systems simply do not have the flexibility and reporting capabilities that computerized versions can deliver.

Types of Computerized Docket Control Systems

There are a variety of computer programs that can be used to schedule and track events for a legal organization. These include generic calendaring/personal information manager programs and case management programs. Most of these programs can be purchased for stand-alone computers or for local area networks. Networked systems, whether generic or legal specific, have the principal advantage of allowing individual users throughout an organization to see and have access to the calendars of other users in the office.

Generic Calendaring and Personal Information Manager Programs

Generic calendaring programs computerize the functions of a paper desk calendar. Since they are generic and can be used by any type of business, they lack many features that are helpful to a legal organization. These types of programs are usually very inexpensive and typically manage only the calendar, things to do, contacts, and e-mail functions.

A generic **personal information manager (PIM)** program consolidates a number of different tasks into one computer program. Most PIMs include calendaring, things to do, a contact database that tracks names and addresses of people, note taking, e-mail, and other tasks as well. Microsoft Outlook is a type of PIM that can come bundled with Microsoft's Office Suite of programs. Outlook is an extremely powerful program. As the generic calendaring and scheduling software market has matured, most new programs are PIMs. PIMs are very popular and convenient to use as they allow a user to organize a number of related tasks into one easy-to-use interface. Generic PIMs are not specifically suited to the needs of legal professionals, but they still have many useful features, and some legal organizations use these. For example, for consistency purposes a corporate law department might use a product like Microsoft Outlook, which can be implemented throughout the corporation, instead of a legal-specific program that only its department can use.

personal information manager (PIM) Consolidates a number of different tasks into one computer program. Most PIMs include calendaring, things to do, a contact database that tracks names and addresses of people, note taking, and other tasks as well.

Overview of Computerized Legal Case Management and Docket Control

Most case management programs offer a variety of features, including the following.

Monthly, Daily, and Weekly Calendar Views

Almost all case management programs have some type of monthly display, which allows the user to get an overview of his or her schedule. In addition to monthly and daily views, most programs allow users to see a weekly view of their schedules as well.

Event Entry Screen

This is where new entries are entered into the case management program. These can include deadlines, things to be done, or appointments. The data entry process for most programs is easy and straightforward. Information that is entered into most entry screens includes the client, matter number, description, date, time, type of entry, place, who the event is for, notes, reminders, and other information.

Perpetual Calendars

Most computerized case management systems have built-in perpetual calendars that allow a person to see and enter data that will be used for many years in the future. Unlike manual calendars, a computerized system does not have to be updated annually (although purchasing updated versions of the software may be desirable). The perpetual calendar is an important feature of a computerized system, since it allows the user to make entries concerning dates that are far in the future, such as a statute of limitations.

Recurring Entries

recurring entry
A calendar entry that recurs.

One advantage of using computerized case management systems is that the user can automatically make recurring entries. A **recurring entry** is a calendar entry that typically recurs daily, weekly, monthly, or annually. For instance, if an office has a staff meeting every Monday morning, the entry could be entered once as a weekly recurring appointment, since most computerized case management systems can make recurring docket entries daily, weekly, monthly, quarterly, and annually. Thus, an entry that would have had to be entered 52 times in a year in a manual system would have to be entered only once in a computerized docket control program.

Date Calculator

Some case management systems have a date calculator that automatically calculates the number of days between dates. For instance, suppose you have 20 calendar days from a specific date to file a motion. The date calculator feature will automatically calculate the deadline. This is useful when you have deadlines that take into account only workdays (i.e., that do not count Saturdays, Sundays, and holidays).

Scheduling Conflict Alert

Some case management systems automatically alert the user to possible conflicts. For instance, if a user mistakenly tries to schedule two appointments for the same date and time, nearly all computerized docket systems will automatically alert the user to the possible conflict. If the user has a conflict, most systems can be overridden and both appointments entered anyway. Some systems have a "lockout" feature that prevents users from scheduling more than one appointment for a given time period.

Some systems even allow the user to enter such information as the individual's regular office hours and days of the week that are usually taken off. If, for instance, an individual's office hours are from 7:00 a.m. to 4:00 p.m. and an entry is made for 4:30 p.m., some systems automatically recognize the problem and alert the user.

Scheduling Multiple Parties

Scheduling free time for an interoffice meeting can sometimes be difficult, since all parties must have an open block of time. Many case management systems that operate on a local area network can automatically bring up dates and times that a group of people have free, thus making scheduling meetings easy.

A computerized case management system also allows other individuals working on a case to see what docketing entries have been made and to find out what is going on in the case. This eases the process of multiple people working on the same case. It also allows for methods of communications between collaborative parties and features passwords and other encryptions to limit the personnel to the key people working on the case.

Centralized and Decentralized Systems

Most case management systems work well in either a centralized or decentralized system. In a centralized system, one person (like a secretary) can make time entries for many individuals; this is beneficial because only one individual is responsible for making the docketing entries. A decentralized system, where the attorney or paralegal enters their own deadlines into the docket program, also works well for some offices.

Automatic Reminders

Most computerized case management systems allow the user to make one entry into the system that also contains the reminder dates. For instance, when an appointment or a deadline is entered into the computer, the system automatically asks the user when they want to be reminded of it. If a reminder date is entered, the computerized method automatically makes reminder entries. This is a great time-saving feature over manual systems in which every reminder must be entered individually.

Calendaring a Series of Events from a Rule

Some case management programs allow a user to enter one event that, in turn, automatically triggers a list of subsequent calendaring events based on court rules. For instance, a complaint is filed. Sixty days after the complaint is filed, according to court rules the complaint must have been served. Therefore, the docketing program automatically enters a deadline to serve the complaint 60 days after the complaint is filed. This kind of feature is very powerful and can be a real time-saver. Many case management programs allow users to program their own court rules into the program or to add on purchased court rule setups.

Reporting

Most computerized systems allow the user to generate a variety of reports that manual systems cannot produce, including daily, weekly, or monthly schedules and things-to-do entries for one person or a group of people. Most systems can also search and sort the entries in a variety of different formats.

Daily Calendar Reports   This is an in-depth listing of a timekeeper's or office's daily schedule. The daily report is sometimes called a day-sheet. Many attorneys and legal assistants use this report every day for an accurate listing of the day's events.

Daily Calendar Report for a Week This is similar to the daily calendar report except that the report shows docket entries for an entire week. Legal assistants and attorneys may want this report at the beginning of the week to get a "snapshot" of what their schedule looks like, so they can plan accordingly.

Per Case Docket Report Most computerized case management systems allow the user to generate a docket report by case—that is, a report showing all the docketing dates for any one case (see Exhibit 7-6). This report can be very helpful in trying to determine how to proceed with certain cases. Exhibit 7-6 provides a listing of all entries for the case *00003-Battise Custody Agreement*. This is particularly helpful when scheduling other events for the same case and for providing details to the client. Keeping clients informed about their cases is very important when it comes to client satisfaction and when it is time for the client to pay the legal bill. A client who is consulted often and kept aware of the progress of the case is more likely to pay the bill and generally is more satisfied than a client who is not notified about their case's progress. This report is very beneficial to clients who want to know what is going on in a case and also to recently assigned attorneys or legal assistants, who would like to see what has happened and where the case is headed.

Exhibit 7-6 Docket Report for a Case

James Adams
Schedule for Custody Agreement
Case Number: 00003

Date	Start	Last, First	Summary	Who	Note
12/28/21	8:30 a.m.	Battise, S.	DISCOVER	AMS	Discovery Deadline
01/02/22	9:00 a.m.	Battise, S.	HEARING	AMS	Hearing on Pending Motions
03/01/22	9:00 a.m.	Battise, S.	C-STATUS	AMS	Status Conference
03/15/22	1:00 a.m.	Battise, S.	PRETRIAL	AMS	Pretrial Conference
03/29/22	10:00 a.m.	Battise, S.	C-SETTLE	AMS	Settlement Conference
04/06/22	8:00 a.m.	Battise, S.	TR PR	AMS	Trial Preparation
04/07/22	8:00 a.m.	Battise, S.	TRIAL	AMS	TRIAL

Number of Events: 7

Past Due Report The past due report prints a listing of all docket entries that are past due (i.e., the deadline or due date has passed) or that have not been marked "Done." The past due report is a safeguard against forgetting or not completing items.

Free Time Report The free time report shows the times that one timekeeper or several timekeepers have unscheduled or open. This is useful when adding scheduling items or when setting up a conference of three or four individuals. Attorneys and legal assistants who have a lot of appointments and court dates also can use this report so they can see when free time is available for scheduling other matters.

Searching

Most computerized case management systems allow the user to search for entries. For instance, if a client calls and wants to know the date of his or her deposition, the user could enter the client's name into the computer and the system would retrieve the entry showing the deposition date.

Advanced Case Management Features

Up to this point, the case management program features we have covered have for the most part been confined to docket control. Now, some advanced case management features will be covered as well.

Case Contacts

Case contacts allow the user to enter people into a contact database (which tracks phone, address, e-mail, etc.), just as in a PIM. The difference is that once they are entered in the database, the person(s) can be linked to a case or cases. So, if a user wanted to see or print a list of co-counsel or opposing counsel on a case, it could be easily done. Also, if the case management system is networked, the legal organization could have one master contact database (linked to cases) for the whole organization. Thus, there would be no duplication in multiple places throughout the legal organization.

Synchronizing with PIMs/PDAs

Most case management systems will synchronize calendars with PIMs (such as Outlook) and personal digital assistants (PDAs). Thus, if a corporate law department wanted to use a case management system, but the rest of the corporation was using Outlook, the two could be set up to share information or synchronize so that all of the entries in the case management program would not have to be entered by hand in Outlook.

Case Diary/Notes

Most case management systems provide a place to maintain a case diary or notes for the file. This allows legal professionals a central place to store their notes, record summaries of phone calls, and much more. A large benefit to case management programs is not only that the information can be stored electronically but that any users in a networked environment can immediately access and use the information at a touch of the button, without having to pull the hard copy of the file. Thus, a good case management system is also a communication enhancement tool.

Document Assembly/Generation

As indicated previously, case management programs store a great deal of information about a case, parties, attorneys, case-related information, case numbers, and much more. Most case management programs can merge that information into a merge document (see Exhibit 7-7). So, a legal professional can automatically generate standard letters, forms, pleadings, and reports right from the case management system without having to reenter any additional data. Most case management systems also work with Word and Word Perfect, so they can merge documents into these programs as well. Also, when a case user creates a

Exhibit 7-7 Sample Document Assembly/Generation Sample

CASE MANAGEMENT DATABASE

Client Name:	First National Bank
Contact Person– First Name:	Sam
Contact Person– Last Name:	Johnson
Client Address:	P.O. Box 1000
Client City:	Philadelphia
Client State:	Pennsylvania
Client Zip:	98934
Client Phone:	943/233-9983
Case Number:	2006-9353
Court:	Philadelphia Superior Court—District 13, Philadelphia, Pennsylvania
Debtor Name:	Philip Jones
Debtor Address:	3242 Wilson Ave. SW
Debtor City:	Philadelphia
Debtor State:	Pennsylvania
Debtor Zip:	98984
Amount Owed to Client:	$25,234
Type of Debt:	Mortgage
Type of Asset:	House at 3242 Wilson Ave SW, Philadelphia, Pennsylvania

Merge function

DOCUMENT TEMPLATE 1—"Complaint"

In the {Court}

{Client name}

Plaintiff

Case No. {Case Number}

{Debtor Name}
{Debtor Address}
{Debtor City}{Debtor State}{Debtor Zip}

Defendant.

COMPLAINT

Comes now the plaintiff, {Client Name}, and states that the defendant, {Debtor Name}, is indebted to the plaintiff in the amount of {Amount Owed to Client} on a {Type of Debt} regarding a {Type of Asset}. Attached to this complaint as Appendix "A" is a fully executed copy of the mortgage above referenced.

MERGED DOCUMENT—"Complaint"

In the Philadelphia Superior Court – District 13, Philadelphia, Pennsylvania

First National Bank

Plaintiff

Case No. 2006-9353

Philip Jones
3242 Wilson Ave. SW
Philadelphia, Pennsylvania 98984

Defendant.

COMPLAINT

Comes now the plaintiff, First National Bank, and states that the defendant, Philip Jones, is indebted to the plaintiff in the amount of $25,234 on a mortgage regarding a house at 3242 Wilson Ave SW, Philadelphia, Pennsylvania. Attached to this complaint as Appendix "A" is a fully executed copy of the mortgage above referenced.

document in the case management system, in many instances it will automatically note this—including the date—in the case diary/notes. A user simply has to indicate what file the document needs to be merged with, and then the user is given a list of documents to choose from, including file reports, letters, memos, and others. Users are, of course, allowed to create their own forms as well.

Other Features

Legal Research Library   Some case management programs give the user a place to store electronic legal research or allow the user to access functions within Westlaw and/or other electronic research tools.

Conflict of Interest   Most case management programs allow the user to do conflict of interest searches. Since the database tracks clients, parties, counsel, and much more case-related information, the conflict search can be very comprehensive.

E-Mail Interface   Many programs now include an e-mail interface that allows users to link e-mails with cases. This is extremely important given the heavy use of e-mails in communicating with clients and handling client matters.

Document Management   Many case management programs can now associate documents with cases. A link can be made between a document/file and a case in a case management program. This allows legal professionals to index and manage case documents from the program.

Time and Billing/Accounting Interface   Many programs share information with timekeeping and billing programs and, in some instances, accounting programs as well.

The Docket Cycle

The docket cycle refers to how information is entered into a case management program. There are three primary ways that information can flow into and out of such a program: a centralized method, decentralized method, and combined method.

Centralized Docket Control Cycle

In a centralized docket control cycle, one person typically is responsible for entering all docket entries into the docket program. This is usually a data entry person or, in some cases, a secretary or paralegal. In this type of system, the first step would be for a user to manually complete a docket slip (see Exhibit 7-8). In the second step, the designated person enters the event into the docket control program. The third step is for reports to be generated, and the last step is for entries to be marked "Done."

Decentralized Docket Control Cycle

In a decentralized docket control cycle, the users enter docket information directly into the computer, controlling their own docket. In this type of system, the first step would be for the user to enter a docket entry into the case management program. Second, the user views or prints reports as necessary, and third, the user marks entries "Done." The advantage of this system is that the user has ultimate control over their own docket; the disadvantage is that the user is doing the data entry instead of a clerk or secretary.

Exhibit 7-8 Sample Docket Slip

ADAMS & LEE   **DOCKET SLIP**

Client/Case Matter: *Sharon Smith* _____ File No.: _____

Event: *Pre-Trial Hearing* _____

Date of Event: *03/15/2022* _____ Time of Event: *10:00 AM – 1:00 PM* _____

Place of Event: *U.S. Ct. House, Div. 8* _____

To Be Handled By: *JQA* _____ Reminder Dates: *03/08/2022* _____

Priority: ① 2 3 4 5 (Circle one, Top Priority is 1).

Slip Completed By: *ct* _____ Date Slip Completed: *02/01/2022*

Notes: *Meet Client at 9:45 at Ct. House* _____

Docket Clerk Use Only
Date Entered in Docket: *02/03/2022*
Entered By: *CTD*

Combined Docket Control Cycle

In a combined docket control cycle, a user can decide whether to enter information into the program or have a clerk or secretary do it. Some docket control programs allow multiple people to enter data into a user's schedule. For example, some networked docket programs allow both an attorney and the staff to enter information into the attorney's schedule. Both have full access to the attorney's calendar.

In this type of system, the first step would be for either the user or a third party to enter a docket entry into the case management program. Second, either the user or the third party views or prints reports as necessary, and third, either the user or a third party marks the entries "Done." In some ways, this is the best of both worlds for the user still has control over their calendar but can delegate the data entry to someone else.

Summary

The practice of law is filled with appointments, deadlines, hearings, and other commitments for every case that is handled. It is extremely important that these dates be carefully tracked for ethical, customer service, and general business reasons. Calendaring is a generic term used to describe the function of recording appointments for any business. Docket control is a law office–specific term that refers to entering, organizing, and controlling all of the appointments, deadlines, and due dates for a legal organization. Case management is a legal-specific term that usually refers to computer programs that not only have docket control but a number of other features, including contact management, document assembly, case notes, document management, and much more.

Ethical issues related to docket control include the duty to competently and adequately prepare for a client's matter, diligently and promptly serve clients, communicate with clients in a timely manner, and to avoid conflicts of interest.

Manual docket control systems include basic calendars and card systems. Computerized systems include generic calendaring and personal information management programs (such as Microsoft Outlook), and docket control/case management programs. Case management programs include a plethora of advanced and powerful features.

Key Terms

Bates stamp	docket control
calendar days	legal malpractice
calendaring	personal information manager (PIM)
case management	recurring entry
Certificate of Service	statute of limitations
continuance	workdays

Practical Applications

1. Your law office currently uses a manual docket system. It works fairly well because the office is small. However, several clients have requested a detailed listing of what is going on in their cases and what is coming up in the future. It takes a staff member quite a while to compile this information. Even though the office's manual system is working, should the office consider a change? What benefits would be realized? Please note that the office is driven by quality and productivity.

2. From time to time, you see new clients who come into the office. On this occasion, you interview a client who has a potential workers' compensation claim. After the client has left, you note that in a month the statute of limitations on the claim will expire. After discussing the case with your supervising attorney, the attorney says that he does not believe that the client has a viable case. Discuss the proper method for handling this situation.

3. Calculate the following due dates.

   a. Motion for Summary Judgment filed 8/1/22; response due 17 days from file date. Court rules use calendar days in this case.
   b. Motion to Compel filed Monday 3/5/22, response due 10 days from file date. Court rules use workdays only in this case. Assume there is one weekend.
   c. Request for Admissions is received 6/1/22, response is due 25 days from receipt. Court rules use calendar days in this case. Response must be mailed by what date?
   d. Request for Publication of Documents is received 12/10/22; response is due within seven days. Court rules use workdays only in this case. Assume there is one weekend and two holidays.

4. Set up and maintain a docket of class assignments for a semester. Use index cards to represent each assignment and file them in chronological order or use a computerized calendaring program. For quizzes and assignments, give yourself a three-day reminder before the assignment or quiz is due, in addition to recording the quiz or assignment itself. For exams or lengthy papers, give yourself three reminders—a 10-day reminder, a 5-day reminder, and a 3-day reminder before it is due—in addition to docketing the deadline itself.

On the Web Exercises

1. Go to the ABA Center for Professional Responsibility Web site at http://www.abanet.org/cpr/home.html, find the ABA *Model Rules of Professional Conduct*, and read and print out the Comments to *Rules 1.1, 1.3, 1.4, and 1.7*.

2. Visit several bar association Web sites (including the Georgia Bar Association) and find three articles on case management, docket control, or a related subject. The mentioned link will take you to a Web site that connects to all state bar sites: https://www.americanbar.org/groups/bar_services/resources/local-bar-resource-directory/.

3. Visit the American Bar Association Technology Resource Center Web site at http://www.abanet.org/tech/ltrc/home.html and review any materials they have on case management software programs.

Case Review

344 P.3d (2015).
In re Disciplinary Proceeding Against Pfefer,

Supreme Court of Washington

February 26, 2015.

Summary

WASHINGTON OFFICIAL REPORTS SUMMARY

Nature of Action: Disciplinary action against an attorney charged with three counts of misconduct stemming from his representation of a client whose personal injury action was dismissed as statutorily time barred as a result of the attorney's neglect and delay. The attorney was charged (1) with violating RPC 1.3 and RPC 3.2 for failing to comply with court-ordered dates and deadlines and for failing to meet with the client in preparation for trial, (2) with violating RPC 1.2(a) and/or RPC 1.4 for failing to consult with the client about a settlement offer and for failing to advise the client that her case had been dismissed, and (3) with violating RPC 1.16(c) and (d) for abruptly withdrawing from representing the client in violation of court rules. The hearing officer found the charges were proved and recommended a six-month suspension from the practice of law for each count and the payment of restitution in the amount of the uncommunicated settlement offer. The disciplinary board unanimously adopted the hearing officer's findings, conclusions, and recommended sanction, although it reduced the amount of restitution and assessed costs and expenses under ELC 13.9.

Supreme Court: Holding that expert testimony was not required to establish the rule violations because the hearing officer was capable of determining the facts and applying the facts to the rules, that the attorney was not denied due process of law by the hearing officer's ruling that his law partner could not serve both as a fact witness and as cocounsel, that the record supported the findings that the attorney committed the charged violations of the professional conduct rules, and that there was no basis to depart from the recommended sanction, the court *suspends* the attorney from the practice of law for six months and *conditions* his reinstatement to practice on his paying restitution to the client and paying costs and expenses to the Washington State Bar Association.

Opinion

En Banc

¶1 **Johnson, J.** — This is a disciplinary proceeding against attorney Matthew Franklin Pfefer, admitted to practice in 2001. Pfefer was hired to represent his client in her personal injury suit. Delay and a lack of diligence characterized his representation. He delayed filing his client's suit until only a few days before the statute of limitations expired. He did not perform discovery. He did not prepare potential witnesses for testimony. He did not comply with court deadlines. He did not tell his client that her case had been dismissed because of his failure to comply with those court deadlines. He did not tell his client that opposing counsel made a settlement offer. He did not give his client notice of his withdrawal, which he made effective immediately. In short, he did nothing to meet his basic responsibility to protect his client's interest, with the result that a viable settlement offer lapsed and her claim is now barred by the statute of limitations.

¶2 Rather than challenge the factual basis of the Washington State Bar Association's (WSBA) three-count complaint, Pfefer's brief to this court raises arguments about due process and unconstitutional vagueness. He does not cite to any testimony, evidence, or argument that the events of his representation did not occur exactly as the hearing officer found. Our own review of the record shows the same—a knowing disregard of fundamental professional duties owed to his client and an indifference to making restitution. The WSBA Disciplinary Board (Board) unanimously recommended that Pfefer be suspended from the practice of law for six months and pay restitution to his former client in the amount of the unaccepted settlement offer. We affirm, suspend Pfefer for six months, and condition his return to practice on the payment of restitution of $5,834.15 to his former client and the payment of costs and expenses to the WSBA.

Factual History and Misconduct

¶3 In February 2006, Ana Ortiz and her minor daughter were injured in an automobile accident. Ortiz hired Pfefer to represent her and her daughter. On February 10, 2009, six days before the statute of limitations would run, Pfefer filed a complaint on behalf of Ortiz and her daughter in King County Superior Court. The court set a trial date of July 26, 2010, a deadline of July 21, 2010 for filing a confirmation of joinder, and a deadline of April 19, 2010 for moving to change the trial date. On the day of the April 19 deadline, Pfefer moved to continue the trial, which was reset to March 21, 2011. The amended order required that settlement/mediation be completed by February 22, 2011 and a joint confirmation of readiness for trial be filed by February 28, 2011. A February 8, 2011 court order reminded both parties of the deadlines.

¶4 Pfefer did little before these deadlines passed. He did not conduct discovery, disclose witnesses, submit the case to mediation (or move to waive it), or exchange exhibits with defense counsel. He did not meet with Ortiz or other witnesses to prepare for trial. Although reminded by a personal phone call from the superior court judge's bailiff, he also did not file the joint confirmation of trial readiness by the February 28, 2011 deadline. Because Pfefer did not file the joint confirmation, the case was not sent to trial. Pfefer did not inform Ortiz that her case was not proceeding to trial. On March 21, 2011, Ortiz appeared at the King County courthouse, unaware that her case had not been sent to trial. Pfefer did not appear; he was evidently in Spokane where he maintained his office. The court dismissed Ortiz's case that same day because Pfefer had failed to meet the court's deadlines.

¶5 On March 24, 2011, opposing counsel offered to settle Ortiz's case for $6,580.06. Pfefer did not communicate this offer to Ortiz.

¶6 On March 31, 2011, Pfefer filed a motion for reconsideration. The court granted the motion, and Ortiz's case was set for a new trial date of June 13, 2011. On May 5, 2011, Pfefer filed a notice of immediate withdrawal, "effective immediately." Ass'n's Ex. A-132, at 1. Pfefer informed Ortiz of his withdrawal by leaving a phone message with one of Ortiz's friends and mailing her a copy of the notice. Ortiz attempted to file an objection in court to Pfefer's withdrawal, but it was struck for lack of proof of service. On May 19, 2011, her case was dismissed. The statute of limitations on her claim then expired.

Procedural History

¶7 The WSBA filed a complaint with the Board under the Rules for Enforcement of Lawyer Conduct (ELC) 10.3, charging Pfefer with three counts of misconduct, and the case proceeded to a hearing. The hearing officer found all three counts were proved: count one, that Pfefer violated Rules of Professional Conduct (RPC) 1.3 and RPC

3.2 by failing to comply with dates and deadlines set out in the May 18, 2010 and February 8, 2011 orders and by failing to meet with Ortiz in preparation for trial; count two, that Pfefer violated RPC 1.2(a) and/or RPC 1.4 by failing to consult Ortiz regarding the settlement offer and failing to advise her that her case had been dismissed; and count three, that Pfefer violated RPC 1.16(c) and (d) for making his withdrawal effective immediately in violation of court rules.

¶8 The hearing officer applied the American Bar Association's *Standards for Imposing Lawyer Sanctions* (1991 & Supp. 1992) to determine the appropriate sanction. For all counts, the hearing officer determined that Pfefer acted knowingly. In weighing aggravating or mitigating factors, the hearing officer found that aggravating factors in ABA *Standards* std. 9.22(d) (multiple offenses) and std. 9.22(j) (indifference to making restitution) applied. He also found that mitigating factors in ABA *Standards* std. 9.32(a) (absence prior disciplinary record) and std. 9.32(b) (absence of a dishonest or selfish motive) applied. Finding that the aggravating and mitigating factors were in equipoise, the hearing officer recommended a six-month suspension on each count.

¶9 The hearing officer also concluded that Pfefer should pay in restitution $6,580.06, the amount of the uncommunicated settlement offer. The Board, by unanimous decision, adopted the hearing officer's findings, conclusions, and recommendation of a six-month suspension. The Board reduced the amount of restitution to $5,834.15, the "amount of the uncommunicated settlement offer less costs directly attributable to Ortiz's case." Decision Papers (DP) at 30. It also assessed costs and expenses under ELC 13.9. Pfefer appeals to this court.

Analysis

Standard of Review

¶10 This court gives considerable weight to the hearing officer's findings of fact. Unchallenged findings of fact are considered verities on appeal, while challenged findings are upheld so long as they are supported by substantial evidence. Conclusions of law are reviewed de novo and are upheld if supported by the findings of fact. *In re Disciplinary Proceeding Against Marshall*, 160 Wn.2d 317, 330, 157 P.3d 859 (2007). An attorney must present arguments why specific findings are not supported by the record and cite to the record in support of that argument. Simply arguing an alternative version of events or an alternative explanation will not suffice to overturn the hearing officer's conclusions. *Marshall*, 160 Wn.2d at 331. Sanctions recommended to this court by a unanimous board will be upheld unless there is a clear reason for departure. *In re Disciplinary Proceeding Against Sanai*, 177 Wn.2d 743, 760, 302 P.3d 864 (2013), *cert. denied*, U.S., 134 S. Ct. 1324, 188 L. Ed. 2d 307 (2014).

Pfefer's Due Process Arguments Lack Merit

¶11 Pfefer, rather than challenging the factual findings that support his sanction, argues that his right to due process was violated by the hearing examiner. According to Pfefer, the hearing examiner improperly considered his own (the hearing officer's) knowledge and experience without the support of expert testimony in concluding that Pfefer's conduct violated the RPC. Because the hearing officer's "secret opinion" was incapable of cross-examination, Pfefer asserts he was denied due process. Resp't-Lawyer's Br. Opposing Disciplinary Bd.'s Decision at 28. In essence, Pfefer argues that expert testimony is required to establish the violations of the RPC. We disagree.

¶12 In *Burtch*, we held that a hearing officer may properly refuse to qualify witnesses as experts if those witnesses lack the ability to assist the trier of fact. ***In re Disciplinary Proceeding Against Burtch***, 162 Wn.2d 873, 890, 175 P.3d 1070 (2008). In that case, we held that the hearing officer did not err in limiting the questioning of two attorney-witnesses because there was no showing that either "lawyer had a specialty in ethics or any other specialty that would assist the trier of fact in this case, the hearing officer, also a lawyer." ***Burtch***, 162 Wn.2d at 890. Pfefer fails to understand that hearing officers are capable of determining the facts and applying the facts and evidence of the case to the RPC and concluding whether an attorney's conduct met the standards established by the rules. The record here contains simple documentary evidence and testimony from witnesses about the history of Ortiz's case, from which the hearing officer determined the facts and drew reasonable inferences in light of the overall testimony and evidence. *See **In re Disability Proceeding Against Diamondstone***, 153 Wn.2d 430, 440, 105 P.3d 1 (2005); ***In re Disciplinary Proceeding Against VanDerbeek***, 153 Wn.2d 64, 82, 101 P.3d 88 (2004). We find no due process or unfairness concerns with this procedure.

¶13 Pfefer also alleges that he was denied due process when the hearing officer ruled that Pfefer's law partner, Robert Caruso, could not serve both as a fact witness and as cocounsel at the disciplinary hearing. Pfefer argues that RPC 3.7 [1] does not apply at disciplinary hearings because the language of the rule states that it applies only "at a trial." *See* Resp't-Lawyer's Br. Opposing Disciplinary Bd.'s Decision at 17. We disagree. The comments to RPC 3.7 state that the purpose of the rule is to protect the "tribunal" from prejudice and confusion. RPC 3.7 cmt. 3. "Tribunal," as defined under the RPC, "denotes a court, an arbitrator in a binding arbitration proceeding or legislative body, administrative agency or other body acting in an adjudicative capacity," evidenced "when a neutral official, after the presentation of evidence or legal argument by a party or parties, will render a binding legal judgment directly affecting a party's interests in a particular matter." RPC 1.0A(m). The plain language of RPC 1.0A(m) and RPC 3.7 support application of RPC 3.7 to disciplinary hearings.

FN1. "(a) A lawyer shall not act as advocate at a trial in which the lawyer is likely to be a necessary witness unless:
"(1) the testimony relates to an uncontested issue;
"(2) the testimony relates to the nature and value of legal services rendered in the case;
"(3) disqualification of the lawyer would work substantial hardship on the client; or
"(4) the lawyer has been called by the opposing party and the court rules that the lawyer may continue to act as an advocate.

"(b) A lawyer may act as advocate in a trial in which another lawyer in the lawyer's firm is likely to be called as a witness unless precluded from doing so by Rule 1.7 or Rule 1.9."

¶14 More fundamentally, Pfefer fails to show on this record that the hearing officer disqualified Caruso at all. Rather, he gave Pfefer a choice: either Caruso could act as advocate and cross-examine two of the WSBA's witnesses (including Ortiz) or he could testify as a fact witness. Pfefer chose the latter. The hearing officer ruled that Pfefer had the opportunity to testify in the narrative, subject to objection, and Caruso was permitted to sit at counsel's table and advise Pfefer throughout the hearing. Because the record shows that the hearing officer did not disqualify Caruso from assisting Pfefer at the disciplinary hearing, we find no error.

Substantial Evidence Supports the Findings of Fact

¶15 Unchallenged findings of fact are treated as verities on appeal, and we give great weight to the hearing officer's determination of credibility and veracity of witnesses. ***Marshall***, 160 Wn.2d at 330. Pfefer challenges only two of the hearing officer's findings of fact. After a full review of the record, we find that the findings of fact are supported by substantial evidence.

¶16 Under count one, the evidence establishes that Pfefer failed to diligently pursue his client's case, in violation of RPC 1.3 [2] and RPC 3.2. [3] He waited over a year after the beginning of representation to file Ortiz's suit, during which time he performed little or no investigation or discovery. After the case was filed, Pfefer failed to comply with any of the deadlines established in the court's February 8, 2011 order requiring completion of the joint confirmation and that the case be submitted to mediation. Despite being reminded by both his paralegal and the superior court's bailiff, he failed to file the joint confirmation by the deadline of February 28, 2011, and because of this the case was dismissed. Pfefer challenges the hearing officer's finding of fact that he found it not credible that Pfefer's reason for failing to file the joint confirmation was due to some confusion about local King County rules. Clerk's Papers (CP) at 201. We agree that Pfefer's conduct was not the product of confusion. Rather, the record amply demonstrates a knowing failure by Pfefer to show reasonable care in Ortiz's case by complying with simple court deadlines. We agree with the hearing officer's conclusion that Pfefer violated RPC 1.3 and RPC 3.2.

FN2. "A lawyer shall act with reasonable diligence and promptness in representing a client."

FN3. "A lawyer shall make reasonable efforts to expedite litigation consistent with the interests of the client."

¶17 Under count two, we find substantial evidence that Pfefer violated RPC 1.2(a) [4] and RPC 1.4 [5] by failing to consult Ortiz about the dismissal of her case and for failing to consult her regarding the settlement offer. Pfefer testified that he believed that the offer was ineffective or a sham, and for that reason he did not communicate the offer to Caruso. The hearing officer found his explanation was not credible. CP at 202. Pfefer challenges this finding. We agree with the hearing examiner. RPC 1.4 requires communication of settlement offers to clients. The "effectiveness" of such an offer is immaterial in regard to an attorney's obligation to inform the client on his or her case. Pfefer informed Ortiz neither of the substance nor the existence of the settlement offer, nor does the record show that Ortiz previously indicated that she would not accept a settlement in the amount offered. Pfefer had provided no evidence or justification in not communicating the offer to Ortiz.

FN4. "Subject to paragraphs (c) and (d), a lawyer shall abide by a client's decisions concerning the objectives of representation and, as required by Rule 1.4, shall consult with the client as to the means by which they are to be pursued. A lawyer may take such action on behalf of the client as is impliedly authorized to carry out the representation. A lawyer shall abide by a client's decision whether to settle a matter. In a criminal case, the lawyer shall abide by the client's decision, after consultation with the lawyer, as to a plea to be entered, whether to waive jury trial and whether the client will testify."

FN5. "(a) A lawyer shall:
"(1) promptly inform the client of any decision or circumstance with respect to which the client's informed consent, as defined in Rule 1.0A(e), is required by these Rules;
"(2) reasonably consult with the client about the means by which the client's objectives are to be accomplished;
"(3) keep the client reasonably informed about the status of the matter;
"(4) promptly comply with reasonable requests for information; and
"(5) consult with the client about any relevant limitation on the lawyer's conduct when the lawyer knows that the client expects assistance not permitted by the Rules of Professional Conduct or other law.
"(b) A lawyer shall explain a matter to the extent reasonably necessary to permit the client to make informed decisions regarding the representation." (Boldface omitted.)

¶18 Similarly, Pfefer proffers no justification for not informing Ortiz that her case had been dismissed. RPC 1.4 requires an attorney to communicate with his or her client, and no excuse or reason was established for this lapse. We have previously addressed this situation and affirmed disciplinary action against an attorney who failed to honestly inform the client of the reason the court dismissed the client's case. *In re Disciplinary Proceeding Against Starczewski*, 177 Wn.2d 771, 780, 306 P.3d 905 (2013) (attorney failed to inform client that case had been dismissed on procedural grounds and later told client that case had been dismissed on the merits). Pfefer's conduct violates the requirements of the RPC because he failed to inform his client that her case was dismissed at all. We agree with the hearing officer's conclusion that Pfefer violated RPC 1.2(a) and RPC 1.4.

¶19 We also uphold the charges under count three, that Pfefer violated RPC 1.16(c) [6] and RPC 1.16(d) [7] by withdrawing from Ortiz's representation "effective immediately." RPC 1.16(c) permits withdrawal following notice to or permission of a tribunal, but only if the lawyer "compl[ies] with applicable law." In this case, that "applicable

law" is Superior Court Civil Rule (CR) 71(c)(1), which mandates that "[t]he attorney shall file and serve a Notice of Intent To Withdraw on all other parties in the proceeding. The notice shall specify a date when the attorney intends to withdraw, which date shall be at least 10 days after the service of the Notice of Intent To Withdraw." Before this 10-day period can begin to run, however, notice must first be served on the client. CR 71(c)(2).

FN6. "A lawyer must comply with applicable law requiring notice to or permission of a tribunal when terminating a representation. When ordered to do so by a tribunal, a lawyer shall continue representation notwithstanding good cause for terminating the representation."

FN7. "Upon termination of representation, a lawyer shall take steps to the extent reasonably practicable to protect a client's interests, such as giving reasonable notice to the client, allowing time for employment of other counsel, surrendering papers and property to which the client is entitled and refunding any advance payment of fee or expense that has not been earned or incurred. The lawyer may retain papers relating to the client to the extent permitted by other law."

¶20 Pfefer's notice of withdrawal, given to the court "effective immediately," violated CR 71(c)(1) because it failed to permit the 10-day period following filing, a period that itself cannot begin to run until service is effective, and proof of service filed, in accordance with CR 71(c)(2). The hearing officer's unchallenged findings established that Pfefer informed Ortiz of his withdrawal only by leaving a message with a friend and mailing a copy of the notice. Pfefer argues that if he did violate CR 71, he was nonetheless in substantial compliance. Immediate withdrawal is not substantial compliance with a procedure that requires, at a minimum, 10 days' notice, especially here where Ortiz's case was facing dismissal based on Pfefer's lack of diligence in complying with the court's scheduling orders and where the statute of limitations would expire shortly after the case was dismissed.

¶21 This evidence also supports the conclusion that Pfefer failed to protect Ortiz's interests in violation of RPC 1.16(d). His immediate withdrawal, filed May 5, 2011, left his client with little chance to pursue her case. Ortiz tried to object in court, but the objection was stricken for lack of proof of service. Ortiz's case was dismissed on May 19, and the statute of limitations ran six days later. It was Pfefer's conduct and his withdrawal "effective immediately" that caused her legal claim to be barred. We agree with the hearing officer's conclusion that Pfefer violated RPC 1.16(c) and RPC 1.16(d).

Sanctions Analysis

¶22 We affirm the hearing officer's and unanimous Board's recommended sanctions against Pfefer. This court applies the ABA *Standards* in all lawyer discipline cases. *In re Disciplinary Proceeding Against Halverson*, 140 Wn.2d 475, 492, 998 P.2d 833 (2000). Under this two-step process, the presumptive standard is first determined by considering (1) the ethical duty violated, (2) the lawyer's mental state, and (3) the extent of actual or potential harm caused by the misconduct. The next step is to consider the application of any mitigating or aggravating factors. *In re Disciplinary Proceeding Against Dann*, 136 Wn.2d 67, 77, 960 P.2d 416 (1998) (quoting *In re Disciplinary Proceedings Against Johnson*, 118 Wn.2d 693, 701, 826 P.2d 186 (1992)). This court reviews sanctions de novo but will uphold a unanimous recommendation by the Board unless there is a clear reason for departure. *In re Disciplinary Proceeding Against Behrman*, 165 Wn.2d 414, 422, 197 P.3d 1177 (2008). Pfefer has shown no reason for departure.

¶23 In his sanctions analysis, the hearing officer concluded that Pfefer acted knowingly under all three counts and caused injury to Ortiz's interests and that of the legal system. We agree. Pfefer's knowing failure to diligently prosecute Ortiz's claim caused her case to be dismissed (twice) and subsequently barred by the statute of limitations. His failure to communicate the settlement offer prevented her from considering acceptance. And his means of withdrawal left his client's interests unprotected.

¶24 The presumptive sanction for Pfefer's misconduct is suspension. The hearing officer determined that ABA *Standards* std. 4.4 applied to counts one and two. ABA *Standards* stds. 4.42(a) and (b) state that suspension is generally appropriate when "a lawyer knowingly fails to perform services for a client and causes injury or potential injury to a client" or "a lawyer engages in a pattern of neglect and causes injury or potential injury to a client." The hearing officer also determined that ABA *Standards* std. 7.0 applied to count three. Under that standard, "[s]uspension is generally appropriate when a lawyer knowingly engages in conduct that is a violation of a duty owed to the profession, and causes injury or potential injury to a client, the public, or the legal system." ABA Standards std. 7.2. We agree with this determination.

¶25 The second step under the ABA *Standards* is to consider any mitigating or aggravating factors. The hearing officer found two aggravating factors [8] and two mitigating factors [9] present. We agree with this determination. Pfefer does not argue that his sanction is disproportionate, nor would we find it to be so in this case.

FN8. ABA Standards std. 9.22(d) (multiple offenses), (j) (indifference to making restitution).

FN9. ABA Standards std. 9.32(a) (absence of prior disciplinary record), (b) (absence of dishonest or selfish motive).

¶26 Pfefer also argues that the amount of restitution should be reduced to reflect his firm's costs but fails to support his argument with any explanation on why such costs are borne by his firm and not by Ortiz. The Board, based on the evidence and argument from Pfefer, reduced the amount of restitution from $6,580.06 to $5,834.15 in order to reflect costs attributable to Ortiz's case. We find that no further reduction is appropriate and affirm restitution in the amount of $5,834.15.

WSBA Costs

¶27 Finally, Pfefer objects to the costs and expenses assessed against him by the chair of the disciplinary board (Chair) under ELC 13.9(a). The WSBA filed a statement of costs and expenses, as required under ELC 13.9(d), listing five headings and the costs associated with each. [10] Pfefer had 20 days from the date of service to file exceptions. ELC 13.9(d)(4). Two days before the deadline, Pfefer filed a blanket objection "to all costs stated by disciplinary counsel as no documentation supports any of these costs." DP at 98. The WSBA had 10 days to reply. ELC 13.9(d)(5). Although not strictly required by the rules, the WSBA provided detailed receipts of all charges. Ten days later the Chair entered the costs under ELC 13.9(e), finding the costs and expenses appropriate.

FN10. (1) "Court reporter charges for attending and transcribing depositions or hearing" in the amount of $4,463.15, (2) "Necessary travel expenses of hearing officers, disciplinary counsel, investigators, adjunct investigative counsel, adjunct trial counsel or witnesses for both investigation and prosecution" in the amount of $1,254.67, (3) "Special mail or delivery charges" in the amount of $10.07, (4) "Other: translation services and court records" in the amount of $1,102.90, and (5) "Expenses under ELC 13.9(c)" in the amount of $3,000. DP at 97. The total claimed is $9,830.79.

¶28 The day after the Chair entered the costs, Pfefer filed a supplemental objection. His supplemental objections challenged virtually every expense, objecting to, for example, mileage reports for disciplinary counsel, [11] lunch expenses, parking, the use of in person questioning of witnesses at the disciplinary hearing instead of performing the hearing telephonically, document fees, and interpreter's services. The Chair did not consider Pfefer's supplemental objections, concluding they were too late.

FN11. Pfefer's supplemental motion to take judicial notice of the distance between the cities of Burien and Seattle is denied.

¶29 We agree with the WSBA that Pfefer's supplemental objections were untimely. Independently, we have reviewed the costs and expenses assessed against Pfefer and find that all costs were "reasonably and necessarily incurred" by the WSBA pursuant to ELC 13.9(b).

Conclusion

¶30 The record amply demonstrates that Pfefer knowingly failed to provide his client with the representation required by the RPC, resulting in injury to his client. Clients expect, and RPC establish, due diligence by attorneys: Pfefer showed little. We adopt the Board's unanimous recommendation, suspend Pfefer from the practice of law for six months, and condition his reinstatement on his payment of restitution to Ortiz for $5,834.15 and the costs and expenses assessed against him under ELC 13.9.

Madsen, C.J., and Owens, Fairhurst, Stephens, Wiggins, González, Gordon McCloud, and Yu, JJ., concur.

Case Review Exercises

1. List each of the attorney's actions in this case that amounted to a lack of diligence, incompetence, or failure to communicate with his client.

2. Discuss how you might have felt if you had been the attorney's client in this matter.

3. What reasons did the Washington Supreme Court give for suspending the attorney?

4. After reading the case, did you tend to agree with the Washington Supreme Court that ordered the attorney to be suspended as decided by the Disciplinary Review Board that recommended a six-month suspension of the attorney? Explain your answer.

Helpful Web Sites

Organization	Description	Internet Address
American Bar Association (ABA)	Association for attorneys. The Web site has a large amount of information and publications relevant to individuals working in the legal profession.	http://www.americanbar.org
ABA Law Practice Management Section	ABA Web site devoted to law practice management issues, including docket control and case management.	http://www.americanbar.org/groups/law_practice.html
ABA Legal Technology Resource Center	ABA Web site devoted to technology. Includes resources and articles.	http://www.abanet.org/tech/ltrc/home.html

Docket Control and Case Management Software

Organization	Product/Service	Internet Address
Abacus Data Systems	AbacusLaw (legal PIM/case management)	http://www.abacuslaw.com
Clio	Full-featured legal accounting software	http://www.goclio.com
LexisNexis	PCLaw/TimeMatters	https://pclawtimematters.com/
Thomson Elite	ProLaw and LawManager	http://www.elite.com/
Gavel & Gown Software	Amicus Attorney (legal PIM/case management)	http://amicusattorney.com/
Lawex Corp.	TrialWorks (legal case management)	http://www.trialworks.com
Legal Files Software	Legal Files (legal PIM/case management)	http://www.legalfiles.com
LegalEdge Software	Case management for criminal defense attorneys, prosecutors, and general law offices	http://www.legaledge.com
ADC Legal Systems, Inc.	Perfect Practice (case management)	http://www.perfectpractice.com
Aderant	Client Profiles (case management) and CompuLaw (case management)	http://www.aderant.com/products/aderant-total-office http://www.aderant.com/products/aderant-compulaw

Suggested Reading

1. *Law Practice magazine*, published by the American Bar Association Law Practice Management Section, https://www.americanbar.org/groups/law_practice/publications/law_practice_magazine.

2. *Paralegal Today* magazine, published by James Publishing, https://www.legalassistanttoday.com/.

3. *Law Office Computing magazine*, published by James Publishing, http://www.lawofficecomputing.com.

Legal Marketing

8

Chapter Objectives

After you read this chapter, you should be able to:

- Explain what marketing is and the purpose of a marketing plan.

- Differentiate between advertising and marketing.

- Identify ethical problems that may arise in carrying out a marketing plan.

- Explain what cross-selling is and why it is important in law offices.

Legal Marketing

Legal marketing is the process of educating consumers on the legal and business activities a firm uses to deliver quality and ethical legal services. Thirty years ago, law office marketing was virtually nonexistent. It was not until the landmark Supreme Court case of ***Bates v. State Bar of Arizona***, 433 U.S. 350 (1977), that this began to change. In ***Bates***, two young attorneys placed an ad in the ***Arizona Republic*** that stated: "Do you need a lawyer? Legal services at very reasonable fees." In response, the Arizona State Bar Association took disciplinary action against the attorneys. The U.S. Supreme Court held that a ban on attorney advertising was a violation of the First Amendment right to commercial free speech and that it was a restraint of trade. Today, attorney advertising is a given. With more than one million attorneys practicing law, the "Why should we market our practice?" question has long been forgotten. The increased competitiveness of the legal field has forced law practices to promote themselves or face the reality of getting left behind by losing business to more aggressive firms. In addition, law offices not only compete against other law offices but also compete against accounting firms when it comes to

legal marketing
The process of educating consumers on the legal and business activities a firm uses to deliver quality and ethical legal services.

handling some types of tax matters, real estate companies regarding real estate transactions, and other types of organizations as well. The only question truly left for a law office is *how* to market itself.

Why Is Marketing Important?

Marketing is the job of everyone who works in a private law office. Your job depends on the firm's ability to find and serve additional clients. Therefore, attorneys and paralegals have a vested interest in the marketing function. Your friends, family members, acquaintances, social groups, and fellow colleagues are worthy of your marketing efforts. Make sure people know the name of the organization you work for, network with other professionals, and be prepared to talk to others about what your law office does. By marketing your firm, you will establish that you have an interest in and loyalty to the firm, and you also will be building some degree of job security. Law offices cannot do business without new clientele.

Marketing Goals

There is a misconception that advertising and marketing are the same thing; they are not. Advertising is simply getting your name out to the public. Marketing, on the other hand, includes advertising, but it is much more: marketing encompasses providing quality services to clients, gaining insight and feedback into client needs, having a good reputation in the community, and exercising good public relations. Law office marketing has focused objectives and goals:

- Educate clients and potential clients regarding the firm's array of services.
- Educate clients and potential clients as to the particular expertise of the firm in certain areas.
- Create goodwill and interest in the firm.
- Create positive name recognition for the firm.
- Create an image of honesty, ethics, and sincere interest in clients.
- Publicize the firm's accomplishments to the profession and community.
- Educate clients on changes in the law, thus creating client confidence in the firm.
- Improve the firm's competitive position in the marketplace.
- Obtain referrals from other attorneys.
- Maintain communication with existing clients.
- Increase client loyalty and retention.
- Increase staff morale and reinforce the firm's self-image.
- Obtain referrals from clients.
- Obtain repeat business from existing clients.

Basic Restrictions on Marketing

There are several restrictions on law office marketing. These restrictions involve ethical obligations and are discussed in depth at the end of this chapter, but the most fundamental restriction is that no matter what the marketing entails, it must not be false or misleading.

The Legal Marketing Plan

A law firm must have a marketing plan before it can begin marketing. A **marketing plan** specifies a target audience the firm is trying to reach, the exact goals that the marketing program is to accomplish, and establishes a detailed strategy of how the goals will be achieved. To reach that target audience, it is important that law offices understand exactly who their clients are (businesses, individuals, government, etc.). Additionally, what legal services will the firm provide and what area of law will the firm practice (general or specialty areas). After that, how will the firm attract clients, ensure the clients receive quality services, retain them, and obtain referrals. Many law offices, even relatively small offices, hire marketing personnel or outsource for consulting, advertising, and other marketing efforts. Depending on the firm, the size will more than likely determine if the firm will employ marketing staff. A solo practitioner will likely have to market themselves, while a large firm (over 20 lawyers) will probably hire marketing staff. Exhibit 8-1 provides a sample job description for a legal marketing director. Due to the increased competition in the legal industry and the continual need for an influx of clients, marketing—as a part of a firm's overall management responsibility—simply cannot be ignored. Much of the research indicates that corporations typically spend from 10 to 13% of their revenues on marketing; law offices spend on average about 2 to 3% of revenues on marketing. However, the trend shows an increase in spending for legal marketing. For example, a small firm with nine attorneys may be spending as much as $60,000 on marketing efforts.

Marketing must be done in an effective manner, and it is important that money not be wasted on efforts that are ineffective for a firm. A well-thought-out marketing plan will help ensure that money, time, and efforts are not wasted. A law firm's marketing plan should include the following:

- Overall goals of the marketing program
- Strategies and activities that will be necessary to achieve the goals (including who, what, when, how, and in what order the activities will be implemented)
- Estimated cost of the marketing program
- Estimated profit the successful marketing program would bring in

The marketing plan and the strategic business plan are related documents. To develop an effective marketing plan, consider the steps presented in Exhibit 8-2. A key component of the marketing plan is to conduct research. The drafter needs relevant information in order to write a good marketing plan, such as what the target group actually wants in the way of legal services; this is a departure from the usual method, which is to provide a target group with what you have to offer. Research in the way of studying competitors, interviewing clients, surveying clients, talking to experts, and really finding out what makes the target group "tick" forms the foundation of a good marketing plan. Another important part of the marketing plan is to develop specific strategies for reaching the target audience in the most effective way. There are innumerable ways to reach a target audience, but finding the most effective way that actually brings clients to the law firm takes thought, skill, and experience. Developing a marketing budget and funding an adequate marketing campaign are also integral parts of the plan.

marketing plan
It specifies a target audience the firm is trying to reach, the exact goals that the marketing program is to accomplish, and establishes a detailed strategy of how the goals will be achieved.

Exhibit 8-1 Marketing Director Job Description

MARKETING DIRECTOR
Job Description

Position Reports to: Executive Director/Marketing Committee/Managing Partner(s)

RESPONSIBILITIES

Overall Responsibility: Position is responsible for developing all aspects of the firm's marketing plan, coordinating all activities related to the plan, and achieving the overall marketing objective.

PRIMARY RESPONSIBILITIES

Interoffice Relations
Collect, prepare, and maintain firm data.
Design or supervise the preparation of mailing lists and client and referral-source databases.
Design, set up, and supervise maintenance of marketing databases that includes development, retrieval, and follow-up activities for members of the legal team.

Media relations
Work with news media, draft press releases, and coordinate for approval and distribution. Prepare placement of lawyer articles for target market publications such as editorial boards and social media Web sites. When applicable, serve as liaison between the firm and public relations counsel. Maintain files for all circulations or publications including previous copies of modified Web site pages on the firms' professionals both internally and externally.

Public relations
Plan and coordinate all of the firm's social- and community-related activities such as seminars and alumni programs. These activities should be designed to give visibility and name recognition to the firm.

Internal communications
Create and facilitate communications between professionals in various practice areas and offices with written and oral vehicles to promote awareness of the firm's marketing activities.

Publications and promotional materials
Responsible for development of newsletters, brochures, Web site materials, and other promotional publications. Prepare directory listings and announcement cards. Place professional advertisements.

Client relations
Develop or supervise client surveys.

Training
Provide or arrange for marketing training for partners and staff.

Proposals and presentations
Assist in preparing written proposals and in-person presentations for new business. Help with the technological aspects of presentation materials and maintain reference files of proposals. Help lawyers rehearse sales presentations.

Budget
Supervise and track a marketing budget and expenditures.

QUALIFICATIONS

Knowledge of
- Law office environment
- Marketing techniques and principles

Ability to
- Coordinate multiple functions
- Communicate with and motivate professionals

EXPERIENCE
Marketing manager in a law or other professional services firm.

EDUCATION
College or course work in marketing, writing, commercial art, or related fields.

Exhibit 8-2 Developing the Marketing Plan

I. Firm Approach

The firm should develop an idea for the type of law it practices, the clients it will serve and the service to provide them, the competition and profitability, all of which will determine the market plan.

II. Target Market and Marketing Plan Objectives

The firm should determine the marketing plan's purpose for reaching a target market, which could be a range of classifications from age, gender, occupation to marital and financial status. Is the firm trying to expand in a new area, increase its size, and maybe even focus on an expertise area of law? In selecting a target market, the firm's marketing plan should include the method for reaching these people.

a. Client Types:

    i. Individuals (impoverished, middle class, wealthy)

    ii. Business Organizations (small or large, private, public or nonprofit)

    iii. Labor Organizations

    iv. Government (local, state, federal, international)

b. Legal Specialty Areas

    i. This can range from Administrative Law to Workers' Compensation Law. Some examples below are areas commonly found; there are many others available.

- Banking Law
- Bankruptcy Law
- Collections Law
- Estates, Trusts, and Probate
- Family Law
- Insurance Law
- Litigation
- Mergers and Acquisitions
- Oil and Gas Law
- Real Estate Law
- Social Security Law
- Tort Law

III. Market Research

Become familiar with the groups' interest and background. The law firms must consider their target groups to determine how they can serve them—what do they want, need, or expect.
a. Study marketing successes and failures.
b. Generate surveys both inside the firm and outside for feedback.

IV. Market Problems and Solutions

The firm should try to anticipate marketing problems and have a plan in place to resolve them—this often includes alternate marketing plans.

V. Marketing Action Plan and Strategy

The firm must have a method in place—a game plan for accomplishing its marketing ideas. How will you deliver the information (mailings, seminars, trade shows)? Who will be responsible for implementing the plan? What is the time frame to reach the target market, and when will the firm adjust time frames to consider market response?

VI. Marketing Budget and Resources

The firm must determine if the resources and finances are available to accomplish the marketing plan. At this point, the firm can proceed as designed or adjust to fit within their budget and resources.

Typical Law Practice Marketing Options and Strategies

The strategies and options that a law firm can use to market their services are many and varied. Exhibit 8-3 shows a number of strategies and marketing alternatives that are available, some of which are described in more detail in this section. One of the most important things an office can do is to actually *track* what marketing techniques are the most successful and then concentrate resources and funds on these methods. When a new client comes into the office, the New Client Questionnaire form should include a question regarding specifically how the client heard about the law firm, and statistics/reports should be maintained to show what sources are the most effective. Future marketing efforts should be based on the results of these reports.

- **Quality legal services**—There's that word again … *quality*. Before a firm can market its services, it must have something of quality to market! Keep in mind that it is always easier to sell a quality product that people want to buy than to sell a product you want to sell. Earlier in this book, it was explained how important existing clients are for bringing repeat business back to the firm and for making referrals to others. This is why quality is so important. Everything a firm does affects quality and therefore its marketing effort. Remember, it's easier to satisfy and keep a client for life by continually meeting and exceeding his or her expectations than it is to have to continually find new clients who stay for a while and then go to a competitor.

An employee who treats clients rudely, a docket control system that does not work, or billing practices that make clients upset in the end are all quality problems. Law office management must ensure quality; marketing and quality are parts of the same equation.

- **Firm Web site**—Operating a firm Web site is a standard marketing practice for most law firms. Solo practitioners have generally been the slowest to move to the Internet. However, in recent years, solo practitioners' presence on the Internet has dramatically increased, most likely due to technology advances, such as Web site builders that are easier and more affordable to maintain. A definite advantage of a firm Web site is that, unlike the office itself, it stays open 24 hours a day, 7 days a week, to local, national, and international customers and clients. A Web site is a particularly good idea for a legal organization with a specialized practice; a firm with a unique niche or specialized practice can reach potential clients anywhere in the world. Many organizations have found the marketing potential of a Web site to be enormous. In addition, because it operates all the time, it is cost effective when compared to other types of marketing alternatives.

    Depending on the information on the Web site, the organization can also provide timely information to current and potential clients. Many legal organizations offer information in their specialty area that would be useful to their clients. Thus, a Web site can provide a service to an organization's clients that hopefully will create goodwill toward the firm.

Exhibit 8-3 Marketing Strategies and Options

- Internet site
- E-mail newsletter
- Online Yellow Pages
- Keyword searching advertising on search engine sites
- Firm brochures and resume
- Hard-copy newsletter
- Promotional materials (folders, pencils, etc., with law office logo)
- Business cards/letterhead/announcement cards
- Subject area information brochures (e.g., tax, auto accidents, etc.)
- Public relations
    - Belonging to boards, associations, and community groups
    - Speaking at public functions
    - Writing articles on legal subjects for the local newspaper
    - Issuing press releases
    - Handling publicized pro bono cases
    - Volunteering in "law day" activities
    - Volunteering staff time to help with fundraisers for community groups
    - Running for public office
- Firm open house
- Public advertising
    - Yellow Page ads
    - Newspaper ads
    - Newspaper inserts
    - Television ads
    - Radio ads
- Client seminars
- Direct mail (not allowable in some states)
- Mining other legal professionals
    - Obtaining referrals
    - Joining legal associations
    - Networking with other legal professionals
- Mining friends, associates, and social contacts regarding the legal services offered
    - Making a call or contact list, including a mailing list
    - Contacting them monthly or quarterly
    - Breakfast, lunch, or dinner engagements regarding their needs and your services
- Mining existing clients
    - Contacting current and past clients monthly
    - Cross-selling
    - Breakfast, lunch, or dinner engagements regarding their needs and your services
    - Personal notes of congratulations for accomplishments
    - Holiday cards
    - Thank-you notes for referrals
    - Reading trade journals regarding a client's business

Most experts say that "content is king." It is extremely important that the content of the law firm Web site be strong, fresh, and changed often. A Web site can also be used for recruiting employees, such as paralegals and other staff. Exhibit 8-4 presents a list of features that can help establish a top-notch law firm Web site.

While firms' Web sites are allowed, there is at least one case where an attorney violated a state's ethical rules by misusing e-mail. In *In re Canter*, Term. Sup. Ct., Nos. 95-831-O-H, etc. (6/5/97), the Tennessee Supreme Court found that an attorney who sent an e-mail advertisement message to thousands of Internet groups and lists (called "spamming") had violated the state's ethical rules. The message did not comply with state rules that required noting that the message was an advertisement, and a copy was not filed with the Board of Professional Responsibility as required.

Exhibit 8-4 Tips for a Strong Law Firm Internet Web Site

Tip	Explanation
List success stories	If the firm has been successful in a matter, tell the story on the Web site. Change the stories on a regular basis. You should not promise the same results, but you can tell the story.
Focus on the client	The whole Web site should be geared to the client. It should be user friendly and meet the needs of the client. It should clearly spell out in layperson's terms what services are available, including resources regarding the subject matters of the areas practiced. It's really about the client, not about the law firm.
List existing clients	Clients like to know that the firm has represented others "like them"; references help.
Demonstrate the firm's experience	Experience counts. Most clients want to know that the firm is an expert in the subject matter of the case they are bringing to the firm.
Keep content up to date	Out-of-date content gives the client no reason to come back to the Web site. Keep it updated and current at all times.
Include a search function	Clients want to be able to quickly find what they need; a search function on the Web site greatly helps in this process.
Make it printer friendly	The Web site should be printer friendly so that clients can print out information as needed.

- **Firm brochure/resume/Web sites**—A firm brochure is typically a pamphlet that informs the general public about the nature of the firm. If the firm maintains a Web site, this information is often integrated on the Web pages in lieu of an actual brochure. In many ways, it is like a resume—some even call it a firm's resume. Firm brochures/resumes often contain the following types of information:

  (a) History of the firm

  (b) Ideology or philosophy of the firm

  (c) Services offered by the firm (e.g., the types of law it practices, specific departments, etc.)

  (d) The firm's fee or billing policies

  (e) Description of the firm's attorneys (background, items of interest, awards, degrees, etc.)

(f)   Description of the firm's support staff

(g)   Address, phone number, Web site address

(h)   Whether the firm has a newsletter or other types of client services

(i)   Notable firm accomplishments

(j)   Important clients the firm has represented (must have client's permission)

Exhibit 8-5 is a firm brochure/Web site page for a law office that has a law practice in several different areas of the law. Firms that practice a wide range of law or large firms typically take a different marketing approach; instead of having one piece of marketing material for the whole firm, they may have separate brochures or Web pages contained on the Web site for each department with material that targets specific industries. Some law firms maintain their law practice within a specific area of law such as health care, bankruptcy, immigration or Social Security law. Exhibit 8-6 is an example of a firm's brochure/Web site page for a law office that has a specialty area law practice.

- **Firm newsletters and e-mail newsletters**—Firm newsletters and e-mail newsletters are a popular way of maintaining contact with clients and generating goodwill. Firm newsletters can be on a single topic, such as real estate, or on a potpourri of topics. Some firms focus on a different legal issue in each issue: family law, real estate, tax, and so on. It is important that the firm knows and understands who its clients are and what type of information would be beneficial to them. Newsletters are also used to inform clients of legislative changes, whether local, state, or national. Newsletters can be produced in-house, by ad agencies, or by purchasing ready-made legal newsletters. With a ready-made newsletter, all the law office has to do is add its logo, firm name, and address. E-mail newsletters are popular because they are relatively low cost and can be distributed immediately.

- **Informational brochures**—These are brochures aimed at informing clients about a specific topic, such as "Why You Need a Will," "What to Do in Case of an Auto Accident," "How Is 'Disability' Defined for Adults by the Social Security Administration," "How to Set Up Your Own Business," or "How to Protect Your Ideas through Copyrights, Trademarks, and Patents." They are informational pieces that are used to inform clients about legal problems, and many firms publish them on their firm Web site.

- **Public relations**—Generating goodwill and a positive public image is a long-standing, successful way that firms have marketed themselves. Attorneys and paralegals can promote themselves and their firms as members of social groups, churches, committees, nonprofit boards, and associations. Speaking at public and association meetings is another way to attract interest and goodwill; other methods of generating and maintaining good public relations include handling pro bono cases and issuing press releases when a firm wins a case or achieves other notable accomplishments.

Exhibit 8-5 Law Firm Brochure—Specialty Area Materials

Printed with permission of Bruno & Bruno, L.L.P.

- **Firm open house**—Some firms hold annual open houses, where clients and visitors can come to the firm and socialize with attorneys and staff members outside the normal pressures of coming to the office with legal problems.
- **Business cards, letterhead, and announcement cards**—Announcement cards are used quite frequently by law offices. An announcement card is

Exhibit 8-6 Law Firm—Webpages for Law Firm Services and Lawyers

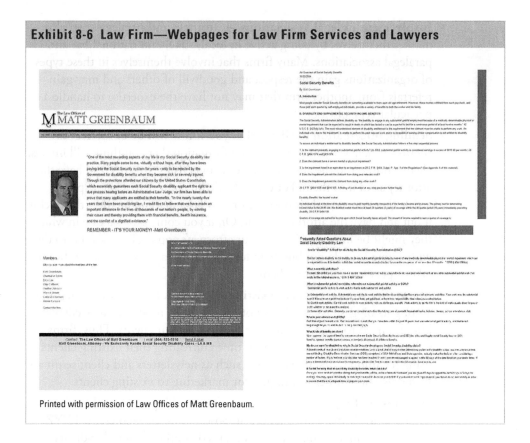

Printed with permission of Law Offices of Matt Greenbaum.

usually a postcard that a firm sends to other firms to publicize a change, such as when new attorneys have been added or firms have merged. Business cards and letterhead are also a frequent way for firms to promote themselves and their staff.

- **Public advertising—yellow pages, newspaper, television, and radio ads**—Public advertisements are another popular form of marketing. They come in all sizes, shapes, and price ranges, and may appear in local yellow pages, newspapers, and television and radio stations.

- **Firm seminars**—Some firms hold seminars aimed at educating their clients or the general public (prospective clients) on legal issues. These seminars may be held on any legal topic that is of interest to clients. Businesses might be interested in the legal issues of hiring, firing, and evaluating employees and employee benefits, and individual clients might be interested in tax planning, trusts and estates, and other issues. Client seminars are usually held for the purpose of creating client loyalty and should be conducted by an attorney.

- **Direct mail pieces**—Some firms send out direct mail pieces aimed at a specific audience. Usually, the pieces are unsolicited; that is, they are sent out to people without being requested. For example, if your firm primarily handles real estate matters, you might send out a letter to all real estate businesses. Note, however, that direct mail is very controversial, especially when the mailing is targeted to a specific group. Ethical rules in some states strictly prohibit targeted mailing under the theory that it is direct solicitation. Attorneys are specifically prohibited from directly soliciting clients.

- **Involvement in legal associations**—Attorneys and paralegals can also market themselves by being active in local, state, and national bar and paralegal associations. Many firms that involve themselves in these types of organizations gain the respect and goodwill of others and may gain referrals from another firm that may not have the expertise to handle a particular type of case.

- **Sending information to clients that you know will be of interest to them**—Whenever you come across information that you think will interest clients, bring it to the attention of your supervising attorney and have the attorney send it to them. For example, if you come across a newspaper article that concerns their business or new laws that might affect them, clip it out and have the attorney send it. Or, if you come across a case in which they might be interested in, get your attorney's approval and send it to them with a note (but do not bill them for it!). Clients appreciate a law office that takes a personal interest in them.

- **Marketing your services to existing clients**—A firm's current clients are among its biggest assets. Firms not only want to market to new clients but also need to keep the business of their current clients. Thus, firms will typically spend a great deal of time cultivating their existing clients using techniques described earlier, such as newsletters and client seminars. Firms also have other techniques for marketing to existing clients.

    (a) **Cross-selling**—Cross-selling refers to selling additional services to existing clients. For instance, suppose a law office represented XYZ business in a tax matter, but XYZ used another firm to handle its personnel disputes. If possible, the law office would like to cross-sell XYZ to use its firm for both the tax matter and the personnel matters.

    (b) **Client questionnaires**—Many firms send out client questionnaires at the end of a legal matter to see how the client felt about the services that were provided. In addition to being a quality-control device, this is also a marketing technique because it is aimed at correcting problems that the client might have had.

    (c) **Keeping the firm's name in front of the client**—What happens if a client's case is completely finished and the client has no other business for the firm at the time? Should the firm forget about the client? No, most firms continue to keep in contact with the client with newsletters, seminars, letters, and holiday cards. Firms want clients to feel wanted and to be reminded that the firm is there to serve them.

    (d) **Developing client relationships**—With whom would you rather do business: friends or strangers? Friends are the unquestionable answer because you trust and feel comfortable with them. This is the kind of relationship that firms want to promote.

    (e) **Thanking clients for referring others to you**—Always send a thank-you letter to clients (or other attorneys) for making referrals to the office.

The Role of the Rainmaker

Rainmaking refers to the ability to bring in new clients to a law office. Sometimes law offices bring attorneys into the firm for the sole purpose of being "rainmakers." Some rainmakers are well connected politically or have

cross-selling
Selling additional services to existing clients.

rainmaking
Bringing in new clients to a law office.

inroads into certain industries. Rainmakers use their influence and skills to bring new clients into the firm. Helping clients achieve their business goals and dreams is often a factor in what makes a good rainmaker. It is important to pay close attention to any issues that affect the clients, which requires a special relationship with them. That relationship gives the clients a sense of security in knowing the attorney is watching out for their best interest. Many private law offices use rainmakers in their marketing schemes.

Marketing—An Ethics Perspective

Although ethical limitations on marketing have eased up over the past 20 years, there are still many pitfalls that can occur from an ethical perspective, including making false or misleading statements in an advertisement, failing to comply with general requirements about advertisements, directly soliciting a client, or putting forth an attorney as a specialist.

False or Misleading Statements   *Rule 7.1* regarding the rules of professional conduct states that attorneys are not allowed to make false or misleading statements in any kind of marketing or advertising piece. They may only promote themselves with advertisements that are completely true.

Thus, when an advertisement discusses a past victory, it must be careful to not create an expectation that the attorney can always achieve the same result, because cases depend on the specifics of each circumstance. Exhibit 8-7 provides several examples of false or misleading advertisements.

Advertising in General   *Rule 7.2* regarding the rules of professional conduct states some general guidelines that apply to all types of advertising, including that an attorney may advertise his or her legal services in the public media or through written, recorded, or electronic communication. The rule generally prohibits an attorney from paying a person who recommends a client to him or her. The rule also provides that any communication shall include the name and address of at least one lawyer or law firm responsible for its content, so that the authorities will know whom to contact if there is an ethical violation. This rule broadly allows lawyers to advertise using virtually any method.

Exhibit 8-7 Examples of False or Misleading Advertisements

Advertisement	Ethical Analysis
A statement of factual results (i.e., "Our firm recently won a $10,000,000 award)—coupled with a promise (i.e., "we can do the same for you.")	This would create an unjustified expectation and would imply that the next case would have a similar result, even though every case is different.[1]
"The Duke Law Firm: Better Than the Rest"; "The Premier Lawyers"; "After you've tried the rest, come to the best!"	Generally, the use of unsupportable, absolute terms is prohibited. It is also false or misleading for lawyers to compare their services to those of other lawyers unless that comparison can be factually substantiated.[2]
"One of the best firms specialized in the immigration and corporate law practice in the Washington, DC area."	Violates *Rule 7.4(a)*, which states subject to the requirement of *Rule 7.1* "a lawyer shall not hold himself or herself out publicly as a specialist."[3]

[1] *Public Citizen, Inc. v. La. Attorney Disciplinary Bd.*, 642 F. Supp. 2d 539 (E.D. La. 2009).
[2] *Id.*
[3] *Attorney Grievance Commission of Maryland v. Runan Zhang*, Misc. Docket AG No. 11, September Term, 2013 (July 21, 2014).

No Direct Solicitation or "Ambulance Chasing" *Rule 7.3* regarding the rules of professional conduct restricts attorneys from directly soliciting persons they do not know either in person, by live telephone, or by real-time electronic means. The rule does not apply if the attorney is soliciting another lawyer, if the person is a family member or a close personal friend, or if the person has had a prior professional relationship with the lawyer. In addition, the rule provides that an advertisement must include the words "advertising material" so that the public clearly understands the nature of the communication.

Direct, in-person telephone contact with individuals that the lawyer does not know is prohibited because of the possibility of undue influence, intimidation, or overreaching when a skilled attorney contacts a layperson. However, prerecorded communications may be acceptable, as the attorney is not "live." This rule also squarely prohibits attorneys from making harassing communication or bothering persons who do not want to be solicited.

A distinction is made in the rule between directly soliciting persons that are known by the attorney, such as family members or past clients, and soliciting unknown individuals. Attorneys and staff may solicit individuals they know. This is quite common, and there is nothing unethical about mentioning to friends and relatives that your law office handles certain types of cases and could help them if the need ever arose. What is prohibited is directly soliciting absolute strangers in person. Written solicitation, such as newsletters, brochures, and—in many jurisdictions—targeted mail, is allowed.

Advertising Fields of Practice and Specialization *Rule 7.4* regarding the rules of professional conduct generally prohibits attorneys from presenting themselves as specialists. Attorneys are allowed to communicate that they practice in a particular field of law, but a lawyer generally cannot state that he or she is certified as a specialist in a particular field unless the attorney has been certified as a specialist by an organization approved by a state authority or the American Bar Association. The word "specialist" has a secondary meaning, implying formal recognition (this rule would not apply in states that provide procedures for certification in particular areas). There are a few stated exceptions in the rule related to patent and admiralty law.

Each state has specific ethical rules about lawyer advertising, so whoever performs the marketing needs to be familiar with the rules of your state. One way to avoid ethical problems is to show the advertisement to the disciplinary administrator for the state before it is run and ask their opinion on the matter.

Summary

Legal marketing is the process of educating consumers on the legal and business activities a firm uses to deliver quality and ethical legal services. Advertising entails getting your name out to the public, whereas marketing encompasses much more. A marketing plan specifies a target audience, sets goals for the marketing program, and establishes detailed strategies for achieving the goals. Marketing strategies and options for law offices include a law firm Web site, brochure/resume, e-mail newsletters, public relation activities, public advertising, law firm seminars, and much more. "Rainmaking" refers to the ability to bring in new clients to the office. Ethical regulations related to marketing include not providing false or misleading information in advertising, not directly soliciting clients, and not allowing an attorney to present themself to the public as a specialist without some kind of certification from an accredited organization.

Key Terms

cross-selling   marketing plan

legal marketing   rainmaking

Practical Applications

1. You and your supervising attorney have just spent 16 weeks in a complicated products liability case regarding vaccine immunization shots for children. Your firm's client contracted the disease from the immunization shot. Your firm received the largest verdict in history for this type of case. Given the success of this case, the firm would like to handle more of these types of cases. When you get back to the office, you are shown a draft of an advertisement that is going to run in newspapers across the country, which reads:

   "MILLER AND HASTINGS Law office SPECIALIZES IN PHARMACEUTICAL CASES! Recently, our firm won a $100 million judgment against the manufacturer of a drug company for producing an unsafe drug. We can win for you too—please call us if you would like us to represent your interests."

   Your supervising attorney asks you for your comment. How do you respond?

2. Your client from the preceding question is ecstatic about the verdict in the immunization case. She learns of your intentions and volunteers to appear in a television ad to do a testimonial about the verdict and the great services the firm provided. What do you think about this?

3. You work in a solo practitioner's office, and the attorney is considering a number of different marketing strategies. One is a high client turnover strategy that includes a high-profile, big television campaign that would presumably generate a lot of new clients. What are your concerns?

4. Your law office is considering placing a yellow pages type of ad. You are to research the issue by looking in the directories under the heading "attorneys." You are to pick out two ads that you like. Consider what it is that you like about the ads and what their messages are. Do the same with television ads. Which attorney ads are the best, and why?

On the Web Exercises

1. Go to the ABA's Information on Professionalism and Ethics in Lawyer Advertising and Marketing home page at https://www.americanbar.org/groups/professional_responsibility/resources/professionalism/professionalism_ethics_in_lawyer_advertising/ and read two ethics opinions related to lawyer advertising/marketing.

2. Using a general search engine, such as http://www.google.com or http://www.yahoo.com, or the ABA's Web site on Information on Professionalism and Ethics in Lawyer Advertising and Marketing, find and print out a copy of *The Handbook on Lawyer Advertising and Solicitation*, published by the Florida Bar Association.

3. The state bar of Texas requires that some marketing material be reviewed by the bar before it is published. Find the advertising review rules and read any "Frequently Asked Questions"

document they may have. Try starting at the ABA's Information on Professionalism and Ethics in Lawyer Advertising and Marketing home page found within the ABA's Web site at http://www.americanbar.org.

4. Go to the ABA Center for Professional Responsibility http://www.americanbar.org/, find the **ABA Model Rules of Professional Conduct**, then read and print out the comments to **Rules 7.1, 7.2, 7.3**, and **7.4**.

5. Visit several bar association Web sites and find a minimum of five articles on legal marketing. The following link will take you to a Web site that connects to all state bar sites: https://www.hg.org/bar-associations-usa.html.

6. Visit the American Bar Association Law Practice Management section http://www.americanbar.org/groups/law_practice.html and review any materials they have on legal marketing.

Case Review

—Doe v. Condon, 532 S.E.2d 879, 341 S.C. 22 (S.C., 2000)

(Cite as: 532 S.E.2d 879, 341 S.C. 22 (S.C., 2000)

Supreme Court of South Carolina.
John DOE, Alias, Petitioner,
v.
Charles M. CONDON, Attorney General for the State of South Carolina, Respondent.
No. 25138.

Submitted May 23, 2000.

Decided June 5, 2000.

Assistant Attorney General Jennifer A. Deitrick, of Columbia, for respondent.

Disciplinary Counsel Henry B. Richardson, Jr., of Columbia, for amicus curiae Office of Disciplinary Counsel.

In the Original Jurisdiction per Curiam.

PER CURIAM: Petitioner sought to have the Court accept this matter in its original jurisdiction to determine whether certain tasks performed by a non-attorney employee in a law firm constitute the unauthorized practice of law. Specifically, petitioner asks (1) whether it is the unauthorized practice of law for a paralegal employed by an attorney to conduct informational seminars for the general public on wills and trusts without the attorney being present; (2) whether it is the unauthorized practice of law for a paralegal employed by an attorney to meet with clients privately at the attorney's office, answer general questions about wills and trusts, and gather basic information from clients; and (3) whether a paralegal can receive compensation from the paralegal's law firm/employer through a profit-sharing arrangement based upon the volume and type of cases the paralegal handles. The Office of the Attorney General filed a return opposing the petition for original jurisdiction.

The Court invoked its original jurisdiction to determine whether the paralegal's activities constituted the unauthorized practice of law, and, pursuant to S.C.Code Ann. § 14-3-340 (1976), John W. Kittredge was appointed as referee to make findings of fact and conclusions of law concerning this matter. A hearing was held and the referee issued proposed findings and recommendations.

We adopt the referee's findings and recommendations attached to this opinion and hold that a non-lawyer employee conducting unsupervised legal presentations for the public and answering legal questions for the public or for clients of the attorney/employer engages in the unauthorized practice of law. See **State v. Despain**, 319 S.C. 317, 460 S.E.2d 576 (1995). We further hold that a proposed fee arrangement which compensates non-lawyer employees based upon the number and volume of cases the non-lawyer employee handles for an attorney violates the ethical rules against fee splitting with non-lawyer employees. **Rule 5.4** of the Rules of Professional Conduct, **Rule 407**, SCACR. (**Jean H. Toal** A.J.; **James E. Moore** A.J.; **John H. Waller, Jr.** A.J.; **E.C. Burnett, III** A.J.; **Costa Pleicones**)

Proposed Findings and Recommendations of the Referee

This is a declaratory judgment action in the Supreme Court's original jurisdiction. The Court referred this matter to me as Referee. Petitioner, a paralegal, has submitted a generalized list of tasks he wishes to perform and has inquired whether performing them constitutes the unauthorized practice of law. Petitioner also seeks a determination of the propriety of his proposed fee-splitting arrangement with his attorney-employer. Despite my repeated offers for an evidentiary hearing, neither party requested a hearing. The record before me is sufficient to address and resolve whether the activities in question constitute the unauthorized practice of law.

I find that a paralegal conducting unsupervised legal presentations for the public and answering legal questions from the audience engages in the unauthorized practice of law. Further, I find that a paralegal meeting individually with clients to answer estate-planning questions engages in the unauthorized practice of law. Finally, I find the proposed fee arrangement is improper and violates the ethical prohibition against fee splitting.

Background

Petitioner submitted the following questions to the Court:

(1) Is it the unauthorized practice of law for a paralegal employed by an attorney to conduct educational seminars for the general public, to disseminate general information about wills and trusts, including specifically a fair and balanced emphasis on living trusts, including answering general questions, without the attorney being present at the seminar as long as the seminar is sponsored by the attorney's law firm and the attorney has reviewed and approved the format, materials, and presentation to be made for content, truthfulness, and fairness?

(2) Is it the unauthorized practice of law for a paralegal employed by an attorney to meet with clients privately in the law office for the purpose of answering general questions about wills, trusts, including specifically living trusts, and estate planning in general, and to gather basic information from said clients for such purposes as long as it is done under the attorney's direction, and the clients have a follow-up interview and meeting with the attorney who would have primary responsibility for legal decisions?

(3) Can a paralegal receive compensation from the law firm he is employed by, through a profit-sharing arrangement, which would be based upon the volume and type of cases the paralegal handled?

Discussion

To protect the public from unsound legal advice and incompetent representation, South Carolina, like other jurisdictions, limits the practice of law to licensed attorneys. S.C.Code Ann. § 40-5-310 (1976). While case law provides general guidelines as to what constitutes the practice of law, courts are hesitant to define its exact boundaries. Thus, the analysis in "practice of law" cases is necessarily fact-driven. The Supreme Court has specifically avoided addressing hypothetical situations, preferring instead to determine what constitutes the unauthorized practice of law on a case-by-case basis. *In Re Unauthorized Practice of Law Rules Proposed by the South Carolina Bar*, 309 S.C. 304, 422 S.E.2d 123 (S.C.1992). I find that Petitioner's proposed actions constitute the unauthorized practice of law and that the proposed fee agreement violates the ethical prohibition against fee splitting.

Our Supreme Court has set forth a succinct standard of the proper role of paralegals:

The activities of a paralegal do not constitute the practice of law as long as they are limited to work of a preparatory nature, such as legal research, investigation, or the composition of legal documents, which enable the licensed attorney-employer to carry a given matter to a conclusion through his own examination, approval or additional effort. *Matter of Easler*, 275 S.C. 400, 272 S.E.2d 32, 33 (S.C. 1980).

While the important support function of paralegals has increased through the years, the Easler guidelines stand the test of time. As envisioned in *Easler*, the paralegal plays a supporting role to the supervising attorney. Here, the roles are reversed. The attorney would support the paralegal. Petitioner would play the lead role, with no meaningful attorney supervision and the attorney's presence and involvement only surfaces on the back end. Meaningful attorney supervision must be present throughout the process. The line between what is and what is not permissible conduct by a non-attorney is oftentimes "unclear" and is a potential trap for the unsuspecting client. *State v. Buyers Service Co., Inc.*, 292 S.C. 426, 357 S.E.2d 15, 17 (S.C.1987). The conduct of the paralegal contemplated here clearly crosses the line into the unauthorized practice of law. It is well settled that a paralegal may not give legal advice, consult, offer legal explanations, or make legal recommendations. *State v. Despain*, 319 S.C. 317, 460 S.E.2d 576 (S.C.1995).

A. Educational Seminars

Petitioner intends to conduct unsupervised "wills and trusts" seminars for the public, "emphasizing" living trusts during the course of his presentation. Petitioner also plans to answer estate-planning questions from the audience. I find Petitioner's proposed conduct constitutes the unauthorized practice of law.

I find, as other courts have, that the very structure of such "educational" legal seminars suggests that the presenter will actually be giving legal advice on legal matters. See, *In Re Mid-America Living Trust Assoc. Inc.*, 927 S.W.2d 855 (Mo.banc 1996); *People v. Volk*, 805 P.2d 1116 (Colo. 1991); *Oregon State Bar v. John H. Miller & Co.* 235 Or. 341, 385 P.2d 181 (Or. 1963). At the very least. Petitioner will implicitly advise participants that they require estate-planning services. Whether a will or trust is appropriate in any given situation is a function of legal judgment. To be sure, advising a potential client on his or her need for a living trust (or other particular estate-planning instrument or device) fits squarely within the practice of law. These matters cry out for the exercise of professional judgment by a licensed attorney. Thus, in conducting these informational seminars, Petitioner would engage in the unauthorized practice of law as a non-attorney offering legal advice.

Petitioner plans to answer "general" questions during his presentation. I have reviewed the Estate-Planning Summary submitted by Petitioner and his attorney-employer. This summary sets forth the subject matter to be covered by the paralegal. Petitioner would present information on, among other things, revocable trusts, irrevocable living trusts, credit shelter trusts, qualified terminable interest property trusts, charitable remainder trusts, qualified personal residence trusts, grantor retained annuity trusts, grantor retained unitrusts, and charitable lead trusts. It is difficult to imagine such specific estate-planning devices eliciting "general" questions or a scenario in which the exercise of legal judgment would not be involved. It is, after all, a legal seminar, apparently for the purpose of soliciting business. [1] To suggest that some "plan" would anticipate all possible questions with predetermined nonlegal responses is specious. And so complex is this area of law that many states, including South Carolina, have established stringent standards for an attorney to receive the designation of "specialist" in Estate Planning and Probate Law. SCACR, Part IV, Appendices D and E. This is the practice of law.

FN1. While this marketing method may raise ethical implications for the attorney involved, the issue before me is whether the activities of the paralegal constitute the unauthorized practice of law. See *Rule* 7.3, Rules of Professional Conduct, 407 SCACR; Matter of Morris, 270 S.C. 308, 241 S.E.2d 911 (1978) (lawyer improperly solicited employment); *Matter of Craven*, 267 S.C. 33, 225 S.E.2d 861 (1976) (an attorney's knowledge that his employee is engaged in solicitation of professional employment for attorney constitutes professional misconduct); *Matter of Crosby*, 256 S.C. 325, 182 S.E.2d 289 (1971) (attorney improperly solicited business). Thus, not only does Petitioner's solicitation of legal clients raise possible ethical concerns for his sponsoring attorney, Petitioner's involvement clearly constitutes the unauthorized practice of law.

I fully recognize the prevailing popularity of "financial planners" and others "jump[ing] on the estate planning bandwagon." (Estate-Planning Summary submitted by Petitioner's attorney-employer, p. 1). This trend in no way affects the decision before the Court. This paralegal would not be presenting the estate-planning seminar as a financial planner. This seminar would be conspicuously sponsored by the paralegal's attorney-employer. The attorney's law firm is prominently displayed in the brochure submitted, e.g., name, address, telephone number, and "Firm Profile." In promoting the law firm and representing to the public the 'legal' nature of the seminar, neither the paralegal nor his attorney-employer can escape the prohibition against the unauthorized practice of law.

B. Initial Client Interview

Petitioner intends to gather client information and answer general estate-planning questions during his proposed "initial client interviews." While Petitioner may properly compile client information, Petitioner may not answer estate-planning questions. See *Matter of Easler*, supra. Petitioner's answering legal questions would constitute the unauthorized practice of law for the reasons stated above. While the law firm in which Petitioner is employed plans to direct clients to an attorney for "follow-up" consultations, a paralegal may not give

legal advice in any event. Moreover, permissible preparatory tasks must be performed while under the attorney's supervision. The proposed after-the-fact attorney review comes too late.

C. Compensation

Petitioner's law firm intends to compensate him based upon the volume and types of cases he "handles." A paralegal, of course, may not "handle" any case. [2] This fee arrangement directly violates *Rule 5.4* of the Rules of Professional Conduct, SCACR 407. [3] This limitation serves to "discourage the unauthorized practice of law by laypersons and to prevent a non-lawyer from acquiring a vested pecuniary interest in an attorney's disposition of a case that could possibly take preeminence over a client's best interest." *Matter of Anonymous Member of the S.C. Bar*, 295 S.C. 25, 26, 367 S.E.2d 17, 18 (S.C. 1998). This compensation proposal arrangement coupled with Petitioner's desire to market the law firm's services via the educational seminars and meet individually with clients creates a situation ripe for abuse. Indeed, the proposal by Petitioner presents the very evil *Rule 5.4* was designed to avoid. Accordingly, I find Petitioner's proposed compensation plan violates both the letter and the spirit of *Rule 5.4* prohibiting fee splitting with non-attorneys.

FN2. The suggestion that Petitioner and the law firm intend for him to "handle" cases speaks volumes about the anticipated role of Petitioner, far beyond the permissible tasks performed by paralegals.

FN3. Nonlawyer employees may certainly participate "in a compensation or retirement plan, even though the plan is based in whole or in part on a profit sharing arrangement." *Rule 5.4(a)(3)*, Rules of Professional Conduct, SCACR 407.

Recommendations

1. Offering legal presentations for the general public constitutes the practice of law.
2. Answering estate-planning questions in the context of legal seminars or in private client interviews constitutes the practice of law.
3. Fee-sharing arrangements with non-attorneys based on volume and cases "handled" by a paralegal violates *Rule 5.4*, Rules of Professional Conduct, SCACR 407.

Respectfully Submitted

/s/ John W. Kittredge Referee April 7, 2000 Greenville, SC

Case Review Exercises

1. Why was the court not persuaded by the paralegal's argument that, because an attorney had reviewed and approved all of the information in the public seminar, there should not be a problem regarding the unauthorized practice of law?
2. The paralegal seemed to argue that, in reality, he or she would be performing a good deed by educating the public on topics such as wills, trusts, and living trusts. Why was the court not persuaded by this argument?
3. If an attorney had been at the seminar, and the paralegal and attorney had jointly conducted the seminar, would the court have arrived at the same conclusion? Why?

4. Did the content of the seminar play a part in the court's decision? Why or why not?

5. The paralegal seemed to make the argument that, because other professionals such as financial planners were giving such advice, the paralegal should be able to as well. Was the decision to create a different standard for paralegals versus other professionals fair and consistent?

6. Read Footnote 2. How does the content of that footnote impact the rest of the decision? Why were the court's conclusions in Footnote 2 important to the case as a whole?

Helpful Web Sites

Organization	Description	Internet Address
American Bar Association (ABA)	Association for attorneys. The Web site has a large amount of information and publications relevant to individuals working in the legal profession.	http://www.americanbar.org
ABA Information on Professionalism and Ethics in Lawyer Advertising and Marketing	ABA Web site devoted to ethics related to attorney marketing.	http://www.americanbar.org/groups/professional_responsibility/resources/professionalism/professionalism_ethics_in_lawyer_advertising.html
ABA Law Practice Today	ABA Web site devoted to law practice management issues, including coverage of legal marketing.	http://www.americanbar.org/groups/law_practice.html
Legal Marketing Association	Nonprofit association for legal marketing professionals.	http://www.legalmarketing.org
Legalmarketingblog.com	Legal marketing blog, including articles and information related to legal marketing.	http://www.legalmarketingblog.com

Suggested Reading

1. Rose, J. (2015). *How to Capture and Keep Clients: Marketing Strategies for Lawyers.* (2nd ed.). American Bar Association.

2. *Law Practice* magazine, published by the American Bar Association Law Practice Management Section, https://www.americanbar.org/groups/law_practice/publications/law_practice_magazine.

3. Hornsby, W. (2000). *Marketing and Legal Ethics: The Boundaries of Promoting Legal Services.* American Bar Association.

4. Siskind, G. & McMurray, D. (2017). *The Lawyer's Guide to Marketing on the Internet.* (4th ed.). American Bar Association.

5. Snyder, T. C. (2021). *Women Rainmakers' Best Marketing Tips.* (4th ed.) American Bar Association.

9

File and Law Library Management

- It was 10 days before Bruce returned from his honeymoon so he could not be asked about the wrongful seizure memorandum prepared. Bruce informed us that Sabrina worked on the memo, but he did not recall where she saved the file or its name.

- After several hours, we located the research file on bankruptcy petition preparers (11 U.S.C. 110) under "11."

- We spent several days looking on each computer hard drive attempting to find the salvage trucks lease purchase agreements involved with the loan refinancing. Eventually, the agreements were found under "templates" on the network drive labeled "salvage trucks." The file name was saved as the first two words listed on the documents.

The Importance of Understanding of File and Law Library Management

Lawyers and paralegals work with hard copy and electronic files every day. It is crucial that they know how to organize, track, and store client files. If a file or parts of a file are lost, misplaced, or misfiled, the effects can be devastating, both to the office and to the client's case. Information must be stored so that it can be quickly found and retrieved. The responsibilities for organizing case files, in most instances, will be that of paralegals and/or staff. However, many lawyers will do their own file organization. In addition, many legal organizations are using automated file management systems. It is important that members of the legal team have a good understanding of automated systems as law firms progress toward a paperless office.

Lawyers and paralegals also must have a basic understanding of law library management. The law library is used to conduct legal research, so it is important that they know how libraries work and be familiar with electronic research resources. Although maintaining the library may be a lawyer responsibility, you could have law offices, especially smaller ones, that have paralegals in charge of maintaining the library. Law libraries have changed drastically in recent years. Increasingly, more information is being stored electronically, so having a good understanding of how to access electronic information and research is critical.

Introduction to File Management

Law offices of all types need a file system that allows them to store, track, and retrieve information about cases in a logical, efficient, and expeditious manner. The outcome of many legal matters depends on the case information gathered, including evidence, depositions, pleadings, discovery requests, and witness interviews. File information generally is worthless unless it is organized and available to the paralegals and attorneys who will use it. File management is a large task, no matter the size of the law practice.

Exhibit 9-1 presents the characteristics of a good file system, whether the system is paperless or hard copy. Each of these areas is vital to a law office, and none can be compromised. A poor file system has some or all of the following problems:

Exhibit 9-1 File System Vital Components

A. **Easy to Learn**—Well-designed file systems are user friendly, simple, and straightforward; anyone can understand it.

B. **Easy to Use**—Well-designed file systems are easily located with quick access and integrate electronic files within the office files' structure.

C. **Easy to Adapt**—Well-designed file systems are easily adjusted as the business environment grows or changes focus.

D. **Comprehensive**—Well-designed file systems are all-inclusive; hard copies and electronic files should contain all relevant case information.

E. **File Integrity**—Well-designed file systems are reliable, dependable, accurate, and sound.

F. **Security Policy**—Well-designed file systems provide a safe environment for both hard copies and electronic files to prevent unauthorized access to specific files as well as the system access.

G. **Retention Policy**—Well-designed file systems have procedures for maintaining and preserving both hard copies and electronic file documents based on required time frames.

1. Files (hard copy and electronic) are lost and cannot be found.
2. Files are messy and disorganized.
3. Office staff is unclear about how the filing system works.
4. Attorneys and paralegals do not trust the file system and keep their own files or keep the office's files in their possession.
5. Staff is constantly aggravated and frustrated over the file system.
6. Large amounts of time and money are wasted trying to find the file and information.
7. Poor-quality legal services are given to clients because of the poor filing system.
8. Electronic file systems are unreliable or do not work.

File management is an important topic because law office management is responsible for providing an effective system that adequately supports its attorneys and paralegals. Files and file systems represent a tool that the attorney and paralegal use to provide their services.

Filing Methods and Techniques

There are different variations or filing methods that accomplish the objectives in Exhibit 9-1. The filing method(s) utilized depends on the particular needs of each law office. These needs may be based on such factors as the number of attorneys in the firm, the number of cases that will be tracked and stored, the type and power of computer hardware and software in use, the size and length of time typical cases are kept open or active, how much paper typical cases generate, the amount of space available for storage, whether the files will be kept in a central location, or whether departments or attorneys will keep their own files.

Each Legal Matter Is Maintained Separately

No matter which filing method is used in a law office, each case or legal matter must be maintained separately. Even if one client has several legal matters pending, each case/legal matter should have its own separate file and should be given its own file number. There is the danger that documents will be misplaced or lost if all documents are commingled.

When matters are commingled, it affects other law office systems, such as conflict-of-interest checking (which determines whether the law office has a conflict of interest), docket control, and billing. Each case should be checked for conflict-of-interest problems, should have its own distinct and separate deadlines entered into the docket control system, and should be billed to the client separately.

Alphabetic Systems

alphabetic filing system
Filing method in which cases are stored based on the last name of the client or organization.

In an **alphabetic filing system**, cases are stored based on the last name of the client or name of the organization. There is a natural tendency to alphabetize because it is a system that most people understand. In addition, staff members do not need to memorize case numbers or use numerical lists: a user knows exactly where the file should be in the drawer.

The larger the number of cases the law office is handling, the more problems it will experience with an alphabetical system. This is because names are not all that unique; many clients may have the same last name. It is not efficient to search through four or five file drawers or cabinets of "Smith" files looking for the right case. It is also not uncommon for clients to have the same first and last names. Other systems, such as a numerical or an electronic system, can track almost infinite number of cases with a unique number and also protect the confidentiality of the client, because the client's name is not the identifier for the file and is therefore not written on all the files. In offices with a large number of cases, an alphabetic system may not be the best kind of filing system; they are difficult to expand and can require constantly shifting files to make room for more.

Numerical Systems

In a numerical filing system, each case or legal matter is given a separate file number. This is similar to when a case is filed with a court; a clerk assigns each action or lawsuit a separate case number. Case identifiers can be, but do not necessarily have to be, composed of all numbers (e.g., 234552). Variations can be used, such as alphanumeric, in which letters and numbers are used. For instance, a letter might be used in the case number to reflect which branch office is handling the case, and two of the numbers might reflect the year the case was filed, such as NO15-990004. The "NO" might stand for the office's New Orleans location, and "15" stand for 2015, the year the case was initiated.

Letters also may stand for types of cases ("PB" for probate, "TX" for tax, etc.) or for a particular attorney—"Patricia Burns," and so forth. Even in a numerical system, however, legal matters for the same client can be kept together. For instance, in the example "NO15-990004," "99" could represent the client's personal number and "4" could mean that this is the fourth case that the office is handling for the client.

Another numerical filing method is to assign a range of numbers to a particular type of case, such as 000–999 for trusts, 1000–1999 for tax matters, and 2000–2999 for criminal matters.

A filing rule that sometimes bears out is that the longer the case number, the more misfiling and other types of errors occur; shorter numbers can also be remembered more easily. Numerical filing solves the shifting problems caused by alphabetical systems. When a new case is taken, the next sequential number is given to the file, and it is stored accordingly. This is different than the alphabetic system, where a new file is stored by the client's name. When the new file is added to the existing drawer in the alphabetical system, the drawer may be full, and then someone must shift or move files to make room for the new addition.

Bar Coding

Bar coding is a file management technique in which each file is tracked according to the file's bar code. Each time a user takes a file, the file's bar code and user's bar code are scanned into a computer. The computerized system then tracks which user checked out which file. When the file is returned, the file's bar code is scanned back into the computer. A report can be generated any time, listing what files are checked out and by whom. Using this system, it

bar coding
A file management technique in which each file is tracked according to the file's bar code.

is possible to find the location of files quite easily. Bar codes are used in many libraries to track the library's collection. Bar coding of law office files works much the same way.

The "Paperless Office" — Electronic Document Management

document management software
Organizes, controls, distributes, and allows for extensive searching of electronic documents typically in a computer-networked environment.

Document management software organizes, controls, distributes, and allows for extensive searching of electronic documents, typically in a computer-networked environment. In a "paperless" office environment, all information is stored electronically. Document management software easily tracks and stores computer files that are already in an electronic format such as word processing, e-mail, and spreadsheet files. It allows a legal organization to file documents electronically so they can be found by anyone in the organization, even when there are hundreds of users spread across offices located throughout the world. Document management software can also accommodate hard copy documents through the use of imaging. **Imaging** uses a scanner to capture an image of a document. That image is stored electronically and can be retrieved later. Given the enormous storage capacities of computers, document management software is the electronic equivalent of a filing room with thousands of file cabinets.

imaging
Uses a scanner to capture an image of a document. The image is stored electronically.

Document management software provides for extensive searching capabilities and allows users to associate files with cases and create profiles of documents for easy retrieval. Document management software tracks files from the time they are opened until they are closed. It also allows many reports to be generated regarding the records that are being kept. Records can be printed regarding files assigned to specific attorneys, types of cases, and more. Many law offices have some kind of document management software; while many are not completely "paperless," most law offices use document management software to some extent. Document management software has many advantages, including the ability to share information across vast distances, excellent tracking and reporting capabilities, reduced instances of misfiling, ability to easily and quickly create a backup copy of information, reduced space and storage costs, and the ability to quickly search and sort information, among others.

Unfortunately, document management also has some downsides. The cost of technology can be substantial, and training of staff is essential. In addition, like any system, a document management system must be maintained and properly administered. Law offices must have procedures and rules for those documents that are saved for long term. Discussion drafts and unfinished documents may need to be stored in a different place. In addition, firms should have a document retention policy that includes both hard copy and electronic documents.

Corporate, Government, and Legal Aid Filing Methods

Corporate law and government departments may arrange their matters differently. They may file matters by subject, by department, or by other means that suit their particular industry or need. Legal services/aid offices typically file cases alphabetically or even geographically, by city or county.

Centralized versus Decentralized

centralized file system
Method in which a file department or file clerk stores and manages all active law office files in one or more file rooms.

A fundamental law office filing consideration is whether the filing system will be centralized or decentralized. A **centralized file system** is where a file department or file clerk stores and manages all active law office files in one or more file rooms. In a **decentralized file system**, files are kept in various locations throughout the law office, such as each department storing its own files or each attorney keeping his or her own files.

A centralized system is typically used when the office has a complex filing procedure best handled by one department or file clerk staff; when the office wants a highly controlled system; or when several attorneys or paralegals work on the same cases. Even though a law office may want a centralized system, the office must first have the physical space to accommodate it. Law offices where a single attorney or paralegal works on each case, such as real estate matters, or needs the case files for long periods of time may use a decentralized file system where the files are located in an individual's office or in a secretarial area. Some offices use a "pod," or team filing system, where several people—perhaps two or three attorneys, a secretary, and a paralegal or two—have offices located close to one another and have their files stored next to them. Some offices may use a combination. Whether an office uses a centralized or decentralized system depends on the size of the office, type of cases handled, and the needs of the personnel involved. Closed files are almost always kept in a centralized location.

decentralized file system
System in which files are kept in various locations throughout the law office.

Opening Files

When a new or an existing client comes into the office with a new legal matter, a new file should immediately be opened. The opening of a file should be standardized and requires certain information about the legal matter. A file-opening form or an electronic version (sometimes called a new client/matter form or case sheet) is customarily completed when opening a new file (see Exhibit 9-2).

The **file-opening form** is used for a variety of purposes, including to check potential conflicts of interest, to assign a new case number and attorney to the matter, to track the area or specialty of the case, to set forth the type of fee agreement and billing frequency in the case, to enter the case in the time-keeping and billing system, to make docketing entries (such as when the statute of limitations in the matter might run), and to find out how the client was referred to the law office. Although file-opening forms are commercially available, most law offices choose to customize the form to reflect their own needs.

Copies of the file-opening form may be sent to the managing partner, other attorneys, accounting department, docket-control department, and the responsible attorney.

file-opening form
A standardized form that is filled out when a new case is started. The form contains important information about the client and the case.

File Format and Internal File Rules

File format (or how case files are set up) and organization depend on the needs of each office. The type of file format will depend on the filing system that is used; for example, vertical file drawers require tabs in different places, while an open-shelf filing system requires tabs on the side.

Many offices use separate manila files as subdivisions in the same case to differentiate information in the same file, such as having files for "Accounting," "Discovery," "Pleadings," "Client Correspondence," and others (see Exhibit 9-3). The individual manila files are stored in one or more expanding files, so that all the files for one case are kept together. Many offices also use metal fasteners to hold the papers securely in place; original documents, however, should not be punched. Instead, they should be maintained separately and a copy put in the regular file. Finally, information is typically placed in each manila file in a chronological order, with the oldest on the bottom and the newest on the top of the file. This gives the user a systematic way of finding information. It is routine to find duplicate and draft copies of documents in a file; however, this makes the organization process more difficult. If duplicates must be kept, they should be in a separate file folder labeled "Duplicates."

Exhibit 9-2 File-Opening Form

New File

Client (Check one)

_____ INDIVIDUAL _____

                    Last   First   Middle Initial

_____ ENTITY _____

            (Use complete name & common abbreviations; place articles [e.g., The at end.)

_____ CLASS ACTION _____

            (File Name, ex.: Popcorn Antitrust Litigation)

Matter (Check One)

_____ NON-LITIGATION

_____ LITIGATION

_____ Approved for litigation by—MUST BE INITIALED by submitting attorney!!

Nature of the Case

Area of law code: _____   Summary of work or dispute: _____

_____

Client Contact (N/A for Class Actions)

Name: _____

Company: _____

Street: _____

City, State, Zip: _____

Telephone: _____

*New Adverse Parties:

_____
_____
_____

*New Related Parties (for Class Actions, Named Plaintiffs Only):

_____
_____
_____

*Will be entered into computer system by Bus. Dept. *AFTER* approval by Managing Partner.

Closed File

Date Closed: _____   Atty. Or Sec. Initials: _____

_____ Attach pleadings and/or file indexes. If indexes are not available, attach brief description of what is contained in the file(s). SEND FILES, THIS FORM, AND INDEX TO FILE ROOM.

	Routing Lists		(Initial)			
	New File:	Date:			Closed File:	Date:
Submitted by	_____	_____			_____	_____
Sec. of Submitting Person	_____	_____			_____	_____

(continued)

(continued)

	Routing Lists	(Initial)		
	New File:	Date:	Closed File:	Date:
Managing Partner	_____	_____	_____	_____
Business Department	_____	_____	_____	_____
File Department	_____	_____	_____	_____
Firm Newsletter	_____	_____	_____	_____
Docket for Litigation	_____	_____	_____	_____

EnviroLaw (Computer Center)   Add? _____
IdeaLaw (Computer Center)   Add? _____
JobLaw (Computer Center)   Add? _____

Billing Address (N/A for Class Actions)
Name: _____
Company: _____
Street: _____
City, State, Zip: _____
Telephone: _____

Team Information (Use initials)
_____ _____ _____   Managing Attorney(s) (for nonlitigation cases only)
_____ _____ _____   Bill Review Attorney(s)
_____ _____ _____   Originating Attorney(s)
_____ Calendar Attorney (for litigation cases only)
_____ Legal Assistant (for litigation cases only)
_____ Secretary to Calendar Attorney (for litigation cases only)

Referral Source (Check one)
_____ Existing Client   _____
                               (Name)
_____ Non-Firm Attorney   _____
                               (Name)
_____ Firm Attorney or Employee _____
_____ Martindale-Hubbell   _____
_____ Other   _____

Fee Agreement (Check those that apply)
_____ Hourly
_____ Contingent _____ %
_____ Fee Petition
_____ Fixed Fee $_____ or Fixed Range from $_____ to $_____
_____ Retainer $_____
_____ Letter of Retainer sent by _____ on _____
                          (Initials)   (Date)

Statement Format (Check those that apply)
Do you want identical disbursements grouped?   _____ Yes _____ No
Do you want attorney hours reflected on each time entry? _____ Yes _____ No
Do you want fees extended on each time entry?   _____ Yes _____ No

---

Conflict Check

Conflict Check Completed By: _____   Date: _____
                          (Initials)

Conflict Check Not Needed: _____
                          (Initials of Submitting Person)

Check One:
_____ No conflicts
_____ Potential conflict with the following existing parties (from computer system):

_____
_____

(Or attach computer printout from Conflict Check System.)

Exhibit 9-3 Typical Subcategories of Files

Accounting

Correspondence with Attorneys

Correspondence with Client

Deposition Summaries

Discovery

Evidence

General Correspondence

Investigation

Legal Research

Memorandums

Notes and Miscellaneous

Witnesses

Color Coding

Color coding files is a simple but effective way to reduce the number of misfiled documents. Files can be color coded in a variety of ways; for example, red-labeled files may be used for probate and green files for criminal matters. Color coding can also be done according to the year the case was opened or according to the attorney handling the matter.

Color coding may be used for cases that are especially sensitive or that need to be kept secure. For example, if the law office is trying to create an "ethical wall" or "ethical screen" to keep a staff member from participating in a case, others can be alerted to the need for security by assigning a certain color of file label to the case. Finally, color coding can be used in an alphabetic filing system—for example, A–E equals blue, F–J equals green, and so forth.

Checking Files Out

In some law offices, where many people have access to files, users are required to check out files electronically (in a process similar to one used in a public library) or to simply leave a large card where the file is stored, showing who checked out the file. It can be quite frustrating to search for a client's file only to discover that someone else took the file home to work on it, or that the file is lost. Tracking the location of files is crucial to an effective file/record management system.

Closing, Storing, and Purging Files

After a legal matter has come to a conclusion and the final bill has been paid, the file is closed and taken out of the storage area of active files. It is boxed up and kept in the office's basement or an off-site storage facility for a certain number of years, until it is destroyed or put on microfilm, microfiche, or stored electronically on CDs or other storage devices.

A closed file is sometimes called a "dead file" or a "retired file." Some offices give the closed case a new number to differentiate it from active cases. The closing of cases represents a problem for many law offices. Attorneys like to have access to closed files in case they someday need the information contained in them. Storage space can be quite expensive, however. Most law offices are continually opening and closing cases, which means that the flow of files never stops and that the required storage area gets larger and larger. Duplicate copies of documents should be removed in order to reduce file storage requirements.

A client must be made completely aware before his or her file is closed. It is strongly recommended that the law firm send a disengagement letter to the client, letting the client know in writing that the file is being closed and that the documents, evidence, or even the whole file can be returned to the client. Electronic records also need to be purged or backed up at the same time that the hard copy of the file is closed.

One solution to storage problems is to purge or destroy files after a certain period of time (see Exhibit 9-4). Some states have ethical rules that also govern file retention. Some law offices purge all files after a certain number of years, such as seven or eight, while others purge only selected files. Destroying hard copy files usually means shredding, burning, or recycling them. Simply throwing them away does not protect the client's confidentiality and should not be done.

Organization of Files

File organization is a large part of what many paralegals do. They must use files on a daily basis; therefore, for most paralegals to become efficient at what they do, they must be able to organize and—in some cases—index case files in a logical and systematic fashion so that they can quickly find information. Case material also must be organized in such a way that others, such as attorneys, can find the information quickly. A file that is a disorganized mess is useless in a law office. For instance, if the paralegal is assisting an attorney at a deposition and the attorney asks him or her to find a specific answer in the discovery request, he or she must be able to locate it quickly. If the paralegal is not familiar with the case, does not have the file organized, or misfiled the document, he or she will not have the ability to find the information quickly, and the client's case may suffer.

File Management and Ethics

There are several ethical questions that should be addressed when considering filing and using filing systems. These issues include performing conflict-of-interest checks before a new case is taken, maintaining client-related property that is turned over to the law office during representation, maintaining trust- and client-related accounting records, returning a client's file to him or her if the client decides to change attorneys, and ensuring that the office's filing system and/or file destruction procedures maintain client confidentiality.

Client Property

Offices should be careful when closing files and especially when destroying files containing documents or other information and items that were given to the attorney by a client. *Rule 1.15* regarding the rules of professional conduct address a law office's duty at the end of a case to give the client the option to pick up information that was delivered to the attorney for representation in the matter. Generally, unless the client consents, a lawyer should not destroy or discard items that clearly or probably belong to the client. In addition, an attorney should be especially careful not to destroy client information until the applicable statutory limitations period has expired.

Exhibit 9-4 Sample Record Retention Periods

Law Office Administration	Retention Period
Accounts payable and receivable ledgers	7 years
Audit reports	Permanently
Bank statement and reconciliations	7 years
Cash receipt books	Permanently
Canceled checks (except for payments of taxes, real estate, and other important payments—permanently)	10 years
Contracts, mortgages, notes, and leases (still in effect)	Permanently
Correspondence, general	5–7 years
Important (significant) correspondence	Permanently
Deeds, mortgages, etc.	Permanently
Employment applications	3 years
Financial statements (year-end)	Permanently
Insurance policies (expired)	10 years
Invoices	7 years
Minutes of directors' and stockholders' meetings	Permanently
Payroll records (after termination)	10 years
Retirement and pension records	6 years
Tax returns	4 years from date issued or paid
Time cards/records	3 years

Clients' Files and Documents—Important Note:

- Retention of a client's file and client-related documents depends on the ethical rules in your state.
- Before destroying a client's file, contact the client to make sure he or she does not want the file or something out of the file.
- When destroying a client's file, burn, shred, or recycle the file to ensure client confidentiality.

Source: Code of Federal Regulations (CFR) and The Sarbanes—Oxley Act.

Duty to Turn Over File When Client Fires Attorney

An attorney also has a duty to turn over to a client his or her file when the client decides to fire an attorney and hire another one. What must be turned over to the client depends on the ethical rules and case law in each state. For example, Rule 3-700(D) of the *California Revised Rules of Professional Conduct* states:

> (a) [An attorney] whose employment has terminated shall … promptly release to the client, all the client papers and property. Client papers and property include correspondence, pleadings, deposition transcripts, exhibits, physical evidence, expert's reports, and other items reasonably necessary to the client's representation, whether the client has paid for them or not.

In most states, the attorney must turn over any documents the new counsel will need to reasonably handle the matter. In some states, such as California, a law office cannot refuse to release a client's file just because the client still owes fees and expenses.

Destruction of Records of Account

Rule 1.15 regarding the rules of professional conduct also address the attorney's duty to maintain financial records related to a legal matter for five years after termination of representation. Law offices should carefully maintain accurate and complete records of the lawyer's receipt and disbursement of trust funds in every case.

Confidentiality

An attorney's duty to maintain the confidentiality of client-related matters should be a factor when considering a law office file management system. Files must be maintained so that sensitive information about a case or client is kept private. The confidentiality rule also does not stop once the case is closed. Law offices should be careful to destroy or dispose of files in a manner consistent with the confidentiality requirements.

Introduction to Law Library Management

Professional librarians may coordinate and manage the law library in medium- to large-sized law offices. In smaller law offices, however, paralegals or associate attorneys may perform these duties. Exhibit 9-5 contains a list of librarian-related duties.

Law libraries are changing. The Internet, CD-ROM libraries, e-Books, and data services such as Westlaw and LexisNexis have forever changed how and where lawyers and paralegals access legal research. Although hard copy books will probably never be completely replaced by their electronic counterparts, most law libraries have gone digital, and this has changed how libraries are managed. Library management used to be centered around purchasing, maintaining, and storing shelf after shelf of books that constantly grew in number. This is no longer the case; many legal professionals do not even need a physical library at all. They can now access a host of electronic legal research at their desk. That said, law firms

Exhibit 9-5 Librarian-Related Duties

- Trains and supervises staff
- Explains research techniques to lawyers and paralegals, and answers questions
- Compiles legislative histories and bibliographies
- Selects and orders books, CD-ROM libraries, electronic database services, and other library resources
- Reviews and approves bills for payment
- Plans library growth
- Catalogs and tracks library resources using computerized methods
- Routes library-related materials to appropriate staff
- Files loose-leaf services and other library-related documents
- Manages check out of books and reshelves material
- Performs or assists legal professionals in legal research, particularly regarding computer-assisted legal research and legal and factual research on the Internet

will always have to provide some type of "library" for their staff, but many firms have moved from the expense of hard copy books to electronic alternatives.

Depending on the structure of the law office, the library may be supervised by a library committee, a managing partner, or an office administrator, or all functions may be controlled by the librarian.

Law libraries generally are thought of as an overhead expense and, regardless of size, are costly to maintain. Proper library management can, however, reduce overhead expenses and increase the quality of services to clients at the same time.

Some paralegals may be put in charge of the law library. Managing a law library may not seem at first like a difficult job, but in many instances it is. Books, periodicals, CD-ROM libraries, electronic databases, and other materials must be ordered on a regular basis to ensure the library is kept current; supplements to books (sometimes called "pocket parts") must be ordered and replaced regularly; the collection must be tracked using some type of computer or card catalog system (this requires quite a bit of time); books must be shelved and maintained; a library budget must be kept and tracked; and from time to time, books must be tracked down and found. Many librarians perform legal research themselves, as well. Proper law library management can be a time-consuming task.

Developing a Library Collection

There are many different types of materials that can be found in a law office library. The office's collection should mirror the type of practice and its specialties. As a law office's practice changes, the library also will need to change to keep information that is current with the needs of the law office. Exhibit 9-6 lists typical types of publications that are found in many law office library collections.

The extent of an office's collection will depend on many factors. Larger offices that have been in existence for many years will have much larger collections than will newer or smaller law offices. Some offices think that most, if not all, research should be performed in their own library, while other law offices that have large collections nearby, such as a law school or state or county law library, may want to keep their costs low and use these resources to the fullest extent possible.

A way to keep overhead costs low in the library is by purchasing electronic databases, e-books, and Internet access; maintaining Westlaw or LexisNexis; and keeping hard copy books and periodicals only as needed. This strategy limits the space requirements needed for most libraries and maximizes the use of computers already on the desks of most staff.

Exhibit 9-6 Possible Holdings in a Law Library

• Case law	• Statutes
• Citators	• Treatises
• Digests	• CD-ROM libraries
• Encyclopedias	• Westlaw
• Index to periodicals	• Internet access
• Periodicals	• LexisNexis
• Reference works	

Electronic Legal Databases

An **electronic legal database** is a database like one found on Westlaw or LexisNexis, which is accessed through the Internet with fee-based services. This database is maintained by the proprietary companies on their Web sites, which is then accessed by the users (lawyers, law offices, etc.) through the Internet. The legal research and resource materials (formerly hard copy books and e-books updated on CD-ROMs) is now updated on the company's Web site. The electronic legal database system has in some cases made law libraries in many law offices nearly obsolete. For example, the complete set of the *Federal Reporter*, which contains federal appellate court decisions from 1880 to the present, takes up more than 150 linear feet of shelf space in a law library, and this does not count the indexes necessary to use the reporters. The same *Federal Reporter* comes on CD-ROM disks, taking up 1 to 2 feet of shelf space, and includes a search engine that allows the user to search for needed material. The same *Federal Reporter* mentioned earlier is now available electronically and downloaded directly onto the office computer system, further reducing the physical library space needed. Updates are simple, and removing or reinstalling CD-ROMs is no longer necessary. Many electronic databases and resources, such as e-books, are compatible with devices such as smartphones and tablets. With a simple download of the resource's application ("app"), you can have access from multiple sources or locations.

CD-ROM and Electronic Legal Libraries   Hundreds and hundreds of CD-ROM and electronic legal libraries are currently available. Many books and periodicals published for the legal industry are available on CD-ROM or in electronic e-book format. This includes everything from criminal and family law to European tax laws, and everything in between. Most of the major legal book publishers, including West, BNA, Matthew Bender, and many others, offer a wide variety of electronic e-book products and online resources.

Electronic Search Engines   Searching electronic databases or CD-ROMs is similar to searching on Westlaw and LexisNexis. Both CD-ROMs and **electronic legal databases** use a search tool that allows the user to utilize terms and connectors including proximity searches, wild card searches, and other searches similar to Westlaw and LexisNexis. Most search engines also have hypertext, which allows a user to go directly to another referenced document immediately (similar to the Internet). For example, if a user is reading a case and another case is referenced, the user can click the mouse on the reference to the second citation, and the computer will immediately take the user to the second case.

Advantages and Disadvantages of Electronic Legal Libraries

There are many advantages to using electronic legal libraries, including the following:

- *Reduced space and expense considerations*—Electronic legal libraries, which may include CD-ROM material, take up a fraction of the space that similar information in book form would. While most law libraries will want some information in book form, there is much information that can be stored on CD-ROMs and database systems. Using electronic law

CD-ROM (Compact Disc – Read Only Memory)
A type of computer memory in the form of a compact disc that is for reading material and cannot be copied.

electronic legal database
A database containing law-related material on the Internet such as Westlaw or LexisNexis. Electronic sources such as e-books may be downloaded or accessed through applications (apps).

library databases further reduces the physically space, since everything is contained within the computer or through the Internet access. This has a tremendous impact on the annual operating cost of a law library for any legal organization. If a law firm or corporate law department can cut the size of its law library in half, it can save a tremendous amount on lease space, shelving, and other items. Because many legal organizations are in the business of making money, this is a very important consideration.

- *Portability*—Unlike rows and rows of books, electronic legal libraries' databases are inherently portable. Users can take the entire body of a state's case law into a courtroom on a laptop or computer and have the information at their fingertips. Additionally, with the Internet connection and e-book sources, you have immediate access to the most current legal information. This can prove extremely beneficial to the attorney or legal assistant.

- *Convenience*—Users can access information on their own computers without going to a library or even leaving their office. In addition, information on electronic database sources, including material found on CDs, can be copied into a user's word processor, just like Westlaw and LexisNexis.

- *Cost*—The total cost of an electronic legal library is often less than for hard copy books or for performing the research online using Westlaw or LexisNexis. It is also more cost effective for anyone who does a significant amount of legal research, because it can usually be done at the person's desk, and in many circumstances, electronic research is substantially faster than using books and indexes.

- *Maintenance*—The cost of maintaining books, and adding and deleting supplements and loose-leaf pages, should not be underestimated, particularly in a large law library. It takes library personnel numerous hours to do this, as compared to updating the law library's Web site database or installing a new CD to replace an old one. As library personnel maintenance time lessens, productivity should increase in other areas, such as the amount of time library staff can spend to assist customers with research projects.

Disadvantages to electronic legal libraries include the following:

- *Maintenance*—Maintenance of the computer software can be an issue: most electronic databases or CD-ROM updates have a monthly, quarterly, semiannual, or annual subscription service that must be purchased to keep them up to date. Electronic databases and CDs require updating and installation; electronic database services must be downloaded to the computer system. In addition, search engines must be upgraded to new versions from time to time. Depending on the environment, such as whether the computers are networked or stand-alone, maintenance can be quite time consuming. Hardware needs (including RAM and hard disk space) as well as networking issues require constant updating to stay current. In addition, the technology involved (including interfacing with a network) must be maintained, the systems may not work, or they may be incompatible. Technical experts must be called in to make modifications, which can be both expensive and time consuming.

- *CD-ROM versus the Internet*—There is some question regarding the long-term validity of CD-ROMs, particularly when compared to the

Internet. CD-ROMs must be continually updated, whereas Internet products never need to be updated because the product is always updated automatically. In most cases, CD-ROMs have been replaced by databases systems accessed online and continually updated online.

- *Training*—Training staff to use electronic legal databases and CDs can be a problem when different publishers, search engines, or applications are used.

Cataloging and Classifying the Collection

Proper classification and organization of a collection are imperative for the office to know what material it has and where it is located. If information is not arranged or organized in such a manner so that attorneys and legal assistants can easily find it without wasting time, the whole purpose of an in-house library is thwarted.

Exhibit 9-7 Modified Library of Congress Classification Numbers

Administrative Law	Constitutional Law
KF5401	KF4501
Agency	Consumer Law
KF1341	KF1601
Appellate	Advocacy Contracts
KF9050	KF801
Civil Procedure	Corporations
KF8810	KF1384
Commercial Transactions	Criminal Law
KF871	KF9201
Conflict of Laws	Criminal Procedure
KF8810	KF9601
Conservation of Natural Resources	Decedents' Estates and Trusts
KF5505	KF746

Cataloging is the process of listing and organizing the inventory of a library. This usually includes giving each book a separate call number and listing the book's author, title, publisher, subject, publication date, and so forth. Some offices classify and catalog their collections according to the Library of Congress classification system or the Dewey Decimal System. The Library of Congress system uses the alphabet for its general divisions. For instance, "K" is the letter that represents American Law. Exhibit 9-7 contains a list of selected Library of Congress legal classifications. Other offices may simply group materials together, such as a tax section, labor section, or real property section. This is sometimes called a "neighborhood" classification system.

Computerized catalog systems can be created using almost any database management program. They are very easy to set up and are very flexible. There are also some commercially available library cataloging systems for many types of microcomputers.

Technology and the Law Library
Computer-Assisted Legal Research (CALR)

Computer-assisted legal research (CALR) uses computers to search the words of cases, statutes, and documents themselves; two familiar legal-information services are Westlaw and LexisNexis.

Because CALR systems use the full text of the document, there is no need for indexes or digests. Instead, the user simply enters common words that describe the issue that might appear in the full text of the case or document, and the system retrieves all cases and documents that meet the request. Since the information is stored on large mainframes, the database can be searched and the documents quickly retrieved. The documents that are retrieved can be read online, can be sent off-line to a printer, or the full text can be downloaded to the user's computer. **Online** means that the user is connected to an information system and is running up charges. **Off-line** means that a user is no longer connected to an information service and that no charges are accruing except possibly a printing or downloading charge. Alternatively, a list of the appropriate cases or documents can be printed or downloaded so that, if the user likes, they can go to a library and examine the full texts.

CALR can be significantly quicker than manual researching techniques. Further, when CALR is used correctly, it can also retrieve cases that might not otherwise have been found using manual methods because of poor indexing or other errors. CALR is faster than manual methods because it is possible to search many databases at once (e.g., searching the case laws of all 50 states on a specific subject). Using manual methods, the user would have to search through several sets of digests, supplements, and indexes.

CALR—in addition to being quicker and sometimes more accurate than manual researching—can also be more convenient. Nearly all legal-information services are available 24 hours a day, unlike many law libraries. Also, the research can be done from the legal professional's office. As mentioned before, when using a law library, it is possible that an important book might already be checked out or unavailable. Sources are always available online with CALR. Another important factor to consider is that new cases are entered into legal-information services usually within a few days of being handed down or decided. Therefore, the information that is available online is almost always more up-to-date than information available in books.

Although CALR is both fast and convenient, it is not free. Most legal-information services charge a yearly subscription fee, along with a fee based on the amount of time a user is connected to their system. Some services also charge a fee for every search that is done on their system. Some services have connect-time charges of more than $200 an hour. In addition, some services have a minimum monthly charge, even if the service is not used. Because CALR is so expensive, new users can run up large bills quickly. Therefore, it is particularly important that new users have a thorough understanding of the CALR system they will be using. This is usually not a problem, because most CALR systems have off-line training tutorials. On the average, though, most legal issues take approximately 15 minutes to research. Most offices bill this expense back to their clients; some even do so at a higher rate than charged to help cover related expenses, such as long-distance charges. The office must be careful, however, to not bill the client for general overhead costs; general overhead costs

online
The user is connected to an information system and is running up charges.

off-line
The user is not connected to an information service and no charges are accruing except possibly a printing or downloading charge.

should already be figured into the office's attorney and legal assistant billing rate, so it would be inappropriate for the client to be billed for them again.

Westlaw

Westlaw is a full-text legal-information service provided by West Group. According to West, it is one of the largest law libraries in the world, with more than 40,000 databases available to its users. It contains cases from all West reporters as well as slip opinions, unreported cases, interactive databases, and much more. This site gives Westlaw users access to an enormous body of legal and nonlegal resources. Many of Westlaw's features are covered here, including its databases, types of search queries, and special features.

Westlaw is most commonly accessed through the Internet and Westlaw-specific proprietary software called with searches through Westlaw Next and West Search.

LexisNexis

LexisNexis is a full-text legal-information service. It was the first online, full-text legal-information service and is one of the world's largest services. LexisNexis and Westlaw are similar in many respects, with a few differences. LexisNexis can be accessed by using a microcomputer and specific proprietary software or by using a microcomputer and a standard Web browser to connect via the Internet.

The Internet

Many, if not most, legal professionals are connected to the Internet and are using it in a variety of ways. Some of the most common include performing legal research, performing factual or business research, using e-mail to communicate with clients and colleagues, accessing court records, and performing marketing functions.

Performing Legal Research on the Internet Performing legal research on the Internet can be done, but it is not at all like researching on Westlaw or LexisNexis. A user can look up, choose, and go to thousands of databases instantly using these two services; there is a uniform search engine and uniform Boolean language; and information is formatted neatly, succinctly, and uniformly. Even with all that, it still takes time, training, and experience to be proficient in Westlaw and LexisNexis.

Very little is uniform when performing legal research on the Internet. You must search for and find information where you can, and you must learn the nuances of many different searching techniques and languages. There is no one central depository of information. As with any kind of legal research, the more experience you have, the better, but it takes time, training, and experience to be good at it.

The following are some strategies to consider when beginning an Internet legal research project:

1. **Consider proper sources to find legal information.** Over the past several decades, research information has dramatically increased. If the user is looking for historic documents, including articles and statutes, or a solid case law background that dates before 1990, the Internet will more than likely have reference to the material. Nearly all traditionally

law libraries include electronic resources, and many have entire sections that are no longer available in hard copy. A user still uses the law library to perform traditional research, but often the Internet is the first stop. The Internet can have rich treasures of information, but you have to look for them. Many resources are free, and others require the user to join or subscribe to a service for a fee to get access, such as Westlaw and LexisNexis.

A cost-conscience legal researcher should start by researching any CD-ROM or electronic legal databases and hard copy books that he or she has, since they are cheap and convenient. The user could then explore the Internet to see what is available online. Again, this is cheap (actually, free) and handy. In some cases, an attorney may have free access to Fastcase, an online legal research tool, available through their state bar association membership. Finally, the user could go to Westlaw or LexisNexis, double-check and confirm the research, fill in any holes, and check citations ("Shepardize").

2. **Clearly understand the legal project and develop a method for completion.** You must know what information is being sought and a method for locating it to avoid wasting time. Because Internet resources are so vast, a user that starts his or her legal research without any direction may lose several hours of productivity "surfing" various Web sites without locating the needed research.

3. **Determine the proper search resources and finding tools.** A user should select search engines and finding tools that match the specific research that will be conducted. It is often difficult to determine what tools are the best suited for researching specific information. There are several good and free legal search resources to use, such as Cornell's Legal Information Institute, FindLaw, the Oyez Project, and Lexis Web.

4. **Consider using a guidebook to locate specific information.** When a user is trying to locate a particular type of material, it is highly recommended to use a legal guidebook. A guidebook provides useful starting points, such as a list with specific legal Web sites by topic, which improves the user's ability to find the information they need. Most major legal publishers have guidebooks available for purchase.

5. **Utilize an online starting point.** When a user is conducting legal research on the Internet, he or she must have a starting point. The starting point is often determined by the user and their technique or experience. Exhibit 9-8 provides a list of search engines, Exhibit 9-9 lists legal research starting points, and Exhibit 9-10 lists factual research starting points.

6. **Get help.** The Internet, along with providing resources for both legal and nonlegal research, also has many helpful tools. Some search engines incorporate methods to inquire like Google's Let Me Google That for You ("LMGTFY") and Ask.com. Additionally, there are listservs and discussion groups, blogs, tweets, and professional Web sites such as the American Bar Association and LinkedIn that offer groups to join providing topic-specific resources. It is more than likely that others have experienced similar Internet research problems. Always remember to be discreet and use proper "netiquette" when asking for help.

Exhibit 9-8 List of Search Engines/Gateways/Databases

Name of Web Site	Web URL (Address)
General Individual/Subject Directory Search Engines	
Ask.com	<http://www.ask.com>
Bing	<http://www.bing.com>
DuckDuckGo	https://duckduckgo.com
Excite	http://www.excite.com
Google	http://www.google.com
Lycos	http://www.lycos.com
Yahoo	http://www.yahoo.com
Specialty Search Engines	
Search (Government)	https://www.usa.gov
Search (Education)	http://www.ed.gov
Pandia Newsfinder (News)	http://www.pandia.com/news
Meta-Search Engines	
Dogpile	http://www.dogpile.com
Profusion	http://www.profusion.com
Zoo	http://www.zoo.com
Library Gateways	
Academic Information	https://www.academicinfo.net/
Digital Librarian	https://the-digital-librarian.com/
The Internet Public Library	http://www.ipl.org
WWW Virtual Library	http://www.vlib.org
Subject-Specific Databases	
Employment Web sites (Monster.com; Indeed.com)	http://www.monster.com; https://www.indeed.com/
Peterson's (college and university Web site)	http://www.petersons.com/college-search.aspx
WebMD (health/medical information)	http://www.webmd.com

Exhibit 9-9 Legal Research Starting Points

Subject	Additional Information	Web URL (Address)
Legal Search Engine/Portal		
Legal search engine/portal	All Law	http://www.alllaw.com
Legal search engine/portal	FindLaw	http://www.findlaw.com
Legal search engine/portal	LawGuru	http://www.lawguru.com
General Starting Points (Including Federal and State Case Law and Statutes)		
Large collection of links to legal resources	HierosGamos	http://www.hg.org
Large collection of links to legal resources	Publiclegal Internet Legal Research Group	http://www.ilrg.com
Law and Policy Institutions Guide	Large collection of links to legal resources	http://www.lpig.org

(continued)

(continued)

One of the best sources of legal information on the Web	Legal Information Institute at Cornell	http://www.law.cornell.edu
Large collection of links to legal resources	Justia—Virtual Chase	https://virtualchase.justia.com/
General and legal-related information	World Wide Web Virtual Library	http://vlib.org/
Federal Government Information, Regulations, and Laws		
FedWorld	Federal information	https://www.webharvest.gov/peth04/20041015000423/www.fedworld.gov
USAGov	Government search engine	http://www.usa.gov
Legal Forms		
Internet Legal Research Group Forms	Free legal-forms database (also includes forms for purchase)	http://www.ilrg.com/forms/index.html
Legal Encyclopedia		
Law About ... (from Cornell Law School Legal Information Institute)	Legal encyclopedia	https://www.law.cornell.edu/wex
Federal Regulations		
Code of Federal Regulations	Database for the code of federal regulations	http://cfr.law.cornell.edu/cfr/

Exhibit 9-10 Factual Research Starting Points		
Subject	**Additional Information**	**Web URL (Address)**
General Web Sites		
Maps	Google Maps	https://www.google.com/maps
Maps	MapQuest	http://www.mapquest.com
Case citation guide	The Bluebook	https://www.legalbluebook.com/
Dictionary/Thesaurus	Merriam-Webster	http://www.merriam-webster.com/
Zip codes	U.S. Postal Service	https://www.usps.com/
National lawyer directory	Martindale-Hubbell	http://www.martindale.com
National lawyer directory	FindLaw	http://www.findlaw.com/
Finding Expert Witnesses		
Expert witnesses	National Directory of Expert Witnesses	http://www.national-experts.com/
Expert witnesses directory	Expert.com	http://www.experts.com/
Expert witnesses directory	JurisPro	http://www.jurispro.com/
Technical advisory service for attorneys	The TASA Group	http://www.tasanet.com
Expert witnesses directory	Almexperts	http://www.almexperts.com
Expert witnesses network	Expert Witness Network	https://expertwitnessnetworks.net/
Finding People, Addresses, Phone Numbers, and E-mail Addresses		
People, addresses, phone numbers, e-mail addresses, yellow pages	Spokeo	**www.spokeo.com**
People, addresses, phone numbers	411.com	http://www.411.com

(continued)

(continued)

People, addresses, phone numbers, e-mail addresses, yellow pages	PeopleSmart	https://www.peoplesmart.com
People, addresses, phone numbers, e-mail addresses, yellow pages	InfoSpace	http://www.infospace.com
People search	ZABA search	http://www.zabasearch.com/
People, address, phone number locator	The Virtual Chase White Pages and Phone Directories	http://virtualchase.justia.com
Other Information About People		
Federal campaign donors	Political Money Line	http://www.politicalmoneyline.com
Family information from census, marriage, Social Security, and other sources	Family Tree Maker by Ancestry.com	https://www.mackiev.com/
Genealogy-related Web site link	Cyndi's List	http://www.cyndislist.com
Listing of military personnel	National Archives	https://www.usa.gov/military-personnel-and-installations
Federal prison inmates	Federal Bureau of Prisons	http://www.bop.gov
Physician list	American Medical Association	https://doctorfinder.ama-assn.org/doctorfinder/
Ancestry database	Ancestry.com	http://www.ancestry.com
Government records database for finding people	Global-Locate by Integrity	https://www.global-locate.com
Public Records (Free)		
Large list of links to finding public information on the Web	Justia Virtual Chase	http://virtualchase.justia.com
Births, marriages, deaths, divorces	Vital Records Information	http://www.vitalrec.com/index.html
Large portal to many Web sites with public records	BRB Public Information Records/Resources	http://www.brbpub.com
Real estate public records	NETR online	http://publicrecords.netronline.com/
Vendors of Public Records (Fee Based)		
Electronic Court Records for cases in Federal Courts	PACER (Public Access to Court Electronic Records) free registration—per page charges.	https://www.pacer.gov
State Court Internet Access to Records	Many state courts have free or monthly fee-based Web site access to records online	Various Web sites in state court locations
Legal Research and Resource for records	WestlawNext by Thomson Reuters	http://legalsolutions.thomsonreuters.com/law-products/westlaw-legal-research
Legal Research and Resource for records	LexisNexis	http://www.lexisnexis.com
News and Directories		
Chicago Tribune		http://www.chicagotribune.com
Los Angeles Times		http://www.latimes.com
New York Times		http://www.nytimes.com
USA Today		http://www.usatoday.com
Wall Street Journal		http://www.wsj.com

(continued)

(continued)

Researching Businesses		
Business service references and information	Library of Congress	http://www.loc.gov/rr/business
Directory of businesses lookup	Superpages	http://www.superpages.com
Business fax lookup	White Pages	http://www.whitepages.com/name/Fax-Number
Business phone/address listings	Bigfoot	http://www.bigfoot.com
Business information and insights	*Dun & Bradstreet*	http://www.dnb.com
Information regarding specific companies	D & B Hoovers	https://www.dnb.com/products/marketing-sales/dnb-hoovers.html
Annual reports for companies	Public Register's Annual Report Service	http://www.prars.com
Electronic Data Gathering of business information required by public companies for filing	Federal Securities and Exchange Commission EDGAR (Electronic Data Gathering Analysis and Retrieval)	http://www.sec.gov/edgar.shtml

Problems with Researching on the Internet   There are inherent problems with researching on the Internet that legal professionals should consider before beginning.

- ***Research on the Internet can take longer to perform.*** This is especially true when looking for cases, statutes, and other primary information, because it is spread over so many different Web sites. Experience is required to know where certain kinds of information reside on the Internet and which Web sites are better than others, especially when looking for historical cases or data.

- ***Research on the Internet must be checked for accuracy and given a citation.*** Unlike Westlaw, LexisNexis, and other fee-based information services, you need to make sure that the data you have collected on the Internet is genuine. You must be able to cite the source of the information.

- ***There are no added features to information.*** The legal researcher needs to remember that cases and other material on the Internet are raw in nature. No additional features typically exist like the case synopsis and keynotes that Westlaw adds to the beginning of a case. For the most part, the information has not been managed, at least not to the extent than it is when using a fee-based service.

Summary

Law offices of all types need a file system that allows them to store, track, and retrieve information about cases in a logical, efficient, and expeditious manner. When considering filing management techniques, each legal matter should be maintained separately and have its own case number. How a law office sets up its case numbering system is up to the office and its own needs. Alphabetical and numerical systems are common.

So many law offices are now moving toward a "paperless" office, where all information is stored electronically. Document management software is a central part of any paperless office. Document management software organizes, controls, distributes, and allows for extensive searching of electronic documents, typically in a computer-networked environment. It can also accommodate hard copy documents through the use of imaging. Imaging uses a scanner to capture an image of a document. That image is stored electronically and can be retrieved later.

Law offices must also decide whether files should be kept in a central location in the office or whether they should be kept throughout the office using a decentralized approach. This is also important for electronically stored files, that is to say, how they are stored within the computer system, either on local networks or in cloud storage.

Most law offices use a file-opening form to help track new cases. Because most offices cannot keep all files indefinitely, an office should close inactive files and destroy the closed files from time to time to reduce file-storage requirements. The *Model Rules* requires that attorneys safeguard client property. Many state rules require that attorneys turn over to a client his or her entire file when the client wishes to fire an attorney and retain new counsel.

Technology has greatly changed law libraries. Now, most if not all legal resources are available online or in computer format. The use of artificial intelligence (AI) has also changed the methods for retrieving, collecting, categorizing, and disseminating information. Most law libraries today include digital legal research tools, CD-ROM and electronic database materials, or e-books, Westlaw or LexisNexis (or both), and the Internet.

Key Terms

alphabetic filing system	electronic legal database
bar coding	file-opening form
centralized file system	imaging
CD-ROM	off-line
decentralized file system	online
document management software	

Practical Applications

1. Your supervising attorney hands you a case file on which she would like you to do some work. It appears from the file that the client saw the attorney on two different cases: the purchase of a piece of property and a medical malpractice matter. When you ask the attorney, she states that the client has recently raised the medical malpractice matter, but that the client's primary focus is on the purchase of a piece of real estate. The attorney also states that she does not think the medical malpractice matter is significant, and that is why a separate file is not being opened. The attorney tells you not to worry about it. To your knowledge, the attorney is not doing any research on the malpractice matter. How would you handle the situation?

2. The solo practitioner you worked for is moving across the country and wishes to close his law practice. The attorney is going to destroy all files related to the law practice because he does not want to have to rent storage space in a city in which he will no longer live. The attorney is getting ready to dispose of the records by hauling them out to the dumpster. What is your advice to the attorney?

3. Your office represents a client who is suing his former partner in a business venture that went sour. Your office has represented the client for two years and has put about 300 hours into the case. In addition, your office has taken five depositions and paid for the transcripts. Your office also has hired an expert witness. The expert witness prepared a report that supports your client's case. The office has about $30,000 worth of fees and expenses in the case. One afternoon, the client comes into the office and gives the receptionist a letter stating that he is terminating the relationship with the law office and that he wants his files returned to him within one week. The attorney in the case states that there is no way he is going to hand over anything until the client pays the office's expenses. The attorney states that because the client has not paid for any work, the files are not legally his, and because the law office fronted the expenses, the law office at least owns the deposition transcripts and expert witness report. How would you handle the matter?

4. The office you work for has recently added six attorneys and three paralegals. The file system is no longer efficient. Finding files is time consuming. You have been asked to come up with a new filing system. The following are some details you should keep in mind when determining the new system:

   - The three tax attorneys want to start their own department. The tax attorneys will shortly move their offices to the basement, and they want to keep their own files so they do not have to run up and down the stairs to get to them. None of the other attorneys use or need access to the tax files.

   - Staff employees can be very reckless about the condition in which they leave files.

   - When a case is opened, all the documents are kept in a large expanding file folder.

   - Documents tend to fall out of the files, and there is little organization to the case files.

   - Many of the attorneys work on cases together and need access to the cases.

   - People are constantly looking through the office trying to find a file.

   - Last week, the accounting department found out for the first time that the office has been handling a case for about four months. The client has never received a bill.

   - The office wants a file system in which it can immediately tell when the case is filed, what type of case it is (the office mainly handles tax, probate, corporate, and general litigation matters), and which partner is responsible for the case (there are five partners).

   Develop a strategy that will help eliminate these problems.

5. The partners in your office are displeased with the way the office's library is being maintained. They say that the library is hemorrhaging money with increased costs, which is crippling the office's profits. Your job is to draw up a plan to bring this situation under control. You have noticed the following:

   - Several copies of books are purchased by different partners and placed on their bookshelves.

   - The library is a mess most of the time. Books are kept in attorneys' and paralegals' offices (they rarely check out the books and then fail to get them back to the library). There is not enough room for the materials the library does have, and books are stacked up on the floor.

   - Many of the materials the library does have are outdated and no longer of use.

   - You asked for several books, and though you know they were ordered, you have not seen them yet.

   - The library has no budget as such; purchases are made when the office thinks it needs them. In addition, when an attorney orders a book, the book is sometimes kept on the attorney's own bookshelf.

   - All library costs, including Westlaw and LexisNexis, are absorbed by the office.

   - The library has no Internet access, although it has been talked about.

   - The library has one old desktop computer that has Westlaw and LexisNexis only.

On the Web Exercises

1. Go to the ABA Center for Professional Responsibility at http://www.americanbar.org, find the **ABA Model Rules of Professional Conduct**, and read and print out the comments to **Rule 1.15**.

2. Using a general search engine, such as http://www.google.com or http://www.yahoo.com, find three manufacturers of legal document management software.

3. Visit five state bar association Web sites and find three articles on one of these areas: filing, records management, record retention, law libraries, or opening/closing clients' files. The following link will take you to a Web site that connects to all state bar sites: https://www.nationallist.com/industry_resources/assoc-state-bar-list/

Case Review

In re Cameron, 270 Ga. 512, 511 S.E.2d 514 (Ga. 1999).

Supreme Court of Georgia.
In the Matter of Johnnie CAMERON (Two Cases).
Nos. S99y0257. S99y0258.
Feb. 8, 1999.

*512 PER CURIAM.

The State Bar filed two Notices of Discipline against Respondent Johnnie Cameron alleging violations of Standards 4 (professional conduct involving dishonesty, fraud, deceit, or willful misrepresentation); 22 (withdrawal from employment without taking reasonable steps to avoid foreseeable prejudice to the rights of the client, including giving due notice to the client, allowing time for employment of other counsel, delivering to the client all papers and property to which the client is entitled, and complying with applicable laws and rules); and 44 (willful abandonment or disregard of a legal matter to the client's detriment) of Bar Rule 4-102(d). Upon Cameron's failure to respond to either of the Notices of Discipline within the time set by Bar Rule 4-208.3(a), Cameron was in default pursuant to Bar ***513** Rule 4-208.1(b) and subject to discipline by this Court. The State Bar has recommended disbarment as an appropriate sanction for Cameron's violations of Standards 4, 22, and 44 of Bar Rule 4-102(d). We agree.

In one disciplinary matter, Cameron was hired by a client to represent him in a Social Security disability claim. The client gave Cameron documents pertaining to the claim and tried to reach Cameron by telephone numerous times. Cameron did not return the client's calls even when the client tried to reach Cameron regarding an appointment scheduled with a physician regarding the client's disability claim. On July 28, 1997, the client spoke with Cameron by telephone and Cameron promised to return the call on July 30,

1997 but failed to do so. After the Social Security Administration scheduled a disability hearing, the client again tried unsuccessfully to reach Cameron. Subsequently, the hearing was postponed when the hearing officer also could not reach Cameron. The client, in making additional attempts to reach Cameron, learned that Cameron's office had been vacated and his home telephone number disconnected. On September 5, 1997, the client wrote a letter to Cameron terminating Cameron's services and demanding the return of all documents. Cameron again failed to respond. Due to Cameron's failure to represent the client, the client was not able to present his disability case to the administrative law judge.

In a second matter, a client hired Cameron on or about November 14, 1997 to advise her on a will and property deeds and gave the original documents plus $50 to Cameron. Although Cameron stated that he would copy the documents and return the originals to the client, he failed to return the documents or to contact the client. The client made numerous attempts to call Cameron at his home and his office but was not able to reach him; she also learned that Cameron's fax number was disconnected. The client and the client's daughter contacted Cameron at his part-time job and requested the return of the original documents. Although in both instances Cameron promised to return the documents on the day of the telephone conversations, he did not keep the appointments or return the documents. In sum, Cameron did not do any work on the client's behalf, did not return any portion of the $50 fee, and failed to return the client's documents.

Although Cameron has no disciplinary history, the State Bar noted the pattern of dishonesty and abandonment evidenced by the two grievances filed and Cameron's failure to respond to the Notices of Investigation as aggravating factors in its recommendation for disbarment. Cameron has failed to respond to disciplinary authorities during the investigation of these matters and the Court finds no evidence of mitigating circumstances.

514 We agree with the State Bar that disbarment is warranted as a result of Cameron's violation of Standards 4, 22, and 44 of Bar Rule 4-102(d). Accordingly, Cameron is disbarred from the practice of law in Georgia. He is reminded of his duties under Bar Rule 4-219(c).

Disbarred.

All the Justices concur.

END OF DOCUMENT

Case Review Exercises

1. List each act committed by the attorney that violated Standard 22 of the state bar rules regarding the "withdrawal from employment without taking reasonable steps to avoid foreseeable prejudice to the rights of the client…."

2. If the attorney had argued that he should not be disciplined because the client had not paid him for the time spent on the case(s) (assuming it was true), would this have changed the outcome of the case?

3. What duty did the attorney have to his client(s) when he moved his office and had his home telephone number and office fax number disconnected?

4. Once the attorney took a part-time job, and assuming he quit the practice of law, what should the attorney have done?

5. Given the fact that the attorney had no prior discipline, do you think disbarment was appropriate?

Helpful Web Sites

Organization	Description	Internet Address
American Association of Law Libraries	Association for law librarians and other information professionals. It provides updates on advances for library resources including technology and Internet legal research advances.	https://www.aallnet.org/resources-publications/publications/law-library-journal/
American Bar Association (ABA)	Association for attorneys. The Web site has a large amount of information and publications relevant to individuals working in the legal profession.	http://www.americanbar.org
ABA Law Practice Division	ABA section devoted to law practice management issues, including file and records management.	https://www.americanbar.org/groups/law_practice/
Association of Legal Administrators	National association for legal administrators. Contains resources and information related to law office management and legal administration.	http://www.alanet.org
Law Technology News and Law.com	Excellent periodical for legal technology issues. Good white papers on technology issues.	http://www.legaltechnews.com/ and http://https://www.law.com/resources

Suggested Reading

1. ARMA International. (2005). *Establishing Alphabetic, Numeric, and Subject Filing Systems*.

2. Cunningham, G. C. (2014). *The Lawyer's Guide to Records Management and Retention*, 2e. American Bar Association.

3. Levitt, C. A., & Rosch, M. E. (2011). *Find Info Like a Pro: Mining the Internet's Publicly Available Resources for Investigative Research, Volume 1*. American Bar Association.

4. Levitt, C. A., & Rosch, M. E. (2011). *Find Info Like a Pro: Mining the Internet's Publicly Available Resources for Investigative Research, Volume 2*. American Bar Association.

Succeeding in the Legal Profession

Attorneys and paralegals must develop good management skills in order to succeed. They need to be accurate and thorough in everything they do. They must be routinely organized, prompt, and prepared. They must be team players and communicate effectively. These skills do not come naturally; most are learned the old-fashioned way: by trial and error over years. Read this section so that you can pick up some good ideas now that will save you from many headaches once on the job. Some of the suggestions may sound simplistic, but they really are not. The suggestions in this chapter come from many attorneys, paralegals, and legal assistants with varied experiences. These suggestions really work, and though some are fundamental, all of them are important.

Accuracy, Thoroughness, and Quality

"Accuracy" and "thoroughness" are easy to say but hard to accomplish. However, high-quality work is vital to the performance of a professional. A law office is a team, and everyone must be able to rely on everyone else; each client is paying for and deserves the absolute best work product the team can provide.

One element of quality work is careful documentation. It is important that, when you talk to witnesses, clients, opposing counsel, or others, you keep written notes of your conversation and send a confirming letter that documents your conversation. Some cases can drag on for years; if proper notes are not kept in the file, vital information can be lost. Keeping proper documentation about the work you have done on a case is very important.

Mistakes happen. If something does slip by, do not try to cover it up. Admit and/or report the mistake, correct the mistake to the best of your ability as quickly as possible, take precautions to make sure it does not happen again, apologize, and go on. Because mistakes are natural and almost inevitable, being accurate and putting out quality work is a daily battle.

Ideas on how to improve the quality of your work include the following:

- *Create forms and systems.* If you do a job more than once, create a system using forms and instructions for yourself. This will evoke memories from the last time you performed the job and speed up the work.

- *Create checklists.* Make a checklist for the jobs you regularly perform. Checklists will keep you from failing to perform specific details of a job that otherwise might be forgotten. In this way, the high quality of your work is maintained.

- *Be careful and complete.* Be prudent and careful in your work. Do not hurry your work to the degree that accuracy and thoroughness are compromised. Your work should always be neat and complete.

- *Keep written documentation and notes.* Keeping proper documentation about work you have done on a case is very important.
- *Take pride in your work.* Do not let work that you are not proud to call your own go out with your name on it.
- *Work hard.* Accuracy and thoroughness are seldom reached by slothfulness. Work hard at what you do, and the quality of the work will always be better for it.
- *Ask for peer review.* If you have a particularly important project due and you have a question about the accuracy of your work, have another attorney, paralegal, or staff member to look it over before you submit it or file it into a court record. While you do not want to become dependent on others or disrupt productivity, sometimes a second opinion can really help, especially if you are new to the organization.
- *Never assume.* Do not assume anything. If you have the slightest doubt about something, check it out, conduct research, make sure that you pay attention to details, and double-check the accuracy of your work.
- *Use firm resources.* Use firm resources, like intranets, brief banks, and tools, to the fullest extent. You will learn from others and your work will be of higher quality if you use the collective knowledge of other experienced staff.

The Assignment

You were assigned a task by a senior partner to draft the necessary documents needed for an important filing with a deadline quickly approaching. You immediately draft the documents and put them on the senior partner's desk for his review. The senior partner thought he told you to "take care" of the important filing. The deadline for the filing the matter was missed. Instead of admitting his error, he blames you for not properly handling the assignment.

When a task is being assigned to you, make sure you understand exactly what the assignment is and what the supervising attorney wants. Be certain that you understand the whole assignment; do not guess or extrapolate. One of the most common mistakes a new attorney or paralegal makes is to not ask questions. It takes a certain amount of maturity to say, "I do not understand," but it is critical. Your supervising attorney will not think any worse of you for it, and your chance of success on the task will be greatly enhanced. It is also a good idea to repeat the assignment back to the supervisor to make sure you understand all the details. If a task is extremely complicated, ask the supervisor to help you break it down into smaller parts. You might say: "This appears to be a good-sized job. Where do you recommend I start and how should I proceed; what steps should I take?"

It is also a good idea to write down your assignment. Have a pencil and a notebook or steno pad with you any time you talk to your supervisor about an assignment. A legal pad can serve as a journal, allowing you to keep all of your assignments in one place. If you record assignments, you will be able to refer back to them later if someone has a question or problem about the work they gave you. Be sure to write down what the assignment is, who gave it to you, any comments the person made about the assignment, and when it is due. Always ask for the exact date an assignment is due, not "sometime next week" or "whenever you get to it." Also be sure to write down when you completed the assignment.

If an assignment gets a little fuzzy to you after you start it, ask the supervisor questions while you are still in the middle of it. Do not wait until the end of the assignment to realize you did something wrong; check in periodically and have the supervisor quickly review it. This is particularly important with large and complex tasks.

Do the following to communicate effectively when receiving assignments:

- *Ask questions when the assignment is given.* Ask questions about the assignment until you fully understand what you are being asked to perform. Be aware that miscommunication problems occur more frequently regarding assignments you have never done before.

- *Repeat the assignment to your supervisor.* Repeat the assignment back to the supervisor to make sure you understand all of the details.

- *Break down complex assignments into small tasks.* Ask the supervisor to help you break complex assignments down into smaller tasks and help you organize the priority of those tasks.

- *Have a pen and paper ready.* Always have a pen and paper (a legal pad works best) with you when you are being given an assignment. It allows you to remember when the assignment was given, by whom, any comments from the supervisor, and when it is due.

- *Always ask for a due date.* Always ask for a specific due date. This prevents miscommunication regarding when an assignment should be completed.

- *Continue to ask questions and check in periodically.* As you work on the assignment, continue to ask clarifying questions and periodically check in with your supervisor to keep him or her updated on your progress.

Preparation and Organization

Successful attorneys and paralegals are organized and prepared for everything they do. Being organized is not hard; it just takes planning and time. Always have an appointment calendar with you so that you can record important appointments and deadlines. In addition, use a "things-to-do" list each day and try to plan and prioritize tasks so that assignments and projects are never late. Begin with the most important assignment you have to do or with the task that has the most pressing deadline. When you are working on projects for two or more attorneys, ask someone to prioritize the tasks for you. If you have a computer program that has organizational features, use it.

The following ideas will improve your preparation and organization:

- *Have an appointment calendar.* Always carry an appointment calendar with you or be sure to constantly update your computerized versions and print out hard copies regularly. This way, if you are caught in the hallway and given an assignment or meeting date, you will know if you have a conflict.

- *Make a "things-to-do" list.* Plan your day in advance, every day. Make a "things-to-do" list and try to complete your list every day, marking off items once they are completed.

- *Prioritize tasks.* When you are preparing your "things-to-do" list, always prioritize the tasks so that you turn in assignments on time. Give priority to assignments that have the most pressing deadlines. If you have a question about what assignment needs to be done first, ask your managing attorney for direction.

- **Be on time.** Always be on time when completing assignments and attending meetings, and always take good notes so that you will remember important facts or information provided in meetings.

Manage Your Time

Are you using your time effectively, or are you wasting it? Time management and organization go hand in hand.

The following ideas can help you manage your time effectively:

- **Set daily objectives.** Always plan your day by setting daily objectives and prioritizing them accordingly. Try to stick to your plan and achieve your objectives every day. Do the most important things first.

- **Do not waste your time on irrelevant tasks.** Do not waste your time on unimportant or unnecessary tasks. When someone walks into your office to talk about an irrelevant subject and you have a job due, politely ask them to come back another time when you are free.

- **Avoid procrastination.** Do not put off what you can do today. Procrastination is unprofessional and leads to dissatisfied clients. Stick to your daily schedule and do not put things off unless you have a good reason.

- **Avoid socializing in hallways.** Socializing is not only a waste of your time, it is also a distraction to others around you. In addition, it looks very unprofessional to clients.

- **Make a timeline or Gantt chart.** When you have a large project, take the time to make a Gantt chart. A Gantt chart is a plan or timeline of projected beginning and ending dates for the various parts of a project. A Gantt chart will help you plan how you will complete the project and will also allow you to track the progress of the work.

- **Have reference material close by.** Lay out your desk and office so that important reference materials are located within arm's reach to minimize time spent looking for things.

Effective Communication with Attorneys

One of your most important tasks will be to establish mutual confidence between yourself and your supervisor. Because attorneys, paralegals, and the members of the legal team must work together very closely, good communication is an absolute necessity.

The following practices will help you maintain effective communication with your supervisor:

- **Always ask questions.** If you do not understand something, ask questions.

- **Listen.** Do not forget to listen carefully when communicating with your supervising attorney. Listen and make notes so that you remember the details you will need to complete assignments.

- *Be confident.* Do not be so intimidated by attorneys that you act timid and fail to communicate. Carry yourself with confidence and authority. When you talk, always make eye contact.
- *Check in.* Check in with your supervising attorney on a daily basis so that he or she is informed of your progress on assignments.
- *Do not make important decisions unilaterally.* Include the supervising attorney in the decision-making process.
- *Establish mutual confidence.* Establishing mutual confidence with your supervising attorney is crucial. Your supervising attorney needs to have confidence in your work, and you need to have confidence in his or her work.
- *Establish your limit of authority.* Ask your supervising attorney what your limit of authority is when making decisions. You need to know as clearly as possible when he or she should be involved in decisions and what types of decisions they are.

The Client Comes First

When you are with a client, he or she should be given your undivided attention. Do not take phone calls, allow interruptions, play with your nails, or do anything else that would take your attention away from the client. Treat each client courteously and respectfully, and as if he or she is the only client you have.

The following measures will help ensure that the client comes first:

- *Give clients your undivided attention.* When you are with a client, be sure that you give the client all of your attention. Do not take phone calls, open mail, or do anything else that would take your attention away from the client.
- *Give clients fast, courteous, respectful treatment.* Treat the client courteously and respectfully at *all* times. Always return clients' phone calls and e-mails as quickly as possible, but never later than the same day, and always try to answer their questions as soon as you can.
- *Treat each client as if he or she were your only client.* A client's case is very important to him or her and should be important to you. Let your clients know that their welfare genuinely concerns you.
- *Serve clients, but do not overstep your bounds.* Do not let your zeal to serve clients cause you to overstep your bounds. Let the attorney answer complex client questions and give legal advice.
- *Maintain client confidence.* Always maintain the strictest standards regarding client confidentiality.

Keep Accurate, Contemporaneous Time Sheets

Attorneys and paralegals keep records of the amount of time spent on each case so that management will know how much to bill the client. Many firms require paralegals to bill a certain number of hours to clients each year or each month, so when you start with a firm always be sure to ask how many hours of billable time you are expected to have per month and annually. Also ask when time sheets are due and when they are monitored for compliance (i.e., weekly, monthly, quarterly). Budget your time so that you know how many billable hours each month, week, or even day you will need to meet your goal, and then monitor yourself on your progress. Do not let yourself get behind, as you will not be able to make it up. If you are given a nonbillable task, delegate the task as much as possible to secretaries and clerks. There are simple techniques to keep accurate time sheets. Always record the necessary information on your time sheet *as the day progresses*. Do not try and go back at the end of the day or week and try to remember what you did; write it down as you perform the work.

Timekeepers, especially new timekeepers, have a tendency to subjectively discount their hours because they feel guilty for billing their time to clients. Record the time you *actually* spent working on a client's case: if it took 6 hours to research a legal issue, record the whole 6 hours. If your supervisor does not believe the finished product is worth that much, he or she can adjust the time billed. Simply put, it is not your call to reduce your hours. Record your actual time and go on.

To keep accurate time records, implement the following measures:

- *Keep track of budgeted and actual billable hours.* Your supervisor may tell you that you are responsible for billing 100 hours a month (i.e., 25 hours a week). You want to be sure every week that the time sheets you turn in to management show as close to the amount budgeted as possible. You need to track this.

- *Keep a time sheet near your phone and computer.* Always keep a time sheet next to your phone or computer so when you pick up the phone or prepare work on the computer, you can record the time for it.

- *Fill out the time sheet throughout the day.* Fill out your time sheet as you go throughout the day instead of trying to play the "memory game" to remember all the things you accomplished.

- *Record the actual time you spent on a case.* Always record the actual time it took you to perform the legal service. Let your supervisor make any decision to adjust or reduce time to be billed to the client.

- *Be absolutely honest and ethical.* Never bill a client for administrative tasks or for time you did not actually spend working on his or her case.

Work Hard and Efficiently

Everyone knows the difference between working hard and coasting. If you work hard, people will respect you and recognize you for it; if you do not, people will recognize this also and typically will resent you for it.

Do not be surprised if you have to work overtime; this is often the case for attorneys and paralegals. The question as to whether paralegals should be paid for overtime is a hot topic; some firms pay overtime compensation and some do not. In any event, if you have to work overtime, do it with a positive attitude. Be honest and sincere. Also try to work as efficiently as possible.

- **_Pull your weight._** Do what is asked of you and produce quality work.
- **_Put in overtime when required._** Be ready to put in overtime when it is required. Try to be pleasant and professional about it.
- **_Work efficiently._** Work as efficiently as possible. If you have access to a computer, it makes sense to use it instead of doing something by hand.

Maintain a Positive Attitude and Team Spirit

A law office is a team that must rely on many different people to work together harmoniously in order to be successful. Approach your job with the goal of being a good team player and helping your team. Put the good of the firm above your own personal interest, and help the firm whenever you can, whether or not it is in your job description.

Good team players help other members of the team by passing along information and cooperating on tasks. They are able to give and receive help when it is needed. Another aspect of being a team player is knowing how to constructively criticize other players. First of all, be cordial and professional. Never criticize another staff member in front of a client, an attorney, or other staff members. Do not become emotional. Politely explain the problem and suggest a reasonable solution for solving it. Treat the other person as an equal. When you are the one being criticized, do not take the criticism personally; look beyond the finding of fault and try to make the adjustments suggested by the firm. Listen carefully and ask questions so that you understand the exact problem.

Your own effectiveness as an attorney or paralegal may depend on how well you work with others at your level within the team. You may strongly dislike some people. You will need patience and interpersonal skills to learn to work with them and develop mutual trust and confidence.

- **_Put the team first._** Always put the needs of the team before your own personal interests. In the long run, what is good for the team is good for you.
- **_Delegate._** Delegate tasks to other team members when possible. Use the team.
- **_Help other team members._** Always remember to take time to help other team members. Otherwise, they will not be willing to help you when you need it.
- **_Share information._** Never hoard information. Pass information along to other staff members, remembering to put the team first.
- **_Constructively and professionally criticize other team members._** Just because you are a team player does not mean you cannot constructively criticize others. Try to be respectful, professional, and nonemotional. Explain the criticism, then suggest ways to fix the problem. Treat others as equals.
- **_Take criticism professionally._** Try to avoid becoming defensive and listen to what is being said. Try to implement the suggestions of the other party as soon as possible.

- *Get along with those you do not like.* You will probably not like everyone you work with. But, for the good of the team, work at relationships and treat all coworkers with courtesy and respect.
- *Know the employees of your firm.* Get to know the employees of your firm and treat all employees as you would like to be treated.

Be a Self-Starter

Self-starters are valuable employees. Self-starters are people who do not need to be told what to do; they see a job that should be done or a need that should be fulfilled and they do the job or meet the need without having to be told. They seek out and volunteer for new work, assume responsibility willingly, and anticipate future needs.

Be flexible, open-minded, and creative; be a problem solver. Do not hesitate to courteously suggest new ways of doing things as long as the idea is well thought out (not off-the-cuff) and would provide the firm with a real benefit over the present way. However, before you try to implement a new idea or approach, be sure that you have researched, organized, and planned the project well in advance and have assessed the chances or risk of failure and the consequences of such a failure. Get others involved in the project, and ask for their help and input; this will help them accept the system later on.

Ideas on being a self-starter include the following:

- *Anticipate.* Anticipate what jobs need to be done or what need is unfilled, and then do the job or fulfill the need without being asked to do it.
- *Seek out and volunteer for assignments.* If a new assignment comes up (especially one with a lot of responsibility), volunteer for it.
- *Be flexible and open-minded.* Always be flexible and open-minded; have a positive attitude. All businesses must change with the times. Be adaptable.
- *Be aware of risk.* Before taking on a new assignment, research, organize, and plan. Assess your chances of success.
- *Get others involved.* Always include others in your development of new ideas. Get their thoughts and feedback. Not only is the information helpful, but people are far more willing to implement an idea to which they have contributed.

Stress Management

A law office is a very stressful place with a great deal of activities, deadlines, appointments, and problems. You must learn to manage your own stress, or it will manage you. Do not be so consumed with your work that you put it above your family or your own happiness. Learn to relax and participate in activities that allow you to do so. A healthy lifestyle and exercise can reduce your stress. You should also consider what causes your stress and how you can change your work environment to reduce it. Being a workaholic will only lead to burnout and frustration. Taking a vacation is also important; everyone needs an extended rest at least once a year.

To manage stress, follow these guidelines:

- *Remember your family.* Do not let your work rule your life. To be a complete person, you must work hard but you also have responsibilities to your family. Try not to go too far in either direction. You need a balance.

- *Participate in relaxing activities.* Learn to relax and participate in activities you enjoy.

- *Exercise.* A healthy lifestyle, with regular exercise, is another good way to reduce stress.

- *Consider your environment.* Consider where your stress comes from and how you can change your work environment to reduce the cause of your stress.

- *Take a vacation.* Take a vacation at least once a year. You need to rest and get away from the office from time to time.

Conclusion

To be successful in the legal profession you must have many attributes in addition to good technical skills. Being a team player, having a positive attitude, working hard, and keeping accurate records are just a few of the skills you must have to succeed.

Everything in this appendix must be considered in light of the corporate culture of the particular law practice in which you are working. *Corporate culture* refers to generally accepted behavior patterns within an organization; this will include the firm's values, personality, heroes, and mores. Most firms have written procedures or staff manuals that contain some of this information. Many policies, however, are never reduced to writing. Make it your business to understand your firm's position and how the firm views its clients, staff, and so on. Understanding how your firm looks at the world is very important.

Glossary

A

activity hourly rate Fee based on the different hourly rates, depending on what type of service or activity is actually performed.

administrative management Management decisions relating to operating or managing a law office, including financial and personnel matters.

administrative task A task relating to the internal practices and duties involved with operating or managing a law office.

Age Discrimination in Employment Act of 1967 Legislation that prohibits employers from discriminating against employees and applicants on the basis of age when the individual is 40 or older.

aged accounts receivable report A report showing all cases that have outstanding balances due and how long these balances are past due.

alphabetic filing system Filing method in which cases are stored based on the last name of the client or organization.

Americans with Disabilities Act of 1990 (ADA) Legislation that prohibits employers from discriminating against employees or applicants with disabilities.

associate attorney Attorney who is a salaried employee of the law firm, does not have an ownership interest in the firm, does not share in the profits, and has no vote regarding management decisions.

attorney or paralegal hourly rate Fee based on the attorney's or paralegal's level of expertise and experience in a particular area.

attorney A licensed professional who counsels clients regarding their legal rights, represents them in litigation, and negotiates agreements between them and others.

attorney–client privilege A standard that precludes the disclosure of confidential communications between a lawyer and a client by the lawyer.

B

bar coding A file management technique in which each file is tracked according to the file's bar code.

Bates stamp Stamps a document with a sequential number and then automatically advances to the next number.

billable time Actual time that a paralegal or an attorney spends working on a case and that is directly billed to a client's account.

billing The process of issuing invoices for the purpose of collecting monies for legal services performed and being reimbursed for expenses.

blended hourly rate fee An hourly rate that is set taking into account the blend or mix of attorneys working on the matter.

bona fide occupational qualification An allowable exception to equal employment opportunity, for example, for an employee to perform a specific job, the employee must be of a certain age, sex, or religion.

boutique firm A small law office that specializes in only one or two areas of the law.

budget A projected plan of income and expenses for a set period of time, usually a year.

C

calendar days System for calculating deadlines that counts all days including weekends and holidays.

calendaring A generic term used to describe the function of recording appointments for any type of business.

case management A legal term that usually refers to functions such as docket control, things to do, contact information by case, case notes, document assembly, document tracking by case, integrated billing, and e-mail.

case retainer A fee that is billed at the beginning of a matter, is not refundable to the client, and is usually paid at the beginning of the case as an incentive for the office to take the case.

case type productivity report A report showing which types of cases (e.g., criminal, personal injury, bankruptcy, etc.) are the most profitable.

cash advance Unearned monies that are the advance against the attorney's future fees and expenses.

CD-ROM (Compact Disc – Read Only Memory) A type of computer memory in the form of a compact disc that is for reading material and cannot be copied.

centralized file system Method in which a file department or file clerk stores and manages all active law office files in one or more file rooms.

Certificate of Service A statement at the end of a court document that certifies or establishes when a document was placed in the mail.

Civil Rights Act of 1964 Legislation that prohibits employers from discriminating against employees or applicants on the basis of race, color, national origin, religion, or gender.

clerks Employees who provide support to other staff positions in a variety of miscellaneous functions.

client confidentiality Keeping information exchanged between a client and law office staff confidential.

client hourly rate Fee based on one hourly charge for the client, regardless of which attorney works on the case and what he or she does on the case.

coaching technique Counseling that focuses on the positive aspects of the employee's performance and explores alternative ways to improve his or her performance.

communication barrier Something that inhibits or prevents the receiver from obtaining the correct message.

communication The transfer of a message from a sender to a receiver.

conflict of interest A competing personal or professional interest that would preclude an attorney or a paralegal from acting impartially toward the client.

contingency fee Fee collected if the attorney successfully represents the client.

continuance Rescheduling an appointment or a court date.

contract attorney An attorney temporarily hired by the law office for a specific job or period. When the job or period is finished, the relationship with the firm is over.

controlling The process of determining whether the law practice is achieving its objectives, holding stakeholders accountable for their goals and making strategy adjustments as necessary so the firm achieves its objectives.

court-awarded fees Fees given to the prevailing parties pursuant to certain federal and state statutes.

criminal fraud A false representation of a present or past fact made by a defendant.

cross-selling Selling additional services to existing clients.

D

decentralized file system System in which files are kept in various locations throughout the law office.

disaster recovery plan A disaster recovery plan includes information on how the law office will rebuild and recover from a total disaster.

docket control A law office–specific term that refers to entering, organizing, and controlling all the appointments, deadlines, and due dates for a legal organization.

document assembly software Creates powerful standardized templates and forms.

document management software Organizes, controls, distributes, and allows for extensive searching of electronic documents, typically in a networked environment.

document management software Organizes, controls, distributes, and allows for extensive searching of electronic documents typically in a computer-networked environment.

E

earned retainer Term for the money the law office or attorney has earned and is entitled to deposit in the office's or attorney's own bank account.

electronic billing When law firms bill clients using electronic means, such as the Internet.

electronic legal database A database containing law-related material on the Internet such as Westlaw or LexisNexis. Electronic sources such as e-books may be downloaded or accessed through applications (apps).

employment-at-will doctrine Doctrine that states that an employer and employee freely enter into an employment relationship, and that either party has the right to sever the relationship at any time without reason.

equal employment opportunity Concept that requires employers to make employment-related decisions without arbitrarily discriminating against an individual.

Equal Pay Act of 1963 Legislation that prohibits employers from paying workers of one sex less than the rate paid to an employee of the opposite sex for work on jobs that require equal skill, effort, and responsibility and that are performed under the same working conditions.

ethical rule A minimal standard of conduct.

Ethical Wall Term for a technique used to isolate the paralegal or attorney with a conflict of interest from having anything to do with a case.

exempt The employee is not required to be paid overtime wages over 40 hours per week.

expert witness A person who has technical expertise in a specific field and agrees to give testimony for a client at trial.

extranet A network designed to provide, disseminate, and share confidential information with clients.

F

facilities management Encompasses planning, designing, controlling, and managing a law office's building or office space.

Fair Credit Reporting Act Federal legislation that governs the use of consumer reports in all employment decisions.

Fair Labor Standards Act (FLSA) Federal law that sets minimum wage and overtime pay requirements for employees.

Family and Medical Leave Act of 1993 (FMLA) Legislation that allows employees in certain circumstances to receive up to 12 workweeks of unpaid leave from their jobs for family- or health-related reasons.

feedback Information sent in response to a message.

file-opening form A standardized form that is filled out when a new case is started. The form contains important information about the client and the case.

financial management The oversight of a firm's financial assets and profitability to ensure overall financial health.

flat fee A fee for legal services that is billed as a flat or fixed amount.

freelance or contract paralegals Works as an independent contractor with supervision by and/or accountability to an attorney; is hired for a specific job or period.

G

Gantt chart A plan or timeline of the projected begin and end dates of a project.

general counsel The chief for a corporate legal department.

groupthink Term for when the desire for group cohesiveness and consensus becomes stronger than the desire for the best possible decision.

H

hourly rate fee A fee for legal services that is billed to the client by the hour at an agreed-upon rate.

human resources management Hiring, evaluating, compensating, training, and directing law office personnel.

I

imaging Uses a scanner to capture an image of a document. The image is stored electronically.

income budget Estimate of how many partners, associates, legal assistants, and others will bill for their time, what the appropriate rates of hourly charge should be, and the number of billable hours each timekeeper will be responsible for billing.

independent legal assistants or legal technicians Services provided to clients in which the law is involved, but individuals providing the services are not accountable to a lawyer.

Interest on Lawyers' Trust Account (IOLTA) An interest-bearing account set up specifically to hold trust funds. The interest that accrues on an IOLTA account is given to a state bar foundation or other nonprofit legal organization for the good of the public.

internal control Procedures that an organization establishes to set up checks and balances so that no individual in the organization has exclusive control over any part of the accounting system.

intranet An internal information distribution system used only by a law firm staff.

L

law clerk A law student working for a law firm on a part-time basis while he or she is finishing a law degree. Law clerk duties revolve almost exclusively around legal research and writing.

law librarian A librarian responsible for maintaining a law library, conducting legal research, and managing library resources.

leadership The act of motivating or causing others to perform and achieve objectives.

legal administrators Persons responsible for some type of law office administrative system, such as general management, finance and accounting, human resources, marketing, or computer systems.

legal malpractice A claim that an attorney breached an ordinary standard of care that a reasonable attorney would have adhered to in that same circumstance.

legal malpractice Possible consequence when an attorney's or a law office's conduct falls below the standard skill, prudence, and diligence that an ordinary lawyer would possess or that is commonly available in the legal community.

legal marketing The process of educating consumers on the legal and business activities a firm uses to deliver quality and ethical legal services.

legal secretaries Employees who provide assistance and support to other law office staff by preparing documents, composing correspondence, scheduling appointments, and performing other tasks.

legal services office A not-for-profit law office that receives grants from the government and private donations to pay for representation of disadvantaged persons who otherwise could not afford legal services.

legal team A group made up of attorneys, administrators, law clerks, librarians, paralegals/legal assistants, secretaries, clerks, and other third parties. Each provides a distinct range of services to clients and has a place on the legal team.

legal technicians People who market their legal services directly to the public.

leveraging The process of earning a profit from legal services that are provided by law office personnel (usually partners, associates, and paralegals).

limited license legal technician In states where legislation has provided, a person qualified by education, training, and work to engage in the limited practice of law in the approved practice area as per the individual state's rules.

M

management by objectives A performance program in which the individual employee and the employer agree on goals for the employee.

management reports Reports used to help management analyze whether the office is operating in an efficient and effective manner.

management The administration of people and other resources to accomplish objectives.

managing partner An attorney in a law firm chosen by the partnership to run the firm, make administrative decisions, and set policies.

marketing plan It specifies a target audience the firm is trying to reach, the exact goals that the marketing program is to accomplish, and establishes a detailed strategy of how the goals will be achieved.

marketing The process of educating consumers on the quality legal services that a law office can provide.

mission statement A general, enduring statement of the purpose or intent of the law practice.

Model Code of Professional Responsibility/Model Rules of Professional Conduct Self-imposed ethical standards for ABA members, but they also serve as a prototype of legal ethics standards for state court systems.

N

negligent hiring Hiring an employee without sufficiently and reasonably checking the employee's background.

noise Any situation that interferes with or distorts the message being communicated.

nonbillable time Time that cannot be directly billed to a paying client.

non-equity partner One who does not share in the profits or losses of the firm but may be included in some aspects of management and may be entitled to certain benefits.

nonexempt The employee is required to be paid overtime wages (time and a half) over 40 hours per week.

O

of counsel An attorney affiliated with the firm in some way, such as a retired or semi-retired partner.

office managers Manager who handles day-to-day operations of the law office, such as accounting, supervision of the clerical support staff, and assisting the managing partner.

office services management It refers to the administration of a number of internal systems and services in a law office. These include mail, copy, fax, and telecommunication services, among others.

off-line The user is not connected to an information service and no charges are accruing except possibly a printing or downloading charge.

online The user is connected to an information system and is running up charges.

organizing The process of arranging people and physical sources to carry out plans and accomplish objectives.

outside counsel Term referring to when corporate and government law practices contract with law offices (i.e., outside of the corporation or government practice) to help them with legal matters, such as litigation, specialized contracts, stock/bond offerings, and so forth.

overhead General administrative costs of doing business, including costs such as rent, utilities, phone, and salary costs for administrators.

P

paralegal managers Oversee a paralegal program in a legal organization, including preparing work plans, hiring, training, and evaluating paralegals.

paralegals As defined by the ABA, is a person, qualified by education, training, or work experience, who is employed or retained by a lawyer, law office, corporation, government agency, or other entity and who performs specifically delegated substantive legal work for which a lawyer is responsible.

partner or shareholder An owner in a private law practice who shares in its profits and losses.

personal information manager (PIM) Consolidates a number of different tasks into one computer program. Most PIMs include calendaring, things to do, a contact database that tracks names and addresses of people, note taking, and other tasks as well.

personnel handbook A manual that lists the formal personnel policies of an organization.

planning The process of setting objectives, assessing the future, and developing courses of action to achieve these objectives.

policy A specific statement that sets out what is or is not acceptable.

powerful managing partner A management structure in which a single partner is responsible for managing the firm.

practice management Management decisions about how a law office will practice law and handle its cases.

prebilling report A rough draft version of billings.

prepaid legal services A plan that a person can purchase that entitles the person to receive legal services either free or at a greatly reduced rate.

pro bono Legal services that are provided free of charge to a client who is not able to pay for the services.

procedure A series of steps that must be followed to accomplish a task.

pure retainer A fee that obligates the office to be available to represent the client throughout the time period agreed upon.

R

rainmaking Bringing in new clients to a law office.

realization Amount a firm actually receives in income as opposed to the amount it bills.

reasonable accommodation Accommodating a person with a disability, which may include making existing facilities readily accessible, restructuring the job, or modifying work schedules.

recurring entry A calendar entry that recurs.

rephrasing A technique used to improve communication by repeating back to a person your understanding of the conversation.

retainer for general representation Retainer typically used when a client such as a corporation or entity requires continuing legal services throughout the year.

rule by all partners/shareholders A management structure in which all partners/shareholders are included in decisions that affect the firm.

rule by management committee/board Management structure that uses a committee structure to make management decisions for the firm.

S

settlement A mutual agreement to resolve a dispute on specified terms.

Sexual harassment Unwelcome sexual advances, requests for sexual favors, and other verbal or physical conduct of a sexual nature that create an intimidating, a hostile, or an offensive working environment. Exhibit 2-13 contains a sample antiharassment policy.

staff attorney An attorney hired by a firm with the knowledge and understanding that he or she will never be considered for partnership.

staffing plan Estimate of how many employees will be hired or funded by the firm, what positions or capacities they will serve in, what positions will need to be added, what old positions will be deleted, and how much compensation each employee will receive.

statute of limitations (also known as prescription) A statute or law that sets a limit on the length of time a party has to file a suit. If a case is filed after the statute of limitations, the claim is barred and is dismissed as a matter of law.

strategic planning Determining the major goals of a firm and then adopting the courses of action necessary to achieve those goals.

substantive task A task that relates to the process of actually performing legal work for clients.

system A consistent or an organized way of doing something.

T

time sheet or time slip A record of detailed information about the legal services professionals provide to each client.

timekeeper productivity report A report showing how much billable and nonbillable time is being spent by each timekeeper.

timekeeping The process of tracking time for the purpose of billing clients.

time-to-billing percentage System of adjusting downward the actual amount that will be billed to clients during the budget process, taking into account the fact that timekeepers are not always able to bill at their optimum levels.

total quality management (TQM) Management philosophy of knowing the needs of each client and allowing those needs to drive the legal organization.

trust or escrow account A separate bank account, apart from a law office's or an attorney's operating checking account, where unearned client funds are deposited.

U

unearned retainer Monies that are paid up front by the client as an advance against the attorney's future fees and expenses. Until the monies are actually earned by the attorney or law office, they belong to the client.

V

value billing A type of fee agreement that is based not on the time spent to perform the work but on the basis of the perceived value of the services to the client.

W

workdays System for calculating deadlines that refers to only days when the court is open.

Z

zero-based budgeting system Procedure that forces everyone in the organization to justify and explain his or her budget figures in depth without using prior years' figures as justification.

Index